# Dictionary of Literary Biography

## Dictionary of Literary Biography Documentary Series

## Dictionary of Literary Biography Yearbooks

# Concise Series

**Concise Dictionary of American Literary Biography,** 7 volumes (1988-1999): *The New Consciousness, 1941-1968; Colonization to the American Renaissance, 1640-1865; Realism, Naturalism, and Local Color, 1865-1917; The Twenties, 1917-1929; The Age of Maturity, 1929-1941; Broadening Views, 1968-1988; Supplement: Modern Writers, 1900-1998.*

**Concise Dictionary of British Literary Biography,** 8 volumes (1991-1992): *Writers of the Middle Ages and Renaissance Before 1660; Writers of the Restoration and Eighteenth Century, 1660-1789; Writers of the Romantic Period, 1789-1832; Victorian Writers, 1832-1890; Late-Victorian and Edwardian Writers, 1890-1914; Modern Writers, 1914-1945; Writers After World War II, 1945-1960; Contemporary Writers, 1960 to Present.*

**Concise Dictionary of World Literary Biography,** 10 volumes projected (1999- ): *Ancient Greek and Roman Writers; German Writers; African, Caribbean, and Latin American Writers; South Slavic and Eastern European Writers.*

Dictionary of Literary Biography® • Volume Two Hundred Forty-Eight

# Antebellum Writers in the South

## Second Series

Dictionary of Literary Biography® • Volume Two Hundred Forty-Eight

# Antebellum Writers in the South

## Second Series

Edited by
Kent Ljungquist
*Worcester Polytechnic Institute*

A Bruccoli Clark Layman Book
The Gale Group
Detroit • San Francisco • London • Boston • Woodbridge, Conn.

Advisory Board for
## DICTIONARY OF LITERARY BIOGRAPHY

Printed in the United States of America

The paper used in this publication meets the minimum requirements
of American National Standard for Information Sciences–Permanence
Paper for Printed Library Materials, ANSI Z39.48-1984. ∞™

**Library of Congress Cataloging-in-Publication Data**

Antebellum writers in the South. Second series / edited by Kent Ljungquist.
    p. cm.–(Dictionary of literary biography; v. 248)
"A Bruccoli Clark Layman book."
Includes bibliographical references and index.
ISBN 0-7876-4665-2 (alk. paper)
1. American literature–Southern States–Bio-bibliography–Dictionaries. 2. American literature–19th century–Bio-bibliography–Dictionaries. 3. Authors, American–Southern States–Biography–Dictionaries. 4. Authors, American–19th century–Biography–Dictionaries. 5. Southern States–In literature–Dictionaries. 6. Southern States–Biography–Dictionaries. 1. Ljungquist, Kent, 1948–   . II. Series.

PS261.A58 2001
810.9'975'09034–dc21                            2001040500
[B]

10 9 8 7 6 5 4 3 2 1

*For my friends and colleagues in the
Poe Studies Association*

# Contents

# Plan of the Series

*. . . Almost the most prodigious asset of a country, and perhaps its most precious possession, is its native literary product—when that product is fine and noble and enduring.*

Mark Twain*

The advisory board, the editors, and the publisher of the *Dictionary of Literary Biography* are joined in endorsing Mark Twain's declaration. The literature of a nation provides an inexhaustible resource of permanent worth. Our purpose is to make literature and its creators better understood and more accessible to students and the reading public, while satisfying the needs of teachers and researchers.

To meet these requirements, *literary biography* has been construed in terms of the author's achievement. The most important thing about a writer is his writing. Accordingly, the entries in *DLB* are career biographies, tracing the development of the author's canon and the evolution of his reputation.

The purpose of *DLB* is not only to provide reliable information in a usable format but also to place the figures in the larger perspective of literary history and to offer appraisals of their accomplishments by qualified scholars.

The publication plan for *DLB* resulted from two years of preparation. The project was proposed to Bruccoli Clark by Frederick G. Ruffner, president of the Gale Research Company, in November 1975. After specimen entries were prepared and typeset, an advisory board was formed to refine the entry format and develop the series rationale. In meetings held during 1976, the publisher, series editors, and advisory board approved the scheme for a comprehensive biographical dictionary of persons who contributed to literature. Editorial work on the first volume began in January 1977, and it was published in 1978. In order to make *DLB* more than a dictionary and to compile volumes that individually have claim to status as literary history, it was decided to organize volumes by topic, period, or

*\*From an unpublished section of Mark Twain's autobiography, copyright by the Mark Twain Company*

genre. Each of these freestanding volumes provides a biographical-bibliographical guide and overview for a particular area of literature. We are convinced that this organization—as opposed to a single alphabet method—constitutes a valuable innovation in the presentation of reference material. The volume plan necessarily requires many decisions for the placement and treatment of authors. Certain figures will be included in separate volumes, but with different entries emphasizing the aspect of his career appropriate to each volume. Ernest Hemingway, for example, is represented in *American Writers in Paris, 1920–1939* by an entry focusing on his expatriate apprenticeship; he is also in *American Novelists, 1910–1945* with an entry surveying his entire career, as well as in *American Short-Story Writers, 1910–1945, Second Series* with an entry concentrating on his short fiction. Each volume includes a cumulative index of the subject authors and articles.

Since 1981 the series has been further augmented by the *DLB Yearbooks,* which update published entries, add new entries to keep the *DLB* current with contemporary activity, and provide articles on literary history. There have also been nineteen *DLB Documentary Series* volumes which provide illustrations, facsimiles, and biographical and critical source materials for figures, works, or groups judged to have particular interest for students. In 1999 the *Documentary Series* was incorporated into the *DLB* volume numbering system beginning with *DLB 210: Ernest Hemingway.*

We define literature as the *intellectual commerce of a nation:* not merely as belles lettres but as that ample and complex process by which ideas are generated, shaped, and transmitted. *DLB* entries are not limited to "creative writers" but extend to other figures who in their time and in their way influenced the mind of a people. Thus the series encompasses historians, journalists, publishers, book collectors, and screenwriters. By this means readers of *DLB* may be aided to perceive literature not as cult scripture in the keeping of intellectual high priests but firmly positioned at the center of a nation's life.

*DLB* includes the major writers appropriate to each volume and those standing in the ranks behind them. Scholarly and critical counsel has been sought in deciding which minor figures to include and how full their entries should be. Wherever possible, useful references are made to figures who do not warrant separate entries.

Each *DLB* volume has an expert volume editor responsible for planning the volume, selecting the figures for inclusion, and assigning the entries. Volume editors are also responsible for preparing, where appropriate, appendices surveying the major periodicals and literary and intellectual movements for their volumes, as well as lists of further readings. Work on the series as a whole is coordinated at the Bruccoli Clark Layman editorial center in Columbia, South Carolina, where the editorial staff is responsible for accuracy and utility of the published volumes.

One feature that distinguishes *DLB* is the illustration policy—its concern with the iconography of literature. Just as an author is influenced by his surroundings, so is the reader's understanding of the author enhanced by a knowledge of his environment. Therefore *DLB* volumes include not only drawings, paintings, and photographs of authors, often depicting them at various stages in their careers, but also illustrations of their families and places where they lived. Title pages are regularly reproduced in facsimile along with dust jackets for modern authors. The dust jackets are a special feature of *DLB* because they often document better than anything else the way in which an author's work was perceived in its own time. Specimens of the writers' manuscripts and letters are included when feasible.

Samuel Johnson rightly decreed that "The chief glory of every people arises from its authors." The purpose of the *Dictionary of Literary Biography* is to compile literary history in the surest way available to us—by accurate and comprehensive treatment of the lives and work of those who contributed to it.

The *DLB* Advisory Board

# Introduction

In a celebrated exchange between Ralph Waldo Emerson and Thomas Carlyle, the former referred to America as "the seat and centre of the British race." Writing in *English Traits* (1856), he dismissed England as "an old and exhausted island" that "must one day, like other parents . . . be strong only in their children." In his famous addresses, "The American Scholar" and "Self-Reliance," Emerson encouraged young Americans to cast off obsolete modes of thinking and expression that were cast in a European mold. In speaking of the new nation as the seat of the British race, Emerson, to be sure, was thinking of New England, but in noting "the prodigious natural advantages" of America, he extended his vision to the entire continent.

Our image of antebellum literary history, shaped by the grandiose tone of Emerson and his disciples, is perhaps a romantic picture of bustling activity in New England, reinforced by influential volumes such as Van Wyck Brook's *The Flowering of New England* (1936) and George Whicher's *Poetry of the New England Renaissance* (1950). Until 1850, however, major publishers in New York and Philadelphia remained the most successful arbiters of literary taste. Boston periodicals, moreover, only found secure footing after the durable successes of the *Knickerbocker,* the *Democratic Review,* and the *Southern Literary Messenger* farther south. The campaign for a distinctive American culture, emancipated from the tyranny of England, was not confined to New England, as reflected in the many articles and manifestos on the subject published in New York. This debate on literary nationalism is perhaps remembered today because two figures, Herman Melville and Walt Whitman, emerged from the clamor surrounding it. It was nevertheless a contentious debate carried out among editors and intellectuals—working for periodicals or participating in private salons and clubs in Manhattan or its environs.

New York City, which tripled in size in the 1840s and 1850s, became America's publishing center in this campaign for a distinctive national literature. Authors, both inexperienced and well traveled in the literary marketplace, flocked to New York during the antebellum period to participate in the activities of the book and periodical trades. After leaving the *Southern Literary Messenger* early in 1837, Edgar Allan Poe, for example, moved to New York City, stayed for more than a year, and pursued magazine work for the "*Monthlies* of Gotham–Their distinguished Editors, and their vigorous Collaborateurs." Harper and Brothers of New York published his first book of fiction, *The Narrative of Arthur Gordon Pym,* in 1838. The publication of the book had been delayed by the financial crisis of the 1830s, and Poe pursued his literary objectives elsewhere, only to return to New York in 1845 to work as a magazine editor and in 1848 to deliver a lecture on "The Universe."

The circumstances surrounding the publication of Melville's *Typee: A Peep at Polynesian Life* (1846), recounted by various commentators, offer further perspective on the multiple crosscurrents in the New York literary world before the Civil War. With the support of Washington Irving, the figure who dominated the New York literary scene, a British publisher had been secured for a narrative of a young sailor's adventures in the Marquesas Islands. If the book first attracted a British imprint, the likelihood of American publication would be enhanced. George Palmer Putnam, soon to become one of the foremost publishers in the United States, arranged to have its proof sheets sent from London back to New York to his firm of Wiley and Putman. *Typee* appeared in 1846 after Evert Duyckinck, who later ascended to a leadership role in the "Young America" group of New York, had served as an editorial evaluator. Complemented by the intervention of New York's most celebrated author, the success of the book was assisted by Putnam, whose name soon rose to prominence with the other great publishing houses of the city: Harper, Scribner, Van Nostrand, and Dodd, Mead. By the end of the decade Putnam was underwriting multivolume editions of the works of both Irving and James Fenimore Cooper. The manuscript of *Typee* was read by Duyckinck, who eventually took the helm of the *Literary World,* and it was reviewed by the young Whitman, clearly attracted to the vigor and energy of the city and beginning his literary career as a contributor to the *New York Aurora* and the *Brooklyn Eagle.*

In *The Raven and the Whale: The War of Words and Wits in the Era of Poe and Melville* (1956), that lively and enduring chronicle of the cliquish battles that divided the literary world of the 1840s, Perry Miller may exaggerate in claiming that "Melville's America . . . consisted almost entirely of the city of New York." Whatever the extent of its influence on the young author, there can be little doubt that his reentry into the environs of New York–the Melville family had lived in the city until his father's financial reversals in the 1820s–marked the beginnings of his education into the vagaries of professional authorship. In all likelihood, many of the challenges and disappointments he experienced as a writer were duplicated in the careers of other literary figures who lived, visited, or wrote in New York in the 1840s, drawn to opportunities of the expanding book and magazine markets.

The careers of these authors underscore the centrality of New York to antebellum literary activity, its influence and attraction for both major and minor figures, and its role in enhancing the profession of authorship and the business of publishing. By the time of their entry into the New York literary world, the booming port city had long ago shed its image as a quaint Dutch town. It had, in fact, become the commercial center of the nation, easily eclipsing Philadelphia, which may have reached the peak of its cultural stature by the War of 1812, for its diversity of publishing ventures. The development of the banking interests in New York and a nascent industrialism were contributing factors in the emergence of a capitalist economy that supplanted the vanished world of Dutch aristocrats. Boston could boast of the prestigious *North American Review,* but by the mid 1840s New York was three times that city's size. "The seat of commerce," reflected a writer in the *Literary World* in 1847, is of necessity "the centre of literary power."

These tangible achievements were obviously a source of pride to local inhabitants. In 1839 the editor Horace Greeley articulated the feelings of many of them when he boasted of the ways in which New York "towered above her sister cities." Similarly, Whitman referred to New York as "the model of the nation." In the face of accelerating and sometimes unsettling geographical, social, and economic changes, however, a more conservative impulse lay behind the work of a group of writers who celebrated the past and local traditions. While businessmen and entrepreneurs trumpeted the commercial prospects of the nation, Irving led a group of New York writers whose satirical essays, histories, and sketches surveyed the region's past. Irving stood for a continuity between Old World values and American culture, and his early works reflected the witty, gossipy style of the eighteenth-century British essayists. His early literary efforts were also collaborative ventures, reflecting the sociability and bonhomie of the group of writers for whom he was to become a model. With his brother William and the young James

Kirke Paulding he produced *Salamagundi; or, The Whim-Whams and Opinions of Lancelot Langstaff, & Others* (1807–1808), a volume of letters, verse, and essays. These miscellaneous papers, as they were called, were infused with the town spirit of Old New York. For his burlesque *A History of New York: From the Beginning of the World to the End of the Dutch Dynasty* (1809) Irving chose the pseudonym Diedrich Knickerbocker, an amateur antiquary who delves into the past of the region in a spirit of comic celebration. In a preface Irving eventually added to the volume, he announced that his purpose was "to clothe home scenes and places and familiar names with those imaginative associations so seldom met with in our own country, but which live like charms and old spells about the cities of the old world." This book, which has been overshadowed by *The Sketch Book* (1819–1820), established the tone for the Knickerbocker group of writers. These writers, steeped in the neoclassical traditions of wit and satire, were also attracted to the emerging Romantic movement in Great Britain, whose heroes were Sir Walter Scott and Lord Byron. In addition to Paulding, other writers sometimes associated with the Knickerbocker school were William Cullen Bryant, Richard Henry Dana, Charles Fenno Hoffman, William Leggett, Nathaniel Parker Willis, Park Benjamin, and Samuel Woodworth. Several of these writers–Bryant, Dana, and Willis–had New England backgrounds, but their literary careers reached maturity in New York. Few writers of the antebellum period could escape the shadow of Irving, whether they imitated, exploited, or burlesqued his narrative voice and strategies. Henry Wadsworth Longfellow, Nathaniel Hawthorne, and John Greenleaf Whittier all contemplated or completed volumes aiming to do for New England what Irving had done for Dutch New York. In surveying the influences on Melville's fiction, scholars have detected Irvingesque echoes even in the audacious *Typee;* one of his later works is titled "Rip Van Winkle's Lilac."

The Knickerbocker school of writers was loosely organized, but many of them interacted socially in private clubs. Throughout the early part of the century many private clubs and voluntary associations that helped to define and shape cultural activity had sprung up. These organizations, depending on their diverse missions, attracted a variety of labels: lyceums, benevolent or humane societies, art or music societies, library societies, debating clubs, and societies for the promotion of useful knowledge. The New York Society Library, the Mercantile Library, and the National Academy of Design attracted the local population as well as visitors from outside the city. The "Club-Mania" of the period, as it was called by the *New-England Galaxy* (16 April 1829), was not confined to New York or New

England and was almost as common in towns and cities of the Middle States and the South. The same periodical summarized the phenomenon by noting "the increase in applications for incorporation, this collecting into associations, this clubbing together of all ages and sexes." Perhaps the most famous literary organization in New York was the Bread and Cheese Club, founded by Cooper in 1822. Irving was made an honorary member in 1826, and some of its members gravitated to the Sketch Club, which cultivated an interest in the pictorial arts. Some Knickerbockers were merchants or businessmen, but for respite from the New York commercial culture many individuals gravitated to the polite atmosphere of private literary salons, where musicians, artists, and poets gathered in a spirit of informal social interchange.

Both Irving and Bryant were also devotees of the theater, and New Yorkers more easily overcame the moral reservations about plays that may have inhibited the cultural life of other regions, most notably New England. English plays were popular fare, but American playwrights perhaps succeeded in gaining greater recognition in New York, where there were six theaters and where some writers were able to exploit their local ties to the city. Poe, whose mother had played leading roles in playhouses in the North and the South, found reinforcement for his lifelong interest in drama when, after being exposed to theatrical coteries in Baltimore and Richmond, he served as an editor for the *New York Mirror* and the *Broadway Journal.* The latter periodical was devoted to the life of the city in all its variety, including the theater, and thus reinforced the image of New York as a cultural alternative to Boston. Just as the clubbing atmosphere of the period stimulated informal literary activity and interchange, these editorial connections provided access to the lively world of playwrights, actors, and artists. In his role as a magazinist Poe reviewed Anna Cora Mowatt's comedy *Fashion* (1849), Willis's melodrama *Tortesa the Usurer* (1839), and Long-fellow's closet drama, *The Spanish Student* (1843). His review of Willis, rather than an evaluation of an isolated performance, can be read as a survey of the status of American theater at the time.

By the time Poe assumed his position with the *New York Mirror,* there were nearly fifty magazines in the city as well as ten daily newspapers, and many writers supported themselves by editing or contributing to periodicals. Poe had commented, "The whole tendency of the age is Magazine-ward," a statement confirmed by the proliferation of periodicals as a staple of Americans' reading habits. In 1825 there were fewer than one hundred magazines in the United States; by 1850 there were more than six hundred.

Many newspapers stressed commerce and politics, but a few—like the *Evening Post,* for which Bryant worked—were hospitable to literature. The *American,* edited by Charles King, was among the first newspapers to devote a page exclusively to literary topics. King's values were refined and fastidious if one compared his publication to the journalistic competition represented by James Gordon Bennett's *New York Herald* and Greeley's *New York Tribune.* To King these papers represented the doctrine "that a newspaper should reflect the living world, as it is, with all its hideous vileness, as well as its rarer virtues—and without too nice repulsion of evil contaminations." To some observers, papers such as the *Herald* relied on sensationalistic reports of murder and mayhem to boost circulation. To others the rise of the penny papers and so-called mammoth weeklies—huge, folio-sized papers that relied on reprinting foreign authors—ushered in an age of cheap literature. The editor of the *New York Review,* Francis L. Hawks, may have had such fare in mind when he derided the "miserable literary trash which surrounds us." The most notorious of the penny papers was the *New York Sun,* edited by Richard Adams Locke (1800–1871). The *Sun* published sensational and fictitious stories in the guise of fact, and Locke's "Moon-Hoax," which appeared in the August 1835 issue, with its narrative of strange creatures and winged bipeds on the lunar surface, was one of the newspaper sensations of the 1830s. Sensing that Locke had ushered in a new and different age in commercial journalism, Poe commented in "The Literati of New York City" (1846): "the object of the journal professed to be that of 'supplying the public with the news of the day at so cheap a rate as to lie within the means of all.' The consequences of the scheme, in their influence on the whole newspaper business of the country, and through this business on the interests of the country at large, are probably beyond all calculation." Many consumers of the new forms of journalism came from the new immigrant population.

This era of professional metropolitan journalism also ushered in the commercialization of print. In an age of increased sensationalism in journalism, editors might exploit colorful topics or appeal to the reader's sense of excitement or novelty by covering trials and murders, discoveries at sea or on the frontier, and developments in the sciences (or pseudosciences). Works of fiction imitated some of the techniques of journalism, and new forms of dissemination included the cheap magazine, the pamphlet, or the pirated novel. In a marketplace in which the written word was seen less as a vehicle of self-expression and more as a commodity, the life of writing seemed uncertain and capricious. If writing were indeed a business, publication was subject to the same economic vagaries that influenced other sectors. The business of publishing was hardly immune from economic uncertainty, and during the depression of the late 1830s, several literary ventures were either curtailed or delayed. Working for periodicals might entail low pay, editorial drudgery, and bitter literary warfare. Periodicals nevertheless represented potential sources of recognition, encouragement, and income to budding writers as they aspired for professional status in a sometimes antagonistic literary marketplace. Some writers felt that periodicals could have a civilizing influence. As a contributor to the *Monthly Anthology* noted in 1805, "periodical publications more than any other, contribute toward the forming of the manners of a people. . . . The papers of Addison, as Dr. Johnson informs us, added not a little to the civility of England."

The *Knickerbocker; or New York Monthly Magazine,* which increasingly espoused urban, cosmopolitan, and traditional values, was influenced by this supposedly gentlemanly tradition of journalism. During the early nineteenth century, magazines functioned as mouthpieces for the opinions of their editors, and once Lewis Gaylord Clark (1808–1873) assumed sole editorial control of the *Knickerbocker* in 1834 (the periodical had been briefly called the *Knickerbacker*), he dominated its contents and tone. Like many of Irving's works, which provided the magazine with its title, the *Knickerbocker* constituted a kind of literary miscellany. A typical issue might include fiction, sketches, travel writing, verse, humor, and reviews. Each issue was usually topped off with a serving from Clark's "Editor's Table," a feature with which readers came to identify. This column included literary gossip and topical humor, though the opinionated Clark could occasionally deviate from his usually convivial tone by serving barbs and insults from his table. Criticism was often reserved for New England writers, particularly the Transcendentalists, whose writings incorporated vague theories or literary fashions imported from Germany. Another target of Clark was Poe, and one can learn much about the journalistic wars of the 1840s by scanning the pages of the *Knickerbocker* from that decade.

Any writing that smacked of foreign corruption was explicitly scorned—the works of Edward Bulwer-Lytton seemed to Clark to have a decadent tone—and the *Knickerbocker* sounded a generally patriotic tone in its early years. One of its paradoxical features, however, was that despite these early nationalistic appeals, the magazine became increasingly supportive and attentive to British writers. *Knickerbocker* writers were conversant with the British essay tradition practiced by Joseph Addison and Richard Steele in the *Spectator* and keenly sensitive to the appeal of urban life. They revered Charles Dickens, and they enthused over later British essayists: Robert Southey, William Hazlitt, Leigh Hunt,

and Thomas De Quincey. If for clarity and transparency of style the model was Addison, for tone—genial, gently playful, and compassionate—the model was Charles Lamb, celebrated by editor Clark as well as by other *Knickerbocker* contributors. In an essay "On Wit and Humor" for the magazine, one of Lamb's keenest disciples, Frederick S. Cozzens, distinguished the intellectual appeal and pungency of wit from the warmth and pathos evoked by the humorist. Cozzens, whose works appeared in the *Knickerbocker* throughout Clark's term as editor, adapted these principles in his own *Sparrowgrass Papers* (1856), a collection of sketches of city dwellers who embark on a sojourn to the country on the banks of the Hudson. Like Frederick W. Shelton's *Up the River* (1853), Cozzens's sketches supposedly offered the attractions of a life close to nature, but their appeal was to the urban (and perhaps suburban) values of the growing readership of the *Knickerbocker,* New Yorkers or suburbanites who might tour or vacation outside the city. Duyckinck in 1853 may have summed up the appeal of this new form of sketch writing when he said of Cozzens's work: "There is a peculiar style of book, genial, humorous, and warm-hearted, which a race of New Yorkers seems sent into the world specially to keep up."

In *Dangerous Pilgrimages: Transatlantic Mythologies and the Novel* (1996) Malcolm Bradbury attempts to revitalize Irving's image as "the originator of the transatlantic dimension to American letters." Irving, to be sure, became the first American author to be hailed in England. *The Sketch Book* did much to transform foreign attitudes to American writing, and his later works popularized an image of the United States abroad. For the other side of this transatlantic dialogue, however, one might consult the pages of the *Knickerbocker* to trace a line of influence from Lamb and the British essayists to Irving and his subsequent American imitators. Clark's editorial hand reinforced this lineage in nonfiction prose by welcoming so many British authors. Though his own creative works were sparse, he did publish an early tale that contrasts rural and urban values by portraying New York as the "London of America." Through his editorial choices at the *Knickerbocker,* particularly by his championing of an Anglo-American tradition, he did much to transform New York into a cosmopolitan cultural center with London as a model.

The perceived gentility of the South appealed to many Northern readers, since the region represented, in Paul Zweig's words in *Walt Whitman: The Making of the Poet* (1984), "an escape from the arduousness of change, too much busy self-reliance." Some wealthy New Yorkers even looked to the South as a region of polite manners, suggestive of a displaced English tone. (During the Civil War, New York acquired the label of a "Copperhead city," sympathetic to the Southern cause.) Despite growing tensions between North and South, Southern romances of the 1830s won the approval of influential editors such as Clark who liked the wholesome message of national pride they inculcated. Of John Pendleton Kennedy's *Rob of the Bowl* (1838), Clark commented: "we rise with a stronger detestation of vice, and a new love of virtue; which make us love our country and our fellow creatures better."

Clark was even more enthusiastic about William Gilmore Simms's *The Yemassee* (1835): "a successful effort to embody the genuine materials of American Romance—such, indeed, as may not well be furnished by the histories of any other country." This tentative and temporary alliance between Northern editor and Southern romancer is not that surprising, given Simms's close relations with many Northern authors. Though he maintained a plantation on the banks of the Edisto River in South Carolina, he frequented New York in the summers (when he was not in New Haven), and he was an admirer of both Cooper, a pioneer in the use of historical materials, and Bryant, who influenced Simms's own verse. He styled himself a Southern ambassador in the North, and his alliance with some Northern editors became stronger when his *Knickerbocker* friends joined him in his opposition to the perceived preeminence of New England authors. Tensions erupted when Rufus W. Griswold and other influential editors omitted all Southern writers from landmark anthologies such as *The Prose Writers of America* (1847). Simms and Clark eventually had a complete falling-out over the issue of literary nationalism, but the former's *Views and Reviews in American Literature, History and Fiction* (1845) offers essential documents in the debate, particularly over various writers' defenses of the use of native materials.

In early issues of the *Knickerbocker* Clark had supported an international copyright law, but he was a moderate on nationalistic issues compared to figures in the "Young America" group, whose most radical spokesman was Cornelius Mathews. Mathews used the pages of the short-lived *Arcturus* to set forth his fervent opinions on copyright laws and the cause of literary nationalism. The journal included serial publication of Mathews's *The Career of Puffer Hopkins* (1842), which aimed to establish New York City as a legitimate setting for works of native genius. Though Mathews and his co-editor, Duyckinck, attracted New England authors like Longfellow, James Russell Lowell, and Hawthorne as contributors, they wanted to make the vigorous cultural life of New York their focus. Rather than the Whig values of polish and refinement, Mathews felt that spontaneity and natural energy were uniquely American traits, which should be hallmarks of the national lit-

erature. These beliefs were heresy to the conservative Clark and his supporters, and Mathews and "Young America" were ridiculed in the *Knickerbocker*. Clark, after all, had spent his editorial career praising the career of Irving, whose works represented continuity between Europe and the United States rather than a distinctive native culture that scorned its Old World roots.

After the failure of *Arcturus* in 1842, Duyckinck enlisted Simms, the young Southerner who by that time had fallen out with Clark. Simms had argued for the compatibility of nationalism and sectionalism and thus drew the ire of Northern editors, who downplayed Southern letters and favored British authors to the exclusion of some regional American materials. Appealing to Duyckinck, Simms wrote, "All your affinities in New York are with the South rather than New England." In an 1845 editorial he recognized the increasing dominance of New York, "the great central city, drawing into her capacious bosom the literary minds of future generations of this country, as certainly as she draws trade and capital." Toward New York "tend writers from all quarters of the country, east and west, north and south." When he edited the *Southern and Western Monthly Magazine and Review* in Charleston in 1845, he hoped to forge an alliance with New York editors in opposition to Boston publishers that favored the literary heritage of New England. In addition to an intensifying dislike for Clark that eventually approached detestation, Simms and Duyckinck shared a common allegiance to the Democratic Party. During a stint as literary editor of the *New York Morning News,* Duyckinck welcomed Simms's attacks that were designed to "disturb even the thrice-drugged conservative North American."

Duyckinck eventually became an unofficial contributor to the *Democratic Review,* edited by John O'Sullivan. Perhaps more than Duyckinck, whose radical impulses may have been tempered by his family's old Dutch roots, his high church Episcopalianism, and his reverence for British authors, O'Sullivan possessed a firm commitment to a democratic culture for the masses. The better-educated classes, O'Sullivan felt, absorbed antidemocratic sentiments because of their obeisance to English culture. In addition to an unwavering espousal of limited government, the *Democratic Review* focused much attention on literary topics and was unwavering in its opposition to the domination by British writers. The best known of O'Sullivan's contributors was Hawthorne, whose *Mosses from an Old Manse* (1846) originally appeared in the *Democratic Review,* and works by Bryant, Anne Lynch, Simms, and the young Whitman also appeared in its pages.

Duyckinck continued to promote his brand of literary nationalism in the *Literary World,* which printed

Melville's "Hawthorne and His Mosses" in 1850, although that periodical moderated its stance on the issue after its first year. When Duyckinck began the *Literary World* in 1847, he was editing two series of books for Wiley and Putnam and maintained close ties with the major authors of the period. When Griswold's *The Prose Writers of America,* an anthology that included Irving, Cooper, Simms, and Mathews, appeared in 1847, the editor included a preface in which he offered a reformulation of the principles of literary nationalism. A work could promote the cause of nationalism by being American in spirit, not necessarily in subject matter. An excess of patriotic zeal, he implied, might be a hindrance to artistic expression. One need not resort to a specific kind of vocabulary or particular subject (in other words, a regional dialect or the American landscape) to promote the cause of American letters. Griswold included in his anthology many popular *Knickerbocker* writers, and he scorned two of the favorites of Young America, Mathews and Simms. Duyckinck responded defensively, but as Miller has noted, *The Prose Writers of America* may have blunted the program and extreme rhetoric of Young America by articulating a conservative brand of literary nationalism, more palatable to the popular taste.

As an anthologist and editor, Griswold was a fairly accurate barometer of popular literary values, and in his role as cultural arbiter he did not limit himself to the genre of prose fiction. Even before *The Prose Writers of America* he had produced a similar collection, *The Poets and Poetry of America* (1842), among other gift books and miscellanies. Few critics today would include Bryant and Fitz-Greene Halleck in a list of foremost American poets, but in the 1840s they were widely listed among "The Copperplate Five," their likenesses reproduced along with those of Longfellow, Dana, and the now-forgotten Charles Sprague on the frontispiece of Griswold's volume. Although his brand of Americanism won the praise of Clark, Griswold's safe editorial choices did not sit well with the adherents of the Young America group, either North or South, nor did they win the approval of those excluded from or slighted in his collections. Poe attacked Griswold on the lecture platform in 1843 and 1844, contributing further to what was already a tense relationship. Their conflicts developed into total rupture as the decade ended and resulted in Griswold's calumnies against Poe's reputation after his death in 1849.

Personal animus prevented Griswold from acknowledging Poe's talents, nor could Duyckinck fully grasp the extent of Melville's genius. As influential editors, both men were in the position to mold literary reputations, but they fell short of taking the measure of two writers now considered central to the American

Renaissance. The term "American Renaissance" was coined by F. O. Matthiessen as the title for his landmark 1941 book, long regarded as the classic description of an unprecedented outburst of imaginative and creative expression in the 1840s and 1850s. Matthiessen correlated American literature with European and classical models. Putting his case for native authors straightforwardly, he noted how so many masterworks of American literature were produced in a condensed time span of the antebellum period. In the 1850s alone Emerson's *Representative Men* (1850) and *English Traits* (1856) appeared, along with Henry David Thoreau's *Walden* (1854) and Hawthorne's major romances, *The Scarlet Letter* (1850), *The Blithedale Romance* (1851), and *The House of the Seven Gables* (1852). In addition to these works by New England authors, Melville's *Moby-Dick* (1851), his *Piazza Tales* (1856), and Whitman's first edition of *Leaves of Grass* (1855) also appeared. Matthiessen used the term "renaissance" rather loosely, but the term invoked the great writers of the English Renaissance, thus imposing greater respectability on the study of American literature. If Griswold and his fellow editors had striven to establish standards of taste for their own period, with Matthiessen's book a new canon of major writings in American literature had been formed.

Though *American Renaissance: Art and Expression in the Age of Emerson and Whitman* had a significant influence on the academic study of American literature in the 1950s and 1960s, scholars, especially in the last decades of the twentieth century, have debated Matthiessen's criteria for inclusion, his nearly exclusive focus on five major authors, and those writers excluded from his overall discussion. Notable by his absence from *American Renaissance* was Poe, who represented to Matthiessen the tragic consequences of isolation, a contrast to those writers who consciously or unconsciously confronted a larger social world. If Whitman's poetry represented an engagement with the ordinary experiences of the common man, Poe's works, according to Matthiessen, suggested an escape from such concerns, a retreat into a realm out of space and out of time. Poe's oeuvre suggested the trappings of an abnormal Romantic temperament, a horror and anxiety generated by a tortured sensibility.

If Matthiessen's treatment of Poe approached caricature, he was fully aware of his own principles of exclusion, as noted in the preface to *American Renaissance.* He acknowledged that his volume could have been titled "The Age of Swedenborg," testimony to a figure whose mystical philosophy inspired Emerson and his circle. The Transcendentalists, of course, were influenced by the spirit of reform that gave rise to a host of social experiments and utopian schemes, several of which were centered in New England communities but which also influenced writers and thinkers in New York. Many American works, including Harriet Beecher Stowe's *Uncle Tom's Cabin* (1852), were directly affected by radical social theories that sparked social upheaval in Europe, particularly the revolutions of 1848. Matthiessen invoked a moderate spirit of democracy consonant with his perceived political ideals of the United States. Of the writers covered in *American Renaissance* perhaps only Whitman embraced radical social change.

Though subsequent scholars of the American Renaissance have critiqued the limits of Matthiessen's treatment, they inevitably use his book as a starting point for their explorations. If he imposed on American literature lines of influence from classical and romantic writing, from Homer to Samuel Taylor Coleridge, subsequent scholars have broadened his perspective on antebellum writing by including humorous and popular authors—for example, temperance advocate T. S. Arthur, Southerners Joseph Glover Baldwin and George Washington Harris, and best-selling novelist Susan Warner. (Matthiessen, noting that his book would stress serious treatments of the common man, acknowledged that the five best-sellers of the antebellum period would not be discussed in *American Renaissance*.) Of the scholars who have explored "another American Renaissance," one that gives just dues to women writers and popular authors, perhaps David Reynolds's *Beneath the American Renaissance* (1988) offers the fullest complement to Matthiessen in its investigation of formulae rooted in the antebellum cultural context.

Another feature of *American Renaissance* is its focus on three New England authors and two New York authors to the nearly total exclusion of Southern literature. The South, to be sure, was less cosmopolitan and more inner-directed during the antebellum period than the North—the region of manufacturing and commerce. If Northern writers faced challenges in gaining a foothold for literary ventures, there were even more severe constraints on those who pursued publishing projects in the South. If Southerners, particularly Virginians, had played a pivotal role in the founding of the new nation, the antebellum period marked a withdrawal to defend regional institutions. As Van Wyck Brooks noted in "South of the Potomac" in *The World of Washington Irving* (1944), the South "was committed to a patriarchal mode of life and a primitive system of industry and labor system where progress was the watchword everywhere else, while its economic mainstay, slavery, an obsolete institution, was opposed to the conscience and professions of the American people." The Nat Turner insurrection of 1831 and growing Northern opposition to slavery hardened the will of many Southerners to defend their institutions.

From an economic perspective Virginia and much of the South retained many of the features of a colonial society until well after the American Revolution and perhaps until after the Civil War. The South, in large measure, retained agriculture as the basis of its economy. (If consumer goods were needed, they were procured elsewhere—either from abroad or from Northern manufacturers.) The South, moreover, lacked urban centers that possessed the commercial status or the cultural amenities to be found in either New York or Boston. If the printing industry did develop—as it did in Richmond, for example—its purpose was to assist in the city's modest commercial development. In addition to ephemeral imprints—newspapers heavy with advertising, handbills, broadsides, and the like—religious and political tracts that responded to local needs constituted the common fare of Southern publishing. Wider distribution of periodicals in an expanding postal system, particularly an increasing number of Northern periodicals with political views inimical to the plantation system of the South, put Southern writers and editors on the defensive or at great disadvantage. The *Southern Literary Messenger* of Richmond has justifiably been called the first substantial literary periodical to succeed in the South, but whatever success it achieved must be gauged against the dozens of failures in periodical ventures in the region. Following the *Messenger,* Southern periodicals such as the *Southern Quarterly Review* promoted causes such as states' rights and slavery and thus consciously stressed opposition to Northern values. When Simms became its editor in 1849, defenses of slavery became more frequent and intense. Later magazines—the *Southern Review* (which helped to give Charleston literary prominence) and *De Bow's Review*—also served to counter Northern propaganda. To the extent that literary content surfaced in these periodicals, it served to complement the political message of the editors.

A cavalier strain seemed to have been kept alive in Maryland, where a spirit of amusement and merrymaking pervaded some of the clubs and private organizations. Unlike the more-sober debating clubs and library societies of the North, songs of the cavalier poets, for example, might be heard in the Delphian Club of Baltimore, which served as a model for a projected volume of satires by Poe, "Tales of the Folio Club." At the Delphian or at the Thespian Club, where Poe's father had gathered with his traveling theatrical companions, those in attendance met for personal enjoyment as well as for supposed public edification. Members gathered in a spirit of conviviality, consumed ample food and drink, and exchanged ideas on literary topics and cultural fashions. Lectures, perhaps more specialized and occasionally more jocular than those sponsored by local lyceums or library societies, were delivered on topics that derived from the interests of club members. Via his Baltimore connections Poe got to know the verses of Philip Pendleton Cooke and Edward Coote Pinkney, the latter quoted at length in "The Poetic Principle" (1848).

Kennedy was a more significant Baltimore author who also gave Poe encouragement. Though active in the public life of Baltimore as a lawyer and promoter of its culture, he maintained ties, via his family connections, with plantations in Virginia. (He was related to the Cookes, Philip Pendleton, the poet, and John Esten, the romancer.) If Irving had evoked the mythic past of the region near the Hudson River, Kennedy established a similar spirit of nostalgia for the post-Revolutionary world of the Old Dominion, in this case, near the James River. Indeed, a clear model for Kennedy's *Swallow Barn* (1832) was Irving's *Bracebridge Hall* (1822). Really a loosely connected series of sketches colored by Kennedy's love for the picturesque, *Swallow Barn* celebrates plantation life through the career of his central character, Frank Meriwether, a country squire. The book includes vaguely chivalric episodes of romance, hunting, and horsemanship, but Meriwether is more of a down-to-earth planter-gentleman rather than a larger-than-life hero. The atmosphere of the book is relaxed and sunny, though at its conclusion Kennedy includes a defense of slavery, which the author sees as beneficial to both races and crucial to the survival of a cherished way of life. Perhaps unwittingly, Kennedy's book marked a divergence with the North, for he included in his leisurely tour of the South an argument that was countered in later years by *Uncle Tom's Cabin* and other works.

*Swallow Barn* established a formula for subsequent literary treatments of the Southern plantation, but Kennedy turned to the genre of historical romance in *Horse-Shoe Robinson* (1835) and *Rob of the Bowl*. The conventions of the historical novel in the United States had been formed with the publication of Cooper's *The Spy* in 1821. If Cooper offered a home-grown model for historical fiction, Kennedy absorbed the romances of Scott. As heroic events of the past were celebrated, the historical novel became a vehicle for furthering the cause of literary nationalism. The public clearly had an appetite for books based on actual circumstances, and no event could outshine the Revolution in importance, especially in the years before and after the semicentennial of the new nation in 1826. For *Horse-Shoe Robinson* Kennedy chose a setting in the Carolinas and Virginia, based on a journey he had made in 1819.

*Swallow Barn* was a series of sketches joined together by the "hooks and eyes of a traveller's notes," as Kennedy noted in a preface to an 1853 edition of the novel, and *Horse-Shoe Robinson* was based on his actual travels. Both books may have capitalized on the growing interest in Southern topics and ways of life, part of a vogue of travel literature. The New Yorker Paulding published *Letters from the South* (1817), and popular novelist Joseph Holt Ingraham offered *The South-West, by a Yankee* (1835). Such fare won ready acceptance with Northern audiences. Of the writers whose careers intersected both the North and the South, no figure wore so many different hats as Simms, whose voluminous works are diverse in genre—he wrote poems, plays, histories, biographies—and in setting, his romances dealing with American as well as European scenery and manners. After submitting verses with a neoclassical flavor to journals when he was a teenager, he produced two volumes of poetry, a genre for which he manifested affection throughout his lengthy career. He tried his hand at Gothic fiction, and he wrote sketches in imitation of Irving. Some of his stories in *The Wigwam and the Cabin* (1845) anticipate the techniques of realism, and Poe thought his "Grayling, or Murder Will Out" (1841) a superior ghost story. Simms's career hit its stride, however, when he took as his subject matter his native South. He had lived in Charleston, absorbed much of its rich history, and had long been a student of his region's past. On his travels he had also been exposed to another aspect of Southern experience—life on the frontier. Inspired by the examples of Scott and Cooper, he wrote a series of "border romances" dealing with historical materials. The first was *Guy Rivers* (1834), soon to be followed by *The Yemassee*, his most widely read work of fiction. In his preface he insisted his work was a romance rather than a novel, and thus shied away from domestic scenes in favor of a wilder setting. In comparing the romance to the epic in his preface, moreover, Simms perhaps sensed that he was adopting the role of mythmaker for his region, much as Irving had done for his beloved New York. In the same year that he published *The Yemassee*, he also published *The Partisan*, the first of his series that cover the vast historical sweep of the Revolution in his beloved South Carolina. A. B. Longstreet's *Georgia Scenes*, recognized as the first significant collection of Southern humor, also appeared in 1835, and the second series of "Georgia Scenes" was published in Simms's *Magnolia* (1842–1843).

Perhaps because the economic and social systems of the South and the North were so different, there has been a tendency to study the literary histories of each region separately. Many nineteenth-century anthologies tended to exclude Southern authors, and during the antebellum period, perhaps only the Duyckincks' *Cyclopaedia of American Literature* (1855) gave any generous recognition to Southern writers. As has already been noted, Matthiessen excluded Southern authors from *American Renaissance*. The suggestions for further reading at the end of this volume should invite further investigation of antebellum authors in regional and national contexts.

*DLB 248* and its companion volume, *DLB 250: Antebellum Writers in New York,* complement *DLB 3: Antebellum Writers in New York and the South* (1978), edited by Joel Myerson. *DLB 3* provided the initial logistical direction, reflected in Myerson's vast editorial and bibliographical experience, for *DLB 248.* The editor is grateful to those contributors from *DLB 3* who agreed to expand, revise, or update their entries for this volume: Bert Hitchcock, James E. Kibler Jr., Jennings R. Mace, Rayburn S. Moore, Donald R. Noble Jr., Miriam Shillingsburg, G. Richard Thompson, Robert W. Weathersby II, and Clyde N. Wilson.

Many colleagues from universities across the United States recommended contributors, and the editor owes special thanks to Ralph M. Aderman, Benjamin F. Fisher, Richard Fusco, Kevin J. Hayes, Etta Madden, Katharine McKee, Joel Myerson, Frank Shuffelton, Jack Wills, Clyde N. Wilson, and S. J. Wolfe.

The completion of this project would not have been possible without the cooperation and collaboration of Wesley T. Mott of Worcester Polytechnic Institute. Throughout the initial phases of planning the table of contents and assigning entries for his own *DLB* volumes on the American Renaissance in New England, Professor Mott shared useful information and helpful suggestions. He also read draft material, and his criticisms helped the editor to construct a stronger introduction for this volume. His generous assistance, along with the gracious help provided by Penny Rock, Margaret Brodmerkle, and Joseph Kaupu at WPI, proved invaluable.

The editor also benefited from attending the International Edgar Allan Poe Conference, held in Richmond, Virginia, in October 1999. Individual papers and sessions on Southern publishing, particularly a session organized by David Rawson, provided background information and insights that were useful in preparing the introduction to the volume. In his role as an editor Poe once contemplated a work, an essential feature of which would be a series of biographical and critical articles on American writers. He envisioned sketches that constituted portraits of "every person of literary note in America," crafted with sensitivity to the individual merits of these authors and written with "rigorous impartiality." Although *DLB 248* does not include entries on every notable author of the antebellum South, the editor is confident that the essential literary values implicit in

Poe's lofty plan are reflected in the biographical profiles prepared by his contributors. He hopes as well that their diligence, care, and, above all, their patience will be rewarded in the publication of this volume.

*–Kent P. Ljungquist*

## Acknowledgments

This book was produced by Bruccoli Clark Layman, Inc. Karen L. Rood is senior editor. Charles Brower was the in-house editor.

Production manager is Philip B. Dematteis.

Administrative support was provided by Ann M. Cheschi, Amber L. Coker, and Angi Pleasant.

Accountant is Ann-Marie Holland.

Copyediting supervisor is Sally R. Evans. The copyediting staff includes Phyllis A. Avant, Brenda Carol Blanton, Worthy B. Evans, Melissa D. Hinton, William Tobias Mathes, Rebecca Mayo, Nancy E. Smith, and Elizabeth Jo Ann Sumner. Freelance copyeditor is James F. Denton Jr.

Editorial associates are Jennifer Reid and Michael S. Martin.

Database manager is José A. Juarez.

Layout and graphics supervisor is Janet E. Hill. The graphics staff includes Karla Corley Brown and Zoe R. Cook.

Office manager is Kathy Lawler Merlette.

Photography supervisor is Paul Talbot. Photography editor is Scott Nemzek.

Digital photographic copy work was performed by Joseph M. Bruccoli.

The SGML staff includes Frank Graham, Linda Dalton Mullinax, Jason Paddock, and Alex Snead.

Systems manager is Marie L. Parker.

Typesetting supervisor is Kathleen M. Flanagan. The typesetting staff includes Jaime All, Patricia Marie Flanagan, Mark J. McEwan, and Pamela D. Norton. Freelance typesetter is Wanda Adams.

Walter W. Ross did library research. He was assisted by Jaime All and the following librarians at the Thomas Cooper Library of the University of South Carolina: circulation department head Tucker Taylor; reference department head Virginia W. Weathers; Brette Barclay, Marilee Birchfield, Paul Cammarata, Gary Geer, Michael Macan, Tom Marcil, Rose Marshall, and Sharon Verba; interlibrary loan department head John Brunswick; and interlibrary loan staff Robert Arndt, Hayden Battle, Barry Bull, Jo Cottingham, Marna Hostetler, Marieum McClary, Erika Peake, and Nelson Rivera.

# Antebellum Writers in the South

Second Series

# Dictionary of Literary Biography

# John James Audubon
*(26 April 1785 – 27 January 1851)*

Arthur Wrobel
*University of Kentucky*

BOOKS: *The Birds of America, from Original Drawings,* 4 volumes (London: Published by the Author, 1827–1838); reprinted, 7 volumes (New York: J. J. Audubon / Philadelphia: Chevalier, 1840–1844); *The Birds of America,* 7 volumes (New York: V. G. Audubon, 1859);

*Ornithological Biography, or, An Account of the Habits of the Birds of the United States of America: Accompanied by Descriptions of the Objects Represented in the Work Entitled The Birds of America, and Interspersed with Delineations of American Scenery and Manners,* 5 volumes (Philadelphia: Dobson, 1831–1839; Edinburgh: Black, 1831–1839);

*The Viviparous Quadrupeds of North America,* by Audubon and John Bachman, 5 volumes (New York: J. J. Audubon, 1845–1854); republished as *The Quadrupeds of North America,* 3 volumes (New York: V. G. Audubon, 1849–1854);

*Audubon and His Journals,* edited by Maria Audubon, 2 volumes (New York: Scribners, 1897; London: Nimmo, 1898);

*Audubon's Western Journal 1849–1850* (Cleveland: Arthur H. Clark, 1906);

*Delineations of American Scenery and Character,* edited by Francis Hobart Herrick (New York: Baker, 1926; London: Simpkin, Marshall, Hamilton, Kent, 1926);

*Journal of John James Audubon Made During His Trip to New Orleans in 1820–1821,* edited by Howard Corning (Boston: Club of Odd Volumes, 1929);

*Journal of John James Audubon Made While Obtaining Subscriptions to His "Birds of America," 1840–1843,* edited by Corning (Boston: Club of Odd Volumes, 1929);

*The 1826 Journal of John James Audubon,* transcribed, with an introduction and notes, by Alice Ford (Norman: University of Oklahoma Press, 1967).

**Editions and Collections:** *The Birds of America,* introduction by William Vogt (New York: Macmillan, 1937);

*John James Audubon: Selected Journals and Other Writings,* edited, with an introduction, by Ben Forkner (New York: Penguin, 1996).

John James Audubon's reputation rests almost exclusively on his achievement as the artist of the monumental *The Birds of America, from Original Drawings* (1827–1838); his sharply detailed, anatomically accurate, and dramatically conceived representations of North American birds won him unqualified admiration and revolutionized all subsequent ornithological art. More recently, however, students of American life and letters are discovering the journals Audubon kept during trips on the Mississippi and Missouri Rivers and, more notably, the "Episodes" or "Delineations." Interspersed with the "bird biographies" in his *Ornithological Biography, or, An Account of the Habits of the Birds of the United States of America* (1831–1839), the "Episodes" offer a firsthand, sometimes fanciful, account of the cultural life and times of the American borderland in the early nineteenth century. A mix of scientific information and personal anecdotes, they include data about the climate, flora, and fauna of different locales as well as descriptions of frontier fetes, Indian hunting parties, lumbermen, and runaway slaves. These writings are increasingly anthologized for their vivid depictions and their enhancement of national themes and myths.

The facts about Audubon's birth, despite his penchant for self-mythologizing, are well established. Born on 26 April 1785 at Les Cayes, San Domingo, he was the illegitimate son of Jean Audubon—a planter, merchant, slave dealer, and naval officer—and Jeanne Rabin, a companion to the family of a retired lawyer. The church records for his baptism on 23 October 1800 give Audubon's name as Jean-Jacques Fourgère Audubon. His father sent Jean and a younger half sister, Rose, to his wife in Nantes in 1788. The couple formally adopted the two illegitimate children in 1794.

Audubon's education was typically bourgeois—a smattering of mathematics, geography, music, and fencing—though the young boy's real interests lay in observing nature and collecting birds' nests and eggs and various curiosities with which to stock his private museum. Audubon's impulse toward collecting was formed under the influence of George-Louis Leclerc de Buffon's monumental *Histoire Naturelle, générale et particulière* (1749–1789), a well-received work despite its stilted wildlife illustrations.

In the fall of 1803, fearing for his son's safety from press gangs seeking soldiers for Napoleon's armies, his father sent Audubon to the New World, his passport showing an anglicized name—John James Audubon—and the Louisiana Territory as his place of birth. He learned English and a trade and became familiar with the operation of Mill Grove, a two-hundred-acre farm near Philadelphia that his father had purchased in 1789. He nevertheless found time to draw the birds and animals he avidly hunted. These formative years coincided with the Enlightenment interest in nature as witnessed by a widespread popularity of Jean-Jacques Rousseau's *Reveries du promeneur solitaire* (1782) and, more immediately, Buffon's *Histoire Naturelle,* in which the birds have an anthropomorphic quality similarly present in some of Audubon's own later renderings.

In the autumn of 1804 Audubon fell in love with Lucy Bakewell, the daughter of an English neighbor. She endured Audubon's restlessness and single-minded pursuit, though her faith was often tested by his artistic endeavors. Notwithstanding Lucy's father's doubts about the young suitor's ability to provide for her security, the two married in April 1807 and set out for Louisville, Kentucky, where Audubon, in partnership with Ferdinand Rozier, opened a mercantile business.

Initially, the couple flourished. Their two sons, Victor Gifford and John Woodhouse, were born in 1809 and 1812, respectively, while their move to Henderson, Kentucky, in 1810 augured a life of middle-class respectability. Affable and handsome, close to six feet tall with hazel eyes and chestnut brown hair worn shoulder length, Audubon established himself as an accomplished swordsman and dancer and an expert huntsman; he also played the flute and violin at parties. Differences in temperament, however, led to the dissolution of the partnership with Rozier in April 1811; Rozier's discipline and focus on business conflicted with Audubon's passion for natural history. In later years Audubon confessed in an autobiographical sketch entitled "Myself" that studying, hunting, and drawing birds provided welcome relief from the irksome responsibilities of business: "birds were birds then as now, and my thoughts were ever and anon turning toward them as the objects of my greatest delight. In short . . . I seldom passed a day without drawing a bird, or noting something respecting its habit" (*Scribner's,* March 1893). Between 1816 and 1820 Audubon's business fortunes steadily eroded, finally collapsing under the blows of two disasters: the building of an ill-conceived saw-and-grist mill and a failed investment in a steamboat.

The pivotal event that nudged Audubon toward his eventual life's work occurred in March 1810, when a Scotsman, Alexander Wilson, carrying two volumes of his projected ten-volume set, *American Ornithology, or The Natural History of the Birds of the United States* (1808–1814), appeared at Audubon and Rozier's store selling subscriptions. Compared to Audubon's eventual achievement, Wilson's birds are stiff and unnatural, lacking in character and richness, while his accompanying text lacks the intimacy of what became *Ornithological Biography*. This encounter provided Audubon with several suggestions: his need to study birds scientifically and methodically, to judge his sketches more severely, and to learn the scientific nomenclature necessary to classify birds by genus and species. Wilson's volumes influenced him in two other significant ways, in that they present the birds in their natural habitat and offer accompanying text about the subject of each panel.

From the summer of 1819 to the following autumn, Audubon desperately attempted to support his family. Faced with limited prospects, he resolved to act on his dreams; on 12 October 1820 he signed on a flatboat as the crew's hunter and set out for New Orleans to build his bird portfolio. The trip provided the materials for his *Mississippi River Journal,* an amalgam published in *Journal of John James Audubon Made During His Trip to New Orleans in 1820–1821* (1929) that, despite its many personal materials, nevertheless provides an important record of frontier America. Together with philosophical ruminations, concerns about the well-being of his family, tallies of his daily bag, and descriptions of flatboat travel, the journal also includes notes on the people he met, botanical and ornithological data, and descriptions of the flatboat crew, frontier settlements, and plantations near Natchez and New Orleans. It offers glimpses of New Orleans and its markets, Latin Quarter, and social life. Disorderly and replete with misspellings, twisted syntax, whimsical capitalizations, and thoroughly ungrammatical constructions, it also captures Audubon's energy and his commitment to the project.

From late in 1821, when Lucy joined him in Louisiana, to the late spring of 1826, when he set out for Europe, Audubon systematically trained himself as a naturalist, scientist, and artist. His stay in the lower Mississippi valley was especially rewarding; the portfolio he assembled eventually accounted for one-quarter of the sketches in *The Birds of America.*

Through the end of 1824 Audubon mounted exhibits of his drawings and delivered lectures before learned societies in major cities. These exhibits failed to attract either patrons or an engraver skilled enough to undertake his massive project, but the praise from knowledgeable men the drawings garnered gave him the self-esteem necessary for him to take the next step–travel to Europe to engage an engraver and enlist subscribers.

Armed with letters of introduction to the mercantile families of Liverpool, he set sail for the city on 27 May 1826. Remaking himself into the romantic figure of an American woodsman with long hair and loose clothing, Audubon readily won over the intellectual and cultural elite of the city: an exhibition of 225 of his

UNDER THE SPECIAL PATRONAGE
OF

Her Most Excellent Majesty,
QUEEN ADELAIDE,

THE

**BIRDS OF AMERICA,**

ENGRAVED FROM

**DRAWINGS**

MADE IN

**THE UNITED STATES AND THEIR TERRITORIES.**

BY JOHN JAMES AUDUBON,

F. R. Ss. L & E.

FELLOW OF THE LINNEAN AND ZOOLOGICAL SOCIETIES OF LONDON; MEMBER OF THE LYCEUM OF NEW YORK, THE NATURAL HISTORY SOCIETY OF PARIS, THE WERNE-RIAN NATURAL HISTORY SOCIETY OF EDINBURGH; HONORARY MEMBER OF THE SCOTTISH ACADEMY OF PAINTING, SCULPTURE AND ARCHITECTURE, &c.

**PUBLISHED BY THE AUTHOR;**

AND TO BE SEEN AT

MR R. HAVELL'S JUN. THE ENGRAVER,
77. OXFORD STREET, LONDON.

MDCCCXXXI.

*Title page for one of Audubon's prospectuses for his* The Birds of America *(1827–1838; from Francis Hobart Herrick,* Audubon the Naturalist, *1917)*

drawings at the Royal Institution drew overflow crowds, while audiences at social gatherings, who had relished James Fenimore Cooper's *The Prairie* (1827), induced him to imitate the calls of American birds, demonstrate Indian war whoops, and relate stories about America and the frontier. Such interest in the New World influenced his later decision to intersperse his bird biographies with "Episodes," sketches and anecdotes about his adventures on the frontier.

Audubon's reception in Liverpool marked the beginning of a three-year tour of England, Scotland, and France, during which he started a subscription book for *The Birds of America.* He held a showing at the Royal Society in Edinburgh in the fall of 1826, read papers before and was elected to various honorary societies, and contributed articles to Scottish scientific journals. More important, Audubon signed a contract with William Home Lizars, a prominent engraver, to prepare the plates for *The Birds of America.* Audubon's plan to produce life-size illustrations that would show his birds to their advantage required him to use double-elephant size paper (measuring 39.5 by 26.6 inches); with its massive scope—eventually numbering 435 plates representing 489 different species of American birds (plus an additional 35 composite plates) in five folio volumes—the project took eleven years to complete, ending in 1838.

After arriving in London in the spring of 1827, Audubon replaced Lizars, whose colorists were on strike, with a new engraver, Robert Havell. He worked on watercolors for Havell to engrave, supervised the work of engraving and colors, solicited and collected subscriptions, and produced oil paintings that he sold to maintain himself. Following three years in Europe, including a two-month stay in Paris in the fall of 1828, he returned to the United States in April 1829 to reunite with Lucy. He added at least two hundred drawings to his portfolio in the ensuing year.

After his return to London, this time with Lucy, in April 1830, Audubon enlisted new subscribers and painted more oils to cover living expenses and publication costs. By October, Audubon also started work on the ornithological biographies, which he intended to be a multivolume text giving scientific information about each of the bird illustrations. He decided to imprint these writings as distinctively his by interspersing technical, ornithological material with more-personal material, namely anecdotes, reminiscences, and tales he had accumulated during a lifetime of pursuing new bird species from Florida to the lagoons of the Texas coast. These "Episodes" or "Delineations of American Scenery and Manners," sixty in number, were to entertain and, more pragmatically, to enhance sales by tapping into the European fascination with the New World. The self-image he portrays in the "Delineations," that of the natural man responsive to instinct as he pursues a vision, appealed to the romantic imaginations of mid-nineteenth-century readers. Another cultivated self-image—that of the frontiersman, explorer, huntsman, self-taught artist, and naturalist—later appears in the fiction of both Robert Penn Warren's *Audubon: A Vision* and Eudora Welty's "A Still Moment" as the artist struggling to sustain his vision.

Based either on his experience or on hearsay, many of the "Episodes" are crafted to heighten their entertainment value or effect. They reflect kinship with the emerging short story, the travel sketch, and, particularly, the Southwest humor writings appearing in fashionable eastern periodicals at the time. Ostensibly firsthand accounts, these writings drew their inspiration from the manners, customs, and behavior of inhabitants of the frontier. Besides promoting the legendary status of such frontier heroes as Davy Crockett and Daniel Boone, this literature also provided important glimpses into frontier folk culture.

Evidence suggests that Audubon initiated a journal of his impressions of the countryside in 1807, as early as his Louisville days; though the early journals appear to be lost, a few of the events in "Delineations" date from this period. One unsettling episode, the ghastly slaughter of a flight of passenger pigeons in 1813 in Henderson, Kentucky, apparently provided Cooper with a similar description in *The Pioneers* (1823). Other "Delineations" include descriptions of Louisville itself, a Fourth of July celebration, a coon hunt, wolf baiting, an escape from a harrowing attempt on the author's life, his horse's terror during an earthquake, his encounter with a runaway slave, and the yellow sky preceding a hurricane and the sulphurous smell in the air afterward. Audubon even makes his own contribution to the Daniel Boone legend with his story "Colonel Boone" from *Ornithological Biography:* Boone spends the night in his cabin (though his physical description of the frontier hero does not limn with what is known of Boone), and in "Kentucky Sports" Boone's celebrated skills with the rifle are exaggerated. Elements of the tall tale are present in "Scipio and the Bear," which describes a hunter pitched six feet into the branches of an overhanging tree by a bear.

Reviews for the first volume of *Ornithological Biography* (1831) were complimentary, noting the welcome difference between the personal style of the text and customary naturalist writing. Audubon's critics, however, cast doubt on its authorship. One of them, Charles Waterton of *Loudon's Magazine,* drew his readers' attention to its "correct and elegant style of composition" and stoutly concluded that it "cannot possibly be that of him whose name it bears." Waterton's charge has a modicum of truth; aware of his shortcomings as a writer, Audubon had enlisted the aid of William MacGillivray, a Scottish naturalist and anatomist, who agreed, for a predetermined price, to copyedit his manuscript. Audubon acknowledged the Scot's contribution in the prefaces to the five volumes of the *Ornithological Biography,* however. MacGillivray's was a masterful job; though he smoothed out paragraphs, regularized capitalization, corrected spellings, and untangled syntax, he succeeded in retaining much of the energetic style and charm of Audubon's original writing.

Audubon was considerably less forthcoming about acknowledging those who painted the backgrounds and vegetation for the plates of *The Birds of America.* He took full credit for the project; however, in all fairness to Audubon, the names of apprentices or assistants for detail or background work, according to custom, were ordinarily omitted.

*Plate 357, the American magpie, in* The Birds of America *(Library, Field Museum of Natural History)*

By the summer of 1831 Audubon could congratulate himself: "I have balanced my accounts with the Birds of America and the whole business is really wonderful. . . ." Reactions to successive volumes of *The Birds of America* seemed to echo those of a French journalist who had first seen the Edinburgh exhibition. Declaring Audubon a: "man of genius," he urged his readers to "imagine a landscape wholly American" depicting "the feathered races of the New World, in the size of life. . . . this realization of an entire hemisphere, this picture of a nature so lusty and strong, is due to the brush of a single man; such an unheard of triumph of patience and genius!" Assessments of Audubon's drawings note the affinity of his depictions with such American artists as John Singleton Copley, Charles Wilson Peale, and Gilbert Stuart, whose works reflect the practice of eighteenth-century portraiture, while those that capture the dramatic or anecdotal moment approximate the works of William Sidney Mount and George Caleb Bingham.

On his return to America in August 1831, Audubon petitioned the government to provide him with financial assistance, a naval vessel, and supplies that would enable him to complete his work. The years from 1831 to 1834 were nourishing for him. On his way to Florida via Charleston, South Carolina, he became acquainted with the Reverend John Bachman, a Lutheran minister and amateur naturalist who became a valued friend, a companion on several expeditions, and a relative by the marriage of his two daughters to Audubon's sons as well as a collaborator with Audubon and his son John on *The Viviparous Quadrupeds of North America* (1845–1854).

In the spring of 1832, with government schooners placed at his disposal, Audubon sailed the St. John's River and Florida's southern coast, the Florida Keys, and the Tortugas looking for new species. These trips and an expedition to Labrador the following summer established Audubon's indisputable ornithological authority—he had a hundred species of birds known neither to Wilson nor to Charles L. Bonaparte in *American Ornithology: or, The Natural History of Birds Inhabiting the United States, Not Given by Wilson* (1825–1833). Henry David Thoreau, in *Natural History of Massachusetts* (1842), was moved to write: "I read in Audubon with a thrill of delight, when the snow covers the ground, of the magnolia, and the Florida keys, and their warm sea-breezes; of the fence-rail, and the cotton tree, and the migrations of the rice-bird; of the breaking-up of winter in Labrador, and the melting of snow on the forts of the Missouri and; owe an accession of health to these reminiscences of luxuriant nature."

Audubon spent the winter of 1836–1837 drawing birds from the skins of some ninety-three species that the ornithologists Thomas Nuttall and John K. Townsend had collected on their expedition to the Columbia River in California. He also started planning with Bachman a collaborative book on American quadrupeds and arranging for the expedition that took him along the Louisiana coast—rich with shorebirds and migrants—to Galveston Bay at the end of April 1837.

In the summer of 1839 Audubon issued two prospectuses: one for a smaller-sized (royal octavo) edition of *The Birds of America,* an edition whose sales were to surpass all other natural history books, and the other for *The Viviparous Quadrupeds of North America.* The latter work was issued in thirty numbers of five plates, measuring 22 by 28 inches (imperial folio) and priced at $10 a number. Eventually, the 150 plates were bound in two volumes and accompanied by three separate books of text written entirely by Bachman, who drew much of his material from Audubon's own papers.

Many of these notes were taken during an eight-month expedition in 1843 up the Missouri River to find species for *The Viviparous Quadrupeds of North America,* though the trip also fulfilled Audubon's lifelong dream of seeing the western territories. He carried with him letters of introduction from the political establishment in Washington, D.C., which had also authorized his party to requisition any needed supplies. They set out in March 1843 from St. Louis aboard a steamer belonging to the American Fur Company in the company of buffalo hunters, whom Audubon described as "the dirtiest of the dirty."

The journal of this expedition, subsequently known as the *Missouri Journal,* follows Audubon's party of five into Indian Territory to Fort Union, what is now North Dakota, near the confluence of the Missouri and Yellowstone Rivers, and back to St. Louis. Though the original manuscript is lost, the version that Maria Audubon published in *Audubon and His Journals* (1897) seems less heavily abridged than other of his writings that she edited. Among other things, the journal is a distressing record of the party's wholesale slaughter of wildlife for sport and out of seeming idleness. Though Audubon registers his own shock at the destruction of the buffalo—"immense numbers . . . are murdered almost daily. . . . But this cannot last . . . and before many years the Buffalo, like the Great Auk, will have disappeared; surely this should not be permitted"—his misgivings were not enough to curb his party's own bloodlust. His journal also vividly describes the hunting and skinning of buffalo; the party's encounters with vari-

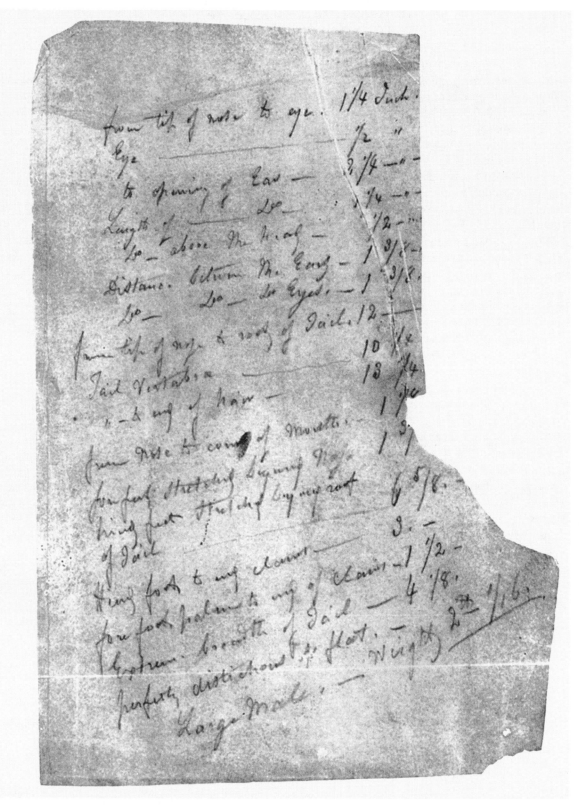

*Audubon's notes about measurement on the reverse of his drawing of a Say's squirrel for* The Viviparous Quadrupeds
of North America, *published from 1845 to 1854 (Boatmen's National Bank, St. Louis)*

ous tribes such as the Riccarees, Gros Ventres, Mandans, Sioux, and Blackfeet; and the affliction of Native Americans with destitution and smallpox. The virulence of the disease was such that many died within a day from the onset of symptoms. An officer at Fort Union estimated the number of deaths among tribes in the vicinity at 150,000. Audubon's several accounts of Native Americans preparing to die are particularly wracking. Rather than endure the suffering and, worse, have tribesmen witness their accompanying physical disintegration, "Men killed themselves, to die a nobler death than that brought by the dreaded disease."

John James Audubon returned in November 1843 to Minnie's Land, twenty-four acres in upper Manhattan on the Hudson River, which he had purchased in the spring of 1841 with profits from *The Birds of America*. He settled down to draw specimens from the Missouri River expedition, with the first folio volume of *The Viviparous Quadrupeds of North America* appearing in 1845; by 1846, when both his mind and eyesight began to fail, he had finished half of the large illustrations. The task of completing the work fell to Bachman and Audubon's sons. Audubon died on 27 January 1851.

**Letters:**

*Letters of John James Audubon, 1826–1840,* 2 volumes, edited by Horward Corning (Boston: Club of Odd Volumes, 1930);

*Audubon in the West,* edited by John Francis McDermott (Norman: University of Oklahoma Press, 1965).

**Bibliography:**

Alice Ford, *John James Audubon* (Norman: University of Oklahoma Press, 1964).

**Biographies:**

Francis Hobart Herrick, *Audubon the Naturalist: A History of His Life and Time,* 2 volumes (New York: Appleton, 1917);

Alice Ford, *John James Audubon* (Norman: University of Oklahoma Press, 1964);

John Chancellor, *Audubon: A Biography* (New York: Viking, 1978; London: Weidenfeld & Nicolson, 1978);

Shirley Streshinsky, *Audubon: Life and Art in the American Wilderness* (Athens: University of Georgia Press, 1998).

**References:**

James H. Dorman, ed., *Audubon: A Retrospective* (Lafayette: Center for Louisiana Studies, University of Southwestern Louisiana, 1990);

Waldemar Fries, *The Double Elephant Folio: The Story of Audubon's Birds of America* (Chicago: American Library Association, 1973);

Alton A. Lindsey and others, *The Bicentennial of John James Audubon* (Bloomington: Indiana University Press, 1985).

**Papers:**

Many of John James Audubon's letters and manuscripts are housed at the American Museum of Natural History, New York City; the American Philosophical Society, Philadelphia; Audubon Memorial Museum, Henderson, Kentucky; Houghton Library, Harvard University, Cambridge, Massachusetts; National Audubon Society, New York City; Princeton University Library, Princeton; and Yale University Library, New Haven.

# Joseph Glover Baldwin

*(21 January 1815 – 30 September 1864)*

Kathryn B. McKee
*University of Mississippi*

See also the Baldwin entries in *DLB 3: Antebellum Writers in New York and the South* and *DLB 11: American Humorists, 1800–1950.*

BOOKS: *The Flush Times of Alabama and Mississippi: A Series of Sketches* (New York & London: Appleton, 1853);

*Party Leaders: Sketches of Thomas Jefferson, Alex'r Hamilton, Andrew Jackson, Henry Clay, John Randolph of Roanoke, Including Notices of Many Other Distinguished American Statesmen* (New York & London: Appleton, 1855);

*The Flush Times of California,* edited by Richard E. Amacher and George W. Polhemus (Athens: University of Georgia Press, 1966).

When Joseph Glover Baldwin published *The Flush Times of Alabama and Mississippi* in 1853, he thought of himself as a lawyer. In the memories of subsequent generations, however, the publication of this volume has overshadowed his varied and illustrious legal career and earned for him a rank as the most literarily skilled of the Southwestern humorists. Nearly fifty years after its publication, W. P. Trent, in his *Southern Writers: Selections in Prose and Verse* (1905), called *The Flush Times of Alabama and Mississippi* "the best book of humorous sketches written in the ante-bellum South," and Samuel Link, in *Pioneers of Southern Literature* (1903), declared: "No man will get all out of life there is for him until he has read 'Flush Times of Alabama and Mississippi.'" Although Link's claim is exaggerated, Baldwin's sketches remain accessible and entertaining, as they both illustrate and challenge traditional expectations for the Southwestern genre.

Joseph Glover Baldwin was born 21 January 1815 near Friendly Grove Factory, Virginia, to Joseph Clarke Baldwin, a textile mill owner, and his wife, Eliza Cook Baldwin. His parents married 6 June 1810, and had seven children, five of whom survived infancy. The families of both parents had been rooted in the Milford, Connecticut, area since the seventeenth

*Joseph Glover Baldwin (from Richard E. Amacher and George W. Polhemus, eds.,* The Flush Times of California, *1966)*

century, but early in the 1800s Joseph Baldwin headed to Virginia to try his luck as an industrialist. There he met Eliza, whose family had earlier immigrated to Virginia. Accounts of Baldwin's success vary, but most conclude that "Jo," as young Joseph Glover Baldwin was known, was sent to work at a young age to help his family financially. Having moved with them around the Virginia countryside—from Friendly Grove Factory to Winchester to Staunton—Baldwin became in his early teens a deputy law clerk in Staunton, where his task was to record court proceedings, surely a factor in his later career selection. He abandoned formal schooling at this point, taking instruction instead from the legal profession.

Baldwin was well read, however. From 1827 until 1829 he was enrolled at Staunton Academy, and he had several years of schooling prior to that, in addition to his mother's careful tutelage. He read the classics of his age: William Shakespeare, Charles Lamb, Sir Walter Scott, Charles Dickens, Joseph Addison, and Richard Steele, the urbane wittiness of the latter two serving as influences on the polished writing style that became Baldwin's signature. Among his own countrymen, Baldwin likely encountered Washington Irving and, later, the staples of Southwestern humor: Augustus Baldwin Longstreet's *Georgia Scenes* (1835) and Davy Crockett's various versions of his own story, possibly authored by Crockett himself.

The Baldwins were staunch in their Whig and Episcopalian allegiances, and the adult Joseph Baldwin followed suit in his political and religious inclinations. He undertook the formal study of law in the law school of his uncle, Judge Briscoe G. Baldwin, with the assistance of his cousin, Alexander H. H. Stuart. He had completed his course of study by age twenty but had to wait until he was twenty-one to obtain his license.

Shortly after his twenty-first birthday, Baldwin briefly embarked on a career in journalism, editing with his brother Cornelius a local paper in Lexington, Virginia, the *Advocate,* and writing intermittently for the *Richmond Whig.* Baldwin's first literary pieces may belong to this era, according to an unfinished, unpublished biography by Cornelius, in which he recalls Baldwin writing a comedic play and publishing several satirical pieces in local newspapers. Political differences likely complicated the brothers' relationship—Cornelius had become a Democrat and so opposed the strong, centralized government that was favored by the Whigs. By March 1836, the *Advocate* had failed, and Baldwin set out for the southwestern frontier, then the states of Georgia, Alabama, Mississippi, and Louisiana, as well as parts of western Tennessee. In April he settled in DeKalb, Mississippi (Kemper County), and became licensed to practice law. Baldwin arrived at the height of "flush times" in the region, a period when the extraordinary rate of land speculation, coupled with the complexities of legal codes in Mississippi, created an unprecedented need for lawyers. In DeKalb, Baldwin earned a reputation as a criminal attorney. In 1889

Reuben Davis, author of *Recollections of Mississippi and Mississippians,* remembered Baldwin's first case: "His speech was marked by the clearest and most convincing logic, rising at times into vivid oratory. It was evident that this modest young man . . . was destined to take no obscure place in his day and generation." Baldwin moved on to Gainesville, Alabama, in 1837, where he established a law practice with Jonathan Bliss that survived until 1850. His experiences in Mississippi and Alabama, along with his travels to other southwestern locations, including Texas, supplied Baldwin's imagination with the stories that later became *The Flush Times of Alabama and Mississippi.*

In the summer of 1839 Baldwin met Sidney Gaylard White of Mardisville, Talladega County, Alabama, daughter of Judge John White. The two married in January 1840 and made their home in Gainesville. They had six children. Three sons survived to adulthood: Alexander White, Joseph Glover Jr., and John White.

In 1843 Baldwin embarked upon a political career. He was elected as a Whig to the Alabama House of Representatives but lost a bid for U.S. Congress in 1848 to the Democrat Samuel W. Inge. Baldwin was also a delegate to the Whig National Convention in Philadelphia in 1848. He and his wife toured northern cities as part of their travels, including New York and Boston. His trip to the North did little to ameliorate the training of his homeland; Baldwin owned at least two slaves in the late 1840s and by 1850 owned as many as six.

In 1850 the Baldwin family moved to a home in Livingston, Alabama, called Villa Vue. In Livingston, Baldwin became the law partner of T. B. Whetmore and likely began writing and compiling sketches about his days as a lawyer during the frontier boom. Between July 1852 and September 1853, eighteen of these sketches appeared in the *Southern Literary Messenger,* a leading regional publication that commanded national attention. In 1853 Baldwin, in consultation with *Messenger* editor John R. Thompson, decided to collect his sketches into a single volume. In July the two men traveled to New York and met with David Appleton of the publishing house D. Appleton and Company. Baldwin entered a contractual agreement with the firm, according to which he would receive 10 percent of the profits from the first edition. *The Flush Times of Alabama and Mississippi* was released on 11 December 1853, comprising seventeen sketches that had previously appeared in the *Southern Literary Messenger* and nine new pieces. In February of the following year the *Southern Literary Messenger* boasted that sales of the first edition were reaching twenty thousand. Although that figure may be exaggerated, the book did exceed the expectations of both the author and the publisher in its popularity, entering ten editions in the nineteenth century and being republished several times in the twentieth.

A reviewer of *The Flush Times of Alabama and Mississippi*, writing in the December 1853 issue of the *Southern Literary Messenger*, called Baldwin's stories and sketches "the very best things of the kind that the age has produced" and praised their graceful style. That style both links them to and separates them from the genre of Southwestern humor to which the critic tacitly refers. That body of writing, concentrated between the years 1830 and 1860, took as its subject life on the southern frontier. Dominated by male writers and characters, bawdy humor, and traditionally masculine activities including hunting, fighting, and gambling, Southwestern humor was written primarily by upper-class observers of frontier life, often from the North, who placed at the center of their tales lower-class characters and then generated amusement at their expense. In fact, Kenneth Lynn, in *Mark Twain and Southwestern Humor* (1959), uses the increasing power of the vernacular voice in the genre to trace the gradual dissolution of aristocratic power structures, culminating in Twain's *The Adventures of Huckleberry Finn* (1885), a novel told completely in the voice of an untutored, lower-class orphan. Like his fellow Southwestern humorists, including Longstreet, Johnson Jones Hooper, George Washington Harris, and Thomas Bangs Thorpe, Baldwin relied on the staples of comic storytelling for his success—a narrator tangentially related to the action at the center of the tale and an audience whose sympathies align more nearly with the narrator than with his subject.

Yet, unlike other Southwestern humorists, Baldwin made scant use of dialect, preferring instead to allow his more sophisticated narrator—easily equated with Baldwin himself—to recount the comic action at the center of the tale. His characters themselves are often a more urbane lot than Harris's Sut Lovingood, for instance, whose dialect renders him sometimes unintelligible and whose naiveté is nearly unparalleled. Baldwin's narrators, rather, are often the most educated in the story; they are lawyers who, like Baldwin himself, have come west to seek their fill in the land of litigious plenty. They seldom speak for themselves, however. Instead, a polished narrative voice recounts the entire tale, leading critics such as Walter Blair in *Native American Humor* (1937) to conclude that Baldwin "writes in a style at times too leisurely, too polished, for an account of the brisk frontier and its rough inhabitants." Other critics, among them Eugene Current-Garcia, convincingly read Baldwin as a social satirist bent on exposing the materialistic urges inciting frontier settlement. In his "Joseph Glover Baldwin: Humorist or Moralist?" (1975) Current-Garcia contends that efforts to interweave Baldwin with other Southwestern humor-

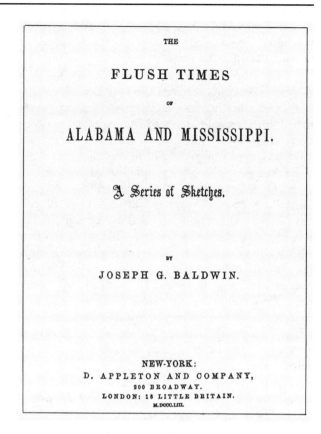

*Title page for Baldwin's 1853 collection of Southwestern humor tales (Thomas Cooper Library, University of South Carolina)*

ists are misguided because his more serious intent and elevated style clearly dinstinguish him. Even Baldwin's publication venue differed from that of his contemporary humorists, who turned most often to the nationally circulated sporting magazine, the *Spirit of the Times*, edited by William T. Porter. Baldwin chose instead the *Southern Literary Messenger*, more staid in tone and reputation than Porter's publication.

Still, the Alabama and Mississippi of Baldwin's fiction is the frontier of Southwestern humor. His characters are often lawyers in a lawless society where the only certainty is that circumstances are likely not what they seem. Baldwin's rustic courtrooms are populated by swindlers, tellers of tall tales, and attorneys whose licenses are the issue of a financial transaction rather than a classroom. In "The Bench and the Bar," for instance, Baldwin describes the southwestern frontier as "a legal Utopia," populated mainly by young men who "had come out on the vague errand of seeking their fortune, or the more definite one of seeking somebody else's." In the final sketch of *The Flush Times of Alabama and Mississippi*, "Examining a Candidate for License," the narrator interviews a potential lawyer. To one question, the candidate responds: "Squire, the Devil himself couldn't answer that, and I guess he's as smart as airy other lawyer." Thus, the legal profession plays a central role in the unprincipled atmosphere of the frontier communities Baldwin describes.

The stories in *The Flush Times of Alabama and Mississippi* can be usefully divided into four thematic categories: comic sketches of individual personalities (some based on real people), serious biographies of figures in the legal community, humorous courtroom stories, and accounts of practical jokes. The first group yields some of Baldwin's most frequently anthologized tales, among them "Ovid Bolus, Esq.," "Cave Burton, Esq., of Kentucky," and "Simon Suggs, Jr., Esq.; A Legal Biography." A lawyer by trade, Ovid Bolus exemplifies the sort of character who survives on Baldwin's frontier. After some debate, the narrator concludes that lying is Bolus's chief vice. He "had long torn down the partition wall between his imagination and his memory," lying most elaborately about his exploits with women. As a swindler Bolus enjoys regular success, until he overworks his schemes and has to beat a hasty midnight retreat, leaving in every home "an autograph, in every ledger a souvenir."

Baldwin's sketch of "Cave Burton, Esq., of Kentucky" is a more fully developed portrait of a consummate storyteller who is both a fixture in his community and an object of its amusement. His nickname is "the Blowing Cave." Burton's "regard for truth was considerable," the narrator notes, "indeed, so great that he spent most of his conversation in embellishing it." Burton is distinguished by his insatiable appetite, which leads him not only to the table with alarming frequency but also to some rather controversial opinions: "for example, he was not satisfied that Esau made as foolish a bargain with his brother Jacob as some think." Oysters are Burton's favorite food, and they constitute the centerpiece for the comic climax of the story. Partygoers at a holiday gathering conspire, before Burton's arrival, to entice him into telling his earthquake story. (Digressions have prevented anyone ever hearing the end of it.) While he is thus occupied, they sneak off one by one and eat all of the oysters. Just as Jim Blaine, a would-be storyteller from Twain's *Roughing It* (1872), never gets around to the story of his grandfather's old ram, Burton loses himself in his own narrative, at last emerging from his tale-telling to learn that his mean-spirited compatriots have tricked him out of any oysters. Constructed as a frame narrative, "Cave Burton, Esq., of Kentucky" typifies the storytelling style typically associated with Southwestern humor. Even the central narrator utilizes comedic exaggeration typical to the genre. Burton's love for oysters is so great, he contends, that a group of men like him "near the oyster banks, would have exterminated the species in a season."

"Simon Suggs, Jr., Esq." is the best of Baldwin's individual character portraits. Baldwin explicitly connects the sketch to early Southwestern humor by making his main character the son of Simon Suggs, from Johnson Jones Hooper's 1845 book by the same name. In his sketch Baldwin crafts a fine comic character of his own, in addition suggesting an intertextual dimension to Southwestern humor and parodying the genre of legal biographies. "Simon Suggs, Jr., Esq." comprises two parts: an exchange of letters between Suggs and a journalist proposing to write his biography and the actual biography they produce. The journalist's letter of solicitation establishes his project of documenting the careers of the greatest American lawmen. Suggs replies that he has provided the requested information; he "got a friend to rite it—my own riting being mostly perfeshunal. He done it—but he rites such a cussed bad hand I cant rede it; I reckon its all korrect tho'." The solicitor turns out to be a swindler himself, requesting $150 to print the piece, which Suggs refuses to pay.

The sketch is written nonetheless and appears next in the volume. It includes the high points of Suggs's rise as a prominent lawyer: outfoxing his own father, a notorious swindler, in a card game; purchasing his law license in Montgomery, Alabama; and establishing his practice in Rackensack, Arkansas, a place filled with such a lawless population that the narrator concedes "the Indians and half-breeds across the border complained of it mightily." Outrageous anecdotes litter the story of his legal career, from witness tampering to engineering jail breaks for his clients. Finally the reader learns that Suggs (who has added the designation "Colonel" to his name) has divorced the woman he originally married for her money in order to wed the daughter of a Choctaw chief so that he can handle the legal business of the tribe.

Baldwin's equating of legal biography and fiction does not prevent him from including several examples of the former in *The Flush Times of Alabama and Mississippi*, curiously embedded in a volume otherwise intended to be funny. Three sketches offer unembellished accounts of the lives and personalities of the southwestern frontier: "Hon. S. S. Prentiss," "The Bar of the South-West," and "Hon. Francis Strother." Anticipating the approach he adopted in *Party Leaders: Sketches of Thomas Jefferson, Alex'r Hamilton, Andrew Jackson, Henry Clay, John Randolph of Roanoke, Including Notices of Many Other Distinguished American Statesmen* (1855), Baldwin weighs both the positive and negative dimensions of Prentiss's and Strother's careers, concluding that profligate living restricted the potential of the first but that Strother was "a gentleman of the Old School with the energy of the New." Stylistically these sketches are similar to surrounding material in that Baldwin incorporates, particularly in "The Bar of the South-West" and "Hon. Francis Strother," comic anecdotes and the language of bemused exaggeration. Their purpose, however, extends beyond humorous storytelling to provide serious documentation of the era. "The Bar of the South-West" seeks to account for the flush times of the 1830s, juxtaposing the intellectual freedom a frontier offers with the unfortunate recklessness that results when moral boundaries are negotiable. Most lawyers in the region, the narrator maintains, were honest men. Baldwin reflects here as well on the legal profession, pointing out that a well-prepared case is far more desirable than a well-orated one.

The lawyers in Baldwin's humorous courtroom stories have yet to learn this lesson, however. In "My First Appearance at the Bar," for instance, the narrator, whose experiences as a Virginian relocated to the West make him an obvious stand-in for Baldwin himself, receives an education in legal procedure and life from the attorney who opposes him, "Sar Kasm," who "had cultivated vituperation as a science." The narrator rises to speak and is soon carried away by his own rhetoric; Kasm systematically dismantles his arguments, however, before branching out to critique his person and the poetry he has written. The idea of a poet convulses the courtroom audience with laughter, suggesting a disdain for polished literature that likely characterized the readers of Southwestern humor. He flees without a backward glance but must concede that his treatment at Sar Kasm's hands taught him to be a successful lawyer, one who concentrates on compiling evidence rather than on staging a show of verbal pyrotechnics in the courtroom.

"How the Times Served the Virginians," one of Baldwin's most frequently anthologized sketches, suggests his own experiences as a young lawyer. Again he describes the allure of the frontier, where "Commerce was king." Virginians, he maintains, found themselves at a distinct disadvantage because the inherent nobility of their natures made them ready targets for the con men from more immoral places, such as Georgia. Baldwin's portrait of his native state and its assumed superiority is comic but suggests as well that Virginia is a distinct place that is rightly a source of pride to its inhabitants. James H. Justus, in his introduction to the 1987 edition of *The Flush Times of Alabama and Mississippi,* calls Baldwin's attitude toward his native land "richly ambivalent"; it is "ancestral but not pious, just as his attitude toward the Southwest is critical but not moralistic."

Practical jokes are central to another subset of Baldwin's tales. Best among this group is "Justification after Verdict," in which the narrator defends Paul Beechim on charges of assault. Typically mild-mannered, Beechim has caned his friend Paul Cousins, saying cryptically after the assault: "How, d—n you, how do you like *that* pine-apple sop?" The narrator gradually pieces together an explanation for Beechim's behavior. He and Cousins had recently been in New Orleans together, and Beechim, originally from Nashville, was taking his social cues from his more cosmopolitan friend. As the two dine in a hotel, Cousins tricks Beechim into dipping his food in his finger bowl, telling him it contains "sop for the pine-apple." When Beechim observes "I think the pine-apple very good, but don't you think the sauce is rather insipid?," the room explodes in raucous laughter. The judge rules that he was justified in later exacting revenge on his playful social tutor.

Baldwin's tales are also insightful interpretations of the 1830s and 1840s, when the stories are set, and the 1850s, when the volume was published. In *The Flush Times of Alabama and Mississippi* he speculates on the rise and fall of the boom era in the southwestern frontier region and identifies in the national character an acquisitiveness and a disregard for others that troubles him. In his observations about the American penchant for land acquired from other countries at whatever literal and moral cost, Baldwin anticipates his later portrayal—in *The Flush Times of California* (1966)—of American dealings with the native population. Baldwin's sketches are laced with references to Native Americans, particularly Choctaws, and to the leaders and the treaties that resulted finally in their removal farther west. Baldwin concludes his portrait of Simon Suggs with the hope that "the Indians live to get their dividends of the arrears paid to their agent," the shifty con artist Suggs. Suggs's self-aggrandizing, self-centered motivations, Baldwin suggests, characterize the general American attitude toward Indians. Suggs and the deceptiveness he embodies appear elsewhere in the volume; in "The Bar of the South-West" Baldwin characterizes the generally outrageous nature of frontier life, exploding:

> And in INDIAN affairs!—the very mention is suggestive of the poetry of theft—the romance of a wild and weird larceny! What sublime conceptions of super-Spartan roguery! Swindling Indians by the nation! . . . . Stealing their land by the township! . . . . Conducting the nation to the Mississippi River, stripping them to the flap, and bidding them God speed as they went howling into the Western wilderness to the friendly agency of some sheltering Suggs duly empowered to receive their coming annuities and back rations!

Although Baldwin's tone is often tongue-in-cheek throughout *Flush Times,* "The Bar of the South-West" is predominantly a serious effort to assess the nature of

*Page from the manuscript for Baldwin's account of his 1854 move west, published in 1966 as* The Flush Times of California
*(The Lester-Gray Collection, Manuscripts Department, Library of the University of North Carolina at Chapel Hill)*

the flush times, and Baldwin's attitudes there serve as a reliable index to his own perceptions.

Elsewhere Baldwin playfully reveals his attitudes toward increasingly serious sectional tensions. Passing references to slavery are frequent and pointed. In "Ovid Bolus, Esq.," for example, the title character breaks an engagement rather than free his slaves as his fiancée's father requests. When the consummate Virginia gentleman, Major Willis Wormley, is welcomed back to his plantation in "How the Times Served the Virginians," the slaves' response is "enough to convert an abolitionist."

Baldwin most directly confronts North-South conflicts in "Samuel Hele, Esq.," the portrait of a lawyer renowned for his unflinching language and similarly inflexible attitudes. Although he is often at odds with his community, in this sketch he does them a service by convincing a New England schoolmarm, Miss Charity Woodey, who has "come out as a missionary of light to the children of the South, who dwell in the darkness of Heathenesse," to return to her coldhearted and misguided home. The narrator is openly insulting in his description of her, labeling her the ugliest woman he has ever seen and declaring that she is "one of those 'strong-minded women of New England,' . . . who, in trying to *double-sex* themselves, *unsex* themselves, losing all that is lovable in woman, and getting most of what is odious in man." Posing as a New Englander himself, Hele approaches Miss Charity, at the instigation of his cronies, one night at a dance and proceeds to regale her with firsthand accounts of the horrors of slavery: he recalls slaves literally being blown up, while white men watch and make bets about whether or not their heads will come off; he tells of black children being sold by the hamperful and of them being drowned like puppies; he explains that the fear of slave insurrection has been mitigated by the monthly donation by each planter of a slave to be lynched or burned as an example to the others. He then tells of a Yankee schoolmistress who was once tarred and feathered for speaking out against slavery and confides in her that he has heard plans are afoot to punish another such interloper, although he is unsure of the target's identity. Miss Charity leaves the next morning, forgetting, in her haste, a letter containing information about slavery and addressed to "Mrs. Harriet S–." The narrator recalls reading similar information in "a very popular fiction, or rather book of fictions, in which the slaveholders are handled with something less than feminine delicacy and something more than masculine unfairness." Baldwin underscores here both what he perceives as the ridiculous nature of northern portrayals of the South and the gullibility of the northern public who reads them. A year after the publication of Harriet Beecher Stowe's *Uncle Tom's Cabin*

(1852), Baldwin's target is unmistakable. In his venom he reflects an increasingly embattled southern perspective and fires a shot on the battleground of the literary Civil War.

Pleased with his new status as writer, Baldwin continued both to publish his work and to practice law, the latter for a brief time in Mobile, Alabama, just before Baldwin and his family headed once more to the frontier, this time to California. Before setting off on this adventure, Baldwin published in the *Southern Literary Messenger* a satirical account of California–"California Flush Times" (November 1853)–and two serious essays, one about Andrew Jackson and another about Henry Clay. John Thompson suggested he use the latter as the basis for a book about politics. Baldwin's critiques of two of the most famous political lives in American history, then, were the seed for the only other book published in his lifetime: *Party Leaders,* copyrighted in 1854 and appearing in 1855. Riding the wave of recognition *The Flush Times of Alabama and Mississippi* had earned him, Baldwin, accompanied by his brother Cornelius, approached Appleton with the manuscript of *Party Leaders* in July 1854; Appleton accepted it, apparently without even reading it, promising Baldwin half of the profits. Cornelius stayed behind to oversee the production of the book, while Baldwin returned to his new home in California.

*Party Leaders* takes as its subject the political lives of five American luminaries. Baldwin's correspondence suggests that this work, rather than *The Flush Times of Alabama and Mississippi,* is the sort of writing by which he hoped to make his literary mark. By placing Jefferson and Hamilton, Jackson and Clay side by side, Baldwin showcases the extremity of opposing views and, without directly stating his intent, suggests that the strengths and weaknesses of each pair have coalesced to shape crucial moments in the evolution of a national identity. Baldwin struggles in the preface to name his book by genre, stating that "he sought to blend interest with instruction" and thus "labored to unite biography with political history; and, by placing rival leaders in antagonism, to make events and principles stand out in bold relief." "The work makes no pretension to research," he confesses. "The events are matters of familiar history. All that the writer has attempted has been a concise narrative of the facts."

The first section, on Jefferson and Hamilton, and the third, on Jackson and Clay, are similarly organized: Baldwin reviews the course of each man's life until the pair intersects. He then describes the nature of their interaction before speculating about its consequences. Of Jefferson and Hamilton, for example, Baldwin observes that "Each was conscious that himself and the other were making history," and of Jackson and Clay,

"If these great rivals agreed in nothing else, they agreed in hating each other with uncommon fervor." He then proceeds to compare the pairs more generally on points as various as politics and writing style. The portrait of Clay is perhaps the most personally conflicted of the lot. Baldwin must acknowledge him as "a dictator" because "there is too much truth in it" to deny, and he concedes that in certain ways Clay's temperament and manner injured the Whig Party as a whole. Yet, evidence of Clay's superiority is undeniably embedded in the fact that "whenever the country was in imminent danger, and could find extrication only in extraordinary resources and wisdom, the public expectation turned to Henry Clay, as its deliverer. . . ."

The section about John Randolph, nestled between the two comparative chapters, reviews his career but also offers an overview of Baldwin's native Virginia and its distinctive nature. Baldwin additionally assesses central events in American history and the character of the American people, including an abbreviated but serious account of the flush times on the southwestern frontier that he had earlier taken as his humorous subject: "every highway teeming with adventurers, swarming in hordes over the land," he recalls; "It seemed as if a new chapter had opened in history, and that the world had been let out of the school of common sense for a holiday of wild commercial insanity."

In the summer of 1854 Baldwin moved to San Francisco, where within a few years he entered a law practice with A. P. Crittenden and Colonel J. B. Crockett, focusing primarily on civil law. Although the flush times in California were subsiding, Baldwin found much to remind him of the southwestern frontier, and he eventually channeled these perceptions into a manuscript. California and its promise of a new frontier had long captured Baldwin's imagination. He wrote about it twice, first in "California Flush Times" and then in a fragment, "The F[lush] T[imes] of California." The latter remained unpublished until 1966, when Richard E. Amacher and George W. Polhemus collected the two pieces as *The Flush Times of California*.

"California Flush Times" is an imaginative picture of the California Gold Rush, composed before Baldwin had ever even visited California and printed in the *Southern Literary Messenger* of November 1853. Amacher and Polhemus compare it to a colonial promotional tract and note its effective use of the staples of American humorous storytelling: understatement, hyperbole, and comic figures of speech. "California Flush Times" is epistolary in form; it proposes to be a letter from "the Author of The Flush Times of Alabama" back to his friend Frank in Alabama and is dated

15 June 1850 from San Francisco, a land where "nothing is impossible and few things difficult."

From the beginning the writer tells his friend that "without a stock of credulity not at all attainable in the old country, it will be impossible for you to believe half of what I say, though, in order to assist belief, I content myself with only stating half of the truth." His tall tales about enormous watermelons become symbolic reflections of the rampant materialism swallowing the countryside: "contracts for new buildings are signed by the light of the fire that is consuming the old," and the ocean itself faces extinction because "some enterprising Yankee will scoop all the water out of it for a quarter of a mile" in order to continue expanding the city. As a lawyer, the writer has profited tremendously. When he first opened his practice, he found it most efficient to make daily appearances on his balcony to dispense advice to the masses and then allow clients to hand up their payments in the form of pouches of gold dust on the end of sticks, in a scene that suggests the deification of the capitalist venture. "How much I made," he concedes, "I never knew—as I never had time to count it. Besides my clerk defaulted for about a flour barrel of the dust." Presumed deception, in fact, unites the people of San Francisco, as "nothing so harmonizes a community as a modest and well grounded diffidence in each other's integrity." Empathy, like honesty, is an outdated virtue in the land Baldwin satirically describes. Jim Screwtite, for instance, forecloses on Tim Sloe because the latter trips and stumps his toe and is a minute and a half late with his repayment. "A good deal of humanity is shown to the poor when sick," Baldwin observes; "if they have no money, they are suffered to die, in the street, a natural death, without interruption."

The social order that emerges from Baldwin's imagined California reverses expectation. The apple stand in front of his office, for instance, is maintained by the Right Rev'd Habbakuk Kent, Professor of Divinity; the laundry man is a former professor of chemistry and belles lettres; and the head waiter at a popular hotel used to be the governor of Rhode Island. Violence is rampant. The speaker has seen his clients lynched, and threats have been made on his own life. In this loss of conventional order, Amacher and Polhemus find Baldwin the Southern Whig gentleman registering the concerns and prejudices of his class about the consequences of unsettled social structures.

"The F[lush] T[imes] of California" is a factual version of Baldwin's move to California in 1854, in the "ebb tide" of the region's "flush times," terms that Baldwin is sometimes credited with coining. "To give some account of this new *epocha* in commercial and social history is the design of these pages," Baldwin remarks, his goal being "to describe the influence of money on men suddenly acquiring it, to show what Society is when every man gets instantly rich or, what is the same thing thinks he is." Woven into Baldwin's observations are several pointed conclusions about the American character. "If the Americans have any weakness it is for land, and if this weakness has any particular weak place it is for other peoples' land," he notes, mentioning specifically the national acquisitions from Spain, France, and native populations. In this essay appears one of Baldwin's rare direct discussions of slavery, in which he concludes that "a crisis of dissolution" will provide the only means of confronting growing sectionalism and bitter debates about the future of Western territories. Although not devoid of humor, Baldwin's attitude here lacks the good nature of his earlier satire, and in his account of the Mexican-American War and in his disparaging references to African American, Jewish, and northern personages, the reader detects the frustrations of an increasingly defensive southerner.

In the late 1850s, the Whig Party now depleted of power, Baldwin became a Democrat. He was elected in 1858 to the California Supreme Court, where he served as associate justice until 1862 and developed an expertise in land, mineral, and water rights, writing nearly two-thirds of the decisions rendered by the court during his tenure. In the late 1850s the Baldwins lived in Sacramento, and in 1860 Baldwin again ran for Congress. He was again defeated. In the early 1860s Baldwin traveled to Nevada to visit his sons, who had become involved in the mining business there and to make some investments of his own. Later, in 1863, he went to Washington, D.C., where he reportedly met President Abraham Lincoln, who told him *The Flush Times of Alabama and Mississippi* was one of his favorite books. This connection did not facilitate Baldwin's request for a pass to visit his family in Virginia; it was denied. Baldwin remained officially neutral throughout the Civil War, although his sympathies likely followed his upbringing, despite his distaste for the fiery rhetoric of both sides. The conflict divided his family, however: his eldest son supported the Union, and his youngest brother died of illness while serving the Confederacy.

At the beginning of 1864 Baldwin was back in California and at work on "The Flush Times of California," although his writing was interrupted by the financial instability that had hounded him at various junctures in his life and by the death of his son, Joseph

Glover Baldwin Jr., at age twenty from tuberculosis. Joseph Baldwin himself contracted tetanus following minor surgery and died on 30 September 1864 at age forty-nine. His legacy remains *The Flush Times of Alabama and Mississippi,* notable not just for its humor and its variations on the Southwestern genre, but also for its self-reflective musings on the nature of American and southern identity.

**References:**

Richard E. Amacher and George W. Polhemus, "Biographical Sketch," in *The Flush Times of California,* edited by Amacher and Polhemus (Athens: University of Georgia Press, 1966), pp. 65–78;

William Braswell, "An Unpublished California Letter of Joseph Glover Baldwin," *American Literature,* 2 (1930): 292–294;

Eugene Current-Garcia, "Joseph Glover Baldwin: Humorist or Moralist?" in *The Frontier Humorists: Critical Views,* edited by M. Thomas Inge (Hamden, Conn.: Archon, 1975), pp. 170–184;

Hunter Dickson Farish, "An Overlooked Personality in Southern Life," *North Carolina Historical Review,* 12 (October 1935): 341–353;

James H. Justus, introduction to *The Flush Times of Alabama and Mississippi,* edited by Justus (Baton Rouge: Louisiana State University Press, 1987), pp. xiii–l;

Mark A. Keller, "The Transfiguration of a Southwestern Humor Sketch: Joseph Glover Baldwin's 'Jo. Heyfron,'" *American Humor,* 8 (Fall 1981): 19–22;

Kenneth Lynn, *Mark Twain and Southwestern Humor* (Boston: Little, Brown, 1959), pp. 115–124;

J. F. McDermott, "Baldwin's 'Flush Times of Alabama and Mississippi'—A Bibliographical Note," *Papers of the Bibliographical Society of America,* 45 (1951): 251–256;

G. F. Mellen, "Joseph G. Baldwin and Flush Times," *Sewanee Review,* 9 (April 1901): 171–181;

Mary Ann Wimsatt, "Baldwin's Patrician Humor," *Thalia,* 6 (Fall–Winter 1983): 43–50.

**Papers:**

The papers of the Joseph Glover Baldwin family were collected in the 1920s by Robert M. Lester and can be found among the Robert M. Lester papers in the Lester-Gray Collection at the New York Public Library.

# Albert Taylor Bledsoe

*(9 November 1809 – 8 December 1877)*

Boyd Childress
*Auburn University*

See also the Bledsoe entries in *DLB 3: Antebellum Writers in New York and the South* and *DLB 79: American Magazine Journalists, 1850–1900.*

BOOKS: *An Examination of President Edwards' Inquiry into the Freedom of the Will* (Philadelphia: H. Hooker: 1845);

*Address Delivered at the First Annual Commencement of the University of Mississippi* (Oxford: Published by Order of the Board of Trustees, 1849);

*A Theodicy; or, Vindication of the Divine Glory, as Manifested in the Constitution and Government of the Moral World* (New York: Nelson & Phillips, 1853; London: Saunders, Otley, 1864);

*A Brief Sketch of the Rise and Progress of Astronomy, in Three Lectures* (Philadelphia: King & Baird, 1854);

*Three Lectures on Rational Mechanics; or, The Theory of Motion* (Philadelphia: Collins, 1854);

*An Essay on Liberty and Slavery* (Philadelphia: Lippincott, 1856);

*Is Davis a Traitor; or, Was Secession a Constitutional Right Previous to the War of 1861?* (Baltimore: Printed for the Author by Innes & Company, 1866); republished as *The War Between the States; or, Was Secession a Constitutional Right Previous to the War of 1861–65?* (Lynchburg, Va.: J. P. Bell, 1915);

*The Philosophy of Mathematics, with Special Reference to the Elements of Geometry and the Infinitesimal Method* (Philadelphia: Lippincott, 1868);

*The Cummins Movement* (St. Louis: Southwestern Book and Publishing, 1874).

OTHER: *Eulogy, on the Life and Character of William Henry Harrison . . . Delivered Before a Meeting of the Citizens of Springfield, Ill., and Its Vicinity, May 1st, 1842* (N.p., 1841).

PERIODICAL EDITED: Editor, *Southern Review*, 1–22 (1867–1877).

SELECTED PERIODICAL PUBLICATIONS–UNCOLLECTED: "The Divine Government," *Quarterly Review of the Methodist Episcopal Church, South,* 1 (April 1852): 280–301;

*Albert Taylor Bledsoe*

"Mr. Bledsoe's Review of His Reviewer," *Southern Literary Messenger,* 23 (July 1856): 20–25;

"Lamon's Life of Lincoln," *Southern Review,* 3 (April 1873): 328–368.

Albert Taylor Bledsoe was certainly among the most versatile men of his generation. An 1830 graduate of West Point, Bledsoe was a soldier, college professor, preacher, lawyer, minor Confederate bureaucrat, and, finally, a magazine editor. He wrote extensively, especially as editor of the *Southern Review,* but was also the author of an historical and philosophical treatise on mathematics that one scholar concluded was still worth reading one hundred years after Bledsoe published *The Philosophy of Mathematics, with Special Reference to the Elements of Geometry and the Infinitesimal Method* (1868). Bledsoe also wrote a volume on religion, but he is best remembered for his defense of slavery and the Southern cause, embodied in *An Essay on Liberty and Slavery* (1856) and *Is Davis a Traitor; or, Was Secession a Constitutional Right Previous to the War of 1861?* (1866). In dozens of articles in the *Southern Review,* Bledsoe continued his arguments for the Southern way of life and economics for more than a decade after the Civil War ended. He is acknowledged as one of the most ardent defenders of the "lost cause."

Bledsoe was born in Frankfort, Kentucky, on 9 November 1809 to Moses O. Bledsoe and Sophia Childress Taylor Bledsoe. Moses Bledsoe was a fun-loving man who moved between occupations such as newspaper editor, general store operator, and minor court official. There were religious officials in his family tree. Bledsoe's mother was the daughter of Samuel Taylor, a Virginia legislator, member of the Kentucky State Constitutional Convention, a planter, and a slave owner. Albert Taylor was the eldest of five children, four of whom survived childhood. He grew up in Frankfort, a frontier town of 1,099 inhabitants in 1810, which included 140 homes, nearly 20 stores, 3 printing offices, a bank, and an Indian threat. Bledsoe was accustomed to slaves—his father owned three and his mother inherited several. The county population was 40 percent black during the 1820s.

He attended private schools briefly in the Frankfort area before he received a West Point appointment in 1825. From all accounts, including his own reminiscences, young Bledsoe had little education before he left for the relatively new military school. Prominent Kentucky politician Robert Letcher sponsored his appointment. In 1825 West Point was a fledgling school under the stern leadership of Syvanus Thayer, consisting of an academy building, two cadet barracks, a mess hall, and some 222 largely undisciplined and often homesick young men. Among Bledsoe's friends were classmates Robert Edward Lee of Virginia, Joseph Johnston, and Meriwether Clark, whose father, William Clark, had explored the West for President Thomas Jefferson, as well as two upperclassmen, Jefferson Davis of Mississippi and Leonidus Polk of Louisiana. Bledsoe was of small frame, for which he earned the nickname "little Bledsoe." Cadets studied mathematics, physics, and engineering, as well as French, drawing, and chemistry. Among the faculty were two individuals destined to play significant roles

in Bledsoe's later life: Edward Courtenay and the chaplain, Charles Pettit McIlvaine. McIlvaine became Bledsoe's mentor as he entered teaching, and upon Courtenay's death in 1854, Bledsoe replaced him on the faculty of the University of Virginia.

As a cadet Bledsoe had to repeat the first year of instruction, barely missing a passing score. He was fond of mathematics. At the end of his second year he stood tenth in his class of approximately sixty-three, a class that included Henry Clay Jr. among its members. He improved in class standing each year until the last term, when he finished sixteenth in a class of forty-two. Discipline, not academics, brought the young man's standing down, as he had received 376 demerits for conduct, which ranked him a poor 207 of 215 students at West Point. He still graduated as a commissioned officer in the army in 1830, some five months shy of his twenty-first birthday. Fellow cadets considered him "persistent and unconquerable"; yet, Bledsoe had a romantic view of duty and honor from his years at West Point. The administration of West Point frowned on reading fiction, and Bledsoe's distaste for the genre and his failure to write fiction may be the two most distinct characteristics he retained from his West Point education.

Fort Gibson was not one of the plum assignments in the U.S. Army of 1830. Situated in present-day Arkansas, the outpost was, according to William Murrell Hays, "remote, exposed, and pestiferous." It was an undesirable post for an officer, particularly one such as Bledsoe, who was unsuited for a military career. He was easily bored, stifled by the administrative routine typical of military service, and had little imagination with which to occupy his mind on such an assignment. Fort Gibson, founded in 1830, was still new but was in poor shape and was located amid the peaceful Osage Indians. One of the fort's neighbors was a storekeeper by the name of Sam Houston. Bledsoe was among the forty officers and five hundred to one thousand men stationed there under the command of Colonel Matthew Arbuckle. Disease rather than Indians was the most dangerous enemy and, after two years, Bledsoe resigned his commission in August 1832. He gave no further thought to a military career.

Having failed at a career in the army, Bledsoe turned to his family for help. He began a two-year study of law in the office of his uncle, Samuel Taylor, a prominent Richmond attorney. This early study of law proved useful for yet another career, although he put the career on hold for several years. Bledsoe recalled that the study of law taught him to examine an issue from every angle and then reach a conclusion. He also developed an appreciation for primary source materials in his legal studies.

He still thought mathematics was a more useful vocation, however, and left Richmond in 1833 to join McIlvaine at Kenyon College in Gambier, Ohio, where his former mentor had become president. Although his job was as a math tutor, he still taught freshman and sophomore mathematics and began the study of theology as well. For the next two years Bledsoe was busy at his studies and teaching duties—in his second year at Kenyon he became an assistant instructor. In 1835 Bledsoe graduated and was ordained in the Protestant Episcopal Church. By August of that same year, he accepted a full-time teaching position at Miami (Ohio) University. The language professor at Miami had died and, although unqualified, Bledsoe sought the position. He was successful only when the mathematics professor accepted the languages position, leaving the math job for Bledsoe. His salary of $600 was further taxed when he married Harriet Coxe, age twenty-five and daughter of a prominent New Jersey family, in April 1836. Her uncle, Tench Coxe, was a Pennsylvania Revolutionary War figure and political colleague of Thomas Jefferson. His wife was also the sister-in-law of McIlvaine. Bledsoe was twenty-six when he married; he and his wife had seven children, four of whom survived childhood.

His stay at Miami, then called "the Yale of the West," was brief. He met and befriended professor William Holmes McGuffey, author of the widely used McGuffey Readers and later a colleague of Bledsoe's at the University of Virginia. At Miami, Bledsoe became involved in a dispute between McGuffey and the president of Miami, Robert Hamilton Bishop, over the issue of student discipline. McGuffey took the issue to the school board of trustees, although no resolution was ever reached. When discipline problems continued, Bledsoe resigned in July 1836. McGuffey followed suit the next year, while Bledsoe began still another career—that of the ministry.

Bledsoe had developed personality traits that marked his later life by age twenty-seven—even his daughter later remembered, as quoted in William Murrel Hays's dissertation, his "irascibility." He was combative, inflexible, often too frank for his own good, immoderate, and arrogant. He did possess, however, a dedication to principle, a trait many friends and colleagues had noted. Beginning in 1837, Bledsoe held four different jobs in the clergy in twenty-five months. He moved first to Sandusky, Ohio, then briefly to Cincinnati, before returning to his native Kentucky. His last move as a member of the Episcopalian ministry was to Cuyahoga Falls, Ohio. As he continued his thorough study of church doctrine, he grew more uncomfortable with its tenets. He found the Ninth and Seventeenth Articles of the Episcopalian Church "utterly inconsistent with the teachings of Christ, as well as with the eternal and immutable dictates of reason." The final straw for Bledsoe and the church was his refusal to baptize infants, and in 1839 he resigned his orders without a job. Bledsoe was of dubious effectiveness as a minister, as his daughter noted: "his reading was monotonous, his delivery poor, and the matter of his sermons were too deep and the length of them too great for popularity or even for usefulness."

Never one to spend time worrying about his career, the former military officer, teacher, and minister decided to open a law office in Carrollton, Illinois, in the summer of 1839. Somewhat dissatisfied with the small town, Bledsoe moved to the capital city, Springfield, in December. When he announced his move to Springfield in the *Sangamo Journal* (27 December 1839), Bledsoe promised: "He will be faithful and punctual in bestowing attention upon such business as may be confided to his care." Bledsoe soon found he was not the only lawyer in Springfield, and one of his colleagues in the legal profession was another Kentucky-born lawyer, Abraham Lincoln.

Springfield was a lively and exciting community in 1840. The 1841 population was only 3,500, and no railroads serviced the capital. Instead, transportation in and out of Springfield was usually by stagecoach. The Panic of 1837 had not been good for business in the Midwest, and Springfield was typical of the slow recovery from economic hardship. Yet, the city was home to county circuit, federal district, and state supreme courts, and lawyers were plentiful. For $4 a week, the Bledsoes moved into the Globe Tavern, where the Lincolns also boarded. When Bledsoe won his first case, one local observer, as quoted by Thomas O'Connor High, remarked that it was "the beginning of a brilliant career before the highest tribunal in the state." Bledsoe's first law partnership, with Jesse B. Thomas, lasted less than a year. Thomas was Lincoln's target in the future president's first political oratory, and soon thereafter Bledsoe and Thomas dissolved their business arrangement. In May 1841 Bledsoe became partners with one of the most respected attorneys in Springfield, Edward Dickinson Baker, who at the time was better known than Lincoln. This partnership lasted three years, but it was not unusual to have such short-term relationships in law offices at that time. Reflecting on a visit to Bledsoe's office on a legal matter, one Springfield resident, Bledsoe's colleague, Samuel Willard, years later recalled that he was "of a logical mind, acute, learned, versatile, able, and even powerful in any field of thought except natural science, in which he was untried." This same man, when asked a hypothetical question of whether Lincoln or Bledsoe would be more suited to the nation's highest political office, remarked: "Bledsoe must be the man."

In six years of practice Bledsoe was indeed a successful litigator. Estimates of his success can be drawn from court records and indicate that he won 60 percent of his cases before the Illinois state supreme court. Bledsoe accepted all kinds of cases—civil and criminal—and argued many slander suits. He was a competent attorney, relying on his memory, logic, and thought before the bench. One biographer, Hays, concluded his extensive education and learning was a liability in representing many Midwestern farmers. Reflecting on her father's business acumen, Sophia Bledsoe Herrick wrote: "his peculiar cast of mind was much better suited to winning cases than to making a good financial showing as a result of his law practice. A lack of business capacity and training, together with a very tender heart for people in trouble, combined to produce a very poor pecuniary result."

During this period, from 1844 to 1846, Bledsoe moved briefly to Cincinnati, where he also practiced law, and then to Washington after his wife became ill. In Washington he went into legal practice with his brother-in-law, Richard Coxe. Bledsoe argued before the United States Supreme Court three times, all unsuccessfully, although the winner in one case is clearly disputable. He and his wife did return to Springfield in time for the December 1846 court term, where records indicate Bledsoe was especially busy in his law practice.

During his Illinois years, Bledsoe jumped into Whig politics. He attended meetings and rallies, served on committees, and began writing editorials advocating the Whig cause. Springfield and neighboring Sangamon County were stubbornly Whig in a largely Democratic state, but the local Whigs elected their candidates to Congress. The tariff, internal improvements, and the National Bank of the United States appealed to many Illinois and Midwest inhabitants, and Bledsoe was often at the head of the charge to promote the party stance. In March 1843, he, Lincoln, and S. T. Logan penned "An Address to the People of Illinois" to define Whig principles and explain party philosophy to the populace. During the 1840 election, Bledsoe was often called upon to speak at party rallies. Despite strong support, the Democratic candidate for president, Martin Van Buren, carried Illinois.

During the summer of 1842 local Clay Clubs were formed in support of Henry Clay, and once again Bledsoe was at the forefront of political activity. He also began writing political editorials for the *Sangamo Journal*, all anticipating the election of Clay in 1844. When he and his family moved to Cincinnati and then Washington over the next two years, Bledsoe's political fires smoldered beneath the surface, only to burn brightly once again after his return to Springfield. In August 1847 the *Sangamo Journal* became the *Illinois Journal*, and

Bledsoe had sole responsibility for the editorial pages. His contributions to the newspaper indicate his developing political philosophy and anticipate his books. He wrote in the *Illinois Journal* that as long as the federal government and the states stayed in "their appropriate spheres of action," the two realms of government would not collide. Rejecting extreme states' rights views, Bledsoe argued that those advocates "seldom fail to look upon the general government with an eye of jealousy and distrust." At this point in his life Bledsoe was advocating the exact opposite of his eventual hard-line political stance. One biographer, Hays, concludes, "From his Editorial chair Bledsoe freely indulged his proclivity for controversy and his bent for philosophical speculation" and later called him a "hair splitting ratiocinationalist."

Yet, during the difficult decade of the 1840s, Bledsoe did not argue in support of slavery, arguments for which history best remembers the fiery Southerner. Illinois was not a hotbed of abolitionism, but Bledsoe wrote in November 1847 that he hoped John C. Calhoun's "powers be not exerted to extend the dominion and the curse of slavery." The next month he wrote to oppose the extension of slavery, "with all its evils to the white and black race," into New Mexico and California. Ten years later, in his controversial and inflammatory (especially in the North) *An Essay on Liberty and Slavery,* Bledsoe ardently defends the institution he saw as a social good, concluding "no fact is plainer than that the blacks have been elevated and improved by their servitude in this country." Such a diametrical change cannot easily be explained in Bledsoe's life.

Bledsoe's views on Lincoln offer insight into Bledsoe and the staunch opinions he held for the rest of his life on the federal union. He used such phrases as "a bundle of contradictions" and "peculiar make and mode of being" to describe his fellow Illinois attorney. In a review of W. H. Lamon's biography of Lincoln, "Lamon's Life of Lincoln," written in 1873, Bledsoe thought little of describing Lincoln as "little like other men" or referring to his "powerful intellect." He thought the president was "one of the most incomprehensible personages we have ever known" and felt Lincoln was "swallowed up in pride." He described the Great Emancipator as a hypocrite in politics and thought Lincoln's seemingly simple ways "were put on for effect of the people." Lincoln, wrote Bledsoe, has a "tendency toward laziness which made him willing to use dishonest measures to gain his end." Considering Bledsoe and his family lived under the same roof at the Globe Tavern in Springfield for three years with the Lincolns, his opinions and views on the future president cannot be entirely dismissed. Lincoln and Bledsoe shared travel, court dockets, legal discussions, and many meals and nights together during the former's early professional years. Yet, Bledsoe, the epitome of the unreconstructed Southerner, took reviewing Lamon's biography as an opportunity to attack the deceased Lincoln, and his objectivity as well as his conclusions are open to considerable debate.

The Illinois years are noteworthy for Bledsoe for one more reason—he began writing seriously for publication. Published in 1845, his *An Examination of President Edwards' Inquiry into the Freedom of the Will* was his first of several major treatises on religion, government, mathematics, and philosophy. President Edwards was Jonathan Edwards, briefly president of Princeton University before his death in 1758, whose writings and preaching established much of the early American religious tradition, and for whom Bledsoe had a great deal of respect. Bledsoe saw his work as a refutation of Calvinism but found Edwards's belief that man is born into a sinful state unacceptable. He termed such a belief "so monstrous a system" and argued that will is not determined. Bledsoe's intent was to expose Edwards and his errors, but to do so he had to prove Edwards wrong and himself right. He falls well short in this regard, although one anonymous reviewer, writing in Bledsoe's own *Southern Review,* which published the crux of his arguments years later in 20 July 1876, felt Bledsoe "laid the great New England giant prostrate in the dust." Another reviewer, writing in the *New Englander* (July 1847), concluded that Bledsoe misread Edwards but that the book included sections that were "usually vigorous and thorough, and many criticisms exceedingly accurate." The book had little popular appeal when published, however.

*An Examination of President Edwards' Inquiry into the Freedom of the Will* is actually a collection of eighteen letters Bledsoe had written to William Sparrow, professor of divinity and church history at Kenyon. Sparrow had been an early mentor to Bledsoe, and they had discussed the issue of free will at length while Bledsoe studied and taught at Kenyon. Bledsoe never mailed the letters but published them as eighteen separate chapters in the book, which he dedicated to Sparrow. Some eight years later he returned to many of his same arguments in another book on religious thought, *A Theodicy; or, Vindication of the Divine Glory, as Manifested in the Constitution and Government of the Moral World,* published in 1853 while he was in Mississippi.

Bledsoe was elected to the chair of mathematics and astronomy at the University of Mississippi in 1848 over sixty candidates. The university opened for its first session in the fall of 1848 with an impressive faculty. Faculty members included President George Frederick Holmes, who later taught at the University of Virginia; A. B. Longstreet, Yale graduate and later president at the University of South Carolina; and L. Q. C. Lamar,

later an American diplomat and leader of the Democratic Party in the South during Reconstruction.

During the 1850–1851 session, Bledsoe was appointed librarian. The problems with student discipline that plagued him at Miami were also evident at the University of Mississippi. Drinking, fighting, going to town, and general misconduct were common on campus. Between 1848 and 1861 there were five incidences of shootings involving students, although there were no deaths. Bledsoe was at the front of those demanding discipline, and in delivering the first commencement address he sternly addressed the students and guests on the depravity of man. For their part, student reaction to Bledsoe was predictable—the 1851 graduating class petitioned for his removal. Reflecting on Bledsoe's death in 1877, a writer using the pseudonym "H" for the *Oxford Eagle* called him "one of the most agreeable men in the social circle who ever lived in Oxford." When he resigned from the Mississippi faculty to take a position at the University of Virginia, the board of trustees wished him well and awarded him a doctor of laws degree.

Most Mississippians around Oxford owned slaves, but the Bledsoes did not at this time, although they depended on hired black labor for domestic work. One of the seeming inconsistencies in Bledsoe's life is his transformation from opposition to slavery, which he so sharply announced in Illinois, to tacit approval of the peculiar institution and later to ardent support. His defense of slavery, *An Essay on Liberty and Slavery,* carries an 1856 imprint, but the book initially appeared in 1855, one short year after he left Mississippi. Obviously, life in Mississippi and others around him had a remarkable effect on Bledsoe, as Hays recounts, "From unqualified opposition to slavery, he came to approve it, if not 'as a practical matter,' at least as necessary for social order; from rejection of the 'extreme' states' rights position, he came to accept the constitutional interpretation espoused by Davis, Holmes, and Longstreet."

His infant son, Albert Jr., died in Oxford, and he had recurring concerns about student discipline at the university, but there is no obvious defining moment in Bledsoe's life that could have altered his stance on slavery so drastically. One possible explanation for his dramatic change is that the national issue of slavery became a constitutional issue for him. Bledsoe, a lawyer whose learning and studious nature were based on reason, was able to make a smooth and logical transition to support slavery in *An Essay on Liberty and Slavery,* in which he joined the ranks of fellow defenders such as Thomas Dew, George Fitzhugh, and William Grayson.

Bledsoe was no doubt held in high regard, and his reputation as a scholar was enhanced with the publica-

# THE SOUTHERN REVIEW.

## No. I.

### JANUARY, 1867.

ART. I.—1. *The Education of the World.* By FREDERICK TEMPLE, D. D., Chaplain in Ordinary to the Queen ; Head Master of Rugby School ; Chaplain to the Earl of Denrigh. Essays and Reviews. Fourth Edition. London. 1862.

2. *The Education of the Human Race.* By Gotthold Ephraim Lessing. From the German. London. 1858.

3. *The Education of Mankind.* An Oration. By Edward Everett, LL. D. Boston. 1824.

4. *The History of Civilization, from the Fall of the Roman Empire to the French Revolution.* By F. Guizot.— Translated from the French by William Hazlitt, Esq. 3 vols. London. 1856.

5. *The Philosophy of History.* By G. W. F. Hegel.— Translated from the German by J. Sibree, M. A. London. 1857.

6. *The Philosophy of History.* By Frederick Von Schlegel. Translated from the German by James Burton Robertson. Fourth Edition. London. 1846.

The Philosophy of History is one of the creations of modern genius. Some writers ascribe the honor of having introduced this new science to Machiavelli, some to Bossuet, some to Vico, some to Montesquieu, some to Herder, and some to other authors. The works of all these men are, indeed, only so many streaks of the dawn, not the full-orbed disk, of the new science. That disk has not, as yet, risen above the horizon. In this instance, as in most others, it takes

2

*First page from the first issue of the magazine Bledsoe founded in 1867 and edited until his death in 1877*

tion of *A Theodicy*. The work was a major treatise following on his earlier studies on determinism and free will. Bledsoe considered *A Theodicy* his major philosophical work, but the book mostly repeats material from his earlier address on Edwards and free will.

As with his earlier work, Bledsoe had to seek a publisher. Sophia Harrick claimed the book sold thirty thousand copies. She also remembered it went through eleven printings and a British edition was published. Another estimate reported the book sold three editions of one thousand copies each in four months, and, by 1876, *A Theodicy* had gone through fifteen or sixteen printings. In *A Theodicy* Bledsoe operates from two basic principles: that God intends for the world to be of a moral order and not a paradise for man and that holiness cannot be necessitated. Neither is an original idea; in fact, both were widely accepted. Bledsoe's treatment of evil is a common approach, and he misses an opportunity to explore the nature of evil in relation to his preoccupation with free will.

Although the book leaves Bledsoe, as some historians have said, short of the first rank of American philosophers, *A Theodicy* did receive some national attention. It also sold well in England. Henry Mansel, the Oxford theologian whom Bledsoe befriended during the latter's years in London, claimed the book changed his own views. The text is still readable, but its lasting influence was limited to Methodists of the American South. John McClintock, editor of the *Methodist Quarterly Review*, stated in an 1854 review that he thought Bledsoe's work "one of the clearest and ablest expositions of the moral government of God" that had ever appeared. In his 1924 book, *Methodists on the March*, Charles C. Jarrell terms *A Theodicy* "one of the profoundest pieces of theological writing of any age." As a more immediate by-product, *A Theodicy* drew more attention to Bledsoe and helped him to land a teaching position at the University of Virginia in 1854.

With letters from friends Jefferson Davis and Robert E. Lee, Bledsoe gained the appointment in June 1854 at a salary of $3,000 annually. When Bledsoe arrived for the fall 1854 term, the institution enrolled five hundred students, claimed a proud tradition traced to Jefferson, and possessed an impressive array of faculty. Both faculty and students enjoyed considerable freedom of expression at the university, and Bledsoe was considered a lenient instructor but one who held his students to rigorous exams. He did revise the mathematics curriculum while at Virginia, dropping arithmetic and moving algebra to the junior year and geometry to the intermediate curriculum. His most significant contribution was the introduction of the history and philosophy of mathematics into the senior year of instruction. Discipline once again occupied much of the attention of the faculty but did not represent the problem Bledsoe had experienced at Mississippi. As the impending crisis over slavery and states' rights moved closer to secession, the students recognized Bledsoe as the one faculty member most closely associated with the Southern cause. He was remembered by one contemporary observer, Mary June Windle, as "an earnest and singlehearted man, who, more than most studious men, forms a connecting link between the past and the future":

> Emphatically a scholar in his habits and tastes, devoted to the labors of his responsible position, avoiding the scenes of public life and popular applause, seeking the highest inspiration in the investigation of his favorite themes, he makes a profound impression on the world than can be readily imagined by those who are sensible to the subtle character of the scholar's influence. We believe that it is conceded that this gentleman is far advanced of his contemporaries, both in the just conceptions of the purposes of education and exact learning.

Bledsoe enjoyed considerable success at the University of Virginia. While there he was recruited to the faculty of the new University of the South and was offered the presidency of the University of Missouri. He declined both positions, but, as his reputation grew, he accepted several speaking engagements. A February 1860 lecture on the "Social Destiny of Man" at the Smithsonian Institution led the *National Intelligencer,* in an article on 15 February 1860, to call Bledsoe a metaphysician who "has no superior in this country." The same article also called his lecture style stiff and awkward. Bledsoe was one of the leading scholars and educators of the South, and in 1856 he became one of the most recognized voices of the region in defense of slavery.

Bledsoe did not own slaves, but his *An Essay on Liberty and Slavery* is one of the major written defenses of the peculiar institution and direct attacks on abolitionists and critics of the constitutionality of slave ownership. Before the essay appeared, Bledsoe's ideas on the institution were sketchy at best. Although he owned no slaves, his parents and in-laws had. There is no evidence he harbored any strong sentiment on the proslavery side; in fact, the exact opposite is true. His experiences in Illinois included a rather strong stand against slavery, but by 1852 there are indications he had given up opposition. Intellectual historian Richard M. Weaver provides one of the best views of Bledsoe in *The Southern Tradition at Bay: A History of Postbellum Thought* (1968), writing that he "had the omnivorousness of mind which seeks strange bypaths of knowledge and finds a challenge in lost causes." Whatever the reason for the transition in Bledsoe during the ten years in which he moved from Illinois to Mississippi to Virginia, in *An Essay on Liberty and Slavery* he holds with former South Carolina governor Stephen D. Miller, who reportedly said in 1829, "slavery is not a national evil; on the contrary it is a national benefit." Abolitionism was also a defining factor in Bledsoe's transformation, as he concluded that emancipation was "admirably calculated to execute plots, murders, insurrections" and that costs associated with emancipation were prohibitive.

His most significant contribution in *An Essay on Liberty and Slavery* is his critique of the philosophy of John Locke and Jefferson's political theory. He is obvious in his admiration for Calhoun, with whom he had not found common ground in earlier years. He looks to Baron Montesquieu and Alexander Hamilton for ideas, as arguably most of Bledsoe's are not original.

Reaction to *An Essay on Liberty and Slavery* was predictable, particularly in the South. An anonymous reviewer in the *Southern Literary Messenger* (May 1856) called the book "the best treatise on Government extant." In the *Richmond Daily Enquirer* for 24 July

1856, Fitzhugh applauded Bledsoe's work but felt he should go even farther. Fitzhugh excused Bledsoe, contending he "has probably left that offensive warfare which the starving, riotous, infidel and revolutionary state of free society invites, to other hands, reserved it for the subject of another book." In *DeBow's Review* (August 1856), Bledsoe's old friend and colleague Holmes was lavish in his praise. He expressed confidence in Bledsoe, who would be "almost certain of the victory when he buckled on his armor to attack the sophisms of Channing, Wayland, and Sumner." Holmes carried this praise to the extreme, claiming "no treatise could be more happily adapted to the function of implanting correct doctrines on the slavery question in the minds of students and guarding them in advance against the subterfuges and lubricities of abolitionist sentiments and reasonings."

Most historians have characterized Bledsoe as one of the voices lacking reason before the outbreak of the Civil War. His writing is generally well conceived, however, and proceeds logically. His use of law and philosophy make *An Essay on Liberty and Slavery* somewhat distinctive among the prewar defenses. The book is still interesting and a remarkable insight into the Southern mind as regionalism rapidly developed into irreconcilable differences and eventually the tragedy of war. Bledsoe's flaw—and the basis of much of his argument—is that his logic was based on the inferiority of blacks, and the fate of his legacy is that of the tragic unreconstructed Southerner.

The war years were not especially hard on Bledsoe, although his daughter reflected that the decision to support the Confederacy "was a very bitter one to him." Bledsoe backed John Bell's candidacy for president. As war approached, students at the University of Virginia expressed staunch support for the Confederacy. After the firing on Fort Sumter the university ceased to offer classes, but the board voted to establish a military school, the School of Military Science and Civil Engineering. The professorship of military science was offered to Bledsoe, who declined in order to accept a commission as a colonel in the Virginia army in 1861. The fifty-one-year-old colonel saw no field service. His daughter claimed none other than Confederate president Jefferson Davis reported Bledsoe's "brains would be of far greater value to the cause of the Confederacy than his arm could be."

Davis appointed his friend and fellow West Pointer to be chief of the War Bureau at the Confederate capitol in Richmond. Davis also neglected to inform Secretary of War Leroy P. Walker of Bledsoe's appointment, and Bledsoe turned out to be a poor choice for the role of war bureaucrat. From the start there was friction between Walker and Bledsoe, and twice Bledsoe resigned his position. Davis convinced Bledsoe to return the first time, but in September 1862 the colonel returned to Charlottesville.

As a minor figure in the Confederate government, Bledsoe was ineffective. "Little Bledsoe" of his West Point years had become "a portly gentleman in a white vest" in the words of John Beauchamp Jones in his *A Rebel War Clerk's Diary* (1866). A Western fiction writer whose books include *Wild Western Scenes* (1841), *The Western Merchant* (1849), *Freaks of Fortune* (1854), and *The War Path* (1858), Jones was a clerk under Walker in the early days of the Confederacy. Jones's diary led some to nickname him "the Pepys of the Confederacy"; the few references he makes to Bledsoe provide a rather accurate portrait of "a fish out of water, and unfit for office." Jones wrote that Bledsoe's ankles were "much too weak for his weighty body," but he could "shuffle along quite briskly when in pursuit of a refractory clerk." Bledsoe's job was routine and his duties too general for an officer. The War Bureau served as a coordinating and clerical agency for the Secretary of War, and he lacked the executive ability to lead it. For two days Bledsoe was acting secretary after Walker's resignation, but after service under two additional war secretaries, Judah P. Benjamin and George W. Randolph, Bledsoe finally resigned in September 1862.

Bledsoe continued to advise Davis, who did not want or need the advice. In the fall of 1863, Bledsoe sailed for England on the *Florida*. The University of Virginia had granted him a one-year leave of absence, and his wife paid for the trip and the more than two years Bledsoe spent in London. The purpose of his trip is unclear, although Bledsoe claimed he was acting upon the request of Davis and Robert E. Lee to research and write a book vindicating the South and the right of secession. Jones bears out Bledsoe's assertion, recording in his diary for 21 August 1863: "I met Prof. A. T. Bledsoe to-day as he was ambling toward the passport office. He said he was just about to start for London, where he intended publishing his book—on slavery, I believe." Jones continued: "at parting I told him I hoped he would not find us all hanged when he returned. I think it possible he has a mission from the President, as well as his book to publish." Although the mission was (and remains) in question, Bledsoe did publish a book on his return. *Is Davis a Traitor?* was published on his return to the United States in 1866, but by then the war was over; Davis was imprisoned; and Bledsoe's lot as an apologist for the Southern cause was cast.

The *Florida* arrived in Wales in October, and Bledsoe traveled to London by train, arriving on 15 October. He did not return for the duration of the war. The *Index*, a Confederate newspaper based in London to arouse support for the Southern cause, announced his arrival, and for almost three years Bledsoe lived an active social life in the city, often dining out, attending the theater, and spending time in research. He contended he needed no introduction. He spent considerable time in the company of members of the Anglican clergy, one of whom—the Reverend Francis W. Tremlett—organized the Society for the Cessation of Hostilities in America after Bledsoe's arrival. He also fraternized with former *Southern Literary Messenger* editor John Reuben Thompson and noted philanthropist William M. Corcoran, both of whom influenced Bledsoe's postwar career as editor of the *Southern Review*. He was also ill for much of his stay in London.

Bledsoe's purpose in traveling to London was to gain access to documents that would support the Southern constitutional right of secession. He contended these sources were unavailable to him in the southern states; yet, he failed to uncover much supporting evidence in London. In spite of this failure he did write to Davis in the fall of 1864 that he "brought many hidden things to light . . . which will show the justice of our cause in new and convincing points of view." He reported to the Confederate president that he had written two volumes, although only the one was published. Bledsoe also wrote a series of four articles for the *Index* on the causes of the war, all in December 1863 and January 1864.

He had left his family in Charlottesville, where his daughters Sophia and Emily were married in his absence. In July 1865 he was terminated from the University of Virginia for "protracted absence." When the war ended, he was still in London and remained there for more than a year, supposedly to gather evidence and write his book. He was known to remark that the South had lost the war and could only be vindicated by the pen. *Is Davis a Traitor?* was privately published in Baltimore by Innes and Company shortly after his return, first to Charlottesville and then to Dinwiddie, Virginia. Bledsoe also launched his apologia for the South, the *Southern Review*, in Baltimore, in 1867.

The question of why Bledsoe went to London in the first place may never be answered. Archdeacon George A. Denison, editor of *The Church and State Review,* offered to pay Bledsoe to publish his research, but the latter declined. Perhaps historians and biographers have relied too heavily on the Jones comment that Davis sent Bledsoe on a mission. This version has certainly found its way into secondary sources. Bledsoe's daughter Sophia hints strongly he went at Davis's behest, but Davis may have simply found it convenient to be rid of his meddling old classmate. Whatever the reason, the resulting book definitely caused controversy in justifying secession.

*Is Davis a Traitor?* is a curious book with a history rooted in Bledsoe's trip to London, his prewar belief in the Constitutional right of secession, and the long-standing states' rights argument. He prefaces his remarks by admitting that by losing the war the South forfeited its right to secede. Instead, Bledsoe turns to the past to argue that secession was an option for the Southern states. In addition, he seeks to vindicate the names of Davis, Lee, General Thomas "Stonewall" Jackson, General Albert Sydney Johnston—all former West Point classmates—and other Southerners. Finally, Bledsoe wrote to fight charges of treason.

The book was published within months after his return from London, so he obviously prepared most of his written arguments before crossing the Atlantic. It was circulated and read—according to Hays, Thaddeus Stevens and Edwin M. Stanton both reputedly felt Bledsoe's arguments were "unanswerable." Bledsoe utilizes reason in his writing but, as Weaver stated, he wrote "in white heat." Although he turns to the writings of Hamilton, James Madison, and Richard Morris, he vehemently attacks statements by Daniel Webster, whom Bledsoe calls "the great expounder," and, to a lesser degree, former Supreme Court justice Joseph Story. To Bledsoe, the Southerner was the noble and brave warrior in contrast to "the rich Northerner, the merchant prince, or the great lord of the loom." He counterattacks any criticism of the South, all in preparation for the work he continued in the *Southern Review,* where he would review the causes and fight the war once again, castigating the North for another dozen years.

Bledsoe's place in history has wavered in the 125 years since his death. Many historians have classed him with other Southern polemicists, where he deservedly belongs. Other characterizations are more ambiguous, however. Scholars have debated the purpose of his trip to London and his superiority to Lincoln as an attorney, for example; they have also questioned whether *Is Davis a Traitor?* rescued the former Confederate president from a trial for treason. This assumption has found its way into biographies, dissertations, and various historical writings but has virtually no basis in history. *Is Davis a Traitor?* is a lively, well reasoned, and even exciting book, but it hardly had any impact on Davis and his legal battles.

By late 1866 Bledsoe's finances were suffering. He moved his family to Baltimore and accepted charity from other family members. He also arranged to publish a magazine, yet still had to supplement his income by teaching at a girls' academy. He also worked as a private tutor. His business sense was never a personal strength, which was evident in the management of what became the *Southern Review.*

The culmination of Bledsoe's career was editing the *Southern Review,* where his "white heat" grew even hotter. One of many postwar magazines designed to vindicate the South, the *Southern Review* featured many articles and reviews written by Bledsoe himself. Edwin Mims, in his multivolume *The South in the Building of the Nation* (1909–1913), quotes Lee as saying to Bledsoe: "Doctor, you must take care of yourself; you have a great work to do; we all look to you for our vindication." Bledsoe, who according to Frank Luther Mott in his *A History of American Magazines: 1864–1885* (1938) had "one of those versatile and many-talented minds that lend themselves easily to work on periodicals," took this great work seriously. The *Southern Review* was an archive of Southern history, culture, and civilization but was also intended to justify the South.

The *Southern Review* was only one of the many literary magazines launched across the South at the time, including *The Land We Love, Southern Magazine,* and the *New Eclectic,* all of which began with a moderate stance on political issues but shifted editorial policies as the role of the South in the nation was questioned and Reconstruction took a radical turn. William Hand Browne, who began as Bledsoe's co-editor on the *Southern Review,* took a militant stance in *Southern Magazine.* The rationale for this explosion in the southern press was articulated by Bledsoe in a 1 January 1867 article: while "the North is sending forth, by ten of thousands, her *Monthlies* and *Quarterlies* exclusively devoted to her own views, it seems but fair and right that the South should also be heard." Bledsoe was, according to Hays "vigorous, passionate, erudite, earnest, sometimes profound, almost always opinionated" and, according to Edwin Mims, "went to work with a stubborn and unconquered spirit, with the idea that sometime in the future all the principles for which the South had stood would triumph." Hays concluded that the editor maintained "remarkably high standards."

A typical issue consisted of eight or nine articles, essentially review essays. Bledsoe did not write the majority of essays, but he was the driving force behind the periodical. As intently as he vilified the North, he wrote "to embalm the memory of Southern heroes"; defending Southerners was his passion in editing the journal. Lee, Davis, Jackson, and Johnston were painted as heroic, long-suffering, and true patriots. Bledsoe's theory that states, not individuals, seceded, was introduced in the pages of the *Southern Review.* He deplored the Northern "fatal grasp" on the South, as he wrote in "Congress versus the Constitution" from issue 4 (July 1868) of the magazine, and in "The Model Republic Credit Mobilier" from issue 12 (July 1876) characterized southerners as a "down-trodden and enslaved people." The North, Bledsoe wrote in "School Histories of the United States" from issue 3 (January 1868), was "determined to remain on the throat of her fallen, bleeding, and helpless victim."

Bledsoe also wrote extensively on blacks and the total failure of the North to grasp the status of the former slaves in the postwar South, holding the line with his arguments in *An Essay on Liberty and Slavery*. He railed against the "pureblindness" of the North on the question of free blacks and expressed pity for the recently freed men and women of color. One of his articles for the first issue ridiculed Harriet Beecher Stowe's *Uncle Tom's Cabin* (1852). Bledsoe used the old theory that blacks were better served in the South than in their native Africa, argued that slavery did not degrade blacks, and theorized that the South and its slave holders had done blacks a service by civilizing them. Yet, he still insisted that slaves were not prepared for freedom, opining in issue 4, for example, that "they have yet to learn the conditions of existence in civil society as independent members." He had little to say about Reconstruction, writing in issue 12 that "The poorest negro was put over Lee's head" by Northern courts, Congress, and state Reconstruction governments. For ten years Bledsoe did not compromise in his defense of the South or his attacks on the North. His editing and writing for the *Southern Review* earned him the epitaph of "the unreconstructed." He loved a good fight, as his good-natured taunt from issue 19 (1876) implies: "Our critics—We have nothing about them, in this number of the Review; but we have several rods in soak for them."

Bledsoe attracted an impressive list of contributors, including Holmes, James L. Cabell, Mary Stuart Smith, William Nelson Pendleton, Paul Hamilton Hayne, Kate Mason Rowland, and Margaret Junkin Preston. Former University of Virginia colleague Basil Laneau Gildersleeve, a Confederate army hero who was injured during the war, was Bledsoe's most frequent contributor. He also drew advertising support from Baltimore merchants, local and neighboring schools, and assorted other businesses.

For all of Bledsoe's efforts, the *Southern Review* was a financial failure as well as a literary enigma. Its subscription list never exceeded three thousand names, and many subscribers simply failed to pay. Bledsoe, and later his daughter Sophia Bledsoe Herrick, addressed concerns to subscribers frequently. In 1876 Bledsoe wrote that fewer than half of the subscriptions were paid and begged subscribers to honor their commitment. Bledsoe's problems were not merely financial, however. Even he realized the "guilty indifference" of southerners to their own literature. Unlike most southern magazines, the *Southern Review* published no fiction, only a handful of poems, and few of the always popular battle accounts. Bledsoe com-

mented on the overall support of the southern press in issue 19, stating that "The patrons who do pay, have, in fact, been worse than the locusts of Egypt on the periodical literature of the South."

In truth, Bledsoe was a poor manager and miserable correspondent. He failed to pay poet Hayne, prompting the South Carolinian to call Bledsoe "an irreclaimable blackguard, and a hypocrite." Hayne wrote to a close friend that "this man is a Pecksniff." Old friend and colleague George Frederick Holmes also failed to receive payment, as did Baptist clergyman John A. Broadus. Only after Sophia Herrick joined the *Southern Review* as co-editor did finances gain some degree of order. She defended her father after his death, calling him in issue 23 (1878) "a man of truth and honesty,—a defense which, had his own hand not been pulseless in death, he need never to have called upon another to make for him." In his "Southern Magazines" in *South in the Building of the Nation,* Mims called Bledsoe a "great titan battling against the spirit of his age." Whichever view one takes of Bledsoe, the *Southern Review* ceased operations within two years of his death and would likely have folded sooner had not the Methodist Episcopal Church provided financial aid, including a regular salary to Bledsoe after 1871. Even such a move did not temper the outspoken editor—some of his most vindictive essays were published after the church assumed some financial responsibility for the magazine.

Immediately after Bledsoe began his efforts to vindicate and rescue the South with the *Southern Review,* he published what he considered to be his best work—*The Philosophy of Mathematics.* First published by Lippincott of Philadelphia in 1868, the book was successful enough to be printed five more times by the same publisher, the latest in 1897. Morris Cohen, one of the pioneer historians of American philosophical thought, suggested that Bledsoe "deserves to be better known." In a footnote in his *American Thought: A Critical Sketch* (1954), Cohen observed that Bledsoe's treatise on mathematics was still worth reading. The book is interesting and lively reading. Bledsoe explores the history of the development of his subject and focuses on the theoretical foundations of geometry and calculus. He also critiques then current mathematics textbooks and offers a strong defense of deductive reasoning. Although at times repetitious, *The Philosophy of Mathematics* represents Bledsoe's penchant for sound scientific reasoning. The work is another example of the author's support of and belief in education.

By the late 1870s Bledsoe was "increasingly irascible" and had alienated many old friends and even his family. Sophia Herrick, who had joined her father as co-editor of the *Southern Review* and continued his work two years following his death, often spoke and wrote bitterly of his last years. Bledsoe suffered a stroke early in 1877 and lingered in poor health until his death on December 8. He was buried in the University of Virginia Cemetery. The *Richmond Christian Advocate* noted his passing on 13 December 1877, reporting "a giant is prone in the dust."

Among the men of his generation, Albert Taylor Bledsoe was certainly one of the most enigmatic. His opposition to Darwinian principles, women's rights, and progressive school textbooks are mere footnotes to the stances he held on the issues of slavery and states' rights. Cohen included Bledsoe among the most versatile of the early Southern philosophers. Mims wrote that "everything for which he battled was destined to be beaten." Others described him as peripatetic, combative, intractable, uncompromising, and irascible. Perhaps the most accurate attempt to describe the "unreconstructed" Bledsoe is found in the pages of *Kentucky in American Letters, 1784–1912* (1913), in which John Wilson Townsend concludes that one can "consider him from a dozen angles, and . . . will not find his like again in the whole range of American history."

## Biographies:

Sophia Bledsoe Herrick, "Albert Taylor Bledsoe," *Alumni Bulletin of the University of Virginia,* 6 (May 1899): 1–6;

John Boyce Bennett, "Albert Taylor Bledsoe: Social and Religious Controversialist of the Old South," dissertation, Duke University, 1942;

Thomas O'Connor High, "Bledsoe's Review: A Southern Apologia," M.A. thesis, Vanderbilt University, 1942;

Willard Murrell Hays, "Polemics and Philosophy: A Biography of Albert Taylor Bledsoe," dissertation, University of Tennessee, 1971;

Bennett, "Albert Taylor Bledsoe: Transitional Philosopher of the Old South," *Methodist History,* 11 (October 1972): 3–14.

## References:

Philip Alexander Bruce, *History of the University of Virginia, 1819–1919: The Lengthened Shadow of One Man,* 5 volumes (New York: Macmillan, 1920–1922), III: 38, 79–87, 142, 262, 316, 344;

Fred Hobson, *Tell about the South: The Southern Rage to Explain* (Baton Rouge: Louisiana State University Press, 1983), pp. 20, 25, 87–88, 91–93, 105, 133, 205, 332;

John Beauchamp Jones, *A Rebel War Clerk's Diary,* edited by Earl. S. Miers (New York: Barnes, 1961), pp. 26, 28, 48, 73, 84, 262;

James B. Lloyd, *The University of Mississippi: The Formative Years, 1848–1906* (University, Miss.: John Davis Williams Library, 1979), pp. 2–21;

John McClintock, "Short Reviews and Notices of Books," *Methodist Quarterly Review, Fourth Series,* 6 (January 1854): 50;

Edwin Mims, *The Advancing South: Stories of Progress and Reaction* (New York: Doubleday, 1926);

Mims, "Southern Magazines," in *South in the Building of the Nation,* 7 (Richmond: The Southern Historical Society Publication, 1909–1913): 437–469;

Frank Luther Mott, *A History of American Magazines: 1864–1885* (New York: Appleton, 1938) pp. 382–384;

Harry E. Pratt, "Albert Taylor Bledsoe: Critic of Lincoln," Illinois State Historical Society, Transactions for the Year 1934 (Springfield, Ill., n.d.);

John Wilson Townsend, *Kentucky in American Letters, 1784–1912* (Cedar Rapids, Iowa: Torch, 1913), I: 171;

Richard M. Weaver, *The Southern Tradition at Bay: A History of Postbellum Thought* (New Rochelle, N.Y.: Arlington House, 1968), pp. 114–122, 133–138, 143–145, 153–158, 161, 166, 187, 244–245, 303, 316, 356;

Mary June Windle, *Life in Washington and Life Here and There* (Philadelphia: Lippincott, 1859).

## Papers:

The largest collection of Albert Taylor Bledsoe's papers is housed at the University of Virginia Library, but there are Bledsoe manuscripts at the Library of Congress, the Virginia Historical Society in Richmond, Houghton Library at Harvard, the Miami University Library (Ohio), and scattered materials in collections of other individuals housed at Duke University Library, the Illinois State Historical Library, the University of Chicago Library, the Mississippi Department of Archives and History, and the Archives of Kenyon College.

# William Wells Brown

*(March 1815 – 6 November 1884)*

Peter A. Dorsey
*Mount Saint Mary's College*

See also the Brown entries in *DLB 183: American Travel Writers, 1776–1864; DLB 50: Afro-American Writers Before the Harlem Renaissance,* and *DLB 3: Antebellum Writers in New York and the South.*

BOOKS: *Narrative of William W. Brown, a Fugitive Slave, Written by Himself* (Boston: Anti-Slavery Office, 1847; enlarged, 1848); republished as *Narrative of William W. Brown, an American Slave, Written by Himself* (London: Charles Gilpin, 1849);

*A Lecture Delivered Before the Female Anti-Slavery Society of Salem, at Lyceum Hall, Nov. 14, 1847* (Boston: Massachusetts Anti-Slavery Society, 1847);

*A Description of William Wells Brown's Original Panoramic Views of the Scenes in the Life of an American Slave, from His Birth in Slavery to His Death, or His Escape to His First Home of Freedom on British Soil* (London: Gilpin, 1849);

*Three Years in Europe; or, Places I Have Seen and People I Have Met. With a Memoir of the Author by William Farmer* (London: Charles Gilpin, 1852); revised and enlarged as *The American Fugitive in Europe. Sketches of Places and People Abroad* (Boston: Jewett / New York: Sheldon, Lamport & Blakeman, 1855);

*Clotel; or, The President's Daughter: A Narrative of Slave Life in the United States. With a Sketch of the Author's Life* (London: Partridge & Oakey, 1853); revised as *Clotelle: A Tale of the Southern States* (Boston: Redpath / New York: Dexter, Hamilton, 1864); revised as *Clotelle, or, The Colored Heroine. A Tale of the Southern States* (Boston: Lee, 1867);

*St. Domingo: Its Revolutions and Its Patriots. A Lecture, Delivered before the Metropolitan Athenaeum, London, May 16, and at St. Thomas' Church, Philadelphia, December 20, 1854* (Boston: Bela Marsh, 1855);

*The Escape; or, A Leap for Freedom. A Drama in Five Acts* (Boston: Wallcut, 1858);

*Memoir of William Wells Brown, an American Bondman, Written by Himself* (Boston: Anti-Slavery Office, 1859);

*Wm. W. Brown.*

*The Anti-Southern Lecturer* (London, 1862);

*The Black Man, His Antecedents, His Genius, and His Achievements* (New York: Hamilton / Boston: Wallcut, 1863; revised and enlarged, 1863);

*The Negro in the American Rebellion: His Heroism and His Fidelity* (Boston: Lee & Shepard, 1867);

*The Rising Son; or, The Antecedents and Advancement of the Colored Race* (Boston: Brown, 1874);

*My Southern Home: or, The South and Its People* (Boston: Brown, 1880).

OTHER: "The American Slave Trade," in *The Liberty Bell*, by "The Friends of Freedom" (Boston: National Anti-Slavery Bazaar, 1848), pp. 231–237;

*The Anti-Slavery Harp: A Collection of Songs for Anti-Slavery Meetings*, compiled by Brown (Boston: Bela Marsh, 1848; Newcastle, U.K.: Blackwell, 1850);

"Visit of a Fugitive Slave to the Grave of Wilberforce," in *Autographs for Freedom*, edited by Julia Griffiths (Auburn, Ala.: Alden, Beardsley / Rochester, N.Y.: Wanzer, Beardsley, 1854), pp. 70–76.

SELECTED PERIODICAL PUBLICATION– UNCOLLECTED: *Miralda; or, The Beautiful Quadroon. A Romance of American Slavery*, revision of *Clotel; or, The President's Daughter, Weekly Anglo-African* (1 December 1860 – 6 March 1861).

Born a slave and lacking any formal education, William Wells Brown occupies a central and remarkably versatile role in the formation of the African American literary tradition. The author of the first novel, the first play, and the first travel book to be published by an African American, he was also a pioneer in the fields of African and African American history, and he wrote one of the most important American slave narratives. Brown matched his literary accomplishments with a long and successful public career as a lecturer for abolition, temperance, and civil rights. Because his prolific writings were often tied to the social causes he advanced, his books are notable more for their rhetorical effectiveness than for artistic unity. His work features many autobiographical elements, which he often renders with fictional techniques, and he frequently borrowed from outside sources, including his own prior publications, to authenticate his material. Though his portrayal of comic figures draws on the minstrel tradition and his light-colored heroines display some of the characteristics of the tragic mulatto, he successfully adapts these conventions to his major themes, which include the destructive effect of slavery on families, the rights of blacks to stay in an America they helped build, the differences between industrial and slave labor, the absurdity of the color line, the hypocrisy of a racist Christianity, and the inconsistency between American ideals and social reality. In addressing these issues he affirmed the strength, courage, and inventiveness of African Americans.

Much of the information about Brown's early life comes from the many autobiographical references in his works as well as from a brief biography written by his daughter, Josephine. According to these sources, Brown was born in March 1815 on a farm near Lexington, Kentucky; he was owned by John Young, a physician, farmer, and politician. His mother, Elizabeth, a strong and capable field slave, had seven children, all by different fathers. She named her youngest son William, but when the Youngs took in an infant relation with the same name they forced him to go by Sandford. Brown's white father, George W. Higgins, was Young's near relative, a circumstance that resulted in both favorable treatment and heightened persecution.

When Brown was still a child, the Youngs moved first to a plantation on the Missouri River and then to one about four miles north of St. Louis. Raised primarily as a house servant and a medical assistant, Brown was occasionally punished by being sent to the fields, where he experienced the cruelty of two overseers. When he was about thirteen, he began to be hired out to a variety of masters, and therefore saw many forms of American slavery. One master, Major Freeland, an innkeeper, gambler, and drunkard, flogged Brown so maliciously that he ran off to complain to Dr. Young, only to be similarly abused. He had a better experience when he worked for the printer and future martyr for the abolitionist cause, Elijah P. Lovejoy, who gave him, as he remembered, "what little learning I obtained while in slavery." In 1832 Brown made three trips to the New Orleans slave market while hired by James Walker, "a heartless, cruel, ungodly" slave trader.

When, shortly thereafter, Brown was given the unusual opportunity of finding a new master, he convinced his mother that they should escape together. Taking flight through Illinois, they were captured and subsequently sold, she to an owner in the Deep South and he to Samuel Willi, a local merchant. The following year Brown became the property of Enoch Price, a merchant and riverboat owner, whose wife sought to keep Brown in place by encouraging him to marry. Brown planned his escape instead, which occurred on New Year's Day in 1834 when he walked off a riverboat in Cincinnati. Suffering from exposure to cold and hunger some days later, he sought the aid of a Quaker named Wells Brown, who helped him along the Underground Railroad. In gratitude Brown accepted Wells Brown's suggestion that he adopt his name, as long as he could maintain his original identity as William.

Feeling safe in Cleveland, then Buffalo and Farmington, New York, Brown supported himself as a handyman, barber, wildcat banker, and eventually as a steamboat steward. In 1834 he married Elisabeth Schooner, with whom he had three daughters, the first of whom died in infancy. While working on Lake Erie, Brown educated himself, read abolitionist newspapers, organized a temperance society, and helped other fugitives escape to Canada.

Brown became a professional abolitionist in 1843, when he began to lecture for the Western New York

Anti-Slavery Society. Although he experienced racial discrimination while traveling he adhered to a grueling schedule, honing his oratorical skills and enhancing his reputation in the movement. Marital difficulties and an eventual separation may have prompted his decision to lecture for William Lloyd Garrison's American Anti-Slavery Society and his Massachusetts Anti-Slavery Society, a shift that caused him to relocate to Boston. Though Brown generally espoused the doctrines of the famous abolitionist, he advocated black suffrage at a time when Garrison's organizations renounced political action, and he argued that slaves had the right to revolt, while the Garrisonians preached nonviolence.

In 1847 Brown published the first edition of his *Narrative of William W. Brown, a Fugitive Slave, Written by Himself.* This slave narrative, which sold more than thirteen thousand copies in six editions in the United States and England, was second in popularity to that of Frederick Douglass, with whom Brown was often compared. While Brown's text follows the conventions of the genre in that it is introduced by a respected white abolitionist, presents scenes of whippings and slave auctions, and exposes the hypocrisy of Christian slaveholding, his account usefully modifies that of his more famous colleague, Douglass. Douglass presents himself as a heroic slave who attains freedom and manhood by courageous self-assertion. In contrast Brown demonstrates how the conditions of slavery often made such a stance impractical. He illustrates this theme early in the text through the story of Randall, a strong and valued slave on Young's plantation, who, like Douglass, resolved to die rather than be whipped. Though he resisted a vindictive overseer, Randall eventually was outnumbered, shot, and savagely beaten. Depicting a world where fortitude is insufficient to overcome an entrenched institution, Brown demonstrates how slavery was best combated with guile and trickery, even if such actions violated conventional moral standards. Brown's portrayal of family life also exhibits a more realistic view of slavery than that of Douglass. Because Douglass was estranged early from his family, he presents himself as an individualistic, self-made man. Brown's narrative illustrates not only the agonizing process by which families were dissolved but also how family loyalty often competed with the desire for freedom.

Anxious to further the work Douglass had begun in England, Brown traveled to Europe in 1849. He served as a delegate to the Paris Peace Congress and began to lecture throughout Great Britain. The Fugitive Slave Law caused him to extend his stay until 1854, during which time he campaigned vigorously against slavery, drew praise for his character and elocution, and emerged as a professional writer.

CLOTEL;

OR,

THE PRESIDENT'S DAUGHTER:

A Narrative of Slave Life

IN

THE UNITED STATES.

BY

WILLIAM WELLS BROWN,

A FUGITIVE SLAVE, AUTHOR OF "THREE YEARS IN EUROPE."

With a Sketch of the Author's Life.

" WE hold these truths to be self-evident: that all men are created equal; that they are endowed by their Creator with certain inalienable rights, and that among these are LIFE, LIBERTY, and the PURSUIT OF HAPPINESS." — *Declaration of American Independence.*

LONDON:
PARTRIDGE & OAKEY, PATERNOSTER ROW;
AND 70, EDGWARE ROAD.
1853.

*Title page for Brown's fictionalized account of the slave progeny of Thomas Jefferson (Special Collections, Perkins Library, Duke University)*

In 1852 Brown published *Three Years in Europe; or, Places I Have Seen and People I Have Met. With a Memoir of the Author by William Farmer,* a collection of twenty-three letters he had sent to friends and abolitionist newspapers about his European experiences. He revised and enlarged the collection, the first travel book by an African American, into *The American Fugitive in Europe. Sketches of Places and People Abroad,* which he published in the United States three years later. These volumes feature an engaging mixture of personal reflections, amusing anecdotes, and descriptions of notable people and places. In addition to verbal portraits of Thomas Carlyle, Benjamin Disraeli, and Harriet Martineau, Brown introduces readers to his friend and fellow fugitive, Ellen Craft, and to Joseph Jenkins, an African jack-of-all-trades whose energy and versatility mirror Brown's own. He also chronicles the Paris Peace Congress, describes the Crystal Palace, and comments on a session of the House of Commons. Throughout both books he exposes the multiple ironies of being an

American fugitive abroad, especially the contrast between the freedom he experiences in Europe and the slavery and racism of the United States. Brown's literary talents were well suited to the loose structure of travel literature, and these books, though they have not been the focus of scholarly attention, were acclaimed by British and American reviewers.

Brown's next book, the first African American novel, received less notice than *Three Years in Europe* but assured him a place in literary history. As critics have observed, *Clotel; or, The President's Daughter: A Narrative of Slave Life in the United States. With a Sketch of the Author's Life* (1853) includes enough subplots to fill a book many times its size, but the central story draws on the popular belief that Thomas Jefferson left some of his own children in slavery. The novel opens with the public auction of Currer, Jefferson's former mistress, and their two light-skinned daughters, Clotel and Althesa. Currer becomes the property of John Peck, a slaveholding minister living near Natchez, Tennessee, yet, Currer dies abruptly of yellow fever. The Natchez section, however, is important for portraying the contending views of the proslavery Peck, his pious abolitionist daughter Georgiana, and the freedom-loving, freethinking Miles Carlton. Georgiana converts to Carlton's way of thinking and then marries him, but after her father dies, she too becomes gravely ill. From her deathbed she resolutely frees her slaves and provides land for them in Ohio. Althesa, meanwhile, goes to New Orleans, where she is purchased by an abolitionist physician who marries her but neglects to emancipate her legally. When both die of yellow fever, their nearly white daughters are sold as mistresses, showing how even the most benign forms of slavery can lead to tragedy.

Intertwined with these plots is the story of Clotel, who stays in Virginia after being purchased as the mistress of Horatio Green. Their initially loving relationship produces a daughter, Mary, but Green eventually succumbs to his political ambitions and marries a woman who forces Mary to serve in their home and demands that Green sell Clotel to a slave trader. After being sold twice more, Clotel escapes and returns to Virginia to free her daughter. Apprehended in the general suspicion surrounding the Nat Turner Rebellion, Clotel is sent to a slave pen in Washington, D.C., within sight of the Capitol and White House. After escaping again, she drowns herself rather than return to slavery. The book ends happily in France with the somewhat contrived reunion of Mary and George Green, a slave whom she freed from jail after he joined Turner's revolt.

Appearing the year after Harriet Beecher Stowe's enormously popular *Uncle Tom's Cabin, Clotel,* like Stowe's book, adapts the conventions of the sentimental novel to the antislavery cause. Revising Stowe's view of slavery and how it can best be ended, Brown organized *Clotel* less for the purposes of fully realizing character and action than to paint broadly the many horrors of the American "peculiar institution." To help him do so, he incorporated many outside sources, including incidents from his own life and from the lives of other fugitives, extracts from speeches, political writings, newspaper reports, advertisements, and even parts of a story by Lydia Maria Child. These disparate elements contribute to the loose structure of the book, but Brown effectively unifies his message through a central irony: that the man who brought forth a nation with the words "all men are created equal" himself engendered a legacy of slavery and tragedy. Mid-twentieth-century scholars criticized *Clotel* for its weak structure and its reliance on nearly white characters; recent critics have more positively explored the advantages of its nontraditional format and its influence on later black writing.

Brown revised and republished his novel three times. Its first American rendition, *Miralda; or, The Beautiful Quadroon,* was serialized in the *Weekly Anglo-African* beginning in late 1860. This version featured many additions and omissions, added a new conclusion, and altered setting, sequence, and characterization. Late in 1864 Brown published a third version, *Clotelle: A Tale of the Southern States,* a shortened version of *Miralda* in which the title character corresponds to Clotel's daughter, Mary, in the original book, and George Green, now called Jerome, changes from a nearly white to a "perfectly black" character. Published ostensibly to inspire and entertain Union troops, the novel no longer links the central female characters to Thomas Jefferson, and it omits some material that might have offended a northern white audience. In 1867 Brown published a final version, *Clotelle, or, The Colored Heroine. A Tale of the Southern States.* Adding four chapters, he carries the action through the end of the war, during which Jerome dies while bravely recovering the body of a white Union officer and Clotelle passes as a Confederate woman to assist Union prisoners. After the war she purchases her former master's plantation. The overall effect of Brown's revisions was to tighten the romantic plot of Mary/Miralda/Clotelle and George/Jerome. These changes give the novel more coherence but make it arguably less powerful as a work of social protest.

After Brown published the first version of his novel in London, he was anxious to continue the fight against slavery in his native land. Friends and supporters purchased his freedom, leaving him able to return and resume lecturing for the American Anti-Slavery Society and the Massachusetts Anti-Slavery Society. He again made literary history in 1856 when he wrote and began reciting what some consider the first African

THE DEATH OF CLOTEL.  *Page* 218.

*Illustration from* Clotel *depicting the moment at which the heroine decides to drown herself rather than return to slavery*

American drama, *Experience, or, How to Give the Northern Man a Backbone*. The text of this play has been lost, but summaries and reviews of it are preserved in the periodical press. *Experience* satirized Nehemiah Adams's proslavery tract, *A South-Side View of Slavery* (1854), by recounting the kidnapping of a northern proslavery minister who, after being sold into slavery, resolves to oppose it upon his release. Reaction to *Experience* was so positive that Brown began to book dates independently of antislavery organizations. Though some abolitionists criticized him for doing so, he argued, "People will pay to hear the Drama that would not give a cent in an anti-slavery meeting."

By early 1857 Brown was performing a second play, *The Escape; or, A Leap for Freedom. A Drama in Five Acts,* which the following year became the first drama to be published by an African American. *The Escape* centers on Melinda and Glen, two secretly married slaves from different plantations. The opening scenes use irony and humor to expose the moral corruption and religious hypocrisy of slaveholding culture. When Melinda's master, Dr. Gains, transfers her to another plantation so that he can more easily seduce her and buys Glen so that he can beat and sell him,

both characters forcibly resist and escape. Gains's slave Cato, a comic character in the minstrel tradition, initially believes his interests lie in cooperating with his master, but he quickly joins Melinda and Glen. Mr. White, an appropriately named abolitionist, conveys the central purpose of the play when he advances from speech-making to assisting the fugitives' crossover to Canada. Though the sensational plot, lofty diction, farcical humor, and limited characters of *The Escape* are typical of nineteenth-century American drama, the play mixes entertainment and abolitionist sentiment with some subtlety.

Brown's personal and professional life changed dramatically as the country moved toward war. His estranged wife died while he was in England, and Brown remarried in 1860. He and his second wife, Annie Elizabeth Gray, had two children, both of whom died early in life. The busy abolitionist also began to practice medicine, which he continued with questionable success for the rest of his life. Just before the Civil War he began to canvass for the voluntary emigration of African Americans to Haiti. His enthusiasm diminished, however, when he found that conditions in Haiti were not as promising as he had been led to believe and when it became apparent that the war would be a protracted struggle.

Once the conflict started, Brown worked hard to ensure that slavery would be the central issue; he recruited black soldiers and denounced the lack of black military officers. Even before the war ended he recognized the precarious position of newly freed African Americans, and, when peace was restored, he openly criticized President Andrew Johnson for not taking stronger measures to protect their freedom. By 1867 he claimed that their position was worse than it had been before emancipation. The best protection, he argued, was the vote. Though in favor of women's rights, he, like Douglass, thought the black vote was so urgent that he did not advocate merging the causes of women's and black men's suffrage.

Brown also published three major historical works in the 1860s and 1870s, all of which of highlighted the rich history and strong character of black people while refuting claims of their inferiority. The first of these, *The Black Man, His Antecedents, His Genius, and His Achievements* (1863), presents fifty-three biographies of those who had overcome adversity and risen by their "own genius, capacity, and intellectual development." Brown follows his opening "Memoir of the Author" with an essay, "The Black Man and His Antecedents," which shows how African peoples led the civilized world during periods of their history, claims that emancipation has been a success in the British West Indies, and demonstrates the courage and love of freedom of black people. Brown also criticized President Abraham Lincoln for his belief in the natural inferiority of African Americans, argued against forced colonization, and predicted that emancipation would only benefit northern industry. He did not expect "the slave of the south to jump into equality"; he hoped only that "he may be allowed to jump into liberty, and let him make equality for himself." *The Black Man, His Antecedents, His Genius, and His Achievements* was praised in abolitionist papers but received mixed reviews from other publications.

The following two historical works did not generate as much public interest. The first of these was a military history, *The Negro in the American Rebellion: His Heroism and His Fidelity* (1867), a book that summarizes the participation of African Americans in the Revolution and the War of 1812 and then discusses how blacks influenced the coming of the Civil War and its outcome, including notable acts of heroism. Brown's next and most ambitious book, *The Rising Son; or, The Antecedents and Advancement of the Colored Race* (1874), traces African civilization, presents theories of racial origin, and recounts the histories of black peoples in Haiti, South America, the Carribean, and the Unites States. It concludes with eighty-one biographical sketches of "Representative Men and Women," some of which appeared in *The Black Man, His Antecedents, His Genius, and His Achievements*. All three of Brown's little-studied histories lack the structure and coherence expected of contemporary historical narratives, but they also show that he was ahead of his time in portraying a distinctive African American culture with important roots in the African past.

Still actively speaking throughout the 1870s, Brown traveled to the South in 1879–1880 for his first visit since he escaped from slavery. The result was his last book, *My Southern Home: or, The South and Its People* (1880), one of the most complex and cohesive of his works. *My Southern Home* includes many of the autobiographical incidents found in Brown's earlier writings, but the narrator is detached and racially indistinct for most of the book. Without overlooking the injustice and cruelty of slavery, Brown infuses his final text with nostalgia, seeking to preserve the folk life of antebellum Southern culture. A common theme is the resourcefulness of slaves. "The negro," Brown summarizes, "would often show his wit to the disadvantage of his master or mistress." While highlighting the adaptability of slave culture and undermining the authority of an already romanticized old order, Brown also seeks to shape the New South by giving a balanced analysis of Reconstruction, exposing the alarming dangers of the post-Reconstruction era, and assuring whites that blacks want their rights protected more than they expect immediate "Social equality." Though he asserts that "The South is the black man's home," he advises, "if he cannot be protected in his rights he should leave." Dropping his neutral narrative pose in the last few chapters, Brown advocates hard work, education, self-improvement, temperance, and racial solidarity in the "glorious work of the elevation of my race."

Brown died on 6 November 1884 in Chelsea, Massachusetts, having lived according to the ideals he advanced. Although his writing, like his public career, has been overshadowed by Douglass's magisterial presence, critics have recently mined the broad range of Brown's work for its diversity, its innovation, and its alternate perspectives on the African American experience.

**Bibliography:**

Curtis W. Ellison and E. W. Metcalf Jr., *William Wells Brown and Martin R. Delany: A Reference Guide* (Boston: Hall, 1978).

**Biographies:**

Josephine Brown, *Biography of an American Bondman, by His Daughter* (Boston: Wallcut, 1856);

William Edward Farrison, *William Wells Brown: Author and Reformer* (Chicago: University of Chicago Press, 1969).

**References:**

William L. Andrews, introduction to *From Fugitive Slave to Free Man: The Autobiographies of William Wells Brown*, edited by Andrews (New York: Mentor, 1993), pp. 1–12;

Andrews, "Mark Twain, William Wells Brown, and the Problem of Authority in New South Writing," in *Southern Literature and Literary Theory*, edited by Jefferson Humphries (Athens: University of Georgia Press, 1990), pp. 1–21;

Andrews, "The Novelization of Voice in Early African-American Narrative," *PMLA*, 105 (January 1990): 23–34;

Andrews, *To Tell a Free Story: The First Century of Afro-American Autobiography, 1760–1865* (Urbana: University of Illinois Press, 1986), pp. 27–29, 144–151, 171–176, 272–274;

Bernard W. Bell, *The Afro-American Novel and Its Tradition* (Amherst: University of Massachusetts Press, 1987), pp. 38–42;

Stephen Butterfield, *Black Autobiography in America* (Amherst: University of Massachusetts Press, 1974), pp. 9–89;

Peter A. Dorsey, "De-authorizing Slavery: Realism in Stowe's *Uncle Tom's Cabin* and Brown's *Clotel*," *ESQ*, 41 (Winter 1995): 256–288;

John Ernest, "The Reconstruction of Whiteness: William Wells Brown's *The Escape; or, A Leap for Freedom*," *PMLA*, 113 (October 1998): 1108–1121;

M. Giulia Fabi, "The 'Unguarded Expressions of the Feelings of the Negroes': Gender, Slave Resistance, and William Wells Brown's Revisions of *Clotel*," *African American Review*, 27, no. 4 (Winter 1993): 639–654;

Paul Gilmore, "'De Genewine Artekil': William Wells Brown, Blackface Minstrelsy, and Abolitionism," *American Literature*, 69 (December 1997): 743–780;

J. Lee Greene, *Blacks in Eden: The African American Novel's First Century* (Charlottesville: University Press of Virginia, 1996), pp. 23–62;

J. Noel Heermance, *William Wells Brown and Clotelle: A Portrait of the Artist in the First Negro Novel* (Hamden, Conn.: Archon, 1969);

Blyden Jackson, *A History of Afro-American Literature, Volume 1: The Long Beginning, 1746–1895* (Baton Rouge: Louisiana State University Press, 1989), pp. 326–342;

Vernon Loggins, *The Negro Author, His Development in America* (New York: Columbia University Press, 1931), pp. 156–173;

Christopher Mulvey, "The Fugitive Self and the New World of the North: William Wells Brown's Discovery of America" in *The Black Columbiad: Defining Moments in African American Literature and Culture*, edited by Werner Sollors and Maria Diedrich (Cambridge, Mass.: Harvard University Press, 1994), pp. 99–111;

Robert B. Stepto, *From Behind the Veil: A Study of Afro-American Narrative* (Urbana: University of Illinois Press, 1979), pp. 26–31;

Alice Walker, "If the Present Looks Like the Past, What Does the Future Look Like?" in her *In Search of Our Mothers' Gardens: Womanist Prose* (San Diego: Harcourt Brace Jovanovich, 1983), pp. 290–312;

Jean Fagan Yellin, *The Intricate Knot: Black Figures in American Literature, 1776–1863* (New York: New York University Press, 1972), pp. 154–181.

**Papers:**

A limited number of William Wells Brown's papers are collected at the Boston Public Library; the Butler Library, Columbia University; the Enoch Pratt Free Library in Baltimore, Maryland; the George Arents Research Library at Syracuse University; the Historical Society of Pennsylvania; the Houghton Library, Harvard University; and the Schomberg Center for Research in Black Culture of the New York Public Library.

# John C. Calhoun

*(18 March 1782 – 31 March 1850)*

Clyde N. Wilson
*University of South Carolina*

See also the Calhoun entry in *DLB 3: Antebellum Writers in New York and the South.*

WORKS: *Speeches of Messrs. Calhoun and Grosvenor upon Mr. Webster's Resolutions; in the House of Representatives of the United States* (Charleston, S.C.: Courier-Office, 1813);

*Speech Delivered in the House of Representatives of the United States, on the [ ] Day of January, 1814, on a Bill Making Further Provision for Filling the Ranks of the Regular Army, Encouraging Enlistments, and Authorising the Reenlistments, for Longer Periods, of Men Whose Terms of Office Are About to Expire* (Alexandria, Va.: Corse & Rounsavell, 1814);

*Mr. Calhoun's Speech on the Loan Bill, Delivered in the House of Representatives of the United States, February, 1814* (Washington, D.C.: Rapine & Elliot, 1814);

*Speech of the Honorable John C. Calhoun, in the House of Representatives, February 4th, 1817* (Washington, D.C., 1817);

*Onslow in Reply to Patrick Henry* (Washington, D.C., 1826);

*Exposition and Protest, Reported by the Special Committee of the House of Representatives, on the Tariff . . . December 19, 1828* (Columbia, S.C.: D. W. Sims, Sate Printer, 1829);

*Correspondence between Gen. Andrew Jackson and John C. Calhoun, President and Vice-President of the U. States, on the Subject of the Course of the Latter, in the Deliberations of the Cabinet of Mr. Monroe, on the Occurrences in the Seminole War* (Washington, D.C.: Green, 1831);

*Mr. Calhoun's Sentiments, upon the Subject of State Rights, and the Tariff; Together with Copies of the Virginia Resolutions of 1798; of the Kentucky Resolutions of 1799; and of the Decision of the Supreme Court of Pennsylvania, Pronounced in 1799, by Chief Justice M'Kean* (Boston: Beals & Homer, 1831);

*Opinions of the Vice President of the United States, on the Relation of the States and the General Government . . .* (Charleston, S.C.: State Rights and Free Trade Association, 1831);

*Miniature by Washington Blanchard (New-York Historical Society)*

*Important Correspondence on the Subject of State Interposition, between His Excellency Gov. Hamilton, and Hon. John C. Calhoun. . . .* (Charleston, S.C.: A. E. Miller, 1832);

*Speeches of Messrs. Calhoun, Webster, and Poindexter in the Senate of the United States on the Revenue Collection Bill* (Washington, D.C., 1833);

*Speech of Mr. Calhoun . . . on the Bill Further to Provide for the Collection of Duties on Imports* (Washington, D.C., 1833);

*Remarks of the Hon. John C. Calhoun, Delivered in the Senate of the U. States, on the Subject of the Removal of the*

*Deposits from the Bank of the U. States. January 13, 1834* (Washington, D.C.: Green, 1834);

*Remarks of the Hon. John C. Calhoun, Delivered in the Senate of the United States, March 21, 1834, on the Motion of Mr. Webster, for Leave to Introduce a Bill to Continue the Charter of the Bank of the United States for Six Years after the Present Charter* (Washington, D.C., 1834);

*Remarks of the Hon. John C. Calhoun, Delivered in the Senate of the United States, April 9, 1834, on the Bill to Repeal the Force Act* (Washington, D.C., 1834);

*Remarks of the Hon. John C. Calhoun, Delivered in the Senate of the United States, May 6, 1834, on the President's Protest* (Washington, D.C., 1834);

*Speech of Mr. Calhoun, of South Carolina, in Senate, January 18, 1836, on the Motion to Refer the Speeches of the President of the United States, Concerning the Relations of the United States with France, to the Committee on Foreign Relations* (Washington, D.C., 1836);

*Speech of the Hon. John C. Calhoun, of South Carolina, on the Abolition Petitions. Delivered on Wednesday, March 9, 1836* (Washington, D.C.: Green, 1836);

*Remarks . . . on the Bill to Regulate the Deposits of Public Money. In Senate, June, 1836* (Washington, D.C., 1836);

*Speech . . . on the Bill to Prohibit Post Masters . . . Delivered in the Senate April 12, 1836* (Washington, D.C., 1836);

*Speeches of Mr. Calhoun of S. Carolina, on the Bills for the Admission of Michigan. Delivered in the Senate of the United States, January, 1837* (Washington, D.C.: Green, 1837);

*Remarks of Mr. Calhoun, of South Carolina, on His Proposition to Cede the Public Lands to the New States . . . February 7, 1837* (Washington, D.C.: Moore, 1837);

*Remarks of Mr. Calhoun, of South Carolina, on the Reception of Abolition Petitions, Delivered in the Senate of the United States, February 1837* (Washington, D.C.: Moore, 1837);

*Remarks of Mr. Calhoun, on the Bill Authorizing an Issue of Treasury Notes: Delivered in the Senate of the United States, September 19, 1837* (Washington, D.C.: Blair & Rives, 1837);

*Speech . . . on Amendment to Separate the Government from the Banks, delivered in the Senate of the U.S., Oct. 3, 1837* (Washington, D.C., 1837);

*Speech of Mr. Calhoun, of South Carolina, on the Sub-treasury Bill: Delivered in the Senate . . . February 15, 1838* (Washington, D.C.: Hamilton & Denham, 1838);

*Speech of Mr. Calhoun, of South Carolina, in Reply to Mr. Clay, on the Sub-treasury Bill. Delivered in the Senate of the United States, March 10, 1838* (Washington, D.C.: Washington Chronicle, 1838);

*Speech of Mr. Calhoun, of South Carolina, in Reply to Mr. Webster's Rejoinder. Delivered in the Senate of the United States, March 22, 1838* (Washington, D.C.?, 1838?);

*Remarks of Mr. Calhoun of South Carolina, on the Graduation Bill. In Senate, Tuesday, January 15, 1839* (Washington, D.C.: Blair & Rives, 1839);

*Remarks . . . on the Bill to Prevent the Interference of Certain Federal Officers in Elections; Delivered in the Senate of the U.S. Feb. 22, 1839* (Washington, D.C., 1839);

*Letter of the Hon. John C. Calhoun . . . in Answer to an Invitation from . . . the Democratic Republican Electors of New York City. . . .* (New York: Jared W. Bell, [1840]);

*Speech of Mr. Calhoun, of South Carolina, on the Report of Mr. Grundy, of Tennessee, in Relation to the Assumption of the Debts of the States by the Federal Government. Senate, U.S. February 5, 1840* (Washington, D.C.: Globe Office, 1840);

*Speech of Mr. Calhoun of South Carolina, on the Prospective Preemption Bill* (N.p., 1841);

*Remarks . . . on the Bill to Distribute the Proceeds of the Public Lands. In Senate Jan. 23, 1841* (Washington, D.C.?, 1841?);

*Speech . . . in Reply to the Speeches of Mr. Webster and Mr. Clay . . . in Senate Jan. 30, 1841* (Washington, D.C., 1841);

*Speech of Hon. John C. Calhoun, of South Carolina, on the Case of M'Leod: Delivered in the Senate of the United States, Friday, June 11, 1841* (Washington, D.C.: Globe Office, 1841);

*Speech . . . on the Report of the Secretary of the Treasury . . . June 21, 1841* (Washington, D.C., 1841);

*Speech on the Distribution Bill, Delivered in the Senate of the United States, August 24, 1841* (Washington, D.C.?, 1841?);

*Speech of Hon. John C. Calhoun; of South Carolina, on the Treasury Note Bill. Delivered in the Senate of the United States, January 25, 1842* (Washington, D.C.: Globe Office, 1842);

*Speech of Mr. Calhoun, of South Carolina, on the Veto Power: Delivered in the Senate . . . February 28, 1842* (Washington, D.C.: Blair & Rives, 1842);

*Speech on Mr. Clay's Resolutions in Relations to the Revenues and Expenditures of the Government, Delivered in Senate of the U.S. March 16, 1842* (N.p., 1842);

*Speech on the Loan Bill: Delivered in the Senate of the United States, Tuesday, April 12, 1842* (Washington, D.C.: Globe Office, 1842);

*Speech in Senate, August, 1842. On the Treaty of Washington* (Washington, D.C.?, 1842?);

*Speech of Mr. John C. Calhoun, of South Carolina, on the Passage of the Tariff Bill: Delivered in the Senate of the United States, Aug. 5, 1842* (Washington, D.C.: Globe Office, 1842);

*Speeches of John C. Calhoun. Delivered in the Congress of the United States from 1811 to the Present Time* (New York: Harper, 1843);

*Hon. John C. Calhoun's Letter to the Hon. W. R. King* (Charleston, S.C.: Walker & Burke, [1844]);

*Speech of Mr. Calhoun, of South Carolina, on the Resolutions Giving Notice to Great Britain of the Abrogation of the Convention of Joint Occupancy. Delivered in the Senate of the United States, March 16, 1846* (Washington, D.C.: Towers, 1846);

*Remarks of Mr. Calhoun at the Meeting of the Citizens of Charleston, Tuesday Evening, March 9, 1847* (Charleston, S.C.: 1847);

*Remarks of Mr. Calhoun, on Presenting His Resolutions on the Slave Question,* February 19, 1847 (Washington, D.C.; 1847);

*Speech on the Bill Making Further Appropriation to Bring the Existing War with Mexico to a Speedy and Honorable Conclusion, Called the Three Million Bill, Delivered in the Senate of the United States, February 9, 1847* (Washington, D.C.: Towers, 1847);

*Speech in Reply to Mr. Turney, of Tennessee. Delivered in the Senate of the United States, February 12, 1847* (Washington, D.C.?, 1847?);

*Speech . . . in Reply to Mr. Benton of Missouri. Delivered in the Senate of the U.S. Feb. 24, 1847* (Washington, D.C., 1847);

*Speech of Mr. Calhoun, of South Carolina, on His Resolutions in Reference to the War with Mexico. Delivered in the Senate of the United States, January 4, 1848* (Washington, D.C.: Towers, 1848);

*Speeches . . . on the 10 Regiment Bill and in Reply to Mr. Davis . . . and Mr. Cass Delivered in the Senate of the U.S. March 16–17, 1848* (Washington, D.C., 1848);

*Speech of Mr. Calhoun, of South Carolina, on the Oregon Bill. Delivered in the Senate of the United States, June 27, 1848* (Washington, D.C.: Towers, 1848?);

*The Address of the Southern Delegates in Congress to Their Constituents* (Washington, D.C.: Towers, [1849]);

*Mr. Calhoun's Address to the People of the Southern States* (Charleston, S.C.: Burke, 1849);

*Speech of Mr. Calhoun, of South Carolina, on the Slavery Question. Delivered in the Senate of the United States, March 4, 1850* (Washington, D.C.: Towers, [1850]);

*The Works of John C. Calhoun,* edited by Richard K. Crallé, 6 volumes–volume 1, *A Disquisition on Government and A Discourse on the Constitution and Government of the United States* (Columbia, S.C.: Johnston, 1851); volumes 2–4, *Speeches of John C. Calhoun, Delivered in the House of Representatives, and in the Senate of the United States* (New York: Appleton, 1853, 1857); volumes 5–6, *Reports and Public Letters of John C. Calhoun* (New York: Appleton, 1857);

*The Papers of John C. Calhoun,* edited by Robert L. Meriwether, W. Edwin Hemphill, and Clyde N. Wilson, 26 volumes (Columbia: University of South Carolina Press, 1959–2000).

**Editions and Collections:** *Speech . . . on the Oregon Bill: Delivered in the Senate of the United States, January 24, 1843* (Washington, D.C., 1843);

*Calhoun: Basic Documents,* edited, with an introduction, by John M. Anderson (State College, Pa.: Bald Eagle, 1952);

*Union and Liberty: The Political Philosophy of John C. Calhoun,* edited by Ross M. Lence (Indianapolis: Liberty, 1992);

*The Essential Calhoun: Selections from Writings, Speeches, and Letters,* edited by Clyde N. Wilson (New Brunswick, N.J.: Transaction, 1992).

John C. Calhoun's significance in the realm of letters is threefold. First, he successfully combined a career of political action with political thought and expression of a high order, in which he resembles the generation of Founding Fathers more than his own or later generations of statesmen. Second, his thought, particularly the part that has usually been summed up as "the theory of the concurrent majority" or "the defense of minority rights," has been perceived by observers of diverse times and viewpoints as including elements of enduring value. Finally, Calhoun was one of the most profound contemporary dissidents from the intellectual main themes of his own time.

From 1811 to 1850–as a representative from South Carolina, secretary of war, vice president for two terms, presidential candidate on two occasions, secretary of state, and senator for fifteen years–Calhoun was a political figure of national power and prominence. Although never predominant in influence, even in the South, he always had to be taken into account. Though he had many admirers, northern as well as southern, his political base was never large compared to that of others, and he never enjoyed the services of an effective party organization or the benefits of any surges of mass popularity such as were experienced by Andrew Jackson or Henry Clay. For most of his career he was either at odds with the leadership of his party or was independent of all parties. Despite the absence of these hallmarks of political power, from the beginning to the end of his forty-year career what Calhoun wrote and said arrested public attention and influenced public opinion. More than any other prominent political figure of his time, his power was literary. What he wrote and said was often as influential as what others did, at a time when deliberation and debate were more salient in the workings of the political process than they later became.

*Floride Bonneau Calhoun, whom Calhoun married in January 1811 (portrait by James A. Bogle; from Charles M. Wiltse,* John C. Calhoun: Sectionalist, 1840–1850, *1951)*

The facts of Calhoun's heritage and early life go far to explain satisfactorily his personality, his political thought, and his literary style. He began *A Disquisition on Government,* the posthumously published summation of his philosophy, with the argument that society, historically and ethically considered, takes precedence over government, and that government is derivative from, secondary to, and supportive of society. This philosophy literally recapitulates the experience of his own family and locale. John Caldwell Calhoun was born 18 March 1782 to Patrick Calhoun, frontiersman and patriot, and Martha née Caldwell at the Long Canes settlement, near present-day Abbeville, South Carolina. He was the fourth of five children. The Calhouns and related families constituted a kith of Ulster Scots who were among the first settlers of upcountry South Carolina less than two decades before the American Revolution. In that situation evidences of government were next to nonexistent. The settlers were not only economically self-sufficient but virtually and spontaneously self-governing and self-reliant in political, ecclesiastical, and military affairs until after the American War of Independence.

Calhoun's independence of mind was further accentuated by the unusual progress of his education. Until he was eighteen, his life was spent on isolated plantations, engaged in farming and field sports. Except for one brief period of schooling at thirteen, his education before eighteen was informal and self-directed. At eighteen he began his formal studies at one of the best secondary schools available, a log-cabin classical academy in Columbia County, Georgia, operated by his brother-in-law, the Reverend Moses Waddel, later president of the University of Georgia. Thus, the twenty-year-old Calhoun who entered the junior class of Yale College in 1802 was physically and mentally mature, economically and socially self-sufficient, confident of his own knowledge and reasoning, quite ready to engage in ideological battle with his elders, and aware of his own potential. Two years at Yale, brief apprenticeships in Charleston and Abbeville law offices, and a year at the Litchfield, Connecticut, Law School, then the best of its kind in the nation, made no impact on his basic qualities of mind and temperament, as is perhaps indicated by the title of his lost Yale commencement address, "The Qualifications Necessary to Constitute an Ideal Statesman."

A brief period of law practice, which he detested and never resumed, and one term in the state House of Representatives were concluded by his election to the U.S. House of Representatives in 1810 and his marriage on 8 January 1811 to a cousin, Floride Bonneau Calhoun, who was the daughter of a wealthy Lowcountry family. His own family, being among the first settlers in the upper part of the state, had acquired valuable lands in a region that was rapidly developing into a profitable center for the growing of cotton, a commodity in great demand by the voracious British textile industry, which supplied much of the world with clothing. Though his means did not place him among the most opulent class of southern planters and northern businessmen and he was often pressed for liquid assets, Calhoun was financially secure as a planter and able to devote as much time and attention as he wished to public life. After his first major speech in the federal House he was announced on 24 December 1811 by the *Richmond Enquirer,* chief organ of the Democratic-Republican Party, to be "one of the master-spirits, who stamp their names upon the age in which they live." Thus, by 1811, before he was thirty years old, he was established as a planter, a family man, and a national politician, which would remain the pattern of his life. In addition, he was intellectually mature and self-confident and widely recognized as a man of extraordinary talent with unlimited possibilities before him.

Calhoun's marriage and rapid rise to prominence were symbolic of the political and social unification of South Carolina, which was consummated at about the same time. A state once critically divided between a Lowcountry gentry—long established, used to predominance, and with ties to Europe and the West Indies—and a more populous and unpolished frontier community of later arrival, became in less than two decades a highly cohesive unit. The cohesion was confirmed and supported by a state constitution, which in its distribution of legislative power gave each group a veto over the other. This arrangement was in part the inspiration of Calhoun's concurrent majority (actually, "the concurring majority" was his usual phrase). He argued repeatedly in many contexts that giving to a minority, where its vital interests were concerned, a defensive veto over the majority did not abrogate democracy or create strife and ineffective government, as might be supposed by superficial observers. Rather, by securing the confidence and cooperation of all parties and their deference to each other, it created a more harmonious and effective consensus of the parts of society than domination by a "mere numerical majority."

The independence of mind early established characterized Calhoun's thought and the manner of its expression all of his life. His was a powerful mind operating largely in isolation and introspection. He traveled little, except on duty, and never went abroad. Most of his life was spent in Washington or at "Fort Hill" (now the Clemson University campus), relatively isolated in the Appalachian foothills, which was his home from 1826. Though Calhoun read widely and was aware of the important intellectual activity of his time—European as well as American, and in philosophy, science, history, and theology as well as economic life and public affairs—his reasoning was always introspective. Presented with a problem as legislator or administrator, he mastered the available knowledge and proceeded to his own conclusions without accepting instruction from anyone or engaging in any give-and-take. His conclusions, whether on the reform of the banking system, the proper policy toward England in regard to the Oregon country, or the strategy with which to confront the abolitionists, were settled by deep reflection and study and could only be changed by new evidence or changing circumstances. They were completely uninfluenced by the opinions of others except to the extent that the opinions of others were factors of the situation to be taken into account. Though this often made him dogmatic and (as commonly charged by opponents in his lifetime) "metaphysical" rather than pragmatic, it also gave him the capacity to take in a larger view than the politician's usual span of vision and thus a certain power of prophecy.

What has been said about the isolated and introspective quality of Calhoun's intellectual life should not be taken to imply that he was of a forbidding or reclusive personality. The most often quoted description of him is that of the English writer Harriet Martineau, who knew him slightly: "a cast-iron man, who looks as if he had never been born, and never could be extinguished." The most-often-reproduced likenesses of Calhoun are those of his later life, haggard with age and illness. Yet, despite the apparently unshakable hold the "cast-iron man" image has upon the popular imagination, the evidence is overwhelming that for most of his life and by most of those with whom he came in contact Calhoun was regarded as handsome, charming, and magnetic. In fact, along with the power of ideas, personal charm was the key to Calhoun's influence. One admirer was convinced that if Calhoun could talk to every man in the United States personally he could carry the day with any measure. Free from the vices of tobacco, drink, and profanity that were nearly universal at the time, fascinating in private conversation, unfailingly courteous and accessible to all ages, sexes, and conditions, he was especially captivating to the opposite sex and to younger men, whom he treated with equality.

In style also Calhoun was independent. The style of his speeches and his public papers differs little from that of his private letters; and the style of his earliest public papers is still evident in his last. Calhoun was almost completely free of the verbosity and ornamentation that were the conventions of his time. The qualities that led fashionable critics in his own era to find him lacking in polish are exactly those that make him now more readable than most of his contemporaries. As stated in *Literary History of the United States* (1948), "his speeches deserve wider reading than they have enjoyed. They are neither dull nor ponderous." Earlier, *The Cambridge History of American Literature* (1917–1921) observed: "Even when discussing subjects which now appear of bygone interest, he commonly struck at fundamentals and at principles with such force and precision that many of his words still have vitality." William J. Grayson, a hostile South Carolinian, wrote in his unpublished autobiography: "Mr. Calhoun's argument was always vigorous, subtle, and with ease. He was never muddy or confused. He was a powerful and skillful debater, not a declaimer or rhetorician. The arts of the rhetorician he seemed to despise. His mode of speaking suited important subjects only."

As an orator Calhoun had neither the impressive majesty of Daniel Webster, the charm and theatrical liveliness of Clay, nor the courtly erudition and wit of Thomas H. Benton, his three chief rivals for attention in the Senate during the 1830s and 1840s. Evaluation of his voice ranged from "harsh" to unremarkable to "silvery and attractive." Many observers found gestures either absent or awkward. Grayson further wrote in this same autobiography: "His manner was abrupt. His sentences were often left incomplete. He cut them short in

*Calhoun during his service as vice president of the United States*
*(portrait by Chester Harding; University of North Carolina*
*at Chapel Hill)*

the heat and hurry of his utterance. His ideas appeared to outrun his words and leave them limping in the rear. His delivery was stiff and without grace, but it was impressive from its intense and eager earnestness. There was a glare, a fire, in his eyes, the fire of a soul that seemed to burn within him. It fascinated the beholder and riveted his gaze."

The predominant characteristic of Calhoun's prose on the printed page is leanness. In the choice of words he preferred the vivid and colloquial to the bookish, giving the prose often an eighteenth-century flavor that was archaic in his own time but that is more natural and enduring than more-studied efforts. His sentence structure is sometimes so sparse that the subject has to be inferred from a previous sentence, a practice that reflects both rapidity of thought and the influence of youthful ingestion of Latin. The words applied by Charles M. Wiltse, Calhoun's major biographer, to his prose, are "concise," "sinewy," "incisive," "compact," "completely ordered," and "defies abridgement." Calhoun never put on a performance. He always sought to persuade rather than to impress. At its most powerful

the prose is that of a man with his back to the wall, striking hard blows. Gaillard Hunt, a biographer, wrote that "he dignified every question he embraced."

James H. Hammond, a sympathetic but perceptive eulogist, wrote:

It was commonly said of his productions that they were characterized by extraordinary condensation. But Mr. Calhoun was often careless in his diction, habitually so in the construction of his sentences. He sought only the words that most clearly expressed his meaning, and left their arrangement apparently to chance. What he did do was go straight to the bottom of his subject, following the slender plummet line of truth until he reached it. Then he built up in a manner equally direct, discarding all extraneous materials; and erected a structure, simple, uniform, and consistent, decorated with no ornament for the sake of ornament, and occupying no more space than was necessary for the purposes in view.

Entering the House of Representatives in 1811, Calhoun in short order became a leader of the young "War Hawks," who succeeded in taking foreign affairs out of the hands of President James Madison's administration and bringing on war with Great Britain. A report written for the Foreign Relations Committee and presented to the House on 28 November 1811 and a speech on 12 December defending the "War Hawks" against the invincible John Randolph of Roanoke established Calhoun as a national figure. The next year, on 3 June 1812, he drafted and presented the report of the Foreign Relations Committee that accompanied and justified the declaration of war. By the end of the war Calhoun was without doubt one of the handful of dominant men in Congress and the Jeffersonian party. His labor and eloquence in providing legislative support for a war unpopular in many quarters caused him to be referred to as "the young Hercules who carried the war on his shoulders." Of interest in this connection are his 14 January 1813 speech on the Army Bill, a 15 January 1814 speech on the dangers of factious opposition, and a 25 February 1814 speech on the Loan Bill. From the beginning Calhoun exhibited his disdain for superficial arguments and policies and showed the ability to penetrate through the smoke of party warfare and transient issues to fundamental questions. He also did not hesitate to condemn major programs of his party when he found them lacking, as in his speech on the merchant's bonds of 8 December 1812 and on the Bill to Repeal the Restrictive System on 6 April 1814.

At the end of the war Calhoun took the leading role in legislation concerning the peacetime military establishment, the currency, and the second national bank chartered in 1816. In an impromptu speech on 4

April 1816, which was to haunt him, he supported the building up of American industry by tariff protection on grounds of equity and patriotism. By a "Bonus Bill," which, though defeated by a presidential veto, gave form to the internal improvements issue that loomed large in American politics for decades, he proposed a federal role in the building of a nationwide network of transportation. This network was to be paid for not by taxation but by a windfall bonus received by the government in chartering the national bank. It was constitutionally justified as necessary to carry out the duty of Congress to provide for the common defense. In a speech on 4 February 1817 Calhoun expounded with fervor on the vast extent and promise of the United States: "We are great, and rapidly, he was about to say fearfully growing. This, said he, is our pride and our danger—our weakness and our strength. . . . Let us then . . . bind the Republic together with a perfect system of roads and canals. Let us conquer space."

By the late 1820s Calhoun was regarded as an opponent of "internal improvements." Though he was accused of inconsistency, his answer was convincing. The internal improvements that were being passed by Congress were not the truly federal plan he had envisioned but a vast logrolling boondoggle that served no national purpose.

From 1817 to 1825 Calhoun was secretary of war in the cabinet of James Monroe. He undertook the post against the advice of friends, who thought it would take him out of the limelight and would be impossible to carry off creditably, and of enemies, who thought him too "metaphysical" for an administrator. The U.S. War Department was the largest and most far-flung of the government departments. Calhoun eliminated the vast administrative and financial confusion left by the war, preserved an efficient professional nucleus in the face of severe retrenchment, and created a bureau system of administration that attracted European imitators. (Volume 5 of *The Works of John C. Calhoun*, 1851–1857, is a convenient source for the most important of Calhoun's reports to Congress as head of the War Department.) The prestige of the West Point Military Academy also dates from his tenure, and he brought a more humane and professional administration to the Bureau of Indian Affairs than had previously existed. Calhoun adhered to the program of Indian removals to the West that had been inaugurated by Thomas Jefferson, but the program as envisioned and carried out by him was gradual and accompanied by efforts at education and settlement, unlike that later carried out by Andrew Jackson, of which Calhoun became a persistent senatorial critic.

Highly regarded in many quarters, talented, ambitious, and at the center of the national government, Calhoun early entered the wide-open field of candidates to succeed Monroe as president when the Virginia dynasty came to an end. He was the youngest man who had even been thought of as a candidate. When it became apparent that his support overlapped that of the popular General Jackson, however, he withdrew. While the presidential votes in 1824 were divided among four candidates and the election had to be decided in the House of Representatives in favor of John Quincy Adams—amid accusations of a "corrupt bargain" by supporters of Jackson—Calhoun was easily elected vice president with the votes of most of Jackson's and Adams's electors.

During his vice presidency, Calhoun established a permanent home at "Fort Hill" on the Seneca River near the town of Pendleton in the Appalachian foothills. Here, he was an avid and successful farmer. The Calhouns had six sons and four daughters, two of whom did not survive infancy. The address "Fort Hill" at the head of a document was universally recognized as identifying Calhoun.

Early in his first term as vice president Calhoun differentiated himself from the doomed Adams administration and joined Jackson's camp. This event was signaled by a newspaper controversy over the vice president's powers and duties in presiding over the Senate, which Calhoun engaged in under the pseudonym "Onslow" with a critic called "Patrick Henry." This critic was either John Quincy Adams or an Adams spokesman. The more important of Calhoun's essays in this controversy were issued in a pamphlet, *Onslow in Reply to Patrick Henry* (1826).

The tariff rates on imported goods were raised in 1824 and again in 1828. Rather than the measure of temporary relief to infant American industries that Calhoun envisioned in 1826, the tariff had become a permanent system of indirect subsidy to manufacturing at the expense of the agricultural interest and the consumer and was increasingly unpopular in the South. In 1828 Calhoun anonymously drafted a report known to history as the "South Carolina Exposition," which was broadcast, although not adopted or immediately acted upon, by the South Carolina legislature, accompanied by resolutions known as the "South Carolina Protest."

The "South Carolina Exposition" argued the unconstitutionality and pernicious effects of the tariff. The Constitution grants Congress the right to levy taxes on imports for the purpose of raising revenue, not for the purpose of protecting manufacturers from foreign competition, it maintained. The effect of such partial legislation was to divide the community into two groups, Calhoun wrote, one of which reaped the benefits while the other bore the burdens. This arrangement undermined the patriotism and fellow feeling necessary for the preservation of the Union.

*Letter from Calhoun to a frequent correspondent, attorney Virgil Maxcy (Maxcy Papers, Library of Congress)*

The fact that this measure was the product of majority rule and not of monarchical or aristocratic dominance did not at all alter the principle that a relationship of master and oppressed was created between the manufacturing section and the agricultural section. Calhoun also suggested that such government-dictated bounty to a certain class would tend to concentrate wealth in that class and lead eventually toward a conflict between capitalists and propertyless laborers in the North. Many later observers have admired Calhoun's grasp of the principles of class conflict involved, though they have often cast these into a frame of reference different from his.

The "Exposition" then outlines a remedy that could be exercised by the oppressed class against such unconstitutional and inequitable legislation as the tariff had been described to be. The remedy was interposition or state veto, known to history by a term not used by Calhoun but applied by its critics: "nullification." Calhoun began with the proposition that the Constitution and the Union were created by the states—that the ultimate power in the American system was that exercised by the people acting through the states. Though this description of the American system was unpopular in later times, it was axiomatic to a majority of Calhoun's contemporaries. Despite this agreement on the first premise, however, he was unable to persuade the majority to follow the next step in his logic. Where differences of constitutional interpretation arose, the final judgment did not lie in the Supreme Court or in any other branch of the federal government, he argued, but in the original creators, the people of the states.

Interposition, as outlined by Calhoun, was to be a peaceful and temporary suspension by a state, within that state, of a federal law judged to be unconstitutional. The purpose of this suspension was not to thwart permanently majority rule but to force a settlement of the disputed point of constitutional interpretation by an appeal to the states. A three-fourths majority of the states could settle the matter by a constitutional amendment that clarified the questioned point. Otherwise, the congressional majority would be obliged to abandon the exercise of the power as unconstitutional. To insure that nullification was not exercised frivolously, it was only to be brought into play after all other remedies had been exhausted and was to be enacted only by an extraordinary convention of the people elected specifically for that purpose, like the conventions that had originally ratified the Constitution.

This program Calhoun defended not as a step toward disunion but as an alternative to it. It would be peaceful because citizens could only be punished by juries of their peers, and because the federal government would not dare inaugurate bloodshed by coercing state officials carrying out the declared will of their people. Calhoun also stressed the intangible benefits. The knowledge that interposition could be invoked would lead the majority to be more considerate to the interests of the minority and, by assuaging their fears, increase the loyalty of the minority. As he put it in a speech on 26 February 1833, in reply to Webster, nullification was not a source of weakness in government. "If we look to mere organization and physical power as the only source of strength, without taking into the estimate the operation of moral causes, such would appear to be the fact; but if we take into the estimate the latter, we shall find that those governments have the greatest strength in which power has been most efficiently checked." Despite disclaimers by Madison, nullification was clearly modeled on the Virginia and Kentucky resolutions of 1798 and 1799, more elaborately defended and more seriously implemented. The ideas were not invented by Calhoun but were skillfully restated by him. Interposition was developed further, after Calhoun had been re-elected vice president under Jackson, in a public letter of 26 July 1831 (usually known as the "Fort Hill Address") and in a letter to Governor James Hamilton Jr. of South Carolina of 28 August 1832; also in papers drafted for the state legislature in December 1830 and November 1831, which were not published until much later.

Meanwhile, two controversies had led to a complete breakdown of relations between Jackson and Calhoun, and Jackson had decided to seek a second term and to adopt Martin Van Buren rather than Calhoun as his political legatee. In 1830 Jackson provoked a new discussion of the controversy that had occurred in 1818 when Calhoun as secretary of war had favored an investigation—some said a punishment—of General Jackson for his unauthorized military attack on the Spanish government in Florida. Calhoun published a defense in two statements appearing in *The United States Telegraph* on 17 and 25 February 1831. The earlier of these statements, with many supporting documents, was issued as a pamphlet: *Correspondence between Gen. Andrew Jackson and John C. Calhoun, President and Vice-President of the U. States, on the Subject of the Course of the Latter, in the Deliberations of the Cabinet of Mr. Monroe, on the Occurrences in the Seminole War.* The second controversy that destroyed friendly relations between the president and vice president was over the social standing of Peggy Eaton, wife of Jackson's close friend and secretary of war, John H. Eaton, who was not received by Floride Calhoun and most other ladies in Washington society for reasons of propriety. After being attacked in print by Eaton, Calhoun reluctantly published a "Reply to John H. Eaton's Address," which first appeared in the press on 19 October 1831.

*Calhoun's office at Fort Hill, in upstate South Carolina (from* Scribner's Monthly Magazine, *April 1881)*

By late 1832 it was apparent that Jackson intended to straddle the tariff issue, and Congress had passed a new tariff bill that included no significant reduction in the rates despite the imminent retirement of the national debt. A South Carolina Convention met in November 1832 and enacted nullification of the tariff laws, effective the following 1 February, thus giving Congress time to summon a constitutional convention. At the same time Calhoun resigned as vice president and was elected to the Senate. In this crisis Calhoun was clearly moved along somewhat unwillingly by the force of opinion in his state, and he saw his role as one of guiding and moderating that opinion. He was aware that he had sacrificed his own political interest, at least in the short run.

Hastening to Washington, where Jackson had already declared the action of South Carolina treason, and pursued by rumors of imminent arrest, Calhoun diligently undertook to defend the state and to defuse the controversy by compromise. At the latter task he was assisted by Clay and the legislature of Virginia. His speeches on 15 and 16 February against the "Force Bill" and on 26 February in reply to Webster on the powers of the federal government were among the greatest of his career. "Does any man in his senses believe," he asked, "that this beautiful

structure—this harmonious aggregate of States, produced by the joint consent of all—can be preserved by force? Its very introduction will be certain destruction to this Federal Union. . . . Force may, indeed, hold the parts together, but such union would be the bond between master and slave: a union of exaction on one side, and of unqualified *obedience* on the other." In the denouement a compromise tariff act was passed providing for a gradual downward revision of the tariff rates over a ten-year period, along with a "Force Act" authorizing the president under limited and specified conditions to employ the armed forces to execute the revenue laws. South Carolina repealed its nullification of the tariff without ever implementing it. Despite a narrow aversion of bloodshed, Calhoun considered nullification a success and a logical unfolding of the principle of the consent of the governed. "The danger of disunion is small: that of despotism great," he remarked later in urging repeal of the Force Act.

From 1833 to 1838, persona non grata to both the Democrats and the Whigs, Calhoun was a freelance statesman, supported only by his own state and a handful of allies in other states, and was able to chart his own course. During this period he presented to the Senate a devastating portrayal of the Jacksonians as unscrupulous spoilsmen without principles or policy, notably in his 13 January 1834 speech on the removal of the deposits; his 6 May 1834 speech on Jackson's protest to the Senate; and the Report on the Executive Patronage of 9 February 1835, along with the speech supporting it on 20 February.

While attacking the Democrats with merciless logic, Calhoun refused to be drawn into alliance with the nationalist Whigs, whom he portrayed as honest but self-seeking and shortsighted in their policies. Taking up the banking and currency questions in a series of speeches, he condemned both parties for lack of a grasp of the real issues involved and accurately predicted the panic of 1837. These speeches prompted the leading historian of the subject, Bray Hammond, to assert that Calhoun understood fiscal and monetary affairs better than any public man of his time. During the same span of years he continued to elaborate a philosophy of government in his speeches: on 9 April 1834 for the repeal of the Force Act; on 2 and 5 January 1837 for the admission of Michigan to the Union; and in his letter to William Smith of Virginia on 3 July 1843 on the Dorr Rebellion in Rhode Island.

Perhaps the most seriously neglected part of Calhoun's thought is that which he devoted to economics, various aspects of which he mastered by hard study. His major speeches in this area constitute an impressive body of work: on the Bill to Continue the Charter of the National Bank, 21 March 1834; on his Bill to Regulate the Deposits of Public Money, 28 May 1836; on the Bill Authorizing an Issue of Treasury Notes, 18 September 1837; on his Amendment to Separate the Government and the Banks, 3 October 1837; on the Bankruptcy Bill, 2 June 1840; on the Loan Bill, 19 April 1842; and on the Tariff Bill, 5 August 1842. In fact, Calhoun made more speeches on banking and currency and government fiscal policy than he did on state rights and slavery.

Prior to 1836 Calhoun showed only a perfunctory interest in the political issue of slavery, having supported the Missouri Compromise. In that year, alarmed by the rising power of abolition, he began the political counterattack that continued the rest of his career, starting with a 4 February report to the Senate on the incendiary publications of the abolitionists and a 9 March speech against the reception of abolition petitions. In defending slavery and rejecting abolitionism Calhoun was no different from all of the South and much of the Democratic Party in the North. In moving from a "Necessary evil" to a "positive good" defense, however, as well as in his tactics, he created a new school. His insistence on the total rejection of abolitionism at the threshold and the total exclusion of the subject from the federal sphere did not carry the day at once, even in the South. Calhoun believed that only complete southern unity and federal noninvolvement could prevent a devastating conflict in the future. In this assertion he was prophetic. Shortly before his death he predicted that a civil war would break out within ten years in the wake of a presidential election. If Calhoun was prophetic he was not pragmatic, for his hard line aroused the antagonism of many Northerners who were indifferent to slavery per se.

In 1838 Calhoun rejoined the Democratic Party, throwing his support to Van Buren, who had essentially adopted his position on banking questions. By 1843, as nullification had faded into the background, he had regained the position in national esteem he held more than a decade before. Admired by many (including Northerners opposed to the rising power of industrialists) for his consistency, freedom from shallow self-seeking, and eloquent elaboration of fundamental principles, he had formulated the policy of his party on many questions of the day. In foreign affairs he had staked out a clear position on the age of Manifest Destiny in such speeches as that on the Treaty of Washington (28 August 1842) and on the Oregon Bill (24 January 1843). Time was on the side of the United States, he said. With firmness, moderation, and statesmanship all its territorial ambitions could be realized without serious conflict.

Calhoun retired from the Senate on 3 March 1843, following which was inaugurated the last serious presidential campaign in his behalf. In connection with this effort Harper and Brothers was persuaded to issue a collection of Calhoun's speeches edited by himself. Although some of the most "nationalistic" of his early speeches were omitted, the editing was light. The chief differences from earlier versions were typographical—capitalization and punctuation practices. Along with the *Speeches* was issued an anonymous *Life of John C. Calhoun, Presenting a Condensed History of Political Events from 1811 to 1843.* Often erroneously asserted to be autobiographical, this book was largely the work of Robert M. T. Hunter, then representative from Virginia, who worked from biographical sketches previously published in pamphlet and periodical form. An estimated eighteen thousand copies of the *Life of John C. Calhoun* were distributed. The *Speeches of John C. Calhoun. Delivered in the Congress of the United States from 1811 to the Present Time* was designed as a companion volume, but problems arose in distribution and probably considerably fewer than eighteen thousand were circulated. In an "Address to his Political Friends and

Supporters," published in February 1844, Calhoun withdrew from the presidential campaign.

In March 1844 he was appointed secretary of state by President John Tyler without dissent in the Senate. Calhoun may be said to have set in motion the diplomatic initiatives that led to the peaceful acquisition of part of the Oregon Territory by the next administration. He had taken up Oregon first, rightly perceiving that the Texas question was insoluble while Mexico thought a war between the United States and Britain was possible over Oregon. Calhoun also completed a treaty for the annexation of Texas; however, his placing the defense of this treaty partly on the slave issue–that the elimination of British influence from the Southwest was necessary to the security of slavery–is usually credited with strengthening the hand of the anti-annexation forces and defeating the treaty.

Disappointed in his hope to continue as secretary of state under James K. Polk, Calhoun reentered the Senate in 1845 and remained until his death. A triumphal tour of the West led to a Senate "Report on the Memphis Memorial" on 26 June 1846, in which he outlined an internal improvements program for the interior, contending that the Mississippi Valley fell within the federal sphere of "foreign and interstate commerce" as much as the Atlantic ports or Great Lakes.

In 1846, when hostilities broke out that led to war with Mexico, Calhoun abstained from the vote on the declaration of war and became an eloquent critic of the war and the Polk administration, although he voted for what was necessary for the forces in the field to maintain themselves. He asserted that the president had unconstitutionally brought on a state of war without the consent of Congress, that there were no objectives to be gained that could not be gained by other means, and that Mexico was the "forbidden fruit," meaning that swallowing her territory would bring no fatal conflicts between the North and the South. He also maintained that society and technology had advanced to such a state that war was disastrous and should only be resorted to in extreme cases.

Perhaps Calhoun appears at his best to later generations in the series of speeches he made during the Polk administration in which he sought to restrain the expansiveness and aggressiveness that had overcome his countrymen: on Oregon, 16 March 1846; on the Mexican War, 9 February, 12 February, and 24 February 1847, and 4 January and 16–17 March 1848; on the European revolutions, 30 March 1848; and on the proposed occupation of Yucatan, 15 May 1848.

The last few years of Calhoun's public life were devoted to the attempt to unify the South within the Union. With such unity, he believed, the South would be able to exercise enough negative power where its vital interests were concerned to preserve the Union from the forces of dissolution. The North, he insisted, should discontinue lip-service allegiance to the Union and show its true allegiance by willingness to carry the burdens, like slavery, as well as to enjoy the benefits. The Union, he said in his last important speech, on 4 March 1850, which had to be read for him by another senator,

> cannot, then, be saved by eulogies on the Union, however splendid or numerous. The cry of 'Union, Union–the glorious Union!' can no more prevent disunion than the cry of 'Health, health–glorious health!' on the part of the physician, can save a patient lying dangerously ill. So long as the Union, instead of being regarded as a protector, is regarded in the opposite character, by not much less than a majority of the States, it will be in vain to attempt to conciliate them by pronouncing eulogies on it. . . . the only reliable and certain evidence of devotion to the constitution is, to abstain, on the one hand, from violating it, and to repel, on the other, all attempts to violate it. It is only by faithfully performing these high duties that the constitution can be preserved, and with it the Union.

The Compromise of 1850, which was the subject of this speech, would not work, he accurately predicted. It should be rejected because it provided unequal treatment of the South in the territories, which would eventually lead to permanent minority status and loss of the means of self-defense. In this speech he also hinted at a constitutional innovation (probably the dual executive that he elaborated upon in his *A Discourse on the Constitution and Government of the United States*) that he intended to propose. Calhoun died a few weeks later, on 31 March 1850, in a Washington boardinghouse.

Aside from the two treatises, *A Discourse on the Constitution and Government of the United States* and *A Disquisition on Government,* published after his death, Calhoun's thought is elaborated in his speeches and public letters and in documents drafted as a legislator or administrator. The standard source has been the edition put together after his death, with family cooperation, by Richard K. Crallé, a Virginia journalist and longtime intimate and disciple. The approximately 150 papers included were judiciously selected. Crallé used both early printed sources and manuscripts. Some of the latter still exist; some do not. Although Crallé was not nearly as intrusive as many editors of the time, the materials nevertheless underwent a moderate amount of stylistic polishing at his hands (the net effect of which was to adulterate the eighteenth-century vigor of Calhoun's natural expression) and some moderate alterations of substance.

In the case of Calhoun's official report and public letters, manuscripts (usually drafts or printer's copies) exist in some cases, in scattered locations. In other cases, the earliest versions are those printed in official documents or in friendly newspapers such as *The United States Telegraph* of Washington, D.C.; the *Charleston Mercury;* or the *Pendleton Messenger,* published in Calhoun's neighborhood. From these early printings they were widely reprinted and adopted into the collected works.

No manuscripts exist of Calhoun's major speeches. In the time of Calhoun and the other great nineteenth-century orators the deliberations of Congress were taken down and published semiofficially by private reporters. Speeches, sometimes after a varying and undetermined amount of revision by the speaker, generally appeared first in Washington newspapers such as the *Daily National Intelligencer, The United States Telegraph,* the *Globe,* the *Madisonian,* and the *Union.* From there they were copied around the country in other papers and later collected into hardbound serial publications such as the *Annals of Congress,* the *Register of Debates in Congress,* and the *Congressional Globe.* Many of the more-important speeches appeared in one or more pamphlet versions, authorized or unauthorized, usually designed for the purpose of distribution to supporters. The publication of such pamphlets offered a further occasion for revision by the speaker, an opportunity that Calhoun seldom exercised except in having third-person, past-tense reports translated to the first-person, present-tense, to give them a greater sense of immediacy. Calhoun made no effort to add literary polish to subsequent printings of his speeches, unlike other orators of the day, notably Webster, though on fairly rare occasions he sought to correct what he considered garbled or inaccurate reports. The text of speeches, generally, were summaries constructed from shorthand notes, and not verbatim reports. Despite occasional complaints of inaccuracy or misrepresentation, the congressional reporters were highly skilled and usually managed to convey faithfully the substance of the speaker's thought and some of the flavor of his style.

For *A Discourse on the Constitution and Government of the United States* and *A Disquisition on Government* no manuscripts exist, and all subsequent versions are based on those prepared and printed by Crallé. Calhoun devoted much of his spare time for the last four years of his life to the two treatises. *A Discourse on the Constitution and Government of the United States* (taking

*Calhoun in 1849 (daguerreotype attributed to Mathew Brady)*

up a little less than three hundred pages in Crallé's edition) is a sophisticated reiteration of the states' rights view of American history and government. Although it was unfinished, the part that exists makes a satisfactory whole.

*A Disquisition on Government* (about one hundred pages in Crallé's edition) is the most considered of Calhoun's works. To his daughter he described it as "nearly throughout new territory" and said that he hoped by it "to lay a solid foundation for political science." Simple and clear in style, the work is complex enough in implications to have provoked many different interpretations. It would be accurate, though not a complete description, to say it is a study of the nature of the consent of the governed in a government of the people. Calhoun saw society as a body made up of organic parts. Each of the parts (those that have come into existence spontaneously by the force of history, not those artificially created or enhanced by government action) ought to be inviolate. They must be allowed to be what they are if the whole organism is to realize its true nature. (The parts are usually thought of as substantial economic interests of the society. Calhoun dealt primarily with economic groups but did not necessarily limit the definition of a minority to economic terms.) It follows that there are things the whole may not do without the willing agreement of the parts, so that in some matters, more vital to itself than to the whole, a part should have an absolute veto. To Calhoun this approach meant not undemocratic obstruction of the majority will but rather a higher fulfillment of the democratic ideal of the consent of the governed.

Vernon Louis Parrington wrote in *Main Currents of American Thought* (1927) that whatever road one traveled one came upon Calhoun standing at the crossroads of the Southern mind. Certainly, for better or worse, history offers few such examples of a thinker who marshaled the ideas of the whole region so effectively, though it is accurate to say that Calhoun led the South only because he sensed and reflected its ultimate tendencies so well.

Some later observers have admired his attempts to sustain the agrarian tradition and create a viable alternative to the hegemony of industrial capitalism. Others have been struck by his early and thoroughgoing awareness of the realities of class conflict, though they have usually deplored if not misunderstood the role that he chose to play in that conflict. Still others have emphasized his original contributions to American political thinking, especially the emphasis on the weaknesses of, and alternatives to, unrefined majority rule. He has thus been seen as the first formulator of the concept of pluralistic consensus that is thought of as a hallmark of modern American democracy.

Judgments of Calhoun the statesman during his own and later times present polar variations from admiration to hatred, as is natural considering the intensity of the historical questions with which he dealt. Literary judgment has been fairly stable, however. Few would deny that Calhoun spoke and wrote with insight and penetration about topics of enduring interest in a style that has worn better than that of most of his political contemporaries, and that his work cannot be ignored in the understanding of his era.

## Letters:

J. Franklin Jameson, ed., *Correspondence of John C. Calhoun, American Historical Association Annual Report for 1899* (Washington: Government Printing Office, 1900);

Robert L. Meriwether, W. Edwin Hemphill, and Clyde N. Wilson, *The Papers of John C. Calhoun,* 26 volumes to date (Columbia: University of South Carolina Press, 1959–2000).

## Bibliography:

Clyde N. Wilson, *John C. Calhoun: A Bibliography* (Westport, Conn.: Meckler, 1990).

## Biographies:

Robert M. T. Hunter, *Life of John C. Calhoun, Presenting a Condensed History of Political Events from 1811 to 1843* (New York: Harper, 1843);

John S. Jenkins, *The Life of John Caldwell Calhoun* (Auburn, N.Y.: Alden, 1850);

Mary Bates, *The Private Life of John C. Calhoun: A Letter Originally Addressed to a Brother at the North, Communicated to the "International Magazine," and Now Reprinted at the Request of Many Personal Friends* (Charleston, S.C.: Walker & Richards, 1852);

William M. Meigs, *The Life of John Caldwell Calhoun,* 2 volumes (New York: Neale, 1917);

Arthur Styron, *The Cast-Iron Man: John C. Calhoun and American Democracy* (New York: Longmans, Green, 1935);

Charles M. Wiltse, *John C. Calhoun,* 3 volumes (Indianapolis: Bobbs-Merrill, 1944–1951);

Margaret L. Coit, *John C. Calhoun: American Portrait* (Boston: Houghton Mifflin, 1950);

Coit, ed., *John C. Calhoun* (Englewood Cliffs, N.J.: Prentice-Hall, 1970);

"An Oration of the Life, Character and Services of John Caldwell Calhoun . . . ," in *Selections from the Letters and Speeches of the Hon. James H. Hammond, of South Carolina* (Spartanburg, S.C.: Reprint Company, 1977);

Merrill D. Peterson, *The Great Triumvirate: Webster, Clay and Calhoun* (New York: Oxford University Press, 1987);

Irving H. Bartlett, *John C. Calhoun: A Biography* (New York: Norton, 1993).

## References:

James L. Anderson and W. Edwin Hemphill, "The 1843 Biography of John C. Calhoun: Was Robert M. T. Hunter Its Author?" *Journal of Southern History,* 38 (August 1972): 470–474;

Guy Stanton Brown, *Calhoun's Philosophy of Politics: A Study of A Disquisition on Government . . .* (Macon, Ga.: Mercer University Press, 2000);

H. Lee Cheek Jr., "Calhoun and His Critics," *Telos,* 118 (Winter 2000): 59–76;

Cheek Jr., *Calhoun and Popular Rule: The Political Theory of the Disquisition and Discourse . . .* (Columbia & London: University of Missouri Press, 2001);

Avery O. Craven, *The Coming of the Civil War* (Chicago: University of Chicago Press, 1957);

William E. Dodd, *Statesmen of the Old South; or, From Radicalism to Conservative Revolt* (New York: Macmillan, 1929);

Peter F. Drucker, "A Key to American Politics: Calhoun's Pluralism," *Review of Politics,* 10 (October 1848): 412–426;

Ronnie W. Faulkner, "Taking John C. Calhoun to the United Nations," *Polity,* 15 (Summer 1983): 473–491;

"'Free Trade; No Debt; Separation from Banks': The Economic Platform of John C. Calhoun," in Robert Paquette and Louis Ferleger, eds., *Slavery, Secession and Southern History* . . . (Charlottesville & London: University Press of Virginia, 2000), pp. 81–100;

Bruno Gujer, "Free Trade and Slavery: Calhoun's Defense of Southern Interests against British Interference, 1811–1848," dissertation, University of Zurich, 1971;

Richard Hofstadter, "John C. Calhoun: The Marx of the Master Class," in his *The American Political Tradition and the Men Who Made It* (New York: Knopf, 1948), pp. 67–91;

Christopher Hollis, *The American Heresy* (New York: Minton, Balch, 1930);

Ralph Lerner, "Calhoun's New Science of Politics," *American Political Science Review,* 57 (December 1963): 918–932;

Pauline Maier, "The Road Not Taken: Nullification, John C. Calhoun, and the Revolutionary Tradition in South Carolina," *South Carolina Historical Magazine,* 82 (January 1981): 1–19;

Theodore R. Marmor, *The Career of John C. Calhoun: Politician, Social Critic, Political Philosopher* (New York: Garland, 1988);

Winston Leigh McKuen, "The Constitution of Man: John C. Calhoun and a Solid Foundation for Political Science," dissertation, Emory University, 1999;

Felix Morley, *Freedom and Federalism* (Chicago: Regnery, 1959);

Vernon Louis Parrington, *Main Currents in American Thought: An Interpretation of American Literature from the Beginnings to 1920,* 3 volumes (New York: Harcourt, Brace, 1927–1930), II: 69–82;

August O. Spain, *The Political Theory of John C. Calhoun* (New York: Octagon, 1968);

John L. Thomas, ed., *John C. Calhoun: A Profile* (New York: Hill & Wang, 1968);

Clyde N. Wilson, "Calhoun and Community," *Chronicles of Culture,* 9 (July 1985): 17–20;

Major L. Wilson, *Space, Time and Freedom: The Quest for Nationality and the Irrepressible Conflict, 1815–1861* (Westport, Conn.: Greenwood Press, 1974).

**Papers:**

The largest collections of John C. Calhoun Papers are at Clemson University and at the South Caroliniana Library of the University of South Carolina. Extant manuscripts number an estimated fifty thousand items and are located in more than fifty depositories.

# George Henry Calvert

*(2 June 1803 – 24 May 1889)*

Thomas S. Hansen
*Wellesley College*

See also the Calvert entries in *DLB 1: The American Renaissance in New England* and *DLB 64: American Literary Critics and Scholars, 1850–1880*.

BOOKS: *A Volume from the Life of Herbert Barclay* (Baltimore: Neal, 1833);

*A Summary of Phrenology, to Accompany the Bust Approved by Dr. Spurzheim* (Cambridge, Mass.: Folsom, 1833);

*A Lecture on German Literature, Being a Sketch of Its History from its Origin to the Present Day, Delivered by Request, before the Athenæum Society of Baltimore on the 11th of February 1836* (Baltimore: Toy, 1836);

*Count Julian; A Tragedy* (Baltimore: Hickman, 1840);

*Cabiro: A Poem . . . Cantos I and II* (Baltimore: Hickman, 1840);

*Miscellany of Verse and Prose* (Baltimore: Hickman, 1840);

*Scenes and Thoughts in Europe. By an American* (New York: Wiley & Putnam, 1846); republished with *Scenes and Thoughts in Europe. By an American, Second Series* as *Travels in Europe: Its People and Scenery, Embracing Graphic Descriptions of the Principal Cities, Buildings, Scenery, and Most Notable People in England and the Continent*, 2 volumes (Boston: Cottrell, 1860);

*Poems* (Boston: Ticknor, 1847);

*Scenes and Thoughts in Europe. By an American, Second Series* (New York: Putnam, 1852); republished with *Scenes and Thoughts in Europe. By an American* as *Travels in Europe: Its People and Scenery, Embracing Graphic Descriptions of the Principal Cities, Buildings, Scenery, and Most Notable People in England and the Continent*;

*Oration, on the Occasion of Celebrating the Fortieth Anniversary of the Battle of Lake Erie; Delivered on the Tenth of September, 1853, in Newport, R.I.* (Cambridge, Mass.: Metcalf, 1853);

*Introduction to Social Science: A Discourse in Three Parts* (New York: Redfield, 1856);

*Comedies* (Boston: Phillips, Sampson, 1856);

*Joan of Arc: A Poem. In Four Books* (Cambridge, Mass.: Privately printed by the Riverside Press, 1860);

*The Gentleman* (Boston: Ticknor & Fields, 1863);

*(from Ida Gertrude Everson,* George Henry Calvert, *1944)*

*Arnold and André: An Historical Drama* (Boston: Little, Brown, 1864);

*Cabiro. A Poem. Cantos III and IV* (Boston: Little, Brown, 1864);

*Anyta and Other Poems* (Boston: Dutton, 1866);

*First Years in Europe* (Boston: Spencer, 1866);

*Ellen: A Poem for the Times* (New York: Carleton, 1867);

*Goethe: His Life and Works. An Essay* (Boston: Lee & Shepard / New York: Lee, Shepard & Dillingham, 1872);

*Mirabeau: An Historical Drama* (Cambridge, Mass.: Privately printed by the Riverside Press, 1873; Boston: Lee & Shepard, 1883);

*The Maid of Orleans: An Historical Tragedy* (Cambridge, Mass.: Privately printed by the Riverside Press, 1873; New York: Putnam, 1874);

*Brief Essays and Brevities* (Boston: Lee & Shepard / New York: Lee, Shepard & Dillingham, 1874);

*Essays Æsthetical* (Boston: Lee & Shepard / New York: Lee, Shepard & Dillingham, 1875);

*A Nation's Birth and Other National Poems* (Boston: Lee & Shepard, 1876);

*The Life of Rubens* (Boston: Lee & Shepard / New York: Dillingham, 1876);

*Charlotte von Stein: A Memoir* (Boston: Lee & Shepard / New York: Dillingham, 1877);

*Wordsworth: A Biographic Æsthetic Study* (Boston: Lee & Shepard / New York: Dillingham, 1878);

*Shakespeare: A Biographic Æsthetic Study* (Boston: Lee & Shepard / New York: Dillingham, 1879);

*Count Rudolf: A Tragedy* (Cambridge, Mass.: Privately printed by the Riverside Press, 1879);

*Coleridge, Shelley, Goethe. Biographic Æsthetic Studies* (Boston: Lee & Shepard / New York: Dillingham, 1880);

*Life, Death, and Other Poems* (Boston: Lee & Shepard / New York: Dillingham, 1882);

*Angeline: A Poem* (Boston, New York: Lee & Shepard / New York: Dillingham, 1883);

*Threescore, and Other Poems* (Boston: Lee & Shepard, 1883);

*Sibyl: A Poem* (Boston: Lee & Shepard, 1883);

*The Nazarene. A Poem* (Boston: Lee & Shepard / New York: Dillingham, 1883);

*Brangonar: A Tragedy* (Boston: Lee & Shepard / New York: Dillingham, 1883);

*Talk about Shakespeare* (Newport, R.I.: Davis & Pitman, 1886).

OTHER: *Illustrations of Phrenology; Being a Selection of Articles from the Edinburgh Phrenological Journal, and the Transactions of the Edinburg Phrenological Society* (Baltimore: Neal, 1832);

Friedrich Schiller, *Don Carlos; A Dramatic Poem,* translated by Calvert (Baltimore: Neal, 1834);

*Correspondence between Schiller and Goethe, from 1794 to 1805,* volume 1, translated by Calvert (New York & London: Wiley & Putnam, 1845);

Joseph Joubert, *Some of the "Thoughts" of Joseph Joubert,* translated by Calvert (Boston: Spencer, 1867);

republished as *Joubert; Some of the Thoughts of Joubert* (Boston: Lee & Shepard; New York: Lee, Shepard & Dillingham, 1876).

Although George Henry Calvert is not central to the American literary canon, his twentieth-century biographer, Ida Gertrude Everson, set him a monument that would be the pride of any American man of letters and has preserved his reputation. Indeed, *George Henry Calvert: An American Literary Pioneer* (1944)—to which any subsequent study is indebted—establishes the authoritative account of Calvert's considerable achievements, while simultaneously bringing the man and his work to life. Calvert's was a writing career that encompassed belles lettres (specifically poetry and drama), travel literature, literary criticism, and reviewing. While he was instrumental in actively promoting phrenology in the United States in the early days of the craze, his most important contribution to the intellectual scene was certainly his mediation and popularization of German letters. Indeed, his connoisseurship and judgment in that area exerted considerable influence upon a reading public fascinated by German writers and thinkers. For this intellectual energy he should be recognized after his poetry and dramas are forgotten.

Calvert (who pronounced the first vowel long, "Cahlvert") was born in Baltimore, Maryland, on 2 June 1803, the great-grandson of the fifth Lord Baltimore, founder of that colony. His unpublished autobiography later recorded that he had been born with six fingers on his right hand. His father, George Calvert of Riversdale (now Riverdale), a few miles from Washington, married Rosalie Eugenia Stier d'Artrelaer, a woman from an aristocratic Belgian family. Her family, lineal descendants of the painter Peter Paul Rubens, came to the United States in 1794 to escape Napoleon Bonaparte. Henri Stier, Rosalie's father, brought with him a collection of paintings that included masterpieces by Titian, Rubens, and Sir Anthony Van Dyck. Rosalie married George Calvert in 1799 and moved to Mount Airy, a plantation house in the Patuxent Valley about twenty-five miles southwest of Annapolis. Former president George Washington was a frequent guest of the family. Calvert was born on this property.

Calvert's cultured mother was an important early influence upon his learning and genteel upbringing. He was sent to Clermont Seminary near Philadelphia, a school where he received a thorough grounding in subjects that covered a spectrum from French to drawing instruction. In 1815, however, he entered the Mount Airy School at Germantown, run by Benjamin Constant. Here the emphasis was on French literature, though he also studied Spanish, music, mathematics, astronomy, Latin, and Greek. He finished his schooling in 1818 with high hopes of entering Harvard College in the fall of that year. Upon failing Greek and Latin, he studied assiduously with tutors until he made up the required work and was admitted to the freshman class after approximately nine weeks of preparation. Among his teachers at Harvard, George Ticknor (professor of French and Spanish), Edward Everett (professor of Greek and Latin), and Edward Tyrell Channing (professor of rhetoric and oratory), left particular impressions upon him. Both Ticknor and Everett had been among the first Americans to bring back news of Germany from their first-hand experiences in Göttingen, from whence they had returned in 1817 in order to inject a new perspective into American university life. During his sophomore year, in 1820, Calvert became caught up in the "Great Rebellion," a student revolt against the strict rules that governed student social life. In the winter of 1821 his mother, at forty-four years old, died, a loss that he felt more keenly in later years.

Of his religious life at Harvard, Calvert recalled in his autobiography that, to avoid the infection of Unitarianism, he would worship at a small Episcopalian church, where he had to pay the college 50¢ for each visit. On the other hand, he never became particularly religious. At Harvard he was occasionally censured for his petty infractions against the Puritanical atmosphere. He enjoyed life, joined the Porcellian Club, and acquired a reputation for his cleverness and good looks. By Calvert's senior year, the influence of George Bancroft, Joseph Green Cogswell, Everett, and Ticknor—all of whom had studied in Germany—began to make itself felt, although he received no formal training in German at college. In his senior year, in 1823, his public association with the student rebellion placed him among the thirty students who were dismissed that spring without their degrees. The son of John Quincy Adams (then secretary of state) was also among the students punished, but protests from Adams on behalf of the students were to no avail. Calvert, however, was finally awarded his diploma in 1855.

After college Calvert set his sights on Europe with the specific goal of studying at the University of Göttingen. He visited his mother's Belgian relatives in Antwerp on the way to Germany, an experience that both impressed upon him his ancestral heritage and instilled in him a suspicion of Roman Catholicism.

Calvert's memoirs recall first impressions of Göttingen mixed with the usual homesickness. Letters of introduction soon provided him access to the social scene, however, where his good manner and spirits made him popular. He began his study of German in earnest and attended lectures on German literature by Georg Friedrich Benecke (Göttingen teacher) Everett, Ticknor, Cogswell, and Bancroft). Calvert, who was

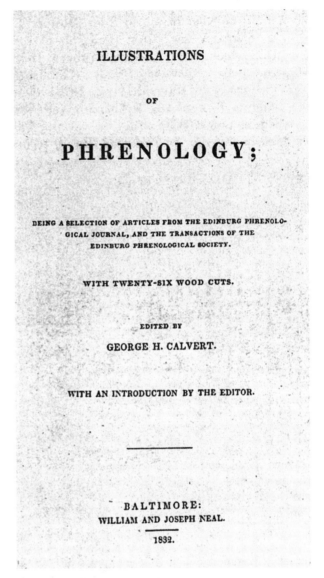

ILLUSTRATIONS

OF

PHRENOLOGY;

BEING A SELECTION OF ARTICLES FROM THE EDINBURG PHRENOLO-
GICAL JOURNAL, AND THE TRANSACTIONS OF THE
EDINBURG PHRENOLOGICAL SOCIETY.

WITH TWENTY-SIX WOOD CUTS.

EDITED BY

GEORGE H. CALVERT.

WITH AN INTRODUCTION BY THE EDITOR.

BALTIMORE:
WILLIAM AND JOSEPH NEAL.
1832.

*Title page for the first American book on the pseudo-science of determining intelligence and character from the shape of a person's skull (Special Collections, Thomas Cooper Library, University of South Carolina)*

the tenth American to register at Göttingen, became part of the small American community and an intimate friend of William Emerson, older brother of Ralph Waldo, who was studying theology. Among his English friends Calvert counted Edward Pusey, who later became a leader in the Oxford Movement. Calvert's professors at Göttingen were friendly and welcoming. His autobiography recalls fond memories of the Old Testament teacher Johann Eichhorn, Friedrich Bouterwek, Friedrich Saalfeld (with whom he formed a friendship), and Georg Sartorius. On his ambitious walking tours he discovered other German cities where friends of his Belgian uncle, Charles Stier, welcomed the young student.

One such walking tour led him to one of the most important and formative encounters of his life. In March 1825 he made his way to Weimar where, unannounced, he paid a call on Johann Wolfgang von Goethe. Calvert's travel book, *First Years in Europe* (1866), presents a vivid account of their meeting: "In 1825, Americans were seldom seen so far inland. In his whole life Goethe had probably not met with six. The announcement of one for the unbusied moments of after-dinner, was I dare say, to the ever-fresh student and universal observer, a piquant novelty. His attitude and expression, as I entered, were those of an expectant naturalist, eagerly awaiting the transatlantic phenomenon."

The seventy-six-year-old writer, who enjoyed the stature of a national living treasure, was gracious and courteous during their half-hour meeting. Their conversation ranged from the professors at Göttingen (who were known to Goethe) to the recent election of John Quincy Adams to the American presidency. Calvert left Goethe a copy of the *North American Review* (October 1824) that included an unsigned essay by Bancroft, the first important piece written on Goethe by an American. In the weeks between 27 March (the day of his meeting with Goethe) to 18 April 1825, when he left Weimar, Calvert circulated through society.

Preferring not to pay the fee required by the university, Calvert never took a degree from Göttingen. Leaving Germany in fall 1825, he made his way to Edinburgh to continue his studies. Once there, however, he did not enroll as a student but spent his time more aimlessly, albeit learning the beauties of English literature. By 1827, after having spent four years in Europe, he decided to return home. He established himself in Baltimore and in 1828 committed himself to a career as a writer. In 1829 he married Elizabeth Steuart, daughter of James Steuart, a Baltimore doctor; their marriage had no issue.

By 1830 the couple was settled in Baltimore, a city in which there were few journals of merit and where literary life did not seem to prosper. As Everson candidly notes, Calvert was also limited by his training; nor did he "possess a highly imaginative talent that impelled him to find expression in creative writing." Perhaps his proficiency in German language and literature served him poorly at first, but he soon began to fill in gaps by reading contemporary English and American literature. While there was no literary companionship in Baltimore, Calvert did gain introduction to the Baltimore Phrenological Society, a group of professors who made up the nucleus of the faculty at the recently founded University of Maryland. Calvert even accepted the Chair of Moral and Intellectual Philosophy at the university. He soon published the first book

in the United States on the subject of phrenology, *Illustrations of Phrenology; Being a Selection of Articles from the Edinburgh Phrenological Journal, and the Transactions of the Edinburg Phrenological Society* (1832).

In 1830 Calvert became joint editor with John T. Ducatel of the *Chronicle of the Times,* a miscellany of popular literature, descriptions of scientific advances, and articles from European journals. For this journal Calvert produced his first translations from the German, specifically from Goethe's *Faust* (1808, 1832). By March 1832 Calvert was the sole editor of the journal, which had changed its name to the *Baltimore Times* in 1831, and was able to place a greater emphasis on literary works.

In 1833 he published his first literary effort, *A Volume from the Life of Herbert Barclay,* a novel with an autobiographical dimension and particular emphasis on German literature. The work includes, for example, Calvert's poem "To Goethe" and translations of two portions of *Faust.* During this period, however, his important contributions to the reception of German literature concern Friedrich von Schiller, a poet whose poverty and lofty ideals brought him greater sympathy with American readers than Goethe's worldly tone and erotic themes. In the July 1834 *North American Review* Calvert gave a positive notice to Thomas Carlyle's *The Life of Friedrich Schiller,* which was published anonymously in Boston in 1833. The following year he published *Don Carlos; A Dramatic Poem,* his translation of Schiller's *Dom Karlos, Infant von Spanien* (1787), which he prefaces with a poem dedicated to another accomplished Schiller translator, Samuel Taylor Coleridge. Harry W. Pfund, who in his "George Henry Calvert: Admirer of Goethe" compared Calvert's English version of Schiller with Coleridge's, concludes: "If the bland verse flows less smoothly than in Coleridge's *Wallenstein,* this is due in part to Calvert's lapses into unusual word order, his involved sentence structure, and certain harsh contractions and elisions, in part to a less powerful command of poetic diction."

Calvert probably resigned his professorship by 1834, the year he joined the editorial staff of the *Baltimore American.* The job, which paid $1,000 per year, entailed much drudgery but did bring him into contact with another writer, John Pendleton Kennedy, who became a good friend. Although Edgar Allan Poe was in Baltimore at this time, no personal contact between the two men can be documented. Poe must have recognized Calvert's promise, for he recommended him to Thomas Willis White, the editor of the *Southern Literary Messenger,* with the result that by 1835 Calvert's pieces were appearing in that journal–specifically, a scene from his drama *Arnold and André* (June 1835) and the essay "German Literature" (May 1836), which had been given as a lecture before the Athenæum Society, Baltimore. This latter piece has greater significance than has heretofore been recognized. Calvert's overview of German literary history would otherwise be unremarkable if Poe had not derived two important pieces of information from the essay.

Poe, whose references to German literature were often either cryptic or generalized in order to conceal his own lack of understanding of the subject, lifts opinions from Calvert's discussion of translations of Goethe's *Die Leiden des jungen Werthers* (The Sorrows of Young Werther, 1774). More important, however, is Poe's obvious borrowing from Calvert in his preface to *Tales of the Grotesque and Arabesque* (1840), where he states that German literature is "not of Germany but of the soul." In his essay in the *Southern Literary Messenger* Calvert had referred to the "wild outpourings" of German literature as "not of Germany only, but of the age," a phrase Poe altered to defend his own writing against charges of imitative Germanism that were being leveled at him by critics. The detail would be less important if twentieth-century scholars had not tried to attribute to Poe expertise in German letters, which Calvert had but Poe lacked. In an 1841 series of installments for *Graham's Magazine*, "Autography," Poe presents short subjective glosses on his contemporaries based ostensibly on an analysis of their handwriting. He writes of Calvert:

> He is essentially a feeble and common-place writer of poetry, although his prose compositions have a certain degree of merit. His chirography indicates the "common-place" upon which we have commented. It is a very usual, scratchy, and tapering clerk's hand—a hand which no man of talent ever did or could indite, unless compelled by circumstances of more than ordinary force. The signature is far better than the general manuscript of his epistles.

Poe, to be sure, made a point of belittling his fellow writers—especially those who possessed talents or training he lacked—and Calvert, perhaps because of his prominence as editor of the *Baltimore American,* does not escape his ire. Calvert, at any rate, does not mention Poe in his own memoirs, which underscores the apparent bad blood between the two men.

When Calvert's father died in 1838, the estate was divided between him and his brother, thereby giving Calvert sufficient independent means to pursue his writing. The disillusionment with Baltimore encouraged him to gravitate toward New England. Elizabeth Calvert and Margaret Fuller had corresponded, and from this friendship came the connection to Ralph Waldo Emerson. Calvert's creative period from around

1820 to 1840 was dominated mainly by European, especially German, literary models.

In 1840 the Calverts again set sail for Europe, this time with a letter of introduction from Emerson to Carlyle. Because the American reading public was eager for travel accounts—a genre in which Calvert excelled—he recorded the experiences of this trip in his anonymously published *Scenes and Thoughts in Europe. By an American* (1846). Nathaniel Hawthorne reviewed the book in the *Salem Advertiser* (29 April 1846), praising especially Calvert's skill in describing art and architecture, although the book (presented in epistolary form) also includes social criticism and political observations. Henry Wadsworth Longfellow introduced Calvert to the German poet Ferdinand Freiligrath, and the two poets corresponded for years. Most interesting are his observations on returning to Göttingen to see the university a pale reflection of its former glory. He is critical of the encroaching political power of Prussia, which was changing the face of Germany and restricting former freedoms throughout the German states. Calvert also describes his visit to William Wordsworth and Carlyle, as well as to the German spa on the Rhine where he became a devotee of Vincent Preissnitz's restorative water cure (known as hydropathy), a treatment that also created a health craze in the United States.

Returning to the United States in 1843, the Calverts moved to Newport, Rhode Island, the following year. Living in this bustling town in relative quiet, he ultimately produced some thirty volumes before his death. The first of these was a translation into lucid, readable English of the *Correspondence between Schiller and Goethe, from 1794 to 1805* (1845). Perhaps more important than the letters themselves, however, was Calvert's defense of Goethe in the preface of this book. Goethe's stock was low in the United States, where the Puritan tradition led Americans to censure the German writer for what was seen as licentiousness. An exception was *The Dial,* in which commentators such as Fuller and Emerson judged Goethe on his merits. Calvert, however, was determined to counter the detraction presented by the clergyman George Putnam in his Phi Beta Kappa oration delivered at Harvard in 1844. American debate on German letters was seldom as heated as this controversy sparked by Putnam's moralizing rejection of Goethe.

In 1847 Calvert contributed poems and German translations to *The Harbinger.* The same year he published his collection *Poems,* a volume that earned the praise of Evert Augustus Duyckinck and John Sullivan Dwight, who was himself an accomplished translator of German poetry. Everson views these poems as a turning point in Calvert's writing, showing as they do an interest in social issues and political affairs far removed from the scholarly task of translating German literature or the gentlemanly activity of recording his travels. His third journey to Europe, from 1849 to 1851, when he revisited familiar places such as Weimar and towns on the Rhine, helped to reinforce interest in social change. The second series of his *Scenes and Thoughts in Europe. By an American* (1852) records the experiences in tones less sentimental or rhapsodic than many travel books by his contemporaries. Calvert intersperses his observations with opinions on the change and unrest that had occurred in the wake of the liberal revolution. He also reaffirms his strong Protestant affiliation through his praise of Martin Luther and opposition to Roman Catholicism.

In Newport, Calvert was a popular public speaker. He involved himself with Democratic party politics, campaigning for Franklin Pierce in 1852 and spreading the socialist ideas of Charles Fourier. He had the reputation of a progressive, particularly in his involvement with the school committee of Newport. When the town renewed its charter, Calvert ran for mayor and won the election. Calvert's writings in the 1860s express his fervent support of liberal causes, such as Giuseppe Garibaldi's struggle in Italy, but offer no public stand on the issue of slavery in the United States.

In 1854 Calvert completed his romantic comedy, *The Will and the Way,* which he had begun earlier in Baltimore. The drama has all the formulae of farce: a masked ball, disguises, two pairs of lovers, banishment, and reinstatement. Calvert gave the play a public reading, but it was never produced. His interest in the drama, however, did not decline. He wrote a second comedy, *Like unto Like,* and published the two texts together as *Comedies* in 1856. Despite the apparently limited readership of Calvert's works, he enjoyed the respect of his contemporaries (Poe's detractions notwithstanding). In *The Cyclopaedia of American Literature* (1881) Evert and George L. Duyckinck offered a generous assessment:

> The literary productions of Mr. Calvert are marked by their nice philosophical speculation, their sense of honor and of beauty, and their pure scholastic qualities. There is a certain fastidiousness and reserve of the retired thinker in the manner, with a fondness for the aphorism; though there is nothing of the selfish isolation of the scholar in the matter. The thought is original, and uttered with firmness.

The 1860s were for Calvert a period of concentrated work. During the Civil War he published *The Gentleman* (1863), a book on a most apolitical subject written in the genteel tradition during highly politicized times. It was one of his most widely read works and brought him considerable popularity. After tracing the origins of the concept of gentlemanliness, Calvert examines specific cases of famous representatives of the type. He concludes that the gentleman possesses qualities of cleanliness, honesty, manners, refinement, breeding, courtesy, and education. Furthermore, a gentleman, observes Calvert, is a man whose "manners are not put on with his dress-coat: they are ingrained and are spontaneous, like his talk." In 1864 Calvert finished the third and fourth cantos of *Cabiro,* a satirical poem in ottava rima begun in Baltimore in 1840. He also published *Arnold and André: An Historical Drama,* an excerpt of which had appeared in 1835 in the *Southern Literary Messenger.*

Calvert wrote three travel books. With the publication of *First Years in Europe* he combined memoirs and travel literature. The work, which uses diaries and letters, is the chief source of information about his life in the 1820s, particularly during his grand tour of Europe from September 1823 to May 1827. It is a humorous account of the academic and social life at Göttingen, including vivid depictions of the German professors and of his stay in Weimar.

The critical response to *Ellen: A Poem for the Times* (1867) was less positive than reviews of Calvert's prose. Even Everson finds in the poem the "mediocrity of much of Calvert's poetry," a trait that can be blamed on stilted diction, Germanic sentence structure, and awkward word choice.

In the 1860s Calvert turned to French culture to translate Joseph Joubert and to write an essay on Charles-Augustin Sainte-Beuve. By the end of the decade, however, he renewed his interest in Goethe, chiefly by encountering George Henry Lewes's *Life and Works of Goethe* (1855), the first biography in English. In 1872 Calvert, referred to by Pfund as "Lewes's disciple," published the first American biography of Goethe, *Goethe: His Life and Works.* Although the book is subtitled "An Essay," it is actually a series of essays. Calvert quotes from Lewes but does not imitate him; the result is a work that popularizes Goethe and brings him to a wider English-speaking public. His cogent, sensitive, and accurate defense of Goethe, at a time when Goethe's reputation was quite low in the United States, is to Calvert's credit. He refused to sit in moralistic judgment of the life and behavior of a man whose literary talent he admired greatly. In 1874 Calvert's *Brief Essays and Brevities* appeared, which includes more criticism on Goethe, as well as several faithful translations of his poems.

In 1875 the young critic Henry James reviewed Calvert's *Essays Æsthetical* for *The Nation* (3 June 1875). It is a significant verdict by a discerning contemporary:

Mr. Calvert occasionally puts forth a modest volume of prose or verse which attracts no general attention, but which, we imagine, find adequate appreciation among scattered readers. We prefer his prose to his verse, and we can frankly recommend this little collection of essays on subjects connected with art and letters. The author's fault, as a general thing, is in his vagueness, and in a tendency to judgments a trifle too ethereal and to a style considerably too florid. We prefer him, therefore, when he is treating to concrete rather than abstract matters, and we have found more edification in the volume before us in the papers on the translators of Dante, on Sainte-Beuve, and on Carlyle, than in the accompanying disquisitions on the Beautiful, on the Nature of Poetry, and on Style. To offer us off-hand, at the present hour, an article on the Beautiful, implies an almost heroic indifference to the tyranny of fashion. Mr. Calvert cares for letters for their own sake, he is a disinterested scholar, and his writing has the aroma of genuine culture. Even the occasional awkwardness and amateurishness of his manner are an indication of that union, so rare in this country, of taste and leisure which allows culture an opportunity to accumulate. The best thing in the volume is the article on Sainte-Beuve, in which the author shows that he had studied the great critic to very good purpose. It is very intelligent and, much of it, very felicitous, and it is filled, moreover, with excellent brief citations.

In the late 1870s Calvert focused on biographical studies, producing three works in this genre. His biography on his ancestor Rubens was the first written by an American. He was helped by his Belgian relatives who supplied him with materials for the project. He never lost his reputation as a Goethe specialist, however, and delivered a spirited lecture to the Goethe Club of New York City in 1877. In fact, the last public lecture that he gave, in 1886, was on Goethe. Closely connected with this interest in Goethe was another project on German literature, the biography *Charlotte von Stein: A Memoir* (1877). This contribution to the literature on Goethe is drawn, as the preface states, from two works that had recently appeared in Germany: the three-volume edition of Goethe's letters to von Stein (1848–1851), edited by A. Schoell; and the biography *Charlotte von Stein, Goethes Freundin* (1874) by Heinrich Düntzer. The letters von Stein wrote to Goethe do not survive. Calvert weaves a sensitive and subjective portrait of this remarkable woman, a central figure in court life at Weimar, liberally adding fictional touches to his narrative to invoke for the reader the emotions of his subject. The work, which is written with great verve and enthusiasm, does not try to hide the author's emotional sympathies for his characters—Goethe being almost as central to the work as von Stein. Goethe enthusiasts praised the work in their reviews; the detractors, on the

GOETHE:

HIS LIFE AND WORKS.

AN ESSAY.

BY

GEORGE H. CALVERT.

BOSTON:
LEE AND SHEPARD, PUBLISHERS.
NEW YORK:
LEE, SHEPARD AND DILLINGHAM.
1872.

*Title page for Calvert's biography of a German author who was widely influential among nineteenth-century American intellectuals (Special Collections, Thomas Cooper Library, University of South Carolina)*

other hand, were critical of Calvert's admiration of the German writer.

In 1878 his pioneering biography *Wordsworth: A Biographic Æsthetic Study* was published. No American had yet written an entire book on Wordsworth, making this biography a cultural milestone. Calvert's taste, which ran to the poets of Wordsworth's generation, had little sympathy for an American contemporary such as Walt Whitman, whose poetry, he felt, could never express eternal truths. Wordsworth, on the other hand, enjoyed almost universal veneration; furthermore, Calvert had visited him twice on his travels to England. The descriptions of these visits give Calvert's work a personal touch. Nonetheless, Wordsworth was known for his antipathy to Goethe—an attitude he did not hide from Emerson, whose own enthusiasm for Goethe was curbed by Wordsworth's rejection of *Wilhelm Meisters Lehrjahre* (1795–1796; translated as *Wilhelm Meister's*

*Apprenticeship,* 1824). While Calvert did not know of that encounter, he also exposed Wordsworth's narrow prejudices. Nonetheless, the book did achieve its goal of gaining American adherents of Wordsworth and won him acclaim as a scholarly biographer for doing so.

Everson describes Calvert's last decade in Newport, Rhode Island, as contemplative. He was both mentally alert, yet understandably disappointed by much of the critical response to his work. He published several volumes of indifferent poetry, among them new editions of earlier publications. He also wrote *Shakespeare: A Biographic Æsthetic Study* (1879), in which he places the playwright even higher in the literary pantheon than Goethe.

*Brangonar: A Tragedy* (1883) was his last verse drama (although the preface is dated 1868). The play is a monument to his revulsion of Napoleon's tyranny. It was never performed, but after publication it received hostile reviews. In his last years, when he had outlived most of his friends, Calvert was mentally active, though his hands were so crippled he could not easily hold a pen. One good friend was the labor activist John Swinton, with whom he exchanged letters. Although isolated in his old age, Calvert did give public lectures and enjoyed public honors. He wrote an "Autobiographic Study" with the apparent aim of publishing his memoirs. The work, which traces his life up to 1840, exists only in page proofs, however. Calvert died at his home in Newport, his wife at his bedside, on 24 May 1889.

**Bibliography:**

Hamilton Bullock Tompkins, *Bibliography of the Works of George Henry Calvert* (Newport, R.I.: Redwood Library & Athenaeum, 1900).

**Biography:**

Ida Gertrude Everson, *George Henry Calvert: An American Literary Pioneer,* Columbia University Studies in English and Comparative Literature 160 (New York: Columbia University Press, 1944).

**References:**

Evert Augustus Duyckinck and George L. Duyckinck, eds. *The Cyclopaedia of American Literature: Embracing Personal and Critical Notices of Authors, and Selections from their Writings, from the Earliest Period to the Present Day,* 2 volumes (Philadelphia: Baxter, 1881), II: 192–198;

Thomas S. Hansen with Burton R. Pollin, *The German Face of Edgar Allan Poe: A Study of Literary References in His Works* (Columbia, S.C.: Camden House, 1995);

O. W. Long, *Literary Pioneers: Early American Explorers of European Culture* (Cambridge, Mass.: Harvard University Press, 1935);

Harry W. Pfund, "George Henry Calvert: Admirer of Goethe," in *Studies in Honor of John Albrecht Walz* (Freeport, N.Y.: Books for Libraries Press, 1968), pp. 117–161;

Henry A. Pochmann, *German Culture in America: Philosophical and Literary Influences, 1600–1900* (Madison: University of Wisconsin Press, 1957);

Edgar Allan Poe, "Autography," in *The Complete Works of Edgar Allan Poe,* 15 volumes, edited by James. A. Harrison (New York: Crowell, 1902), XV: 139–261.

**Papers:**

The largest collection of George Henry Calvert's letters (106) is at the John Hay Library, Brown University. Other letters are in the Butler Library at Columbia University (32 letters and memorabilia), the Houghton Library at Harvard (16 letters), the Milton Eisenhower Library at Johns Hopkins University (9 letters), the Beinecke Library at Yale (6 letters), the Enoch Pratt Free Library in Baltimore (5 letters), and the William Perkins Library at Duke (5 letters). A photostatic copy of his "Autobiographic Study" is at Columbia University.

# William Alexander Caruthers

*(23 December 1802 – 19 August 1846)*

J. Robert Baker
*Fairmont State College*

See also the Caruthers entry in *DLB 3: Antebellum Writers in New York and the South.*

BOOKS: *The Kentuckian in New-York. Or, The Adventures of Three Southerns,* 2 volumes (New York: Harper, 1834);

*The Cavaliers of Virginia, or The Recluse of Jamestown. An Historical Romance of the Old Dominion,* 2 volumes (New York: Harper, 1834–1835);

*The Drunkard: From the Cradle to the Grave. A Lecture, Delivered before the Savannah Temperance Society, at the First Presbyterian Church, Jan. 15, and Repeated Feb. 26* (Savannah, Ga.: Williams, 1840);

*A Lecture before the Georgia Historical Society, at the Unitarian Church, in Savannah, on Tuesday Evening, 14th March, 1843* (Savannah, Ga.: Locke & Davis, 1843);

*The Knights of the Horse-Shoe. A Traditional Tale of the Cocked Hat Gentry in the Old Dominion* (Wetumpka, Ala.: Yancey, 1845).

OTHER: "Daniel Boone," in *The National Portrait Gallery of Distinguished Americans,* 4 volumes, edited by James Herring and James B. Longacre (New York: Bancroft, 1834–1839): II.

SELECTED PERIODICAL PUBLICATIONS–
UNCOLLECTED: "A Musical Soiree," *Knickerbocker Magazine,* 5 (April 1835): 337–339;

"Excerpts from the Portfolio of a Physician. Blushing," *Magnolia: or, Southern Monthly,* 3 (January 1841): 24–26;

"The Ruins of Jamestown," *Magnolia: or, Southern Monthly,* 3 (January 1841): 14–15;

Review of Isabella F. Romer's *Strumer; A Tale of Mesmerism, Magnolia: or, Southern Monthly,* 4 (January 1842): 43–45;

"Excerpts from the Portfolio of an Old Novelist," *Family Companion, and Ladies' Mirror,* 2 (April 1842): 56–57; (May 1842): 79–80; (June 1842): 173;

"Mesmerism," *Magnolia: or, Southern Monthly,* 4 (March 1842): 178–182;

"The Bardolphian Nose," *Orion: A Monthly Magazine of Literature, Science, and Art,* 1 (June 1842): 176–179;

"Excerpts from the Portfolio of a Physician. Love and Consumption," *Magnolia, or, Southern Appalachian,* new series 1 (July 1842): 35–38; (August 1842): 103–108; (September 1842): 177–182.

Though no longer widely read, William Alexander Caruthers remains an important figure in the literary history of the South. Both his near contemporary John Esten Cooke and his biographer Curtis Carroll Davis maintain that Caruthers was the first significant Virginia novelist, but his importance is larger. Though often dwarfed by John Pendleton Kennedy, William Gilmore Simms, and Cooke, Caruthers contributed to the flourishing of Southern fiction before the Civil War. In *The World of Washington Irving* (1944), Van Wyck Brooks goes so far as to assert that "Caruthers was the father" of the Southern romancers. He was undoubtedly one of the creators of plantation fiction and perhaps the first novelist to promote agrarianism.

As an early practitioner of plantation fiction, Caruthers often caricatures blacks, dividing them into solemn, dignified household slaves and boisterous, comic minstrels. Despite these stereotypes of the genre, Caruthers also created slave characters who are more complex than the faithful retainer or the comic folksinger. His concerns about slavery and his interest in the literary uses of slaves' manner of speech anticipate both Charles Waddell Chesnutt and Joel Chandler Harris. Similarly, Caruthers's exploration of the strengths of women prevents his characterization of them from being merely sentimental. Caruthers's women characters may swoon, but they also prove themselves capable and determined. Caruthers's treatment of Native Americans is also complicated, combining clichéd savagery with admiration for the dignity of the Indians and regret at their displacement. Caruthers's entire career is marked by such complexity. While he began his career as a novelist by arguing for the rapprochement of North and South, he went on to define

*Letter in which Caruthers asks Thomas Jefferson to write him a character reference; Caruthers's father managed Jefferson's landholdings around Lexington, Virginia (Jefferson Papers, Massachusetts Historical Society)*

the ideal of the cavalier, which became a potent image for Southern identity both during and after the Civil War. Though he was enamored of this ideal, Caruthers was aware of its weaknesses and limitations.

Caruthers was born on 23 December 1802 to William Caruthers and Phebe Alexander Caruthers in Lexington, Virginia, the fourth of eleven children. A farmer and merchant, William Caruthers was also a local representative for Thomas Jefferson, managing Jefferson's landholdings, including the Natural Bridge. His mother's brother, Archibald Alexander, was a prominent Presbyterian minister who by 1812 was teaching at the College of New Jersey. Caruthers attended but did not graduate from Washington College at Lexington (later Washington and Lee University). He took his medical degree from the University of Pennsylvania Medical School in 1823. That same year he married Louisa Catherine Gibson, who was from Whitemarsh Island off Savannah and who had an inheritance worth more than $40,000, including seventy-nine slaves. Settling in Lexington, the couple soon ran up debts that exhausted Caruthers's own inheritance and his wife's property. His medical practice proved insufficient to prevent his having to declare bankruptcy in 1829.

That year Caruthers moved his family, which included five children, to New York, where he arranged commissions for Lexington merchants and practiced medicine during the 1832 outbreak of cholera. He also began his career as a writer in New York. Davis speculates that he may have reviewed books, and he certainly wrote the entry on Daniel Boone for *The National Portrait Gallery of Distinguished Americans* (1834–1839). Caruthers based this sketch on John Filson's *Discovery, Settlement and Present State of Kentucke* (1784). Like many, Caruthers assumed that the section of Filson's book attributed to Boone was genuine. As a result he made mistakes about dates, Boone's family's religion, and even the spelling of his name. Caruthers's sketch cast Boone as a prophet of the greatness of the nation and as a forerunner of the heroes of Caruthers. Caruthers also wrote "A Musical Soiree" (April 1835), a satire published in the *Knickerbocker Magazine*. Addressing "the unsophisticated inhabitant of the country," Caruthers lampoons the customs and values of city dwellers attending an evening of musical entertainment at a fashionable upper-crust residence in New York. Caruthers claimed to have published books with James Kirke Paulding while he lived in New York, but there is no evidence of these works.

In 1834 Harper and Brothers published Caruthers's first novel, *The Kentuckian in New-York. Or, The Adventures of Three Southerns,* which introduces many of the themes and techniques that occupied Caruthers for his entire career. Thematically, Caruthers is concerned with love and marriage and with the cavalier as a type. Each of his novels works toward one or multiple marriages of young men and women who seem ideally suited to one another but who have been separated either by misunderstanding, social custom, or political power. These men and women, all of heroic stature, contribute to the Southern ideal of masculinity and femininity. His heroes are descended from the cavaliers, whom Caruthers mythologized as the original settlers of the Old Dominion. They may act Byronically, but none is merely a maverick. Each is driven by a prophetic vision of a future national greatness, toward which they strive with considerable energy. Caruthers's heroes and heroines are aided in their matrimonial and political aspirations by a Calvinist sensibility that pervades the novels so that the unregenerate are unequivocally punished, usually with death, while the elect are assured ultimately of being rewarded by divine providence.

While Caruthers's themes are connected with contemporary political issues—sectional conflict, the dangers of slavery, westward expansion, Indian removal, and relations with Mexico—his techniques were influenced by his reading when he returned to Lexington as a newly married man just finished with medical school. Largely literary, his reading was drawn from the small library of the Franklin Society and Library Company of Lexington. In examining the charge sheets for this library between 1823 and 1829, Davis notes that Caruthers read general history and English fiction, particularly Sir Walter Scott, for he withdrew "*The Bride of Lammermoor, A Legend of Montrose, Kenilworth,* the second volume of *Quentin Durward, The Fortunes of Nigel, Rob Roy,* and *The Antiquary.*" He also found Lord Byron appealing and read Miguel de Cervantes in translation. Caruthers was not much interested in Americans; though he checked out James Fenimore Cooper's *The Spy* (1821) and *The Pioneers* (1823), he kept them for only brief periods. His reading led him to employ the techniques of the sentimental novel and to draw heavily on the pastoral and gothic traditions.

For *The Kentuckian in New-York* Caruthers also drew on his travels along the eastern seaboard and on his work among the poor during the cholera epidemic in 1832. The novel is epistolary, a series of letters between two classmates—Victor Chevillere, who travels to New York with his friend Augustus Lamar, and Beverley Randolph, who journeys to Georgia and the Carolinas. Along the way both Chevillere and Randolph comment on the unfamiliar parts of the country that they find. *The Kentuckian in New-York* has also been characterized as an intersectional novel because Chevillere argues

*Charge sheet from the Franklin Society and Library Company of Lexington, Virginia, circa 1827, documenting the books Caruthers borrowed during the early years of his marriage (McCormick Memorial Library, Washington and Lee University)*

repeatedly that each section of the country must learn from and be tolerant of the others:

> The puppyism of Charleston and that of Boston are only different shades of the same character, yet these kindred spirits can in nowise tolerate each other. . . . The mutual jealousy of the north and south is a decided evidence of littleness in both regions, and ample cause for shame to the educated gentlemen of all parties of this happy country. If pecuniary interest had not been mixed up with this provincial rivalry, the feeling could easily have been so held up to that broad light of intelligence, as to be a fertile source of amusement, and furnish many a subject for comedy and farce in after-times.

Insisting that the incipient conflict between North and South could be avoided if each section were to learn more about the other firsthand as he, Lamar, and Randolph are doing, Chevillere advocates nationalism over sectionalism, moderation over anger, and harmony over discord.

Chevillere and Lamar are joined by Montgomery Damon from Kentucky, who accompanies them to New York. Damon is a tall, imposing rustic, comic in both dress and speech. Though Damon is something of the stock character common by the time of Caruthers's novel, he is full of life and confidence, characteristics that Chevillere sees as typical of the West and necessary to correct the moral corruptions caused by the economic structures of both the North and South. On the other hand, he lacks the refinement of the other two sections of the country and is thus unable to distinguish between reality and theatrical drama.

*The Kentuckian in New-York* presents slavery as an impediment to intersectional harmony, but one that cannot be easily resolved. Even though Caruthers hired out the slaves whom his wife owned, he mainly opposed slavery, finding it antithetical to the energetic middle class of the region in which he had grown up and preferring the agrarianism of the small farms in that area. In 1825 he signed a petition to the General Assembly of Virginia to provide funds to transport freed slaves to Liberia because they might help to stir up a slave rebellion. In *The Kentuckian in New-York* Caruthers dramatizes this threat with an attack on Randolph by an anonymous driver, a slave put in charge of others, who was disgruntled by a whipping. The novel suggests another objection to slavery when Randolph contends that slavery had made the slaves unable to take care of themselves.

Caruthers used intermarriage as a symbol of intersectional harmony in *The Kentuckian in New-York*. Each of the three white classmates meets and falls in love with a woman from outside his region as if to enact

Chevillere's insistence on the need for each section to know the other firsthand. Chevillere is captivated by Fanny St. Clair of New York, while Randolph and Chevillere's cousin Virginia Bell fall in love and Lamar courts Isabel Hazelhurst of New York. Before Chevillere's romance can succeed, though, he must solve the mystery surrounding Fanny, who is pursued by a mysterious man who accuses her of murder. Chevillere learns that the man is Fanny's deranged father-in-law, who mistakenly thinks that Fanny poisoned his son with wine at their marriage banquet. Despite this gothic mischief of the crazed father-in-law, Chevillere and Fanny do wed, as do the other couples. Even Damon marries a woman whom he has met in New York. The book ends in an American pastoral at Randolph's home, where the three classmates and their brides celebrate just after Christmas in a parlor presided over by "a full-length picture of General Washington, on the mantel-piece." Raising contemporary social issues, *The Kentuckian in New-York* received favorable reviews.

In his next novel, *The Cavaliers of Virginia, or The Recluse of Jamestown. An Historical Romance of the Old Dominion* (1834–1835), Caruthers took up another contemporary issue—westward expansion. In this historical romance about Bacon's Rebellion, Caruthers is one of the earliest writers to treat Manifest Destiny, even though he may never have heard the phrase, which was used first in 1845. In Caruthers's hand Nathaniel Bacon becomes the first proponent of expansionism when he leads an army against Indians assembled against the colony at Jamestown, driving them beyond the Tidewater. Caruthers asserts that Bacon's Rebellion was a rehearsal for the American Revolution and that both were part of the providential destiny of the country.

Even though Caruthers used Robert Beverley's *History and Present State of Virginia* (1705) and John Daly Burk's *History of Virginia* (1822) as sources for his novel, he was, like all romancers, more interested in his own themes than the historical facts. Caruthers sets the political struggles in the colony at Jamestown, including a rebellion by Cromwellian sympathizers, within the love story of Bacon and Virginia Fairfax, a story complicated by a charge that Bacon is a half brother to Virginia. This charge is made by a mysterious figure called the Recluse who turns out to be Edward Whalley, one of the judges who sentenced Charles I to death. There is little evidence of Puritan revolt at Jamestown or of any of the regicides of Charles I settling in Virginia. Bacon was, in fact, married at the time of the rebellion and from a well-established family, even though Caruthers characterizes him as an unmarried, almost mythic, romantic figure of uncertain parentage.

Caruthers continues his romance narrative with Bacon's capture and torture by the Chickahominies

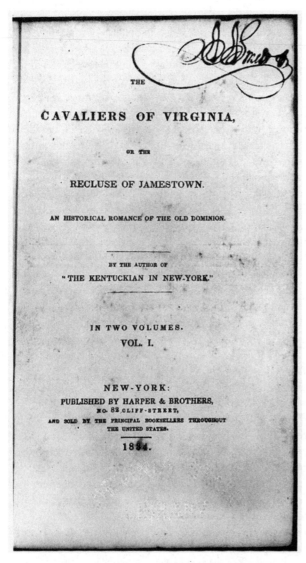

THE

CAVALIERS OF VIRGINIA,

OR THE

RECLUSE OF JAMESTOWN.

AN HISTORICAL ROMANCE OF THE OLD DOMINION.

BY THE AUTHOR OF
"THE KENTUCKIAN IN NEW-YORK."

IN TWO VOLUMES.
VOL. I.

NEW-YORK:
PUBLISHED BY HARPER & BROTHERS,
NO. 82 CLIFF-STREET,
AND SOLD BY THE PRINCIPAL BOOKSELLERS THROUGHOUT
THE UNITED STATES.

1834.

*Title page for Caruthers's fictionalized account of Bacon's Rebellion in 1676 (Special Collections, Thomas Cooper Library, University of South Carolina)*

protesting, "O yes, you will run the long knives through their bodies and then smoke the calumet! You will drive us from our homes, and then you will persuade us to give them up to the white man." Though Caruthers was an advocate of westward expansion, he was also sensitive to the plight of the Native Americans in the path of this growth.

*The Cavaliers of Virginia* expresses a longing for an ideal that Caruthers and others imagined had been lost by the social and political stagnation that had beset Virginia by the 1830s. Bacon embodies this ideal of the gentleman perfectly suited to lead the developing democracy in the wilderness. Caruthers develops the ideal in the battles against the Roundhead insurgents, against the Indian confederation, and against Governor William Berkeley. Each battle demonstrates that the American Cavalier rejects the self-righteousness of the Puritans, the savagery of the Indians, and the self-aggrandizements of the aristocrats. Bacon resists the extremes of all these parties and yet exhibits the self-discipline and intensity of the Roundheads, the dignity and long-suffering of the Native Americans, and the honor and nobility of the Cavaliers. These traits make Bacon a self-reliant figure who cannot only survive on the frontier, but also prophetically direct the destiny of the incipient nation. Caruthers imagines these qualities as almost hereditary, for late in the novel Virginia's father reveals that he is the son of a Commonwealth officer and an English lady.

Davis notes that Caruthers, who had returned to Lexington with his family in 1836, had completed the manuscript for his next novel by 1838 and intended to call it "The Tramontane Order," but he lost this manuscript when a fire destroyed his house in Lexington. Caruthers rewrote the novel when he moved to Savannah the same year and published it serially as *The Knights of the Golden Horse-Shoe* in the literary journal *Magnolia* three years later. In 1845 Caruthers let Charles Yancey of Wetumpka, Alabama, publish the novel with the slightly altered title *The Knights of the Horse-Shoe. A Traditional Tale of the Cocked Hat Gentry in the Old Dominion*. (Later editions of the work used the title with and without the word *Golden*. The 1970 reprint of the novel for the Southern Literary Classics Series used the Yancey text but restored the title used by the *Magnolia*.) Davis speculates that Harper and Brothers was trimming its lists after the panic of 1837 and may have dropped Caruthers. It is also possible that as the intersectional tensions increased in the 1830s, Caruthers, who had pleaded for tolerance, finally took a side, deciding to have a southerner publish his third novel. The decision to let Yancey publish the novel had a serious consequence: Yancey had no means of distributing the book, so it sold badly. Despite its poor sales, Caruthers's third

after the interruption of his marriage to Virginia by the Recluse's charge of incest. In a scene that recalls John Smith's account of being saved by Pocahontas, Bacon is rescued from the Indians when a young Indian woman, Wyanokee, offers to marry him. Wyanokee has lived with the English as a servant to Virginia but has returned to become the queen of her people. Though Bacon finally rejects her offer and marries Virginia, Wyanokee embodies the nobility of the race; when the Indians are defeated and forced to retreat, she speaks eloquently about the calamity that the English settlement posed for the Native Americans: "It leaves room to hunt and plant corn *there* for white men, and finds room *here* to hunt and plant corn, but you do not give the poor red man any hunting ground." Wyanokee graphically describes the English method of settlement,

novel may be his best; the dialogue is less stilted and the action less contrived.

*The Knights of the Horse-Shoe* is the first book to treat Governor Alexander Spotswood and his expedition across the Blue Ridge Mountains, but the novel is largely an historical romance like *The Cavaliers of Virginia*. Caruthers relied on Reverend Hugh Jones's *Present State of Virginia* (1724), Burk's *History of Virginia*, and John Oldmixon's *British Empire in America* (1708). Despite these sources and his correspondence with Charles Campbell and Colonel George Augustine Washington Spotswood, Caruthers adapts history considerably to support his theme of westward expansion. He has hundreds of horsemen make up the expedition when, in fact, there were only sixty-three, and has the horses halt because they lack horseshoes, but on the actual expedition they were shoed before starting out. The threat of starvation and hostile Indians are also Caruthers's invention, as is his having Spotswood's party discover the Valley of Virginia.

In advocating expansionism Caruthers compares Spotswood to Christopher Columbus, suggesting that the governor's expedition was as important as Columbus's initial voyage. Facing both the threat of French extensions west of the mountains and opposition of "the aristocracy of the land," Spotswood mounts an expedition of young gentry, each with fifty followers. While the young men set out with high hopes of glory and treasure, the narrative itself construes their journey as a providential first step in the imperialist expansion of Caruthers's own time. Although Spotswood claims the region in the name of the British king, the narrator suggests that he should have pushed on as far as Mexico.

As with his other novels, Caruthers is also interested in the definition of the gentleman. This aspect of the plot is largely worked out in the character of Frank Lee, who first appears in the colony disguised as his cousin Henry Hall because he has recently supported an effort by Spotswood's half brother to bring Charles, "the Pretender," to the throne of England. Initially employed as the tutor for Spotswood's youngest son, the disguised Frank soon incurs the ire of his own brother, Harry Lee, who suspects him of being an imposter and who is jealous of the attentions he pays to Ellen Evylin. Harry objects that the tutor is no gentleman but a swindler. Despite his protests, Ellen and the governor's daughter Kate sense the manners and virtues of the disguised Lee. In short, they recognize him as a gentleman without knowing his status, as if to suggest that authentic nobility cannot be masked. This plot, which takes up two-thirds of the novel, is finally resolved when Lee is able to reveal his true identity. He then joins the governor's expedition, serving as his chief aide.

Frank is assisted by Joe Jarvis, a Western character like Montgomery Damon; Jarvis provides comic relief with his rough speech and humor, but his practical know-how makes him a valuable asset to the expedition. He suggests hunting parties to supply the expedition with fresh game so that their supplies will not be exhausted. Anticipating that the rough terrain of the mountains will lame most of the horses who have had no need for shoes in the softer soils of the Tidewater, he has a supply of iron placed among the expedition stores. When most of the animals are lamed, he teaches Spotswood and Frank how to shoe them. He also proves himself an adept Indian fighter who saves the expedition from the menace posed by the Native Americans. A complicated character, Jarvis has been compared to Daniel Boone and to Cooper's Natty Bumppo. Although he is a frontiersman at home in the wilderness, he also begins its destruction, becoming the advance guard of a civilization that in cutting down the virgin forests will drive the Indians and game further west. Jarvis's hatred of the Native Americans is similarly complicated. While he rails against Dr. Blair's scheme of schools for young Native Americans as misguided because, in his view, the Indians are incorrigible and incapable of civilization, Jarvis falls in love with Wingina, who ultimately spurns him because she is a queen among her people.

Jarvis's attraction to Wingina fails, but a good portion of the narrative, like all of Caruthers's novels, is concerned with romance. Frank woos Ellen Evylin, while Bernard Moore courts Kate Spotswood. The novel ends with the marriage of these couples and of the real Henry Hall with Eugenia Elliot.

While *The Knights of the Horse-Shoe* did not sell well in Caruthers's lifetime, it has had an important critical afterlife. Davis observes that "Confederate chroniclers such as Thomas C. DeLeon, in *Four Years in Rebel Capitals* (1892), and Dr. Thomas A. Ashby, in *The Valley Campaigns . . .* (1914), envisaged the Spotswood riders as having set the model of valor for those Virginians who resisted Northern aggression during the Civil War."

The rest of Caruthers's writing is limited to magazine pieces and two lectures. In a July 1838 issue of *Knickerbocker Magazine* he published "Climbing the Natural Bridge. By the Only Surviving Witness of That Extraordinary Feat," an account of a trip that Caruthers made to the Natural Bridge with two other students at Washington College in 1818, one of whom, James H. Piper, scaled the bridge. In January 1841 he published a piece on blushing in the *Magnolia*. The following year he argued against mesmerism, reviewing Isabella F. Romer's *Sturmer: A Tale of Mesmerism* in the January 1842

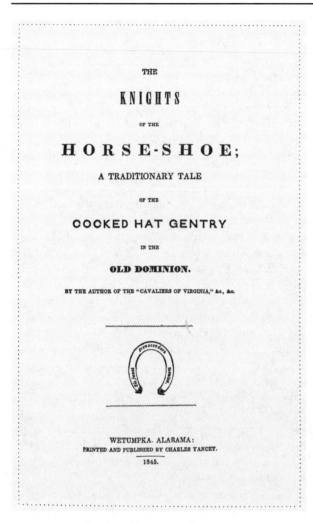

THE

# KNIGHTS

OF THE

# HORSE-SHOE;

A TRADITIONARY TALE

OF THE

## COCKED HAT GENTRY

IN THE

## OLD DOMINION.

BY THE AUTHOR OF THE "CAVALIERS OF VIRGINIA," &c., &c.

WETUMPKA. ALABAMA:
PRINTED AND PUBLISHED BY CHARLES YANCEY.
1845.

*Title page for Caruthers's third novel, a romance based on Virginia governor Alexander Spotswood's 1716 expedition over the Blue Ridge Mountains (Yale University Library)*

issue of the *Magnolia* and writing an article on the subject for the March issue. That year he also published a humorous piece, "The Bardolphian Nose" in *Orion* (June 1842). His most significant shorter writing is "Excerpts from the Portfolio of a Physician. Love and Consumption," which was published in the *Magnolia* in three installments from July to September 1842. This moral tale cautions against the domestic tyranny of a rich and socially prominent wife. Her husband, who has forsaken his childhood sweetheart, is ultimately broken by her scoldings. In 1840 Caruthers lectured on "The Drunkard: From the Cradle to the Grave," which was published as a pamphlet that year. Three years later he lectured before the Georgia Historical Society, of which he was a prominent member. In that lecture he reiterated his call for Southern expansion into western territories: "I feel and believe that our noble and solemn forests, which so lately echoed to the stately tread

of the red warrior, must fall prostrate before the sweeping tide of civilization."

In Savannah, Caruthers continued to practice medicine and to participate in civic organizations. He and his wife joined the Episcopal Church. By the spring of 1846, however, he was stricken with tuberculosis. He died on 19 August 1846. He is thought to have been buried in Marietta, but no grave has been found.

## Biography:

Curtis Carroll Davis, *Chronicler of the Cavaliers: A Life of the Virginia Novelist Dr. William A. Caruthers* (Richmond, Va.: Dietz, 1953).

## References:

Henry O. Cole, "William Alexander Caruthers," thesis, Vanderbilt University, Nashville, 1921;

John L. Hare, "Images of the Family in the Ante-Bellum Virginia Novel," dissertation, University of Maryland at College Park, 1997;

Ian Marshall, "Landscape Aesthetics and Literary History: The Knights of the Golden Horseshoe in Journal, Poem, and Story," *Mississippi Quarterly,* 44 (1990–1991): 69–82;

William R. Taylor, "The Promised Land," in his *Cavalier and Yankee: The Old South and American National Character* (New York: Braziller, 1961), pp. 203–224;

Susan J. Tracy, *In the Master's Eye: Representations of Women, Blacks, and Poor Whites in Antebellum Southern Literature* (Amherst: University of Massachusetts Press, 1995), pp. 23, 24, 39–40, 82–83, 88–89, 92–93, 95, 97–98, 100, 103, 107, 108, 109, 143, 146, 197–200, 213–214, 216, 220;

Simone Vauthier, "When the Dummy Speaks: The Example of William Alexander Caruthers," in *Slavery in the Americas,* edited by Wolfgang Binder (Würzburg: Königshausen & Neumann, 1993), pp. 503–522;

Ritchie Devon Watson Jr., "The Apotheosis of the Cavalier: Caruthers and Cooke," in his *The Cavalier in Virginia Fiction* (Baton Rouge: Louisiana State University Press, 1985), pp. 103–151.

## Papers:

William Alexander Caruthers's letters can be found at Duke University Library; the McCormick Historical Association, Chicago; the Virginia State Library, Richmond; the Georgia Historical Society, Savannah; the National Archives, Washington; the Southern Historical Collection at the University of North Carolina Library; the Cyrus Hall McCormick Memorial Library, Washington and Lee University; and the Huntington Library, San Marino.

# Thomas Holley Chivers

*(18 October 1809 – 19 December 1858)*

James W. Mathews
*State University of West Georgia Emeritus*

See also the Chivers entry in *DLB 3: Antebellum Writers in New York and the South.*

BOOKS: *The Path of Sorrow, or, The Lament of Youth: A Poem* (Franklin, Tenn.: Western Weekly Review, 1832);

*Conrad and Eudora; or, The Death of Alonzo. A Tragedy in Five Acts. Founded on the Murder of Sharpe, by Beauchamp, in Kentucky* (Philadelphia, 1834);

*Nacoochee; or, The Beautiful Star, with Other Poems* (New York: Dean, 1837);

*The Lost Pleiad; and Other Poems* (New York: Jenkins, 1845);

*Search After Truth; or, A New Revelation of the Psycho-Physiological Nature of Man* (New York: Cobb & Yallalee, 1848);

*Eonchs of Ruby, A Gift of Love* (New York: Spalding & Shepard, 1851); revised and enlarged as *Memoralia; or, Phials of Amber Full of the Tears of Love. A Gift for the Beautiful* (Philadelphia: Lippincott, Grambo, 1853);

*Atlanta; or The True Blessed Isle of Poesy. A Paul Epic in Three Lustra* (Macon: Georgia Citizen, 1853);

*Virginalia; or, Songs of My Summer Nights. A Gift of Love for the Beautiful* (Philadelphia: Lippincott, Grambo, 1853);

*Birth-Day Song of Liberty. A Paean of Glory for the Heroes of Freedom* (Atlanta: Hanleiter, 1856);

*The Sons of Usna: A Tragi-Apotheosis, in Five Acts* (Philadelphia: Sherman, 1858);

*Chivers' Life of Poe,* edited by Richard Beale Davis (New York: Dutton, 1952);

*The Unpublished Plays of Thomas Holley Chivers,* edited, with an introduction, by Charles M. Lombard (Delmar, N.Y.: Scholars' Facsimiles and Reprints, 1980).

**Editions:** *Virginalia; or, Songs of My Summer Nights,* edited by E. L. Schwab (Brooklyn: Research Classics, 1942);

*Search after Truth; The Lost Pleiad, and Atlanta,* edited by Charles M. Lombard (Delmar, N.Y.: Scholars' Facsimiles and Reprints, 1976);

*Nacoochee: 1837,* edited by Lombard (Delmar, N.Y.: Scholars' Facsimiles and Reprints, 1977);

*Conrad and Eudora and Birth-Day Song of Liberty,* edited by Lombard (Delmar, N.Y.: Scholars' Facsimiles and Reprints, 1978);

*The Path of Sorrow,* edited by Lombard (Delmar, N.Y.: Scholars' Facsimiles and Reprints, 1979).

SELECTED PERIODICAL PUBLICATION–UNCOLLECTED: "Leoni; or, the Orphan of Venice," *Georgia Citizen,* 17 May–14 June 1851;

Although Thomas Holley Chivers's reputation, if not notoriety, has rested to a degree on his association

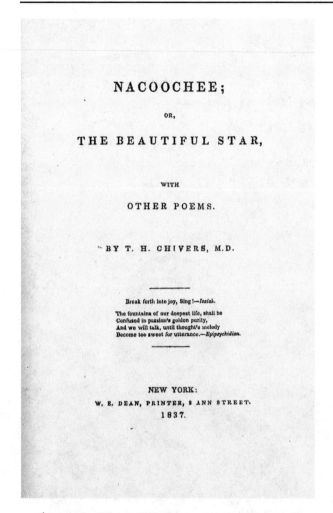

NACOOCHEE;

OR,

THE BEAUTIFUL STAR,

WITH

OTHER POEMS.

BY T. H. CHIVERS, M.D.

Break forth into joy, Sing!—*Isaiah.*

The fountains of our deepest life, shall be
Confused in passion's golden purity,
And we will talk, until thought's melody
Become too sweet for utterance.—*Epipsychidion.*

NEW YORK:
W. E. DEAN, PRINTER, 2 ANN STREET.
1837.

*Title page for Chivers's 1837 book, in which the title poem retells
a story from Georgia Indian folklore (Thomas Cooper Library,
University of South Carolina)*

with and similarity to Edgar Allan Poe, Chivers was a creditable poet in his own right. In his best works his ideas are evocative and his experiments in language and prosody intriguing. His poetry, as he explained in his prefaces and letters and demonstrated in his works, was transcendental, communicating the mystical connection between physical and spiritual reality. Thus, his imagery, often novel, sometimes bizarre, was conceived primarily as a medium to convey the highest truth. Like Poe and Ralph Waldo Emerson, Chivers considered the poet a purveyor of the beautiful, an artist who ultimately revealed the "divine Idea." Unlike Emerson, however, Chivers believed the emotional response to the sounds of poetry to be sine qua non. In his odd, flamboyant style Chivers treated such nineteenth-century conventions as the evanescence of youth and beauty, the glory of freedom, the noble child of nature, the inhospitality of the world, and, paradoxically, the spiritual "correspondences" in natural phenomena. He was a pioneer adapter of American folklore, including

Indian tales and the first of several versions of the "Kentucky tragedy."

Chivers was born at Digby Manor near Washington, Georgia, on 8 October 1809, although his tombstone bears the date 1807. His father, Colonel Robert Chivers, was a wealthy cotton farmer who sired three sons and four daughters, Thomas being the eldest. In 1827 Chivers married sixteen-year-old Elizabeth Chivers, his first cousin, who, soon pregnant, deserted him within the year. In the acrimonious aftermath Elizabeth refused to allow Chivers to see his daughter, and, following years of litigation, he finally secured a divorce in 1836. In the meantime, supported by indulgent parents, he enrolled in the medical school of Transylvania University of Lexington, Kentucky, receiving his doctor of medicine degree in March 1830.

In 1832 Chivers published his first volume, *The Path of Sorrow, or, The Lament of Youth: A Poem,* a kind of apologia of his failed marriage. Composed for the most part during his medical-school days, the eighteen poems in the collection are without distinction except for their evidence of Chivers's early experimentation with a variety of forms and meters. Also while at Transylvania University, he collected material on Jereboam Beauchamp's 1825 murder of Colonel Solomon Sharp to avenge the honor of Ann Cook, a circumstance known as the "Kentucky tragedy." Turning the story into a rather pedestrian blank-verse drama, Chivers published it in 1834 as *Conrad and Eudora; or, The Death of Alonzo,* which he revised during 1838 and 1839 with a new setting and title, "Leoni; or, the Orphan of Venice," and eventually published in the *Georgia Citizen* in 1851. The first of several literary treatments of the story, including Poe's unfinished play "Politian" (1835), Chivers's version is basically true to the facts of the case, although the principals in both versions are little more than caricatures with pseudonyms.

Following his graduation from Transylvania University, Chivers returned to his father's Georgia plantation, Oaky Grove. He practiced medicine for a short time in the vicinity of his home and then during the period from 1830 to 1835 took several trips to the North. Not having to earn his livelihood, he had the money and time to travel and to immerse himself in literature, particularly the work of the Romantic poets. While in New York he made arrangements for the publication of *Nacoochee; or, The Beautiful Star, with Other Poems* (1837), which, in addition to the title piece, includes forty-nine short poems. The title poem, incidents of which came from Georgia Indian folklore as well as Vicomte de Chauteaubriand's *Atala* (1801), tells of Nacoochee, a beautiful Indian maiden, who, although living in an earthly paradise and adored by Ostenee, spurns physical love for celestial perfection. In its denouement the poem dramatizes Emanuel Swedenborg's doctrine of the ultimate separation of "pure spirit" from the carnal. According to Chivers's introduction, a similar attainment is the objective of the poet, who "is capable of giving birth to other beings brighter than himself; and of lifting up his spirit to the presence of those things which he shall enjoy in another state. . . . " In a letter to Poe (27 August 1840) Chivers called this process "Transcendentalism"

> taking the swan of thought, which has floated on the crystalline water of the *familiar* in this world, and giving it wings, whereby it may ascend into the regions of the unfamiliar. . . . What then is inspiration, if it is not a power given to the soul to recognize the beautiful of a truth, which is transcendent in nature, when compared with other truths? We may convey the idea of a heavenly truth by an earthly one—that is, we may make an earthly truth the representative of a truth beyond expression.

Several of the short poems in *Nachoochee* are in accomplished blank verse—an anomaly among Chivers's lyrics—notably "The Death of Time," an apocalyptic vision of the triumphant Christ, and "The Soaring Swan," an extended metaphor of the soul's aspirations.

In November 1837, in New York, Chivers was married again, to Harriett Hunt of Springfield, Massachusetts, and from early 1838 until mid 1842 the couple lived in Middletown, Connecticut, and New York. During this time Chivers published thirteen poems in the *Middletown Sentinel and Witness* and in 1840 began a correspondence with Poe, to whom he sent several poems after receiving a prospectus for the *Penn Magazine* and whom he met in New York in 1845. Chivers and Harriett's first child, Allegra Florence, was born in July 1839 but died from typhoid in October 1842, followed by the deaths of three other children the next year. Two daughters and a son were born later. Chivers's unmitigated grief over the loss of his children looms over his third volume of poetry, *The Lost Pleiad; and Other Poems,* published in 1845.

Comprising mostly elegiac poems written between mid 1836 and late 1844, this volume includes the often-anthologized "To Allegra Florence in Heaven," which Chivers later claimed Poe had imitated in "The Raven." With its monotonous rhymes and artificial, sometimes ludicrous imagery, it is inferior to the title poem, "The Lost Pleiad," a somewhat clinical but touching description of Chivers's daughter ravaged by fever. Certain other poems in the volume, particularly "The Wife's Lament for Her Husband Lost at Sea," "The Soul's Destiny," and "Sonnet: To Isa Sleeping," are not directly autobiographical and are therefore

more quietly moving. *The Lost Pleiad* was reviewed favorably by Poe in the *Broadway Journal* (2 August 1845) and by William Gilmore Simms in the *Southern Patriot.*

Chivers returned to Georgia at the end of 1845, and between then and 1850, he wrote some one hundred lyrics, most of which were published in newspapers and magazines. In the meantime, in 1848, he published a short prose work heavily influenced by Swedenborg, *Search after Truth; or, A New Revelation of the Psycho-Physiological Nature of Man.* In the form of a dialogue between the Seer and Politian (evidently representing Poe), *Search after Truth* purports to give logical proof of the existence of the soul and of its immortality. Interestingly, *Search after Truth* was published in the same year as Poe's philosophical work, *Eureka,* which was less mystical with its hints of modern quantum physics. As a manifestation of Chivers's growing interest in psychic phenomena, he wrote during 1848–1849 several poems and three prose pieces on his own mystical experiences, which were published in *The Univercoelum, or Spiritual Philosopher,* edited by Samuel Byron Brittan.

Perhaps Chivers's most eccentric collection, *Eonchs of Ruby, A Gift of Love* was published in 1851 and reprinted along with several additional poems in 1853 as a gift book under the title *Memoralia; or, Phials of Amber Full of the Tears of Love. A Gift for the Beautiful.* As he wrote in the *Georgia Citizen* (28 June 1851), he chose the word *eonch* instead of *concha* (seashell) simply because of its euphony and *ruby* for its "correspondence" to divine love. In this volume he was at his most inventive in choosing words and phrases for their power of suggestion. The term *eonch* figures prominently in the fourth poem in the volume, "The Lusiad":

> In the sweet time that was floral,
>   With her lips so—
> She this EONCH of sweet Coral
>   Loudly did blow.

Lucy's lover recalls that "Dian, Heaven's sweet Daughter, / [did] Bring to me now / This sweet EONCH, which I taught her / Loudly to blow." In this poem Chivers's predilection for romantic and euphonious proper names was conveniently satisfied by two Georgia rivers that converge in south central Alabama:

> On the banks of Talapoosa,
>   Free from all wo,
> Where it mingles with the Coosa,
>   Southward to flow—
> Rests my beautiful sweet Lucy
>   In her grave low!

*First page of a letter from Chivers to Poe, written shortly after the death of Poe's wife, Virginia*
*(from S. Foster Damon,* Thomas Holley Chivers, Friend of Poe, *1930)*

The first poem in the volume, "The Vigil of Aiden," a tribute to Poe, is replete with terms and phrases suggestive of the better-known poet: "Heavenly Bowers of Aiden," "the old-time Towers of Aiden," "Days of Yore," "forever more," "Flowery Fields Elysian," and "Asphodelian shore," for example. Chivers refers to Poe as "Politian" and Virginia Poe as "Lenore." Several of the poems in the volume are panegyrics, including "The Mighty Dead," which celebrates a procession of noble prophets, patriots, and poets. In a more personal vein, "Avalon" is an impassioned lament for Chivers's oldest son, Eugene Percy, who is now "lying / Beside the beautiful undying / In the Valley of the pausing of the Moon." This volume also includes one of Chivers's simplest and most affective lyrics, "The Shell," four quatrains on the restorative power of sounds emanating from a seashell. Strong suggestions of Poe in theme, language, and meter are present in "Isadore":

> While the world lay round me sleeping,
> I, alone for *Isadore,*
> Patient Vigils lonely keeping—
> Some one said to me while weeping,
> "Why this grief forever more?"
> And I answered, "I am weeping
> For my blessed *Isadore!*"

*Atlanta; or The True Blessed Isle of Poesy. A Paul Epic in Three Lustra* (1853), which, like *Nacoochee,* carries overtones of both Chateaubriand and Swedenborg, is a long narrative poem in three cantos or "Lustra." The Atlanta of the title is another earthly paradise in close proximity to heaven, where Julian, after rescuing Ianthe from Lamorah, achieves physical union with her, symbolizing attainment of the ideal. In this narrative Chivers excels in his lush description of the early primeval setting and of the fanciful Eden Isle. In the preface to *Atlanta* he sets down his requisites for poetry, which are reminiscent of Poe's in "The Poetic Principle" (1850) and "The Philosophy of Composition" (1846). He dismisses the long poem as a contradiction because "no poem of any considerable length, from the very nature of the relations subsisting between the power of the soul to receive, and the impressions to be made, can be pleasing." Furthermore, his preference for concentrated, stunning effects was based on the rationale that "the novel suddenness or rare unexpectedness . . . will confer delight, because, at every appeal made, there will be something new—something the memory of which will not crowd out of the soul succeeding impressions." This assumption accounts for many of Chivers's excesses—unrelieved regularity of meter, strained rhymes, exotic proper nouns, rhapsodic phrases, alliteration, parallelism, incremental repetition, and the ubiq-

uitous refrain. At times, however, when these devices are controlled, they produce a singular aural charm.

Another 1853 publication, *Virginalia; or, Songs of My Summer Nights. A Gift of Love for the Beautiful,* comprises 104 short lyrics, the dominant themes of which are love, sorrow, and joy. Other than the usual depictions of dead girls and Swedenborgian visions, the volume includes several poems of decided merit: "Ganymede," a panoramic vision of American "manifest destiny"; "Apollo," a celebration of divine power; "Pas d'Extase," an ebullient song of hope; "Morcia Funebre," a requiem for Henry Clay, with Poesque onomatopoetic bells; and "The Rising of the Nations," a tribute to liberty, both civil and spiritual. Two poems concern Lord Byron–"Lord Byron's Dying Words to Ada," a commonplace elegy, and "Byron," a tribute to the poet's sacrifice in the cause of Greek freedom. The death of Poe is treated in "The Fall of Usher," which appropriates its subject's versification and vocabulary. In the preface to *Virginalia* Chivers advances a strong defense of the refrain, which "is not only an ornament, but an essence–a life–a vitality–an immortal soul–not a mere profane appendage, but a sacred Symbolical Ensign-imn–a crown of beauty, and a diamond of glory. . . ." Obviously responding to critics of his idiosyncrasies, he declared that "no true Poet ever yet wrote for the Aristarchi of the world–only to show them how little they know–but only for the divine Areopagus of Heaven."

From 1850 to 1852 Chivers was in New York and New Haven, Connecticut, writing "Letters from the North" for the *Georgia Citizen* on literary and social topics. In one letter, dated 8 June 1851, he pointed out the similarities between "The Raven" and "To Allegra Florence in Heaven," and in several he was critical of Horace Greeley and the *New York Tribune* for their abolitionist stand. In 1853 he moved to Boston, where he wrote poems and articles for the *Waverly Magazine,* among which are two under the pseudonym "Fiat Justitia" accusing Poe of plagiarism: "Origin of Poe's Raven" (30 July 1853) and "Poe's Plagiarism" (1 October 1853). Yet, in none of the letters exchanged between Chivers and Poe had there been any mention of plagiarism, and at the time Chivers made his strongest charges he was working on a biography of Poe, which he undertook (but never finished) to counter the scurrilous biography by Rufus W. Griswold. The plagiarism issue has been thrashed about by many critics in Chivers's time and subsequently with no consensus reached. Since Poe's and Chivers's aesthetics were quite similar and borrowings were commonplace in the nineteenth-century literary world, similarities could hardly be avoided.

VIRGINALIA;

OR,

SONGS OF MY SUMMER NIGHTS.

A Gift of Love for the Beautiful.

BY T. H. CHIVERS, M. D.

" Αυτο καθ' αυτο μεθ' αυτου, μονο ειδες αιει ον." — *Plato.*

PHILADELPHIA:
LIPPINCOTT, GRAMBO & CO.
1853.

*Title page for the collection of short lyrics that includes Chivers's tributes to Henry Clay, Lord Byron, and Edgar Allan Poe (Thomas Cooper Library, University of South Carolina)*

In 1855 Chivers returned to Georgia permanently and the next year was asked by a citizens' committee of Washington, Georgia, to prepare a verse oration for the Fourth of July celebration. The result was *Birth-Day Song of Liberty. A Paean of Glory for the Heroes of Freedom* (1856) in laborious anapestic tetrameters. Before he left the North, Chivers had composed a few poems in black dialect, which successfully captured the black personality and voice of the antebellum South. In 1856 Chivers moved from Washington to Decatur, Georgia, and after declining a professorship in Oglethorpe Medical College of Savannah, he completed his final work, the blank-verse drama *The Sons of Usna: A Tragi-Apotheosis, in Five Acts* (1858), one of the first modern treatments of an old Irish legend. In the original the beautiful and tragic Deirdre is betrothed to King Conchobar of Ulster but loves Naoise, son of Usnach. After Naoise abducts her to Scotland, he and his brothers are killed by King Conchobar, and Deirdre kills herself in sorrow. Chivers complicated the plot by adding another love interest and threw over the story a distracting metaphysical veil. Instead of a tragic ending, the poem climaxes with a Swedenborgian apotheosis.

After a short illness Chivers died on 19 December 1858, and since then his merit as a poet has been overshadowed by the Poe controversy. Although his early works received the approbation of contemporary magazine reviewers, he was never a popular writer and was compelled to publish his books at his own expense. He did, however, have a certain following abroad, primarily among the Pre-Raphaelites and symbolists. Thomas Holley Chivers is still known generally for his excesses despite some estimable short poems of moderation and grace.

**Letters:**

*The Correspondence of Thomas Holley Chivers,* edited by Emma Chase and Lois Parks (Providence, R.I.: Brown University Press, 1957).

**Biographies:**

S. Foster Damon, *Thomas Holley Chivers, Friend of Poe* (New York: Harper, 1930);

Charles Henry Watts, *Thomas Holley Chivers: His Literary Career and His Poetry* (Athens: University of Georgia Press, 1956).

**References:**

Charles Lombard, *Thomas Holley Chivers* (Boston: Twayne, 1979);

Alvin H. Rosenfield, "The Poe-Chivers Controversy," *Books at Brown,* 23 (1969): 89–93.

**Papers:**

The major portion of Thomas Holley Chivers's papers can be found in the Henry E. Huntington Library, San Marino, California; the William R. Perkins Library of Duke University; and the John Hay Library of Brown University.

# John Esten Cooke

*(3 November 1830 – 27 September 1886)*

Jack C. Wills
*Fairmont State College*

See also the Cooke entry in *DLB 3: Antebellum Writers in New York and The South.*

BOOKS: *Leather Stocking and Silk; or, Hunter John Myers and His Times: A Story of the Valley of Virginia,* anonymous (New York: Harper, 1854); republished as *Leather and Silk: A Novel* (New York: Dillingham, 1892);

*The Virginia Comedians; or, Old Days in the Old Dominion,* 2 volumes (New York: Appleton, 1854); volume 1 republished as *Beatrice Hallam. A Novel* (New York: Dillingham, 1892); volume 2 republished as *Captain Ralph; A Sequel to Beatrice Hallam* (New York: Dillingham, 1892);

*The Youth of Jefferson; or, A Chronicle of College Scrapes at Williamsburg, in Virginia, A.D. 1764,* anonymous (New York: Redfield, 1854);

*Ellie; or, The Human Comedy* (Richmond, Va.: Morris, 1855);

*The Last of the Foresters; or, Humors on the Border. A Story of the Old Virginia Frontier* (New York: Derby & Jackson / Cincinnati: Derby, 1856);

*Henry St. John, Gentleman, of "Flower of Hundreds," in the County of Prince George, Virginia: A Tale of 1774–'75* (New York: Harper, 1859); republished as *Bonnybel Vane. Embracing the History of Henry St. John, Gentleman* (New York: Harper, 1883); republished as *Miss Bonnybel: A Novel* (New York: Dillingham, 1892);

*The Life of Stonewall Jackson. From Official Papers, Contemporary Narratives, and Personal Acquaintance* (Richmond, Va.: Ayres & Wade, 1863); revised as *Stonewall Jackson: A Military Biography* (New York: Appleton, 1866);

*Surry of Eagle's-Nest; or, The Memoirs of a Staff-Officer Serving in Virginia. Edited, from the MSS. of Colonel Surry* (New York: Bunce & Huntington, 1866);

*Wearing of the Gray: Being Personal Portraits, Scenes and Adventures of the War* (New York: Treat / Baltimore: Morrow / New Orleans: Hummel / Nashville: Kimzey, 1867); republished as *Personal Portraits,*

*John Esten Cooke*

*Scenes, and Adventures of the War, with Thrilling Narratives of the Daring Deeds, Willing Sacrifices and Patient Sufferings Incident to "Wearing of the Gray"* (New York: Treat / St. Louis: Wright, 1871);

*Fairfax: or, The Master of Greenway Court, A Chronicle of the Valley of the Shenandoah* (New York: Carleton / London: Low, 1868); republished as *Lord Fairfax; or, The Master of Greenway Court: A Chronicle of the*

*Valley of the Shenandoah* (New York: Dillingham / London: Low, 1888);

*Mohun; or, The Last Days of Lee and His Paladins. Final Memoirs of a Staff Officer Serving in Virginia. From the MSS. of Colonel Surry of Eagle's Nest* (New York: Huntington, 1869);

*Hilt to Hilt; or, Days and Nights on the Banks of the Shenandoah in the Autumn of 1864. From the MSS. of Colonel Surry of Eagle's Nest* (New York: Carleton / London: Low, 1869);

*Hammer and Rapier* (New York: Carleton / London: Low, 1870);

*The Heir of Gaymount: A Novel* (New York: Van Evrie, Horton, 1870);

*Out of the Foam: A Novel* (New York: Carleton / London: Low, 1871); republished as *Westbrooke Hall: A Novel* (New York: Dillingham, 1891);

*A Life of Gen. Robert E. Lee* (New York: Appleton, 1871); republished as *Our Leader and Defender: Gen. Robert E. Lee* (N.p.: Collins-Campbell, 1889);

*Doctor Vandyke: A Novel* (New York: Appleton, 1872);

*Her Majesty the Queen: A Novel* (Philadelphia: Lippincott, 1873);

*Pretty Mrs. Gaston, and Other Stories* (New York: Orange Judd, 1874);

*Justin Harley: A Romance of Old Virginia* (Philadelphia: Claxton, Remsen & Haffelfinger, 1875);

*Canolles: The Fortunes of a Partisan of '81* (Detroit: Smith, 1877);

*Professor Pressensee, Materialist and Inventor* (New York: Harper, 1878);

*Stories of the Old Dominion from the Settlement to the End of the Revolution* (New York: Harper, 1879);

*Mr. Grantley's Idea* (New York: Harper, 1879);

*The Virginia Bohemians: A Novel* (New York: Harper, 1880);

*Fanchette by One of Her Admirers* (Boston: Osgood, 1883);

*Virginia: A History of the People* (Boston & New York: Houghton, Mifflin, 1883);

*My Lady Pokahontas: A True Relation of Virginia. Writ by Anas Todkill, Puritan and Pilgrim with Notes by John Esten Cooke* (Boston & New York: Houghton, Mifflin, 1885);

*The Maurice Mystery* (New York: Appleton, 1885); republished as *Colonel Ross of Piedmont* (New York: Dillingham, 1893);

*Poe as a Literary Critic*, edited, with an introduction, by N. Bryllion Fagin (Baltimore: Johns Hopkins University Press, 1946);

*Stonewall Jackson and the Old Stonewall Brigade*, edited by Richard Barksdale Harwell (Charlottesville: University of Virginia Press, 1954);

*Outlines from the Outpost*, edited by Harwell (Chicago: Lakeside, 1961);

*John Esten Cooke's Autobiographical Memo*, edited, with a preface, by John R. Welsh (Columbia: University of South Carolina Press, 1969).

OTHER: "The War Diary of John Esten Cooke," edited by Jay B. Hubbell, *Journal of Southern History*, 7 (November 1941): 526–540.

SELECTED PERIODICAL PUBLICATIONS–
UNCOLLECTED:
FICTION

"Peony: A Tale for the Times," *Southern Literary Messenger*, 18 (May 1852): 330–340;

"The Cotton-Mouth," *Appleton's Journal*, 8 (October 1872): 366–370;

"Old Wiley," *Harper's*, 54 (April 1877): 677–686;

"Owlet," *Harper's*, 57 (July 1878): 199–211;

"The Moonshiners," *Harper's*, 58 (February 1879): 380–390;

"The Sumac-Gatherers," *Harper's*, 63 (November 1881): 867–880;

"My Last Match," *Leslie's Illustrated*, 53, nos. 1369 and 1370 (Christmas 1881), 1369: 278; 1370: 310.

NONFICTION

"Thomas Carlyle and His 'Latter-Day Pamphlets,'" *Southern Literary Messenger*, 16 (June 1850): 330–340;

"Recollections of Philip Pendleton Cooke," *Southern Literary Messenger*, 26 (June 1858): 427;

"William Gilmore Simms, Esq.," *Southern Literary Messenger*, 28 (May 1859): 355–370;

"Thomas Jefferson," *Southern Literary Messenger*, 30 (May 1860): 321–341;

"The Author of 'Swallow Barn,'" *Appleton's Journal*, 10 (16 August 1873): 205–206;

"An Hour with Thackeray," *Appleton's Journal*, 22 (September 1879): 238–254.

John Esten Cooke is usually thought of as a writer who ended one literary tradition and initiated another. Beginning his career as an imitator of James Fenimore Cooper and an author of pre–Revolutionary War fiction, Cooke became known, after serving four years as a staff officer in the Confederate army, chiefly as a writer of Civil War novels and biographer of the leading generals of the South. Whereas he had earlier championed the rights of man and included common people as heroes, after the war he became, as did fellow Virginian Thomas Nelson Page, one of the most prominent spokesmen of the Old South movement. In this role Cooke not only lauds the heroism of Confederate soldiers such as Thomas "Stonewall" Jackson, J. E. B. Stuart, and Turner Ashby, unrelentingly romanticizing their exploits, but moves from a prodemocratic to a proaristocratic stance, extolling the virtues of "high-born" Virginia ladies and gentlemen.

One of thirteen children, John Esten Cooke was the son of attorney John Rogers Cooke and Maria Pendleton Cooke, grandniece of Revolution-era judge Edmund Pendleton. Although he was born in Winchester, Virginia, his early years are most identified with "Glengary," a plantation near Charles Town in what is now West Virginia. At Glengary, Cooke developed a love of the woods and fields, which would be reflected in the descriptive passages so characteristic of his novels; here, too, his incipient desire to write and his pro-Cavalier sympathies were reinforced by the influence of his elder brother, the poet Philip Pendleton Cooke, author of *Froissart Ballads, and Other Poems* (1847). When Glengary burned in 1839, the family removed to Charles Town, the site of John Rogers Cooke's law office, and again to Richmond in 1840. Cooke's participation in a literary debating society while a student at the Richmond Academy anticipated both his choice of law as a profession and his ultimate career as a writer.

Cooke hoped to study law at the University of Virginia, but circumstances beyond his control, principally his father's improvidence, forced him to abandon his plans and instead to study privately. In fact, Cooke had never had much interest in practicing law, applying himself instead more enthusiastically to reading the works of authors such as Alexandre Dumas *père*, Alfred Tennyson, and Washington Irving than to his legal studies. Cooke's first published literary effort, the poem "Avalon," appeared in the *Southern Literary Messenger* in November 1848, and, after trying unsuccessfully to balance his two careers for a while, he abandoned law entirely and concentrated on writing.

Cooke's earliest works continued to be published chiefly in the *Southern Literary Messenger*. These were, for the most part, poems, such as his "Eighteen Sonnets" (January 1849), historical sketches such as "Indian Wars of West Virginia" (September 1851), and "Chronicles of the Valley of Virginia" (August–September 1852), and "easy-chair" essays in the manner of Irving and Donald Grant Mitchell, carrying such titles as "Embers of a Wood Fire" and "The End of Autumn." He also showed some talent as a literary critic in "Thomas Carlyle and His 'Latter-Day Pamphlets'" (June 1850) for example, and commentaries on Edgar Allan Poe and Tennyson's *In Memoriam* (1850). Cooke soon became one of the most frequent contributors to the *Messenger* and edited the March 1851 issue.

At this time Richmond had a fairly active literary and social life (William Makepeace Thackeray stopped in the city), and the young Cooke began to immerse himself in this world, engaging in the usual number of hijinks and flirtations but apparently not becoming serious about any of the young ladies. On 7 August 1849 he attended, along with *Messenger* editor John Reuben Thompson, a reading by Poe at the Exchange Hotel. At the same time, however, he maintained a close connection with his relatives in the Shenandoah Valley, generally spending his summers and Christmas holidays there. This habit of keeping one foot in each of these disparate worlds, in fact, seems to have inspired Cooke's first novel, *Leather Stocking and Silk; or, Hunter John Myers and His Times: A Story of the Valley of Virginia,* published in 1854.

While the work is based on an actual account Cooke had gotten from his father, it is quite derivative. Its debt to Cooper is obvious from its title, and its juxtaposing the old frontier world with one of aristocratic gentility owes much to Irving's *The Sketch Book of Geoffrey Crayon, Gent.* (1819–1820), as Cooke himself acknowledged; features of novels of William Alexander Caruthers and Nathaniel Beverly Tucker can also be found in the novel. Set in Martinsburg, Virginia, in the early nineteenth century, the novel, which covers a period of about thirty years, is a weakly plotted work intended to provide a portrait of two types of life in the Old Dominion in the years preceding the author's birth. The natural nobility and solidity of the Natty Bumppo–like title character (whose similarity to Cooper's creation extends even to his use of "Anan?" in response to questions) is contrasted with the social and domestic problems suffered by the genteel society that is replacing his frontier world. Myers, although he appears infrequently in the story, is well drawn and interesting, but the weakness of most of the other characters and the plot (nothing much happens except the pairing of various couples)–combined with the pattern of concealed identities, coincidence, and romanticized action that undercuts so many of his works–condemns this first novelistic effort to mediocrity. Critical reaction to *Leather Stocking and Silk* was generally favorable, reflecting the taste of the times, although one reviewer in a 9 September 1854 issue of *Littell's Living Age* found "the idea of the book . . . better than the execution," quipping, "the bulk of *Leather Stocking and Silk* is in fact linsey-woolsey."

After the publication of *Leather Stocking and Silk,* Cooke began a second novel, "Fairfax," but put it aside when he became more interested in the book that he and most scholars have considered his best work, *The Virginia Comedians; or, Old Days in the Old Dominion* (1854). Based in part, like *Leather Stocking and Silk* and other of Cooke's historical novels, on

"STUART'S RIDE AROUND McCLELLAN.
The gay chase continued until we reached the Tottapotamoi."

*Illustration from Cooke's* Wearing of the Gray *(1867) depicting J. E. B. Stuart's June 1862 maneuver around
General George McClellan's Army of the Potomac, an action in which Cooke participated*

Samuel Kercheval's *History of the Valley of Virginia* (1833), "Fairfax" was completed in 1858 and published serially in the *Messenger* the following year as *Greenway Court; or, The Bloody Ground.* It appeared with minor changes in a single volume in 1868 as *Fairfax: or, The Master of Greenway Court, A Chronicle of the Valley of the Shenandoah.* The inclusion of Lord Fairfax and George Washington in this novel marked the first time Cooke combined fictional characters and historical figures in a work; it also established a pattern of bending the facts of history when it suited his purpose, as in giving the bachelor Fairfax a son.

Cooke's love of colonial Virginia, evident in *Fairfax,* also provided some of the impetus for *The Virginia Comedians.* More immediate was a visit he made in November 1853 to the home of the theatrical Bateman family, whose young daughters Kate and Ellen he much admired, at about the same time he came across a passage in a newspaper column noting that the first performance of a play by "a regular company of commedians," a production of William Shakespeare's *The Merchant of Venice,* had occurred in Williamsburg in 1762. From an idea generated by these incidents, Cooke fashioned the story of Champ Effingham, son and heir of a wealthy planter, whose boredom and arrogance lead him into a destructive,

hopeless pursuit of Beatrice Hallam, the supposed daughter of a theatrical troupe performing in Williamsburg. (Cooke began the first edition with the fiction that the narrator, a descendant of Effingham, was recounting incidents recorded in the latter's papers years after the fact, but dropped it when it became too cumbersome and removed it entirely from subsequent editions.) Spoiled by his position and an Oxford education, Champ, who meets Beatrice by chance on the road, is driven by his ennui and her beauty to court her against her will and the prevailing social realities of the time. In so doing he abandons his intended wife, the passive Clare Lee, and defies his father and public opinion, finally ingratiating himself with Hallam, the manager of the troupe and Beatrice's apparent father, so that he can join the players and press his preposterous suit of marriage with Beatrice. Undeterred by efforts to reclaim him by his young cousin Kate and his fox-hunting friend Jack Hamilton, Champ presses an insulting proposal of marriage on Beatrice, who refuses, and then engages a gang of river ruffians to abduct her. Charles Waters, a young waterman and perhaps the true hero of the first volume of the novel, intervenes; in the melee that ensues, the toughs are killed, Beatrice is thrown into the river (for the second time), and Waters is run through and seriously wounded by Champ, who flees to Europe.

In the second volume (the work was republished in 1892 as two separate titles, *Beatrice Hallam* and *Captain Ralph*), a world-weary Effingham returns from Europe but is destined to play a smaller role, the center of action having shifted to the courtship of Charles Waters's soldier brother and Clare Lee's stronger-willed sister Henrietta. Charles has recovered from his wound, married Beatrice, and moved with her to western Virginia. Here they live happily together for a few short years until Beatrice dies of consumption, a condition aggravated by two drenchings in the James River. In addition to allowing Beatrice to become a sort of martyr, her death frees Charles to spearhead, along with Patrick Henry (who has surfaced periodically in the first volume as the radical and mysterious "Man in the Red Cloak"), the beginnings of the American Revolution in Virginia.

*The Virginia Comedians,* more than any other work, established Cooke's reputation as one of the most important practitioners of the plantation novel in the antebellum South; perhaps only his cousin John Pendleton Kennedy surpassed him in this genre. Moreover, as a social historian he provided a respectable picture of life in colonial Virginia on the eve of the American Revolution. In particular, the reader finds in the character of the introspective, rabble-rousing student Charles Waters the personification of a new egalitarian and rebellious spirit that was to oppose not only the king but also the entrenched, stratified social order in the colonies, particularly in Virginia. Squire Effingham, Champ's father, represents the old hierarchical system: "Every man a vote! Who speaks of it? Who broaches such an absurdity?"; Charles, frequently seen in ideological dialogue with "the Man in the Red Cloak," stands for the new democratic order. Another pertinent characteristic of the novel is that Cooke was the first author of plantation novels to include characters from a cross-section of society and not just aristocrats and servants. The members of the bourgeois Waters family are the most important of these characters, but other castes and occupations are portrayed as well, in the form of Parson Tag, for instance; the Waterses' servant Lanky Lugg and the object of his affections, Donsy Smith; and Donsy's father, the factor of Williamsburg. Lanky and the diminutive slave Mr. Crow also provide comic relief. If Cooke's development of these characters is inadequate, the fact that they are included is significant in itself. *The Virginia Comedians* is also Cooke's longest work, forming, with *Henry St. John, Gentleman, of "Flower of Hundreds,"*

*in the County of Prince George, Virginia: A Tale of 1774–'75* (1859), a trilogy.

*Henry St. John* tells the story of a "Virginia gentleman" who, bored by managing "Flower of Hundreds," the plantation he had inherited at a young age, seeks adventure by embarking on a military career, but instead of being sent to war is installed as the lieutenant of the guard of the boorish, arrogant governor, Lord Dunmore. St. John runs afoul of Dunmore when he brings the child Beatrice "Blossom" Waters, whom he has rescued from the hooves of a carriage horse, into the governor's mansion. When Dunmore is rude and unsympathetic to the child's plight because she is the daughter of the patriot leader Charles Waters, St. John, angered by the governor's intolerable behavior, begins a series of actions that ultimately lead him to resign his position and, gradually, move to an alliance with Waters and the others who support American independence. A second thread in the story is St. John's love for and pursuit of his cousin Bonnybel Vane, who is also the object of the affections of another planter, Lindon, a supporter of the king and St. John's mortal enemy. Typical of Cooke, the union of Henry and Bonnybel is effected only after a duel, an alienation of affections brought about by the duplicity of an unscrupulous seamstress, nocturnal visits to a graveyard, and the kidnapping and attempted forced marriage of Bonnybel with Lindon. As he does with his later Civil War novels, however, Cooke's use of events leading up to Virginia's rebellion against the king–Dunmore's foolish removal of the weapons, powder, and shot from the Williamsburg armory and the people's angry response, for instance– is historically accurate.

Reviewers were enthusiastic about *The Virginia Comedians,* the *Messenger* declaring it "the equal (we think it superior) to any work of fiction put forth the present season" (October 1854) and *Putnam's Monthly* describing it as "a narative no less remarkable for its vigor of description than its dramatic effect" (November 1854). Reactions to *Henry St. John,* however, were mixed. Cooke's friend John R. Thompson, for instance, saw both good and bad in the novel, praising its "purity of sentiment" and finding its style "uniformly as chaste as the sentiment," but also criticized the author for insufficient revision, "ill-contrived plots," and historical inaccuracies. William Gilmore Simms in a 7 December 1859 letter gently tried to steer Cooke away from some of his excesses by advising him, when beginning his next work, to "Give yourself time enough to contemplate your ground & materials full, so as to *design* with a better grasp of the *absolute* in your subject."

Cooke's personal life during the final years of the 1850s was not especially happy. He first experienced an abortive love affair with a young woman from Amelia whom he had seriously considered marrying. More painful were the deaths of three of the people closest to him: his eldest brother, Phil, and both his parents. These losses, along with a natural predisposition for religion, prompted him to seek the solace of the church, and he became a baptized and practicing Episcopalian, a path from which he never strayed. One can see evidence of this inclination in earlier works (in the simple faith of Champ Effingham's young cousin Kate, for instance), but it flavors his work even more strongly after his conversion, perhaps most notably in his biography of Jackson, whose devoutness he greatly admired.

Other than *Henry St. John, Gentleman,* Cooke's output of novels during this period was slight. In addition to the previously mentioned *Fairfax,* he composed a second novel based in part on the young manhood of a famous historical figure, the light-hearted but thin *The Youth of Jefferson; or, A Chronicle of College Scrapes at Williamsburg, in Virginia, A.D. 1764* (1854). Although inspired by Thomas Jefferson's school days at the College of William and Mary and his brief flirtation with Rebecca Burwell ("Belinda" or "Belle-bouche"), an ancestor of Cooke's sister-in-law, the story makes little effort to adhere to historical fact. His only other published book of this period was *Ellie; or, The Human Comedy* (1855), an attempt to write a social novel about childhood poverty in Richmond that amounts to little more than a tract. Cooke also wrote prose articles for periodicals such as *Harper's* and *Putnam's Monthly* as well as for the *Messenger,* in addition to some short stories and poems. As evidence that Cooke had gained some recognition, he was asked to contribute to Appleton's *New American Cyclopaedia,* writing the important entries on Jefferson and Irving.

By the end of the 1850s Cooke was probably the most financially successful writer in the South, firmly established with New York publishers and both southern and northern readers. In spite of his weaknesses, critics were also generally kind to him, with the noteworthy exception of the realist George W. Bagby, who asserted in the *Richmond Whig* on 5 October 1859 that Cooke's eyes were not only "in the back of his head" (a slap at Cooke's habit of setting his novels in the previous century), but that they were "afflicted with a pair of rose-colored goggles of enormous magnifying power." As if to put a capstone on this successful phase of his career, Cooke, in 1859, visited New York at the invitation of Evert and George Duyckinck, where he met some of the luminaries of the day and, notably, spent a pleasant day at Sunnyside with his revered Irving.

Cooke began the next—and most memorable—phase of his life that same year when, as a volunteer with the Richmond Howitzers, he was dispatched to Harper's Ferry during John Brown's raid. Although Cooke had little enthusiasm for perpetuating slavery and no dislike of northerners, he became an ardent supporter of secession upon the election of Abraham Lincoln. By the first Battle of Bull Run he commanded a field piece, having been promoted to sergeant. Before long, however, Cooke was commissioned a lieutenant, becoming Stuart's principal staff officer (Stuart had married Cooke's cousin Flora, daughter of General Philip St. George Cooke, who had remained loyal to the Union). Cooke's first action with Stuart was in the Seven Days' Battle, during which he participated in the cavalryman's famous ride around General George McClellan's troops, and he was soon promoted to the rank of captain. Cooke participated in every major campaign in Virginia, reportedly burying his silver spurs at Appomattox to keep the Yankees from confiscating them. He had been recommended for a majority by Stuart and, in fact, was addressed as "Major" by both Stuart and Robert E. Lee, but, probably because of criticisms of the government in his 1863 biography of Jackson, the recommendation was simply allowed to gather dust.

Beginning with his enlistment, Cooke kept a diary of his military experiences throughout the war. Beginning with the winter of 1862–1863, this diary would provide the raw material for a series of sketches for the *Southern Illustrated News* under the pseudonym "Tristan Joyeuse, Gent." as well as for many of his postwar writings; he also sent dispatches, poems, and prose articles to other Richmond newspapers. In 1863 he wrote the first biography of Jackson, shortly after the death of the Confederate hero at the Battle of Chancellorsville. Cooke had undertaken the work at the request of Richmond publisher Ayres and Wade, although it was pirated almost immediately by Charles B. Richardson of New York. *The Life of Stonewall Jackson* has the advantage of personal knowledge and immediacy, but both it and its postwar revised edition, *Stonewall Jackson: A Military Biography* (1866), suffer from imbalance (Cooke devotes only a few pages to Jackson's entire life prior to the Civil War) and the author's habit of turning all biographical accounts of Southern officers into hagiography. The work is noteworthy as both Cooke's first attempt at biography and the first published biography of Jackson. Both versions have merits: accurate and helpful details, such as General H. P. Bee's bestowal of the

DEATH WOUND OF STONEWALL JACKSON.
" He was then carried to the side of the road, and laid under a tree." His last words were, "Let us cross over
the river and rest under the shade."

*Illustration from* Wearing of the Gray, *a romanticized version of the death of a Confederate general whom Cooke greatly admired*

nickname "Stonewall" at First Manassas; revealing touches of character; and a clear, fast-paced style. The second writing retains much of the original but adds even more pertinent detail and has more objectivity; it also includes eyewitness accounts by other observers in circumstances for which the author was not present, and its anti-Union diatribes have been muted to make it more palatable to northern readers. The work was financially successful, selling three thousand copies the first day.

Cooke wrote little in the final months of the war, pressed by duties and worn down, like most Southern soldiers, by fatigue and resignation to defeat. After Lee's surrender at Appomattox, Cooke briefly entertained the idea of going to New York and then on to Paris, but he quickly acceded to a friend's exhortation to return to the Shenandoah Valley. There he lived for a while at "The Vineyard," the estate of his brother Phil's family, and at other places where he unwound from the war and tried to earn a living by his writing. Unlike some other southern writers, Cooke was able to reopen communication with northern publishers after the war and was soon sending sketches based on his military experiences to the *New York World* and *New York News.* He had

brought with him from the final days of the war the germ of an idea for a novel and, upon completing his revised biography of Jackson, began work on *Surry of Eagle's-Nest; or, The Memoirs of a Staff-Officer Serving in Virginia. Edited, from the MSS. of Colonel Surry* (1866), which became, after *The Virginia Comedians,* the author's best-known and most highly regarded work. In fact, the five-year period following the war was one of Cooke's most productive, the other being the five years before the war's beginning. During these years, along with *Fairfax,* the rewritten Jackson biography, and *Surry of Eagle's-Nest,* he crafted a sequel to the latter, *Mohun; or, The Last Days of Lee and His Paladins. Final Memoirs of a Staff Officer Serving in Virginia From the MSS. of Colonel Surry of Eagle's Nest* (1869); wrote a third Civil War novel, *Hilt to Hilt; or, Days and Nights on the Banks of the Shenandoah in the Autumn of 1864. From the MSS. of Colonel Surry of Eagle's Nest* (1869); published two full-length war histories—*Wearing of the Gray: Being Personal Portraits, Scenes and Adventures of the War* (1867), largely a collection of his sketches from the front, and *Hammer and Rapier* (1870), a compilation of articles that had appeared as "Battles of Virginia" in a monthly periodical, *The Old Guard;* and, after some delay caused by his misinterpreting a modest request by the Lee family, accepted a $1,500 commission from Appleton to write *A Life of Gen. Robert E. Lee* (1871).

All three of Cooke's Civil War novels are listed in their subtitles as "From the MSS. of Colonel Surry," although this character has a central role in only the first. The novel concerns the love of Surry, in some ways an alter ego of Cooke, for May Beverly, to whose home the hero is taken when he is knocked from his horse by a falling limb during a storm. May's coldness toward Surry is later explained by the fact that a marriage has been arranged by May's father and the father of Baskerville, a cowardly fop whom Surry knows and hates. A second plot treats the mortal feud of two former friends, Mordaunt and Fenwick, over the love of Frances Carleton, whom the former has married. The plots intersect as Surry observes a duel between the two in Hollywood Cemetery in Richmond and meets a deranged Frances when he seeks shelter at a mysterious cottage in the wilderness, and on other occasions as Mordaunt relentlessly pursues his seemingly indestructible nemesis. Surry's suit for May is finally successful when Baskerville, having learned of her loss of wealth from the ravages of war, releases her from their engagement. He also learns the history of the enmity of the mysterious, brooding Mordaunt and his rival, Fenwick. While Mordaunt was in England on business, Fenwick had used a forged letter to deceive and manipulate Frances, convincing her that her and Mordaunt's son had died and causing her to lose her mind to "puerperal fever." Ultimately, Fenwick is killed by Mordaunt's faithful servant, Achmed, and Mordaunt reunites with his son, now a volunteer soldier from Maryland, and marries Violet Grafton, a young woman who resembles Frances. A backdrop to all of this sensational action is, of course, the Civil War itself; Cooke describes many incidents from the war in detail and limns from memory portraits of Southern notables—the pious warrior Jackson, the adventurous and affable Stuart singing "Jine the Cavalry," the fearless knight Ashby on his white horse, and the "gallant Pelham," for example. These depictions, too, are reinforced by colorful characters such as Stuart's banjo player, Sweeny; Captain Bogy, with his gourmet meals served up from captured Union wagon trains; and Corporal Hagan.

Because of Cooke's involvement with other projects, *Mohun* was delayed for several years and did not appear in print until 1869, the same year he published *Hilt to Hilt*. The former novel begins where *Surry of Eagle's-Nest* leaves off, its action occurring during the final two years of the war and centering, historically, around Lee, while *Surry of Eagle's-Nest* treats the exploits of Jackson. The plot of *Mohun* is even more convoluted than that of its predecessor, with two families, the Conways and the Davenants, embroiled in a feud that began when the elder Davenant was falsely accused of murdering George Conway. Actually, the crime was committed by Davenant's son, who accidentally killed Conway during a robbery; he subsequently marries Lucretia Conway against her family's wishes, and takes on, at various times, the names Darke and Mortimer. Both are schemers, drawing the title character, Mohun, into a sham marriage with Lucretia and setting into motion the same sort of hostilities between the two men that existed between Mordaunt (a minor character in *Mohun*) and Fenwick in *Surry of Eagle's-Nest*. With the help of the mysterious Nighthawk, a Confederate spy and guerrilla, Mohun finds the marriage certificate of Darke-Davenant (now a Union captain) and Lucretia, enabling him to clear his estate and marry Georgia Conway, and the two villains are killed by Confederate troops. Less successful and more somber in tone than its predecessor, *Mohun* does have the advantage of a wonderfully satiric treatment of hoarders, war profiteers, and malingerers who live comfortably in Richmond while Southern soldiers are suffering the ravages of starvation and disease as well as federal gunfire. *Hilt to Hilt,* set in Fauquier County while Surry is on a tour of duty in "Mosby's Confederacy" in the fall of 1864, uses the same plot device of two former friends, in this case named Ratcliffe and Landon, now caught up in the throes of a mortal feud. It uses the same clanking machinery of the others—including alienation of affections, a faked marriage, and disguises—and is even more sensational, with Landon tearing at his enemy's throat with his teeth in one horrific scene.

Although Cooke's determination to justify the South and glorify its way of life is never far from the surface, the author's ostensible purpose in these works is to endorse a certain kind of honorable behavior: straight dealing, honesty, and compassion. Of course, he found these qualities chiefly in what he called the "Cavalier ideal," but by including a few Confederate villains such as Baskerville and the hoarder Mr. Croaker and by presenting a few Northerners, most particularly General McClellan, in a positive light, he could make the case that he was concerned with principles and not with regions. *Surry of Eagle's-Nest* was well received by both readers and reviewers, although some Northern publications such as the *New York Evening Post* and the *Boston Traveller* attacked its pro-Southern bias and some New England booksellers refused to stock it. Even so, it was Cooke's most successful book, selling close to eleven thousand copies and bringing the author $2,300 by 1871, when it went out of print. In writing it, too, he became the first author of note to treat the Civil War seriously in a novel. Reviews of *Mohun* were mixed. While noting that it shared with other historical romances the fault of mingling fact and fiction, in a review from 28 November 1868 *The States-man* found "nothing vicious or unjust in the tone and temper of the book," and the *New York Record and Indicator* on 5 December 1968 praised its "lofty sentiment, weird and wild adventures, wondrously life-like battle scenes . . . and the comicalities of camp, march, raid and fireside."

Cooke's success in marketing his works during this period allowed him, in September 1867, to marry Mary Francis Page, the daughter of Dr. Robert Page of Saratoga, whom Cooke had met prior to the war and who belonged to a Virginia family as distinguished as his own. The couple lived briefly at Saratoga and then moved permanently to The Briars, an estate Mary Francis had inherited. Here they had three children, two sons and a daughter, and Cooke supported the family partly by farming, which he learned through trial and error, but still chiefly by writing. Although a few signs of bitterness over the war and its aftermath surfaced occasionally, for the most part he enjoyed his idyllic life in the valley with his family and the friends whom he frequently entertained. Although his best work was largely behind him, he continued to write articles and stories for various publications, publishing about fifty such works, as well as novels.

While Cooke's writings in this final phase of his career exhibit most of the same romantic features of his early work and are in some cases even more melodramatic, he does show some evidence of innovation or attempts to move in new directions. A case in point is *The Heir of Gaymount* (1870), once tentatively titled "Truck," which, in presenting a hero who attempts to deal through truck farming with the financial problems wrought by the Civil War, anticipates Ellen Glasgow's *Barren Ground* (1925) by half a century. While, in typical Cooke fashion, the hero Carteret's problems are ultimately solved by finding buried treasure rather than by simply selling wheat and cattle, the book nevertheless includes some good, detailed descriptions of agricultural and marketing practices that the author had learned from experience.

Cooke also tried his hand at writing a novel of ideas in *Professor Pressensee, Materialist and Inventor* (1878), inspired by his having seen a phonograph on a visit to New York with his wife. The narrator, although somewhat awed by the professor's "phonometer," deplores his atheism, using his opportunity to speak into the machine to pronounce a message of refutation for his materialistic views. Not surprisingly, when Pressensee's daughter nearly dies of pneumonia, the scoffer is converted to orthodox religion, now using his scientific skills to improve agricultural machines. Two other novels that also attack religious skepticism, materialism, and unqualified faith in science are *Fanchette by One of Her Admirers* (1883) and *The Maurice Mystery* (1885); the former borrows too heavily from *The Virginia Comedians* (the title character is a reworking of Beatrice Hallam), and the second, an attempt to emulate the tale of ratiocination in the manner of Poe and Wilkie Collins, suffers from poorly drawn characters and an incredible plot. The novelette *Mr. Grantley's Idea* (1879) posits the belief that one can commit a crime, especially in one's youth, without becoming a moral criminal, although its primary interest for modern readers is its excellent portrayal of rural and small-town Virginia life in the nineteenth century.

While Cooke attempted a portrait of contemporary Virginia society in *Pretty Mrs. Gaston, and Other Stories* (1874), most of his other books during this period, *Justin Harley: A Romance of Old Virginia* (1875) and *Canolles: The Fortunes of a Partisan of '81* (1877), for instance, mark a return to his first love, the romantic materials of colonial Virginia. One of these, *My Lady Pokahontas: A True Relation of Virginia* (1885), was based on a story that was particularly dear to the author's heart and, if without much plot, is interesting for his use of a contemporary narrator, Anas Todkill, who writes passable Elizabethan English. Even in his one fictional foray into seventeenth-century English history, *Her Majesty the Queen* (1873), the hero, Edmund Cecil, ultimately makes his home on the York River, reflecting Cooke's theory (later debunked by W. J. Cash) that Virginia was settled largely by Cavaliers who had been defeated by Cromwell's Puritans.

Perhaps the most promising vein in Cooke's works of this final period is to be found in *The Virginia Bohemians* (1880). He had made a previous attempt at local-color fiction with the publication of "The Cotton-Mouth," inspired by a story a former slave brought back from Louisiana, in the October 1872 issue of *Appleton's Journal* and again with "The Moonshiners," set in western Virginia and published in *Harper's* (February 1879). The latter was incorporated into *The Virginia Bohemians*, which also includes well-crafted descriptions of life in a small town in the Piedmont; the characters are better drawn than in many of his other works—the moonshine-distilling mountaineers are among his best—and in spite of some of Cooke's usual romantic claptrap, the work was praised by reviewers, *Harper's* noting its "fresh and unconventional sketches of native character" (July 1880) and *Atlantic Monthly* observing that it "recalls the popular tales of Kennedy" (December 1880). Had Cooke recognized his talent in this mode of writing, he might have earned a higher place for himself in American literary history.

Two other works of this final period, the histories *Stories of the Old Dominion from the Settlement to the End of the Revolution* (1879) and *Virginia: A History of the People* (1883), are also worthy of mention. The former, commissioned by Harper's, is a collection of accounts of important people and events of old Virginia and is essentially a children's book (later adopted as a text by schools in Virginia and West Virginia); its manner is didactic, but, in the words of a reviewer from a 16 August 1879 article in the *Literary World,* it "blends instruction and entertainment in happy proportions." The second, like Cooke's military biographies, is weakened by disproportion, since the greater part of the book is devoted to the pre-Revolutionary era and presents colonial Virginia through the same romantic haze that characterizes those works and Cooke's other Civil War writings, but the work is written with charm and skill. Composed for the American Commonwealths series published by Houghton Mifflin, it sold, over a period of years, more than thirteen thousand copies, more than any of Cooke's other works.

In this final phase of his career Cooke also continued to publish articles and short stories for various periodicals and newspapers, such as *Harper's, Appleton's,* the *Magazine of American History,* the *Detroit Free Press,* the *Winchester Times,* and *The Critic.* Two of the best of the articles are "The Author of 'Swallow Barn'" (16 August 1873), a tribute to his cousin John Pendleton Kennedy, and "An Hour with Thackeray" (September 1879), both appearing in *Appleton's Journal.* Among the best of the fiction Cooke published during this time, in addition to the local-color stories, is "My Last Match" (*Leslie's Illustrated,* Christmas 1881), a story remarkably similar to Jack London's later "To Build a Fire" (1902); typically for Cooke, the story has a happy ending rather than the more tragic and realistic one of London's.

Although his creative powers were flagging noticeably in his final years, Cooke was essentially happy and was able to earn a living with his writing. He had, in spite of the death of his beloved wife, continued to do his best to see that his children were properly brought up and educated and to entertain friends, literary and otherwise, as well as to manage a working farm. In the late summer of 1886, however, he began

to grow weak and lethargic and, after collapsing in his chair, died of typhoid fever three days later, on 27 September. He was buried next to his wife and close to two of his brothers, and, in a final act of reconciliation, his uncle, General Philip St. George Cooke, gave the church at Millwood a stained-glass window emblazoned with a lily, symbolizing at once the Cookes' connection with Bermuda and the peace that had restored to wholeness one of the many American families split apart by the Civil War.

At the time of his death, the type of writing Cooke did had largely fallen out of fashion, the author himself conceding that he was being run out of the field by William Dean Howells and the other realists. He did not realize that he had endured so long as to anticipate the romantic revival brought about by writers such as Robert Louis Stevenson and J. M. Barrie at the end of the century. His better works such as *The Virginia Comedians* and *Surry of Eagle's-Nest* continued to sell for a few years, as did his histories of Virginia, but he gradually fell into an obscurity from which he is unlikely to emerge. Cooke was a good storyteller who wrote, as a rule, in a clear and fluent style, and he is good with descriptive details, particularly of landscape scenes and accounts of action. In *The Virginia Bohemians* and elsewhere he demonstrates that he might have become a competent writer of local-color fiction, but his bent for sensationalism and sentimentality, combined with his need for money, kept him producing second-rate works riddled with hackneyed romantic devices and condemned him to a much lower place in the pantheon of American authors than one feels he might have been capable of occupying. Even so, he produced one of the best colonial novels of the nineteenth century, wrote the first true Civil War novel and the first biography of Jackson, and perhaps had some influence on later movements in American fiction. In his literary corpus, however, Cooke maintained a high sense of personal and professional integrity. Both his works and reports by his friends affirm that, whatever his merits as a writer, John Esten Cooke, like his hero Henry St. John, achieved the status to which he most aspired—that of a Virginia gentleman—in the best sense of the word.

**Bibliographies:**

Oscar Wegelin, *A Bibliography of the Separate Writings of John Esten Cooke, 1830–1886* (Hattiesburg, Miss.: Book Farm, 1941);

Jack C. Wills, "John Esten Cooke," *Bibliography of American Fiction,* edited by Kent P. Ljungquist (New York: Facts on File, 1994), pp. 85–87.

## Biography:

John O. Beaty, *John Esten Cooke, Virginian* (Port Washington, N.Y.: Kennikat, 1922).

## References:

Mary Jo Bratton, "John Esten Cooke and His 'Confederate Lies,'" *Southern Literary Journal*, 13 (Spring 1981): 72–91;

A. Carl Bredahl, "Responding to the 'Airplant' Tradition: John Cooke's *My Lady Pokahontas*," *Southern Literary Journal*, 21 (Fall 1988): 54–63;

Ursula Brumm, "Definitions of Southern Identity in the Civil War Novels of John Esten Cooke," in *Rewriting the South: History and Fiction,* edited by Lothar Honnighausen and Valeria Gennaro Lerda (Tübingen, Germany: Francke, 1993), pp. 169–175;

Carvel Collins, "John Esten Cooke and Local Color," *Southern Literary Messenger,* 6 (January–February 1944): 82–84;

Thomas S. Gladsky, "John Esten Cooke's *My Lady Pokahontas:* The Popular Novel on History," *Southern Studies: An Interdisciplinary Journal of the South,* 23 (Fall 1984): 299–305;

Jay B. Hubbell, "John Esten Cooke," in *The South in American Literature, 1607–1900* (Durham, N.C.: Duke University Press, 1954), pp. 511–521;

Matthew C. O'Brien, "John Esten Cooke, George Washington, and the Virginia Cavaliers," *Virginia Magazine of History and Biography,* 84 (1976): 259–265;

Yvette Salviati, "Du Mythe de la Revolution americaine au mythe sudiste: *Les Comediens de Virginie,* de John Esten Cooke (1854)," *Mythes, Croyances et Religions dans le Monde Anglo-Saxon,* 6 (1988): 97–115;

Eric Solomon, "The Novelist as Soldier: Cooke and DeForest," *American Literary Realism,* 19 (Spring 1987): 80–88.

## Papers:

The largest collection of John Esten Cooke's manuscripts, journals, and letters are held by Duke University Library, Durham, N.C.; the Library of Congress; the New York Public Library; and the Alderman Library, University of Virginia.

# Philip Pendleton Cooke

*(26 October 1816 – 20 January 1850)*

Edward L. Tucker
*Virginia Polytechnic Institute and State University*

See also the Cooke entries in *DLB 3: Antebellum Writers in New York and the South* and *DLB 59: American Literary Critics and Scholars, 1800–1850.*

BOOKS: *Froissart Ballads, and Other Poems* (Philadelphia: Carey & Hart, 1847);

John D. Allen, ed., *Philip Pendleton Cooke: Poet, Critic, Novelist* (Johnson City: East Tennessee State University, 1969).

SELECTED PERIODICAL PUBLICATIONS–
UNCOLLECTED:

FICTION

"The Two Country Houses," *Southern Literary Messenger,* 14 (May 1848): 307–318; 14 (June 1848): 349–356; 14 (July 1848): 436–450;

"Captain Guy; or, The Unpardonable Sin," *Illustrated Monthly Courier,* 1 (2 October 1848): 58–59;

"The Chevalier Merlin," *Southern Literary Messenger,* 15 (June 1849): 326–335; 15 (July 1849): 417–426; 15 (August 1849): 473–481; 15 (September 1849): 569–576; 15 (November 1849): 641–650; 15 (December 1849): 727–734; 16 (January 1850): 42–50;

"A Morning with Cagliostro. From Notes of a Conversation with Mr. Joseph Jenkins," *Southern Literary Messenger,* 16 (December 1850): 743–752.

NONFICTION

"English Poetry," *Southern Literary Messenger,* 1 (April 1835): 397–401; 1 (June 1835): 557–565; 2 (January 1836): 101–106;

"Leaves from My Scrap Book," *Southern Literary Messenger,* 2 (April 1836): 314–316;

"Leaf from My Scrap Book," *Southern Literary Messenger,* 2 (May 1836): 372;

"Old Books and New Authors," *Southern Literary Messenger,* 12 (April 1846): 199–203;

"Dante," *Southern Literary Messenger,* 12 (September 1846): 545–554;

*Philip Pendleton Cooke*

"Living Novelists," *Southern Literary Messenger,* 13 (June 1847): 367–373; 13 (September 1847): 529–536; 13 (December 1847): 745–752;

"Edgar A. Poe," *Southern Literary Messenger,* 14 (January 1848): 34–38;

"The Feudal Armies of France and England," *Southern Literary Messenger,* 14 (June 1848): 362–365.

Philip Pendleton Cooke, an antebellum Romantic writer, is important for his interesting and perceptive essays, as well as his four completed novelettes, which capture much of the spirit and scenery of western Virginia of the 1830s and 1840s. His only collection of poetry, *Froissart Ballads, and Other Poems* (1847), illustrates themes typical of early Southern poetry—the placing of woman on a pedestal, the love of nature, the presentation of problems facing aristocratic society of the Shenandoah region, problems of frontier life in colonial times, and a fascination with the medieval past—themes that appear in his short fiction, as well. He also had a close relationship with the *Southern Literary Messenger* from its beginning.

Cooke was born on 26 October 1816 in Martinsburg, Berkeley County, Virginia (now West Virginia), the son of Maria Pendleton and John Rogers Cooke. The Pendletons and the Cookes, originally from England, were of distinguished backgrounds. After the Revolution, many of the best Tidewater families settled in the Shenandoah Valley. John Rogers Cooke, a lawyer, was one of the framers of the Virginia Constitution of 1830.

Philip was the oldest of thirteen children, only four of whom survived their father. A younger brother, John Esten Cooke, was noted for novels such as *Leather Stocking and Silk* (1854) and *The Virginia Comedians* (1854). John Pendleton Kennedy, a cousin, was the author of *Swallow Barn* (1832) and *Horse-Shoe Robinson* (1835). Another cousin, David H. Strother, used the pen name of "Porte Crayon," and became noted for his illustrations in Union periodicals during the Civil War.

At the age of fifteen, Philip entered Princeton College. Only an average student, he received his degree in 1834, though he was briefly suspended near the end of his college career because of a youthful prank. He became a lawyer but was always under pressure for money.

On 1 May 1837 he married Willianne Corbin Taylor Burwell, who lived with her uncle, Nathaniel Burwell, at a nearby mansion named Saratoga. Uncle Nathaniel built a handsome home for the couple, the Vineyard, two miles from Millwood, Virginia. The marriage produced five children: Elizabeth Lewis (born 22 July 1838), Maria Pendleton (born 15 April 1840), Nancy Burwell (born 27 April 1843), Nathaniel Burwell (born 24 April 1845), and Alethea Collins (born 23 January 1848).

With the death of her uncle, Willianne received a handsome inheritance, and Cooke's financial worries, which had plagued him earlier, were at last over. A lover of the outdoors, Cooke during a hunting trip waded into the icy Shenandoah River to retrieve a

*Cooke's family home, The Vineyard, built shortly after his 1837 marriage to Willianne Burwell*

wounded duck. He developed pneumonia from the exposure and died at the age of thirty-three on 20 January 1850; he was buried in the churchyard cemetery of Old Chapel, near Millwood, Virginia. His wife lived until 1899, though she was blind for the last thirty years of her life.

In a March 1835 issue of the *Southern Literary Messenger* Cooke wrote that the legitimate aim of criticism is "to point out the proper path towards excellence. A true critic effects this by gently and courteously exposing error and lauding beauties where beauties are to be found." He wrote several essays in which he followed this aim. In particular, he evaluated the works of English poets, notably Geoffrey Chaucer, William Shakespeare, Sir Philip Sidney, Edmund Spenser, Percy Bysshe Shelley, and Alfred Tennyson. Cooke felt quite at home in an earlier age of poetry rather than in the modern.

His literary essays reveal his wide reading and his independent, vigorous judgment. Cooke expressed in a 13 October 1843 letter to John Rogers Cooke that he felt the best poetry of men such as John Milton and William Wordsworth is "full of great truths, magnificently uttered." Although prose to him was a lighter form of creation, he did praise some English novelists, notably Sir Walter Scott. He was not especially concerned with American writers, although he had high praise in his essay "Living Novelists" for James Fenimore Cooper, who he believed was the "most creative and most dramatic of our novelists—and the only true poet among them."

Although in his own works he depended for the most part upon the pioneer and plantation life that he knew personally, when it came to choosing the best works of literature he turned to the more romantic and heroic ages of chivalry in Europe. In evaluating him as a literary critic in his *Philip Pendleton Cooke* (1942), John D. Allen wrote that he had "no definite critical theory, consciously employed in the process of estimating an author's qualities. Cooke's mind, it would seem, had little interest in theories in general, in critical and esthetic theories in particular. On the other hand, in dealing with the specific and objective fact, it displayed in its maturity a vigorous good sense which illuminated whatever subject of criticism it chose to examine."

Of greatest interest to scholars have been Cooke's four completed novelettes depicting life in Virginia, all of which were published in the *Southern Literary Messenger*. "John Carper, the Hunter of Lost River" (1848) appeared in three issues of the magazine, from February through April. In all, the seven chapters comprise a total of eighteen pages, for which Cooke was paid $2.00 per page. The attractive novelette is set in a region that the author knew well: the Martinsburg area of the Shenandoah Valley. In addition to the vivid descriptions of the area, the work consists of a love story between two noble people. John Carper is a "brave, truehearted, intelligent man," "a noble specimen of the best class of frontiersman"; six feet, two inches tall in his moccasins, he is "strong as a bear and as longwinded as a wolf." He loves an eighteen-year-old Quaker, Nelly Blake, "the flower of the Lost River maidens." There are problems, however: Nelly's uncle, Joshua Blake, a secret Tory follower, puts obstacles in the way of the lovers. When the Indians in the region capture Nelly, Carper must use all the skills of the frontiersman, aided by his dog, Sharpnose, to rescue her.

"John Carper, the Hunter of Lost River" belongs to the literature of the Indian in America, as do Cooke's poems "The Song of the Sioux Lovers" (*Knickerbocker Magazine*, July 1833), "The Last Indian" (*Southern Literary Messenger*, April 1835), and "The Murder of Cornstalk" (*Southern Literary Messenger*, June 1846). "John Carper" features situations reminiscent of Cooper's Leather-Stocking Tales. Cooke's

narrative style, however, is simple, direct, and vigorous. The action moves swiftly, and the plot is presented without moralizing. Although one Indian is slightly sympathetic, for the most part the Indians are evil stock figures, proud of their race, taking delight in fighting the white frontiersmen and scalping their victims.

"The Two Country Houses" (May–July 1848) is the longest of the four completed novelettes but also the least compact. Originally titled "Mary Hunter of Cotsworth," it has a greater variety of settings than the other three. In addition to giving a detailed picture of life in western Virginia during the 1830s and 1840s, the scene moves to Mississippi and even the city of Paris. Cooke received $61 for the work, which comprised thirty and one-half pages over three issues.

The title of the novelette comes from two houses situated on opposing hills, separated by a stream. One house, Cotsworth, is the home of the Cars; the other, Winisfalen, is the seat of the Hunters. Through a rather complicated genealogy, the heir to the first house, Carabas Car, falls in love with the heiress to the second, Mary Hunter, and asks her to marry him, though they are only fifteen and fourteen years old, respectively. The two gradually drift apart, and Car changes into an irresponsible spendthrift. Mary remains faithful to him despite his faults, however. While living in Paris, Car again is transformed, this time becoming a writer of perceptive articles on international affairs. Eventually he and Mary are re-united. Various situations and other characters reinforce the main plot: a lack of understanding among various family members; a faithful black servant; young men other than Carabas who are not dependable; one young man desiring to marry Mary for her money; several unscrupulous figures, especially a crafty lawyer, Gamil; and a secret will hidden by the lawyer.

Though the two major figures—Carabas Car and Mary Hunter—are two-dimensional and thus not particularly interesting, some of the minor characters do stand out. One of considerable interest is the lawyer, of whom Cooke writes: "It was an eccentricity of Gamil, when fortune favored him, to put out his ruffle to the utmost and load his fingers with rings; but as he became unlucky to suppress these ornaments."

For "The Gregories of Hackwood," which appeared on sixteen and one-half pages in the September and October 1848 issues of the *Southern Literary Messenger*, Cooke received $33 in payment. Set in western Virginia in the 1830s and 1840s, the novelette presents problems facing aristocratic society of the Shenandoah region. The central figure, Miles

Gregory, though once sympathetic, has grown cold and become almost mad with an "insane love of riches." His avarice makes him forget other things and people: his great estate of thousands of acres lies neglected; his home, Hackwood, is falling into decay; his daughters, Joan and Anne, are of little concern; his son, Lewis, blind and with an ill wife and children, receives slight pity. Miles, after giving Lewis a bond to relieve his son's debt, secures it again when he discovers its value. Finally, fearful that his outspoken daughter, Joan, may steal his money, Miles takes his possessions from their hiding place and prepares to leave. Caught in a swollen stream and trapped under his gold, he drowns in six feet of water.

The work has some conventional trappings of melodrama: a miser, a "wily" lawyer named Achilles Wiley, a daughter-in-law dying of a cough, a blind son, a mortgage on a house, even a somnambulist. Yet, the characters are well drawn, especially Miles Gregory, with his "sharp ferret eyes" and his "suspicious, covetous, and fearful nature." In this work Cooke illustrates his excellent gift for dialogue and his ability to keep his plot moving effectively.

The critic David K. Jackson once called "The Crime of Andrew Blair" "a study of a respectable planter with a criminal past." He received $44 for the work, which appeared in the January through March 1849 issues of the *Southern Literary Messenger*. The novelette has two distinct plots. In the first, Andrew Blair, "a man of wealth, talent, political training, and a fair degree of distinction," who lives in a handsome mansion, Lindores, changes during a period of twenty-five years into a "ruin," someone with "an expression of desolate distress" and "a pinch of pain in his sharp features." The reason for the change is not revealed until the end of the work. Blair, earlier in his life, became furious with a colleague, stabbed him, and threw his body in a well. The crime was witnessed by a social inferior, Jack Herries, who blackmailed Blair. Eventually, on his deathbed, Blair reveals his guilt.

In the second plot, Herries forces an unwilling Minny Blair, the niece of Blair and the heiress to his fortune, to agree to marry Herries's shiftless son, Tom. In a remarkable series of events, Tom turns out to be a man of character concerned about Minny's welfare. During a foxhunt Tom tells Minny that she need not marry him; when he almost dies as the result of a terrible fall, Minny declares her love for him.

The settings of western Virginia are suitably described, and the work features an appropriate blending of kind feelings and violence found in much later Southern writing. Many of the characters are skillfully drawn, especially Major Wright, who is devoted to

FROISSART BALLADS,

AND

OTHER POEMS.

BY

PHILIP PENDLETON COOKE.

" Emmi venuta certa fantasia,
Che non posso cacciarmi da la testa,
Di scriver un istoria in poesia
Affatta ignota o poco manifesta."
FORTEGUERRI.

PHILADELPHIA:
CAREY AND HART.
1847.

*Title page for the only published collection of Cooke's verse*

foxhunting and relates long, boring tales about the sport. He has two daughters and is pleased when one, Boadicea, marries a "ruddy young foxhunter with a good property." The other daughter, Araminta, is forced to remain single because her father dismisses her beau, a "young gentleman from town," as "too bad a horseman to marry into his family."

Cooke was working on a fifth novelette, "The Chevalier Merlin," at the time of his death; it was never finished. The existing portion appeared in seven issues of the *Southern Literary Messenger,* from June 1849 through January 1850, but there is no record of how much he received for the work. The work illustrates well a favorite theme of Cooke's—his fascination with the medieval past. The central figure, Merlin Brand, a Norwegian, enters the service of Charles XII of Sweden and takes part in various

*The cemetery at Old Chapel, near Millwood, Virginia, where Cooke is buried*

wars. He meets Czar Peter as well as other "brave and distinguished gentlemen of many countries." Some of his private adventures are also included.

In all, Cooke published thirty-eight poems during his literary career. The editor Rufus W. Griswold, in a letter to John R. Thompson dated 19 February 1850, at one time designated Cooke as "the finest poet that ever lived in Virginia," and he recommended that the Virginian present in one volume some of his best poems. For this volume, *Froissart Ballads, and Other Poems,* in addition to an introductory poem, Cooke selected five ballads patterned after the Frenchman Jean Froissart's *Les chroniques de France, d'Engleterre, et des païs voisins* (circa 1360–1400). In addition, he included eleven miscellaneous poems. Griswold helped Cooke find a publisher, Carey and Hart of Philadelphia. *Froissart Ballads* was dedicated to John Pendleton Kennedy. A total of 750 copies were published in 1847, and in 1848, Cooke recorded that he received $56.40 for the publication. Although it did include some of Cooke's best-known works, it was not widely received.

Cooke, like other Southern poets, places woman on a pedestal, though she may sometimes be just a child. Often she is dead, and the poet grieves because he adored her. Rosalie Lee has "gone to her early rest." Florence Vane, in Cooke's most famous poem, "wast lovelier than the roses / In their prime"; now she is "glorious clay" lying under the "green sod." Elements of nature—the "lilies of the valley and the pansies"—weep for her.

Cooke, again indicative of the Southern poetic tradition, praises nature. In "Life in the Autumn Woods," set in October, the speaker loves "the woods / In this best season" of the year. "What passionate / And wild delight is in the proud swift chase." If someone is grieved, that person can find "a cure in the forest." Nature in "The Mountains" also has healing powers. The work praises the maple, the ash, the pines, the dogwood, the oak, and the hickories. When people have "cares and despairs," they can learn that "nature is a foe severe / To pallid brow, and shadowy fear / And lifts the fallen to valiant cheer."

Furthermore, following other Southern poets, Cooke writes of medieval, often violent times. The woman in "Emily," the introduction to the ballads, with her "temples fair and gliding limbs," loves "ancient lays." The sport of falconry is praised in "The Master of Bolton"; the work depicts jousting scenes, including a knight fighting desperately for the hand of his lady. In "Geoffrey Tetenoire" the title character has wronged Lady Jane; in anger, she tells an admirer, Count Gaston, that she will marry him if he brings her Tetenoire's head. The tables are turned: the count is killed instead, and the evil Tetenoire sends her the head of her lover in a casket.

Finally, the literary life of Cooke paralleled the early development of the *Southern Literary Messenger.* His first contribution to the journal was "A Song of the Seasons," a poem that appeared in volume one, in the January 1835 issue. In all he contributed to forty-four issues. The best-known editors of the *Messenger* during Cooke's lifetime were Edgar Allan Poe, in 1835–1836; Benjamin Blake Minor, who was editor and proprietor from 1843 to 1847; and John Reuben Thompson, editor and proprietor from 1847 to 1860. Cooke exchanged a series of cordial letters with Poe, and he wrote Thompson on 23 October 1849: "Poe always backed me with his praise, and I owe what little repute I possess as yet in the North, more to him than to any other ten men." In response to another letter, dated 20 November 1849, Cooke wrote Thompson that he could find no more than four of Poe's letters, though he probably possessed twenty somewhere. In a remarkable series of letters from Cooke to Minor and Thompson, Cooke expressed his thoughts about the publication of his own works; in addition, these letters also reveal much about the development of the magazine.

During his brief life Philip Pendleton Cooke's primary concerns were providing for his wife and children, his beloved area of Virginia, and his sporting activities, notably hunting and fishing. Notwithstanding Griswold's assessment of his talent, Cooke was scarcely more than a gifted amateur with respect to criticism, short fiction, and poetry. Literature to him was basically recreation. Yet, his works–taken as a whole–have remained of some interest, especially for students of early antebellum Romantic literature.

**Letters:**

Edward L. Tucker, ed., "Philip Pendleton Cooke and *The Southern Literary Messenger:* Selected Letters," *Mississippi Quarterly,* 27 (Winter 1973–1974): 79–99.

**Biographies:**

Rufus W. Griswold, "Philip Pendleton Cooke," *International Magazine,* 4 (October 1851): 300–303;

John Esten Cooke, "Recollections of Philip Pendleton Cooke," *Southern Literary Messenger,* 26 (June 1858): 419–432;

David K. Jackson, "Philip Pendleton Cooke: Virginia Gentleman, Lawyer, Hunter, and Poet," in *American Studies in Honor of William Kenneth Boyd,* edited by Jackson (Durham, N.C.: Duke University Press, 1940), pp. 282–326;

John D. Allen, *Philip Pendleton Cooke* (Chapel Hill: University of North Carolina Press, 1942).

**References:**

Jay B. Hubbell, *The South in American Literature, 1607–1900* (Durham, N.C.: Duke University Press, 1954), pp. 502–511;

Edd Winfield Parks, *Ante-Bellum Southern Literary Critics* (Athens: University of Georgia Press, 1962), pp. 136–157, 302–306;

Edward L. Tucker, "Philip Pendleton Cooke," *Virginia Cavalcade,* 19 (Winter 1970): 42–47.

**Papers:**

The most important manuscript collections of Philip Pendleton Cooke's writings are at Duke University, New York Public Library, Peabody Institute, Boston Public Library, and the Virginia Historical Society.

# David Crockett

*(17 August 1786 – 6 March 1836)*

Lane Stiles
*University of Minnesota*

See also the Crockett entries in *DLB 3: Antebellum Writers in New York and the South; DLB 11: American Humorists, 1800–1950;* and *DLB 183: American Travel Writers, 1776–1864.*

BOOKS: *The Life and Adventures of Colonel David Crockett of West Tennessee,* attributed to Crockett but probably written by Mathew St. Claire Clarke (Cincinnati: E. Deming, 1833); republished as *Sketches and Eccentricities of Colonel David Crockett of West Tennessee* (New York: Harper / London: J. Limbird, 1833);

*A Narrative of the Life of David Crockett, of the State of Tennessee,* by Crockett and Thomas Chilton (Philadelphia & Baltimore: Carey & Hart / London: J. Limbird, 1834);

*An Account of Col. Crockett's Tour to the North and Down East . . . , Written by Himself,* attributed to Crockett but probably written by William Clark (Philadelphia & Baltimore: Carey & Hart, 1835);

*The Life of Martin Van Buren,* attributed to Crockett but probably written by Augustin Smith Clayton (Philadelphia: R. Wright, 1835);

*Col. Crockett's Exploits and Adventures in Texas,* attributed to Crockett but written by Richard Penn Smith (Philadelphia: T. K. & P. G. Collins, 1836; London: R. Kennett, 1837).

**Edition and Collection:** *The Autobiography of David Crockett,* edited, with an introduction, by Hamlin Garland (New York: Scribners, 1923)–includes *A Narrative of the Life of David Crockett of the State of Tennessee, An Account of Colonel Crockett's Tour to the North and Down East,* and *Col. Crockett's Exploits and Adventures in Texas;*

*A Narrative of the Life of David Crockett of the State of Tennessee,* edited by Joseph John Arpad (New Haven: College and University Press, 1972); facsimile edition, with introduction and annotations by James A. Shackford and Stanley J. Folmsbee (Knoxville: University of Tennessee Press, 1973).

*David Crockett ( portrait attributed to Chester Harding; National Portrait Gallery, Smithsonian Institution, Washington, D.C.)*

Perhaps no American traveler of the first half of the nineteenth century was better known to American audiences than David Crockett. Like Daniel Boone before him, "Davy" Crockett stood tall in the national imagination as a paradigm of the frontiersman, a popular type that appropriately had taken early form in travel books. Crockett's popularity and renown, however, far exceeded Boone's, driven by–and, in turn, driving–the production of an extraordinary body of mythmaking literature that elevated Crockett into one of the first and most enduring American mass-culture heroes.

Although more literate than he pretended, Crockett the writer (as opposed to Crockett the self-promoter) played a limited role in the production of this literature. Of the various works attributed to him, all were to some extent ghostwritten, even his autobiography, *A Narrative of the Life of David Crockett, of the State of Tennessee* (1834). Still, *A Narrative of the Life of David Crockett* is a significant historical and literary text—not only the most authentic record of Crockett the man but also one of the earliest and most notable examples of Southwestern humor and a distinctive document of frontier life and politics in the age of Andrew Jackson.

Crockett came by his pioneering spirit naturally. His paternal grandparents had pushed westward from North Carolina across the Appalachian Mountains at the beginning of the Revolutionary War. Both were killed by Indians in 1777, not long after settling in what is now eastern Tennessee. Their son John Crockett escaped the attack and around 1780 married Rebecca Hawkins, who gave birth to David on 17 August 1786 at the Crockett home in Greene County, Tennessee. The Crocketts were poor, even by rural standards, and the young Crockett, who had little formal education, left home early to work and travel. On 14 August 1806, three days before his twentieth birthday, he married Mary "Polly" Finley, with whom he had three children.

In 1811 he moved his family from eastern to middle Tennessee—one of a series of westering migrations that continued to the end of his life. (Like other poor backwoodsmen, Crockett moved as much out of economic need as wanderlust, repeatedly abandoning "sickly" or game-depleted land for newer and richer territories.) Two years later the Creek Indian War broke out, and Crockett volunteered to fight Indians under the command of General Jackson. Shortly after his return from the war, in 1815, Polly Crockett died; within a year Crockett married Elizabeth Patton, a widow with two children.

Crockett was elected to the Tennessee legislature in 1821, and two years later "the gentleman from the cane" (cane was short for canebrake, a rough thicket of canes, typical of the wilds of western Tennessee) was reelected after moving to a new district in the western part of the state. In 1827 he was sent by Tennessee voters to Washington for the first of three nonconsecutive terms in the House of Representatives. Although elected as a Jacksonian, he broke with the president over such issues as public land policy, Indian removal, and the Bank of the United States and soon found himself taken up by eastern Whigs as a conservative countersymbol to Jackson, although he was really more of an anti-Jacksonian than a Whig. After Crockett was defeated for reelection to Congress in 1835 he promptly left Tennessee to explore

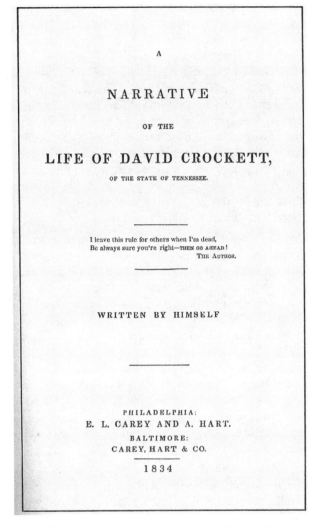

A

NARRATIVE

OF THE

LIFE OF DAVID CROCKETT,

OF THE STATE OF TENNESSEE.

I leave this rule for others when I'm dead,
Be always sure you're right—THEN GO AHEAD!
THE AUTHOR.

WRITTEN BY HIMSELF

PHILADELPHIA:
E. L. CAREY AND A. HART.
BALTIMORE:
CAREY, HART & CO.
1834

*Title page for the most accurate of the several ghostwritten autobiographies of Crockett (Tennessee State Library, Nashville)*

Texas. On 6 March 1836 the forty-nine-year-old Crockett, who had by then joined the cause for Texas independence, was killed by General Antonio López de Santa Anna's forces at the battle of the Alamo.

Crockett's autobiography recounts selected events of his life through his third term in Congress; one of its purposes was to support his campaign for reelection for a fourth term—and perhaps, although Crockett repeatedly denied it, a possible run for the presidency against Jackson's handpicked successor, Martin Van Buren, in 1836. Though rife with anti-Jackson sloganeering, *A Narrative of the Life of David Crockett* is generally, as Crockett asserts in the preface, "a plain, honest, home-spun account" of his life. He does, however, like any good frontier storyteller, stretch the truth occasionally.

Crockett claims, for example, that he writes his own story to correct the inaccuracies of an extremely popular biography released the previous year, *The Life and Adventures of Colonel David Crockett of West Tennessee* (1833), which was republished that same year as *Sketches and Eccentricities of Colonel David Crockett of West Tennessee*. Crockett protests that he does not know the author of the biography. In truth he not only knew but probably also collaborated with the anonymous author, Mathew St. Claire Clarke–a clerk of the House of Representatives and an anti-Jacksonian ally of Nicholas Biddle of the Bank of the United States. Clarke had intended the biography to propagandize for Crockett's reelection, but by exaggerating Crockett's frontier idiom and demeanor he may have hurt as much as helped him–hence, Crockett's disavowal.

*A Narrative of the Life of David Crockett* promises a more authentic Crockett. "The whole book is my own," Crockett declares in the preface, "and every sentiment and sentence in it." Here again Crockett stretches the truth, for he wrote with the help of Thomas Chilton, a congressman from Kentucky, who, like Clarke, was allied with anti-Jacksonian interests and who, like Clarke (but to a much lesser degree), could not resist inflecting Crockett's voice with backwoods solecisms. On the whole, though, Crockett's voice dominates the book, and except for a politically expedient revision of his war record and some confused chronology, the autobiography fairly depicts his life and language (even as it reinforces his emerging legendary status).

As the autobiography of a type of American traveler, *A Narrative of the Life of David Crockett* inevitably involves itself in the discourse of American travel writing. Indeed, the most vividly rendered and carefully detailed passages of the book describe not Crockett's personal and familial life but his travels throughout the South and the West. These travels began early. At age twelve Crockett was hired out by his father to accompany a cattle drive to Rockbridge County, Virginia. A year later he ran away from home to avoid punishment for playing hooky, again hitching up with a drover headed toward Virginia.

He eventually landed in Baltimore, where in the manner of the young Benjamin Franklin, he booked passage to England. (Crockett's book evokes Franklin in a more general way as well–as an early work in the tradition, established by Franklin, of the autobiography of the self-made man.) Unlike Franklin, Crockett never set sail, and after an absence of two and a half years he returned home, so changed his family at first did not recognize him. Crockett narrates both of these early journeys largely in terms of relationships with his various employers–some of whom were considerate and ethical, and some, not–and the hardships he had to endure in these latter cases.

Domestic life intervened, and Crockett did not travel extensively again until he enlisted in the Tennessee militia after the Creek Indians massacred more than five hundred whites and blacks at Fort Mims in the summer of 1813. Crockett's military duty took him southward into Alabama and eventually as far south as Pensacola, Florida. The poorly supplied militia was constantly short on rations, and Crockett spent most of his time hunting and scavenging for food. There were also occasional encounters with Indians, both friendly and hostile.

The callousness of Crockett's accounts of the engagements of his company with the Creeks belies the more sympathetic rhetoric that had been attributed to him a few years earlier in a speech opposing the Indian Removal Act of 1830. For example, Crockett describes what happened after a band of Creek warriors barricaded themselves in a house:

> We now shot them like dogs; and then set the house on fire, and burned it up with the forty-six warriors in it. I recollect seeing a boy who was shot down near the house. His arm and thigh was broken, and he was so near the burning house that the grease was stewing out of him. In this situation he was still trying to crawl along; but not a murmur escaped him, though he was only about twelve years old. So sullen is the Indian, when his dander is up, that he had sooner die than make a noise, or ask for quarters.

The next day the hungry troops found some potatoes in the cellar beneath the burned house and ate them, although, says Crockett, "I had a little rather not, if I could have helped it, for the oil of the Indians we had burned up on the day before had run down on them, and they looked like they had been stewed with fat meat."

For all their apparent racism these accounts do reveal Crockett's egalitarian tendencies. One incident in particular demonstrates his deep-seated distrust of rank and class pretension. Warned of an impending Indian attack, Private Crockett rushes to inform his commanding officer but to his consternation he is ignored. The next day an officer arrives to relay exactly the same warning, and this time the commanding officer immediately musters the troops for a forced march. Crockett complains that the incident "convinced me, clearly, of one of the hateful ways of the world. When I made my report, it wasn't believed, because I was no officer; I was no great man, but just a poor soldier."

After the war Crockett went back to Alabama to look for possible places to settle. One night, near present-day Tuscaloosa, the horses wandered away and he walked more than fifty miles, "wading creeks and swamps, and climbing mountains," trying to catch them but succeeding only in catching malaria. Some Indians helped him to a farm, where he recuperated. His family was astonished when he returned to Tennessee, for his fellow travelers had reported him dead and buried. With characteristic Old Southwest drollness (prefiguring Mark Twain's famous quip about the exaggerated reports of his demise), Crockett notes: "I know'd this was a whapper of a lie, as soon as I heard it."

Crockett's inveterate restlessness is nowhere more apparent than in the final chapters of the autobiography, which deal with his political career. He has little to say about his terms in office but much to say about electioneering for office and bear hunting while out of office. Crockett consistently depicts life on the trail–whether the campaign trail, the trail of wild game, an Indian trail, the trail of fortune, or the trail West–as a series of obstacles to overcome. Travel for Crockett is always a journey of the self: meeting and conquering personal challenges.

Throughout much of the autobiography Crockett mutes the backwoods bragging that he believed had skewed Clarke's characterization of him; but at times, especially in the concluding chapters, something of the legendary, tall-tale Crockett can be glimpsed: the folksy stump orator verbally besting his more learned and better- heeled opponents, the fearless hunter crawling blindly into a dark crevice to kill a bear with only a knife. Crockett's bear-hunting prowess, as described in an account of a particularly successful hunting trip to extreme western Tennessee, is almost incredibly formidable; but even his liveliest hunting stories never sacrifice the simplicity, directness, and believability that firmly ground the entire autobiography. (Testimonials from his contemporaries suggest that Crockett was as good a hunter as he claimed to be.)

The impression *A Narrative of the Life of David Crockett* leaves of its subject is, finally, one of an ingenuous, naturally heroic man of action, fully capable at the age of twelve years of walking seven miles in two hours in knee-deep snow to escape an unscrupulous employer, or at sixteen of crossing a white-capped river in a borrowed canoe on a bitterly cold winter day to make his way home after a long absence, or at thirty-six of crossing a half-frozen, mile-wide, flooded stream on foot in order to fetch a keg of gunpowder so his family could hunt. Generally ignored by critics on its release, Crockett's *A Narrative of the Life of David Crockett* nonetheless proved popular with readers in both the East and the West, selling out its first printing immediately and going into several reprintings in a matter of months, much to Crockett's delight.

Shortly after release of the book in February or March 1834, Crockett abandoned his congressional duties and set out on a tour of the North and the East. He claimed variously that the tour was to promote sales of the autobiography, to rehabilitate his health, or to study northern industrial culture, but the truth was that Crockett was fulfilling a political obligation to his power-

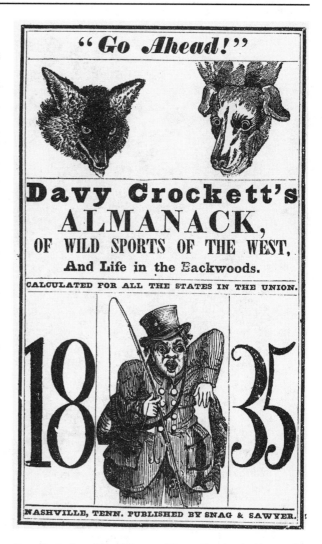

*Cover for the first edition of the annual* Davy Crockett's Almanack, *which featured fantastic tales with Crockett as a larger-than-life hero (American Antiquarian Society)*

ful Whig supporters, who were hoping to exploit his rising national reputation. The tour lasted from 25 April to 13 or 14 May 1834 and included visits to Baltimore, Philadelphia, New York, Jersey City, Newport, Boston, Lowell, Providence, and Camden.

One of the results of Crockett's travels was a book-length assemblage of newspaper clippings, ghost-written speeches, and other documents of the carefully orchestrated tour, titled *An Account of Col. Crockett's Tour to the North and Down East . . . , Written by Himself* and released in March 1835. Despite the claim of the subtitle Crockett's contribution was merely to collect these documents and pass them to the ghostwriter, probably William Clark, a Whig congressman from Pennsylvania. What might have been a humorous inversion of the conventional narrative of the easterner traveling through the

*Illustration of Crockett's West Tennessee home, from the 1835* Davy Crockett's Almanack *(University of Tennessee Library, Knoxville)*

West was in the end little more than a propagandist anti-Jackson, pro-Bank campaign tract.

*The Life of Martin Van Buren,* another pro-Whig work attributed to Crockett, followed a couple of months later. This time Crockett's involvement did not extend past lending his name to the project; the caustic biography of Jackson's vice president was most likely written by Crockett's friend Augustin Smith Clayton of Georgia, another anti-Jacksonian congressman. Both *An Account of Col. Crockett's Tour* and *The Life of Martin Van Buren* fared poorly with the public, as did Crockett's campaign: he lost his bid for reelection to the House of Representatives in August 1835. Shortly afterward on 1 November 1835 Crockett departed for Texas with three friends, traveling down the Mississippi River to the Arkansas River, then west to the Red River, and finally south to San Antonio.

Crockett's death at the Alamo in March 1836 effectively ended his usefulness to the Whig press, but it did not stop the publication of the works ostensibly or nominally written by him. One such narrative was commis-

sioned by Crockett's publishers, Carey and Hart, in the hopes of salvaging the poor sales of *An Account of Col. Crockett's Tour.* The commissioned work–*Col. Crockett's Exploits and Adventures in Texas*–was supposedly based on a diary kept by Crockett that had been rescued from the Alamo, but except for elements from two of Crockett's letters the work was entirely fabricated. Published in early summer 1836, the book was written by Richard Penn Smith. As Carey and Hart hoped, public interest in Crockett increased dramatically after his martyrdom; the back stock of *An Account of Col. Crockett's Tour* was soon depleted, and *Col. Crockett's Exploits and Adventures in Texas* sold more than ten thousand copies in less than a year.

A series of first-person narratives written in Crockett's voice also found popular audiences after his death. These narratives were published in the Crockett almanacs, which began in 1835 while Crockett was still alive and continued for more than twenty years through 1856, more than forty-five issues in all. The Crockett almanacs were largely responsible for the creation of the tall-tale

Crockett–the ring-tailed-roaring, backwoods-screaming half-man/half-alligator, yaller flower of the forest who could hunt bear, kill Indians, and fool Yankees better than any other frontiersman alive. Several of the initial tales in the almanacs were based on stories drawn from Clarke's *The Life and Adventures* and Crockett's *A Narrative of the Life of David Crockett;* for this reason it has often been thought that Crockett actually authored some of the tales, but he did not. Over time the tales became increasingly fantastic, and Crockett was transformed into a kind of mythic superhero. Through the almanacs Crockett's travels continued posthumously; his adventures took him all over the United States and into Central and South America, the Pacific Islands, the Far East, and even outer space, where he saved the planet from destruction by ripping the tail off Halley's Comet.

The legend eventually displaced the man. When such writers as Walter Blair, Constance M. Rourke, and Richard M. Dorson began the twentieth-century reexamination of Crockett in the 1930s, it was quite naturally as a native comic legend and epic folk hero–a point of view that tended to value the tall tales over the autobiography. James Atkins Shackford's definitive biography, *Davy Crockett: The Man and the Legend* (1956), did much to restore the historical Crockett and establish the historicity of *A Narrative of the Life of David Crockett*. More recently, scholars from many disciplines have been interested in the interplay between David Crockett the man and Davy Crockett the legend and in the various historical, cultural, and literary forces that have helped to construct and perpetuate the Crockett legend that now seems to have had more to do with print culture than with folk culture.

While popular interest in Crockett has declined considerably from its peak in the early 1950s, when nearly every young child in America owned a coonskin cap and could sing the words to Disney's "The Ballad of Davy Crockett," the Tennessean shows no signs of disappearing from the pantheon of American legends. *A Narrative of the Life of David Crockett* should remain an important work in the American literary canon for some time to come: as the prototype of an indigenous form of American humor; as a document of colloquial American dialect and usage; as one of the earliest American autobiographies (published only sixteen years after the first American edition of Franklin's autobiography); as a central cultural artifact in the construction of a national type; and as an historical record of the life and times of one of the most popular American heroes.

**Bibliography:**

Miles Tanenbaum, "Following Davy's Trail: A Crockett Bibliography," in *Crockett at Two Hundred,* edited by Michael A. Lofaro and Joe Cummings (Knoxville: University of Tennessee Press, 1989), pp. 192–241.

**Biographies:**

Edward Sylvester Ellis, *The Life of Colonel David Crockett* (Philadelphia: Porter & Coates, 1884);

Charles Fletcher Allen, *David Crockett, Scout, Small Boy, etc.* (Philadelphia: Lippincott, 1911);

Constance M. Rourke, *Davy Crockett* (New York: Harcourt, Brace, 1934);

Edwin Justice Mayer, *Sunrise in My Pocket: or The Last Days of Davy Crockett* (New York: Messner, 1941);

Irwin Shapiro, *Yankee Thunder: The Legendary Life of Davy Crockett* (New York: Messner, 1944);

Walter Blair, *Davy Crockett–Frontier Hero: The Truth as He Told It–The Legend as His Friends Built It* (New York: Coward-McCann, 1955); republished as *Davy Crockett: Legendary Frontier Hero* (Springfield, Ill.: Lincoln-Herndon Press, 1986);

James Atkins Shackford, *David Crockett: The Man and the Legend,* edited by John B. Shackford (Chapel Hill: University of North Carolina Press, 1956);

Mark Derr, *The Frontiersman: The Real Life and Many Legends of Davy Crockett* (New York: Morrow, 1993).

**References:**

Walter Blair, "Six Davy Crocketts," *Southwest Review,* 25 (1940): 443–462;

William R. Chemerka, *The Davy Crockett Almanac and Book of Lists* (Austin, Tex.: Eakin, 1999);

Richard M. Dorson, ed., *Davy Crockett: American Comic Legend* (New York: Rockland Editions, 1939);

Bill Groneman, *Death of a Legend: The Myth and Mystery Surrounding the Death of Davy Crockett* (Plano: Republic of Texas Press, 1999);

Richard Boyd Hauck, *Crockett: A Bio-Bibliography* (Westport, Conn.: Greenwood Press, 1982); republished as *Davy Crockett: A Handbook* (Lincoln: University of Nebraska Press, 1986);

Dan Kilgore, *How Did Davy Die?* (College Station: Texas A&M University Press, 1978);

Michael A. Lofaro and Joe Cummings, eds., *Crockett at Two Hundred: New Perspectives on the Man and the Myth* (Knoxville: University of Tennessee Press, 1989);

Lofaro, ed., *Davy Crockett: The Man, The Legend, The Legacy, 1786–1986* (Knoxville: University of Tennessee Press, 1985);

Lofaro, ed., *The Tall Tales of Davy Crockett: The Second Nashville Series of Crockett Almanacs, 1839–1841,* facsimile edition (Knoxville: University of Tennessee Press, 1987);

Franklin J. Meine, ed., *The Crockett Almanacks: Nashville Series, 1835–1838* (Chicago: Caxton Club, 1955);

Michael J. Mendenhall, *Davy Crockett and the Unconstitutional Welfare State* (Monterey, Cal.: Institute for Constitutional Research, 1990).

# J. D. B. De Bow

*(10 July 1820 – 27 February 1867)*

David A. Rawson
*Worcester State College*

See also the De Bow entries in *DLB 3: Antebellum Writers in New York and the South* and *DLB 79: American Magazine Journalists, 1850–1900.*

BOOKS: *Political Annals of the South* (Charleston, S.C.: Burges & James, 1845);

*Introductory to the First Report of the Bureau of Statistics, of the State of Louisiana* (New Orleans, 1850);

*The Industrial Resources, etc. of the Southern and Western States: Embracing a View of Their Commerce, Agriculture, Manufactures, Internal Improvements, Slave and Free Labor, Slavery Institutions, Products, etc., of the South, Together with Historical and Statistical Sketches of the Different States and Cities of the Union—Statistics of the United States Commerce and Manufactures, from the Earliest Periods, Compared with Other Leading Powers—the Results of the Different Census Returns since 1790, and Returns of the Census of 1850, on Population, Agriculture, and General Industry, etc.,* 3 volumes (New Orleans & New York: Office of *De Bow's Review,* 1852–1853); enlarged, 4 volumes (New Orleans & New York: Office of *De Bow's Review,* 1852–1853); republished as *The Industrial Resources, Statistics, etc., of the United States, and More Particularly of the Southern and Western States; Embracing a View of Their Commerce, Agriculture, Manufactures, Internal Improvements, Slave and Free Labor, Slavery Institutions, Products, etc., of the South* (New York: Appleton, 1854); republished as *Encyclopedia of the Trade and Commerce of the United States, More Particularly of the Southern and Western States; Giving a View of the Commerce, Agriculture, Manufactures, Internal Improvements, Slave and Free Labor, Slavery Institutions, Products, etc., of the South,* 2 volumes (Washington, D.C., 1853; London: Trübner, 1854); republished as *The Southern States, Embracing a Series of Papers Condensed from the Earlier Volumes of De Bow's Review, Upon Slavery and the Slave Institutions of the South, Internal Improvements, etc., Together with Historical and Statistical Sketches of Several of the Southern and Southwestern*

*James D. B. De Bow (from De Bow's Review, June 1867)*

*States; Their Agriculture, Commerce, etc.* (Washington, D.C. & New Orleans, 1856);

*The Seventh Census of the United States: 1850. Embracing a Statistical View of Each of the States and Territories, Arranged by Counties, Towns, etc.* (Washington, D.C.: Armstrong, 1853);

*Statistical View of the United States, Embracing Its Territory, Population—White, Free Colored, and Slave—Moral and Social Condition, Industry, Property, and Revenue; the*

*Detailed Statistics of Cities, Towns and Counties; Being a Compendium of the Seventh Census, to Which Are Added the Results of Every Previous Census, Beginning with 1790, in Comparative Tables, with Explanatory and Illustrative Notes Based upon the Schedules and Other Official Sources of Information* (Washington, D.C.: Nicholson, 1854);

*Mortality Statistics of the Seventh Census of the United States, 1850* (Washington, D.C.: Nicholson, 1855);

*Introductory Remarks on Taking the Chair as President of the Southern Convention, at Knoxville, Tennessee, on the Tenth of August, 1857* (Washington, D.C.: Lem Towers, 1857);

*The Interest in Slavery of the Southern Non-slave-holder. The Right of Peaceful Secession. Slavery in the Bible,* 1860 Association Tracts, no. 5 (Charleston, S.C.: Evans & Cogswell, 1860);

*Tennessee Central or Pacific Railroad: Letters from J. D. B. De Bow, President of the Road, to the Public of Tennessee and Capitalists of the Country Generally* (Nashville, 1866).

OTHER: *De Bow's Commercial Review of the South and West,* edited by De Bow, volumes 1–8 (January 1846–June 1850); volumes 9–13, renamed *De Bow's Review of the Southern and Western States* (July 1850–December 1852); volumes 14–34, renamed *De Bow's Review* (1853–1867).

J. D. B. De Bow is most often remembered as the founder and editor of *De Bow's Review,* a leading platform for proslavery and pro-Southern opinion in antebellum America. Yet, his magazine was more than that: it was an advocate of economic reform in the South in the face of a rapidly changing national economic order. While defending the efficacy of plantation society generally and slavery specifically, De Bow advocated unprecedented public investment in the commercial infrastructure of the region. He argued that such investments were necessary if Southerners were to avert subjection to Northern interests, as was then developing, and return the region to its historic national dominance. The pages of his monthly were a compendium of statistics and articles intended as lessons in political economy for all those who had yet to realize the plight of the South. Thus *De Bow's Review* was not so much a literary journal—as were the contemporaneous *Southern Literary Messenger* and *Southern Quarterly Review*—as it was an educational effort. These lessons, however, proved difficult for most Southerners to embrace, let alone master. By the mid 1850s De Bow had come to believe that the battle for control of the national economy was lost. He argued for secession in the *Review,* making his a conspicuous voice for both slavery and Southern nationalism. After the war, that

advocacy proved an impediment to future success. *De Bow's Review* died shortly after its editor's death, and his impassioned words have since faded from the national memory.

James Dunwoody Brownson De Bow was born on 10 July 1820 into a middle-class, commercial family in Charleston, South Carolina, the principal business center of the seaboard South. His father, Garrett De Bow, was a wholesale grocer of Dutch descent (né De Boog) from New Jersey. In 1800 De Bow married Mary Bridget Norton, daughter of a Revolutionary War hero from Charleston, and they settled in her hometown. Their marriage produced five children before Garrett's death in 1826. At that time De Bow's father had been in sizable financial difficulty, the resolution of which left his mother with scant means to support and educate her children. She insisted that the young De Bow receive the best education possible, however, and begged and borrowed the necessary monies so that he could establish himself in life without a patrimony. As a result of her efforts, De Bow became a widely read scholar, well known among the academic community in Charleston—a circumstance that was of value to him when he lost his mother and older brother to cholera in 1836 at age sixteen. His orphaned state and recognized academic skills gained him admission to the newly established College of Charleston on a scholarship in 1839, after three years spent wandering among various relatives and unrewarding jobs. He graduated at the head of his class in 1843 and was admitted to the South Carolina bar a year later.

Events in the city during the summer of 1844 drew De Bow away from his struggling legal practice into the world of journalism. While in college, he had written pieces for the daily newspaper in Charleston, the *Courier,* with some success. Now his essays appeared in Daniel Whitaker's nationally recognized *Southern Quarterly Review.* The July 1844 issue carried his "Characteristics of the Statesman," a commentary on contemporary political figures favorable to John C. Calhoun, venerated in South Carolina. De Bow's perspective was at once patriarchal and elitist, arguing for government by educated, disinterested statesmen such as Calhoun and not by manipulators of the uneducated masses like Calhoun's nemesis, Andrew Jackson. The essay earned him a regular place in Whitaker's pages, as his views fit squarely with those of several major Southern intellectual figures of his day, many of whom were later important contributors to De Bow's own magazine.

Whitaker had close ties to one of these figures: George Frederick Holmes, a major contributor to his magazine. Holmes, in turn, was part of an informal cadre of Southern intellectuals that included William Gilmore Simms, Nathaniel Beverley Tucker, Edmund

Ruffin, and James Henry Hammond. These men longed for an idealized past, now seemingly lost, when the best-educated men of property ruled American society. They believed that blatant self-interest among politicians and voters had brought the country to the verge of ruin, at least relative to the true "republican" values of the Revolutionary era; the South needed to return to the virtuous models of its heroic past by recognizing the genius of men like themselves and submit democratically to their disinterested governance. This group promoted their views in a growing number of Southern magazines, such as the *Southern Literary Messenger,* the *Southern and Western Monthly,* the *Farmer's Register,* and the *Southern Quarterly Review.* De Bow's education, traditional and conservative as it was, told him that this backward-looking ideology was historically correct; thus he found himself among like-minded individuals who hoped to preserve true "Jeffersonian" ideals against the onslaught of unlettered demagogues. For the rest of his life De Bow demonstrated a marked ambivalence over the tendency of democracy to hinder such just government.

In August 1844 De Bow's newfound popularity among the political leaders of the state accorded him a seat as secretary to an important Democratic Party meeting in Charleston during that presidential election year. This meeting was among the first to urge the creation of a Commercial Convention among the Southern states. Such a convention, it was hoped, would build political unity among those states in the face of growing abolitionist sentiment in the North, while also establishing institutions within the South to encourage projects that improved and advanced Southern commerce. At the head of the list of such projects were the myriad "internal improvements" that had been the political rallying point for trans-Appalachian and Southern farmers since the early days of the Republic. De Bow gravitated to this agenda readily and promoted it himself for many years to come.

Through the winter of 1844–1845 and into the following spring, Southern political and business leaders accumulated commitments to a meeting of the Commercial Convention in Memphis in November 1845. Meanwhile, De Bow was building a reputation for himself in the pages of the *Southern Quarterly Review.* This reputation was capped by an essay that appeared in the July 1845 issue, "The Northern Pacific; California and the Oregon Question," in which De Bow argued for moderation and careful negotiation with Great Britain over the then-disputed Oregon territory; the article received accolades throughout the country for his balanced and thoughtful analysis. The essay was De Bow's last for Whitaker, however. A dispute

with the editor over his scholarship in the "Political Annals of Carolina," from the preceding issue, along with a claim to subscribers of being Whitaker's assistant rather than just a contributor, resulted in his leaving the *Southern Quarterly Review* that September. Yet, that departure had little long-term effect on his reputation. He wrote a series of essays for the *Courier* that fall detailing the need for and purpose of the forthcoming Memphis Convention, the reaction to which brought De Bow election as a delegate to that convention. The response also convinced him that a new commercial magazine dedicated to Southern interests could be sustained, if undertaken. On his way to Memphis, he passed through New Orleans, taking note of its commercial vitality. To De Bow, the business activities and attitudes of the city represented the things that needed to be fashioned throughout the South; they also reinforced his belief that the slave-based agricultural economy of the region was still viable and honorable.

De Bow shared his observations with his fellow delegates in Memphis, finding considerable sympathy and support for his idea of a Southern commercial review. He hoped that such a magazine would operate along the lines of the popular *Hunt's Merchants' Magazine* of New York, a medium providing up-to-date data from which Southern farmers could make informed decisions about their operations. At the same time it would spread word of the reform program the convention proposed and use that program to build a political platform on the coinciding agricultural interests of the South and the West. By the close of the convention, De Bow was determined to proceed and had gained the backing of many of the Southern leaders present in Memphis, Calhoun among them. So he left Memphis not for Charleston, with its ties to the Atlantic coast, but for New Orleans, with its ties to the American interior, believing it to be the best place to start such a magazine. There the *Commercial Review of the South and West, a Monthly Journal of Trade, Commercial Polity, Agriculture, Manufactures, Internal Improvements, and General Literature* made its first appearance in January 1846. The title was shortened to *De Bow's Review of the Southern and Western States* in 1850, before finally settling into the historically recognized *De Bow's Review* in 1853.

Despite this persistence, De Bow's path to success was not smooth. The magazine was frequently in financial trouble, a customary attribute of Southern magazines of the day. Cash was scarce in the Southern economy, especially in rural places away from the urban centers of the region. As a result the plantation economy, at the local level, depended on ledger-credit exchanges of one commodity for another—called in-kind transactions—just as it had in the colonial era. With little cash in circulation, subscriber payments to distant magazine publishers were always problematic, and De Bow's experience was not exceptional. His start-up capital was depleted by the summer of 1847. Lacking sufficient subscription payments to sustain the effort further, he suspended publication for six months beginning that August; a similarly inspired suspension struck the magazine in early 1849. Eventually, De Bow secured the requisite capital to continue, through both new financial backing and improving subscription payments.

One De Bow biographer suggests that some of these financial difficulties were self-inflicted, the result of dividing his energies. On his arrival in New Orleans, De Bow became involved in many civic roles beyond his publishing one. He was a driving force behind the founding of the Louisiana Historical Society and the University of New Orleans, ventures he believed essential to preserving and sustaining Southern culture. His prominence in these ventures led to two prestigious appointments—one public, one private—in 1848. First, he was selected by the university to be its chair of commerce, public economy, and statistics. This post led, in turn, to his appointment as director of the Bureau of Statistics in Louisiana as the most-qualified candidate for the post in the state. Both of these duties drew De Bow away from the offices of the *Review,* an absence that likely contributed to its operating problems. Yet the two suspensions probably also helped him to press his case for Southern economic reform more fully once publication resumed. These breaks gave him the time and the opportunity to amass considerable statistical evidence in support of his arguments, primarily by simply discharging these two appointments. The mass of data he accumulated became the largest of his published works, the three-volume opus, *The Industrial Resources, etc. of the Southern and Western States: Embracing a View of Their Commerce, Agriculture, Manufactures, Internal Improvements, Slave and Free Labor, Slavery Institutions, Products, etc., of the South, Together with Historical and Statistical Sketches of the Different States and Cities of the Union . . . , with an Appendix,* published in 1852 and 1853 and drawn from articles he wrote for the *Review* in the intervening years.

De Bow's evolution from historical analyst and political commentator to statistician was completed, in the public mind at least, in 1853, when he was named superintendent of the seventh federal census, taken in 1850. The appointment was political, based on De Bow's loyalty to the Democratic Party. The election of the Democratic presidential candidate, Franklin Pierce, in late 1852 led to a housecleaning of political appointees left over from Millard Fill-

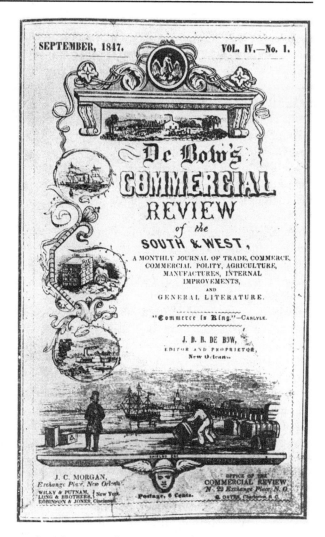

Cover for an issue of the commercial journal De Bow founded in January 1846 and edited until his death in 1867

more's Whig administration in the spring of 1853. The incumbent census superintendent, John C. G. Kennedy, was removed from office without consideration for his masterful handling of the 1850 census, an enumeration that some historians have called the best of that century. De Bow himself was full of praise for Kennedy, whose preliminary reports had found considerable space in the pages of *De Bow's Review.* Thus, when Pierce appointed him to succeed Kennedy, De Bow sought to maintain and extend those standards. The result was the 1854 publication of the most comprehensive set of census statistics ever produced in the United States to that time: *Statistical View of the United States, Embracing Its Territory, Population—White, Free Colored, and Slave—Moral and Social Condition, Industry, Property, and Revenue; the Detailed Statistics of Cities, Towns and Counties; Being a Compendium of the Seventh Census.* This study was followed in 1855 by a comparably exhaustive report on mortality. This second publication completed his responsibilities in Washington, and De Bow was then able to return to New Orleans and his magazine. He was by that time a nationally known figure, however, rather than simply a regional one.

This brief period was thus pivotal in De Bow's life and work. During his Washington years, he married Caroline Poe, cousin of Edgar Allan Poe and part of the Richmond intellectual circle behind the *Southern Literary Messenger*–further evidence of his close ties to the Southern intellectual and political leadership. After leaving Washington he became a widely traveled lecturer, chair of the 1857 Knoxville Commercial Convention, and author of articles on the United States for the *Encyclopedia Brittanica,* as well as editor of his own monthly magazine. Yet, his personal fame came as a result of a deteriorating political situation, a situation he helped to shape with that magazine.

As a result of his census studies, he came to believe that the South was already in an economically inferior position to that of the North, a circumstance that would only increase in the future, particularly as the North grew in population at a rate that exceeded the growth of the Southern population. Yet, his simultaneous analysis of pauperism and mortality in the United States showed that poverty and early death were integral byproducts of the Northern free-labor economy. In his mind, these disturbing characteristics confirmed the immorality of Northern life generally and the hypocrisy of abolitionists specifically. By publishing these opinions in his own review, as well as the data they were based on, De Bow brought down upon himself the wrath of Northern abolitionists and Midwestern "free-soil" interests. As that criticism increased, De Bow's stridency in defending the Southern economy and culture increased as well. Yet, despite the outcry, his message seems to have fallen largely on deaf ears in both the North and the South. Some historians believe that the increasingly strident tone of *De Bow's Review* during the 1850s is not just a response to Northern and abolitionist criticism, but also a display of his frustration at Southerners' unwillingness or inability to follow the reform plan that could save the South, which was detailed monthly in *De Bow's Review*.

Ultimately, De Bow argued that secession was the only course for the South to follow. If the Southern states could not sustain themselves and their way of life within the existing union of sovereign states, then they had every right to preserve their culture and society by leaving that union. The South now needed to be politically independent from a federal system that, because of the changing demographics of the country, was evermore rapidly turning against Southern traditions. For De Bow, and for the many others who agreed with him, there was no inherent moral dilemma in slavery and plantation society. This social system was one that, when run with proper recognition of patriarchal authority, took care of everyone within it, slave or free, from cradle to grave; moreover, the census data showed these beliefs were true despite Northern claims to the contrary. To De Bow and other Southern leaders, the ideals of free labor and free soil were figments of the Northern imagination, not realities of Northern life.

In this regard, De Bow is a perfect representative of the proslavery argument, whether on a moral, political, economic, or legal level. He was not an original thinker, but he was a part of the intellectual discourse that created, refined, and disseminated the proslavery perspective in the 1840s and 1850s. This perspective can be seen especially in his many invitations to other proslavery Southerners–writers such as George Fitzhugh, Edmund Ruffin, George Frederick Holmes, and William Gregg–to make their case in the pages of *De Bow's Review*. As the political position of the South withered through the 1850s, the carefully planned objectivity of his earliest issues slowly and inexorably gave way to the unmitigated partisanship of his wartime ones.

The war years were difficult for all of the South, as well as for De Bow. The capture of New Orleans in 1862 drove *De Bow's Review* out of the city and back to South Carolina, landing first in Charleston and then in Columbia. The disruption of the Southern economy caused by warfare and the naval blockade left De Bow with shortages of cash, paper, and printing supplies, even as he moved his office to safer quarters. As a result he was forced to suspend publication during much of the war, briefly at first in 1862, then almost continuously from late 1862 through early 1866, with only a brief publication of issues in mid 1864. During this period De Bow was appointed to the Produce Loan Board, an agency of the Confederate government that raised revenue for the war effort through the sale of agricultural produce "loaned" to the government by Southern farmers. While his service in this position was exemplary, corruption among subordinates severely limited the effectiveness of the board to raise money, leaving De Bow the focus of intense criticism. Critics also attacked the wealth he made from well-timed investments at the start of the war in companies central to the war effort, which allowed De Bow a degree of comfort that stood as a striking contrast to the privation of most Southerners in the war.

At war's end, De Bow restarted *De Bow's Review* with an eye toward promoting Southern commerce once again, only now within the framework of the lenient Reconstruction policies of President Andrew Johnson. He supported Johnson's approach as a pragmatic one; that leniency was reasonable because of the common interests of North and South, and because of the perceived need to let the South solve the race and labor problems created by Emancipation for itself. De Bow died on 27 February 1867, a month before Radical Republicans in Congress, who wanted to completely reorganize Southern society, seized control of Reconstruction policy through acts passed in March 1867. *De Bow's Review* never regained prestige or authority in the postwar South. The magazine was already in financial trouble at the time of De Bow's death; his wife and editorial staff could not save it, despite three years' worth of effort to do so.

Thus De Bow's legacy centers on his antebellum commentaries, which are abhorred by most modern observers. He is seen as a reactionary rather than a visionary figure. Yet, his basic argument, that Southern economic independence was completely dependent upon the investment in public institutions and modern technology, anticipates in many ways the "New South" perspective of later commentators such as Henry Grady. De Bow essentially argued this view before the war, and Grady argued it afterward. While De Bow can thus be said to be the lost voice of the Lost Cause, he can also be said to be the harbinger of postwar arguments for economic and social reform in the American South.

## Bibliography:

James Adelbert McMillen, comp. *The Works of James D. B. De Bow; A Bibliography of* De Bow's Review *with a Check List of his Miscellaneous Writings, including Contributions to Periodicals and a List of References Relating to James D. B. De Bow,* Heartman's Historical Series no. 52 (Hattiesburg, Miss.: Book Farm, 1940).

## Biographies:

Willis Duke Weatherford, *James Dunwoody Brownson De Bow* (Charlottesville, Va.: Historical Publishing, 1935);

Ottis Clark Skipper, *J. D. B. De Bow, Magazinist of the Old South* (Athens: University of Georgia Press, 1958).

## References:

Drew Gilpin Faust, *A Sacred Circle: The Dilemma of the Intellectual in the Old South, 1840–1860* (Baltimore: Johns Hopkins University Press, 1977), pp. 91, 103, 125;

Paul F. Paskoff and Daniel J. Wilson, eds., *The Cause of the South: Selections from* De Bow's Review, *1846–1867* (Baton Rouge: Louisiana State University Press, 1982).

## Papers:

The bulk of James Dunwoody Brownson De Bow's papers can be found in the J. D. B De Bow Papers at Duke University; many of his letters are scattered throughout the archive collections of his many correspondents as well.

# Eliza Ann Dupuy

## (1814 – 29 December 1880)

Dorri R. Beam

*University of California, Berkeley*

BOOKS: *The Pirate's Daughter,* 2 volumes (New York: Ely & Robinson, 1845); republished as *Celeste: The Pirate's Daughter. A Tale of the Southwest* (Cincinnati & St. Louis: Stratton & Barnard, 1849);

*The Conspirator* (New York: D. Appleton/Philadelphia: G. S. Appleton, 1850);

*The Separation: The Divorce: and the Coquette's Punishment* (Cincinnati: James, 1851);

*The Adventures of a Gentleman in Search of Miss Smith* (Cincinnati: Edwards & Goshorn, 1852);

*Florence; or, The Fatal Vow* (Cincinnati: Stratton, 1852);

*Emma Walton; or, Trials and Triumph* (Cincinnati: James, 1854);

*Annie Seldon; or, The Concealed Treasure* (Cincinnati: Mendenhall, 1854);

*Ashleigh: A Tale of the Olden Time* (Cincinnati: Pearson, 1854);

*The Country Neighborhood* (New York: Harper, 1855);

*The Huguenot Exiles; or, The Times of Louis XIV. A Historical Novel* (New York: Harper, 1856);

*The Planter's Daughter: A Tale of Louisiana* (New York: Fetridge, 1857);

*The Mysterious Marriage: A True Romance of New York Life* (Philadelphia: Peterson & Brothers, 1858);

*Why Did He Marry Her?* (Philadelphia: Peterson & Brothers, 1870);

*Michael Rudolph. "The Bravest of the Brave"* (Philadelphia: Peterson & Brothers, 1870);

*How He Did It* (Philadelphia: Peterson & Brothers, 1871); republished as *Was He Guilty? or, How He Did It* (Philadelphia: Peterson & Brothers, 1873);

*The Cancelled Will* (Philadelphia: Peterson & Brothers, 1872);

*Who Shall Be Victor? A Sequel to "The Cancelled Will"* (Philadelphia: Peterson & Brothers, 1872);

*All for Love; or, The Outlaw's Bride* (Philadelphia: Peterson & Brothers, 1873);

*The Dethroned Heiress* (Philadelphia: Peterson & Brothers, 1873);

*The Gipsy's Warning* (Philadelphia: Peterson & Brothers, 1873);

*The Mysterious Guest* (Philadelphia: Peterson & Brothers, 1873);

*The Hidden Sin. A Sequel to "The Dethroned Heiress"* (Philadelphia: Peterson & Brothers, 1874);

*The Clandestine Marriage* (Philadelphia: Peterson & Brothers, 1875);

*The Discarded Wife; or, Will She Succeed?* (Philadelphia: Peterson & Brothers, 1875);

*A New Way to Win a Fortune* (Philadelphia: Peterson & Brothers, 1875);

*The Shadow in the House: A Husband for a Lover* (New York: J. S. Ogilvie, 1881).

Eliza Ann Dupuy was the prolific and popular author of some two dozen novels published for the mass market in the mid nineteenth century. Often compared with fellow Southerner E. D. E. N. Southworth, although she never quite attained the same degree of success, Dupuy wrote stories that are generally more sensational and lurid than Southworth's. Readers have found that Dupuy's style has little in common with the quiet domestic novels that are most often associated with nineteenth-century women writers. As an April 1855 *Harper's* review of Dupuy's *The Country Neighborhood* (1855) noted, her scenes are generally "set forth in high-wrought language," often inclining toward "an excessive intensity of expression," and her plots are sure to include "situations of exciting interest, portraying the lurid exhibitions of unbridled passion."

Born in Petersburg, Virginia, in 1814, Eliza Ann Dupuy was one of the younger of Jesse Dupuy and Mary Ann Thompson Sturdevant Dupuy's nine children. On her father's side she was descended from one of the oldest Huguenot families in the state. Colonel Bartholomew Dupuy, officer of the guards of Louis XIV and a staunch Huguenot, left France after the revocation of the Edict of Nantes in 1685. He received a land grant from James II and led a small band of Huguenot exiles to Virginia, settling on the James River. Dupuy was proud of her Huguenot heritage and made her ancestor's biography the basis for her 1856 historical romance, *The Huguenot Exiles; or, The Times of Louis XIV.*

Early in Dupuy's life, her family moved to Norfolk, where her father earned a living as a merchant and shipowner. A storm at sea, among other events, caused her father's financial failure, and the family was forced to move west to Kentucky. During this crisis Dupuy began a course of self-education and, out of economic necessity, wrote her first novel at age fourteen. "Merton: A Tale of the Revolution" was reportedly accepted at once for publication, but no copy remains in existence and the publisher is unknown. Any income Dupuy received from this first literary effort was likely of great use to her large family; her father died at about this time, of "disappointment and broken fortune," as Dupuy put it in an undated letter to the firm of Childs and Peterson, compilers of *A Critical Dictionary of English Literature and British and American Authors* (1859).

After the death of her father, Dupuy put her self-education to further use and became a governess for the family of Thomas G. Ellis of Natchez, Mississippi. The Natchez community had a particularly literary bent and proved well suited to a budding author. Ellis was the half brother of Catharine Ann Warfield, who also became a popular author and published in the same mass venues as Dupuy. Like other members of the Natchez literary community, including Warfield; Warfield's sister, the poet Eleanor Ware Lee; S. S. Prentice, the lawyer and orator; and Joseph Holt Ingraham, another hugely popular writer, Dupuy benefited from frequent literary "sessions," in which manuscripts were read aloud and discussed. It was even rumored that Ingraham took one of Dupuy's early manuscripts and, instead of critiquing it, published it under his own name with the title *Lafitte: The Pirate of the Gulf* (1836). Dupuy's charge, Sarah Anne Ellis, must have been inspired by the literary sessions; she grew up to be an author herself and wrote several books under the pseudonym "Filia." While in the Natchez area, Dupuy is also said to have taught Verona Howell, future wife of Jefferson Davis.

By her own account in a letter to Childs and Peterson, Dupuy thought her first effort at a novel was "crude" and "resolved that her next effort should be worthy to be ranked among 'books that are books.'" It is unclear whether Dupuy refers to "Merton" or *The Pirate's Daughter* (1845), her first extant novel. She thus devoted herself "to such studies as are necessary to discipline my mind, and form my task." The result was one of her major successes, *The Conspirator* (1850), an historical novel about Aaron Burr written during her stay in Natchez. Excerpts from the story appeared in the *Southern Literary Messenger* in 1838 with an editorial disclaimer that promised the author was "no conceited

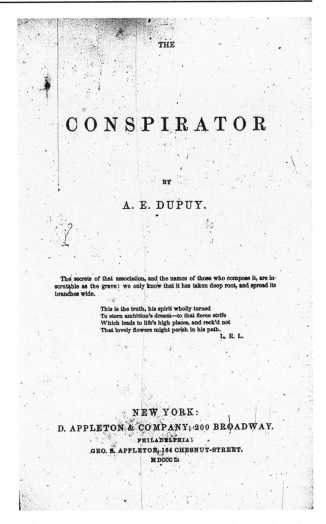

*Title page for Eliza Ann Dupuy's 1850 novel, a fictionalized account of the life of Aaron Burr (Wright American Fiction, microfilm; Woodbridge, Conn.: Research Publications, 1970–1978)*

blue-stocking, no vain belle . . . She meekly tasks her powers to aid a widowed mother in support of a family of helpless orphans." In 1843 the *New World* serialized the work in its entirety, and in 1850 the Appletons published *The Conspirator* as a book, which sold more than twenty-four thousand copies.

*The Conspirator* is a highly fictionalized account of the life of Aaron Burr—here called Colonel Alwin—and his self-destructive ambition, viewed primarily from his daughters' perspectives. Alwin stops at nothing in his treasonous plans to wrest American and Mexican land for himself under the guise of defending the United States from Mexican incursion. Dupuy's readers are only obliquely privy to Alwin's schemes and military maneuvers, however, and learn of them almost solely through their intersection with the daughters' lives.

Nonetheless, the daughters turn out to be central to the negotiations when they find themselves pawns in a series of power exchanges brokered by their father. The primary narrative thread revolves around Julie de Bourg, Alwin's adopted daughter, whose hand in marriage is demanded by the evil Don Pedro Zavala in exchange for the cooperation of the Mexican army. This much-anticipated event is delayed by twists of the plot and finally canceled altogether by the intervention of Julie's long-lost biological father, who arrives just in time to halt the wedding. Meanwhile, Alwin's plans deteriorate because of Zavala's treachery and the vengeful plotting of Theresa, a "wild woman" who is revealed to be the mother of Alwin's first wife–the wife who died of a broken heart when he accused her (wrongly) of infidelity. The final blow to the already broken Alwin occurs on the final page of the novel, just as Theresa prophesies: the apple of his eye, daughter Isabel, is killed by pirates.

Dupuy's plot defies concise summary, but a recurring theme in *The Conspirator* insists that women are the primary victims of men's ambition. Dupuy offers the marriage of Julie to her true love, Charles (Alwin's reviled secret son and Theresa's grandson), as a counterpoint to the havoc Alwin's ambition has wreaked. Unlike Alwin, Charles "valued the joys of domestic life far above the distinctions his acknowledged talents might easily have won. He occupied a high standing in his profession, but he steadily refused to aspire beyond that. The charms of his home were too dearly prized to sacrifice them for a distant and doubtful good." Though many of Dupuy's novels claim to endorse this vision of humble and moderated domestic bliss, the primary focus of her stories consistently ranges far afield of such prosaic scenes into arenas of intense emotion, sumptuous luxury, and exciting events.

During that same period in which *The Conspirator* was published in a variety of formats, other pieces of Dupuy's fiction were appearing frequently in national magazines. By the late 1830s and early 1840s she had placed work in the *Southern Literary Messenger, Godey's Lady's Book,* the *Columbian Magazine,* the *New World,* and a bit later, the *Knickerbocker Magazine.* Gradually she gave up teaching and devoted herself entirely to writing. In the 1850s Dupuy published six novels with Cincinnati publishers before publishing again with a large New York firm.

In 1855 Harper and Brothers published Dupuy's *The Country Neighborhood,* the unassuming title of which belies the turmoil of its vivid and melodramatic plot. Said to be based on "actual life" in the area outlying Natchez, *The Country Neighborhood* is the highly sensationalized story of Lisette, a mulatto woman who is raised thinking she is the only daughter of a wealthy white plantation owner. As such, her marriage is arranged to the son of a neighboring plantation owner,

a young man she loves passionately. Her love is never returned by him, and the marriage is called off when it is revealed that she is the daughter of a slave woman. Thus begins the ever-thickening plot of the intense and haughty Lisette to capture the love of Lenox and vanquish all competitors for his affections. Lisette haunts the romance of Lenox and the sprightly Flora and, through mystical powers and strange poisons, drains Flora of all vitality. Such fascinating villainesses are a primary feature of many of Dupuy's novels. Despite their evil tendencies, they are often the most interesting, because the most developed, characters. Certainly readers quickly lose interest in the wan and wasted Flora. To create Lisette, however, Dupuy flagrantly exploits racist stereotypes–specifically the portrayal of black women as sexual aggressors. Furthermore, Lisette's scheming ends in a harrowing scene of torture that is shocking in its racist and sexist virulence.

Dupuy continued to harness popular prejudice, this time nativist anti-Catholicism, in her next novel, *The Huguenot Exiles,* also published by Harper and Brothers. This historical novel unfolds the personal biography of her ancestor Bartholomew Dupuy, his trials in seventeenth-century France at the hands of the Catholics, and his subsequent flight to Virginia. In this novel, thought by many contemporaries to be her strongest, Dupuy uses her gift for lurid, overwrought descriptive language to characterize Catholics as decadent, avaricious, and perverse. Rosaries and bibles are encrusted with jewels that bespeak the worldly, rather than otherworldly, concerns of their owners. The corpulent priests are ornately attired and sadistic. Dupuy displays a knack for what David Reynolds, in *Beneath the American Renaissance: The Subversive Imagination in the Age of Emerson and Melville* (1988), has called "immoral reform" literature, which was "epitomized by the sexually charged writings of antiprostitution, anti-Catholic, and temperance reformers" of the mid nineteenth century. So graphic and lengthy are the scenes of torture inflicted by the fiendish Catholics that readers may wonder at Dupuy's indulgence in such material. Indeed, in Dupuy's most highly wrought novels, emotional heights are so frenzied that love and rage, desire and revulsion, ecstasy and pain often bleed into each other and become indistinguishable.

Ann Stephens, another popular author who was editing her own *Mrs. Stephens' Illustrated New Monthly* at the time, was full of praise for *The Huguenot Exiles.* Her August 1856 review mused that "this period of history has always seemed to us as affording fine scope and material for the historical novelist, and we have frequently expressed our surprise that so good a period should remain untouched." Assuming the author was a man, she went on to suggest that "there is, perhaps, a little straining, an overdoing in most of his scenes, a piling up of the horrors–while his villains are too unmitigatedly fiendish, and his heroes too saintish, but the effect as a whole is fine. Some of his descriptive passages are absolutely grand."

Apparently Dupuy was grateful for the attention and advice; she dedicated her next novel, *The Planter's Daughter: A Tale of Louisiana* (1857), to Stephens. *The Planter's Daughter* was considered by contemporary critic James Wood Davidson, writing in his *Living Writers of the South* (1869), to be "in an eminent degree sensational." He found the novel "redolent of murders, madness, tears, robbery, revolvers, corpses, and confusions" and asserted that it "trips lightly through the mazes of guilt, blood-and-thunderous declamation, threats, stage love-making, and Italian gallantry." Even though it is indeed full of overwrought emotion and extraordinary acts of man and nature, there is reason to believe that Dupuy heeded Stephens's advice, for *The Planter's Daughter* is actually more low-key than her previous two novels.

Because its title calls to mind Caroline Hentz's successful *The Planter's Northern Bride* (1854), Dupuy's *The Planter's Daughter* might be assumed to respond to Harriet Beecher Stowe's *Uncle Tom's Cabin* (1852), as does Hentz's novel. As publisher's advertisements promised, however, *The Planter's Daughter* is "a Southern novel that is neither Anti-slavery nor Pro-Slavery." An 1857 *Godey's Lady's Book* review expressed relief that Dupuy steered clear of sectional controversy by using "care not to introduce any of those modern devices to obtain an ephemeral popularity which have rendered so many works, north and south, eminently untruthful and ridiculous, and, we may add, destructive to those fraternal feelings which should knit together all of our common country." She may not have engaged the conflict directly, but Dupuy, who resided in the South her entire life, was ardent in her Southern loyalties. She told biographer Mary T. Tardy that "as a southern woman, I would sooner have thrust my hand in a blazing fire than . . . have taken a pen in it to throw discredit on my own people." Though slavery is only a backdrop to the events of the novel, *The Planter's Daughter* resembles more forthright proslavery novels by displaying slavery as a humane institution and slaves as blithely content members of the plantation family.

*The Planter's Daughter* is the story of three adolescent children of a sugarcane planter outside of New Orleans. Dupuy revisits themes from *The Conspirator*–the dangers of male greed and ambition, the silent suffering of unrequited love, the frenzies of male lust, and the victimization of women at the hands of unscrupulous fathers and lovers–but *The Planter's Daughter* is a smoother narrative with interesting twists on the former novel. After the family is ruined by a tornado, a flood, and the planter's foolish market speculations–a series of events that kills both the weak

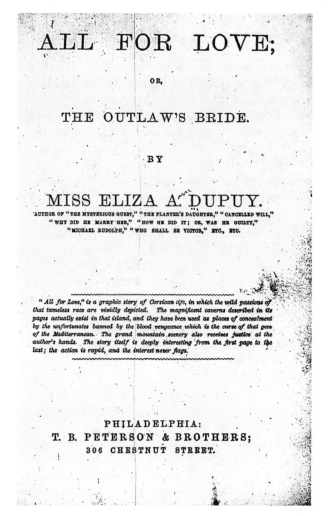

*Title page for Dupuy's 1873 melodrama set on the island of Corsica (Wright American Fiction, microfilm; Woodbridge, Conn.: Research Publications, 1970–1978)*

planter and his foppish son–the women in the family set up house elsewhere and launch a school to support themselves. Meanwhile, perhaps in response to Stephens's review, Dupuy has the villain undergo a reform–but not before he has hastened the ruin of the family in an attempt to gain the hand of the planter's beautiful daughter. At the conclusion, the dying villain admits that he really loves the planter's other, plain daughter, and the two are married as he lies on his deathbed. The plain daughter's love is strong enough to retrieve him from death's door, however, and the couple enjoys a long, happy life together.

At the eve of the Civil War, Dupuy established herself in Flemmingsburg, Kentucky. Unlike many Southern writers, she was able to continue sending stories over the Mason-Dixon Line and placing them in Northern magazines throughout the war, probably owing to her proximity to Cincinnati. One of these magazines was the *New York Ledger,* a family story-paper with immense circulation, and

Dupuy soon became a regular contributor. By 1869 she was under contract to editor Robert Bonner to furnish two stories a year, each five hundred pages long. For the exclusive right to these stories, Bonner paid Dupuy $1,250 per story, or $2,500 a year. Bonner renewed the contract every three years, and Dupuy wrote for him for the last twenty years of her life. She experienced some difficulty getting her *Ledger* serials published as books, because of Bonner's reluctance. Finally, however, Bonner allowed T. B. Peterson and Brothers, publishers of cheap popular novels, to reprint fourteen of Dupuy's serials of the 1860s and early 1870s under new titles.

A shrewd businesswoman with an eye toward managing her career, Dupuy was one of the few authors in Bonner's stable who attempted to bargain with the much beloved editor. She compared her treatment with that of Southworth, star author of the *Ledger,* and questioned the fact that her own books were not given notice in the paper as Southworth's were. She also wondered why her stories were not appearing as she sent them in. For the most part, though, she recognized that her relationship with the *Ledger* was a sound one. As Mary Noel records in *Villains Galore* (1954), Dupuy wrote to Bonner: "I have had offers that sounded finely but none that seemed to me certain of fulfillment—hence I passed them by. As a contributor engaged for the Ledger, I have considered myself certain of retaining my position on the staff as long as I desire to do so." Even in these late years, Dupuy (who had never married) continued to support family members, most particularly a brother who went blind from amaurosis. She kept up her indefatigable pace by writing for four hours every morning.

Her novels for the *Ledger,* many written under the pseudonym "Annie Young," declined in variety as she adapted to the *Ledger* formula and pace. Among those reprinted by T. B. Peterson and Brothers are more historical romances and thrillers. *Michael Rudolph. "The Bravest of the Brave"* (1870) is a fictionalization of the life of Michel Ney. *All for Love; or, The Outlaw's Bride* (1873) is an historical novel involving Corsican vendettas. *The Cancelled Will* (1872) and its sequel, *Who Shall be Victor?* (1872), also claiming a basis in factual events, extend Dupuy's interest in willful, wicked women who stop at nothing to get what they want.

The publishers' preface for *The Cancelled Will* promised that "if this book is sensational, it is of the highest order of that school, for it is pure in all its teachings." While the career of the "fair Nemesis," Nina Gordon, supposedly "founded on facts known to many persons now living," might make for fascinating reading, the publishers claimed that it could also serve as "a warning to many who, like her, rank *success* as the first good in life." Readers had to await the sequel, however, before Nina suffered any

consequences for her lack of scruples. The publishers' disclaimer that "no mother need hesitate to place any of Miss Dupuy's novels in the hands of her daughters" is most likely a reaction to the incipient backlash against popular sensation fiction waged by genteel crusaders in the last quarter of the nineteenth century. The works of Dupuy (as well as of fellow authors Southworth, Warfield, Stephens, and Hentz) were singled out as immoral and artless, and public libraries everywhere embarked on campaigns to purge them from their shelves. This facet of history is partly responsible for Dupuy's current obscurity, but scholars may find interest in her presentation of Southern life to a national audience in the Civil War era; in her representations of slavery and race; and in her extravagant literary indulgence in passions that other women authors, writing in domestic and sentimental veins, actively avoided—lust, violence, and anger.

Dupuy continued to turn out stories in the last five years of her life, despite rapidly failing health and acute eye trouble. She died on 29 December 1880, at age sixty-six, during a stay in New Orleans on the way back from an unsuccessful trip to healing springs in Arkansas. During Dupuy's lifetime, the writing career that she carefully and diligently cultivated carried her to great success and popularity. An obituary in the 13 January 1881 *Boston Evening Transcript* noted that Dupuy "leaves behind her a considerable sum earned by her ever-busy pen," testimony to the absorbing power and popular appeal of her fiction.

**Bibliography:**

James Wood Davidson, *Living Writers of the South* (New York: Carleton, 1869), pp. 174–177.

**Biographies:**

Mary Forrest, *Women of the South Distinguished in Literature* (New York: Derby & Jackson, 1861), pp. 376–385;

Mary T. Tardy, as Ida Raymond, *Southland Writers. Biographical and Critical Sketches of the Living Female Writers of the South,* 2 volumes (Philadelphia: Claxton, Remsen & Haffelfinger, 1870), pp. 28–32.

**References:**

Nina Baym, *Woman's Fiction: A Guide to Novels by and about Women in America, 1820–1870* (Ithaca, N.Y.: Cornell University Press, 1978), pp. 241–243;

Mary Noel, *Villains Galore: The Heyday of the Popular Story Weeekly* (New York: Macmillan, 1954), pp. 88–90, 181.

**Papers:**

The most significant collection of Eliza Ann Dupuy's papers is held by the Special Collections Library at Duke University.

# William Elliott III

*(27 April 1788 – 4 February 1863)*

James Everett Kibler
*University of Georgia*

See also the Elliott entry in *DLB 3: Antebellum Writers in New York and the South.*

BOOKS: *Address to the People of St. Helena Parish* (Charleston, S.C.: Estill, 1832);

*Facts Shewing Mr. Boyce's Claims, with an Examination of Col. Ashe's Report, &c.* (Charleston, S.C.: Miller, 1839?);

*Examination of Mr. Edmund Rhett's Agricultural Address, on the Question "Who Is the Producer?"* (Charleston, S.C.: Miller, 1841);

*The Planter Vindicated: His Claims Examined—To be Considered a Direct Producer: The Chief Producer: And Chief Tax-Payer of South Carolina* (Charleston, S.C.: Burges & James, 1842);

*Carolina Sports by Land and Water; Including Incidents of Devil-Fishing, &c.* (Charleston, S.C.: Burges & James, 1846; revised edition, New York: Derby & Jackson, 1859; London: Richard Bentley, 1867);

*The Anniversary Address of the State Agricultural Society, of South Carolina, Delivered in the Hall of the House of Representatives, November 30, 1848* (Columbia, S.C.: Bowman, 1848);

*Address Delivered by Special Request Before the St. Paul's Agricultural Society, May, 1850* (Charleston, S.C.: Walker & James, 1850);

*Fiesco; A Tragedy* (New York: Trehern & Williamson, 1850);

*The Letters of Agricola* (Greenville, S.C.: Office of the Southern Patriot, 1852);

*Report of the Committee of Agriculture, on the Report of the Hon. William Elliott, Late Commissioner of the State of South Carolina to the Universal Exhibit at Paris* (Columbia, S.C.: Britton, 1855); republished as *Address to the Imperial and Central Agricultural Society of France, Read Before Them at Paris, July 4, 1855* (Columbia, S.C.: Britton, 1857);

*Speech of Mr. Elliott before the Commercial Convention, Held at Knoxville, Aug. 10, 1857, on the Fortifying of Port Royal Harbor, S.C., and the Establishment of a Coaling Station*

*William Elliott III, 1822 (portrait by Thomas Sully; frontispiece for* Carolina Sports by Land and Water *[Columbia, S.C.: The State, 1918])*

*for Large Government Steamers* (Columbia: Carolina Times, 1857).

William Elliott was born in Beaufort, South Carolina, to a family of immense wealth and highest social standing. He was the eldest son of William and Phoebe Waight Elliott. He wrote essays, poetry, verse drama, and political and agricultural pamphlets. He was a planter, legislator, economist, philosopher, and authority on agricultural reform. Yet, he is remembered best for a single work, *Carolina Sports by Land and Water; Including Incidents of Devil-Fishing, &c.* (1846), a well-loved volume of sketches, tales, and essays in bold, manly prose. It is a work that vigorously recounts rattling good adventures in a finely polished style that harks back to the English personal essay of the eighteenth century. It comes from an intellect whose acute powers of discernment are never in question, and whose genial good sense is among the greatest strengths of the volume. Elliott uses baroque flourishes, mock-heroic burlesques, colloquialisms, and classical references in Latin and Greek in stories that blend the fruits of an excellent classical training with folklore and oral yarn.

The paradox of a style that mates ruggedness with grace is explained by the chivalric ideal of Elliott's planter class, whose gentlemanly code prescribed forceful action done with the best grace. Such it was with Elliott's style, and so it was with his life. In his case, truly, the style is the man. *Carolina Sports by Land and Water* mirrors well the high culture in which it was created and is thus a luxuriously rich evocation of time and place, particularly in its "Chee-Ha" plantation sketches. That time is largely the 1830s, and that place is the fields, swamps, tidal waters, and ocean about the southern tip of South Carolina. Through his code of gentlemanly behavior, duty, and accomplishment, Elliott is an excellent representative of the Southern agrarian aristocracy at its highest and most distinguished best.

The Elliott family came to Charleston from Cornwall, England, around 1685 via Barbados. William Elliott I, the author's grandfather, was the first to make Beaufort his home. There he wed Mary Barnwell, of another highly respected family. The author's father, William Elliott II, was a patriot, a public-spirited planter, and a delegate to the state convention that ratified the Constitution. In 1790 he is said to have brought sea-island cotton to South Carolina as he returned home from a trip to the West Indies. It was first grown on his plantation Myrtle Bank, near Beaufort. This long-staple cotton brought premium prices in England and became the basis of fabulous wealth along the coast, where it flourished. The life of the Elliotts was always tied to it.

By the time William Elliott III was born, on 27 April 1788, the family was already a remarkable dynasty, and through his own long and varied career he did his share to enhance the name. The family valued education, clear thinking, and unselfish service to the community, and strongly felt the responsibility to lead both in politics and in furthering learning. Each generation managed to produce without fail members who

showed a conscientious interest in the welfare of the state. Although Elliott wrote, and wrote well, and although he was for many years a statesman, gentleman farmer, and an outspoken advocate of agricultural experimentation, he was primarily a family man, who after his father's death in 1808 became the paterfamilias to whom the family looked for guidance and advice.

Elliott's life was not all seriousness and responsibility, however. At an early age, he acquired a sportsman's taste for hunting and fishing, a love that bore fruit in his most famous literary work. He was a studious youth who enjoyed a good book as well as a hunt; his education was given by private tutors at home and at Beaufort College, from which he entered Harvard as a sophomore in 1807. Although illness forced him to leave school in the winter of 1808, Harvard awarded him a degree in 1810 because of his distinguished record. Before Harvard, he was already fluent in French, and while there he came to be particularly interested in philosophy. As a contemporary biographer for the *Cyclopaedia of American Literature* (1856) put it, "he acquired early a philosophical outlook which enabled him to rise above petty, prejudiced inclinations and which caused him to look for meaning and effect in all issues." He was also something of an athlete and was reputed to be the fastest runner in the college. Apparently, long hunts on the plantation had given him physical strength.

His relationship with his parents was warm and affectionate. His father wrote him letters of counsel, which he heeded. Years later, he was remembered at Harvard for liveliness, gallantry, agreeable manners, and good breeding. He made many friendships in Cambridge that he retained throughout his life.

Elliott returned to Beaufort in 1808 at the age of twenty to help his widowed mother manage their far-flung plantations. She was much help to him until her death in 1855, when well into her eighties she was still managing Myrtle Bank.

Elliott entered politics in 1814 by winning his father's seat in the state legislature. He and essayist and agrarian poet William Grayson went to the legislature together and were close political friends. For the next eighteen years he served St. Helena Parish, but he ended his public career in 1832 when he felt he could no longer represent his constituents with a clear conscience. He had always been a firm opponent of nullification, and Beaufort had become a hotbed of nullificationists. He resigned from the Senate on 1 September 1832 and published his *Address to the People of St. Helena Parish* (1832), considered the best of his political writings. Elliott in fact deserves to be more highly regarded as a writer of pamphlets, perhaps the equal of any during his day. In his work he tried to reason with his electorate concerning the folly of nullification. He opposed the unjust tariff of protection but felt nullification was not the proper remedy. His constituents, however, instructed him by a large majority to vote for nullification; Elliott took exception, arguing that nullification was fatal to the Union and subversive of the government. He contended that the tariff, however oppressive, sprang from a power granted in the Constitution, which by his oath of office he was bound to obey. This reasoning was not satisfactory to his constituents, who, after hearing it, renewed their instructions, whereupon he resigned. In his address Elliott wrote, "You will remember my friendly caution, and look back with regret. When you have struck forward the ball of revolution, can you prescribe its path, and regulate its motion?" Elliott thus proved himself a steady man of conviction who cared nothing for ambition or aggrandizement. He would not sacrifice his principles to save his political career. With his withdrawal, the state lost one of its most articulate planter-politicians.

There were other reasons as well for his resignation. Although the legislature ran for only two months of the year, Elliott had been wearying of the verbal gymnastics of the lawyers, whom he resented as ambitious opportunists. He believed leadership was the responsibility of an enlightened aristocracy acting from reason, but in the legislature the lawyers monopolized the floor of debate, while serious men like himself sat silent. His resignation was not a gesture of arrogance, a trait that was never part of his makeup.

During his political career, he had not neglected other matters. His planting was extensive on lands that spread over a hundred miles. He had become a buyer for all these holdings and spent many hours traveling from one plantation to another in order to supervise. On 25 May 1817 he wed Ann Hutchinson Smith of Oak Lawn Plantation. The daughter of Thomas Rhett Smith Sr. of Charleston, she brought more land to the Elliott empire and a pedigree running back to an original landgrave of the colony. The Elliott lands included three rice plantations, Social Hall or Airy Hall, The Bluff, and Middle Place (all between the Ashepoo and Chee-Ha Rivers); and two cotton plantations (Ball's, near Pocotaligo, and Oak Lawn, near Adams Run). Other Elliott holdings were The Grove, of which Elliott was particularly fond for its beauty–a grove of orange trees overlooking Battery Creek near present-day Port Royal; Shell Point and Ellis, on Port Royal Island; Bay Point, across Port Royal Sound from Myrtle Bank, the scene of Elliott's fishing exploits; Myrtle Bank, his mother's home on Hilton Head Island; Battery Plantation, operated by his sister Mary Barnwell Elliott; Bee Hive and Hope, on the Edisto River; the Ogeechee River lands in Georgia; summer residences at Adams

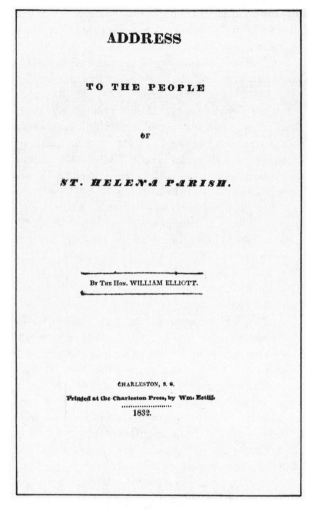

*Title page for the published version of Elliott's speech on the occasion of his resignation from the South Carolina state legislature (South Caroliniana Library, University of South Carolina)*

Run and Bay Point; "Farniente," the mountain home at Flat Rock, North Carolina; and the large townhouse in Beaufort. He was the mayor of Beaufort, and when the Marquis de Lafayette visited the town on 18 March 1825, he presented the welcoming address. In all he had nine children, eight of whom survived to adulthood. He took his daughters to the famous resorts and his sons fishing and hunting. With all his responsibilities, he was never too busy for his family.

In 1828 he was closely associated with his uncle Stephen Elliott in the founding of the *Southern Review* and contributed at least two reviews of works by Sir Walter Scott and Ben Jonson in 1829 and 1830. These essays show that he was well-versed in the English novel and Elizabethan drama and that he particularly appreciated good description and dramatic effect–traits his own writings have in abundance. He was also contributing to the new *Southern Agriculturist*. His first and only known article, in February 1828, was an essay that called for crop diversification and pointed out the shortcomings of a one-crop system.

Elliott began publishing the sketches that became *Carolina Sports by Land and Water* in the *American Turf Register* in 1829. "Fishing Extraordinary" appeared there in December of that year, and "Drum Fishing" was introduced to the public there in 1831. With his withdrawal from politics in 1832, he had more time for planting, travel, sports, and writing. From 1837 to 1838 he published much of what was to be the center of *Carolina Sports by Land and Water* in an excellent new Charleston magazine, the *Southern Literary Journal*. These pieces were "A Wild Cat Hunt in Carolina" (April 1837), "A Day at Chee-Ha" (July 1837), "Another Day at Chee-Ha" (January 1838), "Devil Fishing" (April 1838), and "A Business Day at Chee-Ha" (May 1838). With this last piece, more than half of the volume had been published.

In 1838 Elliott disturbed the even tenor of his life to accept the nomination to run against the incumbent for a Beaufort seat in the legislature and was defeated. In the same year he also addressed the Beaufort Agricultural Society, saying that planters should elect planters to office and that the farmer is the only real producer in the state. This speech aroused two arguments in response. Lawyers attacked Elliott for allegedly trying to poison the planters against them, and Edmund Rhett denied that the planter was the only producer. The controversy with the lawyers lasted but two months, while the Rhett argument continued for more than three years and occasioned several works by Elliott: letters to the *Charleston Courier* and two pamphlets, *Examination of Mr. Edmund Rhett's Agricultural Address, on the Question "Who Is the Producer?"* (1841) and *The Planter Vindicated: His Claims Examined—To be Considered a Direct Producer: The Chief Producer: And Chief Tax-Payer of South Carolina* (1842).

By 1842 Elliott had made the cotton plantation Oak Lawn his principal seat. It consisted of 1,750 acres with a brick great-house built in the early 1700s and approached through a magnificent live oak avenue unsurpassed in the Lowcountry. It was described by contemporaries as one of the noblest seats in the United States. The house was graced by ten acres of roses; and the whole family took pride in the flowers and frequently sent plants and seeds home from their travels. Also surrounding the house were vegetable gardens, orchards, pastures, staple crop fields, and a vineyard. The normal life of the Elliotts was of antebellum opulence. At Oak Lawn, there were twenty-three house servants, a large and constantly growing library, a billiard room, and various musical instruments, which Elliott loved. He also collected art and commissioned Thomas

Sully to paint portraits of family members. The hospitality of Oak Lawn was widely known and enjoyed. Such was home for Elliott—in the winter months. From late February through May the family moved to Charleston. They then summered in the ancestral home in Beaufort, where Elliott's father and mother lived during their younger days and which Elliott inherited shortly after his marriage in 1817. During the months of July through November, Elliott took to the resort circuit.

The squire of Oak Lawn did not lead a life of ease, glamorous as it may seem. As paterfamilias he supervised the activities of the Elliott empire and kept it together. He planned the crops and oversaw the choice of seed and planting on the far-flung lands. As with most of the great planters, Elliott possessed superb managerial skills. He seldom, however, attended the harvest, relying instead on his wife to pass his instructions to overseers. The squire believed in work, and all members of his family, both men and women, were industrious. He frequently cautioned his son at college against indolence. It was a wealthy family, yet not a family of leisure.

Elliott was a successful planter, one of the largest landholders in the South, but, as was the case with most planters, he had little ready cash. His capital was invested in land and more than three hundred slaves. Feeling that the black man's situation improved each generation removed from African savagery, he defended slavery on moral grounds. He adhered to a policy of strict planter responsibility in which there was to be no physical mistreatment or family splitting, careful medical attention, and responsibility for the slave's moral and religious betterment. He also reasoned that the planter of his day had not initiated the institution. He had inherited an English establishment that was now the basis of his economy and not so easily abolished. His solution was the gradual but certain elevation of blacks.

Elliott's principal crops were rice and cotton, but he also grew provisions for self-sufficiency. Attesting to his knowledge as a planter is the fact that his plantations were some of the most fertile and productive in the state. He felt it his duty to share his knowledge of farming with everyone and untiringly passed on his findings through many essays.

As an agrarian, he was regional in scope. For the South he preached crop diversification, self-sufficiency, curtailment of overproduction, and manufacturing. He advocated textile mills and the manufacture of forest products. He demanded agricultural education in the free schools and South Carolina College, and a central agency to collect and disseminate agricultural knowledge. He called for an experimental farm and a survey of mineral resources in the state. As an agricultural reformer, he was a sound thinker a century ahead of his time. Historian Lewis Jones, in his "William Elliott, South Carolina Nonconformist" (1951), feels these accomplishments to be his best.

The state also recognized his abilities and appointed him vice president in the State Agricultural Society. He had been president of the Beaufort chapter for years. His agrarian views are best summarized in his *The Anniversary Address of the State Agricultural Society, of South Carolina, Delivered in the Hall of the House of Representatives, November 30, 1848,* published as a pamphlet that year. Two other pamphlets appeared after similar addresses in 1850 and 1856. While in Paris, he spoke about cotton before the Imperial Agricultural Society on 4 July 1855.

Since 1838 Elliott had also continued to write. He augmented his pieces on drum and devil fishing with essays on angling for sheepshead and bass. To the "Chee-Ha" series he added "The Last Day at Chee-Ha," then rounded off his volume with "The Fire Hunter," "Of the Animals of Chase in South-Carolina," "Of the Birds Which Are the Objects of Sport," and, finally, "Random Thoughts on Hunting." When the new revised edition of 1859 was published, he included one additional chapter, "The Sea-Serpent."

Although he became prominent as an agriculturist of keen insight and a political nonconformist in a time of orthodoxy, he is best remembered for *Carolina Sports by Land and Water,* a volume that consists of lively accounts of his own experiences described in a style that is graceful, clear, animated, graphic, straightforward, and enthusiastic. For many critics, much of the charm of the volume lies in the author's impromptu, playful, personal tone, the genial vein of philosophic reflection which at intervals interrupts the stories of adventure, and the large infusion of wisdom and good sense. The first half of the book deals with fishing exploits; the second with sports of the field, primarily hunts for deer, wildcat, and the game of the swamps and forests along the coast. In one of these hunts he shoots two bears with a single discharge. This feat may seem a tall tale, but his grandson recalls both partridge and deer killed in similar manner during the old sportsman's last years. He remained a crack shot until his death. Although the hunt for a marvelous creature such as the devil fish or spirit deer bears similarities to Thomas Bangs Thorpe's "Big Bear of Arkansas" (1841), the sketches are not tall tales and are graphically accurate. "The Sea-Serpent," added in 1859, is closer to the tall-tale genre and does not fit comfortably into the volume. Although the stories frequently utilize comic relief, they are basically not humorous. Some fall more in the instructional category.

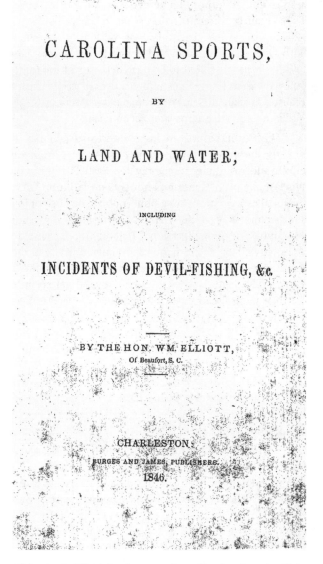

CAROLINA SPORTS,

BY

LAND AND WATER;

INCLUDING

INCIDENTS OF DEVIL-FISHING, &c.

BY THE HON. WM. ELLIOTT,
Of Beaufort, S. C.

CHARLESTON:
BURGES AND JAMES, PUBLISHERS.
1846.

*Title page for Elliott's best-known work, a celebration of sporting life in antebellum coastal South Carolina (South Caroliniana Library, University of South Carolina)*

Elliott only wrote about what he knew because, as he says, the things that the writer "has seen or done, are precisely those which make the liveliest impression . . . and with none other . . . should he attempt the difficult task of interesting the reader." His stories benefit accordingly. His accurately detailed settings place him in company with those writers who were discovering that the American scene was worthy of literature. When one considers the period of composition of many of the sketches, between 1829 and 1838, this fact becomes significant. Elliott must thus be remembered as an early realist, presenting life as it is, without idealizing, sentimentalizing, or prettifying it. He, in fact, precedes Augustus Baldwin Longstreet in this regard by a few years and should be recognized as temperamentally similar to that author. These two first American realists were creating a literature that is remarkably alike in its artistic vision. The early date of the stories that deal with Chee-Ha Plantation and depict Lowcountry plantation life shows Elliott to be a predecessor of the local-color realists. These tales also feature an early use of realistic Gullah dialect, with as skillful a rendering as William Gilmore Simms later accomplished.

Critics have praised his ability to sustain narrative, the enthusiasm for his subject that creates dramatic effect, and his ability to convey the dash of the chase. His last chapter, "Random Thoughts on Hunting," is a personal essay that makes a philosophical defense of the sportsman's way of life. Elliott saw sport as a means of siphoning off "animal passions" that might otherwise be destructive. Further, he wrote, sportsmen must be of the place, not city men who "marshal their forces for a week's campaign" and "who go so far and get so little for their pains." Conservation must be practiced to perpetuate the pastime, which is "noble." Some readers prefer the "Devil Fishing" chapter over the rest; but more critics regard the "Chee-Ha" stories most highly. Jay B. Hubbell, in *The South in American Literature, 1607–1900* (1954), finds "The Fire Hunter" to be his best. Of this story, he writes: "Had Elliott given himself seriously to literature of this kind, he might well have made Simms look to his laurels."

Perhaps Elliott's most wonderfully complex chapter is "A Business Day at Chee-Ha." Its emphasis is on several related themes of profound and universal interest. One is the recognition by a forty-five-year-old narrator of his own mortality, a narrator created by an author whose father had died at age forty-seven. Elliott's most recent critic, Theodore Rosengarten, reduces this chapter to a simplistic racial formula. When the narrator solemnly tells a slave nurse that he does not want to be called "Old Master—at least for two years yet," however, he is not guilt-stricken or gloomy over the institution of slavery and in a rush to leave a slave scene as quickly as possible, but is most likely sobered by a recognition of his mortality and the way that the everyday details to which he must attend are wearing away what time he has left. Elliott's paragraph on transience, presented immediately after this scene, points up this theme clearly.

The narrator's own stated reason for his hurry is that, because it is such a perfect autumn day and a valued hunting companion is ready and urging him to it, he wants to finish business quickly so he can have time to hunt. Ordinarily "Business Before Pleasure" is his motto, he says, thus contradicting Rosengarten's stereotypical depiction of the planter as an indolent and pampered lout. Elliott was not being ironic, for he was

always, from youth to death, a man of great energy, cautioning all in his family against indolence.

Elliott's crowning artistic achievement in this story is his complex use of a younger hunting companion, who, in stripping to swim into the river to retrieve the narrator's shot deer, is imaged as a Greek athlete as he stands naked on the riverbank, the picture of perfect manhood at its most virile—all narrated by an aging, responsibility-beset master, who has to attend to the minutiae of details of whether a slave's pair of shoes fit or whether the cloth has been properly cut to provide both legs of a slave's trousers. Indeed, the narrator must spend much of his time with such unheroic little details as the size of shoes and cloth. Then, old age requires drawing into a smaller physical sphere. One becomes trapped by physical limitations and cannot, perhaps, hunt as strenuously and heroically as when he was young. The story is thus a treatment of both growing old and of coming to grips with one's own limits—a theme in other chapters as well. The "false modesty" to cover the "overweening vanity," of which Rosengarten accuses the narrator, is true modesty, in that he comes to realize that he is finite before an infinite creator and creation—a realization that informs the works of Southern writing in general. It is a mistake not to see Elliott in the context of a larger body of writing, as he was indeed an early founder of this literature.

That the narrator seeks to put responsibilities aside for one day with the certainty of attending them on another distinguishes his culture as antithetical to that of the obsessive, sour Puritan. As Elliott wrote of hunting: "A man without recreation is like a bow kept always taut." Such was the wisdom of Elliott's Southern agrarian heritage. He owned twelve plantations, oversaw them efficiently, and had a family of nine children, to whom he was warmly devoted and who revered him in turn. He was a man of deep learning; a statesman and legislator when his community called on him; an agricultural philosopher and reformer; an unselfish educator of his fellow farmers in new agricultural methods through essays, speeches, and letters; an ardent agriculturist who defended farming as a way of life; and an author of no mean talent and art. Obviously, he was neither ignorant, callous, pampered, indolent, nor hedonistic, as Rosengarten wrongly implies.

Another favorite chapter in *Carolina Sports by Land and Water* is "The Last Day at Chee-Ha." The tale concerns man's destructive willfulness as he again seeks to go beyond the bounds his creator has set for him. It deals with mystery and belief as humanizing agents that work to soften man's cold and clinical empiricism. Elliott pits atheism against belief, misanthropy against jovial fellowship, isolation against community, pride and willfulness against humility and acceptance of limitations, mystery against easy explanation, obsession against good sense–many of the themes of much Southern literature. In the story the appearance of the spirit deer, taken from the folklore of the Chee-Ha area, becomes a central symbolic event. The ghost deer and the characters' various reactions to it bring into focus all the themes of the story. It is a sophisticated, complex, skillfully told story, the depths of which have yet to be plumbed by any of Elliott's critics.

One of the strongest early champions of *Carolina Sports by Land and Water* was George Wauchope, who wrote in the *Library of Southern Literature* (1908–1923) that "Devil Fishing" has never been equaled, and places him with Henry David Thoreau as a naturalist. As for Thoreau himself, his journals reveal that he read *Carolina Sports by Land and Water* but objected to Elliott's killing animals. Most recently, Louis Rubin, in his *William Elliott Shoots a Bear* (1975), finds Elliott an imaginative observer who used social motifs that he might have developed into great literature were it not for the fact that he feared looking beneath the surface. This critical judgment, which uses race and class as the lenses through which to view the book, has influenced the perception of Elliott and his work ever since.

After the 1846 Charleston edition, the book was republished in New York in 1850 from the same plates but with a new prefatory note by Elliott. A second edition appeared in New York in 1859 with illustrations and an added chapter. The stories have both major and minor revisions, including a fourteen-page expansion of "Devil Fishing" and a four-page addition to "The Last Day at Chee-Ha." The 1859 edition was reprinted in London in 1867. A third edition appeared in 1918 published in Columbia, South Carolina, by Ambrose Elliott Gonzales, the author's grandson. Its contents follow the 1859 volume but omit the author's prefaces, while adding an afterword by Gonzales. Reprint editions have appeared in 1963, 1967, and 1994, the last with the "socially conscious" introduction by Rosengarten. It is one of the few early American sporting books that has remained in print almost without interruption.

In 1859 the old sportsman wrote his wife that "if anything that I have written will live after me it will be these 'Sports.' . . . It will be a sort of legacy of honor to my posterity who need not then be ashamed of claiming descent from old 'Venator'!" Simms, in the best contemporary review of the volume, agreed on its permanence. The descriptions of a people's sport, he wrote in the *Southern Quarterly Review*, "will continue to command attention when graver volumes, on what may seem to be more important subjects, have been long forgotten. . . . The sports of a country are somewhat akin to its ballads, and . . . are of more importance than its laws."

In the March 1842 issue of his journal *Magnolia*, Simms remarked that Elliott had completed an historical drama. This work is likely *Fiesco; A Tragedy*, which Elliott privately printed in 1850 and distributed "for private presents to my literary friends." A five-act closet drama for contemplative reading, *Fiesco* is set in Genoa in 1547 and treats the theme of justice. Simms regarded it as "well-written." Like *Carolina Sports by Land and Water*, it shows vitality.

Rubin wrote that *Fiesco* attempts "serious analysis," while *Carolina Sports by Land and Water*, set in Elliott's own day, did not, and regrets that Elliott "did not do with the superb material of his own experience what he attempted to do with his verse drama . . . search out and delineate the human consequences of events described, give definition, and pronounce meaning." *Carolina Sports by Land and Water*, he continues, is only "a record of surfaces." It is true that Elliott did not feel the so-called white man's guilt, as did some thinkers, such as Thoreau. But as Thoreau critic Charles Anderson, in his "Thoreau Takes a Pot Shot at *Carolina Sports*" (1966), says in contrasting them: "as two men living in their times, the palms all go to Elliott. He was gracious and warmly human, Thoreau prickly and cold. He was broad in his interests and deeply involved in the problems of society; Thoreau was narrow, reclusive, and eccentric. He was a public servant; Thoreau almost perversely anti-social. Both were men of principle and integrity, who took their obligations as human beings with proper seriousness, but there is no doubt which of the two is more appealing as a man." Elliott's choice not to lead the introverted life necessary to make his work a *Walden* may be regrettable in some respects, but *Carolina Sports by Land and Water* would then lose other fine qualities responsible for the success of the work for more than a century and a half. One of the most important of these traits is the narrator's warm personality, a presence one does not always feel in abstract or ideological works. Further, *Carolina Sports by Land and Water* provides ample evidence that Elliott was indeed capable of seeing beneath the surface: his interpretations of what he saw there are simply not on the subjects favored by his liberal critics with narrow interests. In 1856, in the *Cyclopaedia of American Literature*, the author of the sketch on Elliott clearly saw that Elliott's "philosophical outlook" had "caused him to look for meaning and effect in all issues." Thus, his insight into Elliott more than a century ago seems to have far surpassed many of Elliott's modern critics.

In the 1850s Elliott was also publishing articles for the *Horticulturist*. Still uncollected are sketches in the *Charleston Courier* under the pseudonyms "Flash," "Venator," and "Piscator." As important as these works, however, is the steady flow of letters to his family begun

*The Elliott home in Beaufort, South Carolina*

during his college years. As Jones states, these letters have a lively style and keen wit: "As a cultured nineteenth century writer of entertaining and well-phrased letters, he stands forth as a noble example. . . . they point out his concern for truth, diligence, and honor." An edition of the many personal letters in the Elliott papers at the University of South Carolina was made available as a dissertation in 1978.

In 1851 Elliott wrote a series of public letters to the *Charleston Southern Standard,* which he collected in 1852 as *The Letters of Agricola.* These letters were an attempt to minimize the emotional appeal of the secessionists through reason and to advocate compromise with the North. His old controversy with Edmund Rhett yielded to a dispute with William Barnwell Rhett, the leading secessionist and Elliott's neighbor in Beaufort. Elliott was habitually affable and charming, but for the Rhetts he had only animosity. He wrote to his wife in 1851 that the secessionists "prostrate themselves before this bellowing mooncalf and swallow all his fatuities as oracles. One who has gulp of this size would swallow a haystack." Like his fellow Beaufort friend and writer William Grayson, Elliott remained consistent as an opponent first of nullification and then of secession. In both stands he was part of an unpopular minority.

In 1853 and 1855 Elliott toured Europe in order to learn about cotton importing and markets, information he made available for the good of the state in a speech before the legislature in 1855. He represented South Carolina at the Universal Exhibition in Paris in 1855. He was in great demand as a lecturer and as spokesman for Carolina planting interests. In March 1857 he journeyed to Cuba to visit his sixteen-year-old daughter, who had married Ambrosio Gonzales, a leader of the Cuba libre movement. On returning home he published a six-part account of his trip in *Russell's Magazine* (1857–1858).

Elliott has two known published poems; five manuscript verses are among the Elliott papers. Doubtless other pseudonymous and anonymous material will come to light with further study. In 1856 Evert Duyckinck mentions "occasional poems, of which a few have seen the light." Elliott's two identified verses postdate this reference, however.

With the outbreak of war in 1861, Elliott cast his lot with the Confederacy. He became politically orthodox as a result of abolition and invasion and backed the cause with his great wealth by subscribing heavily in Confederate bonds. The war played havoc with the Elliott empire. Federal troops seized some of his plantations in 1861 with the occupation of Beaufort early in the war, and his Beaufort townhouse was ransacked in 1862. He moved his wife and daughters to Flat Rock, North Carolina, while all his sons joined the Confederate army. Elliott himself returned to Oak Lawn to try to protect what he could of the Elliott estates. On a trip to Charleston, he died at the Mills House on 4 February 1863 at the age of seventy-four of "an inflamation of the bowels" and was buried at Magnolia Cemetery in Charleston. He had lived long enough to see his world in ruins. The Elliott lands were seized by the government for nonpayment of the direct tax. In 1865 the great-house at Oak Lawn was ransacked and burned by the invading army, its library looted and its grounds laid waste; but the family retained title to it and to some of the other plantations, which they eventually redeemed. However, the agrarian value of place, which Elliott celebrated in his work, had been entirely supplanted by the destruction of war.

As Jones has accurately written, Elliott as family leader set the family's tone and traditions, which continued eighty years after his death and long after the collapse of the family fortunes. The legacy was preserved in the family members of the next generation, particularly in his brilliant grandsons N. G. and Ambrose Elliott Gonzales, intelligent men of conviction who were competent writers of essays and stories themselves, founders and editors of the largest and most influential newspaper in the state, and outspoken critics of emotional politics and corruption in government. His influence as a sportsman is best summed up by George Wauchope in *Library of Southern Literature* (1908–1923), who called him "the model of every Beaufort boy, who for the first time, waded into the surf at Bay Point, to throw his line for bass, or saw with trembling eagerness, the great wings of the devil-fish flash on the broad waters of Port Royal." As a writer, he should be remembered as one of the early realists in the United States and an author whose themes eventually became central to the Southern literature he helped to create. There is no doubt that Elliott's book will continue to delight and become evermore valuable in an age of abstraction and

modern industrial culture. Elliott's slender volume is as "human" a nature book as has been written, and its local base is a springboard to a universality William Faulkner would have understood well. *Carolina Sports by Land and Water* is nothing short of a masterpiece, and one waiting for much wider discovery.

**Letters:**

Beverly Scafidel, "The Letters of William Elliott," dissertation, University of South Carolina, 1978.

**References:**

Charles Anderson, "Thoreau Takes a Pot Shot at *Carolina Sports*," *Georgia Review,* 22 (Fall 1966): 289–299;

Jay B. Hubbell, *The South in American Literature, 1607–1900* (Durham, N.C.: Duke University Press, 1954), pp. 564–568;

Lewis Jones, "William Elliott, South Carolina Nonconformist," *Journal of Southern History,* 17 (August 1951): 361–381;

James Everett Kibler, "Not-So-Intellectual Imperialism," *Mississippi Quarterly,* 48 (Spring 1995): 337–342;

Theodore Rosengarten, introduction to *Carolina Sports by Land and Water* (Columbia: University of South Carolina Press, 1994), pp. ix–lxiii;

Louis Rubin, *William Elliott Shoots a Bear* (Baton Rouge: Louisiana State University Press, 1975), pp. 1–27;

Beverly Scafidel, "William Elliott, Planter and Politician," in *South Carolina Journals and Journalists,* edited by James B. Meriwether (Columbia, S.C.: Southern Studies Program, 1975), pp. 109–119;

[William Gilmore Simms], "Carolina Sports," *Southern Quarterly Review,* 12 (July 1847): 67–90;

B. N. Skardon, "William Elliott: Planter-Writer of Ante-bellum South Carolina," thesis, University of Georgia, 1964;

George Wauchope, "William Elliott," in *Library of Southern Literature,* edited by Edwin A. Alderman and Joel Chandler Harris (Atlanta: Martin & Hoyt, 1908–1923), IV: 1569–1570.

# Joseph M. Field

## (1810 – 28 January 1856)

### Jennings R. Mace
*Eastern Kentucky University*

BOOK: *The Drama in Pokerville; the Bench and Bar of Jurytown, and Other Stories* (Philadelphia: Peterson, 1847).

PLAY PRODUCTIONS: *Tourists in America,* New Orleans, American Theatre, 7 May 1833;

*Coming Out,* New Orleans, American Theatre, 24 May 1833;

*Caesario* (adaptation of the play *Alphonso, King of Castile* by Matthew Gregory Lewis), Mobile, Ala., St. Emanuel Theatre, 9 May 1836;

*Amalgamation, or, Southern Visitors,* St. Louis, St. Louis Theatre, 10 October 1838;

*Victoria, or The Lion and the Kiss,* St. Louis, St. Louis Theatre, 19 October 1838;

*The White House,* New Orleans, St. Charles Theatre, 16 November 1838;

*Bennett in Texas,* New Orleans, St. Charles Theatre, 18 November 1838;

*Plato in Petticoats,* New Orleans, St. Charles Theatre, 19 November 1838;

*Inexpressibles,* Mobile, Ala., Government Street Theatre, 18 March 1839;

*Mademoiselle de Belle Isle* (adaptation of the play by Alexandre Dumas *père*), Mobile, Ala., Chapman's Ballroom, 30 March 1840;

*Catherine Howard* (adaptation of the play by Alexandre Dumas *père*), New Orleans, St. Charles Theatre, 29 April 1840;

*Vot of It?* New Orleans, St. Charles Theatre, 6 May 1840;

*G.A.G., or The Starring System,* New Orleans, St. Charles Theatre, 20 February 1841;

*Boz,* Boston, Tremont Theatre, 21 January 1842;

*Lions Abroad or, Literary Rages,* Boston, Tremont Theatre, 7 March 1842;

*Dr. Heavybevy,* Boston, Tremont Theatre, 12 March 1842;

*Quozziana,* Boston, Tremont Theatre, 14 March 1842;

*Life in China: or, The Feast of Lanterns,* Boston, Tremont Theatre, 21 May 1842;

*Buy It Dear! 'Tis Made of Cashmere,* Boston, Tremont Theatre, 28 May 1842;

*Sardanapalus* (adaptation of the play by George Gordon, Lord Byron), Boston, Tremont Theatre, 4 June 1842;

*Now 'a Days; or, What Next,* Boston Tremont Theatre, 4 June 1842;

*Such as It Is,* New York, Park Theatre, 4 September 1842;

*Nervos-Vitalics; or, The March of Science,* New York, Olympic Theatre, 19 September 1842;

*Antony and Cleopatra,* New York, Olympic Theatre, 1 March 1843;

*1943! or, New Orleans a Century Hence,* New Orleans, St. Charles Theatre, 14 April 1843;

*The 23rd of April,* New Orleans, St. Charles Theatre, 20 April 1843;

*The Artful Dodger,* New York, Bowery Theatre, 4 September 1843;

*1944! or, Mobile, a Hundred Years Hence,* Mobile, Ala., Royal Street Theatre, March 1844;

*1944! or, The Queen City a Century Hence,* Cincinnati, National Theatre, 3 May 1844;

*Foreign and Native,* St. Louis, St. Louis Theatre, 2 June 1845;

*Chevalier de Cronstillac* (adaptation of the novel *Monre au Diable* by Eugene Sue), St. Louis, St. Louis Theatre, 5 October 1845;

*Oregon! or, The Disputed Territory,* New Orleans, St. Charles Theatre, 7 January 1846;

*1946! or, New Orleans 100 Years Hence,* New Orleans, St. Charles Theatre, 4 February 1846;

*Family Ties,* New York, Park Theatre, 19 June 1846;

*How They Do in Washington,* New Orleans, St. Charles Theatre, 7 April 1849;

*Mike Fink, the Last Keelboatman,* St. Louis, St. Louis Theatre, 6 September 1849;

*Married an Actress,* New York, Burton's Theatre, 19 December 1850;

*The Nightingale,* Mobile, Ala., Royal Street Theatre, 25 February 1851;

*The World's Fair or, The Crystal Palace,* Mobile, Ala., Royal Street Theatre, 21 March 1851;

*Dr. Bilboquet* (adaptation), St. Louis, St. Louis Theatre, 19 June 1851;

*Two Dodgers* (probably *The Artful Dodger*), St. Louis, St. Louis Theatre, 5 July 1851;

*Job and His Children,* St. Louis, Varieties Theatre, 25 August 1852;

*Uncle Tom's Cabin: or Life in the South as It Is,* Mobile, Ala., Royal Street Theatre, 30 December 1853;

*Napoleon Crossing the Alps,* Mobile, Ala., Royal Street Theatre, 29 March 1854;

*Griselda; or, The Patient Woman* (adaptation of the play *Griseldis* by Friedrich Halm), St. Louis, Varieties Theatre, 4 September 1854.

Perhaps Joseph M. Field's final place in American letters has yet to be determined because his interests and abilities covered such a wide spectrum. Others have suggested, in fact, that his widely reaching talents kept him from a truly distinguished place in any one area. He was an actor, a playwright, a theater manager, a writer of humorous sketches, and a newspaper editor. Of these endeavors, acting consumed most of his life; yet, given the transient nature of a stage performance, his most enduring legacy will probably be his work as one of the editors of the *St. Louis Reveille* from 1844 to 1850. This newspaper was a fertile field for the writers known as the humorists of the Old Southwest. Often using pseudonyms–Field wrote sketches under the names of "Everpoint" and "Straws"–the Southwestern humorists wrote with a vitality and realism uncharacteristic of most of the writers of the time. Their subjects were the pursuits of the frontier regions: gambling, racing, fighting, courting, and tricking. Their dialogue was often rendered in dialect, and their method of structuring a story frequently employed the frame of sophisticated narrator relating an observed episode or allowing someone else to recount an episode. The *Reveille* attracted many of these writers, including Sol Smith and John Robb. Field's younger brother Matt also contributed to the paper. Some of Field's stories appeared in the *Spirit of the Times,* the premier sporting publication of its day. Short-lived though it was, the *Reveille* will certainly endure as Field's contribution to the spread of Southwestern humor.

Joseph M. Field was the son of Matthew Field Sr., an Irishman with strong Roman Catholic ties who came to England sometime after the Irish Rebellion of 1798. Joe's birth in 1810 has been variously assigned to Dublin, London, and Stockport, England. In 1812 his brother, Matthew Jr., was born in London. In the unpublished "Memoir of the Author," written by Field upon Matt's death, 15 November 1844, he suggests

the family left England for the United States to escape persecution, arriving in New York around 1816. Matthew Field opened a bookshop and published *A Catholic Almanac,* the first in the United States. He died in 1819, leaving a widow with four sons and two daughters to care for. Field may have studied law briefly, but by his teens he was working as a stringer for the *New York Evening Post.*

Though there is chronological overlap, Field's varied life may be examined most conveniently in terms of three general careers: actor and playwright, newspaper editor and writer, and theater manager. As an actor Field's career began in Boston in 1827, where he played for several years, but by 1829 he had moved from bit player to supporting actor. For the 1829–1830 season he began the life of the traveling actor, often rotating between seasons in the South (New Orleans, Montgomery, and Mobile) and the Midwest (Cincinnati, St. Louis, and Louisville).

By the spring of 1834 Field was linked with Sol Smith's acting company in Montgomery, Alabama, a sporadic relationship that lasted most of Field's life. During this season the company also played Columbus, Macon, Augusta, and Milledgeville, Georgia. Smith joined forces with Noah Ludlow in 1835, creating the major troupe in the South and the West for years. In 1835 Smith appointed Field the assistant manager to handle a two-week season in Wetumpka, Alabama, an experience useful to him in 1844 when he began his own career as a manager. Later in 1835 Field jointed the Ludlow and Smith company in St. Louis. On 6 November 1837 he married Eliza Riddle, the leading lady who joined the company in St. Louis in 1836. It appears that Matt Field, also an actor and writer, had actually proposed to Eliza, who then told him about her engagement to his brother. Matt later married Ludlow's daughter, Cornelia. Matt, in his own right, was a colorful figure who wrote sketches of Western travel for the *New Orleans Picayune.* In one stretch he produced eighty-four sketches in fifteen months. Similarly, he wrote many humorous pieces under the name "Phazma." He had drinking and health problems, however, and died and was buried at sea in November 1844.

In the summer season of 1837 in St. Louis, Field played thirty-nine different roles, a fairly routine feat. In one stretch in December 1833, he acted in Richard Sheridan's *The School for Scandal* (1777), Frederick Reynolds's *The Will* and *The Dramatist,* Hannah Cowley's *The Belle's Stratagem* (1780), Susannah Centlivre's *The Wonder: A Woman Keeps a Secret* (1714), and Mordecai Noah's *She Would Be a Soldier* (1819). In a similar passage of sixteen nights in New Orleans in November 1843, Field played fifteen roles, and in December he played fourteen characters. Though Field's repertoire

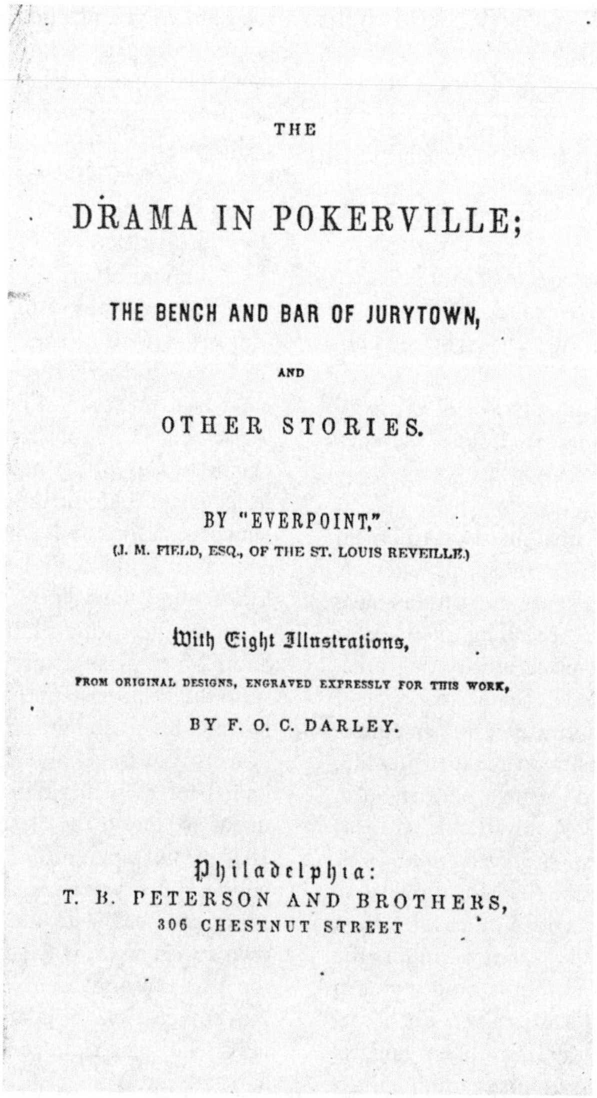

THE

## DRAMA IN POKERVILLE;

THE BENCH AND BAR OF JURYTOWN,

AND

## OTHER STORIES.

BY "EVERPOINT,"

(J. M. FIELD, ESQ., OF THE ST. LOUIS REVEILLE.)

With Eight Illustrations,

FROM ORIGINAL DESIGNS, ENGRAVED EXPRESSLY FOR THIS WORK,

BY F. O. C. DARLEY.

Philadelphia:
T. B. PETERSON AND BROTHERS,
306 CHESTNUT STREET

*Title page for the only published collection of Field's stories (Special Collections, Thomas Cooper Library, University of South Carolina)*

clearly included serious roles, his acting success came from his comic roles. Following the summer season of 1837 in St. Louis, Field and his wife returned to Mobile. On 1 October 1838 Eliza gave birth to Mary Katherine Keemle Field. In her own life, Kate Field continued the family tradition of wide-ranging interests by being a writer, a teacher, a critic, a newspaper reporter, and an actor. She died in 1895. Their second child, Matthew, was born in February 1843 and died at the age of six in the cholera epidemic of 1849.

Between 1837 and 1839 the Fields continued theatrical migrations in the South and the West. During that time, Field acted as supporting star to such genuine stars as Edwin Forrest and J. B. Booth. By May 1839 Field and his wife left Smith and Ludlow

for New York, a venue Field sought to conquer several times during his career. In the summer of 1839 he went to Europe as a reporter for the *New Orleans Picayune*. He was back in Boston by October 1839. Both of the Fields were in Boston for the winter 1841–1842 season. On 1 February 1842 Field, who was known for his addresses, gave one at a banquet in Charles Dickens's honor.

Though he continued to act in New York, appearing at both the Park Theatre and the Olympic Theatre, by 1842 he was devoting more time to writing both plays and humorous sketches. In the New Orleans 1843 season, one year after *Dr. Heavybevy* debuted, he enjoyed considerable success with the play his satiric version of the "scientific" lectures of

Dr. Dionysius Lardner. Field also ran long engagements in New Orleans, Mobile, and St. Louis as a supporting actor for William Charles Macready, the English tragedian. In 1844, with the founding of the *St. Louis Reveille,* Field left the stage for three years.

During his entire career Field wrote plays. His first play, *Tourists in America,* was presented on the New Orleans stage on 7 May 1833. His last verified play, an adaptation, was *Griselda; or, The Patient Woman,* presented at the St. Louis Varieties Theatre on 4 September 1854. Recently, more than fifty titles have been assigned to him and at least six others are thought to be his work. The only manuscripts to survive are *Oregon! or, The Disputed Territory* (1846) and *Job and His Children* (1852). One of his plays, *Family Ties* (1846), won the $500 Dan Marble prize for new American comedy, which focused attention on him as a playwright. Field's plays were usually humorous, often topical. One of his last plays was a burlesque, *Uncle Tom's Cabin: or Life in the South as It Is* (1853), by "Harriet Screecher Blow." Perhaps his most successful play was *1943! or, New Orleans a Century Hence,* first played on 14 April 1843 at the St. Charles Theatre in New Orleans. That play was followed in 1844 by *1944! or, Mobile, a Hundred Years Hence* and *1944! or, The Queen City a Century Hence.* In 1846 he presented *1946! or, New Orleans 100 Years Hence.* Other titles suggest his subject matter: *Victoria, or The Lion and the Kiss* (1838), *Plato in Petticoats* (1838), *Vot of It?* (1840), *Buy It Dear! 'Tis Made of Cashmere* (1842), *Nervos-Vitalics; or, The March of Science* (1842), *How They Do in Washington* (1849). Field's skills as a dramatist were more functional than enduring, if the few examples of his work are any indication; his output is impressive, however, with at least fifty plays in twenty-one years. No doubt the ability to turn out copy quickly was a benefit when he and his brother joined Colonel Charles Keemle in the newspaper business.

On 14 May 1844 the Field brothers and Keemle established the *St. Louis Reveille.* While both Field and his brother had some newspaper experience–Matt had been the assistant editor at the *New Orleans Picayune*–Keemle brought to the project more than twenty years of experience, having worked for the *Indiana Sentinel* and the *Enquirer,* the *Beacon,* and the *Commercial Bulletin* of St. Louis. Matt died shortly after the founding of the *Reveille.* Between 1844 and 1850 Field put his acting career on hold to devote most of his energies to the newspaper. In *The Pioneer Editor in Missouri: 1808–1860* (1958), William Lyon calls the *Reveille* "the most important literary journal in Missouri before the Civil War." The *Reveille* announced that its aim was to "amuse and refine." Suggestive of its involvement in the literary world of its day is a let-

ter Edgar Allan Poe wrote to Field on 15 June 1846, thanking him for his "kindly feeling" toward him and asking Field to condemn an editorial attack on him by Hiram Fuller. Poe's letter suggests that he and Field had met since Poe is concerned that Fuller's editorial will spread a "false impression of my personal appearance": "You have seen me and can describe me as I am." Poe also asked Field to published in the *Reveille* several laudatory editorials from the British press. Field obliged in the 30 June 1846 *Daily Reveille* and the 6 July 1846 weekly edition.

The *Daily Reveille* first appeared on 14 May 1844, with the *Weekly Reveille* beginning on 15 June 1844. Both promoted a type of humor now called the humor of the Old Southwest. Indeed, William T. Porter, editor of the *Spirit of the Times,* the premier showcase for Southwestern humor, published many sketches from the *Reveille.* On 19 May 1849 a fire in St. Louis consumed twenty-three boats, caused three million dollars in damage, and destroyed the *Reveille* offices. Apparently the partners were unable to recover their losses, though they did publish the daily edition until 6 October 1850.

Field's own contribution to the literature of Southwestern humor was the publication of *The Drama in Pokerville; the Bench and Bar of Jurytown, and Other Stories* (1847). *The Drama in Pokerville* includes the usual fare for collections of Southwestern humor and, as befitting the author's livelihood, many of his tales focus on theater life, the title story being a case in point. Field's work, often employing frame stories and dialect, is not in the first rank of Southwestern humor. Frequently the ending to a tale evaporates, and the characters do not approach the vitality of the characters in the work of George Washington Harris or Henry Clay Lewis. Still, "The Drama in Pokerville; or, the Great Small Affair Company" presents a vivid sketch of small-town pretensions and human gullibility. The "aristocrats" of Pokerville long for the implied sophistication bestowed by mingling with "artists." While the townsfolk are the primary targets of the humor in the story, the stage artists also receive their share of ridicule. Mrs. Oscar Dust, leading lady, epitomizes the humbug perpetrated by the Great Small Affair Company. Weighing in at 180 pounds, she frequently refers to the stylishness of her gowns (they are hand-me-downs), the virtue of her daughter at an Eastern seminary (she is on a farm in Kentucky), her "naval man" son (he is a mate on a steamboat), and the success of her career (her notices are vague at best).

The other actors in the troupe are little better, from a drunken singer to a manager, Oscar Dust, who gambles away their earnings. The town has its share of questionable characters, including a young man who was dismissed from West Point; Dr. Slunk, whose title is dubious; a London literary man given to quoting "Chawles" Lamb; and a gallery of tobacco-spitting rogues. The plot that holds the tale together concerns the supposedly precarious moral position of Fanny Wilkins, a young actress in the troupe. The problem is that Mrs. Dust sees Fanny as a stage rival and employs every opportunity to besmirch her character. Mrs. Dust uses Dr. Slunk's unwanted advances toward Fanny to point out the young girl's tainted character. Fanny, for her part, uses the good offices of Mr. Fitzcarol, another actor, to shield her as much as possible from Dr. Slunk's heavy-handed overtures. Dr. Slunk is finally foiled, Fitzcarol is revealed to be a dedicated and brave suitor, and Fanny and Fitzcarol end up in a pretty cottage with a pretty baby.

Several more of the tales focus on the doings of a traveling troupe. In "'Old Sol' in a Delicate Situation," Sol Smith succeeds in subduing a noisy theater patron who objects to Smith's adding lines not in the original play. "The 'Gagging Scheme'; or, West's Great Picture" involves a hoax perpetrated by an out-of-work acting troupe. The town of Skinville is duped into paying to see Benjamin West's "Death on the Pale Horse," a creation actually produced by the scene painter of the troupe. "A Night in a Swamp" recounts an 1834 event in which Smith's acting company is delayed while traveling from Milledgeville, Georgia, to Montgomery, Alabama, because heavy rains have washed out a bridge. Smith's dexterity and inventiveness allow them to secure lodgings when everyone else is reduced to crude camping and also allow them to be first over the newly constructed bridge the next morning.

The rest of the stories cover typical Southwestern humor territory: "Bench and Bar of Jurytown" and "A 'Hung' Jury" concern law and the courts; "Honey Run," "How our Friend B-'s Hair Went," and "An 'Awful' Place" are about politics and campaigning; "Mr. Nobble" and "Stopping to Wood" concern steamboat travel; "A Sucker in a Warm Bath" and "A Resurrectionist and His Freight" center on hoaxes; and "Establishing the Science" and "Ole Bull in the 'Solitude'" are dialect stories. "The Elk Runners" recounts a race that took place in 1818 at the Missouri Fur Company outpost at Council Bluffs, Fort Lisa. The tale deals with the attempt of two runners, D of Kentucky and Mal Boeuf, to kill elk with knives after running them to exhaustion. Field went to some pains to suggest the authenticity of the tale, perhaps a necessity since the two runners

killed sixteen elk and covered seventy-five miles between 8 A.M. and 7 P.M.

Field's other historically based story is "The Death of Mike Fink." Field also included an historically based story, "Death of Mike Fink," a version of the same tale he published in the 21 October 1844 *Reveille*. Field saw it as an attempt to correct the many erroneous accounts of the boatman's end. For his account he drew on the experience of his newspaper partner, Keemle, who had served with the military near the scene of Fink's death. Fink, a guide and trapper, leaves the Mountain Fur Company post because he cannot abide by the rules banning alcohol. He resorts to a life of drinking and carousing accompanied by a young man, Carpenter. In a drunken exhibition of marksmanship, Carpenter wounds Fink while trying to shoot a can off his head. When it is his turn, Mike shoots Carpenter in the forehead. Though Fink claims the death was an accident and that he loved Carpenter like a son, a local gunsmith named Talbot denounces Fink as a murderer. Fink approaches Talbot in an attempt to clear the record but is shot when he fails to heed Talbot's warnings to come no nearer. Talbot later dies while trying to cross the Missouri River in a small boat. In June 1847 the *Reveille* published serially Field's "Mike Fink: The Last of the Boatmen," a more melodramatic version of the same tale.

Field also included three poems in *The Drama in Pokerville*. Two of them, "Establishing a Connection" and "Steamboat Miseries," describe aspects of life on a steamboat, the first dealing with shipboard romance and the second with the problems of getting a good meal. The last poem, "Paternal Gushings," is a sentimental look at wedded bliss and babies.

Though Field wrote many other stories that were never collected, those in *The Drama in Pokerville* are enough to secure his place as a writer of Southwestern humor. His portrayal of the foibles of the human race is characteristic of the genre, as is his attention to the details of frontier life. He presents a land of boisterous doings and colorful characters, no doubt drawn from his own experiences on the Western frontier at midcentury. He adds to that scene an intimate knowledge of the life of the frontier actor, as well.

Following the sale of the *Reveille,* the Fields began the final phase of their lives when they returned to the theater. This time, however, they were managers. Field had some previous experience as a manager while working with Ludlow and Smith, and his long experience with the stage would have provided additional background. In November 1850 the Fields opened the Royal Street Theatre in Mobile. By the spring of 1851 they were in St. Louis managing the St. Louis Varieties Theatre, repeating the seasonal cycle they followed as actors. The St. Louis theater was a constant drain, though the 1852 season was a success. This theater offered variety acts of all sorts, ranging from drama to tightrope performances. The Mobile operation was a more successful venture, including an engagement by the dancer Lola Montez and appearances by the actor and playwright Dion Boucicault and his wife, Agnes Robertson. Field's best year was 1853, though he lost both theaters less than two years later. By March 1855 Field was ill and in debt, primarily from his St. Louis operation. He died on 28 January 1856 of a bronchial infection. Eliza Field died 26 May 1871 on her way to England.

## References:

Alice Adel Beffa, "Joe Field, A Man of the Forties," thesis, Washington University, St. Louis, 1941;

John Michael Heidger, "Family Ties: A Biography of the Fields on the Frontier Stage," dissertation, University of Missouri, Columbia, 1988;

Mark Keller, "St. Louis Reveille," in *American Humor Magazines and Comic Periodicals,* edited by David E. E. Sloane (Westport, Conn.: Greenwood Press, 1987), pp. 244–248;

Grenville Clark King, "'Phazma': A Biography of Matthew C. Field (1812–1844)," dissertation, University of Illinois, 1975;

Noah M. Ludlow, *Dramatic Life as I Found It; A Record of Personal Experience; with an Account of the Rise and Progress of the Drama in the West and the South, with Anecdotes and Biographical Sketches of the Principal Actors and Actresses Who Have at Times Appeared upon the Stage in the Mississippi Valley,* edited, with an introduction, by Francis Hodge (New York: Blom, 1966);

Fritz Oehlschlaeger, "Joseph M. Field," in *Encyclopedia of American Humorists,* Garland Reference Library of the Humanities, no. 633, edited by Steven H. Gale (New York: Garland, 1988), pp. 154–158;

Oehlschlaeger, ed., *Old Southwest Humor from the St. Louis Reveille, 1844–1850* (Columbia: University of Missouri Press, 1990), pp. 11–19;

Solomon Franklin Smith, *Theatrical Management in the West and South for Thirty Years* (New York: Harper, 1868);

Carl Brooks Spotts, "The Development of Fiction on the Missouri Frontier," *Missouri Historical Review,* 29 (1935): 100–108, 186–194, 279–294.

## Papers:

The Joseph M. Field Papers are part of the Ludlow-Field-Maury Collection, Missouri Historical Society, St. Louis, Missouri.

# William J. Grayson

## (12 November 1788 – 4 October 1863)

### C. P. Seabrook Wilkinson
*College of Charleston*

See also the Grayson entries in *DLB 3: Antebellum Writers in New York and the South* and *DLB 64: American Literary Critics and Scholars, 1850–1880.*

BOOKS: *An Oration, Delivered in the College Chapel, Before the Clariosophic Society Incorporate and the People of Columbia, on the 3rd December, 1827* (Charleston, S.C.: Miller, 1828);

*Letter to His Excellency Whitemarsh B. Seabrook, Governor of the State of South-Carolina, on the Dissolution of the Union* (Charleston, S.C.: Miller, 1850);

*To "One of the People"* (Charleston, S.C.: Miller, 1850);

*The Union, Past and Future. How It Works and How to Save It* (Charleston, S.C.: Miller, 1850);

*The Letters of Curtius,* anonymous (Charleston, S.C.: Miller, 1851);

*The Hireling and the Slave* (Charleston, S.C.: Russell, 1854);

*Reply to Dr. Dewey's Address, Delivered at the Elm Tree, Sheffield, Mass. With Extracts from the Same* (Charleston, S.C.: Published by request, 1856);

*The Hireling and the Slave, Chicora, and Other Poems* (Charleston, S.C.: McCarter, 1856);

*The Country* (Charleston, S.C.: Russell & Jones, 1858);

*Marion* (Charleston, S.C.: Privately printed, 1860);

*Remarks on Mr. Motley's Letter in the London Times on the War in America,* anonymous (Charleston, S.C.: Evans & Cogswell, 1861);

*Reply to Professor Hodge, on the "State of the Country"* (Charleston, S.C.: Evans & Cogswell, 1861);

*James Louis Petigru. A Biographical Sketch* (New York: Harper, 1866);

*Selected Poems by William J. Grayson,* edited by Mrs. William H. Armstrong (New York & Washington, D.C.: Neale, 1907);

*Witness to Sorrow: The Antebellum Autobiography of William J. Grayson,* edited by Richard J. Calhoun (Columbia: University of South Carolina Press, 1990).

*William J. Grayson (South Carolina Historical Society)*

SELECTED PERIODICAL PUBLICATIONS– UNCOLLECTED: "The Character of the Gentleman," *Southern Quarterly Review,* new series 7 (January 1853): 57–80;

"What Is Poetry?" *Russell's Magazine,* 4 (July 1857): 327–337.

William J. Grayson came to concentrate on writing only in the final decades of a long and varied career as lawyer, teacher, planter, legislator, government official, and member of Congress. Although the impetus for his most famous poem, *The Hireling and the Slave* (1854), was political, the poems he wrote in the later 1850s are primarily pastoral. He is usually seen as a prosodic dinosaur, an anachronistic Augustan couplet-monger in the age of American Romanticism. Like his friend Hugh Swinton Legaré, Grayson was by education and inclination a classicist, but the caricature of him as a glacial reactionary of narrow views is misleading. He never went abroad, but he was always in touch with English and Continental thought. In his final major writings, two biographies and an autobiography, Grayson looks both forward to the doubtful future of the American republic and backward to the Golden Age of his idyllic Sea Island childhood.

Born seventy miles south of Charleston in Beaufort, the chief town of Port Royal Island, on 12 November 1788, William John Grayson Jr. was the elder and only surviving son of William John Grayson Sr. by his wife, Susannah, daughter of the local merchant Daniel John Greene. Grayson's father had a distinguished career as a Continental officer in the Revolution until his capture at the fall of Charleston in 1780. Intended for a mercantile career by his father, a Yorkshire merchant turned Carolina planter, Captain Grayson opted, as his son did later, for the law. The elder William Grayson did not belong to the grandee level of planter, although through his mother, Sarah Wigg, descendant of an ancient Buckinghamshire family who came to Carolina at the turn of the eighteenth century to prosper and proliferate mightily, he was usefully connected to the Hazzard and Heyward families, and so indirectly to the predominant local planter family, the Barnwells. In the South Carolina in which the poet William Grayson lived and stood for office, family connections were always of the first importance.

The happiest days of young William's childhood were spent with his doting paternal grandmother on her plantation on nearby Parris Island, a subtropical paradise with orange groves and pomegranates in profusion. His life seems to have been entirely uncomplicated until his father died on 10 October 1797, shortly before the boy's ninth birthday. Grayson lost not only a father, but the prospect of life as a planter, for Captain Grayson's estate was found to be heavily encumbered; the son's one inalienable inheritance was membership in the Society of the Cincinnati. The captain's widow secured her financial future when in September 1798 she married William Joyner, a prosperous planter who took charge of his stepson's education. The boy might have reasonably expected to be educated by his stepfather, a widower with four children

of his own, but beyond that his expectations were minimal.

As was befitting his enhanced station, Grayson was sent to school in the North, first to New Utrecht, Long Island, then to Newark Academy. Joyner's good intentions may actually have stunted the lad's intellectual growth, for the eccentric Scottish dominie who ran the New Utrecht academy did not permit his students to use books. Grayson complains in his autobiography, published as *Witness to Sorrow: The Antebellum Autobiography of William J. Grayson* in 1990, that "my mind was deprived of all nourishment and starved for want of food except what a free intercourse with nature gave it." Intercourse with nature remained a vital element of Grayson's life long after he found books and began to write them himself. Despite the schools' shortcomings, his northern sojourn did expose him to the world beyond his harmonious but self-referential Sea Island society.

Originally Grayson was intended for Harvard. Doubtless his career would have been different if he had matriculated there, but instead he returned to South Carolina in 1803 and was enrolled in the Beaufort Grammar School, one of the best in the state. In 1804 he transferred to a private school kept by Milton Maxcy, who first introduced young Grayson to the classical literature that shaped everything he wrote as an adult. Maxcy probably influenced Joyner to send Grayson to the new South Carolina College, of which his brother, Jonathan Maxcy, was founding president. Arriving in Columbia in February 1807, he found the teaching and books for which he had pined on Long Island, and he also made friends he was to keep for life, most notably a young man of Huguenot descent, James Louis Petigru, who remained Grayson's closest friend for more than half a century and whose biography was Grayson's final literary achievement. Petigru graduated with first honors in the class of 1809; illness deprived Grayson of a chance to share those honors with his friend.

Grayson believed that his college education had done nothing to prepare him for adult life, noting in his autobiography: "I became a bachelor of arts with the usual inaptitude of the tribe for any definite or useful employment." Because his patrimony was insufficient to enable Grayson to set up as a planter, his only options, as he saw them at twenty-one years old, were to become an author or a schoolmaster. As the former was not really an option in the rural South in the first decade of the nineteenth century, Grayson drifted into teaching. If he lacked capital, he never wanted for connections, and he soon became assistant principal of Beaufort College, which had opened in 1802 while he was "at the North."

*Sarah Matilda Somersall Grayson, circa 1830 (Collection of Henrietta Barnes Parker)*

He greatly enhanced his financial and social leverage by marriage in January 1814 to Sarah Matilda Somersall, daughter of a wealthy Charleston merchant-planter and granddaughter of a Revolutionary hero and intendant of Charleston, Colonel Daniel Stevens. Maternally she was a Legaré, and thus a cousin to Hugh Swinton Legaré, who after the marriage became her husband's good friend. On her father's side she was a direct descendant of Cotton Mather, so the marriage brought useful contacts not only in Charleston, but also in the first circles of Boston. The marriage was a successful and harmonious partnership, but the parents lost one daughter in infancy, their elder son at a young age and were deeply disappointed in their next son, who died to them when he became a chronic alcoholic. Both surviving daughters married well; the elder daughter, Maria, gave Grayson a home in the last year of his life, and the younger daughter, Sarah, kept his literary flame alive into the twentieth century, bringing out a selection of her father's poems, including some that had never before been published, in 1907.

Throughout his life Grayson made important adjustments to his career in response to a variety of circumstances—even his fertile Indian summer career as belletrist was prompted, in large part, by the publication of Harriet Beecher Stowe's *Uncle Tom's Cabin* in 1852. He drifted into politics almost by accident, when James Hazzard Cuthbert, a connection with whom he shared many cousins, died suddenly during the legislative session in Columbia in October 1813. In November, Grayson was elected to fill out Cuthbert's unexpired term and then reelected in his own right in 1814. He had to give up his seat when in August 1815 he left the state to become principal of the Savannah Academy. After a year in Savannah a malaria epidemic sent the Graysons, now four in number, back to Beaufort. Grayson resumed teaching at Beaufort College until the yellow fever epidemic of 1817, which killed a sixth of the white population of the town, closed the school.

Again finding himself at a loss, he began to study law and was admitted to the South Carolina bar in 1822. The law was for Grayson only a conduit into the much more interesting field of politics. He returned to the South Carolina House of Representatives in 1822 and served there until elevated to the state senate in 1826, where he remained until elected commissioner in equity for the Beaufort District in December 1831. During his latter years in the state senate, and throughout his time as master in equity, Grayson also edited the local newspaper, the pro-Nullification *Beaufort Gazette*. Grayson followed the usual pattern for an ambitious Lowcountry politician: yeoman duty in the lower house, followed by a stint in the senate, then, with luck, connections, and ability, a judicial appointment. He never held statewide office, operating exclusively in the political circles of Beaufort and Charleston. Although he held elected office for a total of seventeen years there was always in Grayson the politician a certain lack of engagement. One senses that he never found politics particularly compelling and was disappointed in himself for not liking it more. His ability to stand back from his actions and view his own life with detachment make him a superb ironist when he surveys his life in his autobiography, but it often made for puzzlement and underachievement in that life itself.

The culmination of Grayson's public career came with his election to Congress in 1832. He served two terms as representative for the Beaufort-Colleton District, during which time he made no great noise in Washington. Partly because he dithered over seeking reelection, he was defeated for a third term in 1836. Grayson returned to South Carolina, not to Beaufort but to the larger pond of Charleston, to regroup, read, and reflect. Like Legaré, he decided to ally himself with the Whigs, and, following their victory in 1840, he too partook of the spoils, being awarded the lucrative and undemanding post of collector of the Port of Charleston, which he held for three presidential terms, until removed by Franklin Pierce in 1853.

Rare among important antebellum Southern writers in his complete freedom from any pressure to write for money, Grayson could afford to please himself—and he did. Soon after he relinquished the collectorship, he purchased "Fair Lawn," a plantation of 4,462 acres, for $100,000 in cash. At this time the celebrated apologist for slavery owned more than a hundred slaves himself. Grayson's writings of the 1850s may usefully be viewed as a variety of sublimated autobiographies. *The Hireling and the Slave* obviously relates to his other late-blooming career, that of large planter, and his 1860 life of Francis Marion is an oblique glance at Grayson's own origins, for in it he revisits the war in which his father fought as an American officer. Finally he turned to biography proper.

Grayson began his productive years as a writer with an 1850 open letter to the secessionist governor, Whitemarsh Seabrook, arguing that the American Confederacy, as he rather confusingly calls it, is unique: "Nothing like it exists, or has ever existed on earth." His predictions are about equally right and wrong; he does not think that Virginia would join a Southern Confederacy, but he assumes that any secession would lead inevitably to war. Grayson spends less time in detailing the supposed benefits of union than in demolishing charges of unconstitutional actions by Congress. At the prospect of solo secession by South Carolina, he finally lets sarcasm jar the pained reasonableness of his argument, wondering whether his state will "stand apart and alone—the San Marino of North America." At the close of the letter, as he evokes his long personal connection with Seabrook, his anguish at the damage politics was inflicting on friendship is evident. That anguish grew in intensity over the troubled decade that followed.

This twenty-page epistle did not exhaust Grayson's ideas about the secession controversy. At the same time he also wrote a curtly titled pamphlet, *The Union, Past and Future. How It Works and How to Save It* (1850). In the following year he collected in book form a series of letters he had published in the *Charleston Courier* as *The Letters of Curtius,* self-consciously evoking his Augustan roots and affinities in this use of a Latin pseudonym, so common in the polemical writing of the eighteenth century. In contrast to the restrained tone of the letter to Seabrook, in *The Letters of Curtius* he lets himself go in exuberant and professedly Swiftian satire, for all the disclaimer in the introduction that the letters "contain nothing which transcends the limits of that calm and temperate irony which has been applied to even higher subjects, by far greater authority."

A somewhat dilatory contributor to Simms's *Southern Quarterly Review,* Grayson, after his removal from the collectorship, was free to play a much more active role in the last Charleston literary journal of the antebellum period. Throughout its brief life, from 1857 to 1860, Grayson was closely associated with *Russell's Magazine.* He wrote the lead article in the debut issue and went on to write essays, reviews, and poetry for the magazine. While his opinions on slavery were orthodox, he clearly enjoyed being outrageously out of date in his literary opinions. His most important critical article, "What Is Poetry?," is a profession of faith in Alexander Pope and the Augustans. In this essay he shows a comic sense of a world turned upside down, where "Poetry becomes prose and prose becomes poetry." Regarding politics he eschewed a comic tone, particularly with disunion in 1860.

The one work for which Grayson is remembered is *The Hireling and the Slave* (1854). Critics have only recently begun to consider this celebrated work as a serious poem, considering elements other than its argument in favor of chattel slavery. If there is nothing original in the argument, or in the verse form employed—Grayson's favorite, the heroic couplet—the combination of the two is novel. An energetic Popean poem of 1,494 lines in two parts, it is consciously archaic in prosody and even pronunciation, as in the end rhyme "join" being pronounced "jine." Grayson does not make extraordinary claims for slavery, rather seeing it as a practical solution that may in time be modified. Devoting slightly more than a hundred often amusing lines to naming names and excoriating specific Northern fanatics, he skewers his satirical targets—Charles Sumner, Horace Greeley, and the unspeakable Stowe. Vernon Parrington wrote admiringly: "With a few dexterous turns of the spit he browns each one nicely like a roasted goose." The benefit of slavery is to civilize, "To tame and elevate the negro mind." He voices the fear that change in the legal relations of white and black would lead to "one bronze coloured breed"—yet, if Grayson is racist, he is no more so than Ralph Waldo Emerson, who held similar views.

In this famous poem about slavery, Grayson is happiest, and most felicitous, when he is not talking about slavery at all. Reverting to pastoral in a deeply felt hymn to his own birthplace, he celebrates the joys of hunting and fishing "Where bold Port Royal spreads its mimic sea." Grayson's writings are distinguished by a feeling for place as profound as that of

*Grayson, circa 1830 (portrait attributed to Samuel F. B. Morse; Collection of Henrietta Barnes Parker)*

any Southern writer of the antebellum period. There is a hint of his growing interest in the heroic figures of the Revolution when mention of neighboring Pinckney Island leads him to an extended tribute to the vanished virtues of its former owner, General Charles Cotesworth Pinckney. Like Legaré, Grayson often has to revert to the Revolution or to Rome itself to find the Roman virtues he admires. Toward the close of the poem he casts a glance further backward, to the Indian past he explores in greater detail in "Chicora" (1856).

At 1,836 lines, "Chicora" is Grayson's longest poem. The title is the Indian word for the region of the poet's birth. Here, as acknowledged in the preface, he enters into territory Henry Wadsworth Longfellow had already marked. This poem is not in heroic couplets, but in octasyllables, a mixture of couplets and linked quatrains, with two long passages in six-line stanzas. He begins by evoking Port Royal in the prelapsarian phase before the advent of the white men, asking "What isles of earth are blessed like

these?" Far less racist than Grayson's writings about African slaves, "Chicora" is notable for its deep sympathy for the vanished Indians, evinced in an attempt to enter imaginatively into their lives and religion. His ear is more sensitive than in any other of his major poems: "The surge is hushed, the waves subside." The poem closes with the destruction of Chicora, through invasion and cultural genocide perpetrated by the Spanish, and a lament for the surviving Indian who must leave "The bright isles of his native land."

The third of Grayson's long poems, *The Country* (1858) represents a significant shift in focus: it is again in heroic couplets, but at 716 lines is only half as long as its predecessors, both of which had celebrated and defended the South. Dedicated to and ending with a tribute to the idealized improving planter, Wade Hampton II, *The Country* is overtly American; at times, in its catalogues of midwestern rivers, it sounds like a bizarre marriage of Pope and Walt Whitman. It subscribes to the Manifest Destiny of Americans who "see and follow far / In western skies, the light of Empire's star." Grayson is almost as fluent as ever, but there is more enjambment and less tightness in the epithets. Few individual lines stand out. The poem suggests that perhaps Grayson's creativity was beginning to flag, or perhaps he was at his strongest only when drawing direct inspiration from his Sea Island childhood.

Grayson's last long poem appears to be based closely on a prose sketch by his friend Simms, "Marion—the Carolina Partisan," which appeared in *Russell's Magazine* in October and November 1858. Concentrating exclusively on Francis Marion's military exploits in 1780–1781, Simms slips into Grayson's favorite pastoral mode, rhapsodizing on the "unexampled beauty" of the Carolina swamps. Part 1 ends with the miraculous conversion by Marion of a young British officer to the cause of the "beautiful virgin" liberty, portrayed almost like an incident from a medieval saint's life. Grayson evidently saw in Simms's historical sketch the possibilities for another long poem, in which he would be freed from the responsibility of providing a detailed narrative of skirmishes. He had recently had experience on a smaller scale of casting prose into verse, when at the request of church authorities he turned the Protestant Episcopal Society's 1857 tract *Appearance and Reality* into what became one of his most popular poems, "A Sunday Morning's Dream." *Russell's Magazine* began serializing Grayson's "Marion" in December 1858; it ran through March 1859. Doubtless it was a relief to Grayson to revert to a day in which sides could be taken so decisively, in which differences were so clear and causes so shining, in which it was noble to be partisan. Grayson finds it impossible to see the struggles of the 1850s as a Manichaean contest between Southern light and Northern darkness. The Tories and British are not the caricatures they were in the Simms "Marion"; allowing that some of the British fought for "loftier ends," Grayson, even in writing about a partisan, can never be as partisan as Simms.

The poem *Marion* (1860) is more a meditation on the life and character of this great man than a connected narrative. Like the later *James Louis Petigru. A Biographical Sketch* (1866), it is an attempt to keep the lamp lit, to preserve the memory of a great man. Like "Chicora," this poem of 1,483 lines, in ten sections of unequal length, is written in octasyllabic couplets, with some passages, fewer than in the earlier poem, in linked quatrains. It is enlivened by strong marchlike rhythms, as in "Souls were the forts of Marion's men." For the first time in his verse Grayson varies couplets with triplets—if not exactly experimenting at the close of his brief but busy career as a writer of longer poems, he was still expanding his repertoire of prosodic devices. Frequently he resorts to footnotes to supply details he cannot fit into his verse. Sections 1 through 9 follow the chronology of the prose "Marion," from the fall of Charleston in May 1780 until the victory at Eutaw Springs in September 1781, but Grayson adds to Simms's materials a coda, "Retirement," in which he idealizes the partisan's rural senescence. This section has clear autobiographical resonances in the poet's own life at "Fair Lawn" in the 1850s. As he did after the first edition of *The Hireling and the Slave*, Grayson made substantial changes to the text of this poem before offering it to the public again, in a privately printed edition, in 1860. The most significant change is the addition at the end of a thirty-nine-line apostrophe to Marion, serene in his fame without the trappings thereof: "Sleep, gallant chief, around thy grave / No sculptured busts nor columns rise." Another contributor to *Russell's Magazine*, Henry Timrod, may have remembered these lines in 1866 when he wrote the most famous of Confederate elegies, "The Magnolia Cemetery Ode."

Grayson's final literary projects were a pair of biographies of South Carolinian military, political, and juridical heroes William Lowndes and James Louis Petigru, both of whom he knew personally, and an account of his own outwardly unheroic life. The biography of Lowndes, written in 1860 at the request of Benjamin Perry, was lost, along with Petigru's house and a sixth of the city, in the last great fire in Charleston, in December 1861. An obvious labor of love, the biography of Petigru is a complement to Grayson's autobiography, the composition of which he apparently interrupted to sketch the life of his friend. In writing of Petigru, Grayson is really writing a sort of counterautobiography or variations on his autobiography, as so much of his friend's life mirrors his own, in the struggles over nullification and the attempt, in the end impossible, to hold the Unionist position against a wronging tide in an increasingly isolationist South Carolina. On a personal level, he could identify with his subject's enduring grief at the death in childhood of a son of promise. Both *James Louis Petigru* and the autobiography employ a distinctive tone, by turns conversational and stately, nostalgic and sharply ironic. Grayson writes what is in effect an elegy for his whole society, in the midst of the war that destroyed it, chronicling both the decline of individual men and of the conditions that had produced Grayson and Petigru.

*Witness to Sorrow* has been considered by some scholars to be one of the great American self-portraits. Its classical restraint and detachment are all the more remarkable considering it was written against the backdrop of Grayson's somber apprehension, from the dark depths of 1862–1863, that the American republic was a failed experiment. A life that began with the American republic—Grayson was born in the year South Carolina ratified the Constitution—draws to a close as that republic seemingly is itself expiring.

Grayson begins his autobiography by invoking Samuel Johnson in the first sentence before delineating the responsibilities of the autobiographer: "He should tell the truth only, but not the whole truth." There are wonderfully incisive miniature portraits of the great egos that he was well placed in the 1830s to observe in action and interaction, including Andrew Jackson, Henry Clay, John C. Calhoun, and John Quincy Adams. Sometimes he writes with a splendid acerbity, as when he speaks of the reminiscences of Thomas Hart Benton: "Yet the vanity is refreshing. It is the least repulsive feature in his character." He views the power of incumbency as a narcotic; yet, he does not even mention his own congressional defeat. Throughout he skips over whole areas of his life; there is not a word on the four years between his service in Congress and his collectorship.

Indeed, after the chapters on his time in Washington there is nothing like chronological narration again. Chapter 11, "Poetry and Poets," constitutes Grayson's most extended literary criticism. He is disarmingly modest about his own literary efflorescence in the 1850s: "It may with reason be asked why I continued to write. It was to have something to do." He moves abruptly from literary study to the battlefield in chapter 12, blaming the war on "Northern folly and madness" while crying plague on Southern politicians and strategists, including President Jefferson Davis. In

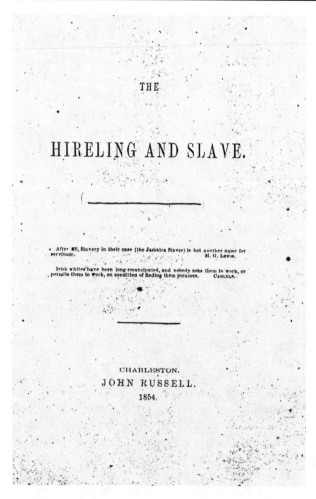

THE

HIRELING AND SLAVE.

After all, Slavery in their case (the Jamaica Slaves) is but another name for servitude.
M. G. Lewis.

Irish whites have been long emancipated, and nobody asks them to work, or permits them to work, on condition of finding them potatoes.
Carlyle.

CHARLESTON.
JOHN RUSSELL.
1854.

*Title page for Grayson's long poem in defense of slavery (South Caroliniana Library, University of South Carolina)*

the final chapter, titled simply "Old Letters," Grayson, fearing the fall and sack of Charleston, sorts his private papers for the flames. The chapter begins: "For some days past I have been living among ghosts, among the shadows of events long past and of persons dead during many years." The letters he reads before destroying "have been able to draw spirits from the vasty deep, the shades of old friendships closed by death, of departed hopes and fears, joys and sorrows, successes and disappointments. I see among them visions of time wasted, opportunity neglected, kindness or love not properly appreciated. . . ." Richard Calhoun's suggestion that Grayson's "War Diary," which he appends to his fine edition of the autobiography, was intended to close that work, is persuasive—the diary form shows that Grayson could no longer detach himself from the terrible things that were going on around him. Such brutal times could not be reduced to beautifully balanced periods.

Grayson's frankest autobiographical writing comes not in the autobiography but in several shorter

poems written right at the end of his life, when he was in his seventies, and which, unlike the autobiography, were probably never intended for publication. In these late lyrics, published in *Selected Poems* (1907), Grayson confesses his belief that his life, like his country, has been a failure, a waste of time and talent: "Buried or lost the talent lent, / Neglected idly or abused." The most candid of these late poems, "Life," reviews his whole life in fourteen six-line stanzas cataloguing his deepest personal disappointments, the private griefs on which he is silent in the stoical autobiography. Perhaps the most moving stanza Grayson ever penned is that on the loss of a loved son to alcoholism:

> The coarse debauch, the reeking bowl,
>   The reeling step, the bloated face
> Debase the mind, imbrute the soul,
>   And blast each youthful bloom and grace.
> What are the wrecks of stormy seas
> To wrecks of hopes and hearts like these?

It is no longer possible to sustain the serene faith he expresses at the close of an earlier and shorter autobiographical review, "Threescore Years and Seven," published in 1855 in the *Charleston Courier*. At the end of "Life" he asks for light from God but takes the hand of his "dear wife" of half a century.

There is always an emotional as well as an intellectual commitment in Grayson's major works. The feeling is genuine; he never merely postures. Richard Calhoun remarks of the autobiography: "It is, in part, pastoral prose poem." Indeed, it may profitably be seen as the grandest of Grayson's poetical productions. Despite his own disclaimers, Grayson's was a poetic life in an age of clamorous prose. That his autobiography should be of a piece with his poems attests to the unity of his writings. They share a shining consistency of thought and artistic purpose the more remarkable given the turbulent times in which Grayson lived—a turbulence to which he bears eloquent witness. His poems are notable for their classical balance, beautiful modulations, and decorous turns of phrase. Grayson is not a master of the miniature; his one published sonnet is not particularly successful. He needs the scope of the longer poem in order to develop his ideas, to paint his landscapes, to evoke pathos. All of his late poems and biographies are in a significant sense elegiac—even his defense of slavery is somehow valedictory.

Grayson could not know when he lamented the Indians' fate in "Chicora" that he too would die a displaced person, far from the Lowcountry he passionately loved. The descendants of the conquering whites who settled the Carolina sea islands were forced to flee Beaufort and the islands when they were seized by

Union forces in November 1861. Much of Grayson's poetry of the 1850s is eerily prophetic of the agonies of the following decade. After enduring the first part of the siege of Charleston, of which he gives a vivid account in the surviving portion of the "War Diary," covering the period from May to November 1862, Grayson reluctantly quit his suffering city in 1863 to stay with his elder daughter, whose husband, Thomas Ogier, was surgeon general of Confederate South Carolina, in the relative safety of Newberry, forty miles north of Columbia. Here, worn out by private and public griefs and doubtless depleted by literary labors impressive for a septuagenarian, William John Grayson died on 4 October 1863, within hours of writing the closing pages of his biography of Petigru.

Since critics have come to recognize that the poetic quality of *The Hireling and the Slave* transcends the poet's politics, it is time to correct the misconception that Grayson is a one-poem phenomenon. A new edition of his poems is needed; indeed, there has never been a collected edition. The autobiography is wonderful, but it is not reliable or complete as a biography. Grayson is so oblique about his own life, and frequently so self-deprecating, that there is surely room for a full-length life of this fascinating and underregarded figure. If anyone in the Antebellum South possessed the tragic sense of life, it was Grayson, a many-sided man who long lived at the center of the intellectual and political life of his times, if not always in step with the tendencies of either.

**References:**

Richard J. Calhoun, "William J. Grayson: Autobiographer," in *Witness to Sorrow: The Antebellum Autobiography of William J. Grayson* (Columbia: University of South Carolina Press, 1990), pp. 1–34;

Jay B. Hubbell, "William J. Grayson," in his *The South in American Literature, 1607–1900* (Durham, N.C.: Duke University Press, 1954), pp. 438–446;

Edd Winfield Parks, "William J. Grayson: Neo-Classicist," in his *Ante-Bellum Southern Literary Critics* (Athens: University of Georgia Press, 1962), pp. 185–192;

Vernon Louis Parrington, "William J. Grayson," in his *Main Currents in American Thought: An Interpretation of American Literature from the Beginnings to 1920,* volume 2 (New York: Harcourt, Brace, 1927), pp. 103–108;

Edmund Wilson, "Diversity of Opinion in the South: William J. Grayson, George Fitzhugh, Hilton R. Helper," in his *Patriotic Gore: Studies in the Literature of the American Civil War* (London: Oxford University Press, 1969), pp. 336–341.

**Papers:**

The manuscripts of William J. Grayson's autobiography and of his "War Diary" are in the South Caroliniana Library at the University of South Carolina.

# George Washington Harris

*(20 March 1814 – 11 December 1869)*

Robert D. Habich
*Ball State University*

See also the Harris entries in *DLB 3: Antebellum Writers in New York and the South* and *DLB 11: American Humorists, 1800–1950.*

BOOKS: *Sut Lovingood. Yarns Spun by a "Nat'ral Born Durn'd Fool.["] Warped and Wove for Public Wear* (New York: Dick & Fitzgerald, 1867); revised and enlarged as *Sut Lovingood's Yarns: Edited for the Modern Reader,* edited by M. Thomas Inge (New Haven: Yale University Press, 1966);

*Sut Lovingood Travels with Old ABE LINCOLN,* introduction by Edd Winfield Parks (Chicago: Black Cat, 1937);

*Sut Lovingood,* edited, with an introduction, by Brom Weber (New York: Grove, 1954);

*The Lovingood Papers,* 4 volumes, edited by Ben Harris McClary (Knoxville: University of Tennessee Press, 1962–1965);

*High Times and Hard Times: Sketches and Tales by George Washington Harris,* edited, with introductory essays, by Inge (Nashville, Tenn.: Vanderbilt University Press, 1967).

**Edition:** *Sut Lovingood Yarns,* facsimile edition, edited by Inge (Memphis, Tenn.: St. Lukes Press, 1987).

OTHER: "Sut Lovegood's Yarns," "The Story of a Shirt," "How Sut Lovegood's Daddy Acted Hoss," and "Sut's Experience with S-o-d-y P-o-u-d-e-r-s," in *The Harp of a Thousand Strings,* edited by Samuel Putnam Avery (New York: Dick & Fitzgerald, 1858).

*George Washington Harris*

The author of one major collection of fiction, George Washington Harris wrote in the tradition of Southwestern humor, with its comic exaggerations, tall tales, rural dialects, and democratic challenges to authority by backwoods tricksters. Popular in his lifetime but never a professional author, he was a businessman and minor political figure who wrote primarily for newspapers and magazines; his work ranged from playful sketches of rural Tennessee life to scathing political satire to the extravagant humor of his most enduring creation, Sut Lovingood, the protagonist of some fifty tales and the titular hero of Harris's 1867 collection *Sut Lovingood. Yarns Spun by a "Nat'ral Born Durn'd Fool.["] Warped and Wove for Public Wear.* Edmund Wilson, in his *Patriotic Gore: Studies in the Literature of the American Civil War* (1962), called the book "by far the most repellent book of any real literary merit in American literature," but generations of readers (and other writers) continue to find in Sut an oddly compelling mixture of vulnerability and power, coarseness and principle–a comic avenger whose goals seem to be the restoration of an orderly social structure and a lusty enjoyment of life.

Though Harris became so closely identified with his most famous character that he was often called "Sut" himself, his life bears little resemblance to the backwoods adventures of the yarns. Harris was born in Allegheny City, Pennsylvania, near Pittsburgh, on 20 March 1814. According to family tradition, his father was also named George and was probably from Virginia; his mother, Margaret Glover Bell, was the widow of Samuel Bell, to whom she had borne a son, Samuel Bell Jr., around 1798. Nothing more is recorded of Harris's parents or of young George until 1819, when his half brother Samuel set up shop as a metalworker in Knoxville, Tennessee, returned to Allegheny City to marry, and brought his bride and five-year-old George to live in Knoxville.

The details of Harris's childhood are sketchy. He certainly had some schooling, at least enough to instill in him a love of reading that later became apparent in his tales. (By 1840 he owned an unusually large personal library of seventy-five volumes, and Milton Rickels, in his 1965 Twayne volume devoted to Harris, has identified references in his work to many writers, including William Shakespeare; William Congreve; Charles Dickens; Robert Burns; George Gordon, Lord Byron; Alexander Pope; and Henry Wadsworth Longfellow.) His formal schooling ended by 1826, when he was apprenticed to Samuel in his jewelry business. That same year the first steamboat arrived in Knoxville, an event so galvanizing that the city commissioned the building of its own boat. The twelve-year-old Harris's response to the excitement was to construct a functioning scale model of the steamboat, which he operated to the delight of the public in a pond at the center of town. Thus, early in his life he seems to have established talents that define his adult career as an author: a meticulous attention to craft and a love of spectacle.

By 1835, his apprenticeship concluded, Harris married the daughter of a Knoxville businessman, Mary Emeline Nance, and became captain of the steamship *Knoxville*, an impressive achievement for a man just twenty-one years old. He continued his career on the river for four years, including service during the forced removal of the Cherokees in 1838. In 1839 he contracted some acreage in nearby Blount County; but at the end of the first year, when the first promissory note came due, Harris was already in financial trouble, and his career as a gentleman farmer was short-lived.

Around 1840 Harris probably published his first writing in the *Knoxville Argus*, a fiercely partisan Democratic newspaper edited by his friend Elbridge Gerry Eastman. What he wrote of the political pieces that appeared in the *Argus* cannot be determined; but Eastman's early encouragement of Harris's writing was acknowledged in the preface to *Sut Lovingood. Yarns.*

Harris remained in Blount County until 1842; a year later, back in Knoxville, he opened a metalworking shop, offering everything from toolmaking to engraving, from patent models to fine jewelry. In that same year Harris published his first identified pieces, a series of sporting letters signed "Mr. Free" that appeared in the magazine edited by William Trotter Porter of New York, the *Spirit of the Times.*

With a wide circulation and an even wider scope—agriculture, literature, drama, and the outdoors—the *Spirit of the Times* offered Harris his first opportunity to craft a vision of life in rural east Tennessee. The "Mr. Free" letters of 1843, three of the four written from "Possum Knob," are miscellanies of rural customs, hunting tales, and purportedly local news, all narrated by the affable Free in a genteel style far removed from the raw dialect that characterizes the Lovingood tales. Harris's letters satisfied Eastern readers' appetite for tales of backwoods horse-racing, corn-shucking, coon-hunting, and quilting, but they had little to distinguish them from many others printed in the *Spirit of the Times*. The epistles are rambling productions, often self-conscious or contrived in their narration; the familiarity of the epistolary format is ill-suited to published letters from Tennessee to New York. Nevertheless, even in this journeyman work Harris's later vividness of description, ear for colloquialisms, and eye for "odd specimens of humanity" are evident.

Harris's first full-length short story, "The Knob Dance—A Tennessee Frolic," appeared in the 2 August 1845 *Spirit of the Times,* two years after his sporting epistles, and marks a dramatic improvement over them in technique and composition. Ostensibly, "The Knob Dance" was occasioned by a published letter from an anonymous Mississippian, who charged that East Tennesseans had no amusements save politics and religion. Harris's persona, now signing himself "Sugartail" after the local name for a donkey, defends the reputation of his region for fun in the broadest terms, "from a *kiss* that cracks like a wagin-whip up to a *fite* that rouses up all outdoors," but places the actual story of the "frolick" in the mouth of an interior narrator, Dick Harlan. While the story itself, of a raucous dance that ends in a drunken brawl, hinges on the thinnest of plots, it captures the energy of the event with rapid dialogue, exaggeration, and an escalating violence that ends harmlessly. There is little differentiation between the voices of "Sugartail" and Dick Harlan; the framed narrative, however, which Harris had begun to experiment with, served him well in his later writing.

Harris continued to write as "Sugartail" for the *Spirit of the Times* in 1846 and 1847, experimenting with narrative strategies and voice and refining his control of plot and delineation of character. "The Snake-Bit Irish-

*Illustration by Justin H. Howard for "Sut Lovingood's Daddy—Acting Horse" in* Sut Lovingood. Yarns Spun by a "Nat'ral Born Durn'd Fool["] *(1867; South Caroliniana Library, University of South Carolina)*

man" (17 January 1846) is a straightforward story of comeuppance, with an overbearing Irishman driven from a hunting camp by pranksters who fasten a deergut "snake" to his breeches. The story was in circulation at the time; "Sugartail" claims it occurred in East Tennessee, and when Harris rewrote it for *Sut Lovingood. Yarns* he recast it to make Sut the trickster. "A Sleep-Walking Incident" is notable for Harris's deft management of two voices, the affected business traveler and the grizzled old man who offers him lodging for the night in a house filled with "three blooming daughters, all shyness and blushing." Predictably, the stranger is driven out at gunpoint after his host finds him "sleepwalking" among the girls; only the conspiratorial help of the host's young son enables the businessman to escape ahead of his outraged pursuer. In such tales, in which plots turn on ethnic stereotypes and tame sexual jokes, the real humor is based upon dialogue, contrasting points of view, the honest lustiness of both men and women, and what later became a trademark of the Sut tales: a restoration of harmony through the expulsion or humiliation of an intruding, self-possessed outsider.

However attractive Harris may have found the literary life, after 1847 there is no record of his publishing

again for nearly seven years. (The *Spirit of the Times* for 12 January 1850 alludes to a Christmas story written by Harris, but it has never been located.) Most likely, Harris's time was taken up with family, commerce, and an increasing activity in statewide Democratic politics. In 1854 he returned to the river as captain of the steamboat *Alida,* and for several months that year he visited the Tennessee mining district of Ducktown as a surveyor. In October 1854 the *Spirit of the Times* carried his first known written work in seven years, a surprisingly sentimental sketch by "Sugartail" titled "How to Marry." A month later Harris published his last story for Porter's magazine, the first to feature the backwoods rascal who made him famous: "Sut Lovingood's Daddy—Acting Horse."

The tale, which opens the 1867 collection of Lovingood yarns, provides a rare glimpse of Sut and his family at a moment of crisis: their plowing horse dead and planting time come, Dad decides to play the horse's role to prompt the others to get to work, and he takes the acting too far. As Sut's mother tells Dad: "Yu plays hoss better nur yu dus husban." Barging through a stand of sassafras, he upsets a hornets' nest, strips off the horsehide disguise, and heads naked for the safety of the creek, kicking and squealing "jis es natral es yu ever seed any uther skeer'd hoss du" as the hornets swarm around him. Sut then becomes his father's tormentor—"Kick em—bite em—paw em—switch em wif yure tail, dad"—before taking off to town, where he tells the story to a crowd lolling on the porch of the general store. Aside from the slapstick elements of Dad's predicament, the tale introduces two important elements of Sut's character: his delight in the agonies that render the powerful powerless, and his view that only a "durned old fool" like his father would violate the laws of nature and common sense to pose as something, or someone, he is not. That Dad so comfortably "acts horse" is a reminder of the bestial nature of mankind—a dualism Sut alternately celebrates and laments in the later stories. In addition, the tale introduces the citified, educated "outside narrator" who frames Sut's story. In later yarns he is called "George," perhaps a thinly veiled persona for the author himself, and he is occasionally a character as well as a scene-setter. In this story his role is merely to prepare readers for Sut's entrance and provide a vivid description of Sut: "a queer looking, long legged, short bodied, small headed, white haired, hog eyed, funny sort of a genius."

Exactly how Harris landed on the character of Sut Lovingood is a matter of speculation. While surveying in Ducktown he met a local character, Sut Miller, often mentioned as a model for Lovingood; Harris may have been playing on "S——l," with which he sometimes signed his "Sugartail" pieces; Sut's last name makes obvious, and ironic, reference to his comic self-image as a ladies' man. Whatever his genesis, in the multifaceted rogue Sut Lovingood, Harris found the character that shaped his literary career, for Sut is appealing, and useful, on a variety of levels that differentiate him from other figures in the Southwestern humor tradition. Unlike Johnson J. Hooper's predatory Simon Suggs, for instance, Sut is not merely "shifty in a new country." Though he clearly relishes bringing down the mighty, he rarely is interested in usurping their power or bilking them of their money; when presented with opportunities to steal and exploit he consistently turns them down, despite his suspicions that he is a fool for doing so. Unlike the narrator in Thomas Bangs Thorpe's "Big Bear of Arkansas" (1841), Sut is more than a genial braggart. His verbal posturing belies his insecurity in a world of flux, human frailties, and treachery: always prepared to run from trouble, Sut perpetrates "skeers" on his enemies while constantly on the lookout for them himself, painfully aware that he acts "in the name, an' wif the sperit, ove plum natral born durn fool." In Sut, Harris had discovered a protagonist, a narrator, a mouthpiece, and a lens through whom he could view the timely, and timeless, qualities of the world around him.

As Edd Winfield Parks notes in his edition of *Sut Lovingood Travels with Old ABE LINCOLN* (1937), Sut is not "by nature" a political commentator. Yet, Harris clearly found him useful as a satiric consciousness for exploring the politics of the day, particularly in the years leading up to the Civil War. Always a frank defender of the Democratic Party and the values of the Old South, Harris must have felt increasingly out of step in Knoxville, where in 1861 a pro-Union convention petitioned for separate statehood to avoid being part of the Confederacy. In 1856 Harris published his first political satire, "Playing Old Sledge for the Presidency," a dream vision in which Sut imagines James Buchanan, Millard Fillmore, and John C. Frémont playing the card game known as "old sledge" or "seven up" to get elected. A straightforward satire with obscure topical references, "Playing Old Sledge" no longer holds much interest, except for establishing Sut as a sarcastic observer.

"Sut Lovingood's Love Feast for Varmints," prompted by Harris's attendance at the state Democratic convention in Nashville in 1859, is a more successful effort. Published in four parts in the *Nashville Union and American* in 1859, the piece satirizes the ragtag political factions that attempted to unseat the Democratic governor by likening the strange alliance to a collection of animals scheming to usurp humanity: "ef they kin do half they wunt tu the coon will be squire, the groun-hog constable, an the wolf preacher, an

humans mus dig roots fur a livin and the he's howl on the cliff when they wants the company ove the she's." Not a dream vision, the piece combines the tall tale and the beast fable, with Sut as the amazed and worried narrator. "Sut Lovingood's Love Feast for Varmints" focuses on state politicians and issues now obscured, but it resembles other Sut tales in its concern for the right order of things, its recognition of the potential bestiality of humans, and its condemnation of pretenders, whether they are wolves changing nature with muskrats or Know-Nothings affecting genuine political savvy.

Harris's most famous satire was also his most bitter, a three-part series in the *Nashville Union* (February–March 1861) that has Sut accompanying Abraham Lincoln to his inauguration in Washington. In part the satire is based on historical fact: warned of a possible assassination attempt in Baltimore, Lincoln passed through the city at night and in disguise, protected by a private bodyguard, and was roundly lampooned as a coward. For the most part, though, Sut's tale is pure invention, revealing "Abe Link-horn" as a drunkard, a tightwad, a political naif, and a fraud. Sut's disguise for Lincoln—an enormous barrel-shaped scarecrow with his face painted apple-red—is a grotesque caricature of the gangly president. There is nothing comic, though, about Sut's feelings when he considers Lincoln in disguise: "I swar just then he minded me ove an orful elephant, called Hanibald, what I wonst seed at a sarcus,— now jist tu think ove this cross barr'd great beastes bein ole ABE, President ove the United States ove North Ameriky. I swar, natral born durn'd fool es I no's I is, I felt shamed, an sorter humbled, an I sorter felt like cuttin ove his throat an a sellin the hay tu pay fur my shame, an drink all the whisky on his carcuss tu make miself feel good agin."

Political satire provided one use for Sut. After the success of "Sut Lovingood's Daddy, Acting Horse" in 1854, however, Harris devoted most of his writing career to developing the character in nonpolitical directions. Twenty-four of these Sut Lovingood tales were revised and collected in the 1867 *Sut Lovingood. Yarns* and are most profitably discussed as part of that later work. Of the rest, many were written during a particularly active period in Harris's life, from 1858 through early 1859. Settled for several months as postmaster of Knoxville, Harris apparently had leisure to write fourteen sketches, letters, and tales that were not collected in 1867. The uncollected materials remained obscure until M. Thomas Inge gathered them in *High Times and Hard Times: Sketches and Tales by George Washington Harris* in 1967.

Among those tales and "letters" are six contributions to the *Nashville Union and American* in June and July 1858. Brief and miscellaneous in their subjects, they do not actually feature Sut Lovingood, despite the fact that they were originally titled as letters and "notes" from him. Probably the editor of the *Union and American* attributed the 1858 pieces to Sut in order to cash in on the popularity of earlier Lovingood tales; it may also be testimony to how closely Harris himself was identified with Sut that letters in his own voice were attributed to Sut's. Whatever the reasons, these pieces do little to advance Harris's reputation as a humorist. The narrator resembles the genteel storyteller of the earlier "epistles," though the topics of the letters—fish stories, drunken Germans, backwoods courts—are a far cry from the sentimental sketches of 1844. Like the true Sut tales, they often turn on exaggeration and dialect humor. Among the more extended is "The Doctor's Bill," published on 10 July 1858, ostensibly a reminiscence of an episode thirty years before in which ignorant locals misunderstand a physician's medical Latin. Inge argues for an actual source for the episode, an anecdote told by a prominent Knoxville doctor. It is more an extended joke than a sketch or tale, and like the other pieces in the *Union and American* series at this time it has none of the raucous satiric energy of the yarns narrated by Sut.

Sut returns as a character and narrator in a series of tales Harris published in the *New York Atlas* from the summer of 1858 through the winter of 1859. Sometime in 1858 Harris traveled to New York City to arrange for publication of a book, most likely the collection eventually published in 1867. Although the project fell through, Harris capitalized on his New York experiences. On 20 June 1858 the *Atlas* carried a Barnumesque announcement promising "THE GREATEST LITERARY FEATURE OF THE DAY," an exclusive series by Sut Lovingood, who has "ranged up and down the Mississippi and Missouri, and hunted 'bar-meat' from Kaintuck to the Rocky 'Mountings.'"

Harris in fact contributed only eight pieces to the *Atlas,* several of them short and negligible. Among the most developed are two chronicling Sut's encounters with New York. The tales are based on an age-old comic premise, the bumpkin's confused confrontation with urban congestion, ethnic variety, and strange technologies. In Harris's hands, however, they are topical sketches, larded with references to celebrities such as P. T. Barnum, Henry Ward Beecher, and Horace Greeley. In "Sut Lovingood Escapes Assassination" Sut recounts to George the "skeers" he suffered in "that cussed, n'isey, skary, strange-lookin' country" called New York. Sut's bizarre travelogue includes stops at Wall Street, Trinity Church, and Lovejoy's Hotel and ends with his escape from "assassination" by a photographer whose camera Sut mistakes for a brass gun, "es big es a quart jug on the bulge, an' all boxed up squar' in some sort ove

black wood." The story continues in "Sut Lovingood's Adventures in New York." Here the humor relies less on misunderstanding than on Sut's xenophobic, often mean-spirited reactions to urban "types," such as the "dandies" he sees on the streets:

> They haint neither man nur 'oman, 'caze they can't talk good nor fight like wun, or kiss ur scratch feelin'ly like t'uther. They seems sorter like a strange wether [a castrated male sheep] what had seed a heap ove tribulashun among an ekal number ove rams an' yews— they's butted about permiskusly by the one, an is snufft at by t'uther; and as they can't fill or feel the instink ove a man, nur do the juty ove an 'oman, they jest settles on a cross-fence atween the two, an' turns inter the wust kind ove fool-monkeys—despised by wun, an 'larft at by t'uther, and the most human view you gits ove 'em, is when they is above you a climbin' up.

These references, like the description of the "duck laiged Jew, what had a nose jist the shape an' size ove a goose-wing broad-axe," are reminders of the offensive bigotry that made stereotyping a staple of American humor. More specifically, though, they reveal Sut's developing aversion to anything, or anyone, he considers unnatural. The New York adventures culminate with an extended caricature of the editor and reformer Greeley, whose outlandish appearance (frequently criticized by his political enemies) so frightens Sut that he routs him with stones. The following day Greeley publishes a news story about the episode, describing Sut (in Sut's words) as "a cross atween a broken-laiged kangaroo and a fust class mowin'-mershean." As Sut is forced to admit, the characterization is not far from the truth: Greeley "sed he believed that crosses yet would be made atween animals an' varmints, an' sutin mersheans, what would perjuce sumthin' tu answer in place of humans—(Dad tried that explite once, durn his pot-headed soul! an' Ise a kerrien the consekenses)." Thus, Harris rescues what could have been merely a recitation of backwoods prejudices by turning the tables on Sut and poking fun at the mutual misunderstandings that result when cultures meet. Significantly, Sut is not uncomfortable with the fact that both he and Greeley are fools. Increasingly, in Harris's worldview, the satiric sword cuts both ways, whether in politics or in human affairs. In a world of fools, moral decisions fall to schemers and buffoons who struggle for the upper hand and maintain their dignity by accepting their nature; the sin, in the *Atlas* tales and the political satires, is to violate the natural order of things by denying one's place in it.

Harris's Lincoln satires in early 1861 were his last known writings for four years. During the Civil War he and his family were on the move. He remained in

Knoxville through November 1861, despite his secessionist views, but was certainly gone by February 1862, when the city was overrun by Union forces. For the next three years the Harris family lived in Chattanooga; Decatur, Alabama; and Trenton, Georgia.

While Harris survived the war, it changed him, as a person and certainly as a writer. He returned to writing Sut stories, again publishing them in the Nashville papers, primarily the *Union and American*. There is clearly an edginess to the tales just following the war, however, which may be a consequence of four years away from writing or may more likely betray a personal sense of anger and disillusionment. "Sut Lovingood, on the Puritan Yankee" (16 October 1866), for instance, is a satiric portrait so bitter it is more properly called invective. In earlier Sut tales evil inheres in denying one's nature; but the Yankee's corruption is that he consistently acts it out: "As the dorg vomits, as the mink sucks blood, as the snail shines, as the possum sham's death, so dus the yankee cheat, for every varmint hes hits gif." Sut bemoans the *Mayflower* landing, berates the Indians for not slaughtering settlers while they had the chance, and indicts New Englanders as frauds literally from cradle (where they suckle at night not because they are hungry but because "stolen meat is sweet") to grave (where even in the finest coffin lurks the "dirt" of corruption). Much of Sut's humor had always turned on hyperbole and incredible violence; in satires such as "Sut Lovingood, on the Puritan Yankee," exaggeration borders on a loss of artistic control. As Sut tells George in the midst of his tirade, "Pass the jug, the subjick is overpowerin me, an I aint quite dun onbuzzumin mysef yet." For two years following the war Harris continued to "onbuzzum" his anger in tales such as "Sut Lovingood's Dream, Tartarus, and What He Saw There" and his sense of loss in the one extant example of his poetry, a sentimental lyric, "The Coat of Faded Grey" (1 July 1866).

He was also reclaiming the comic voice of Sut, however, in all of its prewar manifestations and with some additional, more daring twists, not all of them pleasant ones. "Sut Lovingood's Hog Ride," Harris's first tale published after the war, is arguably the most raucous of Sut's yarns to date, and certainly the most anti-Semitic. In the story, published in the *Nashville Daily Press and Times* (14 September 1865), a drunken Sut, trousers dropped, rides a crazed hog through Ducktown, Sut's exposed privates driving dogs mad with jealousy; when his pants are recovered by a Jewish tailor—a "close clipt, Ch–st killin, hog hatin, bainch laiged son of a clothes hoss"—Sut runs him into a tunnel and terrifies him into returning the clothing by threatening to circumcise him with a table knife. The tale hinges upon juvenile sexual innuendo and the offensive ethnic

*Sut Lovingood and Sicily Burns, the unwilling object of his affections (illustration by W. J. Hennessy; from* The Harp of a Thousand Strings, *edited by Samuel Putnam Avery, 1858; Special Collections, Thomas Cooper Library, University of South Carolina)*

slurs of the time, but it is also a story of Sut's style of justice, for the tailor has marshaled the police and courts against him. The theme of rough justice continues in "Sut Lovingood's Big Dinner Story," first appearing in the *Nashville Union and American* on 10 August 1866. In this prototypical tale of pretension punished, Sut and a young servant girl exact revenge on a social-climbing woman by substituting varmints for food at her dinner party. It was a pattern Harris repeated in a dozen or more yarns to come and helped define an essential quality of Sut's increasingly complicated character: the knight-errant in a world of fools, striking blows against the unnatural, the powerful, and the pretentious. This facet of Sut's personality becomes central in Harris's one great collection of tales, *Sut Lovingood. Yarns.*

The yarns place Sut in a story cycle that reveals his character and the character of the world around him. As Rickels has shown, Harris extensively revised eight previously published stories chosen for the collection, and joined with seventeen new ones they make *Sut*

*Lovingood. Yarns* more than merely a gathering of tales. (Inge's facsimile edition restores a twenty-fifth title, "Sut Lovingood's Chest Story," which was mistakenly omitted from the original printing.) Noel Polk's claim for the book in his "The Blind Bull, Human Nature: Sut Lovingood and the Damned Human Race" (1978)—"among the most ambitious and complex achievements in nineteenth-century American fiction"—may overstate the case. Clearly, though, Harris's yarns, uneven though they are, show the development of his comic sense from the merely colorful or the cruelly hurtful to a more coherent critique of the human condition, tied together by the sensibility of Sut himself, who according to Rickels exhibits "the most complex and fully realized point of view to be found in any of the Southwestern humorists."

*Sut Lovingood. Yarns* begins with a send-up of the traditional book, with Sut and George arguing over the need for a preface and a dedication. Often overlooked in discussions of the book, the "Preface" and "Dedicatory" sections establish the interplay between the scribe (George) and the illiterate narrator, Sut; the thematic relationships of convention and common sense and the linguistic contrast between George's educated diction and Sut's broad vernacular are interwoven throughout the book. As Sut begins the yarns by disagreeing with George's way of creating narrative, so he ends, in the tale "Dad's Dog School," by wresting control of the story from George, who "can't du jestis'" to it. More than simply Sut's naive comic foil, George challenges Sut's power of language. Sut early on wishes he could read and write; he tells George, "I don't like the idear ove yu writin a perduckshun, an' me a-findin the brains," but he is resigned to this sort of exploitation and recognizes the greater power to be found in his narratives, the power to chasten and "skeer" those "hu haint much faith in thar repertashun standin much ove a strain." Thus, when Sut dedicates his book "*tu the durndest fool* in the United States, an' Massachusets [*sic*] too, he or she," he both acknowledges the convention and overturns it by reducing the dedication to absurdity: "TU THE MAN UR 'OMAN, HUEVER THEY BE, WHAT *DON'T* READ THIS YERE BOOK."

Throughout the yarns is interwoven a cast of characters who help lend coherence to the various "skeers" and pranks that undergird the plots of almost all the tales. The corrupt Sheriff John Doltin, who seduces a neighbor's wife, eventually gets his comeuppance in a cycle of four stories. Various innkeepers are Sut's tormentors and victims—like sheriffs, the innkeeper is another exploitative figure whom Sut must expose through trickery. Often, Sut's victims are characterized by excessive appetites for food, drink, sex, or

money. The obese and lazy victim in "Old Skissim's Middle Boy," for instance, is wired up to snakes and firecrackers while he sleeps, awakes in a rage, and attacks his family, leading Sut to spread the tale that he is a murderer and thus ruin his chances to marry the widow he is courting. Perhaps the most notable example of Sut's revenge upon those with unbridled appetites is "Hen Bailey's Reformation." A secret drunkard, Hen mistakenly drinks turpentine and swallows a live lizard while quenching himself with a gourd of water. In a bizarre "cure," Sut and his cohorts stuff a mole up Bailey's pantleg—hoping, they claim, that Hen will mistake it for an escaping lizard; but the mole enters Hen through his anus and chases the lizard out his mouth, and the terrified Bailey afterward joins a temperance society, where "the cussed hippercrit" claims to have been avoiding liquor all along.

Doltin, Skissim, the innkeepers, and Bailey suggest two frequent targets of Sut's pranks: hypocrites who deny their greed, lust, or gluttony, and bullies who flaunt their power without fear of being called to task. Sut's chief nemesis in the yarns significantly combines both hypocrisy and power. In the frequently anthologized "Parson John Bullen's Lizards," Sut plots revenge on the minister who humiliated him when he caught him in the huckleberry bushes with a young woman. Not only does Bullen thrash Sut; the parson also enjoys the hospitality of the girl's home before betraying her to her parents. Sut swears revenge "ontil one ur tuther, ove our toes pints up tu the roots ove the grass." As is often the case with Sut's pranks, revenge means not just defeat but public humiliation on the victim's own terms. Sut attends one of the parson's camp meetings, pretending to be moved to conversion so he can sidle close to the stage; at the moment of Bullen's greatest triumph—the regeneration of the sinner—Sut stuffs lizards up Bullen's pants legs, tormenting him with a real-world equivalent to the devil's serpents of Bullen's sermon. The extended description of Bullen's gyrations, the antics of the lizards, and the crowd's prurient joy when the parson strips off his clothing and runs off in terror is among Harris's most breathless and lively prose. The prank humiliates Bullen, but it also ridicules the hypocrisy of false preaching, reveals the comic possibilities of taking scriptural metaphor literally, uses the crowd's fascination with nudity to critique Victorian prudishness, and restores a chivalrous balance by avenging the young lady's honor.

Tales such as "Parson John Bullen's Lizards" might suggest that the yarns are, as Elmo Howell charges in "Timon in Tennessee: The Moral Fervor of George Washington Harris" (1970), formulaic, simple, and "tirelessly reiterative" stories of Sut's practical jokes. In fact, while Sut is often the avenging trickster,

*Illustration by W. J. Hennessy for "Sut's Experience with S-o-d-y P-o-u-d-e-r-s," later published in* Sut Lovingood. Yarns Spun by a "Nat'ral Born Durn'd Fool.["] *as "Blown Up with Soda" (from* The Harp of a Thousand Strings, *1858; Special Collections, Thomas Cooper Library, University of South Carolina)*

he is sometimes the object of "skeers" himself. At times, the victimization is inadvertent, as in "Sut's New Fangled Shirt." When Betts Carr, his landlady, sees a lawyer in a starched shirt, she washes Sut's in paste. Sut wears the shirt wet, and when the paste dries he can remove it only by tearing off his skin as well. Thus, Sut is literally and figuratively "skinned." The most extended series of mutual trickery involves Sicily Burns, whose story occupies four of the tales. "Blown Up with Soda" recounts Sut's courting of Sicily, whose beauty is described with comic hyperbole: "Three ove her smiles when she wer a tryin ove hersef, taken keerfully ten minutes apart, wud make the gran' captin ove a temprunce s'iety so durn'd drunk, he wudn't no his britches frum a par ove belloweses." Beautiful as she is, Sut recognizes in the strong-willed Sicily "an ekal mixtry ove stud hoss, black snake, goose, peacock britches—an d—d raskil." To dampen his affections for her, Sicily fashions Sut a "love potion" out of baking soda, which leaves Sut

foaming at the mouth and feeling "the bottim ove my paunch cumin up arter hit, inside out."

Sut's revenge begins in "Sicily Burns's Wedding," in which he lets the Burnses' bull loose at the wedding feast, the guests are routed by angry bees, and Sicily and the circuit rider Clapshaw are too swollen with stings to consummate their marriage. Still intent on revenge, Sut catches Sicily having an affair with Doctor Gus Fabin ("Gut Fatty fur short"), a lecherous quack whose "eyes wer like ontu two huckelberrys es tu color and size, stuck deep inter a big ball ove red putty." To give them "both a skeer, an him a little hurtin," in "Sut Lovingood's Chest Story" Sut interrupts their tryst by rigging the Clapshaw house with gunpowder, scaring Fabin into hiding in a trunk, and having him dragged off by a horse with its tail set on fire. "Old Burns's Bull-ride" continues the vengeance, with Sicily's father driven mad after his expulsion from the wedding on the back of "Old Socks," the terrified bull. Thanks to Sut, the wreckage is complete, with Gus Fabin banished,

Clapshaw reluctant to let his bride out of his sight, the Burns family feuding, and Sicily emotionally wasted and sexually cold.

Sut's triumph in the Sicily Burns episodes points out the equivocal nature of trickery in the yarns, for Sut sees himself at last as "the durndes' fool in the mess." In a world of cowards, Sut is most proud of his long legs and their ability to run him out of trouble; in a world of pretense and sham, he freely confesses himself a "nat'ral born durn'd fool." Not merely a collection of comic tall tales in keeping with the "biter bitten" motif of much nineteenth-century humor, *Sut Lovingood. Yarns* depicts a complicated moral world in which the comic fool and the mythical fool-killer are embodied in one character. As Polk has pointed out, Sut's self-deprecation shows his moral superiority to his victims, who lack his capacity for honest self-awareness. Significantly, Sut's triumphs are always temporary: Bullen survives to seek his own revenge, the Burns brothers are actively hunting Sut, and his situation at the end of the yarns is not materially, politically, or economically better than at the beginning. At best, Sut exposes hypocrisy and achieves a satisfying if short-lived revenge; but the corrections are no more permanent than the punishments Sut metes out. (Of all his victims, only one dies—Mrs. Yardley, who is dragged to death by a horse that Sut goads into disrupting her quilting party.) Sut Lovingood's world admits of no easy solutions to the human condition, merely a curbing of the human urge for corruption.

Just as Sut is no mere prankster, so his intentions are usually not merely disruptive. Behind his tricks is a conservative moral and social vision that he shares with his creator. In *Sut Lovingood. Yarns,* particularly, he often condemns those whose selfish excesses threaten proper human relations—including the frank sexuality that he so often celebrates. While the results of his pranks are immediately chaotic, Sut's goals seem to be the restoration of balance and order, civil relations, fairness, even honor. Critics such as David C. Estes have called Sut a mock preacher who points out the fallen, bestial nature of his fellows and punishes the sin of pride, which threatens the social order. Admittedly, Sut's moral values are a far cry from those of institutional religion; at his worst, Sut is racist, cruel, and intolerant. Still, as James E. Caron notes in "Playin' Hell: Sut Lovingood as Durn'd Fool Preacher" (1996), the essentially conservative tenor of the yarns reflects Sut's fundamental belief in standards of right conduct, moral and social. A civilizing force as well as an ethical one, like Harris himself Sut is convinced of the need to maintain a humane order in a world where political power and economic imbalance threaten fundamental liberties and self-determination.

The publication of *Sut Lovingood. Yarns* in the spring of 1867 brought Harris's work to the attention of at least one significant admirer, Mark Twain, whose brief review of the book in *Alta California* (San Francisco) (14 July 1867) commended its humor but predicted—rightly—that Eastern readers "will find it coarse and possibly taboo it." Harris's literary success was undercut, however, by personal tragedy: about the same time as the book appeared, his wife of thirty-two years died. Politically, the unreconstructed Harris was further embittered by the election of Ulysses S. Grant to the presidency in 1868. His final years reflect these changes in his world and his personal life. Wilson has pointed out a "new rancor" in Harris's postwar writings, but it is important to note as well the continuities with his earlier work. Tales such as the slapstick "Sut Lovingood's Big Music Box Story" (1867), in which Sut and his father are terrified by a music box, are examples of an uninterrupted vein of frontier comedy. In addition, Harris returned to political satire with a three-part parody of Grant's campaign biography, "The Early Life of Sut Lovingood, Written by his Dad," published in the *Knoxville Press and Messenger* on 7, 14, and 21 May 1868. "Sut Lovingood's Allegory" (1868) may be the best representation of Harris's late writing and state of mind, however. A reminiscence of old farmer Brakebill, who solves the problem of his "progressive" black billy goat—"a reglar, walkin insult to man, an' beast"—by castrating it, "Sut Lovingood's Allegory" is a thinly veiled racist commentary on the South of the Reconstruction. It also includes Sut's wistful farewell to an antebellum South he recalls as morally and socially "natural," now replaced by a country headed in the wrong directions: "we aint as good as we wer forty years ago. We am too dam artifichul, interprizin an' *sharp*—we know too much."

Though he published several light stories about marital relationships in 1869, Harris brought the Lovingood yarns to a close with "Well! Dad's Dead" in late 1868. The matter-of-fact title belies the complicated emotions of the family as they drag Dad to his grave on a wooden sled pulled by two "borrowed" steers. Ornery to the last, Dad frustrates even this final attempt at family dignity when the smell of his corpse spooks the steers and they bounce wildly toward the graveyard, Dad's body butting the family members onto the roadside. Sut concludes the raucous burial ride by kicking Dad unceremoniously into an open grave. The burlesque funeral and the family's frustrated attempts to be decorous are both broadly comic and touching; for all his rascality, in death Dad prompts tears from Sut's sister Sall and a belated if understated memorial from Sut's mother: "oughtent we to a scratch'd in a little dirt on him, say?" Thus, the father who begins the Lovingood saga by "acting horse" and whose legacy is his son's perverse foolishness perpetuates one final prank on a family that, in turn, buries him crudely and with mock solemnity. "Charm's broke at last," Sut tells his mother when Dad is safely dead. His wry conclusion that the funeral was a rousing success "considerin' the family gittin' hit up" reminds readers of Sut's ironic posture toward all social convention and his self-deprecating recognition that foolishness is not a family trait but an immutable and "nat'ral" fact of the human condition.

In 1869 Harris was remarried in Decatur, Alabama, to a vivacious widow named Jane E. Pride. He was planning a second collection of tales, and on a business trip to Lynchburg, Virginia, in December he made inquiries about its publication. On the return trip, however, he fell seriously ill and was removed unconscious from the train in Knoxville, where he rallied briefly but died on 11 December 1869. Although the official diagnosis of his illness was apoplexy, a local newspaper reported that Harris's final whispered word was "poisoned," leading to intriguing but wholly unsubstantiated speculations about foul play.

As Milton Rickels has noted, *Sut Lovingood. Yarns* remained in print until 1960, and individual pieces appeared frequently in collections of American humor, most notably Walter Blair's *Native American Humor* (1937). Both Twain and William Faulkner acknowledged Harris's influence, as do the many critics who have noted Sut's resemblance to Huckleberry Finn and members of the Snopes family. Academic interest in Harris's writing experienced a revival in the 1960s, beginning with the publication of four annual editions of *The Lovingood Papers,* which include uncollected material and source studies. Rickels's careful study in the Twayne United States Authors Series gave book-length attention to Harris's life and work, emphasizing his complex imagery, irony, manipulation of point of view, and essentially conservative perspective. The pioneering scholarly work of Inge has restored almost all of Harris's work for modern readers with a reliable edition of the uncollected tales, letters, and sketches—*High Times and Hard Times*—and a facsimile of *Sut Lovingood* (1987). Inge and Caron also edited an important collection of critical essays, both reprinted and new, *Sut Lovingood's Nat'ral Born Yarnspinner: Essays on George Washington Harris* (1996).

Harris's reputation remains dependent upon the Lovingood yarns, and the interpretive debate between Brom Weber and Wilson, nearly half a century ago, continues to capture the ambivalence of most readers. Weber defends the "mythic universalities" of the yarns and Sut's representation of "traditional and wholesome values," while Wilson dismisses the "crude and brutal humor," calling Sut "always malevolent and always excessively sordid." Critical discussion has almost necessarily fallen between those extremes, with a deepening appreciation for Harris's verbal acrobatics and skillful development of point of view compromised by reservations about Sut's gratuitous violence, racism, and reactionary definitions of "natural" behavior.

It is therapeutic to remember, though, that any discussion of Sut's yarns must recognize their essential unreality. Like much comic literature, they approximate the human condition by exaggerating it, often with the grotesquerie of a fun-house mirror; the focus of the yarns lies, finally, in Sut's verbal performances, valuable more for the energy of their telling than the verisimilitude of their plots. As Sanford Pinsker points out in an essay collected in *Sut Lovingood's Nat'ral Born Yarnspinner,* Sut "apparently does not expect anybody to believe a word" of his stories, and in his cruelty, hyperbolic "skeers," and fantastic plots he "exists outside all moral boundaries, more akin to the cartoon world of Roadrunners and Wile Coyotes" than to the real world. If the comic abstraction of the yarns makes George Washington Harris unlikely ever to be regarded as a major figure in American fiction, he is generally acknowledged as the most skillful of the Southwestern humorists, thanks to the exuberance of his language and the memorably complex character of his single great creation, Sut Lovingood.

**Bibliographies:**

Jacob Blanck, "George Washington Harris," in *Bibliography of American Literature,* 9 volumes, compiled by Blanck (New Haven: Yale University Press / London: Oxford University Press, 1955–1991), III: 384–386;

M. Thomas Inge, "A Bibliography of George Washington Harris," in *Sut Lovingood's Nat'ral Born Yarnspinner: Essays on George Washington Harris,* edited by Inge and James E. Caron (Tuscaloosa & London: University of Alabama Press, 1996), pp. 315–322.

**Biography:**

Donald Day, "The Life of George Washington Harris," *Tennessee Historical Quarterly,* 6 (March 1947): 3–38.

**References:**

James E. Caron, "Playin' Hell: Sut Lovingood as Durn'd Fool Preacher," in *Sut Lovingood's Nat'ral*

*Born Yarnspinner: Essays on George Washington Harris,* pp. 272–298;

Caron and M. Thomas Inge, eds., *Sut Lovingood's Nat'ral Born Yarnspinner: Essays on George Washington Harris* (Tuscaloosa & London: University of Alabama Press, 1996);

Pascal Covici Jr., "Propriety, Society, and Sut Lovingood: Vernacular Gentility in Action," in *Sut Lovingood's Nat'ral Born Yarnspinner: Essays on George Washington Harris,* pp. 246–260;

Eugene Current-Garcia, "Sut Lovingood's Rare Ripe Southern Garden," *Studies in Short Fiction,* 9 (Spring 1972): 117–129;

Donald Day, "The Humourous Works of George Washington Harris," *American Literature,* (14 (January 1943): 391–406;

David C. Estes, "Sut Lovingood at the Camp Meeting: A Practical Joker Among the Backwoods Believers," *Southern Quarterly,* 25 (1987): 53–65;

Elmo Howell, "Timon in Tennessee: The Moral Fervor of George Washington Harris," *Georgia Review,* 24 (1970): 311–319;

William E. Lenz, "Four Variations of the Confidence Man: Sut Lovingood," *Fast Talk and Flash Times: The Confidence Man as a Literary Convention* (Columbia: University of Missouri Press, 1985), pp. 106–117;

Michael Oriard, "Shifty in a New Country: Games in Southwestern Humor," *Southern Literary Journal,* 12 (1980): 3–28;

Sanford Pinsker, "Uneasy Laughter: Sut Lovingood: Between Rip Van Winkle and Andrew Dice Clay," in *Sut Lovingood's Nat'ral Born Yarnspinner: Essays on George Washington Harris,* pp. 299–313;

Noel Polk, "The Blind Bull, Human Nature: Sut Lovingood and the Damned Human Race," in *Gyascutus: Studies in Antebellum Southern Humorous and Sporting Writing,* edited by James L. W. West (Atlantic Highlands, N.J.: Humanities Press, 1978), pp. 13–49;

Milton Rickels, *George Washington Harris* (New York: Twayne, 1965);

Edmund Wilson, "Poisoned!" in his *Patriotic Gore: Studies in the Literature of the American Civil War* (New York: Oxford University Press, 1962), pp. 507–519.

# Paul Hamilton Hayne

*(1 January 1830 – 6 July 1886)*

Rayburn S. Moore
*University of Georgia*

See also the Hayne entries in *DLB 3: Antebellum Writers in New York and the South; DLB 64: American Literary Critics and Scholars, 1850–1880;* and *DLB 79: American Magazine Journalists, 1850–1900.*

BOOKS: *Poems* (Boston: Ticknor & Fields, 1855);

*Sonnets, and Other Poems* (Charleston, S.C.: Harper & Calvo, 1857);

*Avolio: A Legend of the Island of Cos. With Poems, Lyrical, Miscellaneous, and Dramatic* (Boston: Ticknor & Fields, 1860);

*Legends and Lyrics* (Philadelphia: Lippincott, 1872);

*Address of Col. Paul H. Hayne, of South Carolina before the Ladies of the Memorial Association of Alabama, Wednesday Evening, May 1st, 1872* (Montgomery, Ala.: Barrett & Brown, 1872);

*The Mountain of the Lovers; With Poems of Nature and Tradition* (New York: Hale, 1875);

*W. Gilmore Simms: A Poem Delivered on the Night of the 13th of December, 1877, at "The Charleston Academy of Music," as a Prologue to the "Dramatic Entertainment" in Aid of the "Simms Memorial Fund"* (Charleston, S.C.?, 1877?);

*Lives of Robert Young Hayne and Hugh Swinton Legaré* (Charleston, S.C.: Walker, Evans & Cogswell, 1878);

*The Yorktown Ceremonial Ode* (Charleston, S.C.: Walker, Evans & Cogswell, 1881);

*Poems of Paul Hamilton Hayne: Complete Edition* (Boston: Lothrop, 1882);

*The Broken Battalions* (Baltimore, 1885).

OTHER: *The Poems of Henry Timrod,* edited by Hayne (New York: Hale, 1873).

SELECTED PERIODICAL PUBLICATIONS–
UNCOLLECTED: "Saved by Whom? A Romance of 1782," *New York Weekly,* 26 February–April 1883;

"Ante-Bellum Charleston," *Southern Bivouac,* new series 1 (September 1885): 193–202; (October 1885): 257–268; (November 1885): 327–336;

Eng.<sup></sup> by H.B. Hall & Sons, N.Y.

*Paul Hamilton Hayne.*

"Charles Gayarré," *Southern Bivouac,* new series 2 (June 1886): 28–37; (July 1886): 108–113; (August 1886): 172–176.

Paul Hamilton Hayne was widely known and characterized in the 1870s and 1880s as the "poet laureate of the South," and with the death of William Gilmore Simms in 1870 he quickly became the recognized literary spokesman of the region, a position he maintained throughout the rest of his life, despite Sidney Lanier's brief prominence from 1875 to 1881. After Hayne's death, his reputation declined rapidly and did not begin to recover until the post–World War II period, when scholars and critics gradually reevaluated his work and concluded that he was chiefly important for his contributions as a correspondent and man of letters and, secondarily, as a poet.

Hayne was born in Charleston on 1 January 1830, the son of Paul Hamilton and Emily McElhenny Hayne and a scion of one of the most distinguished families in South Carolina. Colonel Isaac Hayne, a Revolutionary patriot executed by the British, was a collateral kinsman, and two of Hayne's uncles were U.S. senators, one of whom, Robert Y. Hayne, distinguished himself against Daniel Webster in the Senate debate on Nullification in 1830–1831. Before Hayne was two years old, his father, a young naval officer, died of yellow fever, and he was reared by his mother with the help of his Uncle Robert, who, before he died in 1839, taught his nephew to ride and hunt and instilled in him the principles of duty, honor, and integrity.

Hayne attended Christopher Cotes's school, along with Henry Timrod and Basil L. Gildersleeve. There he studied history, mathematics, and the classics, and, on the side, read Simms's romances and Timrod's early poems, an activity for which he was punished by his teacher. His interest in literature flourished, nevertheless, and he read the *Arabian Nights,* Johann Wyss's *The Swiss Family Robinson* (1812–1813), Jean Froissart's *Chronicles* (circa 1361–1400), the poems of Sir Walter Scott, Lord Byron, and Edgar Allan Poe, the novels of Scott and Charles Dickens, and beyond all others, Daniel Defoe's *Robinson Crusoe* (1719). When he was nine years old (according to one account) he began writing verse, and his first poem appeared in the *Charleston Courier* on 11 September 1845. Two years later he matriculated at the College of Charleston and graduated in 1850 with prizes in English composition and elocution. Shortly thereafter, at his mother's urging, he took up the study of law in the office of James Louis Petigru, the former state attorney general.

In the meanwhile he had begun in the late 1840s to contribute verse to the *Southern Literary Messenger,* the *Southern Literary Gazette,* and shortly thereafter, to Northern periodicals *Graham's Magazine* and the *Home Journal.* In May 1852 he married Mary Middleton Michel, the daughter of a French emigré physician in Charleston, and became associate editor of the *Southern Literary Gazette;* he assumed the editorship in the following December and gave up the law in order to focus his efforts on his journal. From this date in his career until his death on 6 July 1886, Hayne, with the steady encouragement and support of his wife and mother and the general opposition of much of the Hayne family, devoted himself to literature. In 1856 his only son, William Hamilton Hayne, was born. The next year Hayne, at the urging of his friends Simms and Timrod, became a founding editor of *Russell's Magazine,* serving in that capacity, with the exception of two or three brief periods, from 1857 to 1860. *Russell's* was the last important Southern literary magazine to be founded before the Civil War, and Hayne was largely responsible for its quality and for its three-year struggle to balance sectional politics with literary standards that transcended geographical boundaries.

At the same time he managed to bring out at his own expense three collections of verse. *Poems* (1855) appeared in November 1854 and is composed mainly of juvenilia, but it also includes an ambitious long poem, "The Temptation of Venus," and a few promising sonnets and short pieces. Hayne's second book, *Sonnets, and Other Poems* (1857), reflects his continuing interest in and increasing mastery of the sonnet form, though its publication in Charleston resulted in less critical attention than the first volume, published by Ticknor and Fields in Boston, received. Consequently, *Avolio: A Legend of the Island of Cos. With Poems, Lyrical, Miscellaneous, and Dramatic* (1860), Hayne's third volume, was published in Boston in November 1859 and is in some respects a collected edition of his verse to date; the title piece is another long narrative, and his best lyrics and dramatic pieces of the prewar period are included.

The imminence of the war, however, not only temporarily halted the development of Hayne's national reputation, but it also brought about the demise of *Russell's;* and Hayne turned to war service (since his health had been delicate for years, his active participation was limited to four months in 1861–1862 as Governor Francis Pickens's aide-de-camp) and to the composition of verse in support of the Confederacy. By 1864 he was able to undertake some serious study of the English poets from Geoffrey Chaucer to Alfred Tennyson, and to complete another ambitious long poem, "The Wife of Brittany," a narrative based upon "The Franklin's Tale" from Chaucer's *The Canterbury Tales* (circa 1375–1400). As a whole, however, the war forced Hayne into uncongenial themes: a fervent supporter of his state and its cause, he was never as successful a writer of patriotic verse as Timrod. It also limited his growth as a poet (he wrote a friend in 1866: "When one is knocked about as I was, deprived of all tranquility, how *can* one compose properly, or artistically?") and ruined him in "fortune and prospects."

In July 1865 Hayne went to Augusta, Georgia, and took a job as news editor of the *Constitutionalist,* but since his fragile health would not allow him to work a ten-hour day, he resigned in October. He then became a freelance writer and editor and moved his family in April 1866 to a cottage near Grovetown, sixteen miles from Augusta, his home for the last twenty years of his life. At Copse Hill, as he later called it, he concentrated on writing and managed at first to wring a precarious and eventually a modest living from contributions to newspapers and magazines, among them *Scott's Monthly, Southern Opinion, Southern Society,* the *South-Atlantic, Home and Farm,* and the *Southern Bivouac* in the South, and the *Round Table,* the *Old Guard,* the *Galaxy, Appletons' Journal, Lippincott's, Scribner's Monthly,* the *Independent,* the *Christian Union, Harper's Bazar* and *Harper's New Monthly,* and the *Atlantic Monthly* in the North. He also served in various editorial and critical capacities on many Southern periodicals, including several of the magazines already named and such newspapers as the *Constitutionalist,* the *Atlanta Sun,* the *Rome* (Ga.) *Courier,* the *Louisville* (Ky.) *Argus,* the *Charleston News* (later the *News and Courier*), the *Columbia* (S.C.) *Register,* and the *Wilmington* (N.C.) *Star.*

Hayne's criticism has never been fully appraised. Edd Winfield Parks's *Ante-Bellum Southern Literary Critics* (1962) by its nature stops short of full-scale treatment, though its general consideration of Hayne as eclecticist and traditionalist characterizes fairly enough his total critical corpus. Hayne thought William Shakespeare, John Milton, and Chaucer the great English poets of the past and William Wordsworth and John Keats the chief bards of the early nineteenth century. Tennyson he considered the reigning poet of the later part of the century. Algernon Swinburne he acknowledged as an important poet, but he was frankly worried about the moral character of his work. Among novelists he loved Scott and Dickens and admired George Eliot, William Makepeace Thackeray, Edward Bulwer-Lytton, Charles Reade, Charlotte Brontë, and Elizabeth Gaskell. As for Americans, he put Henry Wadsworth Longfellow, James Russell Lowell, William Cullen Bryant, John Greenleaf Whittier, and Poe (although he readily admitted Poe's moral limitations) at the top of the New World pantheon. Walt Whitman he scorned. Oliver Wendell Holmes he respected as much for his fiction and essays as for his poetry. Among the fiction writers he liked Nathaniel Hawthorne, Poe, James Fenimore Cooper, and Simms (though he never minimized Simms's weaknesses). He enjoyed Mark Twain's humor, but he apparently did not read *Adventures of Huckleberry Finn* (1885). On the other hand, he despised George W. Cable as a traitor to the South and castigated Henry James and William Dean Howells as devotees of "aesthetic realism," fiction without a "story."

Hayne's own fiction, it may be noted, focused on stories, although he never took them as seriously as he did his poems, criticism, or essays. Nor was there any critical reaction to his fiction, chiefly because Hayne never made any serious effort to collect the stories published in *Russell's* in the late 1850s or in *Appletons' Journal* in the 1870s, or even the novelette, "Saved by Whom? A Romance of 1782," printed serially in the *New York Weekly* from 26 February to 16 April 1883.

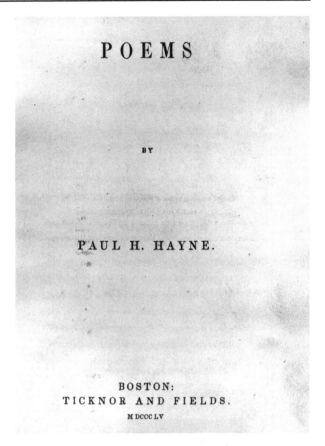

*Title page for Hayne's first collection of verse, including his long poem "The Temptation of Venus" (The Lilly Library, Indiana University)*

Set in Charleston in the last months of the British occupation, "Saved by Whom?" deals with the conflict between patriots and Tories as adumbrated in the affairs of Colonel Phillip Guarre, a leader in "Marion's brigade," and Clara Wentford, his fiancée and daughter of Charles Montague Wentford, a prominent Tory and the "largest land and slave owner in Carolina." Guarre, a Huguenot lawyer and early proponent of "the cause of the provinces," is captured in Charleston at the home of his dying mother, Inez Thirwall Guarre, and despite his vehement denials is unjustly treated as a spy and sentenced to be hanged on the basis of trumped-up evidence. With the help of Larkspur, a blockade runner in disguise as an Anglican priest, and the intervention of his Aunt Helena, twin sister of his mother, with Colonel Balfour, commander of the British garrison in the city, Guarre is cleared of the charges against him, marries Clare, settles in town after the British evacuation in December 1782, and receives a long letter of explanation from his great-uncle Richard Thirwall describing the relationship between the twins and offering a rational explication of supernatural events in which they

*Illustration, from* Poems of Paul Hamilton Hayne: Complete Edition *(1882), of Copse Hill, near Augusta, Georgia,*
*Hayne's home from April 1866 until the end of his life*

were both involved. The affairs of all the characters, major and minor, are finally settled in an epilogue.

As this outline of the plot suggests, "Saved by Whom?" is indeed a "romance" as defined both by Simms in the advertisement to *The Yemassee* in 1835 and by Hawthorne in the preface to *The House of the Seven Gables* in 1851. It is, as Simms would have it, a work that "grasps at the possible," handles extravagantly the "natural romance of our country," and yet includes events that "are strictly true" and based upon historical sources. It recalls Hawthorne's distinction between the romance and the novel that claims for the former "a certain latitude, both as to its fashion and material" and that allows the author to offer a "Legend, prolonging itself . . . to our own broad daylight" and to touch on the "truth of the human heart . . . under circumstances, to a great extent, of the writer's own choosing or creation." Hayne, of course, is mindful of these principles and avails himself of the latitude inherent in them.

Setting, characters, language, and technique are treated rather conventionally, though some exceptions

are observed. Knowing the Charleston area both firsthand and through primary and secondary sources, Hayne offers an account of the scene and background of the period 1782–1783 that is reasonably realistic in the midst of romantic trappings. Many of his characters are literally taken from history–Lord Rawdon, Banastre Tarleton, and Francis Marion among them–and others are fictions based upon actual personages from the appropriate time or near it and known to Hayne or his family. Despite this grounding in fact, Hayne's major characters are mostly stock figures, act in expected ways, and speak a high-toned diction seldom heard except in romantic fiction. The dialect of some minor characters, especially the real-life Gullah of the blacks, is much closer to the language of the area, though perhaps it is nearer to talk in Hayne's own day than in colonial Carolina. As for point of view, Hayne uses the first-person omniscient voice throughout. A well-educated narrator controls the narrative on his own terms and organizes it in a chronology related directly to history, offering at times his own opinion of politics and the war, intervening rarely to explain matters, and dropping occasional footnotes to relate fiction to history.

Hayne's fiction, then, is characteristic of his time and place. He is more interested in story than technique, and his approach is essentially that of nineteenth-century British and American historical fiction from Scott to John Esten Cooke. He is romantic in his attitude toward the past, yet concerned enough about that past and its relation to the present to seek to provide a sound historical context for it. He says on several occasions that he wrote fiction to make money, but despite such an admission, he did not contribute much fiction to the magazines and never made an effort to collect any of it in book form.

In his own day Hayne was viewed chiefly as a poet. The three volumes he published after the war—*Legends and Lyrics* (1872), *The Mountain of the Lovers; With Poems of Nature and Tradition* (1875), and the 1882 complete edition of his poems—led him to be widely considered as the "poet laureate of the South," a sobriquet he earned over the years as literary spokesman for his section on matters social and political as well as literary.

As a consequence of this status, Hayne was frequently asked by organizations and institutions, especially late in his career, for long occasional poems or odes to celebrate or commemorate events such as the centennials of the battles of King's Mountain in 1880 and Yorktown in 1881, the inauguration of the International Cotton Exposition in Atlanta in 1881, the sesquicentennial of the founding of Georgia in 1883, and the centennial of the incorporation of the city of Charleston that same year. Representative of the quality of these pieces is the lyric for the Cotton Exposition, "The Return of Peace," a prophetic tribute to Atlanta, symbolic of the devastated Confederacy, rising from the ashes of "war's remorseless blight" and shaking off the "lotus-languishment of grief" to share with the world at large as "purveyor of divinest charity" a "large and opulent store, / Of all things wrought to meet a nation's need," a mission not unlike that prophesied for the Confederacy by Timrod in "Ethnogenesis" (1861) and "The Cotton Boll" (1861).

Hayne had achieved this standing by the scope, range, and versatility of his production. In addition to the long occasional poems, he had earlier composed several well-received lengthy pieces, including "The Wife of Brittany," Hayne's best-sustained piece of narrative verse, and "Unveiled" (1878), an irregular ode reminiscent of Wordsworth. The tone and characterization of nature in the poem suggest a philosophical kinship with "Tintern Abbey" (1798), and its diction reflects on occasion a Tennysonian cast as the narrator, surrounded by a natural world of brook and mockingbird and "the melted soul of May," seems "to find

remoter meanings; the far tone / Of ante-natal music faintly blown / From out the misted realms of memory; / The pathos and the passion of a dream."

Hayne was even more successful with shorter narratives such as "Cambyses and the Macrobian Bow" (1872), a stark and grim retelling of an incident from Herodotus and the poet's own favorite among the pieces of this length, and "Muscadines" (1876), a sensuous ode, the verbal melody of which derives in part from the "magic juices of the ripened wild fruit of the South." Such a subject indicates Hayne's feeling for the life immediately around him and his home in Georgia, sentiments also demonstrated compellingly in the so-called Copse Hill poems, a series of lyrics—including "Aspects of the Pines," "The Voice in the Pines," "The Pine's Mystery," "Forest Pictures," "Midsummer in the South," and "The Mocking-Bird"—written mostly in the 1870s and contributed mainly to the *Atlantic Monthly*. Though not in the *Atlantic*, "Midsummer in the South" is still typical of Hayne's response to his natural surroundings, including the "gusty flight" of the "swift-winged partridge," the "blithe field-sparrow twittering near," and "the timid dove" whose "faint, voluptuous murmur, wakes / The silence of the pastoral brakes."

The critical response to Hayne's poetry was often favorable, though agreement on his rank in the American pantheon was not always fixed and secure. E. P. Whipple and E. C. Stedman, important contemporary Northern critics, praised his work consistently, and Longfellow and Whittier thought well of him as poet and man. Whittier, for example, wrote Mary Hayne shortly after her husband's death that he was assured a place in the "Valhalla of the country" along with Longfellow, Bryant, and Bayard Taylor. Hayne's poetry, however, has come to seem largely derivative and conventional and expressive of the weakest aspects of an outdated, sterile Romanticism. It is sentimental, unabashedly personal, and frequently lacking in intellectual content. Yet, at the same time, these weaknesses are directly related to some of the strengths in his verse. His work derives sustenance from his sources in Chaucer, Edmund Spenser, Wordsworth, Keats, and Tennyson, and it reflects a versatility in the range of forms, metrical schemes, and techniques employed. Indeed, in this versatility and in the scope and bulk of his production, Hayne is one of the most substantial Southern poets of the century, but for obvious reasons he is not the equal of Poe, Simms, or Timrod, or even Lanier, whose verse resembles his in its penchant for verbal melody and poetic diction; nor has his best work stood the test of time as successfully as theirs.

In the final analysis Paul Hamilton Hayne is likely to be chiefly remembered as a correspondent and

*Hayne in the 1870s*

dence demonstrates a devotion to the profession of letters hardly equaled by Poe or Simms before him or exceeded by such professionals of his own day as James or Howells or Twain. Hayne's commitment was rare in his own section and his resolute determination to pursue a literary career in the midst of discouragement, poverty, and ill health remains noteworthy more than a century after his death.

## Letters:

*A Collection of Hayne Letters,* edited by Daniel Morley McKeithan (Austin: University of Texas Press, 1944);

*The Correspondence of Bayard Taylor and Paul Hamilton Hayne,* edited, with an introduction, by Charles Duffy (Baton Rouge: Louisiana State University Press, 1945);

"A Southern Genteelist: Letters of Paul Hamilton Hayne to Julia C. R. Dorr," edited by Duffy, *South Carolina Historical and Genealogical Magazine,* 52 (April 1951): 65–73; (July 1851): 154–165; (October 1951): 207–217; (January 1952): 19–30;

*A Man of Letters in the Nineteenth-Century South: Selected Letters of Paul Hamilton Hayne,* edited by Rayburn S. Moore (Baton Rouge: Louisiana State University Press, 1982).

## Bibliography:

Jack De Bellis, *Sidney Lanier, Henry Timrod, and Paul Hamilton Hayne: A Reference Guide* (Boston: Hall, 1978), pp. 141–177.

a dedicated man of letters whose devotion to literature in difficult times is exemplary and whose own letters are among the most representative and revealing of the situation of the Southern writer in the period. His voluminous correspondence with his British and American contemporaries is a treasure trove that has yet to be published in full. He wrote to Tennyson, Swinburne, and Reade, and, more regularly, William Black, Wilkie Collins, Jean Ingelow, R. D. Blackmore, and Philip Bourke Marston. Among Americans, he corresponded frequently with Longfellow, Whittier, Holmes, Bryant, Howells, Whipple, Stedman, Taylor, Constance Fenimore Woolson, Lanier, Cooke, and John R. Thompson. His exchanges with Margaret Junkin Preston, Andrew A. Lipscomb, and Charles Gayarré fully express the range and scope of his social, philosophical, and literary views over both long and short periods of time, and his communications with such minor contemporaries as Edgar Fawcett, Maurice Thompson, and Edgar Saltus reveal almost as much. His correspon-

## References:

Charles R. Anderson, "Charles Gayarré and Paul Hayne: The Last Literary Cavaliers," in *American Studies in Honor of William Kenneth Boyd,* edited by David K. Jackson (Durham, N.C.: Duke University Press, 1940), pp. 221–281;

Anderson, "Poet of the Pine Barrens," *Georgia Review,* 1 (Fall 1947): 280–293;

Max L. Griffin, "Whittier and Hayne: A Record of Friendship," *American Literature,* 19 (March 1947): 41–58;

William Hamilton Hayne, "Paul H. Hayne's Methods of Composition," *Lippincott's Magazine,* 50 (December 1892): 793–796;

Jay B. Hubbell, "Paul Hamilton Hayne," in his *The South in American Literature, 1607–1900* (Durham, N.C.: Duke University Press, 1954), pp. 743–757;

Cecil Lang, "Swinburne and American Literature: With Six Hitherto Unpublished Letters," *American Literature,* 19 (January 1948): 336–350;

Sidney Lanier, "Paul H. Hayne's Poetry," *Southern Magazine,* 16 ( January 1875): 40–48;

Daniel M. McKeithan, "Paul Hamilton Hayne and the *Southern Bivouac,*" *University of Texas Studies in English,* 17 (1937): 112–123;

McKeithan, ed., "A Correspondence Journal of Paul Hamilton Hayne," *Georgia Historical Quarterly,* 26 (September–December 1942): 249–272;

Rayburn S. Moore, "'The Absurdist of Critics': Hayne on Howells," *Southern Literary Journal,* 12 (Fall 1979): 70–78;

Moore, "'Courtesies of the Guild and More': Paul Hamilton Hayne and Margaret Junkin Preston," *Mississippi Quarterly,* 43 (Fall 1990): 485–493;

Moore, "'A Great Poet and Original Genius': Hayne Champions Poe," *Southern Literary Journal,* 16 (Fall 1983): 105–112;

Moore, "Hayne the Poet: A New Look," *South Carolina Review,* 2 (November 1969): 4–13;

Moore, "The Land of His Fathers: Paul Hamilton Hayne and South Carolina," *South Carolina Review,* 11 (April 1979): 58–68;

Moore, "'The Literary World Gone Mad': Hayne on Whitman," *Southern Literary Journal,* 10 (Fall 1977): 75–83;

Moore, "The Old South and the New: Paul Hamilton Hayne and Maurice Thompson," *Southern Literary Journal,* 5 (Fall 1972): 108–122;

Moore, *Paul Hamilton Hayne* (New York: Twayne, 1972);

Moore, "Paul Hamilton Hayne," in *Fifty Southern Writers before 1900: A Bio-Bibliographical Sourcebook,* edited by Robert Bain and Joseph M. Flora (Westport, Conn.: Greenwood Press, 1987), pp. 240–249;

Moore, "Paul Hamilton Hayne and Andrew Adgate Lipscomb: 'Sweet Converse' between Poet and Preacher," *Georgia Historical Quarterly,* 66 (Spring 1982): 53–68;

Moore, "Paul Hamilton Hayne and Northern Magazines, 1866–1886," in *Essays Mostly on Periodical Publishing in America: A Collection in Honor of Clarence Gohdes,* edited by James Woodress and others (Durham, N.C.: Duke University Press, 1973), pp. 132–147;

Moore, "Paul Hamilton Hayne and William Gilmore Simms: Friends, Colleagues, and Members of the Guild," in *"Long Years of Neglect": The Work and Reputation of William Gilmore Simms,* edited by John Caldwell Guilds (Fayetteville: University of Arkansas Press, 1988), pp. 166–182;

Moore, "Paul Hamilton Hayne as Editor, 1852–1860," *South Carolina Journals and Journalists: Proceedings of the Reynolds Conference, May 17–18, 1974,* edited by James B. Meriwether (Columbia: Southern Studies Program, University of South Carolina, 1975), pp. 91–108;

Moore, "'A Soul That Took in All Humanity': Hayne on Shakespeare," *University of Mississippi Studies in English,* new series 6 (1988): 199–227;

Edd Winfield Parks, *Ante-Bellum Southern Literary Critics* (Athens: University of Georgia Press, 1962), pp. 227–259;

Parks, *Henry Timrod* (New York: Twayne, 1964);

Margaret Junkin Preston, "Paul Hamilton Hayne," *Southern Bivouac,* new series 2 (September 1886): 222–229;

Thomas Daniel Young, "How Time Has Served Two Southern Poets: Paul Hamilton Hayne and Sidney Lanier," *Southern Literary Journal,* 6 (Fall 1973): 101–110.

**Papers:**

William R. Perkins Library, Duke University, is the chief depository of Paul Hamilton Hayne's manuscripts, correspondence, letters, private papers, diaries and journals, clippings, and personal library. The Perkins Library holdings include "Last Poems of Paul Hamilton Hayne," an unpublished manuscript of selected uncollected verse published after 1882, edited by Mary Michel Hayne and William Hamilton Hayne. The South Caroliniana Library, University of South Carolina, possesses the second most important collection of Hayne papers. Other holdings of significance are those at the Library of Congress, the New York Public Library, the Boston Public Library, and at the libraries of the University of North Carolina, the University of Virginia, the University of Texas, the University of Georgia, Cornell University, Columbia University, Yale University, Harvard University, and Johns Hopkins University.

# James Ewell Heath

*(8 July 1792 – 28 June 1862)*

Boyd Childress
*Auburn University*

BOOKS: *The Lives of Sir Walter and Capt. John Smith; With an Account of the Governors of Virginia to the year 1781,* attributed to Heath (Shepherd's-town, Va.: Maxwell & Harper, 1817);

*Edge-Hill, or, The Family of the Fitzroyals; a Novel* (Richmond, Va.: White, 1828);

*Whigs and Democrats; or Love of No Politics. A Comedy in Three Acts* (Richmond, Va.: White, 1839).

OTHER: Editor, *Southern Literary Messenger,* 1 (August 1834–April 1835).

SELECTED PERIODICAL PUBLICATIONS–
UNCOLLECTED: "A Lecture, Delivered Before the Richmond Lyceum, on Friday Evening, July 13, 1838," *Southern Literary Messenger,* 4 (November 1838): 705–711;

"Death of Thomas W. White," *Southern Literary Messenger,* 9 (February 1843): 65;

"Recollections of James Ogilvie, Earl of Finlater. By One of His Pupils," *Southerner Literary Messenger,* 14 (September 1849): 534–537.

More of a public official than novelist, more politician than playwright, James Ewell Heath is still an important early literary figure in Virginia. Heath's work preceded that of many of his more-noted contemporaries John Pendleton Kennedy, Nathaniel Beverly Tucker, George Tucker, and William Alexander Caruthers, and in many ways anticipated their more successful fiction. He published but a single novel and one rather insignificant play, but his *Edge-Hill, or, The Family of the Fitzroyals* (1828) is an early "plantation novel" and an uncommon work in a society dominated by the issue of slavery.

Although there is no exact record of where, Heath was most likely born in Northumberland County in Virginia, seventy miles east of Richmond on the Chesapeake Bay, to John Heath and Sarah Ewell Heath, on 8 July 1792. John Heath represented Virginia in the third and fourth sessions of Congress but is more

*(from Benjamin Blake Minor, The Southern Literary Messenger, 1834–1864, 1905)*

remembered as one of the organizers and first president of Phi Beta Kappa (at William and Mary College in 1776). The elder Heath also served as attorney for the commonwealth and as a representative in the state legislature. Heathsville, the county seat of Northumberland County, is named for him.

James Heath attended Ogilvie's Academy in Richmond for two or three years (he was in school in

1807). He was elected to the state legislature from Prince William County (northern Virginia) in 1814. He served in the General Assembly three terms before his appointment as state auditor in 1819. Heath remained in the auditor's post for thirty years, until 1849. He was ousted partly as a result of his only effort at writing for the stage, the play *Whigs and Democrats; or Love of No Politics* (1839), although his dismissal came a full five years after the play was first performed in Philadelphia. Heath's first wife was his cousin Fannie Weems, daughter of noted George Washington biographer Mason Locke Weems, known in history as "Parson Weems." Heath was a respected member of the intellectual community in Richmond and Virginia in the first half of the nineteenth century, as he was a founding member in 1831 of the Virginia Historical and Philosophical Society. His name appears on virtually every page of the records of that society's proceedings since he was the first recording secretary. In 1820, following the death of his wife, Heath married Elizabeth Ann Macon, daughter of Colonel William Hartwell Macon of New Kent County. The couple had two children.

Heath's job as state auditor must have kept him busy, if notices in the *Richmond Enquirer* are any sign of his duties. Tax notices of all sorts were common in the pages of the newspaper, and Heath obviously was a full-time public servant. In late 1828 *Edge-Hill* was published in Richmond by Thomas Willis White, a close friend of Heath and founder and first publisher of the *Southern Literary Messenger*. White opened a bookstore in Richmond in 1824 but published few books, *Edge-Hill* and James Mercer Garnett's *Lectures on Female Education* (1824) being the earliest. He is best remembered as the driving force behind the *Southern Literary Messenger*, where another literary figure, Edgar Allan Poe, gained a reputation as a writer, critic, and editor.

*Edge-Hill* is a rather unsophisticated work of fiction that drew little attention in literary circles—in fact, no reviews of the work have been located. Yet, the book is important in many ways, not only because it preceded the work of more-noted Virginia authors, but also because it was the forerunner of the "plantation novel" and an early example of the "Virginia novel." It was adapted as a drama and appeared on the Richmond stage in 1829 and 1831, albeit briefly both times.

Heath's novel is set on Edge-Hill, a James River plantation in Virginia (not far from Richmond) in the early fall of 1781, on the eve of the Revolutionary War battle of Yorktown. Central to the well-developed plot is the Fitzroyal family, headed by the aristocratic Tory Launcelot Fitzroyal; his recently wedded wife, the monied former Mrs. Dashwood; her snobby daughter, Cornelia; and Fitzroyal's only son and heir, Charles, who is the hero of the historical romance. Charles is a college student at nearby William and Mary College and a patriot. His romantic interest is the captivatingly beautiful orphan Ruth Elmore, who resides at Edge-Hill. As the work develops, Charles clashes over political views with his loyalist father and spurns his rightful inheritance for the rebel cause. He also pledges himself to Ruth, who, feeling less than deserving because of her parents' lowly status, gives Charles only lukewarm encouragement. Also central to the plot is Albert Monteagle, Fitzroyal's ambitious, conniving, deceitful nephew. Monteagle emerges as the villain, intent on replacing Charles not only as family heir but also as Ruth's lover.

Along the way the reader meets various historical figures, with whom Heath takes literary license. Among the villains are the hated Benedict Arnold, who appears as paranoid and cowardly; Colonel John Graves Simcoe, leader of the loyalist Queen's Rangers; and the ruthless and much-feared Banastre Tarleton, remembered in the South as "Bloody Tarleton." Not surprisingly, the patriotic Heath portrays the most notorious characters of the Revolutionary era in a poor light. One of the heroes is the Marquis de Lafayette, who not only recognizes Charles as a leader and officer but also plays an important role in reconciling the senior Fitzroyal with his son. Along the way Heath also offers a brief glimpse of Patrick Henry and his oratory.

These historical references are not uncommon in early American fiction, but Heath's portrayal of women as heroic central figures (in the case of Ruth and her ally Harriet Wilton) is, as is his use of a black character not only as a hero but also as a favorite of Lafayette. Such is the role of James, a slave to the Fitzroyals; he serves as a guardian of Charles and a scout for Lafayette and is the one who takes a shot at Arnold and causes his trepidations. These unconventional characterizations place Heath in distinctive company but may well be part of the reason for his lack of recognition as a novelist.

The story develops in an unpredictable manner. Monteagle contrives to separate Ruth and Charles, put the heroine in harm's way, and replace Charles as heir to the Fitzroyal inheritance. Charles joins Lafayette's army, twice successfully leads outnumbered forces against superior British troops, foils imminent capture by Tarleton, and saves Ruth from Monteagle's clutches. More than once James intervenes on behalf of Charles and proves himself invaluable to Lafayette. With college companions Ludwell and Dermot, Charles is a hero and a natural leader of men, and he wins a reputation in the army as loyal and fearless. As the novel ends he has rescued Ruth, regained the confidence (and inheritance) of his father, and helped the American cause in the Revolution. Fitzroyal dies in the end, and Charles

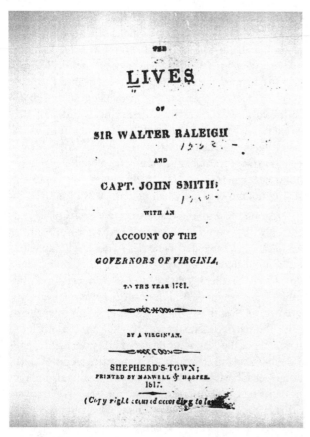

THE

LIVES

OF

SIR WALTER RALEIGH

AND

CAPT. JOHN SMITH;

WITH AN

ACCOUNT OF THE

GOVERNORS OF VIRGINIA,

TO THE YEAR 1781.

BY A VIRGINIAN.

SHEPHERD'S-TOWN;
PRINTED BY MAXWELL & HARPER.
1817.

(Copy right secured according to la

*Title page for an 1817 collection of biographical sketches of early Virginians, attributed to Heath by many scholars (Early American Imprints, second series, microopaque; New York: Readex Microprint, 1980)*

becomes the head of the respected Virginia line and marries Ruth.

If not for the scholarship of Richard Beale Davis, Heath's work may well have continued to be neglected. First in "The 'Virginia Novel' before *Swallow Barn*" (1962) and, later, in *Literature and Society in Early Virginia, 1608–1840* (1973), the distinguished former University of Tennessee professor of American literature has championed Heath. In the latter work he called *Edge-Hill* "much more romantic in tone than *Swallow Barn*" and noting that "it combines stirring events with a plantations setting." Davis also concludes that the novel "clearly anticipates William Alexander Caruthers, John Esten Cooke, and Thomas Nelson Page." He correctly points out Heath's debts to Sir Walter Scott and James Fenimore Cooper and states that "*Edge-Hill* has been forgotten even by those who still read *Swallow Barn* or *The Cavilers of Virginia*." Another historian, Susan J. Tracy, turned to *Edge-Hill* as one of six fictional examples for her *In the Master's Eye: Representations of Women, Blacks, and Poor Whites in Antebellum Southern Literature* (1995). Tracy follows Davis's lead on the insignificance of *Edge-Hill,* but she aptly points out that the status of

women and blacks, especially in the character of James, are unconventional for the literature of the period. Neither Davis, who terms the book "stumbling and uneven," nor Tracy, who subtitled her chapter on Heath "Liberalism Defeated," rank *Edge-Hill* among the leading fiction of the period; yet, Tracy concludes: "What distinguishes Heath from the other authors is his attitude toward slavery and social mobility."

There is ample evidence that *Edge-Hill* was dramatized for the Richmond stage on two occasions. The first enactment of the novel was in June 1829, six months after White published the book in November 1828. The first stage adaptation was in early June 1829. Thomas Flynn and his small group of players performed the "new Melo-Drama dramatized by Mr. Farrell and taken from the celebrated novel of the same title." Bob Farrell was a comedian who also had a part in the drama. Flynn took the part of Charles Fitzroyal. The cast list did not include the slave James. Two years later, in February 1831, *Edge-Hill* was once again dramatized, this time by a Mr. Glascott. Thomas Parnell, who managed the Theatre in Richmond, advertised "An engagement for three nights only with Mrs. Knight to perform the part of Ruth Elmore, with songs, in the new play of *Edge-Hill,* dramatized by a gentleman of this city." The initial enactment drew no reviews, but a review in the *Richmond Compiler* (25 February 1831) praised the second production as "replete with incident, and the language completely characteristic with the feelings of his republican countrymen. The style is flowery and energetic, and calculated to inspire the heart of every freeman." Heath's reaction to the two stage productions, like most of his feelings, is not recorded.

Despite the popularity of historical romances by writers such as Scott and Cooper, *Edge-Hill* did not sell well. Poe praised Heath's work, as did fellow Virginia writer George Tucker, himself a novelist, who ranked Heath with Cooper, Kennedy, and Robert Montgomery Bird. The book was not only a poor seller, but few copies have survived. Tracy mistakenly concludes that the novel is available only on microfilm, but there are a handful of original copies scattered at libraries and historical societies such as those at Duke, Princeton, the Boston Athenaeum, and several in the state of Virginia.

Heath's plot is interesting and his characters well developed. He fails, compared to Cooper, in his descriptions of the natural environment, specifically the James River and the countryside around the capitol at Richmond. Compared to the writings of John Pendleton Kennedy, *Edge-Hill* also falls well short in terms of developing the plantation as a setting–the novel does not mention agriculture, commerce, and especially the peculiar institution of slavery. Although Charles Fitzroyal and Ruth Elmore both visit the slave cabins,

Heath does not actually portray black plantation life. While these shortcomings may have contributed to the lack of the distribution of *Edge-Hill,* the sociopolitical events surrounding the Nat Turner Rebellion in 1831 may also have had an impact, especially in light of Heath's black hero figure, James. The August 1831 slave insurrection accounted for the death of fifty-five white men, women, and children in neighboring Southampton County. The actions of Turner and his band of six followers certainly solidified white attitudes toward free and enslaved blacks and may well have doomed any future literary success Heath anticipated with *Edge-Hill.*

In 1834 Heath's friend and publisher T. W. White launched the *Southern Literary Messenger* and persuaded Heath to serve as volunteer and unpaid editor. White was a Virginia native who had opened his printing shop and bookstore in Richmond ten years previously. He proposed a magazine "Devoted to Every Department of Literature and the Fine Arts" but could ill afford to pay most of his contributors. Notables and writers such as John Quincy Adams, Cooper, Washington Irving, James Kirke Paulding (who was also a contributor to the first issue), and Kennedy all wrote letters of support, but White's call for Southern contributors led to only a few amateur submissions. His resources to pay contributors went to men of letters from the North.

White and Heath wanted a Southern literature, however, and in the first issue (August 1834) editor Heath asked: "Are we to be doomed forever to a kind of vassalage to our northern neighbors—a dependance for our literary food" on Northern magazines and reviews. From the first Heath let it be known that he desired writings that promoted sound reasoning and morals, but, since he had few contributions or contributors, he published some of what he did not like or approve, including the work of Poe. Of Poe's initial contribution, "Berenice—A Tale" (March 1835), Heath wrote "we confess that we think there is too much German horror in his subject, there can be but one opinion as to the force and elegance of his style." In the next issue, Heath once again shared his opinion of Poe's story "Morella," which "will unquestionably prove that Mr. Poe has great powers of imagination and a command of language seldom surpassed. Yet we can not but lament that he has drunk so deep at some enchanted fountain, which seems to blend in his fancy the shadows of the tomb with the clouds and sunshine of life. We doubt, however, if anything in the name of style can be cited which contains more terrific beauty than his tale." Under Heath the *Southern Literary Messenger* did publish some Virginia material, but that practice mostly ended when Heath was relieved of control after nine issues, in April 1835.

Although Poe scholar Robert D. Jacobs, in his "Campaign for a Southern Literature: The *Southern Literary Messenger*" (1969), concluded that "If Heath had remained with the *Messenger* for any length of time, chances are that the magazine would have expired under its own ennui," Heath did his editorial chores after hours and outside his regular auditor's job. Benjamin Blake Minor, in *The Southern Literary Messenger, 1834–1864* (1905), quoted White as saying he "used to go frequently to Mr. Heath's, with letters and contributions, over which they spent nearly the whole night." He added that one particular night they passed the time over a bottle of champagne, "which by no means checked their ardor in the night's work." Minor referred to Heath as "a gentleman of literary culture and a pleasing and graceful writer" and thought Heath "genial and kindhearted," and a "man of taste, judgment, and pure ethical principals." After nine issues, White briefly took over the editorial responsibilities. He was followed, again briefly, by Edwin Vernon Sparhawk, an aspiring poet, before Poe agreed to rescue the *Messenger* in December 1835. Although Poe's editorship was stormy and often unsettling for White, the magazine soon doubled and later tripled in circulation under his imaginative style.

Heath's final literary effort was the play *Whigs and Democrats,* published anonymously in Richmond in 1839 by his friend White. The play is a satire on political party loyalty and election participation set during the Jacksonian era. *Whigs and Democrats* was reportedly staged in Philadelphia in 1844 but never appeared on the Richmond stage. The satire may have cost Heath his state job, but that came in 1849, years after the publication and performance. Heath states in the preface his desire "to show, that our own country furnished ample materials for the drama, without perpetually resorting to foreign nations for characters, customs, and sentiments," as was often the case in American drama. Heath uses natural settings without spectacular or catastrophic incidents, setting his work over two days in the Virginia countryside at the Hickory Tree Tavern on the eve of local elections.

The central characters are the tavern keeper, Roundtree; his daughter Katy; the incumbent representative, Fairweather; his son Henry; and the independent-minded schoolmaster, Supine. As the play progresses, Roundtree, the local Democratic election boss, prepares for the arrival of his assumed friend Fairweather, whose real purpose in his trip is to garner votes and to arrange for Henry to marry the daughter of a neighboring Whig, the aristocratic Worthington. Crude but persuasive, Roundtree pushes the locals to support Fairweather until he discovers the candidate rejects Katy outright as a legitimate mate for Henry.

WHIGS AND DEMOCRATS;

OR

LOVE OF NO POLITICS.

A COMEDY IN THREE ACTS.

J. E. Heath.

To show the very age and body of the time—his form and pressure.
*Shakspeare.*

RICHMOND:
PRINTED AND PUBLISHED BY T. W. WHITE.
1839.

*Title page for Heath's last literary effort, a play satirizing Jacksonian-era politics (Special Collections, Thomas Cooper Library, University of South Carolina)*

Roundtree then influences the voters to turn against Fairweather and not vote. Upon learning of his impending election loss, Fairweather laments to Roundtree that he has been misunderstood, and that certainly Roundtree's daughter is suitable to marry young Henry—only then does Roundtree do another about-face and once again rallies support for the candidate. Heath's characters speak candidly about politics, and their comments would have caused then-seated politicians a certain unrest and embarrassment. Roundtree tells his wife about the local voters: "I can make them wheel to the right or to the left with as much ease as I muster my battalion." Fairweather tells the idealistic Henry that "notions of human equality are mere empty speculations" and counsels: "You must learn to chime in with men's humors, prejudices, and delusions when any advantage is to be gained, flatter them, and remember never to offend, unless you have the power to disarm or defy their resentment." Both characters fully meet their stated philosophies of leadership and electioneering. Even Fairweather's slave Cato can see through his master's politics, as he tells Roundtree's slave Jenny that his master is "as great a palaverer as any in the universe." When Jenny asks for an explanation, Cato simply says "Why one thing 'fore a man's face, and another 'hind his back."

In the end, despite Roundtree's efforts, Fairweather loses the election. In closing, Heath has Fairweather renounce ambition and admit that flattery is "demoralising to them, but must, sooner or later, plant a thorn in our own bosoms to unfit us for the duties as well as for the happiness of life." Supine best summarizes Heath's intent when he opines: "In other words, the whole art of electioneering is conducted upon the principle of *ad captandum vulgus*" or capturing the vulgar masses. The play is an effective satire; yet, with the building political tensions over state's rights and slavery, its lack of local appeal and popularity was never in doubt. In the preface Heath also expresses a desire to ridicule "the despicable acts of demagoguism," which, if unchecked, "will most assuredly endanger our free institutions."

A anonymous reviewer in the *Southern Literary Messenger* (August 1839) applauded the effort to produce a comedy in the state, remarking "this is the first time, we believe, and if not the first—assuredly one of the very few attempts ever made within her borders, in the field of dramatic writing. Well why should not a Virginian try his skills in that department, as well as other folks." The reviewer concluded favorably "Upon the whole, we hope the author will pluck up literary courage, if indeed he lacks it, and delight the public again with some kindred display of his powers."

Although no biographical source on Heath lists it, the Online Computer Library Center and many library catalogues credit Heath with authorship of *The Lives of Sir Walter and Capt. John Smith: With an Account of the Governors of Virginia to the year 1781*. Published in Shepherd's-town by Maxwell and Harper in 1817, the small volume is a brief history of Raleigh, described as possessing "admirable parts, extensive knowledge, undaunted resolution, and strict honor and integrity," and Smith, a "brave, worthy, and adventurous" man. The book also includes notes on the history of the circumnavigation of Africa and a chronology of European discovery. An examination of the volume does indicate one characteristic of Heath's writing—the book is "By a Virginian," the same signature Heath used in *Edge-Hill*. Considering his interest in history, Heath, twenty-five years old in 1817, may well have been the author; the laudatory treatments of Raleigh and Smith are not good writing, however, but simply an effort to preserve a history already well documented by other Virginia and British authors. Heath was likewise the author of many state reports.

After Heath was ousted from state office in 1849, he attained a position as commissioner of pensions in the administration of Whig president Millard Fillmore, a post he filled from 1850 to 1853. On 28 June 1862, at the height of the Civil War, Heath died, probably in Richmond, although with all of the war news, Richmond newspapers did not carry his obituary. Federal census records indicate that Heath had a Richmond residence in 1860 (and in 1830, 1840, and 1850, as well).

Respected in the intellectual circles of Richmond, Heath was never widely recognized as a novelist or playwright in his day. Although he left little in the way of correspondence from which to describe his theory of literature, his writings in and work on the *Southern Literary Messenger* give some evidence of his thoughts. Heath believed that American authors were perfectly capable of providing a distinctive national body of literature. He was careful to avoid harsh criticism, which he considered mean spirited; in the July 1835 *Messenger* he described critics as "the little great men of the world, who have the vanity to conceive that their taste and judgment, (if they have any) is the standard for all mankind, and who snap and bark like the curs who infest our streets." He could, on the other hand, be critical himself, as he wrote in the March 1835 issue: "We can fearlessly recommend the *poetry* in this number,—if not faultless, as at least superior to the carpings of illiberal and puerile criticism." He opposed fairy tales in the magazine as unfit "for the intellectual appetite." He also opposed much of German literature so characteristic of Poe—yet he supported and published Poe. To Heath, the primary value of literature was moral edification, something apparent in *Edge-Hill*. What he lacked in abilities, he compensated for in dedication to work and loyalty.

No other words better describe Heath's minor contributions to American literature than the words of Poe himself, who, in 1841, called him "almost the only person of any literary distinction" then living in Richmond.

**References:**

Richard Beale Davis, *Intellectual Life in Jefferson's Virginia, 1790–1830* (Chapel Hill: University of North Carolina Press, 1964), pp. 224, 248, 265, 309–312;

Davis, *Literature and Society in Early Virginia, 1608–1840* (Baton Rouge: Louisiana State University Press, 1973), pp. 250–254;

Davis, "The 'Virginia Novel' before *Swallow Barn*," *Virginia Magazine of History and Biography*, 71 (July 1962): 278–293;

Robert D. Jacobs, "Campaign for a Southern Literature: The *Southern Literary Messenger*," *Southern Literary Journal* 2 (Fall 1969): 66–98;

Jacobs, *Poe: Journalist and Critic* (Baton Rouge: Louisiana State University Press, 1969), pp. 61–86, 160, 181, 223;

Benjamin Blake Minor, *The Southern Literary Messenger, 1834–1864* (New York: Neale, 1905), pp. 14–15, 20–21, 28, 76, 97, 100, 124;

Martin Staples Shockley, "American Plays in the Richmond Theatre, 1819–1838," *Studies in Philology*, 37 (January 1940): 100–119;

Susan J. Tracy, "Images of Women, Blacks and Poor Whites in Antebellum Southern Literature," dissertation, Rutgers University, 1983;

Tracy, *In the Master's Eye: Representations of Women, Blacks, and Poor Whites in Antebellum Southern Literature* (Amherst: University of Massachusetts Press, 1995), pp. 4, 23–24, 47, 49–50, 54–56, 59, 62–65, 71, 173, 220, 236–240;

Ritchie Devon Watson Jr., *The Cavalier in Virginia Fiction* (Baton Rouge: Louisiana State University Press, 1985), pp. 99–101, 125.

# Caroline Lee Hentz

*(1 June 1800 – 11 February 1856)*

## Miriam Shillingsburg
*Indiana University, South Bend*

See also the Hentz entry in *DLB 3: Antebellum Writers in New York and the South.*

BOOKS: *Lovell's Folly* (Cincinnati: Hubbard & Edmands, 1833);

*An Address Written by the Request for the Lafayette Society of La Grange College* (Florence, Ala.: Florence Gazette Office, 1842);

*De Lara; or, The Moorish Bride: A Tragedy in Five Acts* (Tuscaloosa, Ala.: Woodruff & Olcott, 1843);

*Human and Divine Philosophy* (Tuscaloosa, Ala.: Journal and Flag Office, 1844);

*Aunt Patty's Scrap-Bag* (Philadelphia: Carey & Hart, 1846);

*Linda; or, The Young Pilot of the Belle Creole. A Tale of Southern Life* (Philadelphia: Hart, 1850);

*The Mob Cap and Other Tales* (Philadelphia: Peterson, 1850);

*Rena; or, The Snow Bird: A Tale of Real Life* (Philadelphia: Peterson, 1851);

*The Banished Son and Other Stories of the Heart* (Philadelphia: Peterson, 1852);

*Ugly Effie, or, The Neglected One and the Pet Beauty: and Other Tales* (Philadelphia: Peterson, 1852);

*Eoline: or, Magnolia Vale* (Philadelphia: Peterson, 1852);

*Marcus Warland, or The Long Moss Spring. A Tale of the South* (Philadelphia: Hart, 1852);

*Helen and Arthur: or, Miss Thusa's Spinning Wheel: A Novel* (Philadelphia: Hart, 1853);

*The Victim of Excitement, The Bosom Serpent, etc., etc.* (Philadelphia: Hart, 1853);

*Wild Jack; or, The Stolen Child and Other Stories* (Philadelphia: Hart, 1853);

*The Planter's Northern Bride,* 2 volumes (Philadelphia: Parry & M'Millan, 1854);

*The Flowers of Elocution: A Class Book* (Philadelphia: Desilver, 1855);

*Robert Graham: A Sequel to Linda* (Philadelphia: Parry & McMillan, 1855);

*Courtship and Marriage; or, The Joys and Sorrows of American Life* (Philadelphia: Peterson, 1856);

*Ernest Linwood* (Boston: Jewett / New York: Sheldon, Blakeman, 1856);

*The Lost Daughter and Other Stories of the Heart* (Philadelphia: Peterson, 1857);

*Love after Marriage and Other Stories of the Heart* (Philadelphia: Peterson, 1857);

*The Planter's Daughter: A Tale of Louisiana* (Philadelphia: Hart, 1858).

PLAY PRODUCTIONS: *De Lara: or, The Moorish Bride,* Tremont Theatre, Boston, 1831; Arch Street Theatre, Philadelphia, 7 November 1831;

*Werdenberg; or, The Forest League,* Park Theatre, New York, 24 March 1832;

*Lamorah; or, The Western Wild,* Cincinnati, 1832; Caldwell's Theatre, New Orleans, 1 January 1833.

Northern-born Caroline Lee Hentz was an educator of young ladies and a prolific author of best-selling romantic literature. An author of plays, poems, and stories for magazines, she turned exclusively to fiction in the 1840s. Her most celebrated fictional effort was *The Planter's Northern Bride* (1854), a Southern response to Harriet Beecher Stowe's *Uncle Tom's Cabin* (1852).

Caroline Lee Whiting was of Puritan stock; her ancestor, the Reverend Samuel Whiting, immigrated to Massachusetts in 1636, where his family became prominent. Born in Lancaster, Massachusetts, on 1 June 1800, Caroline was the youngest of the eight children of Revolutionary War colonel John Whiting and his wife, Orpah. The family had deep roots in New England, and three of her brothers had served in the army as officers. On 30 September 1824 she married Nicholas Marcellus Hentz, a political refugee from France, a restless pedagogue, a compiler of French language texts, and the author of a book on entomology. Hentz had been teaching French at George Bancroft's Round Hill School in Northampton, Massachusetts. Caroline Hentz began, two years after her marriage, the sojourn with her husband that took her to live in six southern and western states during the thirty years preceding the Civil War. Though at first writing was a recreational activity, after 1849 she supported the family by writing and attending to her ailing husband.

After a brief tenure at Chapel Hill, North Carolina, where Nicholas Hentz was professor of modern languages, the Hentzes jointly supervised several schools, the first in Covington, Kentucky, from 1830 to 1832. There in 1831 she wrote the Arch Street Theatre (Philadelphia) competition prizewinning tragedy *De Lara; or, The Moorish Bride,* a play about the Moorish occupation of Spain, for William Pelby of the Tremont Theatre in Boston. In 1832 the Hentzes opened another academy in Cincinnati, where her literary ambitions were encouraged by the Semi-Colon Club, in which she probably made the acquaintance of Harriet Beecher Stowe, whose famous work was rebutted in *The Planter's Northern Bride,* among many other works by Southern authors. Hentz was increasingly troubled by the growing breach between the North and the South, and her interest in sectional issues is evident even in her first romance, *Lovell's Folly* (1833), set in "a beautiful valley in New England" invaded by members of the Southern aristocracy. Cincinnati was the scene of an early display of her husband's easily provoked jealousy, reflected as an important theme in several of her novels. According to an autobiography by her son, Charles A. Hentz, a Colonel King, another member of the Semi-Colon Club, improperly sent the vivacious and graceful Hentz a note, which, rather than simply refuse, she attempted to answer. Her husband pretended to go fishing and

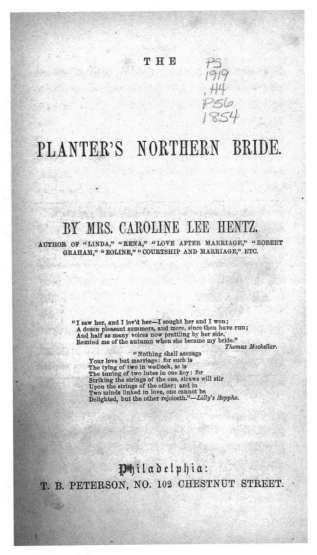

*Title page for Hentz's 1854 novel, one of the many Southern responses to Harriet Beecher Stowe's 1852* Uncle Tom's Cabin *(Thomas Cooper Library, University of South Carolina)*

returned to find her writing a reply. A scene ensued; the family closed their school and moved immediately to Florence in northern Alabama to manage the Locust Dell Academy, a private school that attracted students from throughout the South. They remained in Alabama for nine years, from 1834 to 1843, the most stable period of residence during the Hentzes' marriage.

While preparing lessons and dealing with students, Hentz wrote poems and stories for *Godey's Lady's Book, Magnolia,* the *Southron,* and the *Southern Literary Gazette.* In Florence, Hentz also cared for four young children, supervised her household (the Hentzes never owned slaves), and asked for divine guidance in her revealing, somewhat gloomy diary. The letters, deathbed confessions, and lamentations found later in her novels—often the stock-in-trade of the domestic fiction

*Illustration from* The Planter's Northern Bride

of women—are reminiscent of her Florence diary. The family continued to move, starting another school for females in Tuscaloosa, Alabama, that they ran from 1843 to 1845. Hentz produced a popular collection of short stories, *Aunt Patty's Scrap Bag,* in 1846.

In addition to *Godey's* she also contributed to the *Southern Literary Messenger* and the *Southern and Western Monthly Review.* Other academic posts took the Hentzes to Tuskegee, Alabama, from 1845 to 1848 and to Columbus, Georgia, in 1848–1849. Her literary career began in earnest with *The Mob Cap and Other Tales* (1850). Nicholas Hentz's health failed in 1849, and Hentz was forced to support the family, at first by running the school and after 1851 by her pen. From 1850 until her death the prolific author produced one to three novels per year while attending to her children.

Her novels, at first glance mere Gothic entanglements typical of nineteenth-century fiction, have strong autobiographical roots. For example, the jealous hero of *Linda; or, The Young Pilot of the Belle Creole. A Tale of Southern Life* (1850) and its sequel, *Robert Graham* (1855), vows vengeance on Linda's other suitors and occasionally lapses into unconsciousness during his melodramatic fits of rage. He is, however, converted to religion and, in the sequel, takes her to India as a missionary. Likewise, in *Ernest Linwood* (1856), the hero has a passionate temper that, his mother points out, may be "fatal to the peace of those who love him—fatal to his

own happiness; suspicion haunts him like a dark shadow, jealousy, like a serpent, lies coiled in his heart." Like Graham, Linwood is prostrated by his rage after wounding his wife, Gabriella, and her supposed lover, who turns out to be her cousin. As Nina Baym suggested in her *Woman's Fiction: A Guide to Novels by and about Women in America, 1820–1870* (1984), moreover, her heroines display some of the resilience and desire for personal fulfillment of their creator. In *Linda* the title character endures the loss of both her mother and father but eventually marries her rescuer. In the sequel, Linda and the converted Robert Graham marry after their respective spouses die.

In addition to her rather sensational plots of kidnappings, assaults and murders, shipwrecks, melancholy deaths, abolitionist near riots, drownings, and runaway slaves, Hentz invests her fiction with strong religious and moral sentiments. This strain has personal roots, as may be seen from her Florence diary: "How inextricable are the paths of sin. . . . Would to God I could lay hand on mine & say I had never stooped to deceit." In her fiction she often uses such romantic devices as misplaced or undelivered letters, unrequited love, Byronic influences, and sudden discoveries, often of long-lost kinsmen. Her works—a dozen volumes from 1850 to 1856—were widely read, probably because they are consistently well-written examples of popular literature of the period. During a three-year period more

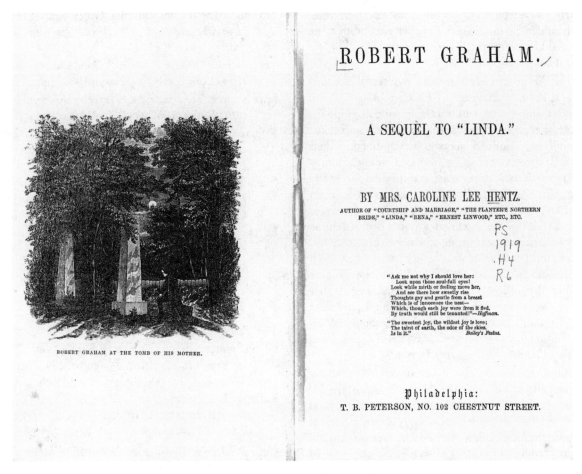

*Frontispiece and title page for Hentz's 1855 novel, in which the hero and his wife go to India as Christian missionaries (Thomas Cooper Library, University of South Carolina)*

than ninety thousand copies of her books were sold, and for twenty years after her death many were reprinted. T. B. Peterson published its "Uniform Edition" of her work as late as 1889.

For the modern reader, Hentz's most important work is probably *The Planter's Northern Bride* for its often compelling style as well as for its commentary on the times. Though this novel is in many ways typical of Southern answers to *Uncle Tom's Cabin,* Hentz's New England background gave an interesting perspective to the South she had grown to love deeply. An important theme in the book, as contemporary reviewers pointed out, was its appeal for allegiance to the entire country, its attempt to mitigate sectional prejudice. Still, other reviewers predictably objected to its idealized portrait of the South, the attempt to portray slavery as a beneficial social arrangement, and its author's refusal to acknowledge the evils inherent in the plantation system. As Elizabeth Moss points out in *Domestic Novelists in the Old South: Defenders of Southern Culture* (1992), "Southern domestic novels fused the conventional Bildungsroman,

or story of development, with the rhetoric of proslavery, veiling an explicitly political message in the dense prose and convoluted plots of the genre; employing language and imagery that were, at first glance, identical to their northern counterparts, they transformed an apparently innocuous romance into an effective propaganda tool." Despite protestations of objectivity in her prefaces, her proslavery arguments emerge in the subsequent narratives. Hentz's careful eye for detail, perhaps enhanced by her own transplantation to the South or her shared interest in her husband's study of natural science, makes this novel, and others by Hentz, remarkable for its local color, especially in setting.

Besides its compelling style and sensational plot, *Ernest Linwood,* the first edition of which sold twenty thousand copies, is notable for the author's early attempt to study irrational psychology. Linwood's mother believes his jealousy to be congenital, his father having acted similarly. Hentz's treatment of the mistaken identities of Gabriella's father and his twin, although potentially an opportunity to study environmental influences on character, never rises above the traditional Gothic reversals and revelations. Still, it is a powerful book.

The figure of Gabriella, who narrates *Ernest Linwood,* and the title character of *Eoline: or, Magnolia Vale* (1852) are interesting and probably autobiographical portraits of repressed feminism–capable, attractive, talented, intelligent individuals who are confined in their roles as women. Gabriella, reared as a simple country girl, marries into the upper class and then discovers she belongs there by birth. Eoline, the heiress who must become a teacher to defy her father's marriage plans for her, at last loves the intended groom. Both of these young women are headstrong to their own detriment; both act out of principle rather than mere custom; both suffer social consequences. Eoline lives happily ever after, but the older Gabriella somewhat regrets her choice of the furious Linwood. In an edition published after the author's death–she died of pneumonia in Marianna, Florida, on 11 February 1856–*Ernest Linwood* was subtitled "The Inner Life of the Author."

Although only a few of her novels are read by modern readers, Caroline Lee Hentz is important for her attempt to treat sympathetically certain irrational psychological characteristics, unhappy marriages, and repressed feminism, and for her efforts to champion the Southern economic and social system in the war of words that preceded secession. Recent scholarship on Hentz has focused on her portrayal of domestic relations in the South and her contributions to popular romantic fiction.

**References:**

Jan Bakker, "Twists of Sentiment in Antebellum Southern Romance," *Southern Literary Journal,* 26 (1993): 3–13;

Ellizabeth L. Barnes, "Mirroring the Mother Text: Histories of Seduction in the American Domestic Novel," in *Anxious Power: Reading, Writing, and Ambivalence in Narrative by Women,* edited by Carol J. Singley and Susan Elizabeth Sweeney (Albany: State University of New York Press, 1993), pp. 157–172;

Nina Baym, *Woman's Fiction: A Guide to Novels by and about Women in America, 1820–1870* (Ithaca, N.Y.: Cornell University Press, 1984), pp. 110–139;

Rhoda C. Ellison, "Caroline Lee Hentz's Alabama Diary," *Alabama Review,* 4 (October 1951): 254–270;

Ellison, Introduction to *The Planter's Northern Bride* (Chapel Hill: University of North Carolina Press, 1970), pp. vii–xxii;

Ellison, "Mrs. Hentz and the Green-Eyed Monster," *American Literature,* 22 (November 1950): 345–350;

Mary Forrest, *Women of the South Distinguished in Literature* (New York: Derby & Jackson, 1861), pp. 265–290;

John S. Hart, *The Female Prose Writers of America* (Philadelphia: Butler, 1852), pp. 151–160;

Robert Hunt, "A Domesticated Slavery: Political Economy in Caroline Hentz's Fiction," *Southern Quarterly,* 34 (Summer 1996): 25–35;

Mary Kelley, *Private Woman, Public Stage: Literary Domesticity in Nineteenth-Century America* (New York: Oxford University Press, 1984), pp. 164–168;

Elizabeth Moss, *Domestic Novelists in the Old South: Defenders of Southern Culture* (Baton Rouge: Louisiana University Press, 1992);

Helen W. Papashvily, *All the Happy Endings: A Study of the Domestic Novel in America, the Women Who Wrote It, the Women Who Read It, in the Nineteenth Century* (New York: Harpers, 1956), pp. 79–94;

Glenda Gates Riley, "The Gentle Subversion: Changes in the Traditionalist Image of the American Woman," *Historian,* 32 (February 1970): 210–227;

Kathryn Lee Seidel, *The Southern Belle in the American Novel* (Gainesville: University Presses of Florida / Tampa: University of South Florida Press, 1985);

Miriam Shillingsburg, "The Ascent of Women, Southern Style," in *Southern Literature in Transition: Heritage and Promise,* edited by Philip Castille and William Osborne (Memphis: Memphis State University Press, 1983), pp. 127–140;

Jamie Stanesa, "Caroline Hentz's Rereading of Southern Pastoralism; or, Pastoral Naturalism in *The Planter's Northern Bride,*" *Southern Studies,* 3 (1992): 221–252;

Stanesa, "Caroline Lee Whiting Hentz (1800–1856)," *Legacy,* 13 (1996): 130–139;

Mary Ann Wimsatt, "Caroline Hentz's Balancing Act," in *The Female Tradition in Southern Literature,* edited by Carol S. Manning (Urbana & Chicago: University of Illinois Press, 1993), pp. 162–175.

**Papers:**

The Southern Historical Collection at the University of North Carolina at Chapel Hill holds the most extensive collection of correspondence and genealogical material relating to Caroline Lee Hentz, including Hentz's diaries and those of her son, Charles A. Hentz. Additional letters can be found in the Overbury Collection, Special Collections Library, Barnard College; Minor Authors Collection of the Clifton Waller Barrett Library, University of Virginia; Perkins Library, Duke University; and the Caroline Hentz Papers, Huntington Library.

# Johnson Jones Hooper

*(9 June 1815 – 7 June 1862)*

David B. Kesterson
*University of North Texas*

See also the Hooper entries in *DLB 3: Antebellum Writers in New York and the South* and *DLB 11: American Humorists, 1800–1950.*

BOOKS: *Some Adventures of Captain Simon Suggs, Late of the Tallapoosa Volunteers; Together with "Taking the Census," and Other Alabama Sketches* (Philadelphia: Carey & Hart, 1846);

*A Ride with Old Kit Kuncker, and Other Sketches, and Scenes of Alabama* (Tuscaloosa, Ala.: Slade, 1849); enlarged as *The Widow Rugby's Husband, A Night at the Ugly Man's, and Other Tales of Alabama* (Philadelphia: A. Hart, 1851);

*Read and Circulate: Proceedings of the Democratic and Anti-Know-Nothing Party in Caucus; or the Guillotine at Work, at the Capital, during the Session of 1855–'56* (Montgomery, Ala.: Barrett & Wimbish, 1855);

*Dog and Gun; A Few Loose Chapters on Shooting, Among Which Will Be Found Some Anecdotes and Incidents* (New York: Orange & Judd, 1856);

*Magnum Opus. The Great Book of the University of Comus. The Paneduct of Our National Hilaritas, Comprising Essays upon the Thirteen Divisions of the Rituals; Sketches of the Tredecim of Doges, Authors of the Plan, and a Monitorial Guide to the Workings of the Fellowship, The Gander-Flight of the Thirteen Doges of Comus,* by Hooper and others (Louisville, Ky.: Published under Direction of the Thirteen Doges / Chicago: Knight & Leonard, 1886).

OTHER: Thomas S. Woodward, *Woodward's Reminiscences of the Creek, or Muscogee Indians, Contained in Letters to Friends in Georgia and Alabama,* edited by Hooper (Montgomery, Ala.: Barrett & Wimbish, 1859).

*Johnson Jones Hooper (Alabama Department of Archives and History)*

Among the host of "Old Southwest" humorists who flourished during the first half of the nineteenth century, Johnson Jones Hooper looms as one of the most important and distinctive. With the publication of *Some Adventures of Captain Simon Suggs, Late of the Tal-* *lapoosa Volunteers; Together with "Taking the Census," and Other Alabama Sketches* (1846), Hooper gave to nineteenth-century literature the epitome of the rascally, unprincipled, conniving, and uncouth backwoodsman, a creation that influenced many other writers, including Mark Twain, and informed the whole American literary tradition of the "confidence man."

While Hooper is associated with Alabama, the state in which he rose to fame as an author as well as attained success as journalist, lawyer, and politician, he was actually a native of North Carolina. Born in the tidewater town of Wilmington on 9 June 1815, he was the sixth child and third son of Archibald Hooper–lawyer, solicitor, and newspaper editor–and Charlotte De Berniere, a cultured, charming woman who claimed to be a direct descendant of seventeenth-century divine Jeremy Taylor. Thus, Hooper grew up in a refined home environment with good parenting. While his two older brothers, George and John, were college educated, Hooper was denied that privilege because of Archibald's losing his editorship of the *Cape Fear Recorder,* a Wilmington newspaper. Hooper was relegated to studying at Wilmington schools and at home under his father's tutelage, where he read voraciously. In 1835 he followed his attorney brother, George, who, after a three-year sojourn in Charleston, South Carolina, had moved to eastern Alabama and settled in Lafayette. The small frontier town was to become Hooper's home, or at least home base, for most of his adult years. He read law in George's office, was appointed census taker of Tallapoosa County in 1840, and married Mary Mildred Brantley, daughter of one of Lafayette's earlier and most prominent settlers, Green D. Brantley. He apparently was admitted to the bar in Tallapoosa County in 1838. The Hoopers had several children, William, Annie, and Adolphus, born in 1844, 1845, and 1849, respectively.

Besides practicing law and riding the court circuit, Hooper followed in his father's journalistic footsteps, becoming editor of the Lafayette newspaper, the *East Alabamian.* He left in 1846 to help manage and edit newspapers in Wetupka and Montgomery, Alabama, but returned in 1849 to Lafayette, where he not only continued his newspaper editing but also made his first try at a political career, running unsuccessfully for the state house of representatives. The last few years of his life were devoted to politics of the Southern cause and attempting to maintain his health, which began to fail in his last years from a bout with yellow fever and exhaustion caused by his intense political involvement and rigorous writing schedule both as journalist and writer of essays and sketches. Among his political accomplishments, he was elected solicitor of the Ninth Judicial Circuit in Alabama from 1845 to 1853 and was elected secretary of the Provisional Confederate Congress in 1861, moving from Montgomery to Richmond when the secessionist government relocated there. He lost the campaign to become secretary of the Senate of the Confederate Congress in 1862, however. Hooper died shortly thereafter, on 7 June 1862, in Richmond and was buried there in Shockhoe Hill Cemetery, while the war, in which he took such fervent interest on behalf of preserving the South, was raging not far from the capital city of the Confederacy.

Hooper's first important foray into the realm of humor, one that caused a stir and captured an audience beyond Lafayette, occurred while he was editing the *East Alabamian.* It consisted of a facetious series of episodes under the title "Taking the Census in Alabama," authored "By a Chicken Man of 1840." Published in the summer of 1843 in his newspaper, the two-part article recounts the hilarious efforts of the protagonist, "Squire," to take count of "the noses of all the men, women, children, and chickens resident upon those nine hundred square miles of rough country which constitute the county of Tallapoosa." The narrative is based loosely on Hooper's exploits of 1840, when, as an assistant marshal, he was assigned to be census taker of the county. "Taking the Census in Alabama" bears some of the most prevalent trademarks of Old Southwest humor, from its depiction of the colorful local characters to including elements of the tall tale. One farm woman's circular, interminable monologue in response to the Squire's census queries anticipates garrulous Simon Wheeler's monologue in Mark Twain's "The Celebrated Jumping Frog of Calaveras County" (1865) as well as the humorous "Jim Blaine's Grandfather's Ram" episode in Twain's *Roughing It* (1872).

The second half of the article introduces one of Hooper's most colorful creations, Old Kit Kuncker of Union Creek, a Jacksonian with a dog named Andy. An inveterate wag, Old Kit is undoubtedly the most distinctive comic character in Hooper's writings except for Simon Suggs. One of the most influential editors of the day, William Trotter Porter, was sufficiently impressed with "Taking the Census in Alabama" to rerun the sketch in the 9 September 1843 issue of his popular New York journal, *Spirit of the Times.* As biographer W. Stanley Hoole observed in *Alias Simon Suggs: The Life and Times of Johnson Jones Hooper* (1952), "Overnight, Hooper left the ranks of the purely local 'funny men,' . . . to become a nationally-read humorist." The circulation of *Spirit of the Times* at this early stage of its existence boasted some sixteen thousand subscribers, and its contents were printed in weeklies nationwide. Thus, Hooper the humorist was exposed to a national audience, and Porter acknowledged his talent and popularity by publishing further stories and sketches by him in the journal.

Within a year after "Taking the Census in Alabama," Hooper began publishing in the *East Alabamian* stories about Captain Simon Suggs of the Tallapoosa Volunteers, the character responsible for his rise to fame as an author. Based perhaps on an actual Tallapoosian, Bird H. Young, as well as being a caricature of Andrew Jackson, Suggs became "Southern humor's most artful trickster before Harris' Sut Lovingood, whom Hooper seems to have influenced," according to

Mary Ann Wimsatt and Robert L. Phillips in *The History of Southern Literature* (1985). Porter was so taken by the Suggs episodes that he delayed the production of his book *The Big Bear of Arkansas* (1843) to include one of the Suggs stories, and influenced his Philadelphia publishers, Carey and Hart, to publish Hooper's novel *Some Adventures of Captain Simon Suggs, Late of the Tallapoosa Volunteers*. A popular success, the book underwent six editions of nearly twelve thousand volumes within five years of its original publication. It remained in print until 1928 and was republished by the University of North Carolina Press in 1969.

*Some Adventures of Captain Simon Suggs, Late of the Tallapoosa Volunteers* is a masterpiece of Old Southwest humorous literature. Simon is a rough-hewn, backwoods shyster whose motto, "It is good to be shifty in a new country," represents his whole ethical makeup. This "new country" was one filled with a wide assortment of stock backwoods types, from outright swindlers to hardened farmwives to itinerant evangelical preachers and worshipers, all of whom offer up a realistic snapshot of the region and times. A parade of exaggerated episodes reveals Suggs at his most boastful, obnoxious self, one who, when leaving home, cheats his own father out of a horse and loads his mother's pipe with gunpowder. There is little by way of redeeming traits in his devious nature. The book is written in the form of a campaign biography, since Suggs is seeking the "Sheriffalty" of his county. It has been called a burlesque campaign biography by critics such as Robert Hopkins, Walter Blair, and Hamlin Hill because it parodies the political biographies of Andrew Jackson. It also adheres to the picaresque tradition, with its roguelike protagonist, episodic nature, the constant traveling from place to place, and the satirical treatment of the various members and groups found in backwoods society.

Of the twelve episodic chapters that make up the volume, two are especially noteworthy: chapter 7, "Simon Becomes Captain," and chapter 10, "The Captain Attends a Camp-Meeting." In the former, Suggs, bolstered by sips of corn whiskey, is chosen leader of the effort against the Creek Indians in 1836, the conniving captain being willing to accept his "commission" because he knows the nearby Creeks are largely passive. Suggs's description of the ideal leader—a "capting that ain't afeard to fight . . . some sober, stiddy feller"—fools the crowd and wins him his post. The only true action on the part of his forces, the "Tallapoosy Vollantares," turns out to be a bungling series of miscues ending with an abortive bayonet charge against an imagined Indian raid that has the men thrusting their bayonets aimlessly into the ground. In "The Captain Attends a Camp-Meeting," a comic scene that influ-

SIMON SUGGS.

*Hooper's best-known character, an unethical backwoods lawyer, politician, and militiaman (from* Some Adventures of Captain Simon Suggs, Late of the Tallapoosa Volunteers, *1846)*

enced Mark Twain's depiction of the Duke and Dauphin in *The Adventures of Huckleberry Finn* (1884), Suggs dupes the camp-meeting congregation into thinking a collection is needed to reform pirates. Once he gathers in the contributions, he retreats to a nearby swamp to pray over the sum, then mounts his horse tethered there and absconds with the money. A vivid depiction of camp-meeting shenanigans—people shouting and rolling on the ground and the preachers embracing the prettiest women—lends both comic and realistic tones to the whole scene. In comparing Hooper's camp-meeting scene with Twain's, Bernard DeVoto writes in *Mark Twain's America* (1932) that whereas Hooper's lacks "the Olympian detachment of Mark Twain and his sketch therefore exists on a lower level . . . , its realism is sharper, its intelligence quite as great, and its conviction considerably greater."

In 1849, while he was running for judge of the ninth circuit in Alabama, Hooper compiled a collection of tales, *A Ride with Old Kit Kuncker, and Other Sketches, and Scenes of Alabama,* published that year. Its 120 pages comprise twenty-two stories. At least half of the episodes had appeared in other publications—mainly newspapers, including Hooper's own. Porter almost immediately reprinted six of the pieces in *Spirit of the Times.* Boosted by the lingering popularity of *Some Adventures of Captain Simon Suggs,* the new book was also successful, and its merits caught the eye of Philadelphia publisher A. Hart, who arranged to republish the volume as *The Widow Rugby's Husband, A Night at the Ugly Man's, and Other Tales of Alabama* (1851). The contents of *A Ride with Old Kit Kuncker* were expanded by several stories, and the order of the original contents of *A Ride with Old Kit Kuncker* was changed. Both volumes consist of backwoods vignettes, one featuring Simon Suggs, who once again plays the con man, this time cheating Widow Rugby's husband out of $50 in order to pay his own overdue inn bills. The two editions rely chiefly on the humor of character and situation, as found, for example, in sketches such as "Dick McCoy's Sketches of His Neighbors," "Jim Bell's Revenge," "The Erasive Soap Man," "The Elephant in Lafayette," "An Alligator Story," and "Montgomery Characters." Exaggerated physical and character traits abound throughout, as well as tall tales—again, all characteristics of Old Southwest humor. Both books also feature tales narrated by an unnamed "Squire" who frames the story with his intelligence and his astute observations of the uncouth characters and often sordid occurrences that characterize the life of the backwoods. While they are interesting miscellanies of incidents and characters, these two collections lack the sustained focus and unified tone, as well as the predominance of a single persona, that make *Some Adventures of Captain Simon Suggs* so effective.

Hooper's life changed considerably when in 1854 he moved to Montgomery, Alabama, to edit the major newspaper, the *Mail.* Although the paper was at first independent, over the next year Hooper turned it into a mouthpiece for the American Party and its offshoot, the Know-Nothing Party. As Hooper matured and prospered as a political essayist in the *Mail,* he consciously tried to distance himself from the Suggs legacy. Hoole wrote in *Alias Simon Suggs* that "by 1856 he is believed to have regretted sorely the identification of his name with that of 'Simon, the shifty man' and wished that he had never published the humorous biography," because as a political aspirant increasingly involved in the Southern cause "his reputation as a 'funny man' was a hazard, a difficult obstacle in every way to his personal advancement and, consequently, he deduced, to the advancement of his beloved region." Thus, in 1855 and 1856 Hooper published two volumes of a different nature from his earlier ones. The first was a kind of political tract, *Read and Circulate: Proceedings of the Democratic and Anti-Know-Nothing Party in Caucus; or the Guillo-*

*tine at Work, at the Capital, during the Session of 1855–'56.* This sixteen-page pamphlet, signed "By an Eye-Witness," is a humorous account of the activity of the newly elected Alabama legislature of 1855–1856, in which the Democratic Party held a two-to-one majority. Hooper, by now an avid Know-Nothing Party advocate, had attended many sessions of the legislature during the fall of 1855 and summarized his observations in this lively pamphlet. He took offense at the caucus system of the Democrats, which excluded the Know-Nothings. While he included humorous passages and even verses berating the Democrats and satirically chided the "enemy" in general, the tone is one of good humor overall.

His second foray into political writing was *Dog and Gun; A Few Loose Chapters on Shooting, Among Which Will Be Found Some Anecdotes and Incidents* (1856). The thirteen chapters constitute a professional sportsman's guide to hunting and the selection and training of a game dog. Although Hooper wrote most of the chapters himself, he also included passages or entire essays from authorities on hunting such as Henry William Herbert ("Frank Forester") and William T. Stockton, who wrote for the *Spirit of the Times* under the pseudonym "Cor de Chase." The volume is well written in a genial, genteel tone, and it found considerable favor with enthusiasts of field sport. It enjoyed some six editions, one of them posthumous, between 1856 and 1871. Despite its serious and professional subject matter and tone, however, its success still did not disengage Hooper from his association with Simon Suggs, much to his regret given his dedication to important political issues.

In 1859 Hooper edited *Woodward's Reminiscences of the Creek, or Muscogee Indians, Contained in Letters to Friends in Georgia and Alabama.* The little book is a volume of essays about "Old Times in Alabama" by General Thomas S. Woodward, a retired army officer from Georgia who settled in Alabama, had fought under Andrew Jackson in the Seminole War, and had been in charge of the Marquis de Lafayette's tour from Fort Mitchell to Montgomery in 1824. Some twenty-six letters were submitted by Woodward to the *Mail* during 1857–1858. Hooper collected the letters and added a preface, and the resulting work was a popular success. Copyrighted in Hooper's name, the volume sold out within a few months of publication in January 1859.

Hooper was also one of the "thirteen doges," all of them members of the Masonic Lodge, who authored *Magnum Opus. The Great Book of the University of Comus. The Paneduct of Our National Hilaritas, Comprising Essays upon the Thirteen Divisions of the Rituals; Sketches of the Tredecim of Doges, Authors of the Plan, and a Monitorial Guide to the Workings of the Fellowship, The Gander-Flight of the Thir-*

Drawing our blanks from their case, we proceeded: "I am the man, madam, that takes the census, and—"  *Page* 151.

*Illustration for "Taking the Census," a story based loosely on Hooper's experiences as a census taker (from* Some Adventures of Captain Suggs, Late of the Tallapoosa Volunteers, *1846)*

teen *Doges of Comus,* a bizarre miscellany published in 1886, more than twenty years after Hooper's death. The book is a satire on Masonic rites and fraternal secrecy filled with a baffling array of weird drawings, nonsensical (to non-Masons) ceremonies, and further burlesques of the organization. Hooper wrote chapter 9, "Thirteen Sages of Antiquity Caricatured." The work adds little to the Hooper canon beyond its curiosity value, however.

Hooper's literary legacy obviously rests primarily with *Some Adventures of Captain Simon Suggs,* one of the most influential works of Old Southwest humor, which Henry Watterson, in his study *Oddities in Southern Life and Character* (1883), proclaimed "a masterpiece." British novelist William Makepeace Thackeray, a contemporary of Hooper's, called him "the most promising writer of his day," as quoted by Hoole in *Alias Simon Suggs.* Fellow humorist Joseph Glover Baldwin, author of *Flush Times of Alabama and Mississippi* (1853), paid tribute to Hooper by writing the good-spirited, parodic "Simon Suggs, Jr., Esq.; A Legal Biography," which appeared as one of the selections in his book.

Hooper's traits as a Southern humorist have been extolled by many readers and critics. Rhoda Coleman Ellison, in *Early Alabama Publications: A Study in Literary Interests* (1947), focuses on Hooper's providing his readers "realistic glimpses of contemporary life in the Alabama backwoods" and calls the sketches of Simon Suggs "a triumph of realism" when compared with other journalistic presentations of the Alabama frontier. She points out that in Alabama fiction of the 1850s characters and issues tended to be conventional and almost uniformly in defense of Confederate ideals; only in *Some Adventures of Captain Simon Suggs* and *Flush Times of Alabama and Mississippi* were "other characters and methods" used in "their portrayal of the Alabama frontier." Franklin J. Meine writes in *Tall Tales of the Southwest* (1930) that "In Simon Suggs, Hooper achieved a powerful character study, bringing to a focus in one character those virulent forces of frontier life." DeVoto, in *Mark Twain's America,* views Hooper as one of the developers of the tall-tale technique that was so influential on Twain, and M. Thomas Inge, in *The Frontier Humorists: Critical Views* (1975), considers the creation of Suggs "the most notable contribution of

America to the literature of roguery," to which James M. Cox in "Humor of the Old Southwest" (in *The Comic Imagination in American Literature,* 1973), adds: "Suggs is, after all, the old picaro reborn as the frontier confidence man." It is left perhaps to Kenneth S. Lynn, in *Mark Twain and Southwestern Humor* (1959), to articulate most perceptively the deep underlying meaning of Hooper's novel. In reading *Simon Suggs,* he says, "one is oppressed by the sense of moving through a darkening world, populated by dehumanized grotesques. . . . sensual and superstitious, gray with fear and green with envy, the people who are taken in by Hooper's confidence man are as morally degraded as he is."

While Johnson Jones Hooper is certainly not a household name, he can be read and appreciated for the lively humor of *Some Adventures of Simon Suggs, A Ride with Old Kit Kuncker, The Widow Rugby's Husband,* and "Taking the Census"; the political satire of *Read and Circulate: Proceedings of the Democratic and Anti-Know-Nothing Party, in Caucus;* or the sporting focus of *Dog and Gun.* His was a life dedicated to his writings, his newspaper editing, his legal career, and to the politics of the antebellum South. While not a major Southern figure such as Twain, William Faulkner, or Eudora Welty, as Paul Somers Jr. concludes in *Johnson J. Hooper* (1984), "Hooper has a secure niche in the history of American literature" as a Southwestern humorist.

**Biography:**

W. Stanley Hoole, *Alias Simon Suggs: The Life and Times of Johnson Jones Hooper* (University: University of Alabama Press, 1952).

**References:**

Walter Blair, *Horse Sense in American Humor* (Chicago: University of Chicago Press, 1942), pp. 103–107;

Blair, *Native American Humor* (New York: American, 1937), pp. 86–88, 308–325;

James M. Cox, "Humor of the Old Southwest," in *The Comic Imagination in American Literature,* edited by Louis D. Rubin Jr. (New Brunswick, N.J.: Rutgers University Press, 1973), pp. 101–112;

Bernard DeVoto, *Mark Twain's America* (Boston: Little, Brown, 1932), pp. 255–257;

Rhoda Coleman Ellison, *Early Alabama Publications: A Study in Literary Interests* (University: University of Alabama Press, 1947), pp. 39, 74–77, 192;

Robert Hopkins, "Simon Suggs: A Burlesque Campaign Biography," *American Quarterly,* 15 (Fall 1963): 459–463;

M. Thomas Inge, ed., *The Frontier Humorists: Critical Views* (Hamden, Conn.: Archon, 1975), pp. 3, 8, 10, 23, 25–27, 29, 31, 60–61, 62, 65, 67, 78, 80, 81, 105–106, 120, 121, 141, 207;

Kenneth S. Lynn, *Mark Twain and Southwestern Humor* (Boston & Toronto: Little, Brown, 1959), pp. 52, 78–87;

Franklin J. Meine, ed., *Tall Tales of the Southwest: An Anthology of Southern and Southwestern Humor, 1830–1860* (New York: Knopf, 1930), pp. xxii, xxiii, xxvii, xxix, 299–301;

John Rachal, "Scotty Briggs and the Minister: An Idea from Hooper's Simon Suggs?" *Mark Twain Journal,* 17 (Summer 1974): 10–11;

Paul Somers Jr., *Johnson J. Hooper* (Boston: Twayne, 1984);

Jennette Tandy, *Crackerbox Philosophers in American Humor and Satire* (New York: Columbia University Press, 1925), pp. 80–89, 95, 99;

Henry Watterson, ed., *Oddities in Southern Life and Character* (Boston: Houghton, Mifflin, 1883), pp. v–ix, 39–91;

Mary Ann Wimsatt and Robert L. Phillips, "Antebellum Humor," in *The History of Southern Literature,* edited by Rubin and others (Baton Rouge & London: Louisiana State University Press, 1985), pp. 136–166;

Norris W. Yates, *William T. Porter and the Spirit of the Times: A Study of the Big Bear School of Humor* (Baton Rouge: Louisiana State University Press, 1957), pp. 44–56.

# Joseph Holt Ingraham

*(26 January 1809 – 18 December 1860)*

## Robert W. Weathersby II
*Dalton State College*

See also the Ingraham entry in *DLB 3: Antebellum Writers in New York and the South.*

BOOKS: *The South-West. By a Yankee,* 2 volumes, anonymous (New York: Harper, 1835);

*Lafitte: The Pirate of the Gulf,* 2 volumes, anonymous (New York: Harper, 1836); republished as *The Pirate of the Gulf; or, Lafitte,* anonymous (London: Newman, 1837);

*Burton; or, The Sieges. A Romance,* 2 volumes, anonymous (New York: Harper, 1838); *Quebec and New York: or, The Three Beauties: An Historical Romance of 1775,* 3 volumes, anonymous (London: Newman, 1839);

*Captain Kyd; or, The Wizard of the Sea. A Romance,* 2 volumes, anonymous (New York: Harper, 1839);

*The American Lounger; or, Tales, Sketches, and Legends Gathered in Sundry Journeyings,* anonymous (Philadelphia: Lea & Blanchard, 1839);

*The Quadroone; or, St. Michael's Day,* 3 volumes (London: Bentley, 1840; 2 volumes, New York: Harper, 1841);

*The Dancing Feather, or The Amateur Freebooters. A Romance of New York* (Boston: Roberts, 1842);

*Edward Austin: or, The Hunting Flask. A Tale of the Forest and Town* (Boston: Gleason, 1842);

*The Gipsy of the Highlands; or, The Jew and The Heir. Being the Adventures of Duncan Powell and Paul Tatnall* (Boston: Redding, 1843);

*Jemmy Daily: or, The Little News Vender. A Tale of Youthful Struggles, and the Triumph of Truth and Virtue over Vice and Falsehood* (Boston: Brainard, 1843);

*Lame Davy's Son: with the Birth, Education, and Career of Foraging Peter. A Tale of Boston Aristocracy. The "Odd Fellow," or the Secret Association; A Tale Portraying the Principles, Character, and Usefulness of the Order of Odd Fellows. Dedicated to the Association of "Odd Fellows" in the United States* (Boston: Roberts, 1843);

*Morris Graeme: or, The Cruise of the Sea-Slipper. A Sequel to the Dancing Feather. A Tale of the Land and the Sea* (Boston: Williams, 1843);

*(frontispiece for* Santa Claus, *1844)*

*Fanny H———; or, The Hunchback and the Roue* (Boston: Williams, 1843);

*Mark Manly; or, The Skipper's Lad: A Tale of Boston in the Olden Time* (Boston: Williams, 1843);

*Frank Rivers; or, The Dangers of the Town. A Story of Temptation, Trial and Crime* (Boston: Williams, 1843);

*The Young Genius; or, Trials and Triumphs* (Boston: Williams, 1843);

*Howard: or, The Mysterious Disappearance. A Romance of the Tripolitan War* (Boston: Williams, 1843);

*Black Ralph: or, The Helmsman of Hurlgate. A Tale* (Boston: Williams, 1844);

*The Beautiful Unknown; or, Massey Finke* (Boston: "Yankee" Office, 1844);

*Theodore; or, The "Child of the Sea." Being a Sequel to the Novel of "Lafitte, the Pirate of the Gulf"* (Boston: Williams, 1844);

*Rodolphe in Boston! A Tale* (Boston: Williams, 1844);

*Biddy Woodhull; or The Pretty Haymaker. A Tale* (Boston: Williams, 1844);

*The Corsair of Casco Bay; or The Pilot's Daughter* (Gardiner, Me.: Atwood, 1844);

*Ellen Hart: or, The Forger's Daughter* (Boston: "Yankee" Office, 1844);

*The Miseries of New York. Or The Burglar and Counsellor* [sic] (Boston: "Yankee" Office, 1844);

*Steel Belt: or, The Three-Masted Goleta! A Tale of Boston Bay* (Boston: "Yankee" Office, 1844);

*Arnold: or The British Spy! A Tale of Treason and Treachery* (Boston: "Yankee" Office, 1844);

*The Midshipman, or The Corvette and Brigantine. A Tale of Sea and Land* (Boston: Gleason, 1844);

*La Bonita Cigarera; or, The Beautiful Cigar Vender. A Tale of New York* (Boston: "Yankee" Office, 1844);

*Estelle: or, The Conspirator of the Isle. A Tale of the West Indian Seas* (Boston: "Yankee" Office, 1844);

*The Silver Bottle; or, The Adventures of "Little Marlboro" in Search of His Father* (Boston: "Yankee" Office, 1844);

*Herman De Ruyter; or, The Mystery Unveiled. A Sequel to the Beautiful Cigar Vender. A Tale of the Metropolis* (Boston: "Yankee" Office, 1844);

*The Diary of a Hackney Coachman* (Boston: "Yankee" Office, 1844);

*Santa Claus: or, The Merry King of Christmas. A Tale for the Holidays* (Boston: Williams, 1844);

*Caroline Archer; or, The Miliner's* [sic] *Apprentice. A Story That Hath More Truth Than Fiction in It* (Boston: Williams, 1844);

*Eleanor Sherwood, the Beautiful Temptress!* (Boston: "Yankee" Office, 1844);

*The Spanish Galleon; or The Pirate of the Mediterranean. A Romance of the Corsair Kidd* (Boston: Gleason, 1845);

*The Clipper-Yacht; or, Moloch, the Money-Lender! A Tale of London and the Thames* (Boston: Williams, 1845);

*Marie; or, The Fugitive. A Romance of Mount Benedict* (Boston: "Yankee" Office, 1845);

*Freemantle: or, The Privateersman! A Nautical Romance of the Last War* (Boston: Redding, 1845);

*Scarlet Feather, or, The Young Chief of the Abenaquies. A Romance of the Wilderness of Maine* (Boston: Gleason, 1845);

*Forrestal: or The Light of the Reef. A Romance of the Blue Waters* (Boston: Williams, 1845);

*Rafael* (Boston: Williams, 1845);

*The Knights of Seven Lands* (Boston: Gleason, 1845);

*Montezuma, the Serf, or The Revolt of the Mexitili: A Tale of the Last Days of the Aztec Dynasty* (Boston: Williams, 1845);

*Will Terril: or, The Adventures of a Young Gentleman Born in a Cellar* (Boston: "Yankee" Office, 1845);

*Norman: or, The Privateersman's Bride. A Sequel to "Freemantle"* (Boston: "Yankee" Office, 1845);

*Neal Nelson; or, The Seige* [sic] *of Boston: A Tale of the Revolution* (Boston: Williams, 1845);

*A Romance of the Sunny South. Or, Feathers from a Traveller's Wing* (Boston: Williams, 1845);

*Paul Deverell, or Two Judgments for One Crime. A Tale of the Present Day* (Boston: Williams, 1845);

*Part II. Paul Deverell; or, Two Judgments for One Crime* (Boston: Williams, 1845);

*Paul Perril, the Merchant's Son; or, The Adventures of a New-England Boy Launched Upon Life . . . Part First* (Boston: Williams, 1845);

*The Adventures of Will Wizard! Corporal of the Saccarapa Volunteers* (Boston: Williams, 1845);

*Alice May, and Bruising Bill* (Boston: Gleason, 1845);

*Bertrand, or, The Story of Marie De Heywode. Being a Sequel to Marie, the Fugitive* (Boston: Williams, 1845);

*Charles Blackford; or, The Adventures of a Student in Search of a Profession* (Boston: "Yankee" Office, 1845);

*The Cruiser of the Mist* (New York: Burgess, Stringer, 1845);

*Fleming Field; or, The Young Artisan. A Tale of the Days of the Stamp Act* (New York: Burgess, Stringer, 1845);

*Grace Weldon; or, Frederica, The Bonnet-Girl: A Tale of Boston and Its Bay* (Boston: Williams, 1845);

*Harry Harefoot; or, The Three Temptations: A Story of City Scenes* (Boston: "Yankee" Office, 1845);

*Henry Howard; or, Two Noes Make One Yes* (Boston: Williams, 1845);

*Mary Wilbur: or, The Deacon and the Widow's Daughter* (Boston: "Yankee" Office, 1845);

*The Mast-Ship: or, The Bombardment of Falmouth* (Boston: Williams, 1845);

*The Wing of the Wind. A Nouvelette of the Sea* (New York: Burgess, Stringer, 1845);

*Paul Perril, the Merchant's Son; or, The Adventures of a New-England Boy Launched Upon Life . . . Part Second* (Boston: Williams, 1846);

*Arthur Denwood: or The Maiden of the Inn. A Tale of the War of 1812* (Boston: Williams, 1846);

*The Lady of the Gulf. A Romance of the City and the Seas* (Boston: Williams, 1846);

*Leisler: or The Rebel and King's Man. A Tale of the Rebellion of 1869* (Boston: Williams, 1846);

*Ramero; or, The Prince and the Prisoner! A Romance of the Moro Castle!* (Boston: Williams, 1846);

*Winwood; or, The Fugitive of the Seas* (New York & Boston: Williams / Louisville, Ky.: Penton, 1846);

*Bonfield; or, The Outlaw of the Bermudas. A Nautical Novel* (New York & Boston: Williams, 1846 / Louisville, Ky.: Penton, 1846);

*The Silver Ship of Mexico: A Tale of the Spanish Main* (New York & Boston: Williams, 1846);

*Berkeley: or, The Lost and Redeemed. A Novel* (Boston: Williams, 1846);

*Mate Burke; or, The Foundlings of the Sea* (New York: Burgess, Stringer, 1846);

*The Mysterious State-Room; A Tale of the Mississippi* (Boston: Gleason, 1846);

*The Odd Fellow, or, The Secret Association, and Foraging Peter* (Boston: United States Publishing, 1846);

*Pierce Fenning, or, The Lugger's Chase. A Romance* (Boston: Williams, 1846);

*The Ringdove: or, The Privateer and the Cutter* (New York & Boston: Williams / Louisville, Ky.: Penton, 1846);

*The Slave King; or, The Triumph of Liberty,* 2 volumes (Boston: Williams, 1846);

*The Spectre Steamer and Other Tales* (Boston: United States Publishing, 1846);

*The Young Artist, and the Bold Insurgent* (Boston: United States Publishing, 1846);

*The Surf Skiff; or, The Heroine of the Kennebec* (New York & Boston: Williams, 1847);

*The Truce; or, On and Off Soundings: A Tale of the Coast of Maine* (New York & Boston: Williams, 1847);

*Blanche Talbot; or, The Maiden's Hand: A Romance of the War of 1812* (New York & Boston: Williams, 1847);

*The Brigantine; or, Guitierro and the Castilian: A Tale Both of Boston and Cuba* (New York & Boston: Williams, 1847);

*Edward Manning; or, The Bride and the Maiden* (New York & Boston: Williams / Louisville, Ky.: Penton, 1847);

*Beatrice, the Goldsmith's Daughter: A Story of the Reign of the Last Charles* (New York & Boston: Williams, 1847);

*Ringold Griffitt: or, The Raftsman of the Susquehannah: A Tale of Pennsylvania* (Boston: Gleason, 1847);

*The Free-Trader; or, The Cruiser of Narragansett Bay* (New York: Williams, 1847);

*The Texan Ranger; or, The Maid of Matamoras* (New York: Williams, 1847);

*Wildash; or, The Cruiser of the Capes: A Nautical Romance* (New York: Williams, 1847);

*Jennette Alison; or The Young Strawberry Girl: A Tale of the Sea and the Shore* (Boston: Gleason, 1848);

*Report upon a Proposed System of Public Education, for the City of Nashville, Respectfully Addressed to the Citizens* (Nashville: Bang, 1848);

*Nobody's Son; or, The Life and Adventures of Percival Mayberry, Written by Himself,* anonymous (Philadelphia: Hart, 1851); republished as *The Life and Adventures of Percival Mayberry: An Autobiography,* anonymous (Philadelphia: Peterson, 1854);

*Man: A Sermon Preached in St. John's Church, Aberdeen, Miss., January, 1852* (New York: McSpedon & Baker, 1852);

*Pamphlets for the People. In Illustration of the Claims of the Church and Methodism, by a Presbyter of Mississippi,* anonymous (Philadelphia: Hooker, 1854);

*The Arrow of Gold; or, The Shell Gatherer: A Story That Unfolds Its Own Mysteries and Moral,* anonymous (New York: S. French, 1855);

*The Prince of the House of David; or, Three Years in the Holy City: Being a Series of the Letters of Adina, a Jewess of Alexandria, Sojourning in Jerusalem in the Days of Herod* (New York: Pudney & Russell, 1855);

*Rivingstone; or, The Young Ranger Hussar. A Romance of the Revolution* (New York: De Witt & Davenport, 1855);

*The Dancing Star; or, The Smuggler of the Chesapeake: A Story of the Coast and Sea* (Boston: Office of the Flag of Our Union, 1857);

*The Pillar of Fire; or, Israel in Bondage* (New York: Pudney & Russell, 1859);

*The Throne of David, from the Consecration of the Shepherd of Bethlehem to the Rebellion of Prince Absalom* (Philadelphia: M. Evans, 1860);

*The Sunny South; or, The Southerner at Home, Embracing Five Years' Experience of a Northern Governess in the Land of the Sugar and the Cotton* (Philadelphia: M. Evans, 1860).

SELECTED PERIODICAL PUBLICATIONS–UNCOLLECTED: "Biographical Sketches of Living American Poets and Novelists. No. 1. Francis William Thomas, Esq," *Southern Literary Messenger,* 4 (May 1838): 297–301; "No. II. James Fenimore Cooper, Esq.," 4 (June 1838): 373–378; "No. III. William D. Gallagher, Esq.," (July 1838): 452–457; "No. IV; William Gilmore Simms, Esq.," (August 1838): 528–535;

"West Point.–A Tale of Treason," *United States Magazine, and Democratic Review,* 3 (July 1838): 235–251; 3 (December 1838): 339–356;

"Dots and Lines,–No. 1; or, Sketches of Scenes and Incidents in the West," *Ladies' Companion,* 11 (May 1839): 38–41; "No. II," 11 (June 1839): 69–71; "No. III," 11 (July 1839): 123–124; "No. IV," 11 (August 1839): 196; "No. V," 11 (September 1839): 243–244;

"The Birth and Nestling of Love. A Short Story in Rhyme," *Godey's Lady's Book,* 19 (September 1839): 120;

"An Evening at Buccleuch Hall; or, The Grenadier's Ghost. A Tale of the Old Stair Head Clock," *Ladies Companion,* 17 (July 1842): 166–171;

"The Bold Insurgent," *Ladies' Companion,* 17 (August 1842): 219–228;

"Lines to the Bunker Hill Monument," *Boston Miscellany of Literature and Fashion,* 2 (October 1842): 187;

"A Brief Review of an Old Magazine of the Last Century," *Ladies' Companion,* 18 (January 1843): 138–141;

"Lafitte–Professor Ingraham's Letter," *DeBow's Review,* 13 (October 1852): 422–424;

"Secrets of the Cells: or, Leaves from My Diary," *Ballou's Pictorial Drawing Room Companion,* 8 (7 March 1855): 162–164; (24 March 1855): 178–179; (31 March 1855): 194–195; (7 April 1855): 210–211; (14 April 1855): 226–227; (21 April 1855): 242–243;

"Elfrida, the Druid's Daughter; or, The Cross Planted in Britain. A Tale of the First Century," *Churchman's Monthly Magazine,* 3 (January 1856): 23–26; (February 1856): 111–116; (March 1856): 138–143; (April 1856): 222–228; (May 1856): 265–270; (June 1856): 330–336; (July 1856): 416–423; (August 1856): 467–473; (September 1856): 539–544; (October 1856): 612–618;

"Sermon. Preached in Trinity Church, Natchez, Whit Sunday, 1858," *Natchez Weekly Courier,* 15 June 1858, p. 3.

The works of Joseph Holt Ingraham are an interesting and occasionally fascinating glimpse into what America wanted to read and would pay for during the twenty-five-year period from 1835 to 1860. As one of the best-selling authors in the United States in the mid 1800s, Ingraham was one of the few American authors to make a living from writing at that time, his works outselling those of Edgar Allan Poe and other better-known authors. Ingraham was a travel writer, a novelist, a magazinist, and, for the last thirteen years of his life, a minister as well. In all areas of his careers he wrote with energy and an eye to details, particularly details of setting. The judgment of history confirms him as a minor writer, however, quite possibly because he wrote too much and planned his work too little.

Named for his prosperous grandfather, Ingraham was born to James Milk Ingraham and his wife, Elizabeth Thurston, on 26 January 1809 in Portland, Maine. His grandfather was a merchant, a shipowner, and a civic leader; little is known of James Ingraham except that he was a merchant and that he had another son, John Philip Thurston Ingraham, who became a minister in the Protestant Episcopal Church. Joseph Holt Ingraham married Mary Elizabeth Odlin Brooks, the daughter of a Natchez, Mississippi, planter, on 24 May 1832. He and his wife apparently had several children, but only one, Prentiss, born 28 December 1843, grew to adulthood. Prentiss, in fact, published even more than his prolific father, gaining most of his fame as an author of dime novels for the publishing company Beadle and Adams.

Because Ingraham kept no diary, used little of his life in his writing, and moved frequently between the North and the South, few biographical details are available. He had no biographer in his own day. He published most of his work anonymously, using "A Yankee" and "By the Author of . . ." on the title pages. In addition, Ingraham was remarkably unaffected by any particular literary ideology or theory; he was not influenced by Transcendentalism, but he did appreciate the beauty of nature, and he had romantic inclinations from the start of his career, most probably because of the conventions established by Sir Walter Scott for the romantic treatment of historical incidents. Nor does Ingraham really fit as a "Southern" writer; he fell in love with the South at the age of twenty-one but used few southern settings in his work and frequently lived in the publishing centers of New York and Massachusetts. What did interest him was the patriotic advancement of American literature, and his phenomenal output of more than one hundred novels and many more than a hundred periodical contributions was most often firmly based on American places and people. He was motivated to tell a good story, often full of action, occasionally with memorable characters, but he started and ended his career with travel writings.

After receiving a good primary education, mostly at the Hallowell Academy in Maine, Ingraham apparently gained some travel experience in his grandfather's merchant ships. He attended Yale College in 1828–1829 but was expelled for an obscure reason and traveled to New Orleans and Natchez, Mississippi. By 1830 he was apparently a junior faculty member at Jefferson College in Washington, Mississippi, probably teaching languages and reading. He was known as "Professor" Ingraham for the rest of his life. This trip by sailing ship to New Orleans and by steamboat up the Mississippi settled Ingraham on his adopted home–the South–and on his career. His first published work was a series of "Letters from Louisiana by a Yankee" published in the *Natchez Courier* from August 1833 through January 1835.

The revised and enlarged letters were published in late 1835 by Harper and Brothers as *The South-West. By a Yankee.* Though the sketches were published anonymously, Ingraham's identity was apparently no secret. He detailed his thirty-one-day trip south, with many observations of life on shipboard, before anchoring at the mouth of the Mississippi River. The traveler was intrigued by New Orleans, its peoples, its languages, its markets, and its cemeteries. The second volume of the work chronicles his ascent up the Mississippi to Natchez, delivers comments on the city and its inhabitants, the plantations, and the slave system; Ingraham includes a description of a visit to a slave market. Poe, in a penetrating review for the *Southern Literary Messenger* (January 1836), commended Ingraham's eye for detail and the fairness with which the new writer discussed the slavery situation in the Deep South. Though travel writing sold well at the time–Ingraham received $300 for *The South-West*–the genre did not become his forte.

With the publication of his next book, his first novel, Ingraham found himself famous. *Lafitte: The Pirate of the Gulf,* published in June 1836 in an edition of 1,500 copies, sold out so quickly that a second and partially revised edition was rushed to press in September. His two-volume melodramatic saga of Jean Lafitte includes some fact, based as it was on the buccaneer's exploits during the battles for New Orleans during the War of 1812, and much fiction. The tale begins along the Kennebec River in Maine with two brothers quarreling over a woman. One kills the other, leaves home, and eventually becomes the corsair Lafitte. Ingraham took some of the characteristics of the Byronic hero–the epigraph on the title page and most of the quotations prefacing each volume are from Lord Byron–and grafted them onto his dark-haired, restless hero with his gnawing remorse and pangs of conscience. Lafitte could have been created by a more modern, psychologically oriented novelist. When he aids General Andrew Jackson at the Battle of New Orleans (a circumstance based on fact), he is still expiating his sins. Ingraham's portrayal of Lafitte is one of his best creations. Melodramatic as the character Lafitte can be, the tension in the portrayal of this antihero is felt and appreciated by contemporary readers. Indeed, *Lafitte* is one of only two of Ingraham's novels that has remained in print. Ingraham received $1,350 for *Lafitte,* a payment that helped him decide to continue novel writing.

Ingraham next wrote *Burton; or, The Sieges* (1838), an absorbing account of Aaron Burr's activities during the early years of the Revolutionary War. The sieges of the subtitle are the military sieges of Quebec and New York, which form the subplot, and the personal sieges laid by Burton against the chastity of three young ladies, which form the main plot. The fact that Burr had died two years previously and that he had been tried for treason under some oak trees on the Jefferson College campus may have influenced Ingraham's choice of subject matter. The first two hundred pages of volume 1, which detail Burton's travels, dangers, and exploits, are the most tightly organized in all of Ingraham's work; Ingraham was

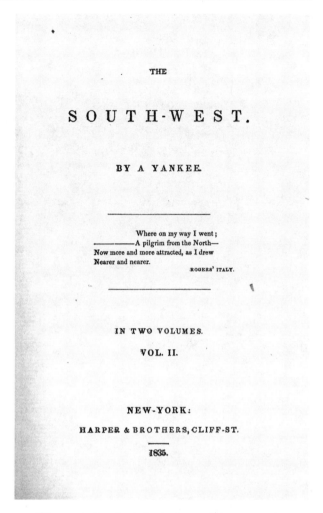

*Title page for Ingraham's first book, a nonfiction account of his travels along the Mississippi River (Thomas Cooper Library, University of South Carolina)*

likely disappointed by the $750 he received from Harper and Brothers for his efforts, however, and he quickly returned to writing a sea tale.

He was paid significantly more ($1,200) for his next two-volume effort, *Captain Kyd; or, The Wizard of the Sea* (1839). This novel is confused and marred by several flaws, however, including improbable coincidences, breaks in the action, characters with a mysterious knowledge of the past, and an abrupt ending that draws all the plot threads to a fantastic close. Based partly on the career of the actual pirate Captain William Kidd, *Captain Kyd* is more derivative than original and not as well plotted as Ingraham's first two fictional pieces. The novel, however, not only sold but was also dramatized for the stage by Joseph Stevens Jones in 1845 in a version that is still extant.

Ingraham's last novel for Harper was *The Quadroone; or, St. Michael's Day* (1840), a pioneer effort in bringing the subject of miscegenation to the general

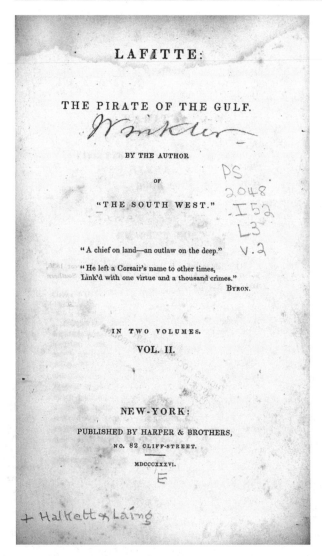

*Title page for volume 2 of Ingraham's first novel, a fictionalized portrayal of Jean Laffite and his participation in the Battle of New Orleans during the War of 1812 (Thomas Cooper Library, University of South Carolina)*

novels, however, his periodical publications are often difficult to identify and locate. Again, much of the work was published anonymously, and there are no extant copies of many of the periodicals in which he published. Though he was not paid well for individual contributions (no one was in this time of no copyright law and multiple reprinting), his total output certainly supplemented his income from his novels, and he apparently had little trouble getting his work in print.

"An Evening at Buccleuch Hall; or, The Grenadier's Ghost. A Tale of the Old Stair Head Clock" (*Ladies' Companion,* July 1842) is a pleasant ghost story much like the quietly humorous tales of Washington Irving. One moral tale, "Harvey Ross" (*Ladies' Companion,* May, June, August 1844), is a hilarious and preposterous story about the evils of chewing tobacco, especially when the juice is spit on the floor. "West Point.–A Tale of Treason" (*United States Magazine, and Democratic Review,* July and December 1838) is a fast-moving story of the treachery of Benedict Arnold. This story was so popular that it became the third Ingraham tale to be dramatized for the stage, in an 1840 adaptation by Joseph Breck. Many of the periodical publications were set in the North since northern publishers put them in print, but Ingraham did write a tale of Bacon's Rebellion in Virginia in 1675, "The Bold Insurgent" (*Ladies' Companion,* August 1842). The longest and most-developed periodical tale that Ingraham wrote was a product of his years as a minister. The *Evergreen,* an Episcopal publication, serialized his "Letters from Adina" from August 1850 through December 1853. Published as *The Prince of the House of David; or, Three Years in the Holy City: Being a Series of the Letters of Adina, a Jewess of Alexandria, Sojourning in Jerusalem in the Days of Herod* in 1855, this work brought Ingraham his greatest fame as a novelist.

Before deciding to study for the ministry in 1847 and becoming an ordained minister in 1852, Ingraham continued to make his living as a novelist. His relationship with Harper appears to have ended after the publication of *The Quadroone,* although the parting of author and publisher was apparently not rancorous. The 1837 financial crunch in the United States had hurt many book publishers, and those who would previously print two-volume romances could make more money by reprinting, in the absence of a copyright law, the work of any writer, English or American. Ingraham offered his work to George Roberts, publisher of the *Boston Notion,* one of the so-called mammoth weeklies that were beginning to reach the public through favorable postal rates and low prices. Such weekly periodicals gave the masses cheap reading matter, which they devoured. The *Notion* published novels in serial format and frequently had several works in progress at once. It

public. Ingraham clears his hero and heroine from any taint of Negro blood in the fantastic close of the novel, but the daring subject matter and its wicked Byronic hero-villain, Garcia Ramarez, are the only interesting features of the work. Ingraham received approximately $800 for this novel, which received mixed reviews.

While the Harpers were publishing his books, Ingraham was also writing for various types of magazines. He kept up a steady flow of fiction, travel writing, poetry, and literary criticism for the *Ladies' Companion,* the *Gentleman's Magazine,* the *Boston Miscellany,* and more than twenty other periodicals. No review of the author's life and work can pretend completeness without a brief overview of this material; as with Ingraham's

*Frontispiece and title page for Ingraham's best-selling work, an 1855 epistolary novel depicting the life of Jesus
(Thomas Cooper Library, University of South Carolina)*

printed the first installment of Ingraham's *The Dancing Feather, or The Amateur Freebooters. A Romance of New York* on 27 November 1841, thus marking the beginning of his most prolific period as an author. *The Dancing Feather* is the story of amateur pirates who occasionally plunder a vessel in order to be able to live the lives of gentlemen in New York City. Published in a single volume in 1842, the novel sold at least forty-seven thousand copies and brought Ingraham to his largest audience.

Boston publishers Edward P. and Henry L. Williams printed eighty of Ingraham's novels during the five years between 1843 and 1847, an output so prodigious that James D. Hart claimed in *The Popular Book. A History of America's Literary Taste* (1961) that these novels accounted for nearly 10 percent of the fiction published in the 1840s. Henry Wadsworth Longfellow, writing in *Life of Henry Wadsworth Longfellow* (1891), commented after a visit with Ingraham in 1846 that Ingraham received more than $3,000 a year for his

work. According to Jay B. Hubbell in *The South in American Literature: 1607–1900* (1954), no other novelist, in the North or the South, was consistently earning that much in the 1840s.

Ingraham's work during this period was, at best, uneven. The number of the novels and the frequency of their publication led the critics to ignore them. Many of them exhibit artistic failings, chief among which was the lack of what Ingraham called "harmonious construction," a phrase Ingraham used in his novel *Morris Graeme: or, The Cruise of the Sea-Slipper* (1845), the sequel to *The Dancing Feather*. He complained in the introduction about constraints imposed by the publishers, which compelled him to abbreviate the plot he had planned, leave out character development, and rush the novel to an early conclusion.

Perhaps especially in light of the torrid pace of production that Ingraham set for himself from 1843 through 1847, he surprised many when, in 1847, he

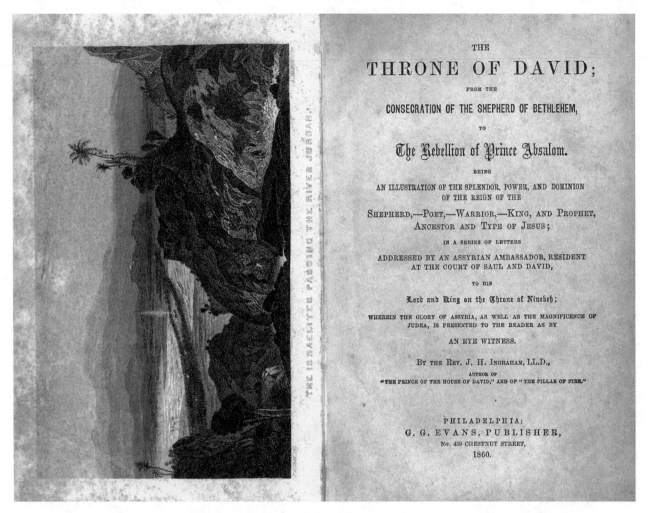

*Frontispiece and title page for Ingraham's novel based on the reigns of Hebrew kings Saul and David (Thomas Cooper Library, University of South Carolina)*

renounced his career as writer and began to study theology in preparation for taking orders in the Protestant Episcopal Church. A careful reader of Ingraham's novels will not be too surprised that the writer would choose the ministry because his work features a firm moral sense, and the name of God is frequently invoked by characters in tight situations.

In 1847 he moved to Nashville, Tennessee, to study theology under Bishop James Hervey Otey. Here he became principal of and teacher at a school for young women, volunteered his services as teacher and minister to the inmates of the Tennessee State Prison, and lobbied for a free public school system for Nashville. He left Nashville in 1851, was ordained a deacon by Bishop William Mercer Green of Mississippi, and was appointed to the missionary post of Aberdeen in northern Mississippi. Bishop Green ordained him to the priesthood on 8 February 1852; Ingraham was then serving a circuit of three towns. In 1853 he accepted a

call to St. John's Church in Mobile, Alabama, where he again became minister to a new church. He served this parish until 11 January 1857. During these years he finished his serial "Letters from Adina" and saw it published in New York as *The Prince of the House of David*. This novel, composed of thirty-nine letters retelling the life of Christ seen through the eyes of the Jewish maiden Adina, was the best-selling book of Ingraham's life and one of the best-selling books in the United States before the Civil War. This romance offered nothing new in technique or writing ability, but the writer-turned-minister had hit on his most popular fusion of fact and fiction, even though he would write only two more biblically inspired novels and a ten-part serial, "Elfrida, the Druid's Daughter," to follow *The Prince of the House of David*. No one seems to have definitive sales figures for the novel: Frank Luther Mott says it sold more than 225,000 copies before the Civil War; as of 1931, according to Don Seitz in "A Prince of Best Sellers," (*Publisher's Weekly,* 21 February 1931), the novel had sold between 4 and 5 million copies, and it has remained in print since then. What Ingraham was paid is not part of the historical record, but he must have received a pittance, for there is no hint that his financial condition changed in any way.

Ingraham's other biblical tales were well received but were not as popular as the first. *The Pillar of Fire; or, Israel in Bondage* (1859) and *The Throne of David, from the Consecration of the Shepherd of Bethlehem to the Rebellion of Prince Absalom* (1860) were both published while Ingraham was rector of a new church in Holly Springs, Mississippi. *The Pillar of Fire* tells the story of the Israelites' deliverance from slavery in Egypt, while *The Throne of David* spans the saga of the reigns of Saul and David.

When the definitive history of biblical fiction in the United States is finally written, Ingraham will deserve a place of prominence. He was held in extraordinary regard as a minister. He raised money for churches, planned them architecturally, helped build them physically, and served them faithfully. His career ended in the vestry of one of these churches, Christ Church in Holly Springs. Civil War tensions gripped the small northern Mississippi town, and Ingraham had taken a pistol to be repaired as a precaution against trouble. The gunsmith, unknown to the minister, loaded the weapon; Ingraham accidentally dropped the loaded gun in his vestry room on 9 December 1860. A chamber exploded, mortally wounding him. He lingered in agony for nine days before dying on 18 December at the age of fifty-one.

Ingraham's last published work was *The Sunny South; or, The Southerner at Home, Embracing Five Years' Experience of a Northern Governess in the Land of the Sugar and the Cotton* (1860), a collection of sixty-nine letters supposedly written by Kate Conyngham, a northern governess and native of a small town near Portland, Maine, about her work in an unnamed town south of Nashville. Ingraham thus ended his literary career as he began it, by writing a travel narrative of the South, its customs, and its people. If he found little to criticize in *The South-West,* he saw even less wrong twenty-five years later. The pleasant condition of the slaves and the kindness of their masters are mentioned repeatedly. *The South-West* is relatively unbiased, romantic travel writing; *The Sunny South* is more emphatically favorable to the region and is an index to its writer's love for his adopted region. Throughout the novel he paints unhappiness and evil coming from Northerners who attempt to interfere in the life of the South.

In a time when debates over the canon in American literature continue to take place, with obscure writers of both sexes being discovered and argued over, the works of Joseph Holt Ingraham bear reexamination. He

THE SUNNY SOUTH;

OR,

THE SOUTHERNER AT HOME,

EMBRACING

FIVE YEARS' EXPERIENCE OF A NORTHERN GOVERNESS

IN THE

LAND OF THE SUGAR AND THE COTTON.

EDITED BY

PROFESSOR J. H. INGRAHAM,

OF MISSISSIPPI.

"Stern winter smiles on that auspicious clime,
The fields are florid with unfading prime;
From the bleak pole no winds inclement blow,
Mold the round hail, or flake the fleecy snow;
But from the breezy deep the land inhales
The fragrant murmurs of the western gales."

PHILADELPHIA:

G. G. EVANS, PUBLISHER,

No. 439 CHESTNUT STREET.

1860.

*Title page for Ingraham's last published work, a collection of fictional letters by a young northern woman working as a governess for a Tennessee family (Thomas Cooper Library, University of South Carolina)*

is clearly not a major writer, but Ingraham could tell a good story. His tales may often lack abstractness and philosophical questionings, but, at their best, they have a physical virility, a directness in portrayal of people, places, and events that is praiseworthy. His talent was limited and undisciplined, but he did not wallow in sentimentality as many other popular writers did. Though his works are of primary value to the literary and cultural historian, they deserve continued study.

**Bibliographies:**

Jacob Blanck, comp., *Bibliography of American Literature,* 9 volumes (New Haven: Yale University Press, 1963), IV: 459–491;

Robert W. Weathersby II, "Joseph Holt Ingraham: A Bibliography of Periodical Publications, Newspaper Writings, and Parish Reports," in *No Fairer Land: Studies in Southern Literature before 1900*, edited by J. Lasley Dameron and James W. Mathews (Troy, N.Y.: Whitston, 1986), pp. 211–225;

Weathersby, "Joseph Holt Ingraham," in *Facts on File Bibliography of American Fiction through 1865*, edited by Kent P. Ljungquist (New York: Facts on File, 1994), pp. 145–148.

**References:**

Alexander Cowie, "Joseph Holt Ingraham (1809–1860)," in his *The Rise of the American Novel* (New York: American Book, 1948), pp. 282–292;

Warren G. French, "A Hundred Years of a Religious Bestseller," *Western Humanities Review,* 10 (Winter 1955–1956): 45–54;

Jay B. Hubbell, *The South in American Literature: 1607–1900* (Durham, N.C.: Duke University Press, 1954);

Albert Johannsen, "Rev. Joseph Holt Ingraham," in his *The House of Beadle and Adams and Its Dime and Nickel Novels: The Story of a Vanished Literature,* 2 volumes (Norman: University of Oklahoma Press, 1950), II: 151–155;

Mark A. Keller, "Joseph Holt Ingraham and 'The Mystery of Marie Roget,'" *Notes on Mississippi Writers,* 15 (1983): 45–56;

Amy Gilman Srebnick, *The Mysterious Death of Mary Rogers: Sex and Culture in Nineteenth-Century New York* (New York: Oxford University Press, 1995), pp. 140–149;

Simone Vauthier, "Jeux Avec L'Interdit: La Sexualité Interraciale Dans Le Roman De Joseph H. Ingraham, *The Quadroone,*" *Recherches Anglaises et Americaines,* 11 (1978): 133–146;

Robert W. Weathersby II, *J. H. Ingraham* (Boston: Twayne, 1980);

Weathersby, "J. H. Ingraham and Tennessee: A Record of Social and Literary Contributions," *Tennessee Historical Quarterly,* 34 (Fall 1975): 264–272.

**Papers:**

Materials related to Joseph Holt Ingraham, including letters and book contracts, are uncollected and scattered throughout various libraries, including the Boston Public Library, Columbia University Library, Historical Society of Pennsylvania, Massachusetts Historical Society, the National Archives, New York Public Library, Pierpont Morgan Library, University of Virginia Library, and Yale University Library.

# John Pendleton Kennedy

*(25 October 1795 – 18 August 1870)*

Judy Logan
*Eastern Washington University*

See also the Kennedy entry in *DLB 3: Antebellum Writers in New York and the South.*

BOOKS: *The Red Book,* in 10 parts, by Kennedy and Peter Hoffman Cruse, anonymous (Baltimore: Robinson, 1820–1821);

*Address Delivered on Behalf of the Faculty of Arts and Sciences on the Occasion of the Opening of the Collegiate Department in the University of Maryland, on the 3d of January, 1831* (Baltimore: Toy, 1831);

*Address of the Friends of Domestic Industry, Assembled in Convention, at New-York, October 26, 1831, to the People of the United States,* by Kennedy, Warren Dutton, and Charles J. Ingersoll (Baltimore: Published by Order of the Convention, 1831);

*Swallow Barn, or A Sojourn in the Old Dominion,* as Mark Littleton, 2 volumes (Philadelphia: Carey & Lea, 1832; revised and enlarged edition, New York: Putnam, 1851);

*Address Delivered before the Horticultural Society of Maryland, at Its First Annual Exhibition, June 12, 1833* (Baltimore: Toy, 1833);

*Address Delivered before the American Institute, at Chatham-Street Chapel in the City of New-York, October 17, 1833* (New York: Hopkins, 1833);

*A Discourse on the Life and Character of William Wirt, Late Attorney General of the United States; Pronounced at the Request of the Baltimore Bar before the Citizens of Baltimore, on the 20th of May, 1834* (Baltimore: Neal, 1834);

*Horse-Shoe Robinson: A Tale of the Tory Ascendancy,* 2 volumes (Philadelphia: Carey, Lea & Blanchard, 1835); republished as *Horse-Shoe Robinson* (London: Bentley, 1835; revised edition, 1 volume, New York: Putnam, 1852);

*Rob of the Bowl: A Legend of St. Inigoe's,* 2 volumes (Philadelphia: Lea & Blanchard, 1838; revised edition, New York: Putnam, 1854);

*Quodlibet: Containing Some Annals Thereof, with an Authentic Account of the Origin and Growth of the Borough and the Sayings and Doings of Sundry of the Townspeople,* anon-

*John Pendleton Kennedy, 1846 (portrait by Matthew Wilson; Peabody Institute Library, Baltimore)*

ymous (Philadelphia: Lea & Blanchard, 1840; revised and enlarged edition, Philadelphia: Lippincott, 1860);

*Defense of the Whigs,* anonymous (New York: Harper, 1844);

*Discourse on the Life and Character of George Calvert, The First Lord Baltimore: Made by John P. Kennedy, before the Maryland Historical Society, December 9, 1845*

(Baltimore: Printed for the Society by J. Murphy, 1845);

*Some Passages in the Life of William Thom: A Lecture Delivered February 4, 1846, before the Asbury Sabbath School* (Baltimore? 1846);

*Reply of J. P. Kennedy to the Review of His Discourse on the Life and Character of Calvert, Published in the United States Catholic Magazine, April, 1846* (Baltimore: Murphy, 1846);

*Memoirs of the Life of William Wirt, Attorney General of the United States,* 2 volumes (Philadelphia: Lea & Blanchard, 1849; revised, 1850);

*Address Delivered before the Maryland Institute for the Promotion of the Mechanic Arts, on the Occasion of the Opening of the Fourth Annual Exhibition, on the 21st October, 1851, being the First Exhibition in the New Hall of the Institute* (Baltimore: Murphy, 1851);

*The Border States, Their Power and Duty in the Present Disordered Condition of the Country,* anonymous (Baltimore?, 1860; Philadelphia: Lippincott, 1861);

*The Great Drama; An Appeal to Maryland* (Baltimore: Toy, 1861);

*The Privilege of the Writ of Habeas Corpus under the Constitution of the United States. In What It Consists. How It Is Allowed. How It Is Suspended. It Is the Regulation of the Law, not the Authorization of an Exercise of Legislative Power* (Philadelphia, 1862);

*Slavery the Mere Pretext for the Rebellion; Not Its Cause. Andrew Jackson's Prophecy in 1833. His Last Will and Testament in 1843. Bequests of His Three Swords: His Solemn Injunction to Wield Them "in Support of Our Glorious Union" against All Assailants, Whether "Foreign Enemies or Domestic Traitors." Picture of the Conspiracy* (Philadelphia: Sherman, 1863);

*Baltimore Long Ago* (Baltimore: Toy, 1864);

*Mr. Ambrose's Letters on the Rebellion* (New York: Hurd & Houghton / Baltimore: Waters, 1865);

*Peabody Institute. Address of the President to the Board of Trustees, on the Organization and Government of the Institute. February 12, 1870* (Baltimore, 1870);

*Political and Official Papers* (New York: Putnam, 1872);

*Occasional Addresses; and Letters of Mr. Ambrose on the Rebellion* (New York: Putnam, 1872);

*At Home and Abroad: A Series of Essays* (New York: Putnam, 1872).

OTHER: *Autograph Leaves of Our Country's Authors,* edited by Kennedy and Alexander Bliss (Baltimore: Cushings & Bailey, 1864).

John Pendleton Kennedy led a full and active life, making contributions to the young nation in many varied contexts. Chiefly a politician and lawyer, he was also a businessman, speaker in the Maryland state legislature, U.S. congressman, assistant secretary of state, secretary of the navy under Millard Fillmore, and a staunch Unionist during the Civil War. Kennedy's career in public life spanned half a century, beginning with his first campaign for public office in 1820 and ending with his 1868 speech in support of Ulysses S. Grant. He campaigned twelve times to represent Baltimore in both the state house and in the House of Representatives in Washington, winning seven times. He was a railroad president and mill owner who helped found the University of Maryland; he was elected an honorary professor of history there and was a provost for twenty years. In and around this busy life, this contemporary of Washington Irving and James Fenimore Cooper wrote three works of fiction that made a serious contribution to the emerging literature of a new nation. Along the way, he gave a boost to the fledgling literary career of Edgar Allan Poe and helped him to obtain the editorship of the *Southern Literary Messenger.* Kennedy was a friend of authors such as Irving, William Gilmore Simms, and William Makepeace Thackeray.

Kennedy's first book, *Swallow Barn, or A Sojourn in the Old Dominion* (1832), is a sort of Irvingesque sketchbook of the aristocratic Virginia plantation life that was at that time already fading from memory. It alternates between soft-edged satire and nostalgic fondness, betraying his mixed feelings about a life he had known from childhood and which was rapidly disappearing, taking with it, he feared, much good along with its less-attractive features. Modern critics find the portrayal and discussions of slavery the most interesting parts of the book. His next venture into the literary world, *Horse-Shoe Robinson: A Tale of the Tory Ascendancy* (1835), an historical romance of the American Revolution, links the two groups that the author increasingly felt must work together if the struggling nation of his own day were to survive: the aristocratic leadership and the commoners who must follow and support. His experience with Jacksonian democracy had left Kennedy concerned about the effects of placing the nation in the hands of an unbridled lower-class populace. Without the order provided by the disciplined upper class, he feared chaos and disintegration. Both books were financial successes, and the character of Horse-Shoe Robinson rivaled for a time the popularity of Cooper's Natty Bumppo. Encouraged by the success of his first two books but hampered by his burgeoning political career, Kennedy struggled to complete a second historical romance, *Rob of the Bowl: A Legend of St. Inigoe's* (1838), set in pre-Revolutionary Maryland. Based on local legends and embroidered with Gothic touches, the book did not sell well, and Kennedy reluctantly abandoned hopes for a sequel and turned his attention to politics.

Kennedy's family heritage–Irish immigrant merchant on one side, Virginia plantation aristocracy on the other–created in him a split identity that influenced his life, his friendships, and his careers in politics and literature. His father, John Kennedy, came to America from Northern Ireland in pursuit of financial opportunities in the family mercantile business begun by his two brothers. He also shared some Scottish ancestors with Irving. His mother, the former Nancy Pendleton, was a southern beauty connected to a thriving plantation clan that prided itself in its seventeenth-century American roots and service in the Revolutionary War.

During Kennedy's early life, his southern ties were stronger, undoubtedly because of the strength of his mother's personality: she insisted that her four children avoid the oppressive summer heat of Baltimore by escaping to her family's plantation, The Bower, owned by his mother's sister and her husband near Martinsburg in what is now West Virginia. His father's business failures in 1809 sealed the necessity of dependence upon his wife's Virginia relations. As he grew older, however, his ties to Maryland and its business community and its concerns overshadowed his southern sympathies.

As a student in private schools and then at Baltimore College, Kennedy studied the neoclassicists, especially Joseph Addison, Oliver Goldsmith, Samuel Johnson, Daniel Defoe, and Laurence Sterne. Sterne's *Tristram Shandy* (1760) and *A Sentimental Journey* (1768) were favorites. His imagination fired, Kennedy filled notebooks with imitations of these authors and dreamed of a career as a writer and satirist. He wrote everything from essays and farces, poems, travel accounts, and journals to sermons and treatises on subjects such as military tactics, engineering, chemistry, and botany. The War of 1812 began five months prior to his graduation, and Kennedy joined the Maryland militia, as became the descendant of Revolutionary War patriots. He participated in several battles, including Bladensburg, where he ran away with the rest in a rout, but managed to rescue a fallen comrade to safety. His experience in battle was helpful when he came to write the battle scenes in *Horse-Shoe Robinson.*

Eager to fulfill his literary ambitions, he penned a series of essays, "The Swiss Traveler," in the style of his literary heroes and using the device of a foreign traveler–in this case, Sidney, a Swiss emigrant–writing about his experiences. They were published in *Portico,* a Baltimore periodical, between February and August 1816. While these essays are little more than a continuation of his college literary imitations, they demonstrate an early commitment to the development of an American literature.

*Kennedy in 1825, around the time he began to write* Swallow Barn *(portrait by Philip T. C. Tilyard; Henry E. Huntington Library and Art Gallery)*

Once out of college and with the war behind him, Kennedy hunkered down to study law with his uncle, Edmund Pendleton, and later under Walter Dorsey, without much enthusiasm. His humorous approach to the foibles of the legal profession emerged in his satiric treatment of lawyers in *Swallow Barn.* After passing the bar in 1816, he resumed his literary avocation in a collaboration with Peter Hoffman Cruse. Together they wrote and published ten issues of a satirical periodical called *The Red Book* between 1819 and 1821. Like its eighteenth-century predecessors such as *The Spectator, The Red Book* took aim at the foibles of society, in this case Baltimore society, especially its female contingent.

The pseudonymously published magazine, while fairly derivative in its humor, style, and focus, was popular, with people eagerly trading speculations as to who the author was. This early fling as an author was cut short when Kennedy won his first election, to the Maryland house of delegates, a position he held for three years. He advocated internal improvements and reforms such as the abolition of imprisonment for debt and spoke out against slavery. Afterward, President James Monroe offered him a coveted diplomatic post in the new republic of Chile, but he turned it down after deciding that such a move would damage his fledgling law practice. His literary aspirations were put on hold as well.

Kennedy married twice, and both marriages helped to draw him further into the mercantile world. He wed Mary Tenant, daughter of one of the most prominent citizens of Baltimore, in 1824. She died in childbirth nine months later, and her infant did not long outlive her. His political life followed this trend of his personal life: in 1826 he ran for the House of Representatives but was defeated. His private and public fortunes revived when Kennedy married again in 1829, this time to Elizabeth Gray. Her father, Edward Gray, was a self-made textile merchant whose fortune assured financial security for the couple for life. Though they had no children, the union was happy. Gray took a genuine liking to his son-in-law, who saw eye-to-eye with him on political and financial issues, and Kennedy apparently admired and enjoyed his wife's father. He came to identify himself with the northern commercial interests that were devoted to the building of bustling cities rather than agrarian villages and to turning a sleepy federation of states into a commercial world power.

Kennedy never completely sundered his southern ties, however. His childhood experiences on the family plantation had instilled a love for the gracious life of leisure and the security of order and traditions, even amid his growing realization that such a life was supported by the insupportable–slavery–and could breed into its adherents less than desirable qualities. While Kennedy was establishing his law practice in Baltimore, his parents settled permanently at The Bower. Even then, the old plantation style of life he remembered from his childhood was passing away. Many of the great Virginia planters had been ruined by the Revolution and had gone west, their lands passing into other hands. This changeover from the old guard is illustrated in *Swallow Barn* in the case of Swallow Barn itself, originally owned by the Hazards. The family had fallen on hard times and was short of ready cash. Frank Meriwether, who owned an adjoining property, marries Ned Hazard's sister and buys the estate, leaving Ned, the rightful heir, on the sidelines.

Thomas Jefferson's presidency had resulted in serious social and economic consequences for those heirs who remained in control of their property. The established Anglican Church was no longer dominant, and the great tobacco farms were broken up by the abolishment of the laws of primogeniture and entail. While a few of the old plantations remained as they had been, many were simply closed, while others were divided up into smaller holdings. The new owners, for the most part, had ideas and ways of doing things that were diametrically opposed to those of the original aristocracy. During a visit to The Bower in 1828, Kennedy wrote to Elizabeth: "How completely the elegancies of society and the best points of a luxurious mode of living have been invaded by a sort of stiff, awkward, and *churchly* morality." Kennedy's divided loyalties echoed the situation in the nation at the time. It too was beginning to feel the tension between the agrarian South and the energetic, commercial North.

Kennedy practiced law, a profession for which he had little love, until 1840 but was spending more and more time as a spokesman for the business interests of the region. During these years between his second marriage and the end of his law career he indulged his literary aspirations, writing three books between 1832 and 1838. There was at that time, particularly in the South, little opportunity for a purely literary career. He was never simply a writer, and his other interests increasingly monopolized his hours and ultimately closed the book on his authorial ventures. Kennedy hoped to use literature to help create an American identity and to stifle the cry that the United States could produce no good authors, that its cultural rawness, lack of structure, and short history provided writers with no suitable materials. Unlike Cooper, Nathaniel Hawthorne, and Henry James, he saw great richness in the regional life and native legends of the nation. "The undercurrents of country-life are grotesque, peculiar and amusing, and it only requires an attentive observer to make an agreeable book by describing them," he wrote in his preface to the 1832 edition of *Swallow Barn*.

Above all he wanted to help Americans to realize the distinctive experience the young nation had undergone and inspire them to properly value its greatness. Each book explores the American past, and in each he sets forth the formula that he hoped would ensure the growth of the nation without losing its stability. While Kennedy's background had caused him to feel pulled in separate directions, he was analytical enough to see the weaknesses and strengths of both its agrarian and commercial traditions. He weaves his theories into his stories. The reader is presented with situations in which the aristocracy with its reliance on established order is combined with the enthusiasm and energy of the lower classes. The result is a stable society that moves ahead without losing sight of its cherished values.

Happily married, his law practice launched, and temporarily freed from political duties, Kennedy finished his first book, begun around 1825. He had planned a collection of sketches of rural Virginia life based upon his childhood experiences but had lacked a unifying device until Irving's use of a narrative frame resolved his dilemma. Still, in many ways, *Swallow Barn* defies classification. In the preface to the 1851 edition he says *Swallow Barn* could be described "as variously and interchangeably partaking of the complexion of a book of travels, a diary, a collection of letters, a drama, and a history." He admits cavalierly in the preface to the first edition: "I might truly say, it is a book of episodes, with an occasional digression into the plot." Following Irving's lead with *Bracebridge Hall* (1822), Kennedy contrived a frame for his story in which Mark Littleton, a New Yorker, is invited to spend part of the summer with his cousin, Ned Hazard, on a southern plantation. Littleton writes to Zachary Huddlestone, a New York friend, describing life at Swallow Barn, and when the recipient responds with lively interest, Littleton agrees to keep a journal and send reports of his experiences in this different but fascinating world. Littleton, a northerner, is an outsider, yet he has connections with the southern clan. He is favorably impressed with what he sees and eager to correct misapprehensions his northern acquaintants have of plantation life. He speaks as a northerner whose prejudices have been shaken; he praises what he sees while at the same time revealing some of the foibles of southern society.

Kennedy's early notes for the book reveal its evolution from simply a comic and satiric sketch into its more solid and serious final form. He had originally planned to call his plantation Hoppergallop House, owned by one Frank Oldstock. The house was described as fallen down and shabby from neglect, decayed and melancholy. He wrote to George Putnam on 3 May 1851 that he had originally planned "to represent an old decayed place with odd and crotchetty people inhabiting it." Later he changed the name to Swallow Barn and gradually it metamorphosed into a dignified southern paradise, the image of The Bower, although he changed the setting to the Tidewater region on the southern shore of the James River near Richmond. He later came to regret even the choice of the name Swallow Barn, thinking it too linked to the earlier decayed state of the house. Significantly, his description of the plantation house is idealized even further in his revisions for the 1851 edition.

Kennedy's first attempt at a frame story employed a young painter as the narrator, whose trip to the plantation was not planned but by chance. His sketches were to be "verbal portraits" of what he saw, but Kennedy was dissatisfied. His substitution of Mark Littleton, who went there as the result of an invitation, as narrator apparently satisfied Kennedy, since he continued to use the name as a pseudonym in his later books. The frame narrative, however, breaks down as the book continues and the two plots develop. The court-

*Kennedy's second wife, Elizabeth Gray Kennedy, in 1835 (portrait by William James Hubard; Sleepy Hollow Restorations, Tarrytown, New York)*

ship between Ned Hazard and Bel, Littleton writes his friend back home, threatens to turn his letters into a novel.

While Kennedy toned down the satire of his setting as his plans matured, he seems to have intensified his satire of some of the characters. Critics have argued whether Kennedy's characters are merely literary stereotypes, updates of neoclassical models, or copies of those of his contemporaries. Others have praised their realism. It appears that both sides are correct. Many of his creations demonstrate characteristics taken from his eighteenth-century literary heroes—among them Henry Fielding, Tobias Smollett, Richard Brinsley Sheridan, Goldsmith, and Sterne—with borrowings from Scott, Cooper, and Irving's character sketches, blended with characteristics of actual people whom he knew, including relatives. His host of quixotic characters includes the feisty Tory sympathizer Isaac Tracy, swamp-obsessed owner of the neighboring plantation; his headstrong daughter, Bel, with her exaggerated notions of romance, chivalry, and style; the foppish and pretentious lawyer, Singleton Oglethorpe Swansdown; and a gallery of stock country characters such as the flighty, prissy plantation tutor; the capable and competent mistress of the plantation; and Meriwether's sister, Prudence, the conventional old maid, with her devotion to religion and temperance societies.

His characters based loosely on real people include Frank Meriwether, master of Swallow Barn, who was modeled on Kennedy's uncle, Philip Clayton Pendleton, whom he admired, and the silly Bel Tracy, who resembles one of his cousins who lived at The Bower, according to his relatives. Parson Chub, the philosophic, book-loving schoolmaster, as Kennedy acknowledged, is partly based upon William Sinclair, a teacher at Baltimore College, where Kennedy was a student. Ned Hazard appears to be a combination of a stock literary character and the author himself, as he shares some of Kennedy's experiences and attitudes. About the author's age, Hazard exhibits many aspects of his personality—frankness, spontaneity, patriotism—and seems to get along with almost everyone. In his youth, like Kennedy himself, he had been "seized with a romantic fever which manifested itself chiefly in a conceit to visit South America, and play knight-errant in the quarrel of the Patriots." He had returned home disillusioned, however, "the most disquixotted cavalier that ever hung up his shield at the end of a scurvy crusade."

Lucretia Meriwether, with her tendency to inflict nasty-tasting malaria remedies on children, is an echo of Kennedy's great-aunt, Mrs. Ferguson, according to Kennedy's reminiscences in Henry T. Tuckerman's *The Life of John Pendleton Kennedy* (1871). Philpot Wart, one of the lawyers involved in the Hazard-Tracy dispute over swampland, is clearly a jest at Kennedy's friend William Wirt, to whom he dedicated the book, perhaps influencing Wirt's reaction to it. In his dedication Kennedy wrote that the book was modeled on Wirt's *The Letters of the British Spy* (1803). Wirt wrote Kennedy a gracious thank-you for his dedication while declaring he had made little headway in reading it, yet he sneered at it in a letter to a friend, denominating it merely a nondescript collection of character sketches written in a "conceited style" with "too much verbiage and too little matter."

While the characters are for the most part a combination of real people and literary stereotypes, critics generally agree that the descriptions of country life deserve high praise for their realism. Jay B. Hubbell, in his introduction to the book, calls *Swallow Barn* "the best picture of Virginia life in the early nineteenth century." In his preface to the 1832 edition, Kennedy wrote that he was attempting to capture "the ordinary actions of men in their household intercourse." Look-

ing back on the book in his preface to the 1851 edition, he said that it was "a faithful picture of the people, the modes of life, and the scenery of a region full of attraction, and exhibiting the lights and shades of its society with the truthfulness of a painter who has studied his subject on the spot." While not true realism in the sense of being an objective recording of an observed scene, the book does offer a great deal more verisimilitude than do most of its contemporaries. *Swallow Barn* is not a romance; it does not rely on mysterious happenings, incredible plot twists, or diabolical villains. It is plausible.

The character sketches that make up the first eight chapters of the *Swallow Barn*—chapter titles such as "A Country Gentleman," "Family Portraits," and "Family Paragons" suggest the pattern—give way to the two intertwined plots that provide the structure for the rest of the book. The narrator learns that Ned Hazard, Littleton's cousin and the brother-in-law of Frank Meriwether, has long been enamored of Bel Tracy, daughter of the owner of the neighboring plantation. Bel has spurned his suit. Ned's bumbling attempts at wooing her and Bel's ridiculously romantic ideas about courtship make for humorous reading. Bel attempts to train a hawk to ride upon her shoulder in the best medieval manner, festooning it with medieval paraphernalia such as leather bewets complete with silver bells, jessups, and a leash and creance.When the bird flies away during her first attempt to fly it, Ned, who is under the influence, swears to find and retrieve it for her. Once he regains his sobriety, he thinks he has made a fool of himself with his rash promise, but Littleton convinces him that he has done exactly what the romantic Bel has been yearning for. He does manage to recover the errant hawk, and Bel is delighted that for once Ned has acted the knightly part. With his thoroughly unromantic nature, however, Ned is forever falling short of the impossible standards set by the heroes of the novels that Bel reads. He is continually offending her refined taste by smoking, engaging in fistfights, or just generally failing to match the fancy language, persistence, and fussy manners of the foppish Swansdown, who impresses Bel. Kennedy drags out their courtship, leaving the issue unsettled by the time Littleton departs for New York; the reader only learns of their marriage in a postscript.

The second plot, the disagreement between Ned and Isaac Tracy over some swampland, takes up the central third of the book, chapters 10 through 27. In 1759 Ned's granduncle had desired to build a flour mill on the small stream that ran between the two plantations. Accordingly, he had secured a deed to the land from Gilbert Tracy, Isaac's forebear, transferring some ground from The Brakes to Swallow Barn for a

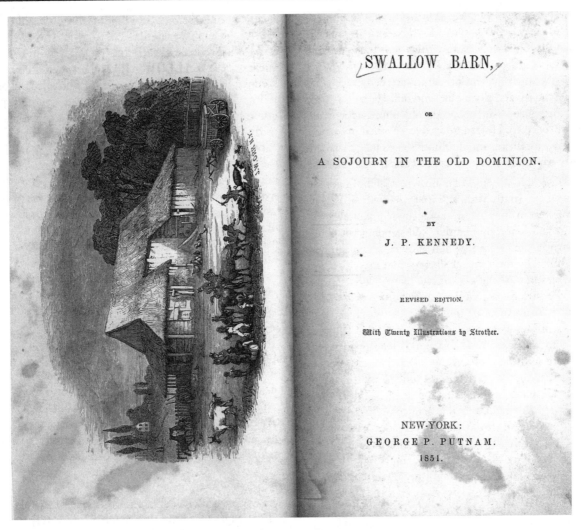

*Frontispiece and title page for the revised edition of Kennedy's best-known work, a fictional*
*Northerner's observations on plantation life in the South (Thomas Cooper Library,*
*University of South Carolina)*

millpond. When the project ultimately failed because the stream did not supply enough power to run the mill, all was allowed to fall to ruin. When Ned decides to drain the land, Tracy goes to court, arguing that the land rightfully belongs to him. The issue is not financial; the land is worthless. What concerns Tracy is the principle of inherited property upon which the southern plantation society was built. To him, it is an issue of family honor.

The courts side with Hazard, but the stubborn Tracy continues to fight. Eventually, Meriwether intervenes, hiring two lawyers, the foppish Swansdown and the wittily wise Wart, to arbitrate the case. Kennedy uses this opportunity to poke fun at the legal profession, making the prissy Swansdown the butt of the jokes. At Meriwether's instigation Wart contrives to have the property awarded to Tracy, even though the law is clearly on Hazard's side. Wart con-

venes court in the middle of the swamp, and by means of some legal obfuscation and the dexterous wielding of some "dog-Latin," declares that the land belongs to The Brakes.

Kennedy obviously enjoyed this mocking parody of legal forms, but the settling of the case left him with twenty-two chapters of the expected two volumes—nearly half of the book–to go. He fills out the remainder with more episodes in Ned's haphazard courtship of Bel, sketches of the surrounding area, and several narrative digressions that are in reality short stories. One of the most memorable of these is a tale told by a poor white, Hafen Blok. Blok had served as a drummer boy during the Revolution, fought Indians, and earned his living variously as a tinker, fiddler, trapper, and in other less savory pursuits. He has a reputation as a teller of marvelous tales, and when he guides the spooked Ned and Mark out of Goblin Swamp, he is invited to tell an appropriately devilish tale. Kennedy's description of Blok is an excellent example of his dexterity at painting with words. Blok is a "short, thick-set, bandy-legged personage, bearing all the marks of an old man, with a strangely weather-beaten face, intersected by as many drains as the rugged slope of a sand-hill. He had a large mouth, disfigured with tobacco, and unprovided with any show of teeth. He had, moreover, a small upturned nose, a low forehead, and diminutive eyes that glistened beneath projecting brows of grizzled and shaggy hair."

Blok's tale about Mike Brown, a light-fingered, swearing blacksmith with a termagant wife, involves visitations from the devil, a close acquaintance of Brown's, and some pranks the "old gentleman" plays on Brown in the swamp. When Brown, feeling he has been insulted by the devil, challenges him to a duel, the devil agrees but asks to choose the place. He goes to a part of the swamp where the fen is dotted with small islands of firm ground and leaps easily onto one. Brown, realizing that the island is so small that the forward momentum required for him to leap to it might propel him into the mud on the other side, chooses to try a straddling approach with one foot on solid ground, the other stretched to the edge of the island. His success depends upon the gentlemanliness of the devil in pulling him to safety, but the devil will have none of it. He is perfectly willing to fight, he says, but if Brown is unwilling to come to the arranged place, it is not his fault. He departs, leaving Brown with no option but to fall into the bog. Brown fails to learn his lesson and soon again, when he is drunk, falls prey to the devil, his adversary pulling an old trick on him. Providing Brown with a long, heavy rake, the devil shows him the reflection of the moon in the water and bids him to rake in the "gold coins" under the surface. Brown's struggles provoke hoots of laughter from the bushes.

Kennedy fills out the book with renditions of other happenings on the estate: a possum hunt and visits to the pasture where Meriwether keeps the blooded horses he raises and to the slave quarters. The latter provides Kennedy with an opportunity for an airing of the southern view of slavery. A calm and kindly master who treats his servants with dignity, Meriwether is the ideal mouthpiece for a dispassionate declaration of the southern case for its peculiar institution. The book winds to a close with the stories of two heroes, one black, one white. During the visit to the slave quarters, Littleton hears old Mammy Lucy's story of her rebellious son, Abe, who later redeems himself by sacrificing his life during a rescue attempt. Then, just before his departure, Mark finds himself in the fine library of Swallow Barn, filled with reverent wonder as he reads the story of the gallant and heroic Captain John Smith.

Kennedy's book begins and ends with Smith, a telltale sign of the author's emphasis.

Meriwether's speech and the juxtaposition of the stories of Abe and John Smith were not coincidental to Kennedy's serious intentions for his book. Living as he did in a border state and with his ties to southern plantation life, he was uneasily aware of the growing danger of disagreements over slavery in the young nation. As early as 1832 he expressed fears that slavery might be the rock upon which the union would break. With this book he hoped to acquaint northerners with the positive aspects of southern life, while at the same time, using gentle satire, urging southerners to examine some of their own foibles. His depiction of slavery, mild even in the original edition, was further softened when he revised the book in 1851 as opposing positions hardened and war seemed more ominous. A slave described as a "flatnosed pigmy" in the 1832 edition becomes a "flatnosed compeer," and Ned's 1832 instruction to old Carey–"Now old gentleman, you have done your duty, so creep into your kennel"–is completely omitted in the 1851 revision.

Slaves are never referred to as such–they are always called simply "negroes"–and they appear to be happy and contented with their lot. The slave owners treat their charges with kindness and concern; no slaves are beaten or abused. A potentially damaging passage in an early draft in which a slaveholder almost strikes a slave who grins when he should not was excised even before the first printing.

Meriwether, explaining slavery in the chapter "The Quarter," argues that while it is "wholly without justification or defense" and is "theoretically and morally wrong," it is a necessary intermediate step in the development of the Negro race, and that to free them at that point in their transition from barbarism to civilization would leave them "in greater evils than their bondage." He compares the dignity and safety they now enjoy to the much worse condition of seamen and soldiers. Meriwether says that it is the job of their masters to "administer wholesome laws for their government, making their servitude as tolerable to them as we can consistent with our own safety and their ultimate good," and that any plan for freeing them must come from the South.

In the meantime, he continues, certain steps could be taken to ameliorate their situation. Families should never be split apart, and some of the more trustworthy older men could be formed into a "feudatory," tenant farmers who could work for themselves. Meriwether then takes Littleton to visit old Mammy Lucy, who tells the story of her rebellious son, Abe, who was banished from the property. Abe reforms while a seaman and willingly risks and ultimately loses his life rescuing some white men. Abe the rebel becomes Abe the hero; he is praised in the language usually reserved for the southern cavalier-hero. The message is clear: slaves are capable of heroism equal to that of white men if only they will avoid rebellion and take their rightful place.

Meriwether voices many of Kennedy's own thoughts about the slavery issue. At the time he was writing *Swallow Barn,* Kennedy himself was briefly a slave owner. When his servant Sam proved untrustworthy, he sent him off to be sold in Virginia and wrote in his journal: "I will never own another slave, and should not have taken this fellow if he had not been given to me by my father." Kennedy was convinced that immediate freedom for the slaves would result in the destruction of the Southern economy as well as harm for the slaves themselves. In a later journal entry he expresses ideas that he had put in Meriwether's mouth: "Manifestly *emancipation* would be a greater evil than the continuance of slavery. I mean, *rapid emancipation.* We should ruin the slave, and make desolate the slave country. Our duty therefore is to mitigate the evil by cautious and discreet treatment of it, and to aid the progress of natural causes in the gradual obliteration of slavery, which is inevitable in the course of the growth of the country."

While slavery is soft-peddled in *Swallow Barn,* Kennedy's approach to Southern whites is multifaceted. Some receive heroic treatment while others are satirized. Kennedy clearly extols the beauties and joys of life at Swallow Barn, with its rides, hunts, dances, and evening storytelling sessions, its cattle-filled hills, rich bottomland, lovely gardens, and lush prosperity ruled with a gentle hand by a wise and caring man, but he also reveals its less pleasing underside: a self-centered, even smug society, proud of its interconnected clans and accomplishments.

Kennedy praises Captain John Smith as the epitome of the Southern gentleman. In one of the earliest sections written for the first edition, Kennedy devotes more than thirty-five pages to this "true knight of Virginia." This section was considerably shortened in the 1851 revision, but the belief that the leadership of such men as essential to the stability of a nation remained central to Kennedy's thinking. The Southern whites whom he celebrates are those who follow the path set out by what Kennedy calls the "Cavaliers," the sixteenth- and seventeenth-century gentlemen-adventurers who first settled Virginia. As J. V. Ridgely notes in *John Pendleton Kennedy* (1966), the merits Kennedy praises had for the most part become central to his own personal value system:

> pride in a long family line; personal honor; love of individual liberty; belief in property as the basis for an enduring social system; chivalric behavior toward women; conservatism in religion and philosophy; participation in the public affairs of the state; dislike of outside interference, especially that of a central government; recognition of an aristocracy of worth, founded upon inherited property and sustained by enslaved Negroes who if properly treated, were far better off than they could be in a state of barbarism.

Qualities such as these continue to live on in men such as Frank Meriwether.

While Meriwether is antagonistic toward business and occasionally holds opinions that clash with Kennedy's own, such as the importance of states' rights, the author presents him in a favorable light; men such as Meriwether were, he felt, the basis of a stable society. Meriwether is "a very model of landed gentlemen": a magistrate, a High Churchman, a man who appreciates aristocracy among horses as well as among men. The danger for such men is that their ideals can degenerate into mere parodies of their original strengths, and they can become too focused on local issues, spurning the larger society and nation. This tendency must be tempered and its horizons broadened if the Meriwethers are to successfully lead the nation rather than merely their own local districts.

In some Southerners, however, many of these ideals had been reduced, over time, to empty formalism. Snobbery replaced rightful pride in one's lineage; weak sentimentalism was all that remained of chivalrous treatment of women; and land ownership became a mere fetish. Concern with one's state could totally overshadow one's ties to the nation as a whole. Kennedy turns from myth building to satire in skewering such types. Isaac Tracy of The Brakes exemplifies all that can go wrong, especially with regard to pride in inherited property and personal honor when he goes to court and almost to war over swampland. That the land is worthless is of no matter; he is convinced that it should be his, and he is willing to go to any lengths to secure it.

As he did in his *Red Book* days, Kennedy saves some of his most satiric wit concerning the degeneration of the Virginia code for the ladies. Bel Tracy, with her ridiculous affectations, is the most conspicuous example. Not satisfied with demanding medieval-style heroism from Ned, she tries to enlist Hafen Blok as her minstrel, complete with a costume for him straight out of Scott's fiction. Ned's traditional ballads, with their emphasis on ghosts, blood, and rough language, give her the vapors, however.

Ridgely praises Kennedy's ability to write dialogue that targets so many romantic foibles, citing a passage in which Prudence Meriwether and Catherine Tracy, both spinsters-in-waiting, moon over the foppish Swansdown. The passage, Ridgely says, manages

I must digress to say a word about Rip's head gear.
He wears a nondescript skull-cap which, I conjecture from some
equivocal signs, had once been a fur hat, but which must
have taken a degree in fifty other callings, for I see it daily
employed in the most foreign services. Sometimes it is a
drinking vessel, and then Rip pinches it up like a
cocked hat; sometimes it is devoted to push-pin, and
then it is cuffed cruelly on both sides; and sometimes
it is turned into a basket to carry eggs from the hen-roost.
It finds hard service at hand-ball, where, like a plastic
statesman, it is popular for its pliability. It is tossed
in the air on all occasions of rejoicing, and now and
then, serves for a gauntlet and is flung, with energy
upon the ground on the eve of a battle, and it is

*Fair copy of a passage from* Swallow Barn *( from Kennedy and Alexander Bliss, eds.,*
Autograph Leaves of Our Country's Authors, *1864)*

kicked occasionally through the school-yard, after the fashion of a bladder. It wears a singular exterior, having a row of holes cut below the crown, or rather the apex (for it is pyramidal in shape) to make it cool, as Rip explains it, in hot weather. The only rest that it enjoys through the day, as far as I have been able to perceive, is during school hours, and then it is thrust between a desk and a bulkhead, three inches apart, where it generally envelopes in its folds a handful of hickory-nuts or marbles. This covering falls down — for it has no lining — like an extinguisher over Rip's head. To prevent the recurrence of this accident, he has tied it up with a hat-band of twine. —

A leaf from Swallow Barn.

John P. Kennedy
Feb. 18. 1864

in one swoop to strike at "intellectual pretension, meaningless legal wrangles, romantic yearnings, rhetorical flourish—in short, the self-revelations of a society which preferred facade to backbone, lofty words and manners to workaday deeds, literary posturing to solid character."

Kennedy finished the book on 31 December 1831, and it was accepted by the Philadelphia publishers Carey and Lea. They first offered to buy the copyright for $500, but eventually the parties agreed upon a 2,000–copy edition of two volumes with good prospects for profits. *Swallow Barn* came out in the spring of 1832, with "Mark Littleton" listed as the supposed author. The book sold well—1,400 copies by December—and the guessing game over the author's identity began immediately, with many concluding that the author was Irving. Kennedy's identity soon leaked out, however, and he was an immediate local celebrity.

When he revised the book in 1850, Kennedy lamented in the preface that "progress" had brought innovation to Virginia and the entire country so quickly. He was appalled at the leveling of stations and regions, seemingly reducing all to a distinctionless if shiny surface. Sounding like a regionalist who sees a culture that he loves sliding into oblivion, he regrets the loss of what was authentic and individual, which was "already . . . dissolving into a mixture which affects us unpleasantly as a tame and cosmopolitan substitute for the old warmth and salient vivacity of our ancestors."

Critical response to both editions of *Swallow Barn* was generally positive. Most remarked on its similarity to Irving's *Bracebridge Hall* and *The Sketch Book* (1819–1820). Reviewers praised the humor and the "fidelity" to actual life in the Old Dominion. Irving sent a noncommittal letter, but the two eventually became friends, and Irving visited at The Bower with Kennedy. Cooper responded with enthusiasm in a letter to their mutual publisher, who quoted Cooper in a letter to Kennedy dated 15 January 1834. The Leather-Stocking author deemed *Swallow Barn* a "clever work" and "unquestionably the work of one of our ablest men," one who could "aspire to a wide reputation." Southern readers of *Swallow Barn* were generally pleased with the depiction of their peculiar institution. The *Frederick* (Maryland) *Examiner,* shortly after the publication of *Swallow Barn,* observed, "There are more Coopers in America than the author of the 'Pilot.'"

Some New England critics, however, responded with much less enthusiasm. The reviewer for the *New England Magazine* chided that slavery deserved only satire, and he lambasted those Virginia gentlemen whom Kennedy held in such high esteem in the July 1832 issue. They "are the most ordinary, trifling, useless generation the world ever saw. To be sure," he wrote,

"they are kind, hospitable, liberal, and honorable, but how are their lives passed? If this work be what it pretends, a Virginian of condition has no use for his time but to pay and receive visits, to attend courts, and to watch the multiplication of his horses and negroes." Although such a life may "conduce to the prosperity of the state," he adds, "deliver us from such a life." While such lives may be satisfactory to themselves, he concludes, they are "very insipid" to the observer. "The whole book is the stillest of still life." English reviewers, who were not always kind to American authors, were surprisingly positive. Kennedy cut out and kept nearly forty reviews that appeared in American and English periodicals.

Carey and Lea eagerly urged him to write another book to capitalize on this interest. Kennedy would have liked nothing more than to have obliged, but once again other duties prevailed, and *Horse-Shoe Robinson* did not appear until 1835. His journal records that he began the book 11 October 1832 but made little immediate headway. His law practice demanded time, and he made several trips to Washington to represent Maryland business interests in disputes over tariffs. Kennedy was a strong protectionist.

In 1833 the new literary lion of Baltimore was asked to help judge a contest sponsored by a local periodical, the *Saturday Visitor.* The unanimous winner was Poe, for his "MS. Found in a Bottle." Then living in poverty with his aunt, Poe sorely needed the $50 in prize money. Kennedy befriended him, helping him to get the position of editor of the influential *Southern Literary Messenger,* and Poe regarded him, as evinced in a 1841 letter to W. F. Thomas, as a genuine friend: "Mr. Kennedy has been, at all times, a true friend to me—he was the first true friend I ever had—I am indebted to him for *life itself*."

The two men continued to correspond. Poe reviewed *Horse-Shoe Robinson* and several times begged Kennedy for money. On at least one occasion Kennedy provided Poe with money for clothes and the use of a horse. When Poe died, Kennedy wrote in his journal for 10 October 1849: "Poor Poe! He was an original and exquisite poet, and one of the best prose critics in this country. His works are among the very best of their kind. . . . He is gone—a bright but unsteady light has been awfully quenched." While Poe's fame eventually overshadowed Kennedy's, at the time it looked as though Kennedy would be the one to outshine Poe. A 1911 novel by F. Hopkinson Smith, *Kennedy Square,* features the two writers as characters and portrays the way they were viewed by their contemporaries. Kennedy, elegantly dressed, is the first guest to arrive at a dinner party given in Poe's honor, but Poe makes a late and drunken appearance, spoiling the party.

Kennedy finished *Horse-Shoe Robinson* in January 1835. He was forty years old and in midcareer. Carey promised him $1,200 for an edition of three thousand copies, and Richard Bentley, the English publisher, agreed to issue it abroad on similar terms, thus frustrating the pirates that had plundered *Swallow Barn*. The book appeared in June 1835. Kennedy dedicated the American edition to Irving and the British one to poet Samuel Rogers. Despite the length of the book, which cut into profits and caused Carey to balk at reprints without some pruning, and sluggish English sales because of what Bentley termed the "anti-Anglican feeling pervading the work," sales overall were brisk and reviews were positive.

For his second book Kennedy tried his hand at historical romance, the most popular genre at the time. Authors such as Cooper, John Neal, James Kirke Paulding, Catherine Maria Sedgewick, and Lydia Maria Child had already written historical romances. Kennedy chose to set his story further back in American history, centering the action around the Revolution. He defended his choice of subject matter in the original preface, writing that until the nation had moved sufficiently away from the war in time, it was not a good subject for fiction because so many of those actually involved in those events were still living. When the nation passed its fiftieth birthday in 1826, however, enough years had passed that tradition and myth had overtaken precise facts, leaving the field open for romancers. The time was ripe for such treatments.

An historical novel allowed Americans to read fiction without feeling guilty because it was based upon truth, an important issue in a country still under the influence of prejudices against fiction. Kennedy claims in his preface: the events "narrated in the following pages, came to my knowledge in the progress of my researches into the personal history of some of the characters who figure in the story," and he assures his readers that one of his reasons for writing is to "illustrate the temper and character of the War of our Rebellion."

Kennedy found a special niche that no one else was mining—with the exception of Simms, but Kennedy was unaware of Simms's plans at the time. Kennedy set his story in Virginia and the Carolinas during the closing years of the war and focused on the British plan to control the southern colonies. The British had turned their attention to the South after failing to conquer the North, where the majority of the early fighting had taken place. As early as 1776 Charleston had been subjected to a ten-hour bombardment, but the southerners had held out, and Charleston was unmolested for two years. When the British again turned their sights on the South, they captured Savannah in 1778; the fort protecting the city had been garrisoned by only nine hundred

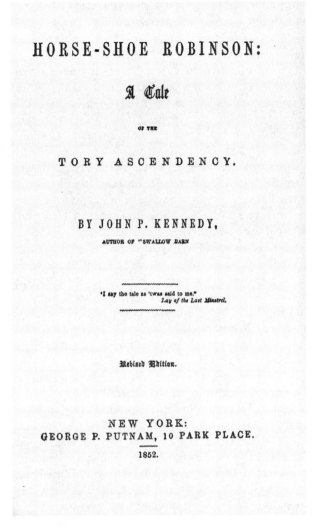

HORSE-SHOE ROBINSON:

A Tale

OF THE

TORY ASCENDENCY.

BY JOHN P. KENNEDY,

AUTHOR OF "SWALLOW BARN"

"I say the tale as 'twas said to me."
*Lay of the Last Minstrel.*

Revised Edition.

NEW YORK:
GEORGE P. PUTNAM, 10 PARK PLACE.
1852.

*Title page for the revised edition of Kennedy's 1835 novel, set in Virginia and the Carolinas during the American Revolution (South Caroliniana Library, University of South Carolina)*

men. Charleston fell in 1780 after a bitter forty-day siege, providing a base of operations for the British from which the British could swarm over the South.

As the subtitle of the book, "The Tory Ascendancy," implies, the many British sympathizers in South Carolina rallied to aid and abet the English armies, making life miserable for those who espoused the partisan cause. The efforts of the Tories were sharply parried by those of the American partisans. The British harassed the southern coast of Virginia and the Carolinas while Francis Marion, nicknamed the "Swamp Fox" by British General Banastre Tarleton, attacked and hounded the British regulars in lightning raids along with Thomas Sumter and other raiders before disappearing into the mazelike cypress swamps. Marion and his men displayed astounding bravery and resourcefulness, despite lack of adequate clothing, food, and shelter. Kennedy saw the clear potential of this situation for historical romance treatment.

Several historical battles are described, including the battle of King's Mountain in October 1780. Chapter 62 vividly and accurately describes the assault, a major achievement of the war in which British Major Patrick Ferguson was killed and his 1,100 Tories were either killed, wounded, or taken prisoner. Other battles include those at Camden, the Cowpens, Guilford Court House, Hobkirk's Hill, Ninety-Six, Eutaw Springs, and the surrender of Cornwallis at Yorktown, Virginia, on 19 October 1781. In some cases Kennedy fictionalizes real events. The capture of Ensign St. Jermyn and his men by Horse Shoe Robinson and fourteen-year-old Andy Ramsay in chapter 22 echoes experiences of Marion and other partisans.

*Horse-Shoe Robinson* illustrates that in many ways the Revolution was as much a civil war as the later war that bears that name. In both cases families were split, and brother fought against brother, neighbor against neighbor. Novelists such as Cooper, Kennedy, and Simms all included this aspect of the war in their work, but Kennedy was the first. He builds the mandatory love story around the issue of conflicting loyalties: a dashing American officer, Arthur Butler, and the daughter of a British loyalist, Mildred Lindsay, are separated first by parental interference and then by his captivity. Characters face choices between the old homeland and the new nation, between father and husband; one of the secrets of the book is that Mildred and Butler have married without her father's consent and are hiding their union from him. Like other heroines of her day, Mildred conforms to the tenets of the school of sensibility, but Kennedy lapses into less melodrama than his contemporaries, and Mildred's intellectual force and resolution make her more believable to modern readers than most such female characters.

Her father, Philip Lindsay, is the quintessential Tory. An early manuscript note concerning him says, "Lindsay's character to exhibit the principles of a man attached to aristocratic rule, and absolutism. A scorn for popular judgment, a disposition to predict the ultimate downfall of a government which rests power in the people." Born in Virginia and educated in England, Lindsay has returned to the United States to live. He attempts to stay neutral while remaining loyal by retreating to his rural mountain home, the Dove Cote. Because of his Tory leanings, his other estates are confiscated; he manages to keep Dove Cote only by turning ownership over to Mildred.

Lindsay loses his son Henry as well as his daughter to the partisan cause. While Kennedy had genuine sympathy for people such as Lindsay—he shares many of his aristocratic assumptions and preferences—the

author is convinced that Lindsay is wrong to abdicate his rightful leadership role. Self-imposed exile is simply not an option for Kennedy. When Lindsay, prodded by Terrell, does finally act, he has waited too long; the partisan cause is in the ascendancy, and he is killed at the battle of King's Mountain. Resisting the oversimplification of portraying all partisans as good and all Tories as bad, Kennedy argues that Lindsay is wrong not so much for his stand but for the fact that he fails to truly take one; he is weak rather than villainous.

Arthur Butler is the ideal foil for Lindsay. Butler too is a southern aristocrat whose lands have been confiscated, but he turns his back on England, identifies himself with the new nation, and fights for the partisan cause. Refusing Lindsay's course of noninvolvement, he believes fiercely that the best hope for the new nation is leadership by aristocrats such as himself. Unlike the usual romance hero, Butler is offstage more than he is on; he languishes in captivity for thirty-eight of the fifty-eight chapters of the book. Butler escapes only once and is immediately recaptured. While this seems an odd scenario for the hero of a romance novel, Butler represents Kennedy's view of the future: the new nation must be led by men such as he once the war is won. He cannot lead alone, however; he needs the aid of the lower classes, represented by Horse Shoe Robinson, if he is to succeed.

Robinson is the real hero of the book, the down-to-earth, lower-class civilian patriot who rides with Butler, escorts and protects Mildred after Butler is captured, tries to keep him from being shot as a traitor by his captors, and aids in his escape. In his introduction to the revised edition Kennedy explains the germ for his story: a trip to South Carolina in 1819 during which he met the original of his eponymous hero and learned the story he was to tell in his book. He describes the then-seventy-year-old Robinson: "What a man I saw! . . . time seemed to have broken its billows over his front only as the ocean breaks over a rock. There he stood—tall, broad, brawny, and erect. The sharp light gilded his massive frame and weather-beaten face with a pictorial effect that would have rejoiced an artist."

Kennedy's delineation reveals the inner man as well as the outer: "His homely dress, his free stride, . . . his face radiant with kindness; the natural gracefulness of his motion; all afforded a ready index to his character. Horse Shoe, it was evident, was a man to confide in." Kennedy emphasizes the probity of Robinson's story and the man's humility: "A more truthful man than he, I am convinced, did not survive the war to tell its story. Truth was the predominant expression of his face and gesture—the truth that belongs to natural and unconscious bravery, united with a frank and modest spirit. He seemed to set no especial value upon his own exploits, but to relate them as items of personal history, with as little comment or emphasis as if they concerned anyone more than himself." Like Mike Brown of *Swallow Barn,* Robinson is a blacksmith, but the name indicates his ironlike physical toughness. In a description of his hero Kennedy writes, "His was one of those iron forms that might be imagined almost bullet proof."

Horse Shoe has much in common with other folk heroes such as Harvey Birch from Cooper's *The Spy* (1821), Mike Fink, Davy Crockett, and Cooper's Natty Bumppo—at the time, Horse Shoe's popularity rivaled Leather-Stocking's—but he is definitely not a carbon copy of any of them. Kennedy's hero is illiterate but wise in the ways of the world; he is witty, companionable, fiercely loyal to his country, even-tempered, and brimming with good will. He is happier and more easygoing than Bumppo. Kennedy says he will tell the story in Robinson's idiosyncratic language with its "peculiar vocabulary and rustic, doric form of speech." Like Leather-Stocking's talk, Robinson's is studded with verbal concoctions such as "Contwistification" and "obstrepolous." While unfailingly polite and chivalrous toward women, he remains, like Bumppo, a confirmed bachelor. Like other folk heroes, Robinson is larger than life. His physique is said to better Hercules', and his exploits are worthy of a superman. He can escape any trap or captivity, outsmart or outtalk any enemy, outdodge any bullet. Like his near-relatives in folk legend, Robinson enjoys a good boast: "My name is Brimstone, I am first-cousin to Beelzebub" is reminiscent of James Kirke Paulding's description of his character Nimrod Wildfire as "half-horse, half-alligator."

According to the introduction, the author sent a copy of the finished book to Robinson. When the book was read to him, Kennedy asserts, the old man replied, "It is all true and right—in its right place—excepting about them women, which I disremember. That mought be true, too; but my memory is treacherous—I disremember." Such detail, which modern critics tend to take with a grain of salt, adds to the air of authenticity that Kennedy sought to create. His insistence that Robinson is a real person who actually fought in the war (and apparently at least that much about the man is true) helps Kennedy establish another layer of authenticity uncommon in historical romances. Usually such books mix real historical characters with fictional ones; Kennedy's story boasts not only those elements but also a real human being who, while he did not gain fame during the war, can be used to link the historical with the fictional. The Horse Shoe Robinson of the book is a bit of both.

While *Horse-Shoe Robinson* is set at an entirely different time than *Swallow Barn,* the two share the same

*Illustration by F. O. C. Darley for the 1852 revised edition of Kennedy's* Horse-Shoe Robinson

central conflict: nationhood has both its positive and its negative aspects. On the one hand it offers a more progressive spirit and a free and open society, but these come at the cost of the loss of roots and the structure, social organization, and family control of property that was inherent in the old system. As Mildred's dilemma dramatizes, to gain a husband one must lose a father. Both books also share Kennedy's concern with the unchecked political power of the common man and the need for social order, which could only be imposed if there were cooperation between the classes. Horse Shoe Robinson alone could not govern successfully; his freedom-loving bent might not be easily tamed and might take him—and the nation—too far in the direction of anarchy.

Critics of Kennedy's day and later rightly praised his powers of description in the book. His minor characters, even though they are literary stereotypes from the Gothic and melodramatic schools, are well drawn and sympathetic, and his accounts of the fighting ring true. Kennedy's familiarity with the area he is describing combined with his love for the picturesque results in Irvingesque effects. Also like Irving, he fills the book with references to the classics, the Bible, old ballads, and William Shakespeare. While the style is more colloquial than Cooper's, it is also, like Irving's, gentlemanly, with genial humor and urbane overtones. In his review of the book in the *Southern Literary Messenger* (May 1835), Poe labels Kennedy's style "simple yet forcible," "richly figurative and poetical," and "altogether devoid of affectation." While Kennedy does rely on coincidence more than necessary, all in all the book is more realistic than most of its day. His use of melodrama is more restrained than Cooper's, and he frequently employs the dramatic rather than the expository method.

Kennedy fabricated no elaborate theories about the writing of literature beyond a love for the picturesque in characters and manners, but he held some strong opinions regarding the writing of history. In "A Legend of Maryland," published in the July 1860 *Atlantic Monthly,* he wrote that what made history the "richest of philosophies" is the "spirit that is breathed into it by the thoughts and feelings of former generations, interpreted in actions and incidents that disclose the passions and motives, and ambitions of men, and open to us a view of the actual life of our forefathers." By seeing them going about their daily business and observing their habits and manners, readers then understand how and why they do things, and then their imagination is "quick to clothe them with the flesh and blood of human brotherhood, and it brings them into full sympathy with our individual nature. History then becomes a world of living figures." While he may have fallen short of this ideal in the writing of *Horse-Shoe Robinson,* he came closer than many of his contemporaries. As Poe concluded, *Horse-Shoe Robinson* is a "book of no ordinary character."

The book was a critical and financial success, even more so than *Swallow Barn.* A second edition was released in the original year of publication and a third the following year. Irving, to whom the book was dedicated, wrote that he read it with "great gusto" and predicted that the public would like it. Lewis Gaylord Clark, a powerful New York editor, urged Kennedy to contribute to *Knickerbocker Magazine,* naming his "own terms of remuneration." Others praised the verisimilitude of the book and were pleased that he celebrated American history. When the book was republished nearly twenty years later, it was still well received. A 15 September 1852 letter to the editor of a New Orleans newspaper praised the book: "As a work of mixed fiction and historical reminiscences, I have never read its superior. The general plot is new, distinct, powerfully worked out and consistent throughout. The characters

are natural–no witches, hobgoblins, or even elfish boys!–no romance inconsistent with real life–no character but what is drawn to the life."

The writer praises Kennedy for sparing the reader any words or deeds that would offend the elderly or "cause a blush on the cheek of the most delicate female" and expresses his boundless admiration for Robinson: "He is the beau ideal of a peasant patriot–a patriot in heart–uneducated–who becomes a soldier from convictions of duty to his country, filled with common sense, as well as mother wit." The writer compares Robinson to Leather-Stocking and concludes that Kennedy's creation is equal to Cooper's.

*Horse-Shoe Robinson* was published in 1835 and *Rob of the Bowl,* Kennedy's next and last novel, in 1838. Between those years Kennedy worked intermittently on his book. This period was also his most active in helping to form the new Whig Party, for which he became a spokesman. Once a follower of Andrew Jackson himself, Kennedy had developed serious doubts about the wisdom of having the country run by the common man, and the Whigs were motivated by opposition to Jacksonianism, especially what they viewed as his usurpation of executive power. Kennedy believed in the things the Whigs championed: commerce, protection of property rights, and a stable economy.

Kennedy ran for Congress on the Whig ticket in 1837. While he tried to focus on strong protectionist legislation, his enemies sought to derail his candidacy by resurrecting old issues such as his earlier support for the Potomac Canal and his refusal of a diplomatic post in Chile. They charged that he was untrustworthy because of his defection from Jackson and the Federalists to the Whigs. They also accused him of having a loose regard for the truth as a writer of fiction and thus unworthy of being entrusted with the public welfare. The vicious smear campaign took its toll: Kennedy lost by two hundred votes.

Several years later Kennedy was still irritated about the way his literary output had been used against him. When similar attacks were mounted against Abel P. Upshur, a Virginian, Kennedy wrote in his journal on 26 September 1841 about the hypocrisy of the "Locos," a nickname for radical Democrat Locofocos: "to sum up his disqualifications he has committed the crime which the Locos consider *my* deepest sin, of writing a novel. . . . I am glad that there is another public man besides myself who can be charged with this atrocity of writing a book. Paulding wrote half a dozen bad novels,–but he was a born Loco and so escaped scot-free."

Despite the continued drumbeat of criticism, Kennedy was still popular in Baltimore, and the following year he was elected to the House of Representa-

Baltimore Mar. 18. 1846

My dear Sir

Messrs Taylor & Co, the publishers, sent me a
few days ago, a copy of Count Julian, in which
I find you have done me the honor of a dedication
I very gratefully acknowledge this kind remembrance, and attach the more value to it as
it comes from "a brother in the art" whose
good opinion affords so fair a motive for
self-gratulation Laudari laudato has been
long admitted as an established excuse for
some little glorification of ourselves, – though
I hope you will acquit me of any very earnest
opinion that my labors (holiday sports rather)
in our common field have entitled me to
the rank which your dedication would seem
to infer. I am no better than a laggard

*First page of a letter from Kennedy to novelist William Gilmore Simms (from the 1937 American Book Company
edition of* Horse-Shoe Robinson)

tives, winning a special election for the seat of the man who had defeated him. He had not held public office for fifteen years. Defeated in 1839, he was reelected in 1840 and 1842 and became chairman of the House Committee on Commerce. While he savored his return to the national scene and his opportunity to champion the causes he believed in, his political life began to completely overshadow his literary hopes; from then on, with the exception of a short period following his 1839 defeat, there would simply be little time for writing much beyond political tracts.

During the 1838 summer recess following his maiden speech in the House, Kennedy finished *Rob of the Bowl*. Set in the "ancient" capital of colonial Maryland, St. Mary's, during the latter half of the seventeenth century, *Rob of the Bowl* is an historical romance based more on legend and invention than on actual historical events. The Rob of the story is loosely based upon tales Kennedy had heard, as he wrote in some preliminary notes, about "a little fellow who had lost his legs and who consequently was strapped in a huge wooden bowl, and I think was called Billy of the Bowl. This worthy flourished, it strikes me, during the Revolutionary war and was connected with some exploit of capturing a small tender which got aground somewhere along the bay shore." Kennedy added that he would "endow him with some faculty of horsemanship, and sometimes describe him in this guise mounted, and with his bowl hung like a shield at his back. He shall be saucy, sarcastic, malicious, envious, &c." "My buccaneer," he continued, "I shall call Cocklescraft and make him a good sailor, a handsome fellow, very brave, wild, dissolute, comic, &c. He shall pretend to some skill in the black art and practice it to make weak people afraid of him. But he shall be rather a favorite with the watermen and others on the bay side on account of his free trading."

Despite the fact that he had previously been applauded for excluding them from his books, Kennedy planned to insert some of the Gothic conventions made famous by stories such as Irving's "The Legend of Sleepy Hollow" and "The Spectre Bridegroom" from *The Sketch Book*. He included a haunted house for Rob and his gang to use, complete with furniture that inexplicably moves about during the night and ghostly echoes of horses and wagons calculated to arouse terror and superstitious dread. To counter this supernatural machinery he planned to give his story a narrative frame to ground it solidly in reality. Though he later jettisoned the frame story, he provided Rob (Robert Swale) with a well-developed sketch of his early career in England that lent an air of authenticity. Kennedy also thoroughly researched the time period, settling eventually on 1681, and visited the area where his story was to be set, all of which added to the verisimilitude of his tale.

When Kennedy had proceeded far enough to open discussions with his publishers about the new book, Carey and Lea responded with mixed signals. While they had no reservations about publishing any romance he might write, they were concerned about the length—the letter refers to *Horse-Shoe Robinson* as "that monster Robinson" whose "vastness was better calculated for fighting than profit." They also protested that the publishing market was weak just then, especially for fiction, and first proposed an edition of three thousand copies, later amending their offer to four thousand copies and a flat payment of $1,600. He had been paid $1,200 for three thousand copies of his last book. After dickering with another publisher, Kennedy eventually agreed to $1,850 for an edition of four thousand copies.

The background for Kennedy's tale is the historical quarrel between the original Roman Catholic landowners of Maryland and the Protestant settlers who were vying with them for control. Although the proprietary, Charles Calvert, Lord Baltimore, was a Catholic, he was tolerant of other faiths, in keeping with the policy of religious freedom in the province. Dissident Protestants, however, continued to stir up trouble, and the situation became quite volatile, occasionally erupting into violence and once leading to the jailing of the Protestant leaders. Lord Baltimore is gracious in victory, treating his defeated enemies with magnanimity. In *Rob of the Bowl* much of this background information is woven into the fabric of a gossip session at a tavern. During the course of this convivial chatter, the reader learns of the various plot complications: a mystery surrounding the fate of the father of the proprietary's secretary, Albert Verheyden, and another surrounding the past of Robert Swale, known locally as Rob of the Bowl, and his suspected connections with a group of smugglers, led by Richard Cocklescraft. Over this basic framework Kennedy lays his web of Gothic touches, including the seemingly haunted fisherman's house. Known as the Wizard's Chapel, the house is the smugglers' headquarters, and these outlaws play upon the superstitious natures of the locals to keep them from discovering their hideaway.

Kennedy supplies the necessary love interest in the persons of Blanche, lovely daughter of an officeholder under Lord Baltimore, and Verheyden. Cocklescraft pursues Blanche, and when his overtures are rebuffed and he realizes that Verheyden is his rival, the swashbuckling smuggler challenges the young man to a duel. To the surprise of all, the gentle Verheyden vanquishes Cocklescraft, and the smuggler decides to cast his lot with the Protestants in order to revenge himself upon the ruling faction. The various mysteries begin to unravel and the plots to intersect when Rob of the Bowl is revealed in an aside to be Verheyden's missing father. When Cocklescraft captures Verheyden, Rob engineers his escape, and later when the smuggler kidnaps Blanche, intending to take her to sea with him, his plans are foiled by Rob's intervention. When Rob is fatally wounded by Cocklescraft, he reveals in a rather bathetic speech that he is the young man's father, and receives his son's forgiveness. Cocklescraft escapes, but Verheyden inherits Rob's wealth—which he employs in helping the poor and other charitable works—and marries Blanche.

Kennedy's amalgam of history, romance, and the trappings of Gothic and sentimental fiction did not fare as well with the public as did his earlier fictional excursions. Critics largely ignored it. Few reviewed the book, and the publishers declined to consider a second edition because of poorer-than-expected sales. So even though Kennedy had left the door open for a sequel by allowing Cocklescraft to escape, the smuggler never sailed again; Kennedy's foray into fiction was at an end.

In this last of Kennedy's three novels, he once again touches on the issue of leadership and the respective responsibilities of the upper and lower classes. The founders of Maryland he classifies as "Cavaliers," honorable, good men who valued tolerance, bravery, and landownership. Kennedy frowned on those who challenged Lord Baltimore's authority not because they were Protestant—he too was one—but because they sought to undermine established authority by rebellion.

The sluggish sales of *Rob of the Bowl* were not Kennedy's sole disappointment. In the election of 1839 he was defeated and lost his seat in the House of Representatives. In his leisure he turned not to historical romance but to satire. *Quodlibet: Containing Some Annals Thereof, with an Authentic Account of the Origin and Growth of the Borough and the Sayings and Doings of Sundry of the Townspeople,* published in 1840, takes satiric aim at the forces of Jacksonian democracy. Named for the fictional village in which his story is set, the book reveals from another angle Kennedy's continual preoccupation with the tension between tradition and progress and his misgivings about the leveling of classes inherent in Jacksonianism. He laments the failure of the upper, aristocratic classes to take their rightful place in leadership roles and his fears about the eventual outcome of unfettered democracy on the lower classes. Vernon Louis Parrington, in his *Main Currents in American Thought* (1927), calls *Quodlibet* "the most vivacious criticism of Jacksonianism in our political history" and ranks it as "one of our few distinguished political satires." Reaction to the book depended upon the reader's political convictions, and the book was not a financial success; the author realized only about $100.

In his attempts to find a creative outlet that would sell, Kennedy turned next to biography. His life of William Wirt, the Baltimore lawyer and writer to whom Kennedy had dedicated *Swallow Barn,* was begun in 1846, but because of the pressures of political life—he was swept in and out of office several times over the next few years—*Memoirs of the Life of William Wirt, Attorney General of the United States* was not published until 1849. Kennedy had figured correctly: a biography was considered more "respectable" than historical romances, and sales were brisk enough to allow a second printing only a month after its initial publication. The profits were still disappointing, however, given the amount of research the book had required. *Memoirs of the Life of William Wirt* eventually went through six editions.

Kennedy's accounting of the returns from his books reveals total sales to have brought in much less than $6,000, small compensation for twenty years of work. His figures include $782.69 for the 1832 *Swallow Barn* (2,000 copies), $1,700 for *Horse-Shoe Robinson* (6,000 copies from two editions), $1,850 for *Rob of the Bowl* (4,000 copies), $100 for *Quodlibet* (1,500 copies), $284.25 for the first edition of his life of Wirt (he split the proceeds with Wirt's widow), and $975 from two subsequent editions totaling 3,750 copies. In addition, his *Defense of the Whigs,* written in 1844, brought him no return for the 4,000 copies printed. When the original publishers showed no interest in reprints, despite Kennedy's repeated urging, the author switched to George Putnam's New York firm in the early 1850s and received 12½ percent for the new edition, the same price commanded by Irving and Cooper.

New rewards awaited Kennedy in the political arena, even though he never again held elective office. President Millard Fillmore appointed him interim secretary of the navy in 1852. In 1860, just before the Civil War, Kennedy wrote *The Border States, Their Power and Duty in the Present Disordered Condition of the Country* in an attempt to influence the North's attitude toward the South. He viewed both the single-minded Northern abolitionists and the equally determined die-hard Southern slavery advocates as grave threats to the Union and urged the buffer states between the two to act as arbitrators and conciliators. Once the war began in earnest, his strong pro-Union stance alienated many who had once viewed him as a friend to the South. His last book-length publication, *Mr. Ambrose's Letters on the Rebellion* (1865), purports to be a series of letters outlining the Northern conservative position. Even though he was no longer an active politician, Kennedy remained committed to the Whig cause and his words commanded respect.

Health woes drove him to travel in search of relief, and he died on 18 August 1870 in Newport, Rhode

Island. In death he was celebrated as a public man rather than as a professional man of letters, but his contribution to American native literature was duly noted if not greatly appreciated in the heyday of William Dean Howells and Henry James. As Ridgely has insightfully noted, what Kennedy should be remembered for is his use of fiction as a vehicle for resolving "the dilemmas which the national experience had created. . . . All of his books are fundamentally concerned with one haunting question: who should lead in a democracy?" Kennedy was "an apostle of progress who nonetheless thought it important to uncover the bonds which linked the present with the past." He stood squarely for inherited property rights, leadership by a native aristocracy, and the stability of an ordered society, but he was also aware of the dangers of stagnation brought on by the overveneration of tradition, disdain of progress, and sectionalism. He used his literary abilities to make his case before the public in a way that he could not as a public figure.

Kennedy's works faded from the public eye during the Gilded Age and did not resurface until the publication of Parrington's *Main Currents in American Thought,* which declared an appreciation for Kennedy's work. In his chapter on Kennedy, Parrington wrote: "He was a man of letters rather than a lawyer, and if he had eschewed politics and law and stuck to his pen, our literature would have been greatly in his debt. Few Americans of his day were so generously gifted; none possessed a lighter touch."

A new edition of *Swallow Barn* appeared in 1929, and *Horse-Shoe Robinson* returned to print in 1937. The first biography of Kennedy since Henry T. Tuckerman's 1871 *The Life of John Pendleton Kennedy* was Edward M. Gwathmey's *John Pendleton Kennedy,* published in 1931, followed in 1961 by both the first reliable modern biography and the first full assessment of Kennedy's work, Charles H. Bohner's *John Pendleton Kennedy: Gentleman from Baltimore* and William R. Taylor's *Cavalier and Yankee.* Both books took full advantage of the collection of his papers that Kennedy had bequeathed to the Peabody Institute Library in Baltimore.

New editions of *Swallow Barn* and *Rob of the Bowl* appeared in 1962 and 1965, respectively, and a new edition of *Horse-Shoe Robinson* in 1962. In 1966 the most recent assessment of Kennedy's contribution to the native literature, Ridgely's *John Pendleton Kennedy,* was published. Recent criticism has centered mainly on *Swallow Barn* and Kennedy's treatment of the slavery issue. Kennedy's reputation appears to be growing and his place in American literary history secure.

**Letters:**

Killis Campbell, ed., "The Kennedy Papers," *Sewanee Review,* 25 (January 1917): 1–19; (April 1917): 197–202; (July 1917): 348–360.

**Bibliographies:**

Jacob Blanck, *Bibliography of American Literature,* 9 volumes (New Haven: Yale University Press, 1955–1991), V: 228–242;

David O. Tomlinson, "John Pendleton Kennedy: An Essay in Bibliography," *Resources for American Literary Study,* 9 (Autumn 1979): 140–170.

**Biographies:**

Henry T. Tuckerman, *The Life of John Pendleton Kennedy* (New York: Putnam, 1871);

Edward M. Gwathmey, *John Pendleton Kennedy* (New York: Thomas Nelson, 1931);

Charles H. Bohner, *John Pendleton Kennedy: Gentleman from Baltimore* (Baltimore: Johns Hopkins University Press, 1961).

**References:**

William L. Andrews, "Inter(racial) Textuality in Nineteenth-Century Southern Narrative," in *Influence and Intertextuality in Literary History,* edited by Jay Clayton and Eric Rothstein (Madison: University of Wisconsin Press, 1991), pp. 298–317;

Jan Bakker, "Time and Timelessness in Images of the Old South: Pastoral in John Pendleton Kennedy's *Swallow Barn* and *Horse-Shoe Robinson,*" *Tennessee Studies in Literature,* 26 (1981): 75–88;

Charles H. Brichford, "That National Story: Conflicting Versions and Conflicting Visions of the Revolution in Kennedy's *Horse-Shoe Robinson* and Simms's *The Partisan,*" *Southern Literary Journal,* 21 (Fall 1998): 64–85;

R. C. Burton, "John Pendleton Kennedy and the Civil War," *Journal of Southern History,* 29 (August 1963): 373–376;

Guy Cardwell, "The Plantation House: An Analogical Image," *Southern Literary Journal,* 2 (Fall 1969): 3–21;

Alexander Cowie, *The Rise of the American Novel* (New York: American Book Company, 1948), pp. 258–270;

Richard Beale Davis, *Literature and Society in Early Virginia, 1608–1840* (Baton Rouge: Louisiana State University Press, 1973);

Rhoda C. Ellison, "An Interview with Horse-Shoe Robinson," *American Literature,* 31 (November 1959): 329–332;

John Lee Hare, "Images of the Family in the Ante-Bellum Virginia Novel," *DAI,* 58 (December 1997): 22–64;

Lothar Honnighausen, "The American Interest in German Romanticism: Washington Irving, John Pendleton Kennedy, and Gottfried August Burger's *Lenoré: A Cultural Studies Approach,*" in *Transatlantic Encounters: Studies in European-American Relations,* edited by Udo J. Hebel and Karl Ortseifen (Trier, Germany: Wissenschaftlicher, 1995), pp. 102–114;

Honnighausen, "Political Landscapes of the Antebellum South: Friedrich Gerstacher and John Pendleton Kennedy," in *Southern Landscapes*, edited by Tony Badger, Walter Edgar, and Jan Nordby Gretland (Tübingen: Stauffenburg, 1996), pp. 57–70;

Jay B. Hubbell, *The South in American Literature, 1607–1900* (Durham: Duke University Press, 1954), pp. 481–495;

Hubbell, Introduction to *Swallow Barn, or A Sojourn in the Old Dominion* (New York: Harcourt, Brace, 1929);

Dean H. Keller, "BAL Addenda: Bird, Irving, Kennedy," *PBSA: Papers of the Bibliographical Society of America*, 74 (1988): 401–402;

John H. B. Latrobe, "Kennedy's Novels," *New York Review*, January 1842;

Ernest E. Leisy, *The American Historical Novel* (Norman: University of Oklahoma Press, 1950), pp. 11, 34, 107, 146;

Leisy, Introduction to *Horse-Shoe Robinson*, by John Pendleton Kennedy (New York: American Book Company, 1937), pp. ix–xxvi;

Lucinda H. MacKethan, Introduction to *Swallow Barn, or A Sojourn in the Old Dominion* (Baton Rouge: Louisiana State University Press, 1986), pp. xi–xxxiv;

John R. Moore, "Kennedy's Horse-Shoe Robinson: Fact or Fiction?" *American Literature*, 4 (May 1932): 160–166;

William S. Osborne, "John Pendleton Kennedy: A Study of His Literary Career," dissertation, New York, Columbia University, 1960;

Osborne, "John Pendleton Kennedy's *Horse-Shoe Robinson:* A Novel with 'the Utmost Historical Accuracy,'" *Maryland Historical Magazine*, 59 (September 1964): 286–296;

Osborne, "'The Swiss Traveller' Essays: Earliest Literary Writings of John Pendleton Kennedy," *American Literature*, 30 (May 1958): 228–233;

Vernon Louis Parrington, *Main Currents in American Thought*, 3 volumes (New York: Harcourt, Brace, 1927–1930), II: 46–56;

Wallace L. Pretzer, "Eighteenth-Century Conventions in the Fictional Style of John Pendleton Kennedy," dissertation, Ann Arbor, University of Michigan, 1963;

J. V. Ridgely, *John Pendleton Kennedy* (New York: Twayne, 1966);

Lewis Simpson, *The Dispossessed Garden: Pastoral and History in Southern Literature* (Athens: University of Georgia Press, 1975);

William R. Taylor, *Cavalier and Yankee: The Old South and American National Character* (New York: Anchor, 1963), pp. 178–193;

David O. Tomlinson, "A Publisher's Advice to Young Authors: John Pendleton Kennedy and Peter H. Cruse Serve a Literary Apprenticeship," *Southern Literary Journal*, 14 (Fall 1981): 56–71;

*Tributes to the Memory of the Hon. John Pendleton Kennedy* (Cambridge, Mass.: Wilson, 1871);

John E. Uhler, "Kennedy's Novels and His Posthumous Works," *American Literature*, 3 (January 1932): 471–479;

Richie D. Watson, "Frontier Yeoman Versus Cavalier: The Dilemma of Antebellum Southern Fiction," in *The Frontier Experience and the American Dream: Essays on American Literature*, edited by David Mogen, Mark Busby, and Paul Bryant (College Station: Texas A&M University Press, 1989), pp. 107–119.

**Papers:**
The largest collection of John Pendleton Kennedy's papers is housed in the George Peabody Department of the Enoch Pratt Free Library in Baltimore. The collection comprises five thousand volumes, including manuscripts of all his books; thirty-five volumes of journals; about four thousand letters to and from Kennedy in thirty-three volumes; seventeen volumes describing trips throughout the United States and Europe; and scrapbooks of newspaper clippings, including many contemporary reviews of Kennedy's books.

# Hugh Swinton Legaré

*(2 January 1797 – 20 June 1843)*

C. P. Seabrook Wilkinson
*College of Charleston*

See also the Legaré entries in *DLB 3: Antebellum Writers in New York and the South; DLB 59: American Literary Critics and Scholars, 1800–1850;* and *DLB 73: American Magazine Journalists, 1741–1850.*

BOOKS: *Letter from the Hon. Hugh S. Legaré on the probable effects of the Sub-Treasury policy on the specie clause, to His Excellency Pierce Butler, Governor of South Carolina* (Washington, 1838);

*Writings of Hugh Swinton Legaré, Late Attorney General and Acting Secretary of State of the United States,* 2 volumes, edited by Mary S. Legaré (Charleston, S.C.: Burges & James / Philadephia: Cowperthwait / New York: Appleton / Boston: Munroe, 1845–1846).

OTHER: "The Study of the Classics," in *The Charleston Book,* edited by William Gilmore Simms (Charleston, S.C.: Hart, 1845), pp. 14–19;

"Hugh Swinton Legaré: German Diaries," in *All Clever Men, Who Make Their Way: Critical Discourse in the Old South,* edited by Michael O'Brien (Fayetteville: University of Arkansas Press, 1982), pp. 89–124.

SELECTED PERIODICAL PUBLICATION–UNCOLLECTED: "Spirit of the Sub-Treasury," *Congressional Globe,* Twenty-fifth Congress, first session, 5 (1837): 236–245.

Hugh Swinton Legaré, cabinet officer, congressman, diplomat, lawyer, orator, editor, and writer, has for more than a century and a half since his death been held up as irrefutable proof that the antebellum South did produce intellectuals of the first rank. It cannot, however, be claimed that his towering intellect was distilled into literature of equivalent elevation. He did a great deal of writing in the course of an incredibly busy life, but Legaré never considered himself a writer; indeed, he sneered in periodical print at Thomas Moore's "determined propensity for book-making."

T. Doney. sc.

*(from* Linda Rhea, Hugh Swinton Legaré: A Charleston Intellectual, *1934)*

The range of his interests, the depth of his reading, the dazzling extent of his linguistic abilities, his polyglot total recall of the riches he absorbed—all provoke wonder in the exclusive fraternity of his modern readers, but there is a sort of freakishness in the compendiousness of his mind. His fluency in so many languages was an obvious advantage when Legaré became a diplomat, yet it is deleterious to any attempt to revive his writings, which are littered with quotations in an almost Poundian profusion of tongues. He reviewed novels, travel narratives, and poems good and bad, but he never embraced belles lettres in his own practice. With minor exceptions, Legaré's surviving writings are of the private and fugitive variety, letters and diaries, or public and occasional, reviews of books long forgotten and speeches in long-expired controversies.

Hugh Swinton Legaré was born on the paternal plantation on John's Island, South Carolina, ten miles south of Charleston, on 2 January 1797. He was the second surviving child and only son of Solomon Legaré Jr. and Mary Splatt Swinton Legaré. His father, of whom little is known, died when Hugh Swinton was two years old; his mother, who was unquestionably the greatest single influence on her famous son, survived until eighteen months before his own death. Both families were prominent, their various branches ranging from comfortably to prodigiously rich. Financially, the Legarés of John's Island were in the middle range of their large family. While they boasted a longer American pedigree, the Swintons had a vastly longer transatlantic one, for the Swintons of that ilk are among the most ancient of Scottish families, stretching back to Berwickshire in the eighth century. Hugh was named for his maternal grandfather, who was in turn the namesake of his uncle, Hugh Swinton, who had come out to Carolina with his brother William in the 1720s. Both branches of the Carolina Swintons soon allied themselves to prominent Huguenot families. The taint of melancholia many of his contemporaries remarked in Hugh Swinton Legaré also afflicted Hugh Swinton, who died in a New York City madhouse in 1759.

Left a widow with an unproductive plantation, little disposable capital, and three small children, Mary Swinton Legaré made the upbringing and launching of those children the main business of her life. Particular care was taken of her son's education, which was rendered the more important by a misfortune that overtook the four-year-old Hugh and to a large extent overshadowed the remainder of his life. When he was inoculated for smallpox, the batch of serum turned out to be tainted, and the healthy and beautiful small boy was reduced to a horribly misshapen and shrunken invalid, who for weeks barely clung to life, was carried about on a pillow by his distraught mother for many months, and did not grow at all for several years. When Hugh began growing again, his arms and legs never attained to adult size, so as a man he was imposing when seated but dwarfish when he rose to speak—a severe disadvantage for an orator. In a classic case of compensation Legaré countered the stunted growth of his body with a prodigious mental development.

From 1803 Mary Legaré engaged a series of tutors for the son whose extraordinary mental gifts were already apparent. Young Legaré received a thorough grounding in Latin and Greek from a Dublin-trained priest, the Reverend Simon Gallagher, who taught at the College of Charleston. When he had absorbed all that Charleston's tutors and the grammar school of the College of Charleston could impart, Legaré was sent to the celebrated academy of John C. Calhoun's brother-in-law Moses Waddel at Williston, where generations of Upcountry and Lowcountry gentry were prepared for the best colleges. He was unhappy there and begged his mother to remove him; she resolutely refused. Again, Legaré soon exhausted the classicists who attempted to teach him what he already largely knew. Entering South Carolina College in Columbia as a sophomore at the age of fourteen in December 1811, he was at once recognized as the greatest prodigy the young college (founded only in 1801) had seen. Legaré compounded his natural intellectual advantages by studying fifteen hours a day; he continued to put in such punishing hours even when in charge of two cabinet departments. The future congressman first shone as an orator in college debates. He had the natural advantage—the solitary physical advantage left to him—of a singularly powerful and pleasing voice, a trait said to be hereditary in the Swinton family. Predictably, he was valedictorian of the class of 1814.

A college graduate at seventeen, Legaré returned to Charleston to study for the bar under his old headmaster at the grammar school, the Scottish-born lawyer and future judge Mitchell King. He lived at home on the John's Island plantation, in whose management he appears to have played little part. Eventually he overdid his studies, and his health, never the best after his early affliction, began to suffer. Obliged to spend a summer away from his books, he went north in 1816 on the first of many such visits; of all Southern luminaries of the antebellum period, he seems to have been most at home "at the North." After some relaxation and the usual spa diversions, including a modicum of romantic dalliance at Saratoga, by the end of August he was in Cambridge devouring the great library of Harvard College. By the time Legaré returned to Charleston at year's end he was suffering from severe eyestrain, and for a time his sister Mary had to read everything aloud to him.

Legaré's career is a mixture of turns that, given his geographical and social position, are predictable, and others that are highly unexpected. Few Carolinians of his day went on, as he did, to study at the University of Edinburgh. Legaré returned to the North in 1818, but only to embark for France to begin a projected three-year course of study on the Continent. His first intoxicating visit to Paris fired his passion for modern languages. Originally, Legaré intended to study at the University of Göttingen, but political turmoil there made him think instead of Leiden; eventually, influenced by his new friend William Campbell Preston, he settled on the University of Edinburgh. The choice, although not his first, was a happy one.

This time was rich in significant beginnings, intellectual and personal, notably his friendship with educator and historian George Ticknor and his passion for the civil law. Alexander Irving's course on civil law was still conducted in Latin. This pedagogical approach was no problem for Legaré, who was able to dispute points with his professor in the language of his lectures. As throughout his life, even when he was doing the work of three men, he found time for society, meeting the aged novelist Henry Mackenzie and shining in the drawing room of the most formidable literary lady of Edinburgh, Mrs. Grant of Laggan. In his 1843 eulogy for Legaré, Preston, his roommate during the Edinburgh year, tells the story, often since repeated, of a twenty-four-hour stint of study: Legaré was found on Sunday morning at the breakfast table, just where he had been on Saturday, apparently unaware that he had been at his books all night. By such behavior Legaré could in effect deny that his problematical body existed, but by the time he rose to national power and cabinet rank he was in continual ill health. After the Edinburgh academic year ended, Legaré went to London, where he was unimpressed by parliamentary debates, and returned to Paris, a city of which he grew particularly fond. His intention was to spend a further year in Italy, but his mother was struggling ever more frantically to manage the plantation on her own, so he cut short his sojourn to take belated charge of the family property. He was not a planter by inclination, and his efforts were not aided by a severe agricultural depression, but he held things together and avoided having to sell the plantation before land prices recovered. In 1822 he cheerfully disposed of his agricultural patrimony, and the three Legarés—mother, son, and unmarried younger daughter—moved into town, to a spacious piazza-girt house, now 76 Bull Street, in the suburb called Harleston Village near the College of Charleston.

In 1820 Legaré was elected to the state house of representatives for the parish of St. John's, Colleton. By November 1822 he was a resident in Charleston, so he had to stand for the urban parish of St. Philip and St. Michael. He was not humiliated at the polls, but he was not elected, either. Legaré is almost always identified with Charleston, but he was not technically (nor perhaps temperamentally) a Charlestonian: he was a Sea Islander, and many who were Charlestonians by birth never forgot that. In Charleston politics he never enjoyed the natural constituency that was his birthright in St. John's, Colleton, but he was elected to city council in 1825, and he did win election to represent St. Philip and St. Michael at his second attempt in 1824, and served in the statehouse until elevated to the attorney generalship on 27 November 1830. By then he had become the friend and political protégé of James Louis Petigru, the leading Unionist in South Carolina, whom he succeeded as the chief legal officer in the state.

His elevation to this at first highly congenial post helped to resolve the conflict between Legaré's intellectual aspirations and the pressures of practical politics. There was always a certain want of practicality in Legaré. He prepared for his legal career with a spaciousness of design his relatively short life was not to justify; he was decidedly overprepared for local tastes when he at last began to practice law at age twenty-five in 1822. Throughout his life, in politics, literature, and law, Legaré tended to intimidate by his superior learning. Perhaps that learning was most usefully employed on behalf of the *Southern Review* during his first period of residence in Charleston. He was among the youngest of the group of Charleston intellectuals who in the autumn of 1827 laid plans for a new review that would serve the political interests and intellectual aspirations of the South. He did not become editor of the *Southern Review* until halfway through its four-year life, but it was with justice known as *Legaré's Review,* for, like his kinsman Paul Hamilton Hayne with *Russell's Magazine* in the late 1850s, he was both editor and chief contributor by default. Cajoling contributors, writing against deadlines, forever struggling to raise money to keep the publication going, he had little time for niceties of style, and he resorted too often to wholesale quotation in his reviews, but after all Legaré had assumed the backbreaking editorial work while serving as attorney general of South Carolina. He could turn his hand to just about any sort of reviewing; his editorial pinch hitting made him versatile, but it wore him out. He might well have written more had he not come to associate writing with drudgery. In an appendix to his *A Character of Hugh Legaré* (1985), Michael O'Brien gives a list of the contributors to the *Southern Review* as definitive as the evidence permits. Legaré had the first word, for the opening article of the inaugural issue, "Classical Learning," is his, as are the final pages of the last, an appendix to the article "Political Economy" which he may have written in its entirety. In between he contributed to at least ten of the twelve numbers of the *Southern Review*. His contributions, twenty-five in all, range from massively learned surveys of classical subjects, Greek and Roman history, literature, and oratory, to reviews of the latest novels by Sir Walter Scott and James Fenimore Cooper and such oddities as an article on "The Siamese Twins" (May 1831). Legaré wrote at least 925 closely packed pages for the *Southern Review,* averaging nearly seventy pages per issue.

When the *Southern Review* finally expired with the February 1832 number, a job offer arrived from Washington, D.C., to fill the gap in the exhausted editor's life. The secretary of state, Edward Livingston, had been impressed when he heard the young attorney general of South Carolina argue a case before the Supreme Court, so he persuaded President Andrew Jackson to offer Legaré the post of chargé d'affaires in the newest European capital, Brussels. Legaré accepted with alacrity an appointment that removed him from the noisome politics of nullification; he was ready to travel again, and his Unionist faction was clearly in decline. After Charleston—with which he was growing disenchanted, as electoral Charleston was to grow of him—Legaré enjoyed the sophistication of Brussels, and he made the most of further opportunities for study and European travel.

Unlike many American envoys, the Southern aristocrat found no difficulty in adjusting to the etiquette and protocol of a European capital. Now he might meet Friedrich von Schlegel, not merely read or review him. In his travel diaries and letters home, Legaré reveals himself as an earnest, self-conscious tourist haunting cathedrals and admiring the works of the Old Masters. The transatlantic Huguenot nursed a guilty fascination for Roman Catholic pomp and ceremony. His concern with the rather dandified figure he cut in Brussels was reflected in endless fussing over the details of his entourage and his wardrobe. He found the time to develop an attachment, perhaps the most serious of his life, to a British noblewoman of exalted birth, Lady Flora Hastings, daughter of a deceased marquis and a Scottish countess in her own right. He picked up languages voraciously, perfecting his German, adding Dutch and Romaic for good measure, and even learning enough Polish to appreciate poet Adam Mickiewicz. His linguistic arsenal was now fully stocked, but Legaré had no project that required all this ammunition. Had he found a fit subject, he might be remembered as another John Lothrop Motley, an American historian, rather than as perpetrator of another set of unreadable nineteenth-century "Remains." He was not, however, some alienated Jamesian wanderer. Absence may have kept him out of touch with the details of American politics, but it strengthened his commitment to the American experiment in democracy. From Brussels he wrote home to his beloved mother: "I have learnt to be *an American,* to feel an interest in my country, and to be proud of my privileges as one of its citizens."

As he had in 1832, Legaré fell on his feet when he resigned his Brussels posting and sailed for Charleston. Immediately upon his arrival in August 1836 he found himself nominated for Congress on the Unionist ticket. In November he defeated the incumbent, a man with one of grandest political and social inheritances in Charleston, Henry Laurens Pinckney, who had fallen afoul of the powerful Calhoun. Like William John Grayson, who was defeated for reelection just as his friend was elected, Legaré was somewhat bemused by Congress, for all he enjoyed the social opportunities of Washington. The House of Representatives afforded him a fit venue for his most exalted flights of oratory. His speech of 13 October 1837 on the Sub-Treasury bill was a triumph of oratory but a disaster as a political gesture, for it infuriated Calhoun. Legaré was admired as a speechmaker by John Quincy Adams, but his towering ambition was not satisfied. In 1838 he stood again, defying conventional wisdom that the disfavor of Calhoun was the kiss of political death in South Carolina. In his reelection bid Congressman Legaré was defeated by one of his closest friends, Isaac Holmes; he took Holmes's victory as a betrayal. As he admitted afterward, Legaré was effectively defeated by himself, by a miscalculation of the odds against him that led the member for Charleston District to decline to go back to Charleston to campaign in person. Instead, he took a summer tour of the Hudson River Valley and Cape Cod.

Deeply wounded, and at a loss for what to do, Legaré returned to Charleston and turned again to the practice of law. He kept returning to his legal briefs, expecting in due course to be offered another plum position—and he always was. As a Broad Street lawyer, he finally began to make some money, much of which he lent to his mother and to his elder, and disastrously married, sister. He also returned to writing, penning three massive articles for the *New York Review* on Roman legislation, the constitutional history of Greece, and his hero among orators, Demosthenes. The high-water mark of his career at the bar was the celebrated lawsuit growing out of the sinking of the steamship *Pulaski, Pell and Wife v. The Executors of Ball,* which came to trial early in 1840. The case was complicated, with a great deal of money at stake, but also with sensational and pathetic elements that Legaré played for all they were worth. Legaré's team won; the oddity no one seems to have noticed is that he was acting against the executors of his own first cousin, Hugh Swinton Ball. With nothing to lose by it politically, he spent more time in the North, summering with the Ticknors on Cape Cod and exploring New York State and New England. Nursing his resentment against the city that had turned him out of office and severing local ties one by one, Legaré was

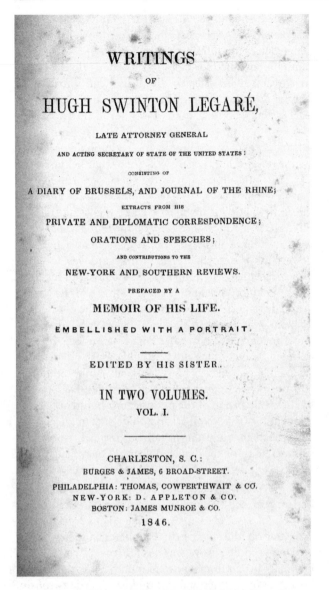

*Title page for the posthumously published edition of Legaré's*
*private and public writings (Thomas Cooper Library,*
*University of South Carolina)*

hinted through well-placed friends that a diplomatic posting to Europe might be most agreeable. In the event, on 11 September 1841, while he was watering at Newport, Legaré found himself nominated to be attorney general of the United States. The appointment furnished him with an excuse to make the final break with Charleston; he brought his mother, his unmarried sister, and the domestic servants to Washington and set up house there. The post of attorney general was then a part-time one, so Legaré carried on a private practice as well. During his second Washington period Legaré argued four cases before the Supreme Court as a private lawyer and eleven as attorney general. His record was impressive: he won ten of these fifteen cases.

By January 1843, Legaré, the one-time ghost-editor of the *Southern Review,* began ghosting for Secretary of State Daniel Webster. Now the politically isolated President Tyler's closest confidant, Legaré was, on Webster's formal resignation, appointed secretary of state ad interim on 5 May 1843, becoming perhaps the only man in American history to hold two cabinet portfolios simultaneously. The added burden was too much for his failing health. Reluctantly, he left his desk in mid June to join Tyler and the rest of the cabinet for a round of speechifying celebrating the dedication of the Bunker Hill Monument in Charlestown, Massachusetts. Taken ill soon after reaching his hotel, the acting secretary of state was moved to the nearby house of his old friend Ticknor. Here he calmly made his will, sorted his official papers for return to President Tyler, and, after three days of agony from the last of many intestinal blockages, died peacefully in the arms of his friend of a quarter century on 20 June 1843.

The corpus of Hugh Swinton Legaré's published writings is dwarfed by the many projects he did not complete. He was invited to write for the *North American Review* but never found time to prepare a piece for that exalted organ. His long-cherished ambition to prepare an edition of the Renaissance legal philosopher Heineccius died with him. His later writings were dashed off in the intervals between his political appointments and offices. There are not enough samples from his final decade to suggest whether his writing style might eventually have changed as radically as did his politics. Some of Legaré's best writing for the *Southern Review* comes in his long disapproving look at *Travels in North America, in the years 1827 and 1828* (1829), by a Scottish naval captain, Basil Hall. He may have met Hall at one of Petigru's celebrated Sunday evening dinners. Legaré hijacks the occasion of this 1829 book review to deliver a withering indictment of the inadequacies of American higher education. Correctly predicting the inevitable ascendancy of the American language, he anticipates some of Ralph Waldo Emerson's most striking ideas of

effecting an untidy divorce from Charleston. He campaigned in upstate New York for the Whig ticket, seemingly willing to do almost anything to get away from Charleston. His new political allegiance helped to stabilize a life with a deteriorating sense of direction.

Having served the Whigs effectively in the 1840 presidential contest, Legaré expected to be rewarded with an appointment. By December he had his eye on the attorney generalship, but President William Henry Harrison paid a debt to Henry Clay by appointing John J. Crittenden instead. The unexpected accession of John Tyler to the presidency when Harrison died one month after his inauguration gave Legaré another chance. This time he

the mid 1830s. He lacks Emerson's charm, but his thinking is clearer. The supercilious assessments of American society of yet another upper-class British tourist who, as Legaré describes in "Hall's Travels in North America," "went about sketching, scribbling, sneering, scolding to our very faces" lead Legaré in the *Southern Review* (November 1829) to the territory of Emerson's "The American Scholar" (1837) and "Self-Reliance" (1841): "we do defer too much to English criticism, and suffer ourselves at once to be governed and to be made unhappy by it. We have too much national vanity, and too little of the far nobler feeling of national pride. There can be no true greatness either in individuals or in multitudes without self-reliance." This review also includes Legaré's major discussion in print of "the peculiar domestic institutions of the Southern States." His defense of slavery is expectably legalistic, but he also characterizes it as a practical solution to a peculiar problem, reminding his readers that "all virtue is relative, and consists not in visions of ideal perfection, not in a puling and sickly sentimentalism, but in making the most of our situation, whatever it may be, for purposes of improvement and benevolence."

Legaré's massive two-part review in the *Southern Review* (May 1830, 1831) of Moore's edition of the *Letters and Journals of Lord Byron: With Notices of His Life* (1830), which runs to more than a hundred pages, is by far his most substantial exercise in literary criticism. It is also a moral inquest on the poet. He ranks Byron the third figure in English literature, inferior only to William Shakespeare and his revered John Milton. In these pages, more than in any other of his, the reader enjoys the spectacle of Legaré plucking his illustrations from the well-stocked shelves of his polyglot mind, swinging with assured ease from Sophocles to Horace to Dante to Voltaire. Between May 1830 and May 1831 Legaré changed his mind completely about Moore, if not about Byron. Pronouncing the first volume a "disappointment," he announced in the first sentence of his review of the second that it was "one of the most interesting books in the language." Legaré might, and evidently did, identify with many aspects of Byron's background and experience—both were melancholy aristocrats with mortifying physical disabilities, fatherless at an early age, raised by a Scottish mother. He writes from his own psychological perspective in observing of Byron: "His destiny was a cruel tantalism. He possessed signal advantages—but every blessing was dashed with bitterness, and the suffering from what was withheld was more than the enjoyment from what he possessed." This assessment is notable for an epigrammatical turn rare in Legaré's writings: "But Byron's only refuge from despair is in desperation." In the second review Legaré expresses his delight in Byron's letters and softens his

censure of Byron the man, contemplating him more in sorrow than in anger: "It is scarcely possible to read these letters and not feel disposed rather to deplore the fate, than rebrobate the conduct of the writer." He interrupts his review for a long discursus—long even by Legaré's standard—on the nature of Greek tragedy, liberally laced with quotations from Plato, before closing with an appreciation of *Manfred* (1817), which he pronounces Byron's masterpiece, again finding it chords his own anxieties, as it adumbrates "that dreariest of all solitudes, the utter loneliness of the blighted heart."

There is also a strong hint of sublimated autobiography in Legaré's 1828 review of the posthumously selected writings of the Charleston lawyer and literary dabbler William Crafts, which sounds the first note of disenchantment with the intellectual resources and aspirations of Charleston. The reviewer turns this look at Crafts—exactly ten years his senior—into a justification of his own protracted preparation for the practice of law, so different from that of Crafts, who was undone by "his suicidal indolence." The career of Crafts is a cautionary tale, for instead of endeavoring "to acquire knowledge of the law" by severe and unremitted study—the only price at which it can be had—he ridiculed those who did so, as mere plodders that had forfeited all claim to the reputation of men of genius." But at age thirty-one, Legaré was not much more successful than Crafts had been: he was in the legislature, and he had been elected to city council, but his literary output was even more meager than that of Crafts. He could boast only of a few printed orations. Many of the sentences he writes about this embarrassing book would later be applicable to Legaré himself: "We remember what he was, and what he was expected to become." He too was presented to posterity in the form of "remains" culled by a well-meaning but inept editor.

The "German Diaries," as retitled and reedited by O'Brien in his *All Clever Men, Who Make Their Way: Critical Discourse in the Old South* (1982), are the freshest, funniest, and most accessible pages of Legaré's prose. There is an unconscious comedy in the self-portrait of the peripatetic chargé d'affaires as a fussy hypochondriac tourist with cultural indigestion, exclaiming "I am tired of palaces" or suspiciously tasting unfamiliar food and trying to survive Berlin dinner parties without offending "my horror of all strangeness." With Schlegel, he is at last on equal terms intellectually—or at least philologically. He always notices pretty women, but he is seldom deeply excited by the landscapes through which he travels, only noting the occasional "impetuous, brawling stream." There is much musing on his reading; after all, reading was an important part of Legaré's every day for more than forty of his forty-six years. He throws off staccato literary judgments, despatching Samuel Johnson in seven words: "Dr. J. is a horribly bad writer." The "German Diaries" are most valuable for their detailed accounts of Legaré's visits to the famous in the German principalities, which tantalizingly furnish the menus of his conversational feasts, but not the taste of the talk. The entry on his visit to the Prussian foreign minister Johann Peter Friedrich Ancillon includes perhaps the most characteristic sentence in the thirty-page diary: "Then a discussion of Tacitus' Latinity." The German tours were really Legaré's debut as an intellectual.

In his reviews Legaré repeatedly expresses his preference for a plain style. His own style can scarcely be said to be plain, yet it is seldom pompous, never overelaborate, sometimes refreshingly acid. His points are always massively oversupported, however, and too often he strays from the subject in gargantuan digressions. Much of his prose seems to be positively gasping under the weight of the author's vast learning. Vernon Louis Parrington, in his *Main Currents in American Thought: An Interpretation of American Literature from the Beginnings to 1920* (1927), wryly exclaims, "How many outlandish authorities were contained in the huge inkwell on his desk it is idle to conjecture." One never penetrates the carapace of his scholarship; Legaré's learning was a form of insulation in life, and it has proved so in death as well.

It is hard to think of an antebellum intellectual who was less interested in religion. In Swinton and Legaré, this John's Island native inherited two strands of Calvinism. He was more a Swinton than a Legaré, an agnostic Calvinist who retained the outlook without the theology, the tone without the substance. His was the most Scottish mind among the major figures of the mid-nineteenth-century United States. Throughout his life the Scottish influence was more important than has been acknowledged—in his family heritage, in mentors such as King, in his close reading of Scottish Common Sense philosophy, and in the lingering effects of his Edinburgh education, even in his "last attachment" to a half-Scottish noblewoman. A great legal scholar who awed the learned Justice Joseph Story, he was in effect a Scottish advocate manqué, a votary of the civil law that did not exist in the United States.

A lonely man made lonelier by his learning, he endured intense intellectual isolation in Charleston, especially after the loss through their deaths of sparring partners such as Thomas Smith Grimké. Yet, paradoxically, Legaré, happy in the world of ideas, happiest strolling the shady lanes of philology or Renaissance legal theory, was also excited, at least latterly, by politics—and, after September 1841, by real political power. His scholars have been too ready to dismiss Legaré as an indifferent or even incompetent politician. He actually learned something from his bitter defeat in 1838;

he never made himself so vulnerable again, nor did he ever make such an elementary miscalculation.

He possessed that talent rare in a conservative politician, an ability to reinvent himself. O'Brien supposes that "the Legaré of 1830 would have been appalled at the Legaré of 1840, in and coping with the Agora of Harrison's Whig democracy." If he had stood for the highest office in 1844, as many in the spring of 1843 already expected him to do, he would have campaigned in a different manner. He was after all a magnificent orator, who showed in *Pell v. Ball* that he could play adroitly to the galleries. Legaré seems never to have been comfortable with the degree of popular persuasion required of an American politician of his day, yet he died on a cabinet public-relations jaunt. No one who knew him well ever accused Legaré of having the common touch, but he took to the stump with gusto in 1840. As perhaps the only Southern politician who was at the time widely trusted and respected in the North, he might have been able, if not to reconcile North and South, at least to postpone their separation. In his last years he found a new ability to beat political barbs into ploughshares. He probably died before receiving the letter from Calhoun, written from Calhoun's South Carolina plantation on 7 June 1843, in which the overbearing senator ended a routine request with a sprig of olive: "I avail myself of the occasion, to express the hope, that your temporary appointment to the State Department may become, permanent, if that post should be prefered [*sic*] by you to that of Attorney General."

Legaré's career never advanced by a clear trajectory; it is full of embarrassing pauses and unexpected leaps. Often changes of direction were imposed on him by an engineered appointment, for example, or an unsought election. For much of his life Legaré filled the shoes of literally or politically dead men. Twice he was unexpectedly elected to office; twice he was surprisingly defeated for reelection. Both an under- and an overachiever, he never found the proper medium that would involve all of his learning, nor the ideal appointive or elective office. After his extended honeymoon with Charleston in the 1820s, he never found another place in which he felt entirely at home. His entire life may be viewed as a preparation for service on the U.S. Supreme Court, a position to which he probably would have risen had he lived a few years longer. He went much further in politics than a latter-day intellectual of his weight might have been expected to do. He had many opportunities to retire to the groves of academe, but he spurned all offers of college professorships and presidencies, including invitations to head the state colleges of South Carolina and Kentucky.

Buried first in the Ticknor family vault and then in Mount Auburn Cemetery in Cambridge, Hugh Swinton Legaré was brought in 1858 and reburied in Magnolia Cemetery under a great deal of marble. This monumental tribute perhaps indicates the extent to which he was perceived as marmoreal in his own day. O'Brien's excellent attempt in *A Character of Hugh Legaré* to liberate the man from the marble is still just that. Legaré always saw himself as a personage and maintained his reticence in his writings, systematically filtering out personality, except in some of the intimate letters, which, like those of his semi-hero Byron, give a flavor of what his brilliant talk must have been like. His letters collected in the two-volume *Writings of Hugh Swinton Legaré, Late Attorney General and Acting Secretary of State of the United States* (1845–1846) are certainly deficient in charm, but they were bowdlerized by a doting but prudish sister, Mary S. Legaré. O'Brien complains that "his *Writings* contain a bare and bizarre sampling of his correspondence." The best hope for a revival of interest in Legaré would appear to be an edition of his letters, which would give a far better sense than scattered reviews and articles of the multiple layers of the man's acquaintance and the variety of his intellectual and political interests.

Legaré loved learning for its own sake, and he apparently never thought of collecting his writings. The two volumes of his writings are also a monument, a sort of literary inurnment stiffening further what was already decidedly stiff. Paul Hamilton Hayne, in "Hugh Swinton Legaré," from a January 1870 issue of the *Southern Review,* savaged the *Writings of Hugh Swinton Legaré* as "simply *execrable*" and "a species of sepulcher in which the bright genius of Legaré lies buried." Even in the 1870s Hayne could not interest anyone in a more representative edition of Legaré's writings. As writer, as politician, as lawyer, Legaré is several of the great might-have-beens of nineteenth-century America. His friend and first biographer, Edward W. Johnston, wonders "how much, in the full twenty years of life due, he would have achieved . . . useful to his times and memorable to others." The life of this real-life counterpart of George Eliot's Casaubon in *Middlemarch* (1871–1872) was one of preparation for works that were not written, offices that he did not live to hold. Hugh Swinton Legaré's was an unfinished life, and any account of it must partake of that incompleteness.

## Biographies:
W. C. Preston, *Eulogy on Hugh Swinton Legaré* (Charleston, S.C., 1843);

Edward W. Johnston, "Biographical Notice," in *Writings of Hugh Swinton Legaré, Late Attorney General and Acting Secretary of State of the United States,* 2 volumes, edited by Mary S. Legaré (Charleston, S.C.: Burges & James / Philadelphia: Cowperthwait / New York: Appleton / Boston: Munroe, 1845–1846), I: v–lxxii;

Paul Hamilton Hayne, *Lives of Robert Young Hayne and Hugh Swinton Legaré* (Charleston, S.C.: Walker, Evans & Cogswell, 1878);

Linda Rhea, *Hugh Swinton Legaré: A Charleston Intellectual* (Chapel Hill: University of North Carolina Press, 1934);

Michael O'Brien, *A Character of Hugh Legaré* (Knoxville: University of Tennessee Press, 1985).

## References:
Jay B. Hubbell, "Hugh Swinton Legaré," in his *The South in American Literature, 1607–1900* (Durham: Duke University Press, 1954), pp. 263–274, 945–946;

Michael O'Brien, "Politics, Romanticism and Hugh Legaré: 'The Fondness of Diasppointed Love,'" in *Intellectual Life in Antebellum Charleston,* edited by O'Brien and David Moltke-Hansen (Knoxville: University of Tennessee Press, 1986), pp. 123–151;

Edd Winfield Parks, "Hugh Swinton Legaré: Humanist," in his *Ante-Bellum Southern Literary Critics* (Athens: University of Georgia Press, 1962), pp. 23–50, 268–276;

Parks, "Legaré and Grayson: Types of Classical Influence on Criticism in the Old South," in his *Segments of Southern Thought* (Athens: University of Georgia Press, 1938), pp. 156–171;

Vernon Louis Parrington, "Hugh Swinton Legaré: Charleston Intellectual," in his *Main Currents in American Thought: An Interpretation of American Literature from the Beginnings to 1920,* volume 2 (New York: Harcourt, Brace, 1927), pp. 114–124;

John R. Welsh, "Southern Literary Magazines, IV: An Early Pioneer: Legaré's *Southern Review," Southern Literary Journal,* 3 (Spring 1971): 79–97.

## Papers:
Hugh Swinton Legaré's papers are held at the South Caroliniana Library, University of South Carolina, Columbia; National Archives; Library of Congress; Southern Historical Collection, University of North Carolina, Chapel Hill; South Carolina State Archives, Columbia; and the Perkins Library, Duke University.

# James Mathewes Legaré

*(26 November 1823 – 30 May 1859)*

C. P. Seabrook Wilkinson
*College of Charleston*

See also the Legaré entry in *DLB 3: Antebellum Writers in New York and the South.*

BOOK: *Orta-Undis, and Other Poems* (Boston: Ticknor, 1848).

OTHER: "The Collected Poems of James M. Legaré," in *That Ambitious Mr. Legaré,* by Curtis Carroll Davis (Columbia: University of South Carolina Press, 1971), pp. 150–313.

SELECTED PERIODICAL PUBLICATIONS–
UNCOLLECTED: "Going to Texas," *Southern and Western Monthly Magazine and Review,* 2 (December 1845): 396–402;

"Pedro de Padilh," *Graham's Monthly Magazine,* 37 (August 1850): 92–97; (September 1850): 144–148; (November 1850): 305–310; (December 1850): 372–381;

"Ninety Days," *Graham's Monthly Magazine,* 38 (January 1851): 54–61; (February 1851): 78–87;

"Deux Oies, Vertes," *Graham's Monthly Magazine,* 38 (April 1851): 304–323;

"The Lame Girl," *Sartain's Union Magazine,* 9 (August 1851): 106–114;

"Miss Peck's Friend: A Novel in Ten Chapters," *Putnam's Monthly Magazine,* 1 (May 1853): 539–546; (June 1853): 618–629; 2 (July 1853): 45–60;

"Fleur de Sillery," *Knickerbocker Magazine,* 44 (October 1854): 390–400; (November 1854): 494–503;

"Cap-and-Bells," *Harper's Magazine,* 27 (November 1863): 775–785; 28 (December 1863): 36–50; (January 1864): 184–192.

James Mathewes Legaré was born into a prominent family in a city–Charleston, South Carolina– where birth has always been a major consideration, but his attitude toward that advantage, as toward much about his native city, was always ambivalent. Although there was a certain stature accorded to any member of the Legaré (pronounced *luh-gree*) family, the branch to

*James Mathewes Legaré, circa 1855 (engraving by Capewell and Kimmel; from* The Knickerbocker Gallery *[New York: Hueston, 1855])*

which this poet belonged was the least prosperous and least well-connected one. James Legaré was fifth in descent from the original Huguenot immigrant. As his own full name and that of his father's third cousin, Attorney General Hugh Swinton Legaré, indicate, after five or six generations in the United States the French blood had been much diluted; indeed, all of Legaré's direct male ancestors after the immigrant Solomon L'Egaré had married women of English descent.

The poet's father, John Doughty Legaré, married his second cousin Mary Doughty Mathewes. The first of their three children was born in Charleston on 26 November 1823 and named for his maternal grandfather, a local factor. The John D. Legarés probably lived with James Mathewes for the early years of their marriage; not until 1835 does John Legaré have his own address in the city directory. John Legaré changed occupations with bewildering frequency—one of the ways in which his son resembled him. A ne'er-do-well who fretted the fringes of politics, retail, agriculture, and journalism, John Legaré twice served as editor of the *Southern Agriculturalist,* the periodical the Agricultural Society of South Carolina established in 1828. Like his son, John Legaré was drawn to scientific experiments, in his case cross-breeding livestock, fruits, and vegetables. In a radical change of direction, John Legaré ran a spa hotel at the Grey Sulphur Springs in southwestern Virginia for the first half of 1834, then returned to Charleston to another round of unsuccessful commercial enterprises, including an agricultural and horticultural "Repository."

Records of the grammar school then run by the College of Charleston indicate only that James Legaré left in 1832. It is not known where he completed his preparation for college, but he was evidently sufficiently well prepared to enter as an upperclassman. Fortunately for the financially feckless John Legaré, the city council reconstituted the local college as the municipal College of Charleston in 1837, just in time for his elder son to get a good college education at a much reduced rate. James Legaré probably matriculated in 1840; the records for the period just after reorganization are incomplete. It was a small college, but with high standards and a talented intake: among Legaré's contemporaries were young men who later won renown in journalism, literature, politics, and diplomacy—Augustin L. Taveau, James D. B. DeBow, William Henry Trescot, and William Porcher Miles, who was valedictorian of Legaré's class of 1842.

Immediately upon graduation on 22 February, Legaré embarked on a course unusual for a Charlestonian of his time: he went on to another college for further study, not of medicine or law, but of languages and literature. On 12 March 1842 he was enrolled at St. Mary's College in Baltimore. He remained there for sixteen months, pursuing a linguistically challenging course of study that included French, German, Spanish, and Greek, as well as the Latin in which he was already proficient. In addition to his crowded academic schedule Legaré took up painting and began to write verses with some success. Perhaps the most significant event in Legaré's life during his time in Baltimore was the sudden death of Hugh Swinton Legaré on 20 June 1843, which elicited from his young kinsman the first of his poems to show more than mere genteel facility. The lure of extracurricular activities proved too strong for the easily distracted young man, for he did not graduate at commencement in July 1843, receiving instead a

"1st Premium of diligence" for his oil painting and an honorary certificate for his academic work. Failure to follow through became one of the leitmotifs of Legaré's short life.

Legaré returned to Charleston in late July 1843 with no graduate degree and no clear career plans but with a great deal of enthusiasm for writing verses and painting landscapes in oils. He also brought home the makings of an elaborate hoax, which first brought him, if not fame, a whiff of notoriety. Early in March 1844 a workman at a property on Anson Street that had formerly belonged to the Legaré family dug up a small iron box, dated 1682, which contained a parchment family tree, written in Latin and elaborately blazoned, taking the Legaré family back to their noble origins in 912 A.D. The *Charleston Courier* reported this "interesting discovery" on 15 March. In an era of ingenious hoaxes and stories about hoaxes, notably those by one of Legaré's favorite living writers, Edgar Allan Poe, the discovery of the Legaré parchment was taken up by newspapers in Boston and Baltimore. This elaborate genealogical spoof, carefully plotted in Baltimore, where he purchased the parchment and had the iron box made, is a defining incident of Legaré's life, combining as it does his artistic flair, his linguistic skill, his turn for writing improbable fiction, and his interest in history. Most of all it illustrates how much of his ingenuity was misspent, deflected into the arcane or trivial. The bogus genealogy shows a Janus-faced approach to being a Legaré: he was glad of the advantages conferred, but also impatient of the pretensions of his wealthier and haughtier relations, such as Colonel James C. W. Legaré, who was furious when he discovered that the genealogy was a hoax. Legaré's compulsion to debunk aristocratic pretensions fuels the satirical thrusts of his later fictions published in magazine form, in which he ridicules the most exalted local families, turning august Rutledges into Rutridges.

Legaré began exhibiting his paintings and publishing verses in minor periodicals such as *The Rambler*. He also embarked on the study of law in a desultory fashion in the office of a fellow Huguenot, James Louis Petigru, who was the most eminent attorney in Charleston and who had been a close friend of Hugh Swinton Legaré. Petigru's law office turned out more prominent poets than lawyers; both Paul Hamilton Hayne and Henry Timrod also studied with him. Legaré made more headway as writer and painter than in his professional preparations. He had made measurable progress when no less an editor than William Gilmore Simms included his most ambitious early poem, "Du Saye," in his gift miscellany, *The Charleston Book,* in November 1844. By May 1845 Legaré had accumulated enough work to consider publishing a volume. He approached

*Legaré's house in Aiken, South Carolina*

Simms, who annotated the advice-seeking letter with the comment "A young writer of considerable talent." Just as things were going well for him artistically (if nowhere financially), however, Legaré's health began to fail. In 1844 throat problems and exhaustion obliged him to spend the summer in the mountains of north Georgia. He enjoyed the scenery but did not regain his strength; before winter was over it was clear that he was suffering from tuberculosis. He fought the disease for fourteen years of increasingly precarious life.

In the first half of 1846, partly with Legaré's health in mind—the long, humid Charleston summer was merciless to pulmonary complaints—and partly in response to further financial reverses, the entire family of five moved to the small resort village of Aiken, more than a hundred miles away in the Sand Hills near the Savannah River. At first Charleston remained home, and the family viewed their relocation as a temporary exile: Legaré wrote to Rufus W. Griswold on 31 May 1846 from Aiken that "we cannot consider it a home." The Legarés' outlook gradually changed. For a time the higher elevation and drier climate arrested the progress of Legaré's disease. His father declared bankruptcy and accepted a government appointment, the postmastership of the village, in which he was succeeded briefly by his elder son in 1852. Legaré supported himself by writing prose and verse for a variety of periodicals, by painting, and—

least successfully—by starting a finishing school for young ladies. In 1847 a periodical project, the "Journal of Literature: European and American," was stillborn.

Legaré continued to publish his verse in periodicals, collecting his contributions in 1848 in his first and only volume, which bears the inaccessible title *Orta-Undis, and Other Poems*. The prominent Boston firm of Ticknor printed 500 copies and sent 150 of them to John Russell, the leading bookseller in Charleston. The historian A. S. Salley, according to the critic Curtis Carroll Davis, reported finding more than 100 of these copies still unsold in a secondhand bookstore in Charleston around 1900. If the public ignored the little volume, major periodicals did review it: fourteen notices, most of them at least mildly favorable, some positively enthusiastic, were published between April 1848 and October 1849 in venues ranging from Boston to New Orleans. By May 1849 the volume had earned only $23.59 for its author, who was in desperate need of funds. Legaré turned to fiction, with better financial but with vastly inferior artistic success.

After a leisurely courtship Legaré married a young lady with literary leanings from nearby Augusta, Georgia, Ann C. Andrews, on 20 March 1850. The newlyweds settled into a three-room cottage on the grounds of the senior Legaré's home and made of it the sort of impossibly pretty bower in which Legaré's love poetry abounds. In this abode, christened "Turtle-Dovey," the childless couple doted over a series of exotic pets, including a mockingbird whose cage dominated the sitting-room. This room also featured a fountain, for which Legaré rigged up a power device to keep the water flowing. Increasingly he frittered his dwindling energies on such inconsequential ingenuity. At the same time he was conducting a long-distance literary wooing of the most successful poet in the country, Henry Wadsworth Longfellow. His correspondence with Longfellow was of enormous importance to the intellectually isolated Legaré; at one stage the audacious younger man suggested that they collaborate.

The year of his marriage was Legaré's busiest as a writer of fiction. With some overlaps, he wrote poetry first, then fiction, then abandoned both to pursue his scientific interests. Essentially he had given up poetry by 1850, with one stray poem, "The Lighthouse," following around 1856. Legaré became fascinated with mechanical invention about 1847. Eventually this new interest displaced his writing and painting altogether. By 1852 he had set up a laboratory, where he pursued his idée fixe, an air-powered engine. In the rough order of their discovery, his inventions were a plastic fiber he called "plastic cotton"; an ivory-frame composition to replace the glue-and-whiting composition used by frame-makers; an encaustic tile for floors and roofs; a light, cushionless reading chair; and a cheap, waterproof glazier's putty. Legaré fashioned pieces of elaborate and unattractive furniture out of plastic cotton, some of which won first prize in the "household furniture" category of the Charleston Industrial Fair of 1856. In the following year a whole section of the fair was devoted to Legaré's inventions, but none of them achieved any commercial success. The Panic of 1857 led to the suspension of apparently promising negotiations with a New York firm for production of his ivory-frame composition.

Legaré's poetic output was not large: in *That Ambitious Mr. Legaré: The Life of James M. Legaré of South Carolina, Including a Collected Edition of His Verse* (1971) Curtis Carroll Davis collected forty-nine poems comprising about 130 pages. There is little, if any, development: the least forgotten of his poems, "To a Lily," dates from 1845. More than half of his output consists of poems to or about idealized women. The next largest group celebrates nature, in panorama ("Toccoa") or in close-up ("To a Lily"); perhaps his best poems are those in the latter category. He also wrote moralizing tales in verse; one historical verse tale, "Du Saye"; a solitary elegy for his kinsman the attorney general; and "Thanatokallos," a reply to the most celebrated poem by William Cullen Bryant, "Thanatopsis" (1817). His romantic and nature categories frequently overlap, as he likes to paint his ladies in rural landscapes. He adopts the female point of

view in "The Hemlocks," in which, as even in his earliest effusions, art is seen as the vehicle of romantic conquest. He does an extraordinary amount of walking in his poems—as much as his Concord contemporary Ellery Channing, whom he also resembles in his arboreal passion.

As a poet Legaré had the courage of his idiosyncracy, as in the engaging battiness of "Georgia," which is really nonsensical. Already in "Du Saye" (originally published in 1844) he displays a healthy tendency not to meet expectations: the romantic couple are both dead by the end of the tale. Long before Ezra Pound, he peppers his texts with foreign words and phrases. Rather vain of his linguistic skills, Legaré uses Latin not merely in titles such as "Loquitur Diana," but for the entire text of the title poem of the volume. Even more strikingly, in the "Woman of Canaan" four of the six stanzas end in New Testament Greek. A facile rhymester, Legaré likes to flaunt his facility, as in the octosyllabic triple rhymes of "Janette"; yet, sometimes he has the wisdom not to rhyme at all, or risks off-rhyme, as with "pines" and "nuns" in "The Book of Nature." In "The Welcome Rain" there is an interesting two-foot start to the stanzas:

But now I know,
How over sodden graves meek blossoms blow,
Luxuriant the more for what's below.

He indulges in an amount of metrical experimentation unusual for his day, making bold use of an irregular, hemistich-like short line in "Last Gift." The eleven-syllable bias to the lines in "Thanatokallos" makes for a sort of loosened blank verse, rendering the tone conversational, for all heavy moralizing of the message.

Legaré's theology is far more orthodox than his prosody; his poetry suffers greatly from a tendency to offer religious consolations. His piety, however sincere, is too often in the foreground for the good of his poems: "And thou shalt clearly then perceive / That God did only make thee grieve / More elevated faith to leave." Even in "Ornithologoi," one of his best poems, he preaches "For God loves all, and does not give / Life only, but the means to live." Jesus turns up at odd junctures, as in the final lines of "The Trouvére's Rose." Legaré often falters or retreats into pious clichés at the close of his poems, as when in "Janette" he prays, "GOD grant us all our sins to know."

The sound of Legaré's poems is quite distinctive. Almost all of his lyrics attest the acuteness of his ear. One of his gifts as a poet is an ability, at least occasionally, to transform the trite into something memorable: "The path still winds, the brook descends, / The skies are bright as then they were. / My Amy is the only leaf / In all that forest sear." He has a good rate of success in

of birds, some of which he merely describes, some of which he anthropomorphizes and allows to speak at length. In the encounter of raven and lamb, narrated by the former, startling realism breaks in on the pastoral territory reminiscent of William Wordsworth:

> Down its white nostril bubbled red
> A gush of blood; ere life had fled,
> My beak was buried in its eyes,
> Turned tearfully upon the skies—
> Strong grew my croak, as weak its cries.

The poem is not for the squeamish: "In either hand around he slings / An anguished trunk with panting wings, / Then off the headless carcass flings." Sentimental passages lauding the lady's rescue of nestlings mingle with the gore. While this poem is particularly complex in its shifts of tone and voice, Legaré could also write with a winning simplicity, notably in what is apparently his last poem, "The Lighthouse." Its concluding stanza is at once neatly turned and from the heart:

> Give, O blind world, your loud applause
> To men renowned through blood and tears—
> 'Twas not for *that* he gave his life
> And these are not among his peers.

This poem is a fit conclusion to Legaré's dozen years of poetic activity, not least in its evocation of one who keeps to his post, who dies bravely striving—as, with his own failing health in latter years, did Legaré.

Legaré completed seventeen stories, ranging in length from a one-page sketch to two ten-chapter novellas. Davis, the only close student of Legaré's fiction to date, recognized six roughly chronological genres: Western stories, humor, historical romance, adventure romance, domestic sentimentalism, and satire. Legaré sets his stories in locations he never visited, but settings and plots are equally unrealistic. Reminiscent of William Makepeace Thackeray but with a Southern accent, the satire is the most interesting, if not perhaps the most successful, of his fictional genres. Some of his stories appear to have been quarried from unfinished novels. Two of the weakest, "The New Aria" and "The Lame Girl," won best story prizes from their respective periodicals, *Richards Weekly Gazette* and *Sartain's Union Magazine*. For all his tales read as though they were spun out without premeditation, the writing of fiction did not come easily to him. He complained in a 22 May 1850 letter to John R. Thompson, editor of the *Southern Literary Messenger:* "I cannot write more (in my miserably slow way—rewriting whole pages over and over, and making them often worse than at first!) . . ." The stories fill columns, and presumably they paid enough to fill his larder, but they did little more then, and they do nothing for the

*A "plastic cotton" hall tree designed and fabricated by Legaré (Charleston Museum, Charleston, South Carolina)*

forcing blossoms from the barren soil of cliché, but there is more grace than force in his lyrics. In "Loquitur Diana" the commonplace is gilded in one of the poet's many descriptions of moonlight: "And saw in eddies of the river / Thy arrows fall and shiver." In "Last Gift" he props the tired timbers of the theme of conferring immortality through art.

In "Ornithologoi," at 336 lines Legaré's longest poem, he begins with his usual image of a lovely lady in a lush landscape but then turns his attention to a variety

modern reader. It is impossible to take seriously characters with names like "Miss von Waddlevurst" or the Gossamer family—a coinage perhaps unconsciously ironic, for his characters are flimsy as gossamer. There is no real intercourse between Legaré's fictions and his life; the tales are escapist as much for him as for his genteel lady readers. Yet, in "Cap-and-Bells" (*Harper's Magazine,* November 1863) he exclaims impatiently, "What fools we are to cry over sham troubles when we have so many of our own." This tale's arresting character, an American heiress who wrecks on the reefs of the European aristocracy, is a remote anticipation of Henry James's Baroness Munster in *The Europeans* (1878).

Removal from Charleston changed the whole complexion of Legaré's fledgling literary career. It perhaps contributed to his originality and taste for technical experimentation and it certainly gave him different landscapes to paint in oils and verse, but it also removed him from fellowship with other artists, from the congenial circles and genial criticism of Russell's Bookstore. There was a literary society in Aiken, in which Legaré was active, but it could scarcely compare with the intellectual offerings of Charleston. Even in his small village Legaré was too much insulated by his doting wife and adoring parents. At this period most Legarés married cousins more or less close, or at least kept within the pale of the planter aristocracy. Legaré's marriage to an Augusta girl with no Lowcountry connections helped to seal the break with his native city and some of its ways. When he did visit his birthplace in the 1850s, it was in connection with exhibitions of paintings or of new fire-resistant roof tiles.

As he was dying, Legaré continued to seek funding for his scientific experiments. His last letter, written a fortnight before his death, is to former senator James Henry Hammond, imploring at great length for financial sponsorship of the air-engine, which he continued to hope might bring success to a life chiefly rich thus far in unfulfilled promise. During the last decade of his life Legaré became an increasingly convinced Episcopalian. At his death he was senior warden of the local church, St. Thaddeus, in whose churchyard he was buried the day after his death on 30 May 1859.

Legaré was too ethereal to be a professional literary man in the South of his day; he nursed the satirical impulse but lacked the stiletto wit necessary to the writing of effective satire. Pursuing the chimera of his air-engine, he turned aside from the one path in which he might have won lasting fame. Paradoxically, he tried hard to be popular in his fiction while seemingly striving in precisely the opposite direction in his poetry, with polyglot vocabulary and Latin titles. If his poems are never tedious, his stories are invariably so. In his fiction he demonstrates no

talent to animate his industry, whereas in the poetry he went his own way; he had things to say and found novel ways in which to say them.

Jack of too many genres, amateur of all arts and professional of none, Legaré undoubtedly dissipated his energies in too many directions. It is, however, doubtful whether he could ever have turned all of his aptitudes to the service of poetry; the nervous energy and capriciousness that make his verse interesting also undermined his commitment to letters. The poems are often excessively tender, but they are seldom silly. Some of the most arresting lines in antebellum poetry are to be found in Legaré's poems, as, for example, "Down in the meadows of the heart" in "The Reaper." He was a man with an amateur's commitment in most of his endeavors who lacked the independent means of a Charleston gentleman. As with his admired kinsman Hugh Swinton Legaré, any attempt to measure his achievement wakes a strong sense of unrealized possibilities. His final decade was spent in increasingly bizarre byways—the plastic-cotton furniture, the double steam engine—far removed from poetry. There is in Legaré's best poetry an engaging quirkiness, coupled with a surprising sharpness, a sense of Nature "red in tooth and claw" and at the same time lyrically lush, pretty but potentially deadly. The high incidence in his work of the unexpected—in sentiment, in detail, in phrasing, in stanza-form, in prosody—makes James Mathewes Legaré among the freshest of all antebellum poets, South or North.

**Biography:**

Curtis Carroll Davis, *That Ambitious Mr. Legaré: The Life of James M. Legaré of South Carolina, Including a Collected Edition of His Verse* (Columbia: University of South Carolina Press, 1971).

**References:**

Curtis Carroll Davis, "Fops, Frenchmen, Hidalgos, and Aztecs: Being a Survey of the Prose Fiction of J. M. Legaré of South Carolina (1823–1859)," *North Carolina Historical Review,* 30 (October 1950): 524–560;

Davis, "The Several-Sided James Mathewes Legaré: Poet," *Transactions of the Huguenot Society of South Carolina,* 57 (1952): 5–12.

**Papers:**

James Mathewes Legaré's library is preserved in the collection of his younger brother Joseph John Legaré in the Charleston Library Society. His letters are widely scattered; the largest and most important collection of them is among the Henry Wadsworth Longfellow Papers at Harvard.

# Henry Clay Lewis

## (26 June 1825 – 5 August 1850)

Jennings R. Mace

*Eastern Kentucky University*

See also the Lewis entry in *DLB 3: Antebellum Writers in New York and the South.*

BOOK: *Odd Leaves from the Life of a Louisiana "Swamp Doctor,"* as Madison Tensas (Philadelphia: Hart, 1850).

Henry Clay Lewis is one of the most distinctive and intriguing of those writers classified as humorists of the Old Southwest. He is remembered as the creator of Madison Tensas, M.D., the Louisiana "Swamp Doctor." The Southwestern humorists, prominent among them Augustus Baldwin Longstreet, Johnson Jones Hooper, and, perhaps the best-known, George Washington Harris, portrayed frontier regions often characterized by raw humor, violence, and dialect. Lewis clearly followed that tradition, but there is in his work an uncommon pushing of the boundaries of what is humorous. Indeed, many of his sketches deal with subject matter so gruesome that the reader is left to question the source of the laughter evoked.

The publication of *Odd Leaves from the Life of a Louisiana "Swamp Doctor"* (1850) established his reputation as one of the most-popular Southwestern humorists, though the author's identity was unknown. The promise obvious in the collection was cut short when Lewis drowned in 1850. In the twenty-five years of his life he climbed from field hand to doctor and left behind a collection of vivid sketches.

Lewis, whose ancestors were French and Italian Jews, was born in Charleston, South Carolina, on 26 June 1825, the seventh child of David and Rachel Solomon Lewis. According to some accounts, David Lewis came to the United States in 1777 with the Marquis de Lafayette and fought in the Revolutionary War. Around 1829 the Lewises moved to Cincinnati, where Rachel Lewis died in 1831. Shortly after her death Henry Lewis was sent to live with an older, married brother, Alexander. From this point on, Lewis's life followed a varied and somewhat tumultuous path. If the autobiographical elements in his sketches from *Odd Leaves from the Life of a Louisiana "Swamp Doctor,"* primarily among them "My Early Life," are any indication, his life with his brother was unpleasant and eventually led him to escape to the Ohio River at age ten. No doubt the year or so he spent on steamboats provided a rich source for later sketches. Apparently Lewis worked at a variety of shipboard jobs until he ended up on a boat traveling the Yazoo River between Vicksburg and Manchester–later named Yazoo City–Mississippi.

In Manchester, Lewis was reunited with another brother, Joseph, who was a successful merchant there. With the prospect of receiving an education supported by Joseph, Lewis gave up the river and settled with his brother. The panic of 1837 wiped out Joseph's finances, however, and Lewis found himself at work in the cotton fields for five years. This reversal of fortune was one of several that followed Lewis throughout his life. Having missed an opportunity to become a printer's apprentice, in 1842 he was finally placed as an apprentice to Washington Dorsey, a physician. In October 1844 Lewis left Yazoo City for the Louisville Medical Institute in Louisville, Kentucky, perhaps one of the best medical schools in the South and certainly boasting a distinguished faculty.

From a literary standpoint, one of the most important events in Lewis's life occurred during the summer of his first year of medical school. The 16 August 1845 issue of the *Spirit of the Times,* the premier sporting journal of the day, printed his "Cupping on the Sternum," which he submitted under the pseudonym "Yazoo." This story of a hapless medical apprentice was a forerunner of the sketches later related by Madison Tensas in *Odd Leaves from the Life of a Louisiana "Swamp Doctor,"* though this particular sketch did not appear there.

While Lewis was back at Louisville for his second term in October 1845, Dorsey died. The death was a loss to Lewis in several ways, since he had a deep regard for his mentor and he anticipated Dorsey's help in establishing a practice after he earned his M.D. In March 1846, at age twenty, Lewis completed requirements for his M.D. and returned to Yazoo City to begin a practice. Competition for cases forced him to accept a practice in remote Madison Parish, Louisiana. Once established on the Tensas River in Madison Parish, Lewis began building a profitable practice and gained some of the social prominence he seemed to crave. Here he came face-to-face with the frontier character he vividly portrayed in later sketches.

In addition to financial success and an established place in the community, Lewis also experienced literary success. Five of his sketches were published in the *Spirit of the Times*, all under the name "Tensas." William T. Porter, editor of the *Spirit of the Times*, recognized in him a writer of some talent and took time to suggest improvements in Lewis's sketches. His literary fortunes took another turn in May 1847 when "A Leaf from the Life of a 'Swamp Doctor'" appeared in the magazine. This sketch marks his first use of the term "Swamp Doctor." By the end of 1848 he appears to have had the idea of a collected series of sketches to be published in book form.

By early 1849 Lewis was living in Richmond, Louisiana, an environment quite unlike the rough existence on the Tensas. Here he entered a partnership with Dr. George Shadburne and mingled with the most influential residents of Richmond. Though the exact reason is uncertain—politics, alcoholic high spirits, or Lewis's admittedly short temper are the most likely possibilities—Lewis appeared before the Richmond court on charges of assault and battery.

In March 1850, after several delays, A. Hart of Philadelphia published *Odd Leaves from the Life of a Louisiana "Swamp Doctor,"* which features the most fully developed portrayal of the persona "Madison Lewis." Lewis, though a young man, presents Madison as an old "Swamp Doctor" who recounts his experiences as a young medical student and budding doctor. Of course, the character of the young doctor was much closer to the actual age of the author. For this reason it is tempting to consider some of the sketches in an autobiographical light. Indeed, many of the facts known about Lewis's life—his struggles as a young man, his medical studies, his life in Louisiana—are reflected in his tales.

The publication of Lewis's book was closely followed by a cholera epidemic that ran through the parish in the summer of 1850. On 5 August 1850 Lewis, who had been treating patients, drowned while trying to ford a flooded bayou near Richmond. Apparently his horse became tangled in submerged willow branches and took the bachelor doctor, who could not swim, to his death. By the time of his death he had amassed the significant estate Madison Tensas sought.

Though his output was modest, Lewis's *Odd Leaves from the Life of a Louisiana "Swamp Doctor"* remains one of the best collections of sketches written by a Southwestern humorist and assures him a place in American literature. The best source for biographical information about Lewis's life is John Q. Anderson's *Louisiana Swamp Doctor: The Life and Writings of Henry Clay Lewis, Alias "Madison Tensas, M.D."* (1962). Recent examinations of his work also reveal that he was much more than merely a humorist. His edgy flirting with the boundaries of what is humorous makes him intriguing and distinctive. The tales included in *Odd Leaves from the Life of a Louisiana "Swamp Doctor"* provide a spectrum of the types of Southwestern humor sketches, ranging from traditional subjects, to those specific to the medical profession, to subjects distinct from all of Southwestern humor. In terms of traditional tales, Lewis's "A Tight Race Considering" recounts a wild horse race between a friend's mother and the local parson. By the end of the race both contestants have been stripped of their clothes and end up naked in the meetinghouse. "A Rattlesnake on a Steamboat" deals with a boasting foreigner, in this case an English sailor, who proclaims his fearlessness in the face of various serpents. The appearance of a real rattlesnake, brought on board by the young doctor, makes the sailor jump overboard. One of Lewis's most popular tales, "The Indefatigable Bear-Hunter," is part of a long line of Southwestern stories about bear hunters, the most famous of them all being Thomas Bangs Thorpe's "The Big Bear of Arkansas" (1841), a sketch mentioned in Lewis's tale. Lewis's bear hunter, Mik-hoo-tah, is obsessed with hunting and the place in history his hunting exploits might earn. The fact that Mik lost a leg to a bear does not completely slow him down; he once more joins the hunt and manages to kill a bear by clubbing it with his wooden leg. This story, told in dialect by Mik, presents a frontier character reveling in his skill as a hunter and linking his hunting to his happiness in life.

Lewis's tales dealing with the medical profession but generally following the tradition of the Southwestern humorists focus on the young doctor's struggles to find a practice and the odd cases that come his way. "My Early Life" and "Seeking a Location" trace the doctor's youthful difficulties and trou-

"My cloak flew open as I fell, and the force of the fall bursting its envelope, out, in all its hideous realities, rolled the infernal imp of darkness."—*Page 137*.

" The way that bar's flesh giv in to the soft impresshuns of that leg, war an honer to the mederkal perfeshun for having invented sich a weepun."—*Page* 175.

*Illustrations by F. O. C. Darley for "Stealing a Baby" and "The Indefatigable Bear-Hunter" in Lewis's*
Odd Leaves from the Life of a Louisiana "Swamp Doctor"

bles in establishing a practice. "Being Examined for My Degree" details the subterfuge Tensas uses to deflect the questions of his examiners and pass the exam without having studied. Other tales recount "cupping" (a practice that attempts to draw blood by placing heated glass cups on the patient) an Irishman, dealing with "aristocrats" from Virginia who fear contracting a "common" disease, curing a slave of feigned fits, and discussing the difference between the city physician and the country doctor.

Finally, his most distinctive tales feature frequent raw realism and a steady eye on the human mind under pressure. No doubt the trained physician was only too familiar with the ailments that rifled the human body. In several of these tales an apparently humorous sketch in the typical mode of the genre takes an abrupt and nightmarish turn. In "The Day of Judgment" Tensas and some rowdy acquaintances decide to disrupt a camp meeting where the worshipers await the end of the world. Dressed in flowing white robes and carrying torches, the young men descend on the meeting. They create an added authentic touch of the apocalypse by soaking a mule in turpentine and setting it aflame. The expected pandemonium ensues. The story ends with a grim

portrait of the suffering mule, however: "The stream was nearly reached; with ecstasy the poor brute beheld the glistening waters; he sped on with accelerated steps—one more spring, and he would find surcease of anguish 'neath their cooling waves. But he was destined never to reach them; he fell exhausted on the brink, vainly endeavoring, with extended neck, to allay his fiery thirst; as the flame, now bereft of fuel, sent up its last flickering ray, the poor mule, with a low reproachful moan, expired." Thus, typical material for the Southwestern humorists—the camp meeting—follows the expected path until the end, when the reader is quickly brought face-to-face with the hard reality of the prank.

If Lewis is willing to redirect the expected pattern of a sketch, he is also willing to present sketches that push the boundaries of humor. In "The Curious Widow" Lewis recounts the attempts of several medical students to thwart their landlady's habit of rummaging through their belongings while they attend class. Having cut the face off a hideously disfigured cadaver, they cover it in several layers of wrapping, place it in a coat pocket where the landlady will see it, and hide to observe her reaction. The widow finds the package, eagerly unwraps it, and, contrary to what the young medical students expect, coolly remarks that this isn't likely to frighten someone who had slept with a drunken husband for twenty years. In "Stealing a Baby" Tensas, the young medical student, steals a dead baby from the morgue so he can dissect at leisure in his room. His plan is compromised when he runs into his sweetheart, who is being trailed by her father, unhappy with his daughter's choice of a beau. Tensas and Lucy attempt to hide, but a dog chases them from their spot; Tensas slips on the icy pavement; and the dead baby flies out from his coat. The courtship is quickly over.

Two additional sketches illustrate the distinctiveness of Lewis's work. Both these sketches are part adventure yarn, part psychological journey. "Valerian and the Panther" starts with a humorous look at the Spiffle family, prolific swamp-dwellers given to violence and telling stories in their dialect. The story moves beyond the merely humorous when the doctor begins his journey home, however. Lost and worried about spending the night in the swamp, Tensas spurs his faithful horse, Chaos, in an attempt to cover as much ground as possible before darkness sets in. He increases his speed when he hears the scream of a panther. Convinced that he will be overtaken and eaten, he plans to kill himself with poison rather than suffer that fate. In a sort of crazed fear Tensas resorts to biting his horse's neck to urge him on and finally decides that if he sacrifices his horse the panther will be diverted long enough for him to escape. To that end he cuts the horse's carotid artery. Covered with the noble horse's blood, Tensas turns to find the panther leaping for him. On impulse, instead of drinking the poison he pours it into the panther's mouth and, under the stress of the moment, faints. When he regains consciousness, he finds the panther dead, its jaws clamped tightly on the valerian—a sort of catnip—he carried for medical purposes.

The last sketch in *Odd Leaves from the Life of a Louisiana "Swamp Doctor"* is "A Struggle for Life," and it provides a fitting close to a collection of stories that, though firmly based in the traditions of Southwestern humor, are distinguished especially by their occasional probing of the mind. In fact, other than the initially carefree tone of this particular narrative, there is little humor in the sketch. Summoned once again into the swamp to treat a patient, Tensas must follow the Negro dwarf sent to guide him, but he is no ordinary guide. Tensas describes him as looking like an ape or "ourang outang." His face sports a pair of tusks on either side of a double harelip. Deep in the swamp, Tensas is attacked by the dwarf, now crazed by a drink of brandy Tensas had given him.

The scene that follows is reminiscent of Edgar Allan Poe's exploration of mental states, with Lewis providing a detailed description of Tensas's feelings as the powerful dwarf chokes the life from him. Tensas, who now believes he is dead, speculates on the mutability of the body and reviews his past life. Just then, however, he revives and discovers that the dwarf, in a drunken rage, has rushed into the flames of the campfire and been burned to death. This last sketch recounts another escape from the forces of the natural world, a world often dangerous and deadly.

*Odd Leaves from the Life of a Louisiana "Swamp Doctor"* merited some six printings in the nineteenth century and at least three more in the twentieth century, suggesting that it transcends the genre. Lewis was driven by the urge to succeed against significant odds, struggling from riverboat to cotton field to swamp to prominence. He was also a writer concerned with craftsmanship, who altered many of the tales between their publication in the *Spirit of the Times* and *Odd Leaves from the Life of a Louisiana "Swamp Doctor."* Henry Clay Lewis, dead at age twenty-five, left behind one volume of tales, but those tales are so vivid and unusual that they set themselves far apart from all other tales from the Old Southwest and reveal an author of unusual power.

**Bibliography:**

Nancy Snell Griffith, comp., *Humor of the Old Southwest: An Annotated Bibliography of Primary and Secondary Sources* (New York: Greenwood Press, 1989), pp. 128–135.

**References:**

John Q. Anderson, "Folklore in the Writing of 'the Louisiana Swamp Doctor,'" *Southern Folklore Quarterly,* 19 (December 1955): 243–251;

Anderson, "Folkways in Writing About Northeast Louisiana Before 1865," *Louisiana Folklore Miscellany,* 1 (1960): 18–32;

Anderson, "Henry Clay Lewis, Alias 'Madison Tensas, M.D., the Louisiana Swamp Doctor,'" *Bulletin of the Medical Library Association,* 43 (January 1955): 58–73;

Anderson, "Henry Clay Lewis, Louisville Medical Institute Student, 1844–1846," *Filson Club Historical Quarterly,* 32 (January 1958): 30–37;

Anderson, "Louisiana 'Swamp Doctor,'" *McNeese Review,* 5 (Spring 1953): 45–53;

Anderson, *Louisiana Swamp Doctor: The Life and Writings of Henry Clay Lewis, Alias "Madison Tensas, M.D."* (Baton Rouge: Louisiana State University Press, 1962);

Edwin T. Arnold, "Facing the Monster: William Gilmore Simms and Henry Clay Lewis" in *William Gilmore Simms and the American Frontier,* edited by John Caldwell Guilds and Caroline Collins (Athens: University of Georgia Press, 1997), pp. 179–191;

Arnold, introduction to *Odd Leaves from the Life of a Louisiana Swamp Doctor* (Baton Rouge: Louisiana State University Press, 1997), pp. xi–xlvi;

Richard Boyd Hauck, *A Cheerful Nihilism: Confidence and "The Absurd" in American Humorous Fiction* (Bloomington: Indiana University Press, 1971), pp. 44–48;

M. Thomas Inge and Edward J. Piacentino, eds., *The Humor of the Old South* (Lexington: University Press of Kentucky, 2001), pp. 4, 38, 45, 47, 48, 52, 62, 63, 64, 66, 67, 68, 78, 79, 80, 199, 210, 211;

Charles Israel, "Henry Clay Lewis' *Odd Leaves:* Studies in the Surreal and the Grotesque," *Mississippi Quarterly,* 28 (Winter 1974–1975): 61–69;

Mark A. Keller, "'Aesculapius in Buckskin': The Swamp Doctor as Satirist in Henry Clay Lewis' *Odd Leaves,*" *Southern Studies: An Interdisciplinary Journal of the South,* 18 (Winter 1979): 425–448;

Piacentino, "Contesting the Boundaries of Race and Gender in Old Southwestern Literature," *The Southern Literary Journal,* 32, no. 2 (Spring 2000): 116–140;

Piacentino, "Henry Clay Lewis," in *Cyclopedia of American Humorists,* edited by Steven H. Gale (New York: Garland, 1988), pp. 280–284;

Milton Rickels, "The Grotesque Body of Southwestern Humor," *Critical Essays on American Humor,* edited by William Bedford Clark and W. Craig Turner (Boston: Hall, 1984), pp. 155–166;

Alan H. Rose, *Demonic Vision: Racial Fantasy and Southern Fiction* (Hamden, Conn.: Archon, 1976), pp. 25–38;

Rose, "The Image of the Negro in the Writings of Henry Clay Lewis," *American Literature,* 41 (May 1969): 255–263;

Arlin Turner, "Seeds of Literary Revolt in the Humor of the Old Southwest," *Louisiana Historical Quarterly,* 39 (1956): 143–151;

Edward Watts, "In the Midst of a Noisome Swamp: The Landscape of Henry Clay Lewis," *Southern Literary Journal,* 22, no. 2 (1990): 119–128.

# Augustus Baldwin Longstreet

*(22 September 1790 – 9 July 1870)*

E. Kate Stewart
*University of Arkansas at Monticello*

See also the Longstreet entries in *DLB 3: Antebellum Writers in New York and the South; DLB 11: American Humorists, 1800–1950;* and *DLB 74: American Short-Story Writers Before 1880.*

BOOKS: *An Oration Delivered before the Demosthenian & Phi Kappa Societies of the University of Georgia, at the Commencement of August, 1831* (Augusta, Ga.: Lawson, 1831);

*An Oration Delivered in the City of Augusta, on the Centennial Birth-Day of George Washington* (Augusta, Ga.: Lawson, 1832);

*Georgia Scenes, Characters, Incidents &c, in the First Half Century of the Republic* (Augusta, Ga.: Sentinel Press, 1835; reprinted, New York: Harper, 1840);

*Address Delivered before the Faculty and the Students of Emory College, Oxford, Ga. by Augustus Baldwin Longstreet, President of That Institution, at His Inauguration, 10th February, 1840* (Augusta, Ga.: Thompson, 1840);

*Eulogy on the Life and Public Service of the Late Rev. Moses Waddell, D. D.* (Augusta, Ga.: Chronicle & Sentinel Office, 1841);

*Letters on the Epistle of Paul to Philemon, or the Connection of Apostolical Christianity with Slavery* (Charleston, S.C.: Jenkins, 1845);

*A Voice from the South: Comprising Letters from Georgia to Massachusetts, and to the Southern States* (Baltimore: Western Continent Press, 1847);

*The Letters of President Longstreet . . . The Alien and Sedition Laws and Virginia and Kentucky Resolutions of 1798 and 1799 . . . The Democratic Platform of 1852* (New Orleans: Office of the Louisiana Courier, 1852?);

*Know Nothingism Unveiled. Letter of Judge A. B. Longstreet, of Mississippi, Addressed to Rev. William Winans* (Washington, D.C.: Congressional Globe, 1855);

*Fast-Day Sermon: Delivered in the Washington Street Methodist Episcopal Church, Columbia, S.C., June 13, 1861* (Columbia: Townsend & North, 1861);

*Shall South Carolina Begin the War?* (Charleston, S.C., 1861);

*Augustus B. Longstreet*

*Master William Mitten; or, A Youth of Brilliant Talents Who Was Ruined by Bad Luck* (Macon, Ga.: Burke, Boykin, 1864);

*Valuable Suggestions Addressed to the Soldiers of the Confederate States* (Macon, Ga.: Soldiers' Tract Association of the Methodist Episcopal Church, South, 1864);

*Stories with a Moral Humourous and Descriptive of Southern Life a Century Ago,* compiled and edited by Fitz R. Longstreet (Philadelphia: Winston, 1912).

SELECTED PERIODICAL PUBLICATIONS–
UNCOLLECTED: "From out of the Fires," *Nineteenth
Century Magazine* (December 1869): 543–624;
"Old Things Become New, I," *Nineteenth Century Magazine* (January 1870): 839–851;
"Review of Gov. Perry's Article on John C. Calhoun," *Nineteenth Century Magazine* (January 1870): n.p.

In his sketch "The Dance" Augustus Baldwin Longstreet relates that the meal "consisted of plain *fare,* but there was a profusion of it." Tracing his career, one might be inclined to relate similarly about Longstreet: a profusion of plain fare. During his seventy-nine year span, Longstreet distinguished himself as lawyer, judge, politician, writer of both expository and creative prose, Methodist minister, and college president. Although he succeeded in all of these endeavors, Longstreet is best remembered for his humorous, often earthy, sketches in *Georgia Scenes, Characters, Incidents &c, in the First Half Century of the Republic* (1835). Scholars credit these tales with influencing local color and realistic fiction of the later nineteenth century. Writers in subsequent generations, most notably Mark Twain and William Faulkner, looked to the works of Longstreet for some of their inspiration. The Native Georgian, as he would style himself, captured well the essence of life in the antebellum South. Despite the fact that his total yield of creative enterprises consisted of less than thirty humorous sketches and a novel, scholars continue to find Longstreet worthy of critical inquiry.

Born on 22 September 1790 in Augusta, Georgia, to William and Hannah Randolph Longstreet, young Gus weighed a reported seventeen pounds. His parents had migrated to Georgia from New Jersey in 1785, along with several of their friends. With its rich and abundant soil, the region offered the Longstreets more prosperity than they might have achieved in the Northeast.

Apparently a homely child, young Longstreet had to vie for attention in a family in which he was one of six siblings. Practical jokes and petty mischief constituted his primary means of attention-getting, and he continued to ply these talents in his early years of schooling at the Richmond Academy. He showed intellectual promise early, having learned to read and write rather ably by the age of eight years. His foundational education both at the Richmond Academy and at the Hickory Gum Academy in Edgefield, South Carolina, though, failed to interest him, and his antics often caused him to serve time on the dunce stool. His deportment sank to such depths that Longstreet for a time was considered mentally unstable.

Acting on the advice of friends, William and Hannah Longstreet sent their son to the Waddell School in Willington, South Carolina, in 1808. By the time Longstreet matriculated at his school, Moses Waddell had already gained prominence as a Presbyterian minister and educator. One of Waddell's prize students, John C. Calhoun, had studied with Longstreet for two years before attending Yale and graduating first in his class. Because they revered the Calhouns, the Longstreets entertained hopes that their son would follow in Calhoun's footsteps. Indeed, Waddell in large measure began Longstreet on his successful career.

Following in Calhoun's path with no small encouragement from the Calhoun family, Longstreet entered Yale in 1811 as a junior. Because New Haven and Augusta were roughly the same size–with a population of about five thousand people–the southerner felt relatively comfortable in his new environment. He later noted, in fact, that his two years at Yale were among the happiest of his life. After graduating in 1813, Longstreet, again duplicating Calhoun, studied law with Tapping Reeve and James Gould, prominent Litchfield, Connecticut, judges. As he had in New Haven, Longstreet apparently became the charm of the social circle with his talent for regaling audiences with stories about his native Georgia.

Completing his education in 1814, Longstreet returned to Georgia. He was admitted to the Georgia bar on 26 May 1815 and promptly became a judge in the Richmond County circuit. His travels as a judge took him to Greensboro in neighboring Green County, where he met Frances Eliza Parke, whom he married on 3 March 1817. Because his wife's family was wealthier than his, the newlyweds settled near Frances Longstreet's people. In 1821 Longstreet was elected as representative to the Georgia Assembly from Green County, and in 1822 he was elected judge of the Superior Court of the Ocmulgee District.

Had not a double tragedy occurred in 1827, Longstreet might well have continued in Georgia politics. That year, though, his son Alfred and his mother-in-law died within two days of each other. The calamity caused him to withdraw from the congressional elections and to sink into a depression. Neither Longstreet nor his wife had been active in the church until this dual loss, but they joined the Methodist Church in 1827.

Longstreet's next career move took him into journalism. In 1834 he became the owner and editor of the *States Rights Sentinel,* based in Augusta. In that paper Longstreet published the humorous sketches he began writing in 1830, which comprise *Georgia Scenes, Characters, Incidents &c, in the First Half Century of the Republic* (1835). The newspaper also served as the vehicle through which Longstreet could air his political and social views. The name of the *States Rights Sentinel* puts forward plainly some of Longstreet's political agenda. As evidence of his states' rights bent, he had published around 1833 a subsequently lost review of the *McCulloch v. Maryland* (1849) case, in which John Marshall had determined that Congress had "implied powers." Longstreet believed that such a notion infringed on states' rights, and as a strict constructionist he believed further that the decision violated the Constitution.

Although his political writings are not without interest, Longstreet's legacy was established when the *Sentinel* published in book form his newspaper sketches. Longstreet chose to remain anonymous, designating merely that *Georgia Scenes* was penned by "a Native Georgian." Perhaps recognizing that his work did not typify contemporaneous literature, Longstreet included a preface to the first edition in which he outlined his rationale for and methodology in the work.

Longstreet characterizes the sketches in *Georgia Scenes* as "nothing more than fanciful *combinations* of *real* incidents and characters," noting further that he enhanced scenes that might be "dull and insipid" by adding some of his own adventures, be they truth or fiction. In language that anticipates Mark Twain's assurance in *The Adventures of Huckleberry Finn* (1884) that he told mostly the truth with some stretchers, Longstreet notes that he exaggerates some details, combines selectively the details of several genuine episodes, and just plain invents others.

The "Native Georgian" creates a delicate balance between verisimilitude and fabrication and gives readers little direction in distinguishing between the two. Perhaps, though, readers may glimpse at the methodical madness in the sketch "The Character of a Native Georgian." The vignette illustrates Longstreet's declared purpose in *Georgia Scenes,* to depict accurately the fiber of those living in and around Augusta.

Lyman Hall, the narrator of the sketches in *Georgia Scenes* featuring men, introduces readers to Ned Brace. Although he qualifies that he cannot vouch for the truth of all the accounts about Brace, Hall establishes him as something of a Georgia everyman, a representative of the whole. Brace's primary character trait is his propensity for playing practical jokes and observing people's reactions to them. Hall recounts a business trip that the two took to Savannah and tells of Ned's insane antics, such as adopting strange eating habits at a boardinghouse and convincing a Frenchman that he is in fact a fellow Georgian. Readers meet Ned again in "A Sage Conversation," related by Abram Baldwin, who narrates the stories about women. In a casual conversation with three worthy matrons about marriages, Brace shares nonchalantly that the strangest union he knew was that of George Scott and David Snow. He continues to praise the strength of the marriage, noting also that the two "raised a lovely parcel of children." After Baldwin and Brace retire for the night, Mrs. Barney, Mrs. Shad, and Mrs. Reed continue the conversation, speculating about how two men joined in marriage could have children. After proposing various theories, the three go to other subjects. The next morning they ask Ned for a few more details, and he notes that the

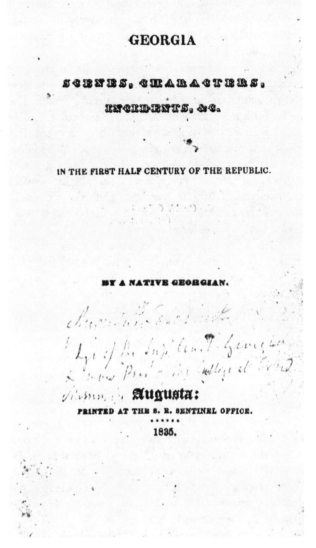

*Title page for Longstreet's best-known work, a collection of sketches about rural Georgia society (South Caroliniana Library, University of South Carolina)*

men were widowers with children when the two married. The explanation satisfies everyone—with the possible exception of the readers.

On the surface these sketches present the exploits of a genial buffoon; at another level, though, Longstreet reveals his artistry in *Georgia Scenes*. Readers are never quite sure if the narrators Hall and Baldwin are the author's alter egos or if the other characters are. Like the rollicking trickery in "The Horse-Swap" or "The Wax-Works," Longstreet in his tales engages readers in scams that cause them no harm but deliver at times a questionable bill of goods.

That fact notwithstanding, Longstreet does offer keen observations about the human race. The nineteen sketches in *Georgia Scenes* take readers into the boardinghouse and the schoolroom, onto the dance floor, and into the highways and hedges of rural Georgia. Through the eyes of Baldwin or Hall, readers survey the foibles and triumphs of women and men as they participate in social enterprises.

Modern audiences may well be disconcerted by Longstreet's depreciation of ethnic and social groups who were shunned as equals in the antebellum South. The author captures with some accuracy the racial and class distinctions in the society, although he has noted that much of the material is exaggeration. In both "The Character of a Native Georgian" and "The Fight," for instance, the fictional narrator, Hall, relates disturbing incidents of mistreatment of African Americans and "Georgia crackers," a euphemistic term for poor Southern whites. Readers see Longstreet at his worst here.

At his best, though, Longstreet portrays the common insecurities and shortcomings that beset all individuals irrespective of racial, cultural, and regional lines. In "The Dance" Baldwin exposes both his inability to recall accurately the past and his self-importance when he is sure that the fetching Polly Jackson is one of his old flames. She recollects Baldwin not at all, even when he tries to impress her with his expertise on the dance floor. Weeks after the dance, Polly still has no recollection of him. Interestingly, though, she can retrieve memories of all of Baldwin's boon companions.

Some of Baldwin's comeuppance appears justified in light of his revelation that he is returning to a frontier outpost of the state from the city. Although he grew up in the locale, he shows a degree of disdain for the unsophisticated bumpkins, having himself, he imagines, developed a degree of urbanity. His healthy ego presumes that Polly would naturally remember him.

Growing up, Longstreet would have been aware of the Southern class system. His family was not exactly wealthy, but neither were they poor. This social vantage, perhaps, led him to recognize that the Southern aristocrats were esteemed, yet that they could also be supercilious. With its bittersweet ending, "The 'Charming Creature' as Wife" reveals the dangers of forsaking practicality for haughtiness. Baldwin's nephew George becomes enamored of Evelina Smith, whose parents sent her to a Philadelphia finishing school because they prized her great beauty far more than her natural intelligence. Because of the attention she received as a "charming creature," Evelina early on cultivated pride and vanity as her most notable character traits. The end result was that she was ill equipped to be a farmer's wife, and hers and George's marriage proves so unsatisfactory that the hapless husband turns to drink.

While Baldwin exposes the dangers of feminine pride and vanity in "The 'Charming Creature' as Wife," "The Song," "The Ball," and "The Mother and Her Child," Hall reveals the perils of masculine pride and van-

ity in such tales as "The Fox-Hunt," "The Shooting-Match," "Georgia Theatrics," and "The Gander Pulling." Serving as the narrator of each, Hall reveals his own social awkwardness in "The Fox-Hunt," as his roommate Baldwin does in "The Dance." In the other three tales he exposes the Southern male's propensity for competition and physical confrontation.

A less uppity individual than Baldwin, Hall can, nevertheless, bring humiliation on himself when he puts on airs. He had read romanticized accounts of foxhunts and anticipated eagerly his opportunity to participate in one. From his old, docile horse, Smooth-Tooth, to his inability to judge the fox's physical state by its tail, Hall is ill equipped to join the sport. His desire to be a part of this event, which served as a mark of gentility, gets the better of him, however. Hall also experiences humiliation in "The Shooting-Match," where he has the great misfortune of meeting on the road Billy Curlew and his rifle, Soap-stick. Curlew had heard of Hall and his shooting expertise from his father, and he insists that the narrator accompany him to a shooting match. Reluctantly, Hall must participate in the competition, where he at first is ridiculed for his shooting ability. A chance shot, though, salvages his male ego.

"Georgia Theatrics" may have been inspired partially by Longstreet's childhood; as quoted in John Donald Wade's biography, he notes that in his younger days he aspired to be the best fighter in the county. Hall relates his shock at hearing a brutal fight, replete with crude language and excessive violence. The stunned narrator discovers that a solitary eighteen-year-old was merely practicing fisticuffs by staging a mock confrontation with himself. Through Hall, Longstreet also studies the propensity for male competition and violence on the frontier, ultimately a matter of pride and vanity. Less successfully, "The Fight" and "The Turf" also explore these same flaws.

Although it too involves male competition, "The Gander Pulling" differs in intent from the others. On the surface the yarn focuses on one of those rural entertainments that centers on the abuse of animals. The competition, which involves suspending a greased gander upside down and having men on horseback pass under the fowl and attempt to pull off its head, possesses little genuine humor. The setting of the contest, though, lends credibility to the story. The promoter of the gander pulling sets the competition at the junction of four Georgia towns, Augusta, Springfield, Harrisburg, and Campbellton. The towns espouse different political views, and bringing them together in an inane activity undercuts the importance of their political ideology.

*Georgia Scenes* established firmly Longstreet's literary reputation and fostered the development of local color and realism as literary genres. In his preface Longstreet apologizes for the "coarse, inelegant, and sometimes ungram-

Another would "buss her" because she was George's wife

*Illustration for "The 'Charming Creature' as Wife" in* Georgia Scenes

matical language," but he defends its use for the sake of accuracy in depicting the life of Augusta, Richmond County, and its environs. The individuals whom Longstreet introduces in *Georgia Scenes,* characters he likely met traveling about as he executed his judicial duties, enchanted Georgians, the general public, and even Edgar Allan Poe, who offered high praise for the work in a review for the March 1836 *Southern Literary Messenger.* Admitting that he laughed "immoderately" over *Georgia Scenes,* Poe praised Longstreet for his insight and understanding of "character in general, and of Southern character in particular." Without doubt, the Native Georgian achieved his principal objective.

In 1838 Longstreet exchanged his judicial circuit for the ecclesiastical circuit. From all accounts Longstreet never fully recovered from the death of his young son in 1827; many believe that the event lead him into the Methodist ministry. When he entered his pastoral career, he put aside his careers in law and writing and devoted himself fully to the ministry. He helped care for yellow fever vic-

tims in 1839, but his career as a full-time preacher was abbreviated when he accepted the presidency of the burgeoning Emory College.

Assuming the presidency of a church-sponsored college gave Longstreet the opportunity to combine his advocacy of strong academics and moral teaching. His presidential inaugural address, issued as a separate volume in 1840 and reprinted in Oscar Penn Fitzgerald's biography of Longstreet, reveals clearly his notion that the two complemented each other. The oration also reveals Longstreet's other ideals of love of state and country and fidelity to man's and God's laws. As president of Emory he believed himself a guardian of youth. He viewed his appointment an honor and took seriously his commitment to the trustees of the college. Although some of the students complained that his sermons were insipid, Longstreet did receive praise as an able college administrator in his eight years at Emory.

After he began his career as a college president, Longstreet never devoted himself to writing as he had done prior to the publication of *Georgia Scenes*. Yet, he did not abandon totally his pen. Between 1842 and 1844 Longstreet wrote six or so other sketches that appeared in the *Mirror,* the *Southern Literary Messenger,* and primarily the *Magnolia: or, Southern Monthly.* Though they are not without some merit, these sketches never garnered the praise of the earlier tales. Less humorous and more somber than their predecessors, they push perhaps too vigorously morality and political conservatism.

Perhaps the best of the later sketches, "Darby Anvil" (*Mirror,* 30 October 1839) relates the saga of an unqualified person who manages to be elected to political office. The local blacksmith, Anvil, reluctantly enters the race for the state legislature at the behest of his wife, who sees an elective office as a means to financial security. Anvil, who is described as possessing "shrewdness and low cunning," knows little of the legislative process. His ignorance of the law becomes apparent in his debate with his lawyer opponents. Although he lacks their education, the blacksmith manages to hold his own in debates with them because he declares that he is one of the people, unlike his upper-class opponents, and must work for a living. Anvil's campaign rhetoric anticipates the stratagems adopted by the Southern politicos of the early twentieth century, the type whom Robert Penn Warren portrayed vividly in Willie Stark of *All the King's Men* (1946). Anvil wins his race but lets success go to his head and sells out early on to unscrupulous individuals who demand favors. Financial security eludes him, and he ends up losing what little he had.

Longstreet studies both politics and journalism in "The Gnatville Gem," a sketch first published in the *Magnolia* in June 1843. Asaph Doolittle goes to Gnatville proposing to set up a newspaper. In gauging the attitudes of the community, Doolittle discovers that most of the citizens are Jeffersonian Republicans and that a scanty number are Federalists. The would-be editor had been reared a Federalist but is willing to switch allegiances in order to succeed. A political war erupts in the *Gnatville Gem,* as Doolittle christens the paper, and the town is split apart because of the acrimonious debate. The editor is forced to leave town, and only a religious revival can restore the community. Reminiscent of "The Gander Pulling," "The Gnatville Gem," with less skill than the former, targets the folly of narrow-mindedness and pernicious political hostilities.

In "Julia and Clarissa" (*Magnolia,* September–October 1843) Longstreet renews his attack on superficial society by taking stabs at Julia's mother, Mrs. Carp, and her daughter, who hope to arrange a marriage between the son of the family and an heiress. The two women's primary design, of course, is to enhance their own social status regardless of what their machinations might do to the welfare of others. As he develops the story, Longstreet attacks

also overly permissive parents, whom he believed were destroying Georgia society by allowing their raucous children a free hand. Longstreet later expanded this theme in *Master William Mitten; or, A Youth of Brilliant Talents Who Was Ruined by Bad Luck* (1864), in which he re-uses characters from "Julia and Clarissa." The issue of undisciplined children concerned him enough that he broached it in a sketch from *Georgia Scenes,* "The Mother and Her Child," which exposes a mother who blames others for her child's crying without seeking a cause for it, and in "Family Picture," one of the later sketches first published in the *Mirror* in 1838. In "Family Picture" Longstreet adopts a more positive stance by exhibiting the Butlers, who have something of the right notion about child rearing because they combine love and discipline.

Possibly the more overt moralizing in these later tales accounts for the fact that Fitz R. Longstreet, the author's nephew, anthologized some of them in *Stories with a Moral Humourous and Descriptive of Southern Life a Century Ago* (1912). The fact, though, is inescapable; these later works simply lack the artistry of those found in *Georgia Scenes.* Since Longstreet had entered other professions, he may not have had time to devote to creative endeavors. His darkening political vision and the changing times may also account for the more melancholy drift.

At the same time that he wrote these sketches, Longstreet also produced several works that modern readers find disturbing. In 1844 Longstreet attended the General Conference of the Methodist Church in New York. He discovered that the denomination was sharply divided over slavery. A product of his upbringing, Longstreet supported slavery and believed that servitude was the proper station in society for African Americans. At the sometimes acrimonious General Conference he articulated plainly his views on the divisive issue. Following the meeting, he published *Letters on the Epistle of Paul to Philemon, or the Connection of Apostolical Christianity with Slavery* (1845) and *A Voice from the South: Comprising Letters from Georgia to Massachusetts, and to the Southern States* (1847). Both of these works defend slavery as a biblical principle, one of the most common justifications of the institution that antebellum Southerners offered. These publications are distinct from Longstreet's otherwise consistent commitment to humanitarian causes.

In 1848 Longstreet resigned from Emory, anticipating that he would become president of the University of Mississippi. A dispute among some of the trustees of the latter institution over having an ordained minister as head of a secular college caused a delay in his appointment. Rather, in 1849 Longstreet became president of Centenary College in Louisiana, another Methodist school. Centenary did not live up to Longstreet's expectations, however. The students were unruly, and Shreveport was truly a frontier settlement. His tenure there lasted five months.

*Illustration for "The Fox-Hunt" in* Georgia Scenes

The trustees of the University of Mississippi reconsidered their position on hiring a minister for the presidency, and Longstreet took the helm of the ten-year-old institution in 1849. He expected the student body to be more sophisticated than the one at Centenary, but he discovered instead rowdy planters' sons who had grown accustomed to lax leadership. Longstreet managed to bring discipline to the campus in short order, however, and the institution experienced remarkable growth during his tenure. The students christened him "Old Bullet," according to some sources, because his head was shaped like a cannonball. They may, however, have been making a reference to Longstreet's story "The Horse-Swap," which features the trading of a horse named Bullet, who has an incurable sore on his back.

Because of his own educational background, Longstreet was well qualified to bring discipline to the rowdies. He himself had been a student whose deportment was often found wanting. His tutelage under Waddell transformed him into a serious, dedicated pupil. Longstreet, too, was already wise to the tricks of collegians, having written on the battle of wills between a teacher and his charges in "The Turn Out" from *Georgia Scenes.*

Longstreet did in fact bring decorum to the University of Mississippi, but he also expanded his political activism, which did not ultimately have a positive effect on his presidency. In 1855 he carried on a verbal war with the Reverend William Winans over the American Party, or the Know-Nothings. When the Whig Party began to lose ground in the South over the slavery issue, many of its members saw the American Party as a viable alternative. The Know-Nothings had banded together because of their belief that those with Anglo-Saxon roots constituted true Americans, as well as their suspicion of immigrants, especially Irish Catholics. To carry out their objectives the members of the party often resorted to intimidation and shrouded themselves in secrecy, hence the name "Know-Nothings."

Despite his advocacy of slavery, Longstreet was taken aback by the Know-Nothings; he objected particularly with their use of bullying, their animosity toward Catholics, and their advocacy of unionism. Never one to keep silent on what he deemed important issues, he spoke and wrote against the Know-Nothings. Some individuals, especially some of the trustees of the University of Mississippi, disagreed with his outspokenness, believing that Longstreet was using his position at the university for political gain. These protestations, though, were not sufficient to keep him from a lively exchange in the *Natchez Courier* with his fellow Methodist clergyman Winans. Longstreet's responses to Winans were gathered into a pamphlet and published as *Know Nothingism Unveiled. Letter of Judge A. B. Longstreet, of Mississippi, Addressed to Rev. William Winans* in 1855.

The trustees who were skeptical about Longstreet as president from the onset began to suspect that their reservations were well founded. Not only was he a political activist, but he had also become a land speculator, amassing large tracts of land in and around Oxford. By this time Longstreet had likely become enough of a curmudgeon that merely placating trustees would not be possible; thus, he tendered his resignation in July 1856. He might well have retired in ease, but in November 1857 he accepted the presidency of the University of South Carolina.

Although Columbia at this time was a well-established city in sharp contrast to Jackson, Louisiana, and Oxford, Mississippi, Longstreet encountered the same sorts of boisterous students that he had found at Centenary and the University of Mississippi. Again he brought a measure of discipline to the campus despite the resistence of the student body. His efforts were not nearly as successful as they had been at the University of Mississippi, however. Students at South Carolina staged a demonstration against their president that echoed the one in "The Turn Out." Longstreet's administration was merely adequate; his greatest accomplishment in these years, with the Civil War brewing, was, therefore, the serial publication of *Master William Mitten* in the *Southern Field and Fireside* (2 May–November 1859). The novel was published in book form in 1864.

Longstreet began *Master William Mitten* in 1849 during his brief tenure at Centenary. He suggested that the novel was inspired by his outrage at those parents—particularly the mothers of two of his students—who indulged their children's every whim, but he had entertained the notions he considers in *Master William Mitten* perhaps since his own youth. The novel chronicles the ultimate fall of a gifted young man who has an overindulgent mother and no discipline. Early in his schooling, Mitten begins lying to his teacher, Mr. Markham. He first tries to weasel out of his recitation by feigning illness. Later he hides his textbook in a thicket, claiming that he lost it. Markham observes the latter indiscretion, however, and administers a caning. Rather than counsel her son, Mitten's mother defends him each time. Mitten continues his deceptions at Princeton, wooing two women and becoming engaged to both. Eventually he is dismissed from college because of gambling and comes to ruin.

Longstreet teaches overtly the moral lesson that in order to enjoy success in life young people must be taught discipline, morals, and responsibility. Mitten fails because he lacks these qualities; some of his classmates who lack his advantages but possess these traits ultimately succeed. Longstreet tolerates deception with more amusement in

*Georgia Scenes* than he does in *Master William Mitten*. In "The Horse Swap" dissimulation is a part of the game when seasoned con artists barter blemished goods. More similar to *Master William Mitten*, "The Wax-Works" tells of a group of would-be hedonists who revel so copiously that they are unable to pay their tab. To raise the capital they devise a bogus sideshow. Although both narratives from *Georgia Scenes* involve chicanery, no one comes to ruin in them. His addition of tragic consequences in *Master William Mitten* illustrates Longstreet's growing melancholic vision.

Under the influence of Waddell, Longstreet developed the basic principles of pedagogy that he employed consistently as a college administrator. His theories about teachers being the guardians and guides of youth, which he expressed in his inaugural address at Emory, became his practice throughout his academic career. When he encountered the spoiled, raucous students at Centenary, the University of Mississippi, and the University of South Carolina, Longstreet considered first improper parental guidance as a likely source of the problem. He addressed this issue throughout his fiction, most notably in *Master William Mitten* but in sketches in *Georgia Scenes* as well. The difference in the later work is that the message becomes more pointed and grave. By the time he wrote the novel, Longstreet was more caustic and likely less amused by the weaknesses of the Southern aristocracy. His growing political activism in troubled, unsettled times, too, may have cast a darker shadow over his message.

His words to the graduating class of 1859 at South Carolina reflect well his inquietude about the times. Longstreet notes that they were leaving the institution at "the most portentous period" in the history of the United States. In the speech, which even some of his friends termed a diatribe, he reiterates some of his defenses of slavery and the Southern solutions to it. Calling Northerners "insatiable harpies," he cites tariff laws and the War of Mexican Succession as exemplars of violations of states' rights. Longstreet proffers no solution to the ideological war, but instead he encourages secession of the Southern states.

As an ardent proponent of states' rights, Longstreet in some measure favored the Southern states going off on their own. When faced with the reality of impending war, though, he questioned the wisdom of this course of action. In *Shall South Carolina Begin the War?* (1861) he encourages South Carolina officials to be judicious in drawing battle lines. He did not shun verbal battles, but he saw physical combat as injudicious and unnecessary. As ardently as he had defended slavery and states' rights, he did not think that they need cause bloodshed. Longstreet even avers that he would "cheerfully surrender the power of speech and of hearing" to prevent war.

Students at South Carolina set out for war in November 1861, however. With the departure of both student body and the consequent end to his position as the elder statesman of college administrators, Longstreet returned to Mississippi, where he still had substantial holdings in Oxford. Although he believed that the South should engage in the war only in the event of "dire necessity," Longstreet supported avidly the Southern cause after the Civil War began. His son-in-law L. Q. C. Lamar and his nephew, General James Longstreet, kept him informed about events of the conflict, and he participated vicariously by offering advice on strategy to his nephew. His intense interest in the war could have endangered him. In a special article for the *Charleston Daily Courier* in 1861, P. O. Bryan, who managed the telegraph office in Washington, D.C., reported on Confederate spying. In his article Bryan alluded to a letter Longstreet may have written to an unspecified Thompson in which he inquired about the movement of Union troops in the South. Nothing apparently came of this newspaper story, but it does indicate Longstreet's keen interest in the progress of the war.

Since he was physically too old to enlist, Longstreet served by writing *Valuable Suggestions Addressed to the Soldiers of the Confederate States* (1864). If readers remembered "The Militia Company Drill" from *Georgia Scenes,* they could certainly question his qualifications and perhaps his attitudes toward the military. His thoughts to the soldiers, though, encouraging them in the face of fear and exhorting them to remain steadfast to the cause, reflect well his characteristic inspirational writing. *Valuable Suggestions* echoes Longstreet's presidential address at Emory.

With the burning of their home in 1862, the Longstreets moved to Oxford, Georgia, and then to Columbus, with their daughters and their families. Ever the teacher, Longstreet became involved once again in education by establishing interracial Sunday schools and mathematics classes in both Charleston, South Carolina, and Enon, Alabama. In 1865 he returned to Oxford, Mississippi, nearly half of which was destroyed during the war.

Like many fellow Southerners, the Longstreets accepted painfully the reality of the "lost cause." They were surrounded by their children and grandchildren in Oxford and settled into an amicable environment. Longstreet and his wife celebrated their fiftieth wedding anniversary in 1867; from all accounts theirs had been a harmonious union. When Eliza Longstreet died in October of the next year, Augustus experienced a sadness that duplicated his grief over the death of their small son in 1827.

As he had following the death of Alfred, Longstreet found a measure of consolation in religion. He preached occasionally and wrote a book-length manuscript, "A Correction of the Canonized Errors of Biblical Interpretation," which was never published and was later lost in a fire at the home of his literary executor and grandson-in-law,

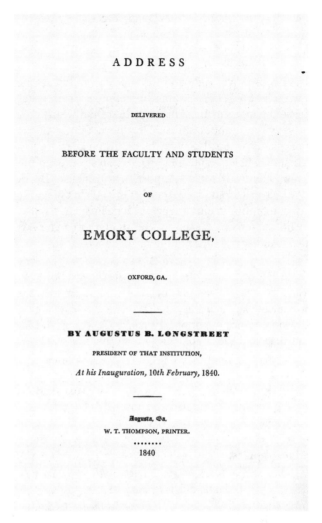

*Title page for the published version of the speech Longstreet delivered when he was inaugurated as president of Emory University in 1840 (Thomas Cooper Library, University of South Carolina)*

Edward Mayes. He also contributed four articles to *Nineteenth Century Magazine* around this time. A recollection of the war years, "From out of the Fires" (December 1869), offers a defense of the Southern cause. The article presents no particularly startling revelations, but it is perhaps important because it reflects well the attitude of many members of the Southern aristocracy who longed for their romanticized antebellum life. In January and July 1870 *Nineteenth Century* printed "Old Things Become New," a rather rambling autobiographical sketch in two parts. In "Review of Gov. Perry's Article on John C. Calhoun" (January 1870) Longstreet takes issue with the Reconstruction policies of Governor Benjamin Franklin Perry, defends his lifelong friend Calhoun, and maintains his advocacy of states' rights.

Longstreet remained active until his peaceful death on 9 July 1870. He is buried in the St. Peter's

Cemetery in Oxford, Mississippi, the same place of interment of his literary descendant William Faulkner. A year after Longstreet's death James Jackson offered at Emory a flowery eulogy to him that states in part: "I love his memory; and had I the ability I would entwine a wreath of *immortelles* around his coffin, as deathless as the soul which inhabited his body here, and which now surveys the beauties and inhales the fragrance of the glory-land. As it is, I may lay by on his honored tomb a few simple flowers gathered by affection's hand and fragrant only with love." A poem by Sallie A. Broek attached to Jackson's effusion begins: "What shall we say of him—our genius bright– / The Christian, scholar, patriot, statesman, / Who gave fresh glory to a glorious age, / And added lustre to that age's light?"

Likely few, if any, critics would express the same sentiments of these two eulogists. Most scholars, however, will accede that Augustus Baldwin Longstreet merits a prominent place in literary studies because of his talents in drawing distinctive portraits of native Georgians and his influence on the local color and realistic milieu.

**Letters:**

Jimmy Ray Scafidel, "The Letters of Augustus Baldwin Longstreet," dissertation, University of South Carolina, 1976.

**Bibliographies:**

Atlanta Public Library, *Augustus Baldwin Longstreet: Pater litterarum* (Atlanta: Public Library, 1955);

Jacob Blanck, *Bibliography of American Literature,* 9 volumes (New Haven: Yale University Press, 1955–1991) VI: 1–5.

**Biographies:**

Oscar Penn Fitzgerald, *Judge Longstreet: A Life Sketch* (Nashville: Methodist Episcopal Church, South, 1891);

John Donald Wade, *Augustus Baldwin Longstreet: A Study of the Development of Culture in the South,* edited by M. Thomas Inge (Athens: University of Georgia Press, 1969).

**References:**

Patricia Beam, "The Theme and Structure of *Georgia Scenes,*" *Journal of English,* 15 (September 1987): 68–79;

Margaret McDiarmid Gooch, "Point of View of the Frontier Spirit of Baldwin, Longstreet, Hooper, and G. W.

Harris," dissertation, University of North Carolina, 1967;

C. Hugh Holman, *The Roots of Southern Writing: Essays in the Literature of the American South* (Athens: University of Georgia Press, 1972), pp. 76–77;

Jay B. Hubbell, *The South in American Literature, 1607–1900* (Durham: Duke University Press, 1954), pp. 666–669, 947–948;

M. Thomas Inge, *The Frontier Humorists: Critical Views* (Hamden, Conn.: Archon, 1975), pp. 85–104;

Kimball King, *Augustus Baldwin Longstreet* (Boston: Twayne, 1984);

James B. Meriwether, "Augustus Baldwin Longstreet: Realist and Artist," *Mississippi Quarterly,* 35 (Fall 1982): 351–364;

Michael Oriand, "Shifty in a New Country: Games in Southwest Humor," *Southern Literary Journal,* 12 (1980): 3–28;

Robert L. Phillips, "The Novel and the Romance in Middle Georgia Humor and Local Color: A Study of Narrative Method in the Works of Augustus Baldwin Longstreet, William Tappan Thompson, Richard Malcolm Johnston and Joel Chandler Harris," thesis, Chapel Hill, University of North Carolina Press, 1971;

Henry O. Robertson, "The Antebellum Southern Humorist and the Whig Perspective: Baldwin, Thorpe, and Longstreet," M.A. thesis, Louisiana State University, 1992;

Scott Romaine, "Negotiating Community in Augustus Baldwin Longstreet's *Georgia Scenes,*" *Style,* 30 (1996): 1–25;

Lucy B. Sitton, "Naturalism in the Works of Augustus Baldwin Longstreet," M.A. thesis, University of Oklahoma, 1949;

Wilson Snipes, "The Humor of Longstreet's Persona Abram Baldwin in *Georgia Scenes,*" *Studies in American Humor,* 4 (Winter 1985–1986): 277–289;

Marion Isabel Zula, "Augustus Baldwin Longstreet: Humorist," M.A. thesis, University of South Carolina, 1940.

**Papers:**

The library at Emory University houses more than one hundred letters, manuscripts, and other papers of Augustus Baldwin Longstreet, dating between 1844 and 1860. The University of South Carolina holds twenty-six items, most of them letters.

# Orlando Benedict Mayer

*(24 February 1818 – 16 July 1891)*

James Everett Kibler
*University of Georgia*

See also the Mayer entry in *DLB 3: Antebellum Writers in New York and the South.*

BOOKS: *Luther and the Children* (Columbia, S.C.: South Carolina Lutheran Synod, 1883);

*Malladoce, the Briton. His Wanderings from Druidism to Christianity,* edited by John A. Chapman (Richmond, Va.: Everett Waddey, 1891);

*John Punterick. A Novel of Life in the Old Dutch Fork,* edited by James Everett Kibler (Spartanburg, S.C.: Reprint Company, 1981);

*The Dutch Fork,* edited by Kibler (Columbia, S.C.: Dutch Fork Press, 1982).

OTHER: "Dr. Jacob H. King and Nicholas Summer, Esq.," "The Physicians of the Country," and "Rev. Herman Aull," in *The Annals of Newberry: In Two Parts,* by John A. Chapman and John Belton O'Neall (Newberry, S.C.: Aull & Houseal, 1892), pp. 453–454, 557–562, 658–664;

"'The Innocent Cause, Or How Snoring Broke Off a Match.' A Tale of Hog-Killing Time," "Snip–A Tale," "The Easter Eggs; A Tale of Love, Poetry, and Prose," "The Corn Cob Pipe: A Tale of the Comet of '43," "Little Dassie, or 'The Burning Pine-Knot's Fitful Flare,'" in *Fireside Tales: Stories of the Old Dutch Fork,* edited by James Everett Kibler (Columbia, S.C.: Dutch Fork Press, 1984), pp. 35–44, 59–73, 99–115, 117–131, 141–153.

## SELECTED PERIODICAL PUBLICATIONS– UNCOLLECTED:

FICTION

"A Sunday Evening in Germany," *South Carolinian,* 5 November 1847;

"Batchelor's Hall–A Glimpse," *South Carolinian,* 15 February 1848;

"Aberhot Koselhantz, the Wizard Gunsmith. Story of the Dutch Fork," *Russell's Magazine,* 1 (May 1857): 144–152;

*Orlando Benedict Mayer*

"The Voice, the Hand, and the Silhouette, Being the Title of a Manuscript Found in a Stove," *Russell's Magazine,* 1 (August 1857): 455–460; (September 1857): 521–533; 2 (October 1857): 69–78; (November 1857): 144–151;

"My Landlady's Story," *Russell's Magazine,* 3 (August 1858): 437–441;

"The Dutch Fork. Number 3 and 4," *Newberry Herald,* 29 March, 26 April 1883;

"The Two Marksmen of Ruff's Mountain," *Southern Bivouac,* 2 (November 1886): 361–367; (December 1886): 417–423; (January 1887): 469–474.

NONFICTION

"Letters from Europe," *South Carolinian,* 8, 15 May; 19 June; 3 July; 14 August 1845;

"Do de Woders of Lexington," *South Carolinian,* 28 July 1848;

"Obituary of Thomas Jefferson Summer," *South Carolinian,* March 1852;

"Report on the Endemic Diseases of Newberry, Read Before the Newberry Agricultural Society," *Southern Agriculturist,* 1 (June 1853): 165–167;

"Fireside Revisitings," *Newberry Conservatist,* 6, 13, 20 April; 4, 11, 25 May; 8 June; 6 July; 3, 17 August 1858;

"Johnston's New Map of the Republics of North America," *Newberry Rising Sun,* 13 October 1858;

"Obituary of Henry Summer," *Newberry News,* 18 October 1878;

"Pinnacles of Remembrance: Being Recollections of Travel in Europe Forty Years Ago," *Newberry College Stylus,* 1 (January–June, October–November 1884).

Orlando Benedict Mayer was born near Pomaria, in present-day Newberry County, South Carolina. A rustic humorist whose work was mostly published anonymously or pseudonymously, Mayer is only now being discovered and, it seems, deserves to rank high among writers of Southern backwoods humor. He also figures strongly as a precursor of the local-color movement.

Hans Ulrich Mayer, the author's great-grandfather, came to Pomaria from Germany in 1752. Both he and his son, Johannes Adam Benedict, fought in the South Carolina militia during the Revolutionary War. Johannes Benedict, the author's grandfather, married the daughter of the Colonel Adam Summer whom Mayer describes in his history of the community as the pioneer settler of the area. Johannes became a well-to-do farmer and blacksmith and owned large holdings of land on the Broad River. He had one son, Adam, the author's father. Orlando Mayer was born on 24 February 1818 to Adam Mayer and Mary Counts (Koonts) Mayer, and he had three sisters, Frances, Susannah, and Elvira.

The Dutch Fork area of South Carolina was settled by German and Swiss Protestants in the mid 1700s. It was named after the *Deutsch* (German) people living in the fork between the Broad and Saluda Rivers. During Mayer's childhood the area was still largely isolated from its English-speaking neighbors. German language, customs, and folklore and Lutheranism were all the community knew. Mayer spent his boyhood on his grandmother Mayer's farm, where he was born. Here he listened to her and her old friend Ommee Lohner carry on lively conversations and spin tales of the old days. Many were stories of witches, wizards, goblins, and practices that had their origins in pre-Christian German myth. Mayer later used them as the basis of some of his own stories, such as "Aberhot Koselhantz, the Wizard Gunsmith. Story of the Dutch Fork" (1857). Mayer's *The Dutch Fork* (1982) has a graphic description of these days of his childhood.

As a barefoot farm boy in a homespun shirt with old-fashioned ruffles, Mayer visited Columbia, the state capital, thirty miles away and was made fun of by the town boys. Similarly, his characters who venture from their home are also constantly made aware of their separateness. One character, for example, who had always been proud of his German name, is hurt to find that in another district a family of English background ridicules its strange sound. In Mayer's work, the sons and daughters of the Dutch Fork are ill at ease until they return home.

In the time Mayer was growing to manhood his home was undergoing tremendous change, however—a time of transition ideal for producing a writer. English replaced German in the pulpits of churches of the area and likewise became the preferred language in schools. Mayer still recalled old people luxuriating in the mother tongue every time they got together, but the children of his generation were brought up to speak English. He was eager to dramatize these changes in his fiction and wanted to transmit knowledge of the old ways to the later generations who would not know these customs otherwise.

He was a member of St. Johannes Lutheran Church on Crim's Creek, Pomaria. Attached to the church was a school supported by the church and its members. Here Mayer began his elementary education in 1824, alongside his best friend and distant kinsman, Adam G. Summer, who himself later became a writer of humorous sketches and, as an editor, figured largely in Mayer's life and career. At St. Johannes, Mayer was particularly adept at language, and literature was a part of the curriculum. In later years he remembered dramas performed on the school porch "converted into a palace or prison by quilts borrowed from beds in the neighborhood." Summer also recalled their training in diverse fields, with their master teaching William Shakespeare and then taking them outside to study the plants and trees that grew in the virgin oak forest around St. Johannes. Both men wrote kindly of these school days in their stories. Their training was sound, and the two entered the Classical Academy of the Lutheran Seminary in 1834, some forty miles from home. In 1834 the school had nine students. Its purpose was to prepare young men in classical studies for admission to the seminary. The principal of the classical department was the Reverend Washington Muller. While Mayer attended, both the academy and seminary held classes in the same building. Little is known of his days in Lexington, South Carolina, except that his father moved there to operate a business and built his own mother a house, next to the courthouse, that she ran as a hotel. Mayer's father died later that year at the age of thirty-seven.

Mayer then entered South Carolina College, from which he graduated in 1837 at the age of nineteen. He studied literature under Henry Junius Nott, himself a writer of humorous sketches published as *Novellettes of a Traveller* (1834). He studied sacred literature under James Thornwell and Stephen Elliott, classics under I. W. Stuart, and attended lectures by Thomas Cooper, William Ellet, Francis Lieber, and Thomas Twiss. After graduation he learned medicine under Drs. Toland and Wells of Columbia and journeyed to the Medical College at Charleston, from which he graduated in March 1840. His thesis was on inguinal hernia. The year before, Mayer had wed Mary Davis, daughter of a wealthy planter near Monticello, across the Broad River from Newberry County. She died sometime in 1840, and Mayer was emotionally devastated. In some ways he never recovered.

After the death of his wife and four years of medical practice at Pomaria, he decided to renew his studies for three years in Europe. He debarked at Charleston for Liverpool on 25 April 1844, and after a passage of forty-two days arrived on 12 June. He studied medicine in Edinburgh until November 1844, then went to Paris, continuing his studies there for fifteen months, until 20 February 1846. A. G. Summer's brother Thomas joined him in Paris at Rue de la Harpe, No. 101, while Summer himself was studying agricultural chemistry. Mayer then took a German tour and stayed at Heidelberg to study language—as always, a great interest. After Heidelberg, he went to Giessen to study chemistry under the well-known Dr. Leibig. From Giessen, he went to Mannheim on 28 September 1846. He then continued on to Berlin for medical studies before returning home in February 1847, to continue practice in Pomaria that April.

Through this extensive training, Mayer had become a master of French and German and was, according to one contemporary, "well up" in Latin and Greek. He had by no means neglected literature and was a reader of catholic tastes. The allusions in his works are from every literary period and show a wide knowledge, particularly of the eighteenth century. They also reveal a good knowledge of art and music. A history of the Lutheran Synod of South Carolina called

*Drawing by John C. Dennis of the St. Johannes Lutheran Church in Pomaria, South Carolina, where Mayer received his early education (from* The Dutch Fork, *1982)*

him "a classical scholar of rare attainments, . . . a talented musician, being an authority on vocal music, and himself a composer of no small ability."

Having returned from Europe with, as he said, "the materials for many sketches," Mayer began publishing fiction based on his European travels. His first known sketch, "A Sunday Evening in Germany," appeared in the *South Carolinian* on 5 November 1847. Mayer's literary reputation, however, rests primarily on his humorous tales with Dutch Fork settings and character types, which he wrote for newspapers and magazines such as the *South Carolinian*, Paul Hamilton Hayne's *Russell's Magazine,* and the *Southern Bivouac.* Like his contemporary, Henry Clay Lewis of Louisiana, a country doctor and humorist of some renown, Mayer managed to balance the demanding responsibilities of a physician with his avocation as an author of comic tales.

Mayer's life at this time may be glimpsed in his humorous novel *John Punterick. A Novel of Life in the Old Dutch Fork,* which, though written later, is set in June

1847 and describes a gathering of tellers of comic tales, of which Mayer and A. G. Summer are part. There was apparently an informal Dutch Fork school of humorists who were aware of the tradition and were active in furthering it. The frame presents a remarkable firsthand picture of this coterie of yarn spinners in action. These gentlemen, who were planters, farmers, or doctors and not professional writers, took turns swapping tales at such casual gatherings as the one Mayer describes, held under the trees at Pomaria Plantation. A. G. Summer (under the name Vesper Bracket in the novel) speaks in the fashion of his newspaper essays, and Billy Summer likewise talks as he does in the columns of his brother's paper.

Mayer's most important and representative literary works generally place him in the school of Southern frontier humor. His first known humorous stories were published in the *South Carolinian,* the weekly newspaper edited by A. G. Summer, who was also writing humorous tales, several of which were republished in the New York–based *Spirit of the Times.* During his tenure as editor of the *South Carolinian* between 1845 and 1848, Summer, who has been called a kind of Southern William Trotter Porter, not only published South Carolina humorists such as Mayer but also reprinted some of the sketches of many of the best-known humorists of the 1840s, including Johnson Jones Hooper, William Tappan Thompson, Thomas Bangs Thorpe, George Washington Harris, Sol Smith, Joseph Field, and John S. Robb. As one of the contributors for the *South Carolinian,* Mayer likely read these writers. In fact, Mayer knew Thompson, whom he and Summer entertained in Columbia in 1848, the same year that Mayer published his first humorous tale.

This story, "'The Innocent Cause, Or How Snoring Broke Off a Match.' A Tale of Hog-Killing Time," appeared in the *South Carolinian* of 25 January 1848 under the pseudonym "Haggis" and exhibits most of the ingredients familiarly associated with the frontier tall tale: the frame device, lively and earthy dialect, exaggerated descriptions, graphically animated action, incongruous situations, and an eccentric rustic prankster. Employing the epistolary format that Thompson skillfully used in *Major Jones's Courtship* (1843) and a rogue whose traits suggest a close literary kinship to Harris's Sut Lovingood, Mayer creates in his chief character, Belt Seebub, more commonly and humorously known as Belzebub, a likable prankster-fool whose antics provide an entertaining and engaging story of rural courtship. Incongruities abound, the most humorous being in some of Belt's exaggerated figurative renderings of character and incident. For instance, while sharing a room for the night with a snoring Kentucky hog driver, whom he regards as a meddlesome, unwanted competitor in his quest for a country girl's affections, Belt resorts to unflattering hyperbole to create a comic effect: "He lay flat upon his back, with his hed berried in the piller, his eyes sot and half open, and his underjaw hung down tel his tongue could be seen as dry as a swinged pig tail. In fact, his mouth looked like a steel trap set for an otter and baited with a piece of dried beef." When the Kentuckian's snoring becomes so loud that Belt cannot sleep, he expediently places the end of a stovepipe over the man's face. The resulting noise, which Belt ludicrously asserts "was sumthin between the howl of lettin off steam and the scream of a circular saw cutting through a hard pine-knot," causes fright and pandemonium among the farm animals, and the soot blown through the stovepipe soils the clean white petticoats drying on the clothesline and creates major mayhem among the female population.

"Snip–A Tale," Mayer's second humorous work of short fiction and his first to employ a discernible Dutch Fork setting and German dialect, was likewise published under the signature of "Haggis" in the *South Carolinian* on 5 September 1848. It delineates with genial humor the character of a horse named Snip and the role that he plays in a rural family—focusing on a Dutch Fork wedding and the customs that it involves. In part the humorous incongruity of the tale depends on the juxtaposition of Haggis's allusive and stilted rhetoric, which sometimes approaches lyricism, and the vividly unrestrained, realistic dialect of the rural characters of the Dutch Fork. Yet Haggis, the native Dutch Forker, does not exhibit, as do other genteel raconteurs of frontier humor, a conspicuously condescending attitude toward these characters or their eccentricities. Following the manner of backwoods comedy, Mayer includes several slapstick situations. At the outset, when a wagon belonging to the Wimples, a local farm family, becomes bogged down in the mud, Snip, a steed more reliable for courting purposes than for strenuous work, refuses to pull it out of the mire. Attempting to coerce the horse, young Joe Wimple falls "flat upon his back, leaving an impression in the mud, from which a very correct cast of his proportions could have been taken."

"Snip" is at once backwoods humor and local color but rises above both genres with its universal characters. In fact, these three characteristics, with a strong predilection for the latter, mark all of Mayer's humorous works. His approach to character almost always comes through a good-natured realization that man is often a foolish, even absurd creature owing to his vanity, stubbornness, pride, selfishness, and hypocrisy. Unlike Mark Twain, Mayer was never to denounce bitterly "the whole damned human race" but instead pointed out its foibles and laughed at them. Mayer's love of humanity is never in doubt. As a physician he was always praised for his kindheartedness, patience, and unselfishness, and these qualities show through his warm humor. He was never blind to men's faults, however, and as a result he never idealizes. While possessing endearing traits, Mayer's characters can also be incredibly pigheaded.

This focus on character, particularly on the humorous and absurd aspects thereof, seemed to grow during his career. Another story of the rustic humor variety and exhibiting humorous incongruity in characterization, "The Easter Eggs; A Tale of Love, Poetry, and Prose" is a lengthy piece that first appeared in the *South Carolinian* on 27 October 1848. Focusing again on Dutch Fork courtship customs and contrasting the vernacular and formal literary stylistic modes, the humor of the tale is most graphically exemplified by the reenactment of the "big brag" or "ring-tailed roarer" motif involving a conflict between two rival suitors of a rural lass. Interestingly, this scene, complete with the use of accentuated gesture and phrasing (one of the suitors remarks to the other, "my mammy is as good a man as ever trod shoe leather!" and then springs into the air, striking "his heels together three times before he touched the earth"), anticipates similar confrontations between raftsmen in other frontier humor.

Two months after the appearance of "The Easter Eggs," Mayer published another long story in the *South Carolinian*, "The Corn Cob Pipe: A Tale of the Comet of '43," which exhibits several close parallels to Washington Irving's "The Legend of Sleepy Hollow" (1819). Indeed, Irving has been called one of the most important literary influences on Southern backwoods humor as a whole, and there is little doubt Mayer was conforming to the pattern of his genre in this tale. "The Corn Cob Pipe," which is often acclaimed Mayer's single best work of short fiction, is another story of courtship characterized by frequent comic incongruity. The plot of the tale, appropriate to situation comedy, centers around a conflict between a young Dutch Fork farm girl and her parents regarding whom she should marry. Whereas they desire that she marry the genteel schoolmaster, Isom Jones, her own personal preference is Abram Priester, a young farmer "of athletic proportion." To accomplish her objective the girl contrives a scheme for blowing up her father with a cob pipe filled with gunpowder, a stratagem that, when executed, results in the schoolmaster's being erroneously blamed as the culprit and his subsequent rapid disappearance "from the neighborhood like the pedagogue of Sleepy Hollow." As Leland Cox wrote in "Realistic and Humorous Writings in Ante-Bellum Charleston Magazines" (1975), in "The Corn Cob Pipe" Mayer's "ability to deal frankly and humorously with the violent power struggles that sometimes occur between children and

parents" is central to an understanding of his art. Mayer's story, while delineating customs, actually concerns the lengths to which a young woman will go to get the man whom she has chosen. Cox continues that the story goes beyond its model and that "the rubric of 'local color' can only become a pejorative term when applied to a story such as this."

This first year of Mayer's writing career was thus among his most fertile, no doubt partly because of the circumstances in which he found himself. During 1848 Mayer, Summer, and two others had kept in Columbia what Mayer called "a Batcheler's Hall." Mayer writes that two of these men (likely he and A. G. Summer) had been "rocked in the same cradle, played together in the same puddle, and have been flogged by the same stick." Here Summer invited writers such as William Gilmore Simms and the Georgia humorist William Tappan Thompson to dine and talk about writing. Mayer lost this valuable stimulus and means to sharing literary ideas when Summer retired from the newspaper on 31 December 1848. Despite his literary successes, Mayer regretted these years as frivolous. He must have been something of a blade.

In 1849 Mayer moved to the county seat town of Newberry, where he practiced medicine and, according to one of his contemporaries, "lived, honored and useful" for more than forty years. There and throughout the state, he became known as an eminent physician. His personality seemed especially well suited for practicing among the rural and small-town inhabitants of his native place, for as another has described him, he was known as a "jolly extrovert who enjoyed practical jokes."

In 1851 Mayer was wed a second time, to Caroline "Carrie" N. DeWalt, described by contemporaries as a "remarkably handsome, vivacious, gentle, and gracious lady" of Newberry, and they lived in the old DeWalt home on Main Street. The couple had two sons, Orlando Benedict Mayer Jr. and Eugene Adam, and four daughters, Mary, Caroline, Catherine, and Alice, before the wife's death in 1861.

Summer's literary influence on Mayer yielded to that of Paul Hamilton Hayne, a genteel author much different from the rustic school of humorists in which Mayer had been nurtured. Mayer's next known work was "The Music Girl of the Rue de la Harpe," published in Hayne's *Russell's Magazine* of April 1857. This story draws on his experiences in Paris and is in the serious, genteel mode of Irving, Edgar Allan Poe, and German Romanticism. In "Aberhot Koselhantz, the Wizard Gunsmith. Story of the Dutch Fork," published in *Russell's* in May 1857, Mayer again uses native folk customs, legends, superstitions, and local dialect to create a story of merit. The plot of the tale revolves

*Mayer, circa 1850s (from* The Dutch Fork, *1982)*

around the title character's supernatural ability to cast immobilizing spells on persons attempting to harm his family. When British soldiers attempt to molest Koselhantz's wife and daughters, Mayer shifts the tale into the fantastic mode, with the gunsmith casting a spell that turns the intruders to stone. Once they are freed from the spell, the story becomes a semifarcical comedy of errors as they unsuccessfully attempt to complete their sinister actions.

"The Voice, the Hand, and the Silhouette, Being the Title of a Manuscript Found in a Stove," published in the August through November 1857 issues of *Russell's Magazine,* is set in Germany and reverts to the style and Gothic mode of "The Music Girl of the Rue de la Harpe." The stories with European settings are inferior to his Dutch Fork narratives. They are, however, an aspect of his career that cannot be dismissed, because he continued writing in this vein until his death. Mayer's next contribution to *Russell's* was a rewritten version of "The Corn Cob Pipe" in the May 1858 issue; his last, "My Landlady's Story," appeared in the August issue. This sketch is set in Edinburgh and is a suspenseful tale of demonic possession. It is perhaps the best of his European stories.

Under the pen name "Obadiah Haggis," Mayer published a ten-part series, "Fireside Revisitings," in the *Newberry Conservatist,* edited by his friend Bill

Nance. These chatty essays concerning Revolutionary war battles in South Carolina appeared from April to August 1858.

Mayer's finest work of long fiction, *John Punterick,* was begun around 1860. The first half, titled "Mirthful," was published in 1981. In 1996 a second half of the novel, titled "Mournful," was acquired by the South Caroliniana Library and rests in manuscript there. The "Mournful" half is set in and around Paris and follows the melancholy, genteel, Gothic mode of Mayer's other European fiction; but in "Mirthful," Mayer's native cultural influences run strong. At its beginning, set in 1847, several friends have gathered to swap stories of character, of past community events that have shaped the present, and of changing times. The tradition is of the oral narrative—relaxed, discursive, sometimes episodic, but always redolent of good common sense, friendly humor, and frank, realistic observation of character. Fritz, one of the characters in the frame, proposes to read a manuscript in his possession, a semihumorous satire of the Horatian ilk that mildly ridicules the foibles and frailties of the society in transition. Though most of the characters in the novel, including John Punterick, are near caricatures, they nonetheless reveal Mayer's shrewd insights into human nature. His title character, the first man to leave the Dutch Fork and thus break the "talismanic charm" that bound the community together, is a representative man of the modern era, of the new rootless American society that is replacing the old traditional culture to which he stands in marked contrast. He is materialistic, hedonistic, and self-centered. Unlike the typical man of the old community, he does not care about tradition, communal ties, or neighbors. He cares nothing for place or sense thereof. Money, comfort, and self-indulgence are his aims. Mayer also provides a humorous view of a host of less serious human foibles in his minor characters, who suffer variously from hypocrisy, superstition, stubbornness, obsession with trivial matters, meddlesomeness, and monomania, to name only a few. Yet, Mayer does not fail to portray their strengths, so the novel, like the best of his finest short comic fiction, again provides a rounded study of human nature.

The "Mirthful" section of *John Punterick* thus offers good insights into human nature, its strengths as well as weaknesses, and considers the broad implications of change on the value of the society. The Dutch Fork becomes a microcosm of the modern world, and the main character becomes an everyman. *John Punterick* is thus an important literary work from one who had evidently thought long and deeply. Here, Mayer is at the same time a social historian and a realist who sees through hypocritical shams and presents human nature without idealization. He depicts his characters' follies and faults with warm understanding and never despises those who have them. In this work, Mayer's literary realism seems to have been most closely influenced by Henry Fielding. Like that novelist, whom he quotes occasionally, he good-naturedly depicts his characters' follies as the true source of the ridiculous. Jonathan Swift is another literary forebear, but Mayer never uses Swift's bitter invective. Mayer was remarkably well-read; a quick survey of his literary allusions provides rather staggering results. His favorites were Robert Burns, Lord Byron, Thomas Chatterton, Swift, Irving, Poe, Shakespeare, Sir Walter Scott, Alexander Pope, John Milton, John Dryden, Fielding, folk ballads, Virgil, Homer, Johann Wolfgang von Goethe, Thomas Gray, William Cowper, Miguel de Cervantes, Edmund Spenser, Oliver Goldsmith, and Charles Dickens, but these represent only a few of his antecedents. His chief influences in humor were Fielding, Irving, Swift and the oral and written Southern backwoods humor tradition.

Mayer had been one of eighteen original board of trustees members responsible for creating the new college in Newberry. They began their work in 1856 as a building committee, and when Newberry College opened in 1859 Mayer became a member of the first faculty, as professor of chemistry, botany, mineralogy, and geology. John Bachman, a Lutheran minister, naturalist, and friend of John James Audubon, was also a lecturer at the Lutheran school and became a friend of Mayer while Bachman served as the president of the first board of trustees. Mayer, Bachman, and the Summer brothers were all thus instrumental in founding the new school. Mayer remained on the faculty until 1868, when the college was destroyed by occupation forces after the war. It moved to Walhalla, South Carolina, and returned to Newberry in 1877, at which time Mayer became a lecturer on physiology and hygiene. During the 1860's, Mayer produced little fiction. He is said to have published some humorous stories in the local papers, among them "Old Nick" and "Jes Middlin, Mass Ben," but these have not yet been located.

As a physician in the foremost rank of his profession, Mayer's medical essays were highly regarded, and he was sought for counsel in critical cases. A contemporary wrote of him that he "did not seek the applause of men, or he could have obtained a world-wide distinction in his profession, and also in literature, in which he took great delight. He did not seek wealth, or he might have grown rich. . . . He was pure-hearted, honest, overflowing with generosity and kindness . . . a truly religious man, one of the most faithful and devoted students of the Bible I have ever known; a firm believer in it as the Word of God, making it the rule of his life. He was a consistent member of the Lutheran Church, but not a bigot–an humble, pious, devoted Christian. His

faith was childlike, taking God at his word. . . ." Another biographer noted that he was a lifelong "defender of the faith of the Lutheran church." In the *Newberry Herald and News* for 22 August 1905 J. M. Crosson recalled Mayer as a "beloved, intellectual, polished Christian gentleman." During the later years of his medical career he went into practice with his son, O. B. Jr., who became president of the South Carolina Medical Association. Mayer's son terminated this partnership, however, because his father would never discuss the patient's payment of bills. The son had a large family to support, however, and so set up his own practice. The son's own biographer writes that his home influence was the chief factor in his success and in the shaping of his character.

After retirement Mayer continued to perform difficult surgery when requested. During his last decade he was busy rewriting some of his early stories, such as "The Corn Cob Pipe," "Aberhot Koselhantz, the Wizard Gunsmith," and "The Easter Eggs." In spring 1883 he published a rough, chatty series of reminiscences called "The Dutch Fork" in the *Newberry Herald*. Later in that year he published with the South Carolina Synod of the Lutheran Church a pamphlet, *Luther and the Children,* given out at the commemoration of the four hundredth anniversary of Luther's birth, at Bethlehem Church, Pomaria, 10 November 1883. On the occasion Mayer led the singing of "Ein Feste Burg" in German as a member of a special choir. In 1884 he wrote a series of reminiscences of his European travels of the 1840s, which he published in the Newberry College literary magazine, the *Stylus*.

Several significant new works of fiction appeared in the last decade of Mayer's life. "The Two Marksmen of Ruff's Mountain" (written in 1884 and published in Hayne's *Southern Bivouac* in November 1886) is set in the Dutch Fork during the Revolution. A quasi-humorous work, with the plot centering around the vengeance of two brothers against a villainous British murderer, the tale indicates that Mayer was still influenced by the frontier tall tale. He portrays two rustics, one superbly skillful in rifle marksmanship and the other incredibly adept at throwing stones, displaying "such power and dexterity that he could, without fail, strike a bullock dead, at the distance of twenty-five paces." Both resemble the archetypal demigods of the frontier tradition, such as Paul Bunyan and Davy Crockett. "The Two Marksmen" is a good work that ranks high in the canon.

In 1885 Mayer traveled to Bath, England, where he visited in the home of a Captain Simpson. He took a hiking tour to Salisbury Plain to view Stonehenge and returned home abruptly in August 1885. During the last days of his life he was writing a novel, *Malladoce, the*

*Briton. His Wanderings from Druidism to Christianity,* in which he uses his Stonehenge experiences, complete with the strange apparition of a couple on a white horse that he had there–the vision that sent him hurrying back home. Mayer died in Newberry on 16 July 1891 before he could finish the novel. He had completed and revised the first part, and John A. Chapman, to whom he had talked about the story, completed it. It was published in late 1891. Like all Mayer's stories on serious topics set outside the Dutch Fork, it does not quite measure up to the humorous, realistic sketches but can be grouped instead with the competent *Russell's* gothic-romance tales of the 1850s, such as "The Music Girl of the Rue de la Harpe," "The Voice, the Hand, and the Silhouette," and "My Landlady's Story."

Another important creation of his last year was a revision and republication of his 1883 series, *The Dutch Fork,* as an expanded seven-part, warmly humorous and nostalgic reminiscence of the old times. It appeared in 1891 in the *Newberry Herald and News.* He had intended to publish this history in book form later in the year, interspersing his short stories of Dutch Fork, as he says, "for the purpose of portraying" in fiction the events, customs, and traditions of the history. Such a project would be squarely in the local color fashion popular at this time. He promised also to "revise the sketches entirely, and make large additions to them of materials purposely withheld, and much that has come recently to my knowledge." Although a friend reported that Mayer had finished revising his sketches "on the day before he was taken with his fatal sickness," his death prevented him from seeing this volume through the press. Celebrating the past as a simpler and better time, *The Dutch Fork,* which was eventually published in 1982, exploits some of the same subject matter–customs, lore, and superstitions as well as the contrast between genteel and rustic and the modern and the traditional–found in Mayer's earlier and best humorous fiction.

Also just before his death in 1891, Mayer gave to the editor of the *Herald and News* the Dutch Fork story "Little Dassie," which was printed posthumously. This sketch reveals that in his last years Mayer had drifted toward sentimentality but that his old love of realistic characterization was still with him. As his letters to Hayne reveal, the loss of his wife, a son and daughter, and best friends A. G. Summer and William Nance had deepened a melancholy that was always a facet of his character. Death had been much on his mind during the 1880s. Mayer's personality thus shows a dichotomy: he was a jolly humorist who knew the meaning of sadness and cultivated melancholy, and a doctor who had often faced death, yet found its reality difficult to accept.

One final work of interest is Mayer's journal, which he kept for a long period of his life. This manuscript, which he said was the source of many of his stories, has not been located. It still existed in 1891, when he reports using it in writing "Little Dassie." Here he recommends keeping such a notebook to each country doctor, who would by the age of forty thereby become "a wise acre and warmhearted humorist," an apt description of the author himself. The manuscript was said to be in sad repair, having "afforded accommodations to a matronly mouse up to the third and fourth generations" and was "legible (shame to me) only here and there."

It should also be noted in passing that the old doctor was also a prolific poet. Some of his poems, as a contemporary put it, "were preserved but never published in book form." Only one poem is proved to be his: "Song. O! the Ship Is the Harp of the Storm," published in the *South Carolinian* of 5 November 1847 and signed "Haggis." Some of the unsigned poems, as well as a verse translation of Friedrich Schiller, in the *Newberry Conservatist* in 1858 were no doubt also from his pen, but cannot be conclusively identified. Likewise, it is reported that he had "rendered many of the German hymns and sonnets into English verse, requiring the exercise of fine poetic taste as well as good knowledge of the German." Some of these still exist in a manuscript notebook. Since work on Mayer is in its infancy, future investigation may reveal poems and additional works of fiction as well. A close friend reported that Mayer, at his death, left unpublished manuscript "stories and sketches fully equal" to his published works. One of these was likely the two-part *John Punterick,* but the others are unknown.

Although a local historian wrote that during his day Mayer "acquired celebrity as a writer," his fame must have been almost entirely limited to his community. He made no impression on the literary establishment of his day. Other than his coterie of fellow Dutch Fork humorists, only Hayne, who published his works in *Russell's* and the *Southern Bivouac,* seems to have taken notice of him. This lack of attention did not concern Mayer, who was not ambitious for literary fame and more times than not published his works without attaching his name to them, or, as in the case of *John Punterick,* circulated them among friends without publishing at all. His indifference to notoriety is perhaps explained by one of his favorite poems, Gray's "Elegy Written in a Country Churchyard" (1751), which stresses the short and simple annals of the little man. Even though he was a celebrated physician, he was devoted to his rural community and its folk traditions–traditions that were preliterary and passed on in ways other than through the celebrity of the printed word. Mayer was well aware of the valuable role of oral narrative and of the bard as creator of legend that captures essential truths that give a people a sense of identity. His abiding interest in character might best be expressed in the words of a figure in Mayer's last story. In "Little Dassie," Big Dave, the gentle rustic, is fond of saying, "Human natur, Doc, is more amazin than the seasins."

As Edward Piacentino has recently written, Orlando Benedict Mayer deserves to be elevated to a more prominent position in the ranks of the Southern rustic humorists. Certainly his humorous novel, *John Punterick,* is a work of literary merit, and several of his humorous stories–"The Innocent Cause," "Snip–A Tale," "The Corn Cob Pipe," "The Easter Eggs," "The Two Marksmen of Ruff's Mountain," and "Aberhot Koselhantz, the Wizard Gunsmith"–are of the first rank and therefore may be favorably compared with similar tales penned by some of the more prominent humorists of the antebellum frontier school. As these works attest, Mayer was a good prose stylist, a shrewd student of human nature, and a sophisticated, entertaining, and technically competent storyteller who possessed a keen ear for dialect and fond appreciation for the rustic customs and traditions of his little postage stamp of native soil. Above all, he simply had a wonderful way with words. Interest in Mayer's works has recently been stimulated with publication of editions the "Mirthful" section of *John Punterick, The Dutch Fork,* and some of his stories. With the likelihood that still more of his work will be discovered and republished, Mayer in time may receive a well-deserved reevaluation.

## References:

John A. Chapman, *The Annals of Newberry: In Two Parts,* by Chapman and John Belton O'Neall (Newberry, S.C.: Aull & Houseal, 1892), pp. 567–568;

Leland Cox, "Realistic and Humorous Writings in Ante-Bellum Charleston Magazines," in *South Carolina Journals and Journalists: Proceedings of the Reynolds Conference, University of South Carolina, May 17–18, 1974,* edited by James B. Meriwether (Spartanburg, S.C.: Reprint Company, 1975), pp. 177–205;

J. M. Crosson, "The Newberry of Days That Are Past," *Newberry Herald and News,* 22 August 1905, p. 1;

James Everett Kibler, "The Dutch Fork of Mayer's Fiction," *Names in South Carolina,* 30 (Winter 1983): 24–31;

Kibler, "'The Innocent Cause, Or How Snoring Broke Off a Match': A Sketch from the Dutch Fork School of Humor," *Studies in American Humor,* 2 (Winter 1983–1984): 185–194;

Kibler, Introduction to *John Punterick, A Novel of Life in the Old Dutch Fork,* by O. B. Mayer (Spartanburg, S.C.: Reprint Company, 1981), pp. ix–xix;

Kibler, Introduction to *The Dutch Fork,* by Mayer (Columbia, S.C.: Dutch Fork Press, 1982), pp. vii–xv;

Kibler, Preface to *Fireside Tales: Stories of the Old Dutch Fork,* edited by Kibler (Columbia, S.C.: Dutch Fork Press, 1984), pp. 1–4;

Kibler and Edward Piacentino, "Orlando Benedict Mayer," in *Encyclopedia of American Humorists,* edited by Steven Gale (New York: Garland, 1988), pp. 315–320;

"Orlando Benedict Mayer," in *Cyclopedia of Eminent and Representative Men of the Carolinas of the Nineteenth Century* (Madison, Wis.: Brant & Fuller, 1892), I: 323–324;

Piacentino, "Backwoods Humor in Upcountry South Carolina: The Case of O. B. Mayer," *South Carolina Review,* 30 (Fall 1997): 79–85;

Piacentino, "Letter from O. B. Mayer to Paul Hamilton Hayne," *Mississippi Quarterly,* 50 (Winter 1996–1997): 117–123.

# Louisa S. McCord

*(3 December 1810 – 23 November 1879)*

Richard C. Lounsbury
*Brigham Young University*

BOOKS: *My Dreams* (Philadelphia: Carey & Hart, 1848);

*Caius Gracchus. A Tragedy in Five Acts* (New York: Kernot, 1851);

*Louisa S. McCord: Political and Social Essays,* edited by Richard C. Lounsbury (Charlottesville: University Press of Virginia, 1995);

*Louisa S. McCord: Poems, Drama, Biography, Letters,* edited by Lounsbury (Charlottesville: University Press of Virginia, 1996);

*Louisa S. McCord: Selected Writings,* edited by Lounsbury (Charlottesville: University Press of Virginia, 1997).

OTHER: Frédéric Bastiat, *Sophisms of the Protective Policy,* translated by McCord (New York & Charleston: Putnam, 1848); republished as *Sophisms of the Protection* [part 1 of *Essays on Political Economy*] (Chicago: Western News, 1869); republished as *Sophisms of the Protectionists* (New York: Putnam, 1870).

*Louisa S. McCord (Collections of the Georgia Historical Society)*

Louisa S. McCord defended women's traditional role and yet believed, and in "Slavery and Political Economy" (1856) wrote, that "the positions of women and children are in truth as essentially states of bondage as any other." She exalted slavery as a civilizing force and the protection of the slaves, and she informed a Northern visitor that "she would prefer to have $25,000 in good bank stock rather than $100,000 in negroes and plantations." She praised women as "the conservative power in the world" and praised her native state, South Carolina, for its principles "among the most conservative in all the country," and she wrote a tragedy in which the Roman heroine can conserve nothing amid the ruin killing her son. Burdened, while still in her twenties, with the care of a large household, McCord then superintended a plantation that came to be recognized as a model and reared and educated her own three children; yet, she wrote of her "effortless life," which was, "to a restless mind, a weary fate to be doomed to; and as no other door is open to me, I may

as well push on at this"–"this" being a desire for fame as a poet and tragedian, augmented, then overwhelmed, by a zeal to defend Southern society with her pen, until troubled eyesight and civil tumult blocked up even her obdurate ambition. On the losing side, she did not tolerate loss; she would not regret what others preferred regretting; and like her, her legacy has been too able, too vigorous, too various to be ignored.

She was born Louisa Susanna Cheves on 3 December 1810 in Charleston, South Carolina. She was the fourth of fourteen children. Her father, Langdon

Cheves, was the only child of a Scottish immigrant and Loyalist. With the independent fortitude that Louisa came to admire in her father, Cheves clerked in a general store and taught himself the law, until, having developed a large and remunerative practice, he became the state attorney general and, at the time of Louisa's birth, had just been elected to the U.S. House of Representatives. He had married in 1806 Mary Elizabeth Dulles, whose father was a wealthy Charleston merchant and whose mother had inherited several plantations in South Carolina and Georgia. Thus, Louisa was a child of the professional, mercantile, and planter classes of her region. She immediately became more broadly acquainted, however—first with the federal capital, where her father became Speaker of the House and whence, in 1814, the family was forced to flee the marauding British; and then, in 1819, with Philadelphia, to which Cheves moved his large family upon being appointed first president of the Bank of the United States by President James Monroe.

In Philadelphia with her elder sister Sophia, Louisa received the finest education that a father of Cheves's station and fortune could procure. She studied French, in which she became proficient. She was not content with the subjects conventionally taught to young ladies, however. One day, hiding behind a door and working problems while her brothers were being tutored in mathematics in the next room, she was apprehended by her father. Of all his children Louisa was always to be the closest to Cheves in intellect, a position he recognized by bequeathing to her his library; and now he acted accordingly, ordering that henceforth Louisa should be instructed along with her brothers in subjects usually the province of boys. Her education was not formal only. In Philadelphia she was brought to understand, for the first time, the ignorance of the South in Northern minds and the difficulty of combating that ignorance. She remembered the occasion, "one of our earliest trials in life," in the *Southern Quarterly Review* (January 1853), in a review of Harriet Beecher Stowe's *Uncle Tom's Cabin* (1852), the work that, to her mind, most destructively evinced that ignorance:

> Our first entrance upon school being made in one of our Northern cities, we found ourselves, before the first week of probation was over, the object of some comment among the younger members of the establishment, and were finally accused, by the leader of the little faction, of coming from the land of negrodom. To this charge, we, of course, could but plead guilty, wondering, in our little mind, what sin there could be in the association. A portion of our iniquities we soon had revealed to us. "Father's cousin's wife's sister was at the South once, and she knows all about how you treat your negroes! She knows that you feed them with cotton-seed,

and put padlocks on their mouths to keep them from eating corn while they are in the field." Vainly we protested; as vainly reasoned. Authority was against us, and the padlock story vouched by "father's cousin's wife's sister, a very nice lady, that always told the truth," was swallowed by the majority, and received in our Lilliput community with as undisputed credence as Mrs. Stowe's brother's account of the fist "calloused by knocking down niggers" will be gulped down by her admirers.

In 1829 the Cheves family returned to South Carolina. Leaving politics behind as he had left behind the law, Cheves took up rice and cotton planting, at which he prospered as always. His wife's health was not prosperous, however. When Sophia Cheves was married in 1830, Louisa took over many of the duties of plantation mistress and manager of a large family. After her mother's death in 1836, all of those duties became her concern. "I feel," she wrote to Sophia, "as I wander about the house and have to take her place in a thousand things as if I were doing wrong all the time." By the standards of her society she was late to marry, in May 1840 at twenty-nine years of age. Her husband, David James McCord, was a lawyer of some standing, thirteen years her senior. He had edited a series of South Carolina law reports; he was also a newspaper editor and banker. He was a widower, whose eldest daughter had been married to Louisa's younger brother Langdon in December 1839. Unlike that occasion, the wedding of Louisa to McCord, as her disappointed sister Anna wrote to a cousin, "was about as quiet an affair as could well take place. . . . We thought of getting up a picnic or something of the kind, but our plans here were also frustrated, for Mr. McCord was obliged to return to Columbia the day after he was married on business." A son was born to the McCords in April 1841 and named Langdon Cheves McCord; two daughters followed, Hannah in 1843 and Louisa in 1845. The family made its home at Lang Syne plantation, about thirty-five miles south of Columbia, which in 1841 Cheves gave to Louisa in her own right when distributing his properties among his children.

Visitors from as far away as Canada commended the elegance and style of living at Lang Syne and the prudence and dedication of its management. In 1845 a young physician from Quebec traveling for his health, Edward Dagge Worthington, stayed at Lang Syne for two months. After morning inspection of the slaves' quarters as he recalled in her 1894 letter, his hostess "would take me off for a gallop through the open to some high point commanding a view of the country. . . . She was a tall *queenly* woman, and a very queen at heart; motherly and kind. She treated me as though I were an over grown boy." The McCords divided the year

MY

DREAMS.

BY

LOUISA S. M'CORD.

Clarior è tenebris.

'Tis to create, and in creating, live
A being more intense, that we endow
With form, our fancy; gaining as we give
The Life we image, e'en as I do now.
CHILDE HAROLD.—Canto 3d.

PHILADELPHIA:
CAREY AND HART.
1848.

*Title page for McCord's first book and only collection of poems
(South Caroliniana Library, University of South Carolina)*

between Lang Syne and Columbia, where in 1849 they built a house across from South Carolina College. They shared interests in politics and political economy, working, as their family liked to remember, at matching desks in the library at Lang Syne. David James McCord, for the most part retired on account of uncertain health, fostered his wife's literary interests, writing a preface to *Sophisms of the Protective Policy,* her translation of the French economist Frédéric Bastiat's *Sophismes économiques,* and supervising the publication of her book of poems, *My Dreams.* Both books appeared in 1848.

*My Dreams,* at first, seems to be the more characteristic work of a literary lady in 1848. It is a collection of forty-five poems mostly in lyric meters, with some, the longest poem among them, written in blank verse. Yet, they are mysterious poems, and not only because

almost nothing is known of the context and sequence of their composition. Certainly they delight in invention, in playing with common themes in multiple ways and varying meters both within and among poems. The placement of poems indicates sure care for the effect of the whole.

Behind the craftsmanship, however, the poems are rigorously detached. McCord uses the first person rarely, preferably to narrate or engage in dialogue. Loneliness is a favorite theme, but seldom personalized; many poems, on the other hand, seem to accept solitude as the price of rising, of soaring above something that clings from below. Sometimes it is tempting to conjecture autobiographical hints. McCord wrote in letters of her restless mind; in "The Fire-fly," the poet addresses her subject: "What though thou, like me, must find–/ Born to Earth, doomed to regretting– / Vainly that the restless mind / Seeks to soar, its birth forgetting?" "The Comet," invoking the "lone stranger through the sky," might invoke also the woman whose amalgam of ambitions, abilities, and duties at once demanded and resisted fulfillment:

Or art thou but some wandering discontent?
Some thought, which may not find a resting-place,
Fixed to one constant round of endless change,
For ever wandering, and for ever doomed
To wander on alone; teaching itself
To suffer; gnawing itself, and bringing home
Its direst misery? a misery
Of loneliness unshared, which nought can know
And nought can pity?

The eerie ballad "Poor Nannie" focuses on four characters. The first, a "tardy labourer" returning home during a December storm, is frightened by strange, seemingly supernatural cries. The cries, it transpires, come from a young woman who, having deserted her aged father to run off with a suitor, now travels through the icy tempest to see her father on his deathbed. The morning after the storm the father wakes: his daughter is dead by his bed; he dies beside her. Visiting the common grave of father and daughter, the fourth character, the suitor "who like a serpent crept, / And stole her from her father's home," then rides away to forget the woman whom he had betrayed. The dedicatory poem of *My Dreams* is addressed to Langdon Cheves for his "hope-inspiring praise" nourishing his daughter's poetry, a phrase that echoes Nannie's comment about her own father: "And happy was I with his praise, / The greatest pleasure that I felt."

McCord's translation of Bastiat's *Sophismes économiques* was her first contribution to the study of political economy. She entered this study with some circumspection, first by means of translation, then, in her essay "Justice and Fraternity" (*Southern Quarterly Review,* July 1849)

*McCord's home in Columbia, South Carolina, built in 1849 (South Caroliniana Library, University of South Carolina)*

combining translation with commentary, and followed in "The Right to Labor" (*Southern Quarterly Review,* October 1849) with a preponderance of commentary and independent disquisition. John Seely Hart printed excerpts from these essays in his *Female Prose Writers of America* (1852), with a note that their author was "one of the few women who have undertaken to write on the difficult subject of political economy." The rarity of her contribution was expanded in Sarah Josepha Hale's *Woman's Record* (1855), which observed that McCord had "distinguished herself in what may be styled political literature, a species of writing seldom attempted by woman."

By that time McCord had contributed long and polemical articles on women's roles, slavery, and Southern politics to the *Southern Quarterly Review, DeBow's Review,* and the *Southern Literary Messenger.* While these were her three constant subjects, the occasions might vary widely. She suspected that books arguing against polygenesis of the human species were covert attacks on racial slavery. Horrific descriptions of the English poor in Charles Kingsley's *Alton Locke* (1850) suggested to her that English abolition-

ists might better occupy themselves with the misery in their own country. She defended her father's position in the South Carolina secession crisis of 1850–1851 in the article "Separate Secession" (*Southern Quarterly Review,* October 1851). Her "Enfranchisement of Woman" (*Southern Quarterly Review,* April 1852) answered the British radicals John Stuart Mill and Harriet Taylor Mill; "Woman and Her Needs" (*DeBow's Review,* September 1852) sought to expose the muddy thinking and dishonest arguments of so-called moderate feminism. Henry C. Carey's *The Slave Trade, Domestic and Foreign: Why It Exists, and How It May Be Extinguished* (1853) was vitiated by the author's bizarre notions of political economy; worse, as she wrote to Carey himself, "it is,–excuse my saying so,–of a class of works which do us more harm than the most violent abolitionist attacks; assuming the ground of a wrong where wrong does not exist, and with laboured argument upon false grounds, forcing to fearfully practical conclusions."

Stowe's *Uncle Tom's Cabin* provoked McCord's most sustained reaction. The novel itself had engendered many, usually laudatory responses from the British press, and

McCord took up the charge of refuting these responses as well. She identified her foes as a motley assortment of feminists, abolitionists, and sentimental, hypocritical aristocrats; what they all had in common was a presumptuous ignorance, a foolish contempt for natural law. Herself no orthodox Christian, McCord nevertheless judged Christianity to be the bulwark of civilization and a deistic God to be the guarantor of the natural law that must be the base of rational and stable society. That law decreed slavery as the best protection for slaves against the superior intelligence and cunning of their masters and women's subordination as the only guard against the superior strength and violence of men. "There is evil in God's blessed world (why, God only knows), but there is also good–deep, earnest good–for those who will seek it deeply and earnestly. Below the nauseous froth-scum of sickly philanthropy and new-light Christianity, runs, quiet but clear, the pure stream of God-given reason and common-sense humanity. Ladies and reviewers, *God is God, but ye are not his prophets.*" More and more she despaired of converting her opponents or saving those whom they corrupted. There was no common ground of rational discourse.

Even with her plantation duties, the college gossip in Columbia, and her campaign in defense of Southern institutions, McCord was often restless. Columbia itself was deserted and oppressed with heat in the summer. She and her family traveled northward, to Narragansett Bay in Rhode Island and the spas in western Virginia. In summer 1851 she met diarist Jane Caroline North at Red Sweet Springs. "Mrs. McCord paid us a visit this afternoon. . . . she is a masculine clever person, with the most mannish attitudes and gestures, but interesting and very entertaining." At White Sulphur Springs, Maryland novelist John Pendleton Kennedy encountered "several South Carolinians . . . ridiculously distempered with nullification and Disunion." David McCord, predicting civil war, "is the most moderate of them–though I am told his wife, who has lately written a tragedy called 'Gracchus,' is not."

McCord's *Caius Gracchus. A Tragedy in Five Acts* was published in spring 1851. *DeBow's Review* of October 1852 pronounced it "a brilliant anomaly in our literature." To be sure, women in the United States had written plays on classical, and specifically Roman, themes before. Besides two adaptations of Edward Bulwer-Lytton's 1834 novel *The Last Days of Pompeii* (by Charlotte Barnes in 1835 and Louisa H. Medina in 1844), there were Mercy Otis Warren's *The Sack of Rome* (1790), Margaretta Bleecker Faugeres's *Belisarius, A Tragedy* (1795), and *The Roman Tribute; or, Attila the Hun* (1850) by Elizabeth Oakes Smith, whose book *Woman and Her Needs* (1851) McCord later reviewed. These predecessors were few enough; moreover, all had written on incidents from the Roman Empire, perhaps because the domestic atmosphere of a court suited better the domestic role of women. Only McCord chose her subject from the Roman Republic, thereby imitating a male playwright such as Robert Montgomery Bird, whose popular tragedy *The Gladiator* (1831), dealing with the slave revolt led by Spartacus between 73 and 71 B.C., had little space for female concerns or his female characters.

By choosing to treat political turmoil in the late second century B.C., McCord certainly took advantage of the opportunity to speak in roles otherwise denied to her, placing, for example, two long formal speeches in the mouth of her hero, Gracchus, famous for his oratory. She did not deny space to her women characters, however; indeed, her choice of subject entailed the presence of perhaps the most celebrated of Roman Republican women, Cornelia, legendary mother of the Gracchi and daughter of Scipio Africanus, conqueror of Hannibal and the Carthaginians in the Second Punic War. Cornelia's son Gaius Gracchus (or "Caius," as McCord spelled it, according to the nineteenth-century preference), elected as tribune, vows to continue and extend the progressive reforms advocated by his brother, Tiberius Sempronius Gracchus, who during his own tenure as tribune had been murdered by a gang of senators and their clients. Gaius's opponents are forced to outbid him with the people, who in particular are jealous of their citizens' rights, which he proposes to extend within Italy. Although reelected once, Gaius loses his bid for a third term, and in the riots that ensue he is killed along with many of his supporters. His failure and death are the subject of McCord's play.

Gaius's own tragedy is illustrated by that of his wife, Licinia, and Cornelia. McCord's chief source was the Greek biographer Plutarch's lives of the two Gracchus brothers, but in form the play is most influenced by McCord's admiration for William Shakespeare–its diction and versification are his–and in particular by *Coriolanus* (1607–1608), in which the hero's mother, Volumnia, and wife, Virgilia, are made to play off him and each other. An even closer parallel is found in John Dryden's *Cleomenes* (1692), which takes as its hero the Spartan king whom Plutarch chose as parallel to Gaius Gracchus in his series of Greek and Roman lives. In Dryden's play, as in McCord's, wife and mother debate the course of action proper to a woman during a political crisis, albeit their case is even more critical: whereas Cornelia survived her sons in honored retirement, the mother of Cleomenes, along with her grandchildren, was executed after her son's death.

Yet, despite these influences, and any exerted by Marie-Joseph Chénier's *Caius Gracchus* (1792), Vincenzo Monti's *Caio Gracco* (1800), or James Sheridan Knowles's *Caius Gracchus* (1815, 1823), McCord's Cornelia and Licinia face predicaments very much their author's own. Licinia vacillates between rushing forward to join her husband in the public arena and withdrawing him to the unpolitical seclusion of the home. Cornelia, on the other hand, restrains her daughter-in-law from the first course and urges the folly of the second. She admits and embraces the necessity of public life for her son, yet she counsels prudence and restraint in that life. It is a difficult, eventually an impossible, compromise, both for her and for him; it fails as utterly as Licinia's last plea to her husband (the scene was a favorite among Baroque painters) to retreat to the safety of their household; and it fails through a tragic irony alien to the rhetorically useful certainty of McCord's polemical essays on women's roles. Like the chorus in Greek tragedy, Cornelia is the moral compass by which the action is to be judged, yet is powerless to intervene. The role of chorus, indeed, is what McCord believed woman most suited to play, and must bear. "As to my productions being *closet dramas*," she wrote in 1848 to her husband's cousin William Porcher Miles, whom she had asked for criticism of some drafts of her work, "what else can a Woman write? The *world of action* must to her be almost entirely a closed book." Cornelia breaks out of the role of chorus, however. Near the end of the play, as Gaius Gracchus despairs, his mother comes to him—McCord's innovation, not in Plutarch—and urges him to strive onward even in the face of sure disaster. When he agrees, she speaks her last words to her son:

> Then once again farewell! These bursting tears
> Now come to show the woman's heart, whose boldness,
> Your sickly resolution to upbraid,
> Usurped the man. Oh! were they tears of blood,
> Feebly they'd speak my anguish.

Adopting Cornelia's resolution as his own, Gracchus strives onward—to a miserable death, stabbed in the back by one of the commoners whose condition he had labored to raise.

In July 1851, the *Southern Quarterly Review,* while it allowed that "a tragedy by a Southron, and a lady, is surely no such ordinary event, that we should pass it with indifference," found the matter insufficiently tragic—the Roman people were a rabble, Gracchus a rabble-rouser—and the verse insufficiently sweet and exquisite because its author's "mental attributes," though these included force, vigor, eloquence, were nevertheless "all masculine." The reviewer in the *Southern Literary Gazette* of 28 June 1851 agreed but praised that *Caius Gracchus* was "characterized by more than common vigour of style, and displays, indeed, a masculine energy of thought and utterance quite *germain* to the theme"; and *DeBow's Review* wrote that "South Carolina has produced the only American poet whose productions may be said to belong to the elder school; which appeal to the intellect more than the fancy, and are marked by such sinewy strength of thought and expression as to be stamped at once with a character of

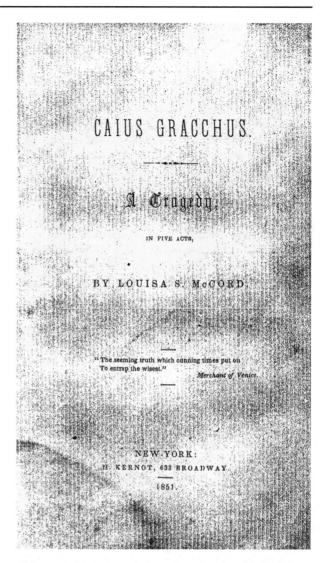

*Title page for McCord's tragic drama, set against the political turbulence of the Roman Republic (South Caroliniana Library, University of South Carolina)*

originality. . . . She is wholly unlike any of her sisters of the lyre, and writes with a terseness, vigor, earnestness, and masculine energy, which show her to be altogether of a different order."

McCord's Cornelia, further, was soon taken by those who knew her to be a portrait of herself. James Wood Davidson, acquainted with McCord from being a tutor to her children in the early 1850s, in his *Living Writers of the South* (1869) described her as having a mind "Roman in its cast, and heroic in its energy, . . . in person Mrs. McCord might personate Cornelia herself." At one point in her diaries Mary Chesnut misremembered the title of her friend's play (she called it "The Mother of the Gracchi") and in another place recorded a visit to Cheves McCord at his mother's house in Columbia:

He had been badly wounded at Second Manassas, in both the head and the leg.

Mrs. McCord went at once to Richmond and found he was still at or near Manassas Junction. She went to Mr. Miles to get her a passport to go down for him. He said the thing was impossible. Government had seized all trains, and no passports were given. "I let him talk," said Mrs. McCord, "for he does it beautifully. That very night I chartered a special train. We ran down to Manassas and I brought back Cheves in triumph. You see he is nearly well, with our home nursing."

"Mother of the Gracchi," we cried.

David McCord died in May 1855. In the autumn Louisa's brother Charles died at the age of thirty, of fever contracted after returning too early to his plantation on the coast. The unexpected news precipitated a stroke in Langdon Cheves, who did not recover; rather, he had begun his long decline into senile dementia, passed at McCord's house in Columbia. "My feelings towards my Father," she wrote in a letter of 1876, "have through life been almost those of worship, rather than simply of affection"; and she endured grimly, sometimes despairing, her father's long deterioration, much of it recorded in a series of letters to her brother Langdon, from the delusions of its beginning—he thought Louisa was conspiring to cheat him—to the slack imbecility of its end. His death, in June 1857, brought further distress, a lawsuit among his children from which McCord tried unsuccessfully to hold aloof. Its aftermath lingered into 1860, when she declared her willingness to accept whatever settlement was agreed upon by the others, except "as regards negroes I cannot consent to receive any more, for I am almost out of my senses with those that I have, and with my now permanently established defective vision, am entirely unfit for learning anything about planting concerns. . . . To embarrass myself with more would be wretchedness to them and death to me."

Symptoms of severe eyestrain had appeared after her husband's death; treatment—she was forbidden to read and spent much of her days in a darkened room—and travel in 1856 and 1857 did not improve her condition. In July 1858 she departed for Europe with her son and her daughter Louisa. She wrote home that specialists in Paris had brought guarded improvement: "My eyes face light better than they did, but I do not think mean ever to let me use them as I wish and have been accustomed to do." An energetic tour took up the rest of her European visit, to England and to Scotland as far as the Orkneys, to the Netherlands, Germany, and Switzerland. In Paris she and her son attended a reception at the court of Napoleon III; in Italy she joined her children for an ascent of Mount Vesuvius, was in Rome for Holy Week and an audience with Pius IX, and traveled to Florence to consult with the sculptor Hiram Powers, to whom she intended to give the commission of a colossal bust of Langdon Cheves, with smaller copies, for the Cheves family monument in Charleston. Her dilatory brother Langdon, however, had failed to send ahead of her the death mask and other materials. The time was not wasted; Powers carved a bust of Louisa McCord herself, in Roman garb, a likeness that her daughter Louisa later judged the best surviving of her mother.

Returning to the United States on 26 October 1859, the McCord family learned of John Brown's raid on Harpers Ferry, Virginia, ten days before. According to her daughter Louisa, "My mother said, 'There goes then this glorious Union.' . . . I remember the shock it gave me and the way my brother looked as he said 'Oh no, don't say that.' . . . She answered him, 'Yes, you will see–this is not the end of it, we will be forced to assert ourselves.'" South Carolina seceded from the Union on 20 December 1860. Four days later McCord wrote to Powers explaining the event. It was revolution, she knew, and she hoped it would be bloodless, although she also knew, "a bloodless revolution (an unheard of event in history) can scarcely be expected." When war broke out in April, she was carried away by popular sentiment enough to welcome, she wrote to her brother Langdon, the "glorious affair of Fort Sumter, and truly it would seem to have set old Lincoln crazy. Did ever any stupid animal ever so set fire to its own nest! He has given us Virginia already, and how much else will follow?"

The romance of war attracted her only briefly. To a group of ladies, Chesnut among them, disputing over the name to be given to a new Confederate gunboat, she said only, "Let it be 'she-devil,' for it is the devil's own work it is built to do." She turned over Lang Syne immediately to the cultivation of provisions and outfitted at her own expense a company of soldiers under her son's command. In Columbia she became the first president of the Soldiers' Relief Association and of the Soldiers' Clothing Association. The principal focus of her zeal was fixed in June 1862, however, when buildings of South Carolina College were converted into a hospital for the surge of wounded already taxing Confederate resources. Soon her command there, although voluntary and unofficial, caused some disquiet, as reported in a letter by the wife of one of the doctors: "I remember once saying to my husband, 'St. Julien, two ladies were here today, who said they wondered at your letting Mrs. McCord manage your Hospital.' He answered abruptly, 'The more she manages the better, every bit of her that isn't enthusiasm is common sense.'"

Profiteers and blockade-runners, ladies to whom nursing seemed a form of flirting, and the incompetence and timidity of certain generals of the Confederacy were objects of McCord's scorn and blunt speaking. "Mrs. Preston and I whisper," said Chesnut. "Mrs. McCord scorns whispers." Her strength was not hardness, as those close to her knew. Chesnut described how McCord bade a sol-

_Tuesday_ night _March 5th 1856_

I send the above my dear Brother, as an excuse for what I fear you will consider my persecution of you. It is an attempt of our dear old Father to write something; I believe a letter to you. — He is very anxious to hear from you & evidently much irritated with _me_ because he does not do so. He seems to think it is _my fault_. I offered to write for him but he would not allow me to do so, & when he found he could not write, then says he will send down June with a message. — Indeed he wished to send him today, and with difficulty has been prevented. — He is much irritated, much displeased, & is altogether in a far more painful condition than when you saw him. — Could you not my dear brother, write or even cause Charlotte to write, if it be but 2 lines, say every week? It would I think assist in soothing Father. — My position is here so intensely distressing that you must excuse me if I press upon you more urgently than you think right. — I know you have troubles, I know you have

_First page of a letter from McCord to her younger brother, Langdon Cheves Jr. (South Carolina Historical Society)_

*Bust of McCord by Hiram Powers, which McCord posed for in Florence, Italy, in 1859 (South Caroliniana Library, University of South Carolina)*

dier charge to her account the cost of a wooden leg, after the surgeon had told him to do without. "Hospitals are hard places," she wrote to Chesnut in 1863, "in which Women may be comforters but Doctors too often are tyrants." Her daughter remembered the constant effort to comfort, and the toll it took. "My mother knit" clothing for the soldiers "day and night, walking, driving, under all circumstances. When troubles and sorrows came thick and fast and sleep came no longer to comfort her, I used to wake at night and listen to the click, click of her needles, and shudder at the groans and sobs that accompanied them when she supposed no one heard her."

McCord's sorrows continued throughout the war, however. Her brother John's only son was killed; her sister Sophia lost two sons in one month; her brother Langdon was killed while superintending the fortifications of Charleston Harbor. Cruelest was the blow coming in January 1863, when her own son, wounded at the second Battle of Manassas the previous August and apparently convalescent, died after a botched operation to remove a bullet from his skull. Finally, in February 1865, her house

in Columbia was looted by Federal troops and she herself robbed of her father's watch and nearly throttled by those trying to force their way past her upstairs, where her daughters were hidden. It might have been worse, had not the looters been interrupted by an officer sent by the general in charge of the city to take over her house for his headquarters. The general's presence saved the house from the burning of the city, but it was looted again upon his departure; and Lang Syne was also plundered.

At the end of the war her daughter Louisa was married to a friend of her dead brother's, Augustine Smythe of Charleston. Smythe made an attempt to restore Lang Syne for his mother-in-law's support, but this plan proved unworkable. By that time Hannah, too, had married, and, without children to be responsible for, McCord sold Lang Syne in 1870. No longer able to tolerate Reconstruction in South Carolina, she fled northward, eventually settling in Canada, summering in Cobourg on Lake Ontario and spending the winters in Drummondville, Quebec, not far from Montreal, where she had McCord relations. Hannah's death in 1872 after the birth of her second child only worsened her sorrow, however. "An old Lady here of 85," McCord wrote to her son-in-law Smythe in 1874, "deliberately pitched herself headforemost into a well the other day. If I were not as firm to my principles, as you sometimes want to quarrel with me for being, I would feel some days mightily inclined to follow her example." Finally, after six years away, McCord returned to her birthplace, making her home with the Smythes.

While away, she had not forgotten the South. She did what she could to set the record straight, in a world which she knew had a short memory, and that memory inaccurate. In 1867 she had made a sworn affidavit before a committee of Columbia citizens investigating the causes of the fire of 1865. In 1873 she had visited Charleston to depose a second account of her experiences during the Federal occupation, for commissioners examining, in accordance with provisions of the Treaty of Washington, claims for damages incurred by foreign nationals during the war. Having retired to Charleston, she turned to the preservation of her father's memory. A nephew had requested her to write an account of him, of which her narrative down to his early years as a lawyer and some scattered and disconnected notes survive. She commissioned an obelisk to be raised at the Cheves family plot in Magnolia Cemetery and composed the inscriptions for its base. In 1878 she wrote to Hiram Powers's son, Preston Powers, to renew the commission for a bust of her father.

Taking thought for her own future, too, she purchased the house adjacent to the Smythes and was planning extensive renovations with a contractor when, in November 1879, she fell ill with what was diagnosed as "gout in the stomach." The pain was great; the physician gave her up; to her daughter, who asked if she was willing to die, she replied, "Willing, my child? *Glad*–glad to rest." After suffering for five days, she died on 23 November. The obituary in the *Charleston News and Courier* was a few lines only, ignoring her service to the Confederacy and making no mention of her writings. The omission would not have surprised her. Even her revered father, she had written to Preston Powers, was "now almost forgotten in the scramble which follows our noble but disastrous war." Only twenty-two years had passed since his death, but "in such a country as ours now is, that is enough to stamp into oblivion every thing worth remembering. . . . My world is dead and in the past."

## References:

Susan A. Eaker, "'A Dangerous Inmate' of the South: Louisa McCord on Gender and Slavery," in *Southern Writers and their Worlds,* edited by Christopher Morris and Steven G. Reinhart (College Station: Texas A & M Press, 1996), pp. 27–40;

Elizabeth Fox-Genovese, *Within the Plantation Household: Black and White Women of the Old South* (Chapel Hill: University of North Carolina Press, 1988);

Jessie Melville Fraser, "Louisa C. McCord," M.A. thesis, University of South Carolina, Columbia, 1919;

Eugene D. Genovese and Fox-Genovese, "Slavery, Economic Development, and the Law: The Dilemma of the Southern Political Economists, 1800–1860," *Washington and Lee Law Review,* 41 (Winter 1984): 1–29;

Archie Vernon Huff Jr., *Langdon Cheves of South Carolina* (Columbia: University of South Carolina Press, 1977);

Mary Kelley, "Designing a Past for the Present: Women Writing Women's History in Nineteenth-Century America," *Proceedings of the American Antiquarian Society,* 105 (1995): 315–346;

Richard C. Lounsbury, "*Ludibria Rerum Mortalium:* Charlestonian Intellectuals and Their Classics," in *Intellectual Life in Antebellum Charleston,* edited by Michael O'Brien and David Moltke-Hansen (Knoxville: University of Tennessee Press, 1986), pp. 325–369;

Louisa McCord Smythe, comp., *For Old Lang Syne: Collected for My Children* (Charleston, S.C.: Lucas & Richardson, 1900);

Margaret Farrand Thorp, *Female Persuasion: Six Strong-Minded Women* (New Haven: Yale University Press, 1949).

## Papers:

The largest collection of Louisa S. McCord's letters and documents is located in the Langdon Cheves I Papers, Langdon Cheves III Papers, Dulles-Cheves-McCord-Lovell Papers, and Smythe-Stoney-Adger Papers at the South Carolina Historical Society, Charleston. Other McCord papers can be found in the Rachel S. Cheves Papers and Ann Heatly Reid Lovell Papers at the Manuscript Department, William R. Perkins Library, Duke University, Durham, North Carolina; the Francis Lieber Papers at the Henry E. Huntington Library, San Marino, California; the Edward Carey Gardiner Collection, Henry C. Carey Section, at the Historical Society of Pennsylvania, Philadelphia; the Hiram Powers and Powers Family Papers in the Archives of American Art, Smithsonian Institution, Washington, D.C.; the Cheves Family Papers, Francis Lieber Papers, James Henley Thornwell Papers, Williams-Chesnut-Manning Families Manuscripts, at the South Caroliniana Library, University of South Carolina, Columbia; the William Porcher Miles Papers at the Southern Historical Collection, University of North Carolina, Chapel Hill; the Preston Family Papers at the Virginia Historical Society, Richmond; and the Lyman C. Draper Manuscripts at the State Historical Society of Wisconsin, Madison.

# Maria Jane McIntosh

*(1803 – 23 February 1878)*

Esther Lopez
*University of Rochester*

See also the McIntosh entry in *DLB 239: American Women Prose Writers, 1820–1870*.

BOOKS: *Blind Alice; or, Do Right If You Wish to Be Happy,* as Aunt Kitty (New York: Dayton & Saxton, 1841);

*Florence Arnott; or, Is She Generous?* as Aunt Kitty (New York: Dayton & Saxton, 1841);

*Jessie Graham; or, Friends Dear, but Truth Dearer,* as Aunt Kitty (New York: Dayton & Saxton, 1841);

*Ellen Leslie; or, The Reward of Self-Control,* as Aunt Kitty (New York: Dayton & Newman, 1842);

*Grace and Clara; or, Be Just as Well as Generous,* as Aunt Kitty (New York: Dayton & Saxton, 1842);

*Conquest and Self-Conquest; or, Which Makes the Hero?* anonymous (New York: Harper, 1843; London: Bruce & Wyld, 1844);

*Woman, an Enigma; or, Life and Its Revealings,* anonymous (New York: Harper, 1843; London: Bruce, 1843);

*The Cousins: A Tale of Early Life,* as Aunt Kitty (New York: Harper, 1845);

*Praise and Principle; or, For What Shall I Live?* anonymous (New York: Harper, 1845; London: Routledge & Warne, 1850);

*Two Lives; or, To Seem and to Be* (New York: Appleton, 1846; revised, 1847); republished as *Grace Elliot; or, To Seem and to Be* (London: Thomas Nelson, 1853);

*Aunt Kitty's Tales* (New York: Appleton, 1847);

*Charms and Counter-Charms* (New York: Appleton, 1848);

*Woman in America: Her Work and Her Reward* (New York: Appleton, 1850);

*Evenings at Donaldson Manor; or, The Christmas Guest* (New York: Appleton, 1851);

*Letter on the Address of the Women of England to Their Sisters of America, in Relation to Slavery* (New York: Crowen, 1853);

*The Lofty and the Lowly; or Good in All and None All-Good* (New York: Appleton, 1853); republished as *Alice Montrose; or, The Lofty and the Lowly: Good in All and None All Good* (London: Bentley, 1855);

*M. J. McIntosh*

*Emily Herbert; or, The Happy Home* (New York & London: Appleton, 1855);

*Rose and Lillie Stanhope; or, The Power of Conscience* (New York: Appleton, 1855);

*Violet; or, The Cross and the Crown* (Boston: Jewett, 1856);

*Meta Gray; or, What Makes Home Happy* (New York: Appleton, 1859);

*A Year with Maggie and Emma: A True Story* (New York & London: Appleton, 1861);

*Two Pictures; or, What We Think of Ourselves, and What the World Thinks of Us* (New York: Appleton, 1863);

*Violette and I,* as Cousin Kate (Boston: Loring, 1870);

*The Children's Mirror: A Treasury of Stories,* as Cousin Kate (London & New York: Thomas Nelson, 1887).

As a best-selling author of women's domestic fiction, Maria Jane McIntosh enjoyed great popularity. A native Southerner who spent most of her adulthood in the North, McIntosh was in a key position to comment on the major issues of her day. Like many domestic novelists, McIntosh scorned the women's rights movement; her heart always in the South, she believed that women should use their influence in the domestic sphere to better the condition of the nation as a whole. She took pride in her willingness to present balanced portraits of both the North and South in the chaotic years before the Civil War. McIntosh's major work of nonfiction, *Woman in America: Her Work and Her Reward* (1850), explicates the philosophy implicit in her novels; shorter works of nonfiction define her proslavery position. Although most were never published, she also wrote poems. Despite the renewal of interest in nineteenth-century American women writers, McIntosh continues to receive scant critical attention, perhaps because her proslavery stance offends contemporary critics.

The daughter of Lachlan McIntosh, a descendant of the eminent McIntosh clan and a prosperous plantation owner and lawyer, and his fifth wife, Mary Moore Maxwell McIntosh, Maria Jane McIntosh was born in Sunbury, Georgia, in 1803. Raised primarily by her mother, as her father died when she was three years old, she began her education under her mother's tutelage and continued it first at a coeducational academy in Sunbury and later at Baiden's Bluff Academy in McIntosh County. Taking over the management of the plantation after the death of her invalid mother in 1823, she sold the estate in 1835 and moved to New York to live with her half-brother, Captain James McKay McIntosh. After investing her money in securities and losing it all in the Panic of 1837, McIntosh embarked on a writing career at the suggestion of a friend and wrote prolifically to support herself throughout the next two decades.

McIntosh's books were widely read in both the United States and England, and several of her works were translated into French. Emulating Samuel Griswold Goodrich's "Peter Parley" tales, she wrote as Aunt Kitty, and her moralistic children's stories were so familiar that Julia D. Freeman, under the pseudonym Mary Forrest, commented in her *Women of the South Distinguished in Literature* (1865) that "countless were the curly-headed darlings who blessed her in their nightly prayers, and carried her, a last sweet thought, into dreamland." McIntosh's domestic fiction, some of which was published anonymously, sold extremely well: *Two Lives; or, To Seem and to Be* (1846) had seven editions in less than four years; *Charms and Counter-Charms* (1848) had eight, with sales of about one hundred thousand.

One significant element in McIntosh's success was her ability to tap into contemporary moral concerns. In *Woman's Record* (1870) Sarah Josepha Hale wrote that "her style is easy and graceful, and her first object is evidently the maintenance of pure morality and religion." For example, in McIntosh's *Conquest and Self-Conquest; or, Which Makes the Hero?* (1843), her first moral fiction for young men, the temperate navy midshipman Frederic Stanley wins the hand of his ladylove while his lazy friend is sent home in disgrace. Although the plot seems overly didactic to modern readers, a writer to the "Gossip about a few Books" section of the *Southern Literary Messenger* (April 1844) praised the novel, writing, "Except for Miss Edgeworth and the author of 'Sandford and Merton,' I do not know a writer who has so happily portrayed true heroism."

A brief perusal of the titles of McIntosh's works testifies to her fondness for contrast. For example, *The Lofty and the Lowly; or Good in All and None All-Good* (1853), a proslavery novel written in response to Harriet Beecher Stowe's *Uncle Tom's Cabin* (1852), contrasts the chivalrous South with the industrialized North. Several of McIntosh's domestic fictions employ pairs of heroines, sometimes using the familiar trope of blonde opposed to brunette to indicate interior differences. Many of her heroines are orphans who temporarily support themselves and other family members by working as governesses or seamstresses until they marry. Despite McIntosh's reliance on comparison and contrast, her plots are often complex. In *The Female Prose Writers of America* (1852) John Hart noted that "it will be obvious to everyone familiar with Miss McIntosh's writings, that she is a delineator entirely of mental life"; twentieth-century critics such as Nina Baym have also lauded this ability.

*Woman, an Enigma; or, Life and Its Revealings* (1843), published anonymously, is McIntosh's first domestic fiction. It takes up what was a persistent theme for her: a woman's search for identity. McIntosh credited her "habit of self-reliance" to her education at the academy in Sunbury; similarly, her heroines develop through a combination of education and life experience. In *Woman, an Enigma* Louise de La Valliere, born and raised in a convent, is engaged to a sophisticated marquis, the Duc de Montreval. Hoping that she will acquire more polish and worth in her fiancé's eyes, she goes to Paris before the wedding, only to be mistakenly scorned as a flirt when they re-unite. Refusing to marry her, Montreval offers her a trust, which she declines.

WOMAN IN AMERICA:

HER WORK AND HER REWARD.

BY

MARIA J. McINTOSH,

AUTHOR OF "CHARMS AND COUNTER-CHARMS," "TO SEEM AND
TO BE," ETC. ETC.

"The ancients looked towards the land of the setting sun as to a land of
promise, where the earth puts forth fruits for eternal life; and surely the home
of the Hesperides must have features and beauty of its own, and a calling not
known to the old world."

F. BREMER.

NEW YORK:

D. APPLETON & COMPANY, 200 BROADWAY.

PHILADELPHIA:

GEO. S. APPLETON, 164 CHESNUT-STREET.

M DCCC L.

Title page for McIntosh's book-length argument against the women's
rights movement (Special Collections, Thomas Cooper
Library, University of South Carolina)

She supports her mother as a governess, and when she meets Montreval again he finds her quite changed: "he had known her a sensitive girl, appealing by her timidity and tenderness to the hearts of others; he saw her, with no less feminine gentleness, show a modest, unpresuming dignity and repose of manner—something that seemed to say she had '—the conscience of her worth that would be wooed and not won.'"

Montreval is now sufficiently impressed to marry her. McIntosh's focus on Louise's newfound confidence clearly implies that her failure was not her naiveté but her eagerness to submit to Montreval's wishes. By attempting to become the woman she thought he wanted she compromised her character, thereby diminishing her potential influence in the domestic sphere.

The first novel published under her own name, *Two Lives* was part of the "new wave" of best-selling novels by women. Like *Conquest and Self-Conquest,* the novel pairs characters to further explore the themes investigated in *Woman, an Enigma.* While not overtly autobiographical, *Two Lives,* like many of McIntosh's works, reflects her deep and abiding passion for her Southern childhood home. As the novel opens, cousins Grace and Isabel, like McIntosh before them, are preparing to move from the South to New York in the wake of Grace's father's death: "To-morrow they were to leave their beloved home in the warm, friendly, South for one in a colder clime—and the dwellers in that clime for whose society they must exchange that of their kind, indulgent, aunt, might not they prove that 'the cold in clime are cold in blood?'" Promising her aunt to devote herself to Grace, Isabel renounces the proposal of a young, southern minister, Falconer, believing that Grace also loves him. Falconer is only interested in Isabel, however, so he leaves and Grace becomes engaged to another. Despite the "sharp, arrowy, thought, which had darted into Isabel's mind— 'the happiness of my life, and perhaps, of *his* has been sacrificed to a fancy,'" she quickly forgives Grace. Meanwhile, their uncle Elliott has lost all his money, so Isabel gives music lessons to support him until Falconer returns and marries her. As in *Woman, an Enigma,* the lesson is that women should not sacrifice their own best interests for another.

One of McIntosh's most popular novels, *Charms and Counter-Charms* is also one of her most ambitious. Freeman gushed that the novel "seems to have concentrated the strength of her artistic and womanly nature. It is threaded with veins and nerves, as if she had dipped her pen in living hearts, and written on, and on, because the electric tide would flow." *Charms and Counter-Charms* contrasts the life of Evelyn and her husband, Euston Hastings, with that of her friend Mary and her husband, Everard Irving. The bulk of the novel, however, focuses on Evelyn's unhappy marriage. Initially engaged to Everard, Evelyn instead marries the more worldly Hastings and quickly becomes totally dependent upon him. Taking up with Evelyn's friend, Mrs. Mabury, he abandons her in disgust and goes to Europe. Evelyn follows and finds Hastings alone, having already parted with Mrs. Mabury. Telling her that he "will never yield again to any woman the power to torture with which the name and position of a wife endows her," Hastings consents for her to remain with him only if she agrees to "fill a wife's place without a wife's name."

In circumstances perhaps suggested to McIntosh as a result of her own experiences with her mother, Evelyn nurses Hastings through an illness, thereby developing her self-esteem enough to motivate her to leave him. Like the titular heroine of Charlotte Brontë's *Jane Eyre,* published the previous year, Evelyn realizes that "I had forgotten Him, beloved,–I had forgotten that the universe held any being greater, nobler than thou." Not surprisingly, given McIntosh's other novels, after she leaves Hastings, he decides to acknowledge the marriage. Moreover, after the death of their daughter, he becomes a Christian. The moral significance of Hastings' conversion is perhaps best demonstrated by Freeman's inclusion of this episode in her sketch on McIntosh.

McIntosh's only long work of nonfiction, *Woman in America* outlines her domestic philosophy and explicates her resistance to the women's rights movement. Although Freeman argues that "her ideas upon the subject are in strict accordance with her life," contemporary critics such as Baym, Bashar Aliki, and Elizabeth Moss detect an underlying tension between McIntosh's stated intentions, her failure to marry, and her writing career. McIntosh calls for "American women . . . to rectify the errors of American society." To illustrate her vision of American womanhood, she divides women into types, contrasting the self-centered Flirtilla with the noble Egeria, who selflessly promotes the education of everyone in her household according to their own aptitudes. In keeping with this philosophy, women's missions vary according to their region. In the West it is to Americanize the immigrant population; in the South, to Christianize the slave and motivate the aristocracy to see the value of work; and in the North, to combat the monetary mode of life.

*The Lofty and the Lowly,* published in two volumes, is McIntosh's longest work and the one that most clearly reflects her Southern heritage. Written after the Compromise of 1850, the preface announces her "desire to remove some of the prejudices separating the Northern and the Southern United States, by a true and loving portraiture of the social characteristics of each. To do this for the South, required, of course, the introduction of negro-slavery; and though with a painful consciousness that she was nearing the elements of strife, the author has endeavored to sketch it as it appeared to her during an acquaintance with it of more than 20 years." Volume one opens as the Northerner Thomas Browne and Southerner Colonel John Montrose receive news of the death of Charles Montrose, the former's brother-in-law and latter's brother; their differing reactions to the news immediately serves to characterize each region. Browne, a wealthy businessman, knowing that his sister and her children are practically penniless, writes to Montrose that he will "incur the trouble" of settling his brother-in-law's estate. Since he never approved of his sister's marriage to an "indo-

lent" Southerner, the destitution of his sister and her family fails to surprise him, and he and his family express little grief.

In contrast, Montrose and his family grieve openly and passionately; moreover, "the mean Yankee" Browne's suggestion that the children lead "a life of toil" appalls him; he writes to his sister-in-law that "You cannot, I feel assured, deny me the only consolation I can know under the pressure of this heavy sorrow. . . . Your children are henceforth mine–and you must relinquish to me all care for their future maintenance and settlement in life." Although McIntosh no doubt believed that she represented accurately the vices and virtues of both the South and the North, the lush portrait of the plantation in the absence of an equally gushing description of Browne's home implies that the vices of the South are far more bearable than those of the North. As volume one concludes, Montrose is dying, surrounded by his family and several of his "people." He calls for his minister but is answered with "Mr. Dunbar aint here, maussa; will you hear poor Cato pray?" Montrose, who has instructed his slaves in religion, is clearly designed to banish the memory of Stowe's villainous Simon Legree.

Volume two, which opens with the death of John Montrose, is particularly concerned with slavery. Montrose dies unaware that his son Donald's large gambling debt, acquired at the hands of Northern swindlers, has accumulated to the extent that it forces a mortgage of the estate. Returning to the North after Montrose's death, Mrs. Charles Montrose and her daughter, Alice, find themselves with only Alice's embroidery to support them until they send for Cato, who, after being freed, offered to go North with them. After his arrival he works selflessly on their behalf. He encounters an abolitionist, Sampson, who questions Cato about his "bondage"; thinking of God, Cato replies that "we all in bondage to bery hard maussa, work we day and night neber stop tell we fall down and dead." Sampson misinterprets his answer, however, and leads a mob of abolitionists to the Montroses' cottage. This development allows McIntosh to characterize abolitionists as villainous meddlers ignorant of Southern practice. Cato's choice to remain with his master's family even after he is freed and McIntosh's description of various slave families who "dressed in their best" and showed "little anxiety, either in countenance or manner, for the result of the allotment about to be made" as they are valued after Montrose's death are obviously refutations of Stowe's argument that slavery destroys families.

The inclusion of Robert Grahame, who owns a textile mill yet remains a gentleman because his actions are motivated by benevolence and not greed, mediates McIntosh's otherwise harsh portrait of Northern industry. He first rescues Alice and her mother, then proceeds to teach Donald about finances, allowing him to settle his debts and efficiently manage the plantation. Alice's marriage to Robert and the marriage of Donald and Robert's sister, Mary, symbolize the peaceful domestic union of the nation McIntosh still hoped was possible, a belief shattered by the advent of the Civil War.

Baym, in *Woman's Fiction: A Guide to Novels by and about Women in America 1820–1870* (1993), argues that "because of the complexity of its social portraiture, it is probably the most rewarding of her books, despite its length, for a twentieth century reader." Elizabeth Moss's argument in *Domestic Novelists in the Old South: Defenders of Southern Culture* (1992) for a uniquely Southern domestic tradition focuses in part on *The Lofty and the Lowly,* implying that Baym's observation is correct. Moss maintains that although McIntosh tried to discourage sectionalism, the novel itself encourages it because she does not succeed in offering a balanced picture of the North.

McIntosh's last domestic novels, *Violet; or, The Cross and the Crown* (1856) and *Two Pictures; or, What We Think of Ourselves, and What the World Thinks of Us* (1863), break with her earlier fiction in that her view of feminine independence is less celebratory. This change may be because of a keenly felt awareness that self-reliance involves a certain amount of struggle; as Baym notes, unlike her heroines, McIntosh's work was not interrupted by the timely appearance of a husband. *Violet* fails to mention the South, perhaps because McIntosh now despaired of a domestic resolution to the problems of the nation. The title character is at the mercy of her real father and her adoptive one, who argue over her suitors until a happy accident results in her marriage to a handsome Englishman, implying that for women, the alternative to work is accepting men's control over their lives.

In 1859 McIntosh accompanied her nephew, John Elliot Ward, American minister to China, and his family to Liverpool. After traveling in Europe, she spent the remainder of the year in Geneva with Ward's wife while he pursued his work. According to Freeman, Switzerland offered her a "haven of rest, which the overwrought brain . . . required." Returning to New York in 1860, she began teaching at the school of Henrietta Haines and worked on *Two Pictures, or, What We Think of Ourselves, and What the World Thinks of Us,* her final novel. Like *Violet,* it reveals a certain degree of weariness. The novel opens with what may be read as McIntosh's own lament: "Home, home, I had many resting places–but I have had, and can have, but one home." Like all of McIntosh's heroines, Augusta Moray suffers a series of misfortunes before marrying

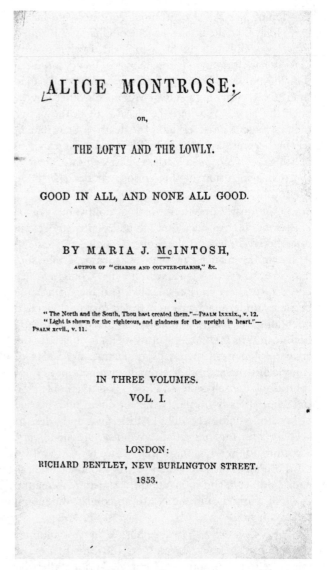

*Title page for volume one of the British edition of McIntosh's novel contrasting the lives of a Northern and a Southern family connected through marriage (Special Collections, Thomas Cooper Library, University of South Carolina)*

the heir to the plantation on which she grew up. The final scene, in which Augusta reads a review of *Uncle Tom's Cabin* and contrasts "the picture of the vulgar and beastly tyrant just presented her with the image enshrined so reverently in her heart," betrays some cynicism; the "parting word to the reader" is similarly pessimistic. McIntosh urges readers to remember that "What may be the world's portraiture of you, then, you may esteem as of little moment. It may be all fair and lovely, it may be all dark and hideous; it scarcely *can* be just." Perhaps the advent of the war caused McIntosh to doubt whether or not women were really capable of exerting any influence.

After reestablishing her financial independence, McIntosh founded something of a salon and gave readings of her work. Leaving New York for New Jersey in ill health, she lived with her niece and namesake, Maria McIntosh Cox, in Morristown, until her death on 23 February 1878. Although McIntosh's rather melodramatic style and didacticism attract a limited audience today, her work is perhaps most valuable to contemporary readers for its portrayal of a divided nation. McIntosh's defense of Southern culture suggests, as Moss argues, that regional differences are present in domestic fiction. Moreover, though many scholars may find McIntosh's proslavery fiction distasteful, its defense of the "peculiar institution" is valuable to scholars interested in women's roles in ideological debates surrounding slavery.

## References:

Bashar Akili, "Maria Jane McIntosh, a Woman in Her Time: A Biographical and Critical Study," dissertation, University of Technology, Loughborough, U.K., 1990;

Nina Baym, "Maria McIntosh," in *Woman's Fiction: A Guide to Novels by and about Women in America 1820–1870,* second edition (Urbana & Chicago: University of Illinois Press, 1993) pp. 86–109;

Julia D. Freeman, as Mary Forrest, *Women of the South Distinguished in Literature* (New York: Richardson, 1865), pp. 163–183;

Sarah Josepha Hale, *Woman's Record; or, Sketches of All Distinguished Women; or Woman's Record, from the Creation to A. D. 1868. Arranged in Four Eras. With Selections from Authoresses of Each Era,* third edition (New York: Harper, 1870);

John S. Hart, *The Female Prose Writers of America* (Philadelphia: Butler, 1852), pp. 63–75;

Elizabeth Moss, *Domestic Novelists in the Old South: Defenders of Southern Culture* (Baton Rouge: Louisiana State University Press, 1992);

M. T. Tardy, *The Living Female Writers of the South* (Philadelphia: Claxton, Remsen & Haffelfinger, 1872), pp. 223–229.

## Papers:

Maria Jane McIntosh's papers are not archived at one university, but several libraries hold at least one letter or manuscript. These libraries include the Beinecke Rare Book and Manuscript Library at Yale University; The Lilly Library at Indiana University; the Boston Public Library; the John M. Olin Library at Cornell University; the Wollman Library at Barnard College; the Haverford College Library; the Historical Society of Pennsylvania at Philadelphia; the John Hay Library at Brown University; and the Alderman Library at the University of Virginia.

# A. B. Meek

## (17 July 1814 – 1 November 1865)

### Bert Hitchcock
*Auburn University*

See also the Meek entry in *DLB 3: Antebellum Writers in New York and the South.*

BOOKS: *An Oration Delivered before the Society of the Alumni of the University of Alabama . . . Dec. 17, 1836* (Tuscaloosa, Ala.: Slade, 1837);

*A Poem Pronounced before the Ciceronian Club and Other Citizens of Tuscaloosa, Alabama, July 4, 1838* (Tuscaloosa, Ala.: Ciceronian Club, 1838);

*The Southwest: Its History, Character and Prospects: A Discourse for the Eighth Anniversary of the Erosophic Society of the University of Alabama* (Tuscaloosa, Ala.: Baldwin, 1840);

*Jack-Cadeism and the Fine Arts: A Discourse before the Literary Societies of La-Grange College, Alabama, June 16, 1841* (Tuscaloosa, Ala.: Slade, 1841);

*Americanism in Literature: An Oration Before the Phi Kappa and Demosthenian Societies of the University of Georgia, Athens, August 4, 1844* (Charleston, S.C.: Burges & James, 1844);

*An Address before the Baymen's Society of Mobile . . . Nov. 29th, 1852* (Mobile, Ala.: Register Job Office, 1853);

*The Claims and Characteristics of Alabama History: An Address before the Historical Society of That State* (Tuscaloosa, Ala.: Warren, 1855);

*The Red Eagle: A Poem of the South* (New York: Appleton, 1855);

*Romantic Passages in Southwestern History; Including Orations, Sketches, and Essays* (New York & Mobile, Ala.: Goetzel, 1857);

*Songs and Poems of the South* (New York & Mobile, Ala.: Goetzel, 1857);

*The Progress and Principles of Odd Fellowship: An Oration before the Grand Lodge of the State of Alabama, and the Subordinate Lodges in the City of Mobile . . . April 26, 1859* (Mobile, Ala.: Thompson, 1859).

OTHER: John G. Aikin, comp., *A Digest of the Laws of the State of Alabama, Containing all the Statutes of a Public and General Nature, in Force at the Close of the Session of the General Assembly, in January, 1833 . . . With an Appendix . . . and . . . Supplement . . . 1835,* includes contributions by Meek (Tuscaloosa, Ala.: Woodruff, 1836);

*A Supplement to Aikin's Digest of the Laws of the State of Alabama, Containing All the Unrepealed Laws of a Public and General Nature Passed by the General Assembly since the Second Edition of the Digest, up to the Close of the Called Session of April, 1841,* compiled by Meek (Tuscaloosa, Ala.: White & Snow, 1841);

"The Journal of A. B. Meek and the Second Seminole War, 1836," edited by John K. Mahon, *Florida Historical Quarterly,* 38 (1960): 302–318.

A. B. Meek, lawyer, legislator, editor, orator, historian, and poet, stands among the first of Alabama writers both in time and influence. Well known in literary circles of the South, he was an intellectual, cultural, and political leader of his state for two and a half decades before the Civil War. Although something of a dilettante who never got what he considered his most important work into print, he affords as interesting, impressive, and pure an example of the romantic literary nationalist as the Old Southwest of the nation had to offer.

The son of Anna McDowell and Samuel Mills Meek, a physician and minister, Alexander Beaufort Meek was born on 17 July 1814 in Columbia, South Carolina, and moved with his family to Alabama in 1819. Here, except for short residences in Athens, Georgia, and Washington, D.C., he made his home for more than forty years, first in Tuscaloosa and then Mobile, the cultural centers of the state. In 1863 he moved to Columbus, Mississippi, where, still close by his cherished Tombigbee River, he died two years later on 1 November 1865. Never a father, he was twice married, first to Emma Donaldson Slatter in 1856, and after her death, to Eliza Jane Cannon in 1864.

A lawyer and newspaper editor by profession, government attorney and judge by official appointment, and state legislator and presidential elector by public vote, the six-foot, four-inch, two-hundred-and-forty- pound Meek was also by nature and cultivation a pleasant, attractive social companion and a popular occasional orator by frequent demand. Returning home from the University of Georgia, Meek had become a member of the first graduating class of the University of Alabama in 1833. Two years later he was admitted to the state bar and assumed management of the *Flag of the Union,* a Democratic Party newspaper. In 1836 he was a volunteer officer in the Florida Seminole War and held a brief appointment as state attorney general. Later, after a private law practice, he was appointed county judge but failed to win subsequent election. A supporter of James K. Polk and member of the Electoral College of 1844, Meek received a U.S. Treasury Department appointment in Washington before being named the U.S. attorney for south Alabama and moving to Mobile in 1846. Apparently at this time he turned down the professorship of English literature at his alma mater. In Mobile, Meek held several legal positions, including probate judge, and for five years was an editor of the *Mobile Daily Register.* He was elected to the state legislature in 1853, where he was instrumental in establishing a public-school system for Alabama, and was reelected in 1859, becoming Speaker of the House. As an 1856 elector on the James Buchanan ticket he was named president of the U. S. Electoral College. A distinguished member of a highly conspicuous Alabama delegation, he attended the fateful 1860 Democratic National Convention in Charleston, South Carolina.

Meek's extensive professional, public, and personal activities proved serious obstacles to his calling as a writer, particularly as a poet and creative spokesman for the beauties of the United States and Alabama in literature. Partly by virtue of his other prominent roles, Meek's was a literary voice that was listened to. Finally the voice was more oratorical than artistic, however, and his message more one of admonishment than of embodiment.

Although his poetry was widely published in antebellum Southern periodicals and at least seven of his orations appeared as pamphlets, Meek was late in achieving book publication of his literary work. He had long sought a publisher for *The Red Eagle: A Poem of the South,* which was finally brought out by Appleton in 1855. His two other book-length works, excluding a digest of Alabama laws, were collections published in 1857: *Songs and Poems of the South,* a selection of previously published poetry, and *Romantic Passages in Southwestern History,* an assemblage of orations, sketches, and essays, about half of which had appeared earlier. *The Red Eagle* secured immediate

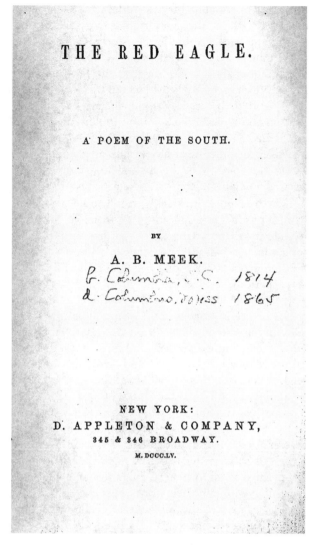

Title page for Meek's long poem based on the life of Creek Indian leader William Weatherford (South Caroliniana Library, University of South Carolina)

and continuing favorable attention in the North as well as the South, and public reception of the 1857 collections necessitated three reprintings of each within the year.

For Meek's Southern literary generation the acknowledged modern masters were British: Sir Walter Scott, Lord Byron, and Thomas Moore especially, and, as less predominant models, Robert Southey, Samuel Taylor Coleridge, Percy Bysshe Shelley, Thomas Campbell, and John Keats. Meek's romantic convictions were established early and were often in evidence through both assertion and example. Love of woman, nature, and country or section, inseparable in some important ways and yet each reflecting a separate important aspect of his romanticism, became his prevailing themes. Although the first was ultimately to be the least significant, Meek, who remained a bachelor until he was forty-two years old, owed much of his local fame to verse tributes and lover's complaints to members of the other gender. Despite his apparently being smitten by a belle of the West, said to be Jessie Benton, during his days in Washington with the Polk administration, the "girl of the Sunny South," as he makes clear in a "song" of that title, remained unrivaled in the poet's mind. For Meek the South was the natural home of angelic, celestial woman, "poetry's sunniest, fondest dream."

A true poet, in Meek's eyes, would also be a natural product and reflection of his native land and would make important use of all the beauty and romantic possibilities immediately around him. In the lead article for the first *Southron,* a short-lived literary periodical Meek edited in 1839, he passionately articulated, as he would continue to do, the untapped literary riches of the beautiful natural scenery, the character of the original Native American inhabitants, and the romance inherent in the historical discovery, exploration, and settlement of his region. What he had to say about the materials and possibilities for Southern literature was, however, only part of the larger picture he drew most definitively in his "Americanism in Literature" address to a University of Georgia audience in 1844. Although he professed to be displeased with the "tendencies and achievements" of American literature thus far, the great native influences at work, must eventually produce great national art, he argued. Calling attention to the distinctive physical, social, historical, and political features of the country, he found only self-imposed impediments to the achievement of a significant American literature.

Since "the most potent influence of Americanism in Literature" was for Meek "the form and spirit of our political institutions," the relationship of national to sectional patriotism for this self-conscious Southerner is particularly noteworthy. Nowhere is the tension better evidenced than in the long occasional poem commemorating the Fourth of July, 1838, published in *Songs and Poems of the South* as "The Day of Freedom." One of Meek's best-known pieces, "The Land of the South" is a short-rhymed poem embedded in the blank-verse "The Day of Freedom." Its stirring, ominous, concluding pledge of the poet's life for the Southern cause led to frequent separate reprintings, without its integral introduction in the longer poem. In that first part, elaborating his lesson "To love alike all portions of our land," Meek warns of human selfishness and dwells upon the invaluable common possessions of all Americans. Likening the American union of sovereign states to the solar system, he expresses belief that displacement of any of the individual "orbs" would turn the inspired system into a disastrous "wreck" and "make even Heaven's high angels grieve!"

Reluctantly, Meek gave his final political loyalty to his state and region. In "The Day of Freedom" he had recognized that the locale of one's youth would naturally and rightly be loved the most, and such love effectively dictated his literary efforts as well as his civic judgements. *Romantic Passages in Southwestern History,* he writes in its preface, is a "guide-book to an almost uncultured territory, in which the Historian, the Novelist, and the Poet may find the richest materials and incentives for the highest exercise of their respective vocations." Mainly the historian in this volume, he takes pains to note that "romantic" in the title was "intended to indicate rather the peculiar character of the incidents, the manner of their arrangement, and the coloring of the style, than any want of authenticity in the facts narrated." Still close in time to some of its most romantic if bloody incidents, Meek took the role of Alabama historian seriously. He noted with pride the recognition of his researches by historian George Bancroft, and, though finally unfinished and unpublished, a definitive volume of Alabama history was his lifelong work.

In his role as creator of verse, Meek wrote about an organic local "poetic Faith" in the preface to *Songs and Poems of the South:*

> The poetry of a country should be a faithful expression of its physical and moral characteristics. The imagery, at least, should be drawn from the indigenous objects of the region, and the sentiments be such as naturally arise under the influence of its climate, its institutions, habits of life, and social condition. Verse, so fashioned and colored, is as much the genuine product and growth of a Land, as its trees or flowers. It partakes of the raciness of the soil, the purity of the atmosphere, the brilliancy of its skies, its mountain pictures, and its broad sweeps of level and undulating territory. The Scenery infuses itself into the Song; and the feelings and fancies are modulated by the circumstances amid which they had their birth.

Meek's literary theory and practice, his impulses to both poetry and history, and his various romantic inclinations merge most completely in *The Red Eagle.* Dedicated to William Gilmore Simms, this three-canto, 1,824–line production of varying verse forms has as its hero William Weatherford, the mixed-blood military leader of the Creek Indians during the Alabama wars of 1813. That Weatherford commanded the force that massacred hundreds of men, women, and children at Fort Mims did not prevent the poet from recognizing his eloquent nobility. Meek's most ambitious effort, this long, epical poem had a generally favorable contemporary reception. Noting the influence of Moore's *Lalla Rookh* (1817) on the work and praising the poet's nature imagery and gorgeous scenery painting, Meek's friend William Russell Smith also recognized in his *Reminiscences of a Long Life* (1889), however, that the romantic, visual excesses of the poem left the mind lethargic. As Smith perceptively noted, Meek had tried to make lyric poetry out of basically historical, nonpoetic material. Thus Weatherford, or Red Eagle, according to Smith, becomes more lover than warrior and "is shorn of much of his majestical proportions" because he is "cut off at the knees by the lyrical sword." Modern readers have reported finding the poem flowery and melodramatic despite being engaged by the dramatic story. A few, however, have unexpectedly found themselves admiring Meek's love of names and landscapes–and, occasionally, excellent lines of poetry.

The most well-received and enduring portion of *The Red Eagle* is, like "The Land of the South" in "The Day of Freedom," a short poem or song embedded in the longer work. In this case the passage truly is a song, featuring the *Terra-re!* call of the Southern bluebird, which, like several other of Meek's lyrics, became popular, was set to music, and was often reprinted. Although Smith praised his sonnet of invocation to voluptuous Southern spring in *The Red Eagle,* Meek wrote to Simms in an 18 May 1847 letter that the sonnet at its best is still but "poetry in the pillory." High praise of poetry, as he thought of Simms's work, would be to liken it to "the gushing and reckless warblings of our wood-birds in the morning."

One of Meek's most popular poems was "The Mocking Bird," considered by some persons to be the best of the many Southern poems on the subject. It, no less than his "Elegy on a Mocking Bird Killed by a Cat," however, indicates how much Meek was pilloried by literary convention and how far away he was from recklessness. Regular in form, most of his most-anthologized pieces such as "The Mocking Bird" are Southern in subject. The poem that brought him the most personal gratification probably is "The Fated City," which is about Pompeii. Almost certainly his best-known and most frequently reprinted piece was "Balaklava"–inspired by an incident of the Crimean War, initially attributed to the English poet Alexander Smith, and frequently compared with Tennyson's "The Charge of the Light Brigade" (1854).

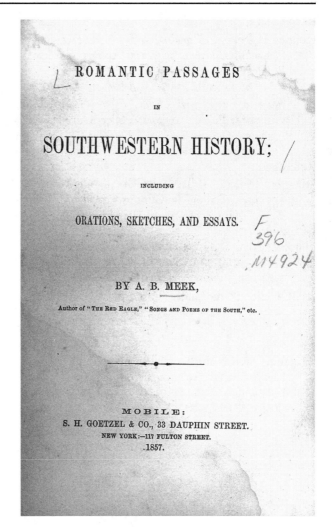

*Title page for Meek's regional guidebook for "the Historian, the Novelist, and the Poet" (Thomas Cooper Library, University of South Carolina)*

Later generations have not found either the intellectual or poetic genius that many of his contemporaries saw in A. B. Meek. Meek recognized the difference between potential and accomplishment, knew his problem, and was aware of his shortcomings. "My sympathies are all literary," he wrote to Simms, "though my habits are anything else." In the preface to his *Songs and Poems of the South,* he had declared himself "not a Poet, by profession or ambition," and had composed, he said, "only at long intervals, or at the instigation of trivial or transient causes." Meek did, however, realize the ambition for his literary labors as he expresses it in the preface: to develop "more gifted capacities . . . and wreathe into the garlands of a graceful and becoming literature" the richness of his nation and, especially, of its Southland.

**Biographies:**

Herman C. Nixon, *Alexander Beaufort Meek: Poet, Orator, Journalist, Historian, Statesman* (Auburn: Alabama Polytechnic Institute, 1910);

Robert H. McKenzie, *Alexander Beaufort Meek: Pioneer Alabama Lawyer and Literary Figure* (Tuscaloosa: Center for Public Law and Service, University of Alabama, 1983).

**References:**

Philip D. Beidler, "A. B. Meek's Great American Epic Poem of 1855; or, the Curious Career of *The Red Eagle,*" *Mississippi Quarterly,* 51 (Spring 1998): 275–290;

Margaret Gillis Figh, "Alexander Beaufort Meek, Pioneer Man of Letters," *Alabama Historical Quarterly,* 2 (Summer 1940): 127–151;

Jay B. Hubbell, "Alexander Beaufort Meek," in his *The South in American Literature, 1607–1900* (Durham, N.C.: Duke University Press, 1954), pp. 624–629, 950;

Robert H. McKenzie, "Law and Literature in Antebellum Alabama: Two Case Studies in Applying the Humanities to Public Policy," *Southern Studies,* 22 (Fall 1983): 302–313;

Charles Hunter Ross, "Alexander Beaufort Meek," *Sewanee Review,* 4 (August 1896): 411–427;

S. S. Scott, *The Mobilians; or Talks about the South* (Montgomery, Ala.: Brown, 1898), pp. 121–128;

William R. Smith Sr., *Reminiscences of a Long Life* (Washington, D.C.: Smith, 1889), I: 315–344;

Benjamin Buford Williams, "Alexander Beaufort Meek, Poet and Historian," in his *A Literary History of Alabama: The Nineteenth Century* (Rutherford, N.J.: Farleigh Dickinson University Press, 1979), pp. 39–57;

Williams, "Two Uncollected Civil War Poems of Alexander Beaufort Meek," *Alabama Historical Quarterly,* 25 (Spring–Summer 1963): 114–119.

**Papers:**

The A. B. Meek Collection at the Alabama State Department of Archives and History, in Montgomery, is the largest gathering of such materials. It includes manuscripts, journals, letters, and miscellaneous items. A second noteworthy holding, though not greatly extensive, is at Duke University. The University of Alabama, Tuscaloosa, also has a Meek collection, which includes some manuscripts and letters and copies of biographical documents.

# Edward Coote Pinkney

*(1 October 1802 – 11 April 1828)*

Rayburn S. Moore
*University of Georgia*

BOOKS: *Rodolph. A Fragment* (Baltimore: Robinson, 1823);

*Poems* (Baltimore: Robinson, 1825);

*The Life and Works of Edward Coote Pinkney,* edited by Thomas Ollive Mabbott and Frank Lester Pleadwell (New York: Macmillan, 1926).

In a life that lasted less than twenty-six years, Edward Coote Pinkney pursued a naval career, practiced law, held a professorship, edited a newspaper, and published enough verse to complete two slim volumes, *Rodolph. A Fragment* (1823) and *Poems* (1825). These works and particularly the song "A Health" (1824) led Edgar Allan Poe to declare in "The Poetic Principle" (1848) that had Pinkney "been a New Englander, it is probable that he would have been ranked as the first of American lyrists," but Pinkney's brief life was over before American poetry had advanced beyond the work of William Cullen Bryant in the 1820s. Nevertheless, Pinkney's poems, especially the songs and lyrics, have earned for him an honored niche in the history of Southern and American poetry.

Pinkney was born in London, the seventh child of Maryland parents, William Pinkney, U.S. commissioner and later minister to the Court of St. James, attorney general of the United States, and senator from Maryland, and Ann Maria Rodgers Pinkney, the sister of Commodore John Rodgers of the U.S. Navy. His early education was in England, where he was being prepared for Eton when his father resigned his post in 1811 and the family returned to Maryland and settled in Baltimore. There he attended St. Mary's College as a day student, and in November 1815, at the age of thirteen years, he was appointed a midshipman in the navy with the help of Commodore Rodgers.

Pinkney served on active duty until 1824, chiefly in the Mediterranean and the Caribbean, where he participated in operations against pirates and was cited for bravery. He also got into trouble over matters concerning his honor, however, and was reprimanded and court-martialed for "disrespect to a superior officer" in

*(frontispiece for* The Life and Works of Edward Coote Pinkney, *1926)*

May 1820. After the death of his father in February 1822 Pinkney was assigned to shore duty in Baltimore, where, after failing to secure further sea duty, he began writing poems and preparing for a career in law. In January 1823 he published his first poem, "Serenade," a song addressed to Mary Hawkins, whom he was unsuccessfully courting at the time, and shortly thereafter *Rodolph,* a composition in the manner of Lord Byron and Thomas Moore, was published as an octavo pamphlet that sold for 25¢.

The following October, Pinkney, offended by some slanderous remarks about his dead father in *Randolph* (1823), an anonymous novel purportedly written by John Neal, challenged Neal to a duel. When Neal refused to acknowledge and "disavow unequivocally in writing" his comments or to fight, Pinkney posted handbills throughout the city describing Neal's cowardice. A year later, in October 1824, Pinkney's resignation from the navy was accepted, and in the same month he married Georgiana McCausland, the daughter of a well-known Baltimore businessman and the inspiration for his verse from 1823 onward. During this period he was admitted to the bar and began to practice law in the city, though he continued to compose lyrics from time to time, as *Poems,* his first collection, indicates.

Early in 1826 he was appointed to a nonteaching position as professor of rhetoric and belles lettres at the University of Maryland, but when his legal and professorial work failed to provide an adequate living, Pinkney went to Mexico to seek a commission in the Mexican navy under Commodore David Porter. He did not receive an appointment but instead contracted a serious disease in Mexico. He returned to Baltimore in ill health and, in December 1827, became founding editor of the *Marylander,* a newspaper established by supporters of President John Quincy Adams. During the next four months Pinkney consistently promoted and defended Adams's causes and attacked Andrew Jackson's positions, but his health deteriorated after his sojourn in Mexico and he died on 11 April 1828, less than six months before his twenty-sixth birthday.

Because of Pinkney's short life, his literary production is limited compared to that of any of his contemporaries of consequence. He published his first poem and his first book—actually a pamphlet—at the age of twenty and his last poem at the age of twenty-five. His longest piece, *Rodolph,* is a "fragment" of only two parts and twenty-three stanzas. Many of his lyrics are brief; they frequently deal with themes of love and time and celebrate women and their beauty. These early songs are often addressed to Hawkins, who failed to respond to his advances, and to McCausland during and after their courtship. They remind many readers of poems by the seventeenth-century Cavalier bards, but Thomas Ollive Mabbott and Frank Lester Pleadwell maintain that they really owe more to Byron, Moore, Sir Walter Scott, and William Wordsworth. Other writers familiar to Pinkney, according to Mabbott and

Pleadwell, include, among the Greeks, Homer, Herodotus, and Plutarch and, among the Romans, Terence, Virgil, Cicero, Horace, Ovid, Livy, Seutonius, and Pliny the Younger. He also knew the works of Geoffrey Chaucer, William Shakespeare, John Milton, John Dryden, Thomas Carew (the only Cavalier poet Pinkney quotes in the *Marylander*), Alexander Pope, Jonathan Swift, Laurence Sterne, Samuel Johnson, Robert Southey, Samuel Taylor Coleridge, and Percy Bysshe Shelley. Among American poets, he read Fitz-Greene Halleck and may have known some of the work of Philip Freneau, Bryant, and William Gilmore Simms.

Whether or not Pinkney knew Cavalier poetry well, many of his poems, such as "Serenade," "A Health," and "On Parting," include the qualities of melody, wit, and urbanity usually associated with the seventeenth-century lyrics gentlemen poets addressed to ladies. "Serenade" is a case in point. The song illustrates succinctly Pinkney's promise and accomplishment along these lines, as its final stanza demonstrates:

> Look out upon the stars, my love,
>   And shame them with thine eyes,
> On which, than on the lights above,
>   There hang more destinies.
> Night's beauty is the harmony
>   Of blending shades and light;
> Then, lady, up—look out, and be
>   A sister to the night!—

Reminiscent in tone, theme, and imagery (especially in its use of hyperbole) of Romeo's soliloquy before the balcony scene in act 2 of Shakespeare's *Romeo and Juliet* (circa 1595–1596) and of Ben Jonson's "Song: To Celia" ("Drink to me only with thine eyes") from *The Forrest* (1616), the lyric nevertheless stands on its own and is noteworthy not only for its early appearance in Pinkney's career (he had just turned twenty years old at the time) but also for its attainment at this early stage in the development of American poetry, a period during which Freneau and Bryant were well established on the scene and Halleck was beginning to emerge in his own right.

"A Health," Pinkney's best-known poem, shares the qualities embodied in "Serenade" but is more serious in tone and purpose, as its putative address to his wife may imply. In the convention of celebrating a lady's health and beauty, the poem takes its place with the best of its kind in Anglo-American song.

> I fill this cup to one made up of loveliness alone,
> A woman, of her gentle sex the seeming paragon;
> To whom the better elements and kindly stars have given,
> A form so fair, that, like the air, 'tis less
>   of earth than heaven.

Proceeding to establish the lady as a "paragon," the speaker characterizes her affections, feelings, and passions as they are etched in his memory through her "bright face" and echoing "voice," leading him to wish that "on earth there stood some more of such a frame, / That life might be all poetry, and weariness a name." In "The Poetic Principle" Poe praised "A Health" for its "brilliancy and spirit" and for "the poetic elevation which it induces," and more recent scholars—including Mabbott, Jay B. Hubbell, Edd Winfield Parks—have generally agreed.

Other lyrics owe a debt to Wordsworth, as, for example, does another of his pieces addressed to his wife, "To [Georgiana]" (1823), which a line in the poem explicitly links "With Wordsworth's 'She was a Phantom of Delight'"—a "portraiture of Thee," the speaker acknowledges:

> . . . , Time, may mar
> All meaner sculpture of my mind,
> But in its darkness, like a star,
> Thy semblance shall remain enshrined.

Moreover, the "Song" that begins "Those starry eyes" suggests Wordsworth's Lucy poems:

> Those starry eyes, those starry eyes,
>  Those eyes that used to be
> Unto my heart, as beacon-lights
>  To pilgrims of the Sea!–

At the same time, this imagery harks back again to Romeo's overture to Juliet in act 1 of Shakespeare's play.

Some verse, on the other hand, displays a vein of sadness and melancholy inherent in English poetry since the sixteenth century. "On Parting" (1823), another piece composed for Georgiana Pinkney, reflects this strain:

> Time,–envious time,–loves not to be
>  In company with mirth,
> But makes malignant pause to see
>  To work of pain on earth.

This tone and mood are also intimated in "The Widow's Song" (1825)–"I burn no incense, hang no wreath / On this, thine early tomb"–and in the well-known "Song" (1825):

> We break the glass, whose sacred wine
>  To some beloved health we drain,
> Lest future pledges, less divine,
>  Should e'er the hallowed toy profane.

"Song" ("I need not name"), composed around 1823 and addressed presumably to Mary Hawkins, provides another variation on this theme:

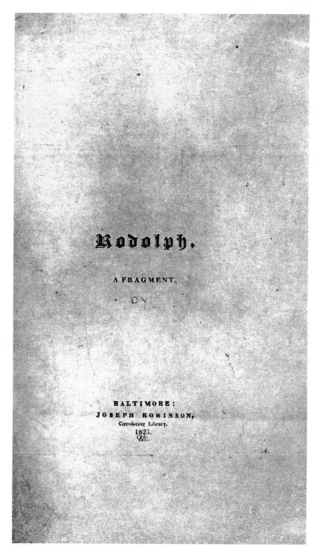

*Title page for Pinkney's long poem influenced by the works of Lord Byron (from* The Life and Works of Edward Coote Pinkney, *1926)*

> I pledge thee, and the empty cup
>  Emblems this hollow life of mine,
> To which, a gone enchantment, thou
>  No more wilt be the wine,–Mary.

On occasion Pinkney turns to action, as in "Song" ("Day departs") from 1825, a stirring balladlike account of two lovers leaving "loveless halls." The speaker urges his love to "Come, come–affection calls– / Away at once with me," and assures her, despite the threat of "kinsmen,"

> I'll keep thee, dear,
>  In safety as we ride,–
> On, on my heart is here,
>  My sword is at my side!

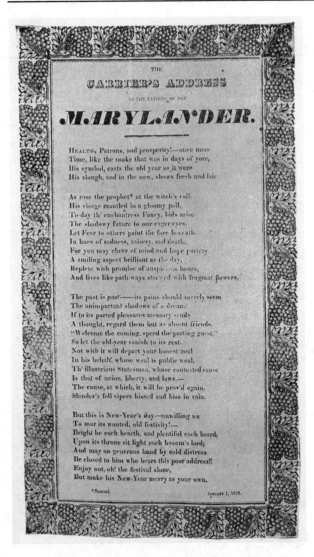

HEALTH, Patrons, and prosperity!—once more
Time, like the snake that was in days of yore,
His symbol, casts the old year as it were
His slough, and in the new, shows fresh and fair.

As rose the prophet* at the witch's call,
His visage mantled in a gloomy pall,
To-day th' enchantress Fancy, bids arise
The shadowy future to our eager eyes.
Let Fear to others paint the face beneath,
In hues of sadness, misery, and death;
For you may cheer of mind and hope portray
A smiling aspect brilliant as the day,
Replete with promise of auspicious hours,
And lives like path-ways strewed with fragrant flowers.

The past is *past*——its pains should merely seem
The unimportant shadows of a dream:
If to its parted pleasures memory sends
A thought, regard them but as absent friends,
"Welcome the coming, speed the parting guest,"
So let the old-year vanish to its rest.
Not with it will depart your honest zeal
In his behalf, whose weal is public weal,
Th' illustrious Statesman, whose contested cause
Is that of union, liberty, and laws,—
The cause, at which, it will be prov'd again,
Slander's fell vipers kissed and hiss in vain.

But this is New-Year's day—unwilling we
To mar its wonted, old festivity!—
Bright be each hearth, and plentiful each board,
Upon its throne sit light each bosom's lord;
And may no generous hand by cold distress
Be closed to him who bears this poor address!!
Enjoy not, oh! the festival alone,
But make his New-Year merry as your own.

*Samuel.                              JANUARY 1, 1828.

*Broadside with Pinkney's New Year's poem for subscribers to the* Marylander, *the newspaper for which he served as founding editor beginning in December 1827 (from* The Life and Works of Edward Coote Pinkney, *1926)*

Paradox and irony, qualities of seventeenth-century verse, come into play from time to time in Pinkney's lyrics. "Evergreens" (1825) provides a fine example of the paradoxical relationship between light and shadow, summer and autumn. The resulting imagery embodies a moral reflection that has been often quoted:

Thus thoughts that frown upon our mirth
 Will smile upon our sorrow,
And many dark fears of to-day
 May be bright hopes to-morrow.

A slightly longer poem, "Italy" (1824), represents his feeling for the country his father revered and taught him to appreciate. It reveals concurrently the narrator's passion for his "Beloved" and for "the land which lov-ers ought to choose," "that delightful spot" where "nature is delicate and graceful," where art shows "Her sculptured marbles, and her pictured walls," and where "the speaking ruins in that gentle clime / Have but been hallowed by the hand of time."

A longer and more forceful piece, "The Voyager's Song" (1825) is Pinkney's most successful ode. Composed of six ten-line stanzas, the lyric is a kind of dramatic monologue in which Ponce de León exhorts his men to seek Bimini, a possible location of the fountain of youth. In words similar to those used by Alfred Tennyson's Ulysses in his 1842 poem of that title to rally his followers to "seek a newer world" and to "sail beyond the sunset," de León harangues his crew:

Onward, my friends, to that bright florid isle,
The jewel of a smooth and silver sea,
With springs on which perennial summers smile
A power of causing immortality.

The great theme, to be sure, is the triumph over time by means of the "wondrous waters" with their promise of "perpetual life." Along the way the speaker turns from his men to talk with "Miranda"–the beautiful one who typifies the "brave new world" alluded to by Prospero's daughter Miranda in Shakespeare's *The Tempest* (1611)–and contemplates a "green eternity" with her:

The envious years, which steal our pleasure, thou
May'st call at once, like magic memory, back,
And, as they pass o'er thine unwithering brow,
Efface their footsteps ere they form a track.
Thy bloom with wilful weeping never stain.
Perpetual life must not belong to pain.
For me,–this world hath not yet been a place
Conscious of joys so great as will be mine,
Because the light has kissed no face
 Forever fair as thine.

*Rodolph,* Pinkney's longest poem, was published first as a pamphlet in 1823 and in a revised and augmented but still incomplete form in 1825. It comprises two cantos and 554 lines in a style established by Scott, Byron, and Moore. Rhyme schemes vary from stanza to stanza, but the couplet dominates throughout. A narrative of lawless love and murder in the Byronic mode, the poem focuses on the psychological state of its hero and provides the poet with an opportunity to display his own intellectual interests and learning in allusions and references to a wide range of ancient and modern lore, not unlike Poe's attempts to embody such materials in "Tamerlane" (1827) and "Al Aaraaf" (1829). *Rodolph* remains, however, in the final analysis, a "fragment" and not so consequential an achievement as his short poems.

These lyrics constitute a body of work that entitles Edward Coote Pinkney to consideration as a significant poet of the 1820s. "Serenade," "A Health," "Evergreens," "Song" ("We break the glass"), "The Widow's Song," and "Song" ("Day departs") are close to a certain kind of artistic perfection and establish a voice assuredly Pinkney's own. His limited canon—the poems cover ninety-eight pages in the Mabbott and Pleadwell edition of his work—may make him a minor poet, but his best poems are finely crafted, musical, intriguing, and aesthetically satisfying.

## Letters:

"Letters," in *The Life and Works of Edward Coote Pinkney,* edited by Thomas Ollive Mabbott and Frank Lester Pleadwell (New York: Macmillan, 1926), pp. 14–28, 33–34, 35–36, 49, 74–75.

## Bibliography:

Thomas Ollive Mabbott and Frank Lester Pleadwell, "Bibliography," in *The Life and Works of Edward Coote Pinkney,* edited by Mabbott and Pleadwell, pp. 219–223.

## Biography:

Thomas Ollive Mabbott and Frank Lester Pleadwell, "Memoir," in Pinkney, *The Life and Works of*
*Edward Coote Pinkney,* edited by Mabbott and Pleadwell (New York: Macmillan, 1926), pp. 1–92.

## References:

Eugene L. Didier, "Pinkney: First of American Lyricists," *New York Times,* 11 January 1902, p. 27;

Evert A. and George L. Duyckinck, eds., *Cyclopedia of American Literature* (New York: Scribner, 1856), pp. 338–341;

Jay B. Hubbell, *The South in American Literature 1607-1900* (Durham: Duke University Press, 1954), pp. 301–304, 954–955;

Wrightman F. Melton, "Edward Coote Pinkney," in *Library of Southern Literature,* edited by Edwin A. Alderman and others (Atlanta: Martin & Hoyt, 1909), pp. 1063–1067;

Melton, "Edward Coote Pinkney," *South Atlantic Quarterly,* 11 (October 1912): 328–336;

Charles H. Ross, "Edward Coate [*sic*] Pinkney," *Sewanee Review,* 4 (May 1896): 287–298;

J. P. Simmons, "Edward Coote Pinkney—American Cavalier Poet," *South Atlantic Quarterly,* 28 (October 1929): 406–418;

C. Michael Smith, "Edward Coote Pinkney (1802-1828)," in *Fifty Southern Writers Before 1900,* edited by Robert Bain, Joseph M. Flora, and Louis D. Rubin Jr. (Westport, Conn.: Greenwood Press, 1987), pp. 359–364.

# Edgar Allan Poe

*(19 January 1809 – 7 October 1849)*

G. R. Thompson
*Purdue University*

See also the Poe entries in *DLB 3: Antebellum Writers in New York and the South; DLB 59: American Literary Critics and Scholars, 1800–1850; DLB 73: American Magazine Journalists, 1741–1850;* and *DLB 74: American Short-Story Writers Before 1880.*

BOOKS: *Tamerlane and Other Poems. By a Bostonian* (Boston: Thomas, 1827);

*Al Aaraaf, Tamerlane, and Minor Poems* (Baltimore: Hatch & Dunning, 1829);

*Poems, By Edgar A. Poe. Second Edition* (New York: Bliss, 1831);

*The Narrative of Arthur Gordon Pym, of Nantucket . . . ,* anonymous (New York: Harper, 1838; London: Wiley & Putnam, 1838);

*The Conchologist's First Book; or, A System of Testaceous Malacology . . .* (Philadelphia: Haswell, Barrington & Haswell, 1839);

*Tales of the Grotesque and Arabesque,* 2 volumes (Philadelphia: Lea & Blanchard, 1840);

*The Prose Romances of Edgar A. Poe* (Philadelphia: Graham, 1843);

*Tales* (New York & London: Wiley & Putnam, 1845);

*The Raven and Other Poems* (New York: Wiley & Putnam, 1845; London: Wiley & Putnam, 1846);

*Eureka: A Prose Poem* (New York: Putnam, 1848; London: Chapman, 1848).

**Editions and Collections**: *The Works of the Late Edgar Allan Poe: With Notices of his Life and Genius,* edited by Rufus Wilmot Griswold, 4 volumes (New York: Redfield, 1850–1856);

*The Complete Works of Edgar Allan Poe,* edited by James A. Harrison, 17 volumes (New York: Crowell, 1902);

*The Narrative of Arthur Gordon Pym,* edited by Sidney Kaplan (New York: Hill & Wang, 1960; revised edition, Urbana: University of Illinois Press, 1990);

*The Poems of Edgar Allan Poe,* edited by Floyd Stovall (Charlottesville: University Press of Virginia, 1965);

*Edgar Allan Poe (daguerreotype by Samuel W. Hartshorn; Brown University Library)*

*Collected Works of Edgar Allan Poe,* edited by Thomas Ollive Mabbott, 3 volumes (Cambridge, Mass.: Belknap Press of Harvard University Press, 1969–1978);

*The Narrative of Arthur Gordon Pym,* edited by Harold Beaver (New York: Penguin, 1975);

*The Short Fiction of Edgar Allan Poe: An Annotated Edition,* edited by Stuart Levine and Susan Levine (Indianapolis: Bobbs-Merrill, 1976);

*The Annotated Tales of Edgar Allan Poe,* edited by Stephen Peithman (New York: Avenell, 1981);

*Collected Writings of Edgar Allan Poe,* edited by Burton R. Pollin, 5 volumes to date (Boston: Twayne / New York: Gordian, 1981);

*Essays and Reviews of Edgar Allan Poe,* edited by G. R. Thompson (New York: Library of America, 1984);

*Poetry and Tales of Edgar Allan Poe,* edited by Patrick F. Quinn (New York: Library of America, 1984);

*The Narrative of Arthur Gordon Pym,* edited by J. Gerald Kennedy (New York: Oxford University Press, 1994);

*The Narrative of Arthur Gordon Pym,* edited by Richard Kopley (New York: Penguin, 1999).

From the perspective of more than a century and a half, the achievements of Edgar Allan Poe as a man of letters are extraordinary. He may be regarded without too much exaggeration as the single most important influence on the development of an entire poetic tradition in Europe at the end of the nineteenth century: the Symbolist movement. He had a major impact on the writing of fiction in the United States and, indeed, the world. Although his critical reception has been marked by strong disagreement over the intrinsic merit of his writings, his achievement in poetry, criticism, magazine journalism, and fiction is at least historically impressive. As a professional man of letters in a young country, Poe tried in his career to unify the sophisticated and disparate roles of poet, writer of fiction, theoretical critic, practical critic, reviewer, journalist, editor, and philosopher.

Poe's life and career were always strongly marked by self-division, perhaps appropriate for one born in the North and reared in the South. His adult life alternated between Boston and Richmond, in ever-decreasing pendulum swings from the coastal cities of New York, Pennsylvania, and Maryland, to rest motionless in the streets of Baltimore. He was born on 19 January 1809. His mother was a minor actress named Elizabeth Arnold married to a sometime actor and reputed alcoholic, David Poe. By the time Edgar was three years of age, his father had mysteriously disappeared from the scene, and Elizabeth Poe was on her deathbed in Richmond, Virginia. Poe and his older brother, William Henry, and younger sister, Rosalie, were suddenly orphans. At her death Poe's mother left him an inscription on a sketch she had made of Boston Harbor: "For my little son Edgar, who should ever love Boston, the place of his birth, and where his mother found her best, and most sympathetic friends." The South became Poe's first love, however, and Richmond the city he called home. Yet, in early youth, alienated from his foster father, John Allan, a Richmond merchant, and from Southern society, Poe fled north to Boston, where his first book, *Tamerlane and Other Poems* (1827), appeared anonymously as "By a Bostonian."

Biographers have always found this beginning powerfully suggestive of the major tensions and divisions in Poe's life and literary career. Indeed, one of the more-coherent explanations of Poe's fragmented life is that which casts him as an actor imitating various personalities. Poe, as the orphaned child of itinerant actors reared in the home of a tyrannical and unloving foster father, is said to have felt a lack of roots and self-identity. This lack of identity is supposed to have caused him to assume various unsuitable masks, or guises, and to spend his life in role-playing. He even refers to himself at least twice as a literary *histrio,* a player.

The player analogy clearly pertains to the earliest models for his fiction, that of *Blackwood's Edinburgh Magazine,* which developed a cult of personality around its editors and contributors, who under code names played to a special audience of the intellectually elite. In another dimension, even Poe's satire and parody are supposed to show how dependent on imitation and playing he was for literary inspiration. In his poetry Poe is said to have borrowed not only the symbols of British Romantic writing but also the personalities of the Romantic poets. Poe played (so the theory goes) Lord Byron in his earliest poems, then Thomas Moore, Percy Bysshe Shelley, and Samuel Taylor Coleridge. Yet, at the same time that he played the role of the dreamy Romantic poet, he also played the contradictory role of the mechanical calculating machine. Toward the end of his career he played the mathematical critical theorist of such works as "The Philosophy of Composition" (1846) and the "Review of Twice-Told Tales by Nathaniel Hawthorne" (1842), as well as the superanalytical French detective hero of "The Murders in the Rue Morgue" (1841) and "The Purloined Letter" (1845).

The player analogy seems to explain a good deal, but there are some cautionary considerations. First, the idea of the writer as role-player leads to an easy and potentially reductive model that underplays the fact that all human beings are contradictory and have a natural tendency to play roles. One of the most popular interpretations of Poe's life and works has been a more or less Freudian interpretation of the traumatic centrality of his loss of his mother and subsequent mother figures. This assumption carries an attendant theory of Oedipal conflict with his absent father and with his foster father, along with other male rivals in the professional literary world. The model often presumes an overly simplistic logic of direct cause and effect that can lead to exceedingly naive psychoanalytic and literary judgments based on superficial and even erroneous biographical interpretation. In Poe's case the difficulty in interpretation is compounded when psychoanalytic critics downplay the trajectory of his professional career, the economics of the publishing market, and the day-to-day considerations of earning a living by one's pen (such as proofreading and meeting deadlines). It is further compounded by some

*Poe's foster mother, Frances Keeling Valentine Allan (portrait by
Thomas Sully; Valentine Museum of Richmond)*

critics' minimal knowledge of the literary conventions of
the author's time. In the Romantic era, for example, evocation of such things as the death of a beautiful loved one
or instances of premature burial or the use of opium were
staples of popular fiction, and they do not necessarily
reflect the psyche of the author in a direct, one-to-one
way.

Rather than sentimentalized or Freudian guesses
about Poe's dark psyche, it is more useful to focus on his
insistent quest for a vocation, deliberately modeled on the
pattern of the great British magazinists and poet-critics of
the latter eighteenth and earlier nineteenth centuries. The
frustrated desire of his driving ambition—as much as any
of the Freudian speculations about him—explains some of
the contradictions and tensions in the public and private
life of the enigmatic genius whose great promise was
never fully realized. Toward the end of his career, Poe
wrote in the preface to *The Raven and Other Poems* (1845):
"Events not to be controlled have prevented me from
making, at any time, any serious effort in what, in happier circumstances, would have been the field of my
choice. With me poetry has not been a purpose, but a
passion . . . ." The events and circumstances were that he
had lived and worked under grinding poverty all of his
adult life and had made himself into the most famous

magazine editor and critic in the United States and one
of the best-known writers of fiction in the country. In his
reviews and theoretical pieces Poe had always ranked
poetry higher than any other genre or mode, attaining in
his view to the closest proximity with the Ideal, with
Beauty, with God. Poetry in the United States, however,
with the exception of that of Henry Wadsworth Longfellow, did not buy bread.

This idea of the poet within Poe struggling with the
professional man of letters encompasses the idea of Poe
as strongly rooted yet rootless and restless, orphaned and
adopted, divided between North and South, and divided
in himself. Poe can be seen as a kind of Byronic wanderer acting out various adopted roles in quest of a persona adequate to a vision of himself in life and in art.
The basic conflict Poe faced was this sense of a vocation
analogous to a religious calling versus the sense of a
worldly profession. If Poe brought to the profession of
letters a poetic based on his idealistic concept of the calling of poetry, the poetic came to inform the professional
and worldly calling of journalism and letters. The
worldly came to inform the later poems, which are more
fictionally and dramatically conceived than the early lyrical poems. Simultaneously, he came to feel a greater and
greater apprehension of collapse in both the worldly and
otherworldly spheres of the imaginative life. In a real
sense, the literary career of Poe begins and ends with his
failed quest to become a major Romantic poet.

Another problem with the psychoanalytic
approaches is that not all the facts of Poe's life fit the
interpretation equally well. Despite the violent disagreements and final estrangement, Poe was fortunate in
many ways to have John Allan, the self-made practical
businessman, as a foster father. When Elizabeth Poe died
in Richmond, the family was split up among various
Richmond friends. William Henry had been left in the
care of David Poe's father, celebrated for keeping the supply lines open for the Marquis de Lafayette and others
during the Revolution. Rosalie was taken into the home
of William Mackenzie and his wife. Three-year-old
Edgar came under the care of Frances Keeling Valentine
Allan, who, childless and in ill health, treated him as her
own. Her husband, John Allan, for all his sometimes
excessive thrift and temper, did well by the boy for the
next fifteen years. He seems to have been prepared to
bring up his young charge not only in prosperous circumstances but also as an heir to a large fortune. Allan
knew the value of an education, and he was determined
to give the boy the best available. He sent Poe to two
good Richmond academies and continued carefully to
oversee his education into young manhood.

Allan saw that Edgar was well instructed when in
1815 they went to England, where Allan hoped to
enlarge his business operations. In London he took quar-

ters in Russell Square, Bloomsbury. He arranged for Poe to attend the Dubourg sisters' boarding school and for two years paid for several extra privileges: a bed separate from the dormitory, laundry service, mending, pew rent, advanced writing lessons, and a variety of books. Frances Allan declined in health, and eventually Allan sent her to the Gloucestershire countryside to make use of the health waters. He sent Poe, now nine, to the more advanced school of the Reverend John Bransby in the village of Stoke Newington, then outside the city limits of London. Once more Allan paid for extra comforts (again a separate bed) and slipped the boy extra pocket money, contrary to the wishes of the schoolmaster, who thought Poe spoiled. Spoiled or not, Poe excelled in his studies, especially in Latin and French.

The firm of Ellis and Allan began to suffer reverses, and in June 1820 the family set sail for home. By August they were reestablished in Richmond, though in less prosperous circumstances than before. Nevertheless, Poe was enrolled in Richmond academies where he could associate with the sons of the genteel society of the city. He was not accepted as an equal, however; he was taunted about being the son of actors and about his unconventional position in the Allan household. In the winter that Poe turned fifteen years old, he learned that Jane Stith Stanard, the mother of his friend Robert Stanard, had a brain tumor, which caused her periods of mental abstractedness. She seems to have represented to him an ideal of womanly grace, and he was fond of calling her "Helen." When she died in the spring, Poe was distraught and is reported to have visited her grave frequently. As with the memories of his mother, combined with his natural concern over Frances Allan's deteriorating health, idealized womanly beauty was once again associated with illness, death, and loss.

Poe had begun to write poetry. He composed poems to several young Richmond girls; Allan seems to have liked these efforts, but Poe's schoolmaster advised him not to have them printed. Poe also composed satires, including one on the Junior Debating Society, of which he was a member. Allan at this time is said to have enjoyed walking and reading with Poe. He was himself fond of poetry, with the exception of Byron. He admired William Shakespeare and could recite passages from memory. Allan's admiration for and indulgence of his foster son are reflected in one recorded remark: "Edgar is wayward and impulsive . . . for he has genius. . . . He will someday fill the world with his fame."

Poe was considered intelligent and talented at school, if a little prone to get by on brains rather than by study. He read Ovid, Caesar, and Virgil in Latin, followed by Homer in Greek, and then by Horace and Cicero in more-difficult Latin. His facility with languages was such that he could translate even the hardest classics

at sight. Poe was gifted in athletics and had a penchant for acting. For example, he was remembered at school to have declaimed with fiery scorn the famous speech of Cassius from act 1, scene 1 of Shakespeare's *Julius Caesar*. It is suggestive that the one performance by young Poe that is recorded by his contemporaries in specific detail is of the ironic and disdainful, ambitious and restless Cassius.

Allan, meanwhile, was having more ill luck, and finally the Ellis-Allan firm was dissolved. Allan was a womanizer, and one affair had brought him an illegitimate son, Edward Collier, for whom he tried to provide as well as he did for Poe. Considering his reduced circumstances, Allan had a worrisome number of obligations. Poe apparently felt the reduction in social status keenly; he had been educated for and grown accustomed to expect a more or less genteel life. This change in circumstance, perhaps combined with embarrassment over Allan's love affairs, seems to have led to quarrels with his foster father. Frances Allan also seems to have quarreled with Allan frequently, and Poe is said to have joined in on her side. Yet, Poe's adolescence does not seem to have been particularly unusual—he was moody, and by turns defiant, sociable, and given to solitude—nor was Allan's response to the challenge to his authority by an adolescent boy out of the ordinary. A deep rift began to develop at this time, however. Allan, as stated in a 1 November 1824 letter to Henry Poe, was beginning to find the boy "sulky & ill-tempered" and without affection or gratitude.

A turn of fortune eased matters temporarily. Allan's uncle, William Galt, died, leaving him an estate of several hundred thousand dollars. Allan bought a large house in a fashionable part of Richmond and had Poe privately tutored for entrance into the University of Virginia, in Charlottesville. Poe, now in improved circumstances, called on an attractive fifteen-year-old girl, Sarah Elmira Royster. At first he was well received. They had a brief adolescent courtship (much romanticized by biographers) and may have become engaged before he registered at the university in February 1826.

Now seventeen years old, Poe enrolled in the schools of ancient and modern languages, where he was to study the classics, along with French, Spanish, and Italian. He was also supposed to enroll in mathematics, and when he did not, the pragmatic Allan was angered. Allan had given Poe $110 to cover expenses, but it was exhausted the first day, so that Poe immediately incurred indebtedness. He could not resist affecting the pose of a young Virginia gentleman of means and ran up a staggering debt of some $2,000 in gambling debts and in charges with the local merchants. Despite his troubles, Poe did well in classes and seems to have been well enough liked by his fellow students. He had a talent for drawing and is said to have covered the walls of his room with charcoal sketches; some were imitations of illustrations in a volume of Byron, and others were caricatures of the professors. He also read aloud to his friends from his growing stock of manuscripts. When he took final examinations in Latin and French, he stood in the second rank in Latin and in the first rank in French.

But Poe's irresponsibility otherwise had alienated his foster father. Allan went to Charlottesville and paid the debts he considered legitimate but not those that Poe regarded as the debts of honor of an aristocratic Virginia gentleman. Back in Richmond for Christmas, he must have felt that he was ostracized not only in the Allan household but also in Richmond society. When he inquired after Elmira Royster, he was told by her parents that she was out of the city. It is not fully clear what happened, but she had in fact become engaged to Alexander B. Shelton. Allan meanwhile refused to send Poe back to the university. In early spring Poe and Allan had a fierce shouting match, and Poe stormed out of the house. He established a mailing address under the name of "Henri Le Rennent" at a local tavern, where he wrote Allan of his determination to seek a "better treatment" in the "wide world" than Allan had given him. Then, in a typically adolescent gesture, having defied and insulted Allan, he asked him for money to go north. But Allan's patience was exhausted; he wrote back pointing out Poe's debt for his upbringing and education. Poe's role as an indulged son was at an end. On 3 April 1827, penniless and in disgrace at home, the eighteen-year-old "Virginia gentleman" set out for Boston.

The record of Poe's whereabouts immediately thereafter is sketchy, but en route to Boston he apparently visited his brother and other friends in Baltimore. By the end of May he had enlisted for a five-year stint in the army under yet another assumed name, "Edgar A. Perry." He began training with Battery H of the First Artillery at Fort Independence, Boston Harbor. Meanwhile, he had arranged to publish his first book, *Tamerlane and Other Poems. By A Bostonian*. In these early poems Poe experimented with a variety of standard verse forms, though he was much less concerned with metrically regular lines than he came to be in the later incantatory poems that Ralph Waldo Emerson disparaged when he called Poe "the jingle man." The themes and attitudes expressed in *Tamerlane* are especially important for an adequate understanding of Poe's writings. For one thing, it was in poetry above all that Poe sought (however mistakenly) to distinguish himself. For another, the book is instructive in placing Poe in the tradition of Romantic poetry.

Byronic models are useful formulations for Poe. The major themes of *Tamerlane* are the lost joy and lost visionary experience of youth, desire for unworldly

dreaming as a refuge from pain or dull reality, and scorn for one's own worldly pride and ambition, all combined with an indefinite sense of some higher truth and purity residing beyond this world in the realm of the far stars. Hovering about all existence is a vague sinister threat, from nature, from the mind, or both. The tone of the poems, however, is surprisingly varied underneath the dominant melancholy. In the preface and the notes Poe indulges in a good deal of ironic fun. For example, he comments that the poems "savour too much of Egotism" because the author has so little experience of the world that he has had to write from his own heart. Moreover, he disdains to correct the many faults of these "youthful" productions, despite the practice of his predecessors in poetry, and "amend them in his *old age*." The preface is the first of Poe's many half tongue-in-cheek statements about himself and his work. He probably had been at work on the poems from before his fourteenth year, as he claims, but he also doubtless had revised them carefully through his eighteenth, as would be consonant with his inveterate habit of revision and re-revision throughout his career.

The title poem, which comprises slightly more than half the volume, is a dramatic monologue addressed to a "holy friar" by a dying Mongol conqueror who had left his childhood love to pursue his "Ambition" and who has now returned to his little village to discover the girl dead and childhood's dream flown. It is hard to resist drawing direct biographical parallels with Poe's circumstances at the time, such as with his own willful pride that caused him so much trouble with Allan, and especially with the unlooked-for loss of Royster. But the poem is more centrally an imitation of Byron's *Manfred* (1816–1817) in style, tone, and theme. It is striking that Poe's first published work is a half-ironic dramatization (a deathbed confession) focused on Tamerlane's self-disgust and sense of loss, which center around the death of a beautiful woman—features characteristic of his later work. The nine shorter lyric poems comprising the rest of the volume (under the title "Fugitive Pieces") seem rather more personal, though they too are highly self-conscious manipulations of literary conventions: "To–" ("Song"), "Dreams," "Visit of the Dead," "Evening Star," "Imitation," "In Youth Have I Known" ("Stanzas"), "A Wilder'd Being" ("A Dream"), "The Happiest Day–The Happiest Hour," and "The Lake." Especially prominent is the theme of the intertwining of lost love with the infinite regression of all perception into one dream behind another, in tension with the sad celebration of the dreaming imagination, wherein "visionary" perception is always combined with a "dark alloy . . . powerful to destroy / A soul that knew it well."

To move from the imaginative world of these dreamy, sorrow-laden poems to the outward life of the young army private consumed with daily artillery practice is startling and suggests in another way the dual existence Poe led. The poet-soldier trained all summer and assisted in the commissary before becoming company clerk. On 8 November 1827, Battery H was transferred by sea to Fort Moultrie, South Carolina, nine miles from Charleston. (Nearby Sullivan's Island seems to have provided the setting for some of Poe's later work, notably "The Gold-Bug.") He became friendly with Colonel William Drayton, who introduced him into the genteel society of Charleston. On 1 May 1828 Poe was promoted to the rank of artificer.

Meanwhile, Frances Allan had grown seriously ill, and John Allan at last inquired after Poe. The army was now aware of Poe's true identity, and the regimental colonel tried to effect a reconciliation with Allan. Apparently, Allan and others encouraged Poe to think of becoming an officer by entering West Point as a cadet. But a formal reconciliation with Allan was necessary before the commanding officer would discharge Poe from the enlisted ranks. By 15 December 1828 the regiment had transferred to Fortress Monroe, Virginia, on the James River. There Poe went to work in the adjutant's office. On 1 January 1829 he was promoted to the rank of sergeant major, the highest noncommissioned rank in the army. Because of his intelligence and education, and apparently also because of great self-discipline, his progress had been extraordinarily rapid. After a month's illness, he wrote Allan in February. He pointed out that since he had already had a year of university training and nearly two years of practical military experience, his entrance to West Point would probably be a mere formality. He added that he thought the course of study there something "I could run thro' in 6 months."

Frances Allan died 28 February 1829, the third such loss in Poe's young life. He was given a ten-day leave and arrived in Richmond the day after the funeral to find Allan considerably mellowed. They apparently agreed that Poe should enter West Point, and Allan gave him some clothing and money. Poe's next letter from Fortress Monroe is addressed to "Pa" and signed "affectionately." On 15 April, Poe paid Sergeant Samuel "Bully" Graves $25 down and gave him a note for another $50 to act as his substitute in the army, as was the custom for discharge at the time, though Graves's fee was excessive. Poe arranged for letters recommending his appointment to West Point; one of his officers wrote that "his habits are good and intirely [*sic*] free from drinking." During the next several months, while Poe was on his own and without pay from the army, Allan repeatedly sent him money, but the newly established cordial relations once more began rapidly to break down.

In May 1829 Poe looked in on his family in Baltimore. He found that his grandmother was the mainstay

*Poe's foster father, John Allan (Poe Shrine, Richmond)*

not only of his brother, Henry, but also of her daughter, Maria Clemm, and her two children, Henry and Virginia, who were eleven and seven years of age. While in Baltimore, Poe submitted a sheaf of new poems to the Philadelphia firm of Carey, Lea, and Carey, which agreed to publish them in a volume if Poe would make good any losses. Poe immediately wrote asking Allan to help him put himself "*before the eye of the world.*" He suggested that the cost would not exceed $100; he added, seemingly in an effort to mollify Allan further, that he had "given up *Byron* as a model." Allan by this time possessed habitual skepticism about Poe's handling of money, and Poe tried to explained his sudden loss of funds by claiming that on 25 June his cousin Edward Mosher had robbed him of $46 and that he had made good the $50 note to his army substitute, Graves. Poe was lying, at least about the latter, as Allan was shortly to find out. Three weeks later he again asked for money and pleaded with Allan to give him an indication of his present feelings toward him.

Without substantial support from Allan for a new book-length volume, Poe was forced to withdraw his manuscript from the Philadelphia publishers. He submitted it instead to the Baltimore publishers Hatch and Dunning, who in December 1829 brought out *Al Aaraaf,*

*Tamerlane, and Minor Poems.* In addition to "Al Aaraaf," which is Poe's longest nondramatic poem (more than four hundred lines), the volume included in a section titled "Miscellaneous Poems" seven new works: "Sonnet–To Science," which stood as the introduction; "Preface," which was later titled "Romance" in a much-altered version and then further revised to stand as "Introduction" to Poe's third volume of poetry (1831); "To–" ("Should My Early Life Seem"), "To–" ("The Bowers Whereat, in Dreams, I See"); "To the River"; "To M–" ("O! I Care Not that My Earthly Lot"); and "Fairy-Land."

"Sonnet–To Science" is an important poem in its own right, possibly one of the best Poe ever wrote, but it also serves well as the introduction to "Al Aaraaf." On a literal level the poem is a lament for the passing of the traditional and beautiful myths of poetry, which have been made obsolete by the "dull realities" of science. In this sentiment the poem is consistent with those of *Tamerlane* in its retreat from the objective external world and its celebration of the subjective inner world; again the visionary power of the creative imagination has somehow suffered a loss. But insinuated under the surface statement of the poem is an ironic structure that leads to an affirmation of the poetic imagination after all.

The apparent conflict between science and imagination, reality and dream, truth and poetry, is part of the sustaining thematic framework of "Al Aaraaf." The poem continues the imagery of dreams and stars from the earlier volume. It is a dream vision of the far-wandering star where poetic myths, banished from earthly realities, still have ethereal existence. The poem is generally regarded as Poe's most difficult. It also provides a key to his aesthetic worldview and a gloss on many other of his works. Key to it is the concept of an otherworldly midregion where all is counterpoised in stasis, except, possibly, for the passion of transitory love.

Poe had written Carey, Lea, and Carey in May that the dramatic world of the poem was derived from "the Al Aaraaf of the Arabians, a medium between Heaven & Hell where men suffer no punishment, but yet do not attain that tranquil and even happiness" that "they suppose" to be found in heaven. He continues that he has located this realm in "the celebrated star discovered by Tycho Brahe which appeared & disappeared so suddenly" between 1572 and 1574. Brahe had described in *De Nova Stella* (Copenhagen, 1573) the appearance of the star near a rectangle of four other stars in the constellation of Cassiopeia (which accounts for the four suns in the sky of Poe's Al Aaraaf). This star, Poe writes, "is represented as a messenger star of the Deity" on "an embassy to our world."

In part 1, Nesace, the ruling angel of the star, silently prays in adoration of the beauty belonging to the higher heaven. Although the form of God is unknown, it is hinted at by the form of man, whose mind is made in his image. Nesace waits for a "sound of silence" that all nature speaks in tune with the "music of the sphere." It is the "eternal voice of God" commanding nature to "wing to other worlds" and bring warning to those proud star realms that threaten to fall, as did the guilty race of earth. Part 2 opens with a description of a mountain temple. Nesace enters to sing summons to her subjects. She invokes Ligeia, the music of harmony of nature, to awaken the sleeping spirits of Al Aaraaf. While the spirits gather, two lovers hold back, failing to hear the summons clearly because of their passion. One of these, named Angelo, is the spirit of the earthly artist, Michelangelo. Angelo bends his "dark eye" upon the earth and tells his lover, Ianthe, that such monuments as the Parthenon recall to him that there is more beauty in the intellect than in physical passion and that he half wishes "to be again of men." Ianthe reminds him of the beauty of their present "brighter dwelling-place" and of "woman's loveliness" and "passionate love." Angelo then tells of a sensation of falling, rather than rising, to Al Aaraaf at the moment of his death. He also had a perception of the earth hurled into chaos in an apocalyptic fusion of all time in a panoramic moment.

Who speaks the penultimate paragraph is unclear, but it is likely Ianthe's response. The spirits are likened to the "fire-fly of the night"; they simply come and go without asking any reason beyond the "angel-nod" of Nesace, who, in turn, is responding to some summons from her God. Time, it is said, never unfurled a wing over a fairer world than the earth, but when Al Aaraaf's beauty appeared in its sky, the star and the earth trembled reciprocally before the guilty "heritage of men." The two lovers then seem to fall toward eternal sleep, not having responded to Nesace's call:

> Thus, in discourse, the lovers whiled away
> The night that waned and waned and brought no day.
> They fell: for Heaven to them no hope imparts
> Who hear not for the beating of their hearts.

"Al Aaraaf" is a midworld in a series of infinitely regressive dreams of a higher reality–a half-realized Platonic idea of absolute Beauty. The divine is known only through beauty via the imagination, which is the god-like part of man. Even in this "deep sky," however, as in the yet deeper heaven, the "terrible and fair, / in beauty vie," in an eternity of which we feel but the shadow. The spirit beings whom God's messenger, Nesace, has known have only dreamed of God's "Infinity" as a "model of their own." Through beauty (Nesace) and harmony (Ligeia) the will of God is indefinitely communicated to man. Only faint understanding

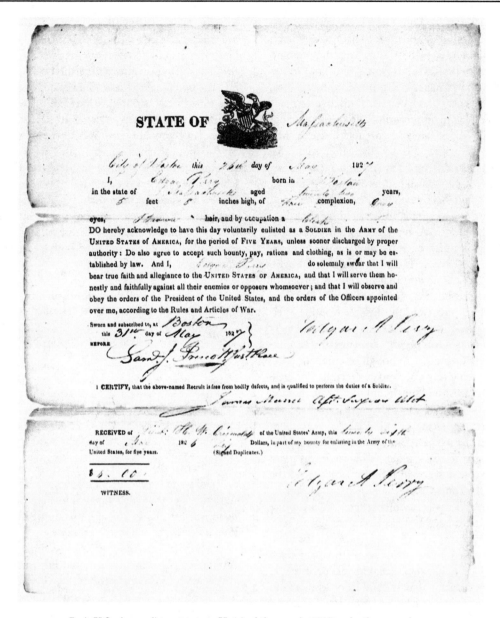

Poe's U.S. Army enlistment papers. He joined the army in 1827 under the assumed name
"Edgar A. Perry" (National Archives, Military Services Division).

of such things is to be found on earth; earthly science confuses truth and falsehood, and fuller knowledge is refracted, through death, from God's infinity. Although the poetically imagined star-world of the angels hints of the true beauty, even in this star-world passion–which is too earthly for pure poetry and beauty–intrudes. This world too is flawed; the only release is to sink into oblivion. "Al Aaraaf" is an invented cosmological myth codifying the implications of the earlier poems "Evening Star," "Stanzas," and "A Dream." It anticipates Poe's later prose-poem dialogues about the creation and destruction of the earth, "The Conversation of Eiros and Charmion" (1839), "The Colloquy of

Monos and Una" (1841), and "The Power of Words" (1845). It anticipates as well his book-length cosmological treatise, also a prose poem, *Eureka* (1848), in which Poe attempts to reconcile various contraries of existence under the proposition of a fundamental paradox that annihilation is built into the origin of existence. The other poems of the volume continue the themes of transitoriness, lost love, lost joy, unreal dreams–with a touch of defiance here and there. Of these, "Romance" (one of Poe's favorite works) and "Fairy-Land" both include burlesque elements in varying degrees.

The publication of *Al Aaraaf, Tamerlane, and Minor Poems* doubtless made waiting for acceptance to West

Point somewhat easier for Poe. Allan finally invited Poe to visit him in Richmond, and Poe seems to have lived with him through January 1830. In March the appointment came. On 3 May 1830, however, Sergeant Graves asked Allan for the remaining $50 that Poe owed him; Allan was extremely annoyed with discovering yet another lie from Poe. In defense Poe wrote Graves that general confusion reigned in the household because "Mr. A is not very often sober." Shortly thereafter Allan discovered this letter and completely severed relations. At this time, however, he was still supportive; he equipped Poe for West Point and gave him money. Poe took entrance examinations in June and was enrolled 1 July with pay of $28 a month. Also about this time, Elizabeth Wills bore Allan illegitimate twins–while he was proposing marriage to Louisa Gabriella Patterson, who accepted him on the condition that he reform certain of his ways. They were duly married the following October. During the summer Poe went through the routine exercises of encampment, which is the first training of new cadets. The academic term began 1 September. He studied French and mathematics. Although he complained to Allan about not being sent appropriate texts, he did well. He came to stand third in French and fifth in mathematics among the cadets.

But something went wrong. Poe ran into debt again; as always, he asked Allan for money, but it was not sent. He began to drink alone in his room. In good fellowship he wrote a series of satiric caricatures of the officers, which the cadets appreciated, but by Christmas Poe's academy career was essentially over. Allan wrote him that he never wanted to hear from him again, having seen his letter to Graves. Poe rehearsed his own grievances and asked Allan's permission to resign from the academy. If Allan would not send formal permission, it was his intention deliberately to disobey orders so as to be dismissed by court-martial. Poe missed roll call and refused to go to church or to classes. An unsubstantiated tradition has it that he once turned out for roll call on the parade ground dressed in nothing but his military cross-buckstraps. On 27–28 January 1831, Poe was court-martialed; his formal dismissal date was 6 March. Meanwhile, he solicited, with official permission, subscriptions from the cadets for a new book of poems. Most of those subscribing apparently were under the mistaken impression that the volume would include Poe's caricatures of the officers.

In February, Poe, now twenty-two years old, left West Point for New York, where he contracted a bad ear infection. Once again he asked Allan for help, this time in a letter in a shaky hand. He also wrote Colonel Thayer, the commandant at West Point, for a recommendation to the Marquis de Lafayette so he could go to Paris to join the Polish Revolution. In April the New York pub-

lisher Elam Bliss brought out *Poems By Edgar A. Poe. Second Edition,* dedicated to "the U.S. corps of cadets." The book is not quite what its title implies; it included only a few lines from previously published poems, incorporated into the two longer works "Tamerlane" and "Al Aaraaf," and nine "new" shorter works. The volume also has a critical prefatory essay, "Letter to Mr.–," which begins "Dear B–," probably an invented person, though possibly his publisher Bliss. This essay is Poe's first critical statement; in it he states a poetic credo derived in part from Coleridge. Whereas he admires Coleridge, he attacks William Wordsworth. He also is opposed to the metaphysical in poetry, though what he means by the term is unclear. Using "indefiniteness" as a key, Poe asserts that a poem is opposed both to a work of science and to a work of romance:

> A poem . . . is opposed to a work of science by having, for its *immediate* object, pleasure, not truth; to romance, by having for its object an *indefinite* instead of a *definite* pleasure, being a poem only so far as this object is attained; romance presenting perceptible images with definite, poetry with *in*definite sensations, to which end music is an *essential* since the comprehension of sweet sound is our most indefinite conception. Music, when combined with a pleasurable idea, is poetry; music without the idea is simply music; the idea without the music is prose from its very definitiveness.

In "Letter to B–" one can see more definitely the significance of Ligeia (the spirit of harmony and melody) in "Al Aaraaf," later to be developed into a famous definition of poetry as the "Rhythmical Creation of Beauty" in "The Poetic Principle" (1848) and other essays.

"Mysterious Star" is a new introduction to "Al Aaraaf" emphasizing the otherworldly quality of the star-world, with its dream gardens and dream maidens. The new "Introduction" to the volume as a whole, however, sounds a quite different note, and it is important in understanding Poe's complex attitude toward himself and his work. In part it suggests the self-pitying aspect of the Byronic pose. Moreover, the new poem includes some of the most notorious lines in all of Poe's poetry:

> I could not love except where Death
> Was mingling his with Beauty's breath–
> Or Hymen, Time, and Destiny
> Were stalking between her and me.

These lines have been seized upon by Freudian critics to demonstrate that Poe could not love except when the woman was dead or dying. But such a reading ignores the romantic conventions of the poetry of the time, and the philosophical statement the poem makes about romantic awareness of the constant presence of death in human affairs. More important, such an interpretation ignores the ironic and even parodic elements of the poem. For in "Introduction" a long middle section presents a wry rendering of the "perversity" of the "visionary" spirit. This ironic portrait comes suspiciously close to self-mockery and is at least gentle mockery of all visionary romantic spirits.

The two contrary impulses of the 1831 collection–the visionary dreams of lost joy and beauty and the satire burlesque of such poetry–almost pull the volume in two. For example, "Fairy-Land," in a key of self-parody and satire similar to the "Introduction," is followed by what is often regarded as Poe's finest lyric, "To Helen," a hymn to womanly beauty admired for its classical allusions and images, for its mellifluous, melodic use of alliteration, assonance, and consonance, and for its idealized picture of woman standing elevated in a window niche, holding a lamp as a guide to the holy regions. Another of Poe's most famous poems, "Israfel," appears in this volume. The theme is the superiority of other worlds to the earthly for the poet. The speaker of the poem suggests that if Israfel would trade places with him, the angel might not "sing so wildly well"; but if the earthly poet were transported to the star realm a "bolder note" might swell. The dramatic situation of "The City in the Sea" is based on the story in Genesis 19 of the destruction of the five cities of sin on the plain surrounding the Dead Sea. According to tradition, the waters of the Dead Sea change colors three times a day as the rays of the sun fall at different angles; the ruins of the Cities of the Plain are visible just under the surface of the water and even, in dry weather, protrude out of the water. A standard reading of Poe's landscape is that it prophesies that an earthquake will tumble down the ruins that are still standing sunken in the lake. As the city settles downward–perhaps into its own reflection–hell seems to rise upward to "do it reverence."

Poe was fortunate enough to receive a couple of favorable reviews for the 1831 *Poems* in the local papers. Although he was trying to establish himself on the New York literary scene, he returned to Baltimore in May 1831, where he applied for an editorial position with the *Federal Gazette,* vacated by his cousin Neilson Poe. He failed to get the appointment and applied for a teaching position in a local boys' school, which he also failed to get. He moved in with Maria Clemm, her children, and Grandmother Poe. For the next four years Poe lived in Baltimore, supporting himself meagerly by odd jobs (such as copyediting and news reporting) and by an occasional sale of a story. By 1833–1834 he was in desperate circumstances, apparently starving and in ill health. But he kept writing. In 1831–1832 his first fiction began circulating in the presses. The bulk of it was satiric and humorous, displaying almost the opposite impulse of the

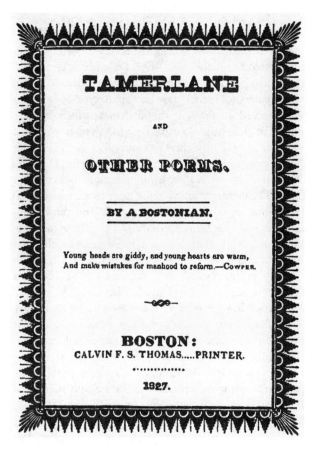

Title page for Poe's first collection of poems, published soon after his alienation from his family and from Richmond, Virginia, society (Huntington Library)

early poems, though, as indicated, the ironic and satiric element had begun to manifest itself in the poetry.

In June 1831 the *Philadelphia Saturday Courier* announced a contest for fiction with a prize of $100. Poe sent five tales that were part of a larger interconnected sequence. That August, William Henry Poe died of consumption, just before the devastating cholera epidemic that raged through Baltimore in September. In October, Poe wrote Allan of his regret at their estrangement, remarking that although he was poor and in debt, he was not this time asking for assistance. By November he had apparently received some kind word from Allan, and true to form, Poe immediately asked Allan for $80 to pay a mysterious debt. (Allan sent no money until January.) The *Courier* editors awarded the contest prize to Delia S. Bacon for a tale called "Love's Martyr," but they began to publish Poe's five stories: "Metzengerstein," "The Duke de L'Omelette," "A Tale of Jerusalem," "A Decided Loss" (the first version of "Loss of Breath"), and "The Bargain Lost" (the first version of "Bon-Bon"). These were at regular intervals throughout 1832, from January to December.

Poe's satiric intent in some of these stories seems to have been only vaguely comprehended, for the satire frequently depended on specific acquaintance with certain literary works of the day. "The Duke de L'Omelette" must have puzzled most of the *Courier* readers. A sensitive French nobleman dies in a paroxysm of disgust when served an ortolan without paper ruffles. Finding himself in Hell, he plays cards with the Devil to win back his soul, succeeds by cheating, and takes his leave with the remark, in French, that if he were not the Duke de L'Omelette he would have no objection to being the Devil. The literary context of the tale reveals the story to be a satiric parody of the literary style and the elegant manners and cultural pretensions of a contemporary editor, Nathaniel Parker Willis. Poe exaggerates the bad imitation of the "silver-fork" style of Benjamin Disraeli in Willis's preciously written column, "The Editor's Table," in the *American Monthly Magazine*. "A Tale of Jerusalem," in which the Jews, besieged in the Holy City by Pompey's legions, bargain for a sacrificial lamb but are given a pig instead, also seems rather pointless and unpleasantly anti-Semitic. The tale, however, is a satire on the rage for didactic historical novels set in the Holy Land, parodying in particular Horace Smith's *Zillah, A Tale of the Holy City*, a three-decker published in 1828.

"The Bargain Lost" (later called "Bon-Bon") tells the story of a philosopher chef who, while completing an absurd metaphysical treatise, gets into a drunken conversation with the Devil. The Devil is a gourmet—of philosophers' souls. The chef offers his own soul for his Satanic Majesty's delectation only to be turned down. The satiric point of the tale, with its metaphysical conversation, plentiful references to classical authors, and other recondite allusions, seems to be mockery of German metaphysics and pretended scholarship in contemporary fiction. Similar pretense, as well as the whole genre of "sensation" tales or "intensities" featured in *Blackwood's Magazine,* along with transcendentalism, are the major satiric targets of "A Decided Loss" (later titled "Loss of Breath"). The "predicament" of the narrator is that he has lost his breath while cursing his wife. He tries to get along without the faculty of speech that his "loss" engenders by practicing the "Indian" dramas then popular on the American stage, for these plays require only "froglike" tones, looking asquint, showing of teeth, working of knees, shuffling of feet, and other "unmentionable graces which are justly considered the characteristics of a popular performer." While searching for his breath, the hero is beaten, accused of various crimes, hanged, partially dissected, and entombed—all the while conscious of his "sensations." The tale is not without some effectively grisly scenes of horror, but the absurdities of the story are obvious and its subtitle ("A Tale à la Blackwood") points to the object of satire.

Whether "Metzengerstein" is a parody or a straight Gothic tale of terror is more equivocal. A hereditary feud between an old Count and a young Baron is given a bizarre twist when the Count is burned in a fire and apparently transformed into a horse at the same time that the figure of a horse disappears from a tapestry. The young Baron captures the horse and rides him night and day in a frenzy. A fire then breaks out in the Baron's castle, the horse carries him into the fire, and the smoke from the ramparts rises into the shape of a horse. "Metzengerstein" is clearly the most somber and horrific of the *Courier* group. Some critics, however, have found enough exaggerations and incongruities—such as the confused curse, the dense narrator (who at one time praises death by consumption), the melodramatic style, the possible delusion of the Baron—to suggest that if the tale is not direct satire, it may yet be a hoax. With its equipoise balance of absurdity and supernatural horror, the story presents a basic problem of interpretation not only in and of itself but also for Poe's other fiction.

During the year that the *Courier* published these tales, Poe must have continued to work at odd jobs while he continued to write both poetry and fiction. But the year is nearly a blank in terms of scholarly knowledge of his life. There is a story that he enlisted in the army again, under yet another assumed name, that some of the officers recognized him, and that, embarrassed to have a former cadet in the enlisted ranks, they forced him out. Then there is the romantic story that Poe told about himself some years later. He claimed that in his youth (about this time) he had gone to Europe, managed to get to St. Petersburg, Russia, and intended eventually to join the Greek Revolt. He ran out of funds and was sent back home courtesy of the U.S. minister. The story seems to have been a fabrication to enhance his Byronic image with his public. Similarly, a story extant in manuscript and ascribed to Alexandre Dumas père about Poe's visiting him secretly in Paris seems to be spurious. It is also told of Poe during these years that he cut a melancholy but dashing figure in his West Point coat, charming the Baltimore ladies with his gray eyes, dark hair, melodious voice, and gracious manners. It is known that he wrote poems for their autograph albums in the early 1830s, sometimes using the same poem several times for different ladies. Also in these years Poe met an eighteen-year-old woman named Mary Starr (also known as Devereaux). They are supposed to have become engaged; if so, the match was quickly broken off.

In May 1833 Poe wrote to Joseph and Edwin Buckingham, the publishers of the *New England Magazine,* about a collection of sequential stories tentatively titled "Eleven Tales of the Arabesque." This never-published collection Poe apparently intended as a large-scale parody. He included with his letter to the Buckinghams, as representative of the collection, his tale "Epimanes" (later called "Four Beasts in One—The Homocameleopard"). It is the story of a Syrian tyrant who runs wildly through the streets of Antioch disguised as an animal until the beasts become indignant at the imposture and break out of their cages and lead a protest march through the city. The tale is an overtly comic work with many satiric thrusts at American democracy and nineteenth-century concepts of progress. The whole series of tales, Poe explained, was not only an imitation of contemporary styles of tale writing but also a burlesque of current modes of criticism:

> They are supposed to be read at table by the eleven members of a literary club, and are followed by the remarks of the company upon each. These remarks are intended as a burlesque upon criticism. In the whole, originality more than anything else has been attempted. . . . If you like the specimen which I have sent I will forward the rest at your suggestion—but if you decide upon publishing all the tales, it would not be proper to print the one I now send until it can be printed in its place with the others.

The "Eleven Tales of the Arabesque" were probably the five tales published in the *Philadelphia Saturday Courier* in 1832, to which he now added six tales submitted to the *Baltimore Saturday Visiter* in response to an announcement of a prize contest: "Some Passages in the Life of a Lion" (revised as "Lionizing"), "The Visionary" (revised as "The Assignation"), "Shadow," "Epimanes," "Siope" (revised as "Silence"), and "MS. Found in a Bottle." Poe also submitted a poem, "The Coliseum." The poem, which, like "The City in the Sea," is an evocative description of the ruined pride of an ancient architectural structure, won an honorary second prize. "MS. Found in a Bottle" won first prize of $50. The tale is based on the legend of the *Flying Dutchman,* the phantom ship doomed for eternity to roam the seas. The narrator initially suffers a shipwreck, but at the moment of apparent destruction he is thrown high into the rigging of a gigantic ship that has been growing in the South Seas like a living organism. The phantom crew ignores the new passenger from the world of the living, and the rest of the narrative is rendered with an atmosphere of dreaminess that makes it difficult to be sure whether the events are real or the delusion of a man driven mad. His exaggerated, melodramatic narrative breaks off just as the ship is poised at the brink of a maelstrom—or is it perhaps the southern of the two fabled entrances to the center of the earth at the poles? Throughout, the narrator feels he is on the verge of some great discovery, but the revelation is withheld, and the ship merely goes "down." Both the tale and the poem were published in the *Visiter* in October

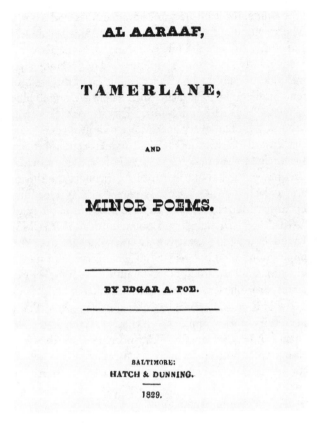

AL AARAAF,

TAMERLANE,

AND

MINOR POEMS.

BY EDGAR A. POE.

BALTIMORE:
HATCH & DUNNING.
1829.

*Title page for Poe's second collection of poetry, including "Al Aaraaf," generally considered his most difficult poem (New York Public Library)*

1833, along with an advertisement for subscriptions to a volume to be called "Tales of the Folio Club."

The "Folio Club" is an expansion of the scheme of the "Eleven Tales of the Arabesque," which, like the earlier project, was never published as an interconnected whole. Critics have come to regard the "Folio Club" plan as centrally important for a full and balanced view of Poe's art in fiction. The "Folio Club" survives in a fragmentary manuscript that includes only the preface and the concluding tale, "Siope" ("Silence"). This manuscript is all that remains of a relatively lengthy collection of tales that Poe unsuccessfully sent to various publishers over the next three years.

The Folio Club (perhaps modeled on the Delphian Club, a Baltimore literary society) is a "Junto of Dunderheadism" that meets once a month at dinner for a reading by each member of "a short tale of his own composition." The author of the best tale becomes president for the month; the author of the worst tale provides dinner and wine for the next meeting. The writer of the preface represents himself as making an exposé of the club after attending his first meeting. Although some of the members' tales may at first seem no more ridiculous than the standard Gothic and sensational fiction popular at the time, most of the stories are parodies and satires. The intention of the club, the narrator says, is "to abolish Literature, subvert the Press, and overturn the Government of Nouns and Pronouns." The membership includes, besides the newly elected author of the preface, ten "most remarkable men," such as "Mr. Convolvulus Gondola," "De Rerum Natura, Esqr.," "Mr. Solomon Seadrift who had every appearance of a fish," and "Mr. Blackwood Blackwood who had written certain articles for foreign magazines." A good deal of scholarly speculation has ensued about which of the fictitious "authors" are to be assigned to various tales (such as Horribile Dictu to "Metzengerstein," Chronologos Chronology to "A Tale of Jerusalem," and Solomon Seadrift to "MS. Found in a Bottle"), as well as critical debate over the implications of the "Folio Club" manuscript for Poe's intentions in his earliest tales—about how serious, satiric, comic, or ironic these works were intended to be.

This critical debate has special pertinence to Poe's next story, for example, much admired for its somber fatality. After receiving the *Visiter* prize, Poe met the novelist John Pendleton Kennedy, a member of the award committee. Kennedy helped Poe select from among his tales a story called "The Visionary" (retitled "The Assignation") for submission to *Godey's Lady's Book*. *Godey's* published the tale in January 1834; it was Poe's first publication in a journal of wide circulation. In Venice, a Byronic stranger and a married countess make a suicide pact, but the narrator of the tale is unaware of the situation until the end. The narrator describes with awe and puzzlement the odd behavior of the stranger and the sumptuous appointments of his palatial apartment. The mysterious stranger remarks incongruously at one point that "to die laughing" would be the most glorious of deaths, even though he also says that his spirit is "writhing in fire." Reference to an Altar to Laughter in ancient Sparta is countered by reference to the grinning masks at Persepolis, from the eyes of which adders writhe. The tale balances sinister passion with comic wryness; a satiric element is added by a pun on the name Thomas More. The thrice-repeated name is a clue that the tale is a parody of the Romantic poet Thomas Moore, who wrote an adulatory account of his visit to Byron's Venice apartment in 1819 and who edited Byron's letters in 1830. The whole tale plays on Byron's intrigue with Countess Guiccioli, though no names are given in the text. The parodic aspect of the tale is further underscored by the "Folio Club" scheme, for its most likely author would be the unlikely Convolvulus Gondola (a humorous reference to Venice's canals).

Sometime early in 1834, Poe seems to have gone to Richmond to see Allan. According to tradition, when Allan's second wife told him that his foster father was too ill to receive him, Poe pushed past her and went upstairs;

the bedridden Allan raised his cane at him, and Poe left without a word. Allan died 27 March 1834. In his will he provided for everyone, including his illegitimate children, but not for Poe.

The friendship with Kennedy, meanwhile, was proving to be one of the lucky events in Poe's life. When subscriptions to "Tales of the Folio Club" did not materialize, Kennedy generously recommended the book to his own publishers (though they eventually replied that a volume of such tales would not be profitable). Kennedy's major contribution to Poe's career was to introduce him to the editors of the *Southern Literary Messenger*, which had been established just a few months before in Richmond, Virginia. Poe submitted his tale "Berenice." The *Messenger* accepted the story (published March 1835), asked for more contributions, and offered Poe regular reviewing assignments.

Poe had also been writing a play, a blank-verse imitation of Renaissance tragedy. Never finished, it was published as "Scenes from 'Politian': An Unpublished Drama," a blank-verse imitation of Renaissance tragedy. Poe seems to have based the action on a famous affair known as the "Kentucky tragedy." In 1825 Jereboam O. Beauchamp stabbed Colonel Solomon P. Sharp to death in obedience to a wish from his bride to avenge her prior seduction by Sharp. Poe's version sets the action in late-fifteenth- or early-sixteenth-century Rome; his characters are Italian aristocrats with names such as Lalage, Alessandra, Jacinta, and Baldazzar, intermixed with historical figures such as Castiglione (in the role of Sharp) and Politian (in the role of Beauchamp), though the parallels with the "Kentucky tragedy" are relatively faint.

With the death of Grandmother Poe in July 1835, the government pension that was the mainstay of the family ceased, and by 18 August, Poe was in Richmond in search of some permanent employ. T. W. White, publisher of the *Southern Literary Messenger*, agreed to take him on trial for a month at a salary of $10 a week, to be supplemented with payment (by the column) for any contributions Poe made to the magazine. He had at last secured a professional literary position.

But all was not well with Poe. According to White, he was subject to fits of despondency and at times drank to excess. Maria Clemm's letter after barely two weeks separation could hardly have contributed to his equanimity. She wrote from Baltimore suggesting that Virginia would be taken into the home of cousin Neilson. Poe promptly and somewhat hysterically wrote to ask for Virginia's hand in marriage. He was twenty-six and Virginia, thirteen. This circumstance has led to the view of Poe as somehow perverted, having an unnatural interest in little girls. Actually he was drawn more to older women, and the circumstances of his proposal to Virginia do not suggest much erotic interest. In fact, years later Poe wrote that he never consummated the marriage. This too has been taken as evidence of psychological abnormality–that he was impotent. Such a conclusion is presumptive. That he loved Virginia seems clear, but it was at this time probably in a brotherly way. His letter to Maria Clemm (29 August 1835) suggests anguish over what threatened to be the final breakup of his already fragmented family.

In September 1835 Poe abruptly left his position with the *Messenger* and returned to Baltimore, where he took out a license to marry Virginia. Indeed, they may have been married in secret at this time. He then wrote White about the possibility of regaining employment with the *Messenger*. In reply, White wrote a friendly but firm letter: "it must be expressly understood by us that all engagements on my part would be dissolved, the moment you get drunk." On 3 October, Poe brought Virginia (whom he called "Sissy") and her mother to Richmond, where they took rooms in a boardinghouse for $9 a week, leaving only a single dollar from his salary. Anything extra came from his writing.

From the time the *Messenger* had printed his first story in the spring of 1835 through the spring of the following year, Poe contributed to it revised versions of his first seven stories, eight new poems, and seven new stories. From the fall of 1835 through the fall of 1836 Poe wrote more than one hundred reviews and editorials for the magazine, including a column on current literary events. He also wrote a series of half-satiric sketches of famous literary figures, the "Autography"; under the pretense of analyzing signatures, Poe filled the series with hidden jokes of various kinds, from ethnic slurs to printer's puns. This literary output was in addition to the chores of soliciting and reading manuscripts, keeping up a large correspondence, acting as a copyist for White, copyediting manuscripts, proofreading galleys, and in general overseeing the production of the *Messenger*. Poe was so good at his job that White rapidly (though anonymously) turned over the magazine to him, so that as of December 1835 Poe was de facto editor. To the December 1835 issue alone he contributed excerpts from "Politian" and more than two dozen reviews on a wide variety of subjects. Whatever his problems with depression and drinking, he was a hardworking writer and editor.

In addition to the tales reprinted from the *Courier,* the *Visiter,* and *Godey's,* Poe published from March 1835 to March 1836 the new tales "Berenice," "Morella," "Some Passages from the Life of a Lion" ("Lionizing"), "Hans Phaall," "King Pest the First. A Tale Containing an Allegory," "Shadow. A Fable," and "Epimanes" ("Four Beasts in One"). Three of these are on the surface terror-ridden Gothics. "Morella" tells the story, in highly evocative, highly cadenced prose, of the reincarnation of a mother in the form of her daughter (at least according to the distraught husband). "Shadow" is a revelation of the impending finality of death; during a seancelike wake a shadow guest speaks with the voices of a thousand departed souls in an eerie climax. "Berenice," however, is more problematic. The narrator, who is a visionary born and brought up in his mother's library, has developed a grotesque obsession with his loved one's teeth. These concrete and specific objects somehow represent the idea of Berenice to him. When she "dies," the narrator breaks into her burial chamber to retrieve her teeth. She has been buried alive in a cataleptic fit. The narrator is only dimly aware of the situation and pries the teeth out of the still-living woman. The final image of the thirty-two gory teeth scattered about the floor of the library acts as an objective correlative of the narrator's "monomania." As with "Metzengerstein," because facets of the tale approach absurdity, some critics have felt that "Berenice" is a "Folio Club" parody of a contemporary style of storytelling.

In fact, Poe himself commented obliquely on the matter. "Berenice" was the first tale he had published in the *Messenger,* and White had complained that the story had too much "German" horror. In defense Poe had written White that "Berenice" was merely typical of the kind of tale that sells magazines. White was not to take the tale so seriously, since it "originated in a bet" that he "could produce nothing effective on a subject so singular." He continued: "The history of all Magazines shows plainly that those which have attained celebrity were indebted for it to articles *similar in nature–to Berenice.* . . . I say similar in *nature.* You ask me in what does this nature consist? In the ludicrous heightened into the grotesque: the fearful coloured into the horrible: the witty exaggerated into the burlesque: the singular wrought out into the strange and mystical."

All but the last formulation in the series applies to the grotesque, semigothic tale, "King Pest the First." Two drunken sailors come upon a weird group of people in a plague-infested area of London near an undertaker's business. King Pest is a tall thin man with an abnormally high forehead; Queen Pest is a lady whose mouth gashes across her face from ear to ear. The others include a lady whose nose dangles below her mouth, a man with bladderlike cheeks, a man with huge elongated ears, and a man with enormous goggle eyes. They are drinking wine from human skulls, beneath an inverted skeleton chandelier, coals glowing in its skull. The sailors are invited to drink to the coming of Death. When they refuse, the court of King Pest tries to drown them in a barrel of ale. The sailors subdue the men and carry off the women. Although the fusion of the grisly and the comic has puzzled many readers, an underlying satiric allegory (mentioned in the subtitle) unifies what seems an otherwise

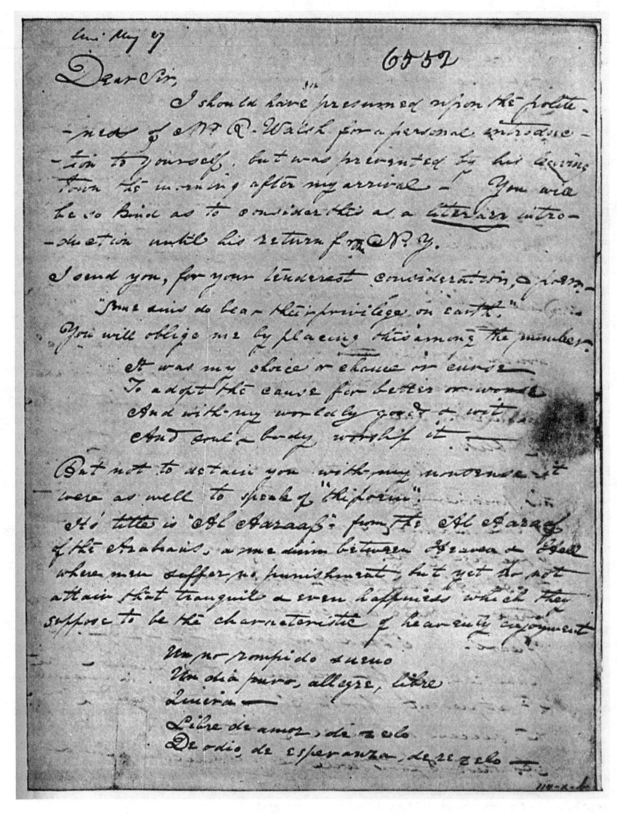

*Letter from Poe to Philadelphia publisher Isaac Lea, circa 27 May 1829, explaining the meaning
of the poem "Al Aaraaf" (Library of the Drexel Institute)*

pointless tale. The characters are burlesques of Andrew Jackson and his "kitchen cabinet" so that the tale is in large part political satire.

Satire also underlies the puzzling tale "Some Passages in the Life of a Lion." The large-nosed narrator, having completed a treatise on "Nosology," is lionized by artsy society. He becomes so vain that he demands a fee of £1,000 for the privilege of portraying his nose on canvas. When he is insulted by the men in the group, he challenges one to a duel and shoots off the fellow's nose. To his chagrin, he finds that the artsy ladies now lionize his rival, who is the more interesting for having "no proboscis at all." The satiric point of the tale becomes clear when one sees the thrusts at specific literary figures: the British novelist, Edward Bulwer-Lytton; the patroness of the arts, Lady Blessington; the Irish poet, Thomas Moore; and the Scots editor of the *Edinburgh Review,* Francis Jeffrey. The tale is notable for its specifically sexual humor, usually not so blatant in Poe. The remaining *Messenger* story, "Hans Phaall," has stimulated interest among science-fiction readers, who see it as an early prototype of space travel. It is also basically framed as a satire and comic hoax. Poe does experiment, however, with the illusion of verisimilitude in the speculative details given about the journey, which is accomplished rather improbably in a balloon. Perhaps his concern for Defoe-like verisimilitude is the cause of the unusual length of the tale (it is the third longest of Poe's fictions).

In all these tales, Poe claimed to have "book-unity" always in mind and had sent them as a unified sequence to Kennedy's publishers for book publication; and when they had been returned as unprofitable, he had sent them as a group to Harper and Brothers. On 3 March 1836 the New York novelist James Kirke Paulding wrote to White regarding Poe's manuscript. Although Paulding disclaimed any influence with the firm, noting that they had an independent editorial reader, he told White that they had communicated to him their reasons for declining Poe's manuscript: the stories had been so recently published in the *Messenger* "that they would be no novelty—but most especially they object that there is a degree of obscurity in their application, which will prevent ordinary readers from comprehending their drift, and consequently from enjoying the fine satire they convey." Emphasizing this point, Paulding commented: "For Satire to be relished, it is necessary that it should be leveled at something with which readers are familiar." The same point was made by Kennedy and by Harper and Brothers when the firm returned his manuscript in June.

Poe would not give up the "Folio Club" scheme, however. By September 1836 he had expanded the number of tales and narrators to seventeen. In a letter to the Philadelphia publisher Harrison Hall, Poe stated that all the tales recently published in the *Southern Literary Messen-* ger were part of the "Folio Club" series: "They are of a bizarre and generally whimsical character. . . . The seventeen tales which appeared in the Messenger are supposed to be narrated by the seventeen members. . . . As soon as each . . . tale is read—the other 16 members criticise it in turn—and these criticisms are intended as a burlesque upon criticism generally." At this time Poe had actually published only fourteen tales in the *Messenger*. It would seem logical therefore to conclude that the other three tales were among those published immediately following the fourteen in the *Messenger,* and that Poe had originally intended them for the *Messenger.* The most likely seeming candidates are the overtly comic and parodic "Von Jung," "How to Write a Blackwood Article," and "A Predicament." The last two mentioned are companion tales, the second being an illustration of the first, and so might be construed as by one "Folio Club" author. Scholars have, however, made cogent arguments for other, later tales.

Meanwhile, Poe was pouring out critical reviews, of which several are important for an understanding of his developing literary principles. Among the more generally significant in the first series, published in the *Messenger* in December 1835, are the reviews of Kennedy's *Horse-Shoe Robinson* (1835), the Classical Family Library *Euripides* (partially borrowed from August Wilhelm von Schlegel), Theodore S. Fay's *Norman Leslie* (1835), E. S. Barrett's *The Heroine; or Adventures of Cherubina* (1814), and William Godwin's *Lives of the Necromancers* (1834). The review of *Norman Leslie* is a classic example of Poe's unrelenting attack on the type of literary clique, especially in the North, that overpraised or "puffed" the works of its own set. The *New York Mirror* had been breathlessly announcing the coming publication of Fay's novel. Poe's review begins:

> WELL!—here we have it! This is *the* book—*the* book *par excellence*—the book bepuffed, beplastered, and be-*Mirrored:* the book "attributed to" Mr. Blank, and "said to be from the pen" of Mr. Asterisk: the book which has been "about to appear"—"in press"—"in progress"—"in preparation"—and "forthcoming." . . . For the sake of everything puff, puffing and puffable, let us take a peep at its contents!

> Norman Leslie . . . is, after all, written by nobody in the world but Theodore S. Fay, and Theodore S. Fay is nobody in the world but "one of the Editors of the New York Mirror."

He goes on to analyze the characters, plot, style, and grammar of the novel and finds them all wanting. Such reviews began to earn Poe the title of the "tomahawk man" from the South, while the circulation of the *Messenger* began to increase.

POEMS

BY

EDGAR A. POE.

TOUT LE MONDE A RAISON.—ROCHEFOUCAULT.

SECOND EDITION.

New York:
PUBLISHED BY ELAM BLISS.
1831.

*Title page for Poe's third collection of verse, which includes several of his best-known visionary poems (Library of the University of Pennsylvania)*

After his first review, for example, the friends of the wounded author charged Poe with "regular cutting and slashing." Poe could certainly be caustic enough. Seizing upon the title of Laughton Osborn's *Confessions of a Poet* (1835), Poe wrote: "The most remarkable feature in this production is the bad paper on which it is printed. . . . The author has very few claims to the sacred name he thought proper to assume." But Poe pointed out later, that he did not "regularly" slash; in fact, he claimed that most of his reviews were favorable. A good example is the review of Barrett's *The Heroine,* a piece important for what it suggests about Poe's literary values. *The Heroine* is a lighthearted parody of the conventions of the Gothic romance and of the character of the sentimental heroine. Poe wrote of it: "There are few books written with more tact, spirit, *naïveté,* or grace, few which take hold more irresistibly upon the attention of the reader, and none more fairly entitled to rank among the classics of English literature. . . ." Even though it is a "mere bur-

lesque," its "wit, especially, and its humor, are indisputable. . . ." Such praise throws further light on Poe's own early fiction, his interest in humor, and the "Folio Club" question.

In the next series of critical reviews for the *Messenger* (published January 1836), the most important pieces include Poe's discussion of three volumes by women poets, William Gilmore Simms's *The Partisan* (1835), and a republication of *Robinson Crusoe.* But while discussing the poetry of Lydia Howard Sigourney, Poe mentions in passing that Coleridge's *Christabel* (1816) is "entitled to be called *great* from its power of creating intense emotion in the minds of great men." This idea continues the affective theory of poetry first begun in "Letter to B——," which Poe developed into the famous critical definitions of the 1840s. The next step in the theory is a concern for "proportion." Poe comments that in long poems, that is, in a poem of "magnitude," the "mind of the reader is not, at all times, enabled to include in one comprehensive survey the proportions and proper adjustment of the whole." In the long poem the reader is pleased with successive accumulation of "pleasurable sensations inspired by . . . individual passages during the process of perusal." In the briefer poem such as Sigourney's, however, the effect is dependent on "the contemplation of the picture *as a whole.*" Thus its effect will depend on the precise "adaptation of its constituent parts, and especially upon what is rightly termed by Schlegel, 'the *unity or totality of interest.*'" Poe was shortly to decide that a long poem, such as John Milton's 1667 *Paradise Lost* (which he had found wearisome in "Letter to B——"), is a contradiction in terms. Poe develops these ideas step by step, review by review.

The same concern for unity of effect in fiction is evident in his review of Simms. He notes Simms's lapse of taste in giving the minute details of a murder committed by a maniac, a seemingly puzzling remark for the author of "Berenice." When he charges Simms with "a love for that mere *physique* of the horrible which has obtained for some Parisian novelists the title of the 'French convulsions,'" however, he is pointing to a disjuncture between the content of certain scenes and their function in the overall design of the novel. Simms achieves only external semblance of horror rather than a pervading atmosphere of horror. Related is Poe's enthusiastic praise for a new edition of Daniel Defoe's *Robinson Crusoe.* He adduces three reasons for the continued popularity of the book. First is "the potent magic of verisimilitude" with which the author permeates his narrative. This quality is then combined with the author's power of "*identification*—that domination exercised by volition over imagination which enables the mind to lose its own, in a fictitious, individuality." The third reason for the popularity of the book is the subject matter: the "idea of man in a state of perfect isolation," he says, has exerted a constant fascination for readers.

April was the month of one of Poe's most revealing and important reviews, that of Joseph Rodman Drake's *The Culprit Fay* (1835) and Fitz-Greene Halleck's *Alnwick Castle* (1827), collections of poems of a certain romantic sort, which Poe minutely dissected. He began by tracing American criticism from initial "servile deference to British critical dicta" to present-day American chauvinism. Now, he claimed, Americans suffer under the "gross paradox of liking a stupid book the better, because, sure enough, its stupidity is American." Neither Drake nor Halleck are truly poetical for Poe. He parodies Drake's attempt to "accoutre a fairy" by rewriting several lines in which he mechanically substitutes different animal and plant metaphors, one-for-one, with those of Drake, concluding that "the only requisite for writing verses of this nature . . . is a tolerable acquaintance with the qualities of the objects to be detailed, and a very moderate endowment of the faculty of Comparison."

The difference between the poems of Drake and Halleck and those poems that are truly poetic—such as *Christabel,* Shelley's *Queen Mab* (1813), Milton's *Comus* (1637), and Dante's *Inferno*—is the difference between mere "Fancy" and true "Imagination." Imagination, Poe writes, is the "soul" of poetry and springs "from the brain of the poet, enveloped in the moral sentiments of grace, of color, of motion—of the mystical, of the august—in short of the ideal." Although the imagination may modify, exalt, enflame, purify, or control "the *passions* of mankind," there is no "inevitable" or "necessary co-existence" of true imagination and the passions. The passions are earthly; poetry is spiritual. Poetry is so ethereal it cannot even be defined. "Its intangible and purely spiritual nature refuses to be bound down within the widest horizon of mere sounds," that is, by mere earthbound words. Yet, although poetry cannot be defined, it can be recognized: "If, indeed, there be any one circle of thought distinctly and palpably marked out from amid the jarring and tumultuous chaos of human intelligence, it is that evergreen and radiant Paradise which every true poet knows, and knows alone, as the limited realm of his authority—as the circumscribed Eden of his dreams."

Poe uses two phrenological terms to get at the essence of true poetry. The functions of "Veneration" and "Ideality" both point to some power or realm superior to the present earthly human condition. Poetry, he says, is "the sentiment of Intellectual Happiness" on earth and "the Hope of a higher Intellectual Happiness hereafter," and he singles out Shelley's "Hymn to Intellectual Beauty" (1817) as the poem most nearly describing these aspirations and possessing such ideality.

A careful reading of the specific lines that he isolates for criticism in the works of Drake and Halleck reveals that as a practical critic Poe works by binaries, in which an indefinite opposite is implied by certain images, such as "twilight" by "day," and that he rejects out of hand, as simply unpoetic, any references to the world of labor, money, trade, or business. Yet at the same time that he values vagueness and ideality, he also insists on a logical preestablished pattern for the whole work. A similar attitude and methodology may be observed in his August review of an anthology of British poems called *The Book of Gems* (1836), in which he comments on ethical or moral elements in poetry and makes revealing comparisons of such poets as John Donne, Abraham Cowley, Wordsworth, and Coleridge. The two tendencies of his thought—toward ideal indefiniteness and patient, step-by-step organization—are further underscored by Poe's analysis in the same issue as the Drake-Halleck review of the famous "mechanical" chessplayer then being demonstrated in America by J. N. Maelzel. In contending that it worked via a concealed human being underneath the table, Poe gives a sequence of deductive reasons, proceeding as though inductively, that resembles the method of C. Auguste Dupin, the prototype of Sherlock Holmes that Poe invented five years later in "The Murders in the Rue Morgue."

In May 1836 Poe took out in Richmond a second license to marry Virginia; after the ceremony they went on a two-week trip to Petersburg, Virginia. Poe now decided to demand payment from the U.S. government of the $40,000 his grandfather had contributed to the Revolutionary cause. But since his grandmother had died before Congress passed the bill allowing such claims, none of the Poe family ever collected on the debt. In the August *Messenger,* Poe printed thirteen of his reviews along with a column titled "Pinakidia," a miscellany of sayings and quotations from encyclopedias and other sources. Although primarily filler, the column is of value for indicating the topics to which Poe's interest was drawn.

In the June 1836 number, Poe praised the unknown author of *Watkins Tottle,* a collection of sketches "by Boz"—an American reprint of the early work of Charles Dickens. During the course of the review Poe defends the "brief article" as different from and perhaps better than the "sustained effort" of the novel. He observes that "unity of effect" may be somewhat foregone in a mere novel, but not in the brief article. Novels, he decides, are generally remembered not for their whole design but for "detached passages." As an example of the unity of effect of the short article he copies out the whole of Dickens's sketch "Gin Shops." In September he reviewed Dickens's *The Pickwick Papers* (1836–1837) favorably, reprinting all but the first few paragraphs of the tale "A Madman's Ms." Reviews such as these, both the positive and the negative, caused the circulation of

*The Clemm home on Amity Street in Baltimore,
where Poe lived for a time in the 1830s*

the *Messenger* to increase—from 500 to more than 3,500 during the year and a half Poe was associated with it (at least so he claimed)—and made the magazine a nationally recognized force in American letters.

Poe began drinking again, however, and in September 1836 White gave him a month's notice. Apparently, Poe made him some sort of promise, and White reinstated him. In the October issue of the *Messenger* Poe reviewed a British story, James F. Dalton's "Peter Snook," in which he praised the work for its design. In opposition to the prevailing romantic ideas of his time, and in modification of his comments on Drake, he stated that originality is not "a mere matter of impulse or inspiration"; instead, to "originate, is carefully, patiently, and understandingly to combine." This review seems to be an early statement of the principles more emphatically articulated in the 1840s in his review of Nathaniel Hawthorne and in "The Philosophy of Composition"; but it also may have some bearing upon the jigsaw-puzzle way in which he was putting together *Arthur Gordon Pym,* his only novel.

By December, White and Poe were at odds again, and for whatever reasons—renewed drinking on Poe's part, dissatisfaction with his low salary, disagreement over editorial policy (White later said he felt "cramped

by him in the exercise of my own judgment")—they severed relations at the end of 1836. Poe's last contributions to the *Southern Literary Messenger* were in the January and February 1837 issues: five reviews, including important discussions of Washington Irving and William Cullen Bryant, and two installments of his novel-in-progress.

In February 1837 Poe moved to New York, where he first rented a place in Greenwich Village and then a place farther south, where Maria Clemm could take in boarders. In response to an inquiry from a new annual, the *Baltimore Book,* he sent them "Siope—A Fable," a tale that develops the theme of solitude in a kind of inverse Eden. An unstable world with shrieking water lilies, lowing hippopotamuses, and rocks engraved with letters that spell "Desolation" is described by a Demon to the narrator as one in which there was never any rest. Here poisonous flowers constantly writhed and blood streamed from the skies—until the Demon cursed the land with silence and stasis. Then the solitary man inhabiting this world at last knew terror. At the end of his description the Demon laughs at the narrator, while a lynx comes out of a cave and stares steadily into the Demon's face. The tale has been admired as an apocalyptic tone-poem, and certainly on the surface it is portentous enough. It is part of the "Folio Club" manuscript, however, and carries the subtitle "(In the Manner of the Psychological Autobiographists)" as a clue to some specific model. The tale has some close parallels with the opening of Benjamin Disraeli's *Contarini Fleming* (1832), which was subtitled *A Psychological Auto-Biography,* as well as with Edward Bulwer-Lytton's story "Monos and Daimonos" (1830). Both writers were favorite satiric targets of Poe.

Poe placed "Von Jung" ("Mystification") with the *American New Monthly Magazine,* where it was published in June. The sketch is a comic piece in which Baron Von Jung, noted for "mystification" (that is, practical jokes and hoaxes), is more or less insulted by a student named Johann Hermann, an expert duelist. The baron writes that Hermann should consult the ninth paragraph in an obscure Latin text. Hermann does and replies that he is now entirely satisfied. Von Jung then reveals to the narrator that the passage referred to is a burlesque about a duel between two baboons and that it includes a hidden cryptographic joke. He observes that Hermann is so vain that he would never admit that he could not understand a text on dueling. The characters of Von Jung and the sinister jokester in "Hop-Frog, or the Eight Chained Orangoutangs" (1849) have been seen by biographical critics as revealing self-caricatures of Poe that complement the self-characterization in Roderick Usher and others of his sort. If so, the two major tendencies of Poe's personality are clearly drawn. The only other writing Poe seems to have had significantly advanced at this time was his "Arabia Petrea" review of J. L. Stephens for the

*New York Review,* which was not published until October 1837. Poe consulted with Professor Charles Anthon of Columbia College for help with Hebrew characters pertinent to the work, which resulted in a new friendship. Poe then worked fake Arabic and Hebrew words into the editorial conclusion of *The Narrative of Arthur Gordon Pym,* in which rock writings and even the chasms of the island of Tsalal, near the South Pole, as seen from above, spell out a mysterious message.

Little is known of Poe's life in New York in 1837 and the first half of 1838 except that it was not easy. It is said that the family lived on bread and molasses for weeks at a time. There is an unsubstantiated story that Poe worked as a printer and studied lithography. In 1837 political change was in the air; the Whigs, with whom Poe associated himself, defeated the Jacksonian Democrats, giving Poe some hope of a political appointment. During this time Poe finished *The Narrative of Arthur Gordon Pym,* which he sent to the Harpers. They agreed to publish it by the following summer.

Given his increasing disparagement of long works in both poetry and prose, it is surprising that Poe began at this time a novel-length piece. Kennedy, Paulding, and publishers had advised him to create longer work if he wanted to sell to a large audience; perhaps that incentive was the initial motivation for *The Narrative of Arthur Gordon Pym.* Although the book received a few favorable notices in America and had a vogue in Britain for a while as a "factual" account of an extraordinary voyage, it has been generally dismissed by critics and readers. It has seemed unduly obscure, especially in its mystifying editorial frames and its inconclusive conclusion. Moreover, it has seemed episodic to the point of disorganization. Poe himself later called it "a very silly book," though precisely what he meant by that is unclear. Recent criticism, however, has come to see it as central to the Poe canon, a key to his worldview, and possessing structural symmetry and thematic consistency. This view is not unchallenged, however; a good deal of critical controversy rages over the book. T. O. Mabbott, editor of the Harvard edition of Poe's works, has gone so far as to say that the chief importance of the novel seems to be that "it is supposed to have inspired to some extent Melville's *Moby-Dick.*"

The first two installments appeared in the January and February *Messenger.* It was not published as a whole until July 1838. Poe had a good deal of time to reconsider and refine the work—as indicated by the small alterations of early chapter breaks for suspense and changes of the time sequence for symbolism and symmetry (so that the main narrative extends from spring to spring, for example). For the book version, "Pym" writes an editorial preface in which he comments that "Mr. Poe," a well-known editor, had written a narrative based on Pym's experiences more than a year earlier; since these initial episodes were well received by readers, he now offers the rest of the story himself. The reader should have no trouble, he says, in seeing where Poe's style and his own diverge.

Four sea journeys structure the temporal episodes, two in small boats, enclosing two in larger vessels. The sequence of enclosures, descents, lapses into states of dream and unconsciousness, and the consequent emergences from these, suggests a series of metaphoric deaths and rebirths—what one critic (Paul John Eakin) calls a "Lazarus" plot. Yet, the world of *The Narrative of Arthur Gordon Pym* is one of repeated revolutions of order in which survival is by chance alone. The characters habitually or instinctively dissemble; they are subject to misperception and recurrent fits of "perversity" (the impulse to self-destructive acts). Deception, masquerade, treachery, and illusion constitute the norms of Pym's world.

In the first episode two boys, Pym and Augustus Barnard, go for a drunken sail during a storm and are run down by a whaler. Pym is rescued after being pinned to the hull by a bolt through his neck and submerged for some five to ten minutes, so that the reader is immediately faced with an improbability or absurdity. The experience so whets Pym's appetite for adventure that he has "visions" of "ship-wreck or famine," a clue to his "perverse" character. He admits also to lifelong "deceit" and "hypocrisy."

In the second episode he stows away on the *Grampus,* a whaler commanded by Augustus's father. Augustus has prepared a coffinlike, iron-bound box for him in the dark, tomblike hold. Here Pym spends most of his time sleeping; he succumbs to a continuous nightmare of demons, bright-eyed serpents, empty deserts, rows of leafless trees with twisting roots immersed in black water that cry in silence to heaven for mercy. Augustus eventually reaches Pym, but rescue from entombment must wait, for there has been a mutiny and most of the crew has been murdered.

A mutiny develops among the mutineers, however, and one Dirk Peters befriends the boys. When Pym throws a fright into the mutineers by masquerading as a murdered sailor returned from the dead, Peters and the boys are able to take control. They spare only one man, Parker. A storm forces them to cut away the masts, leaving the ship helpless. Three days later, a "Dutch" ship, all black, bears down on them. A figure leaning over the rail nods and smiles, but it is a corpse, the ship a plague ship, the smile that of death.

For seven days they drift south, when the *Jane Guy* picks them up. A storm drives them farther south; in October they put in at "Christmas Harbor" on "Desolation Island" in the Indian Ocean. Here Pym studies the flora and fauna, noting especially the geometric configu-

*Poe's aunt, Maria Clemm, whose daughter, Virginia, Poe married in 1836 (from the daguerreotype formerly owned by Annie Richmond)*

ration of the rookeries formed by the black and white penguins and white albatrosses. In November, Pym's dates become inconsistent as he chronicles the voyage farther south. He recounts the voyages of earlier explorers and feels mounting excitement over some impending revelation or discovery. Instead of growing colder the farther south they proceed, it grows warmer.

On 19 January (Poe's birthday) they land on the island of Tsalal. A hundred ebony natives greet them. Their chief, Too-Wit, leads a small party aboard the *Jane Guy,* and they examine the ship with childlike wonder, though Pym suspects their demeanor is affected for the white men's benefit. Ashore the white men find a land much different from the world they know. Everything is of a dark hue. The water is striated or veined, each layering a different hue. The black natives display a nervousness over things white. While Pym, Peters, and another sailor are exploring a large fissure in the hills, a violent earth tremor knocks Pym unconscious. Pym and Peters find each other in the dark and climb laboriously to the surface and daylight, where they discover that the blacks have led the other sailors down a deep gorge and buried them in a rock slide. The natives have also taken the ship, which now explodes, and a thousand black bodies fall like rain from the sky. Others of the natives have discovered the body of a white furry creature with scarlet

teeth and eyes, which they enclose in a circle of stakes, crying "Tekeli-li" at it.

Pym and Peters hide until mid February, when they descend a deep chasm of black granite. They discover a pattern to this and two other chasms—a straight line entering into a loop—except that the third chasm ends in a cul-de-sac of hardened clay and shells. Carved in its wall are figures: one seems to be a man pointing; others look like letters of a strange alphabet. A few days later they climb down the south face of the mountain, and Pym has an irrational desire to fall—a fit of perversity. He is saved by Peters, however. They surprise five of the blacks, kill four, and take one prisoner. Stealing a canoe, they drift farther south.

Gray vapor appears on the southern horizon; the water grows warm and milky. When Pym takes out a white handkerchief, their black prisoner shudders in horror and goes into a convulsive fit, which draws his lips back from his perfectly black teeth. A numbing dreaminess sets upon them while fine white powder or ash falls. Above, the sky is dark, but out of the ocean comes a luminous glare. A veil of white vapor ranging the whole extent of the southern horizon begins to assume some distinctness of form, as though it were "a limitless cataract, rolling silently into the sea from some immense and far-distant rampart in the heaven." "Gigantic" and "pallidly white" birds fly from beyond the veil, uttering the cry "*Tekeli-li.*" A chasm opens in the white vapor, and there arises in their pathway a huge human figure, shrouded, the hue of whose skin is "of the perfect whiteness of the snow."

Here the narrative breaks off; the revelation is withheld. An appended editorial note explains that Pym died suddenly and that the last chapters are missing. There follows some speculation on the possible meanings of the shapes of the chasms and letters on Tsalal: the first suggests an Ethiopian word meaning "to be shady," the second an Arabic word meaning "to be white," followed by an Egyptian word meaning "the region of the south." There is no further comment.

One interpretation of *The Narrative of Arthur Gordon Pym* is that it is basically a book that Poe tried to pass off as a tale of real adventure (thus the preface about "Mr. Poe" and "Mr. Pym"). Some readings emphasize satiric and ironic elements in the structure, especially those matters that seem to be calculated contradictions or absurdities. Others suggest that Poe was in a hurry, needed to fill a lot of pages, and merely wanted to create a sensation with a narrative of a journey to the South Pole reporting "evidence" of an ancient civilization. A biblical reading may be grafted onto this interpretation by reference to Poe's "Arabia Petrea" review and the controversy over the nature of the curse on the land of Edom, along with specific biblical echoes in the text of *The Narrative of Arthur*

*Gordon Pym.* By such speculation, the name "Tsalal" and other vaguely Arabic and Hebrew words in the text suggest "Psalemon" and the dispersed tribes of the ancients.

A racist interpretation may be added to these readings from the implications of the favorable review of two books on slavery in the April 1836 *Messenger.* Some scholars think the review is by Poe, though others attribute it to Judge Beverley Tucker; and indeed in a letter to Tucker (2 May 1836) Poe explains some cuts in the "Slavery" review, confirming Tucker's authorship. In fact, recent scholarly investigations into American cultural attitudes toward race in the era between 1820 and 1850 suggest that Poe was no more racist than the ordinary white person of his day and considerably less racist than the average Southerner. Nevertheless, the racist reading of *The Narrative of Arthur Gordon Pym* (and other works such as "A Predicament," "The Gold-Bug," and "Hop-Frog") remains popular with critics of the 1980s and 1990s. By this interpretation, *The Narrative of Arthur Gordon Pym* is an allegory of race relations in the United States, one that predicts, through recovery of mythic history, the increased hatred between black and white, and as well hints of the abandonment of a cursed land by whites. In this reading Tsalal is metaphorically hell; the blacks are the damned. The eternal hostility of black and white was prefigured in the Creation when God "divided the light from the darkness."

In nonracist terms, critics have made the identification of Tsalal with hell the main metaphor of an archetypal interpretation. Pym is the mythic hero who advances toward a higher state of knowledge and purity by coming to understand the basic unity of the universe, which he does by the archetypal descent into hell. The sea journey is a complementary Jungian image of a voyage into the recesses of the human psyche. By journeying inward into the collective unconscious, Pym travels back to the origins of creation.

Another coherent view suggests that Pym's journey is purely regressive. He moves away from the complex world of business and family toward a primal world that is increasingly simple. Pym learns that the division between mind and body is false; the mind is one with bodily thirst and hunger. Perceptions are frequently false; the color of the world becomes simplistically split into black and white at the same time that the steady increase of whiteness to all things suggests an original unity to creation that negates shape, distinction, and perception. The traditional meaning of whiteness is intellectual or spiritual illumination. Pym's perception is of a negating white blank, wherein the "oneness" of the universe is fused with "nothingness." At the end of Pym's journey, rather than the traditional blackness of death, there arises up in a "shroud" the blinding white light of revelation—of void.

The American poet Richard Wilbur, in "The House of Poe" (1959) and elsewhere, has argued that the central proposition in Poe is that annihilation is built into creation and that the poet abets the design of the universe in writing of death and regression to the primal unity of nothingness. Since, in Poe's mythology, the universe is in a collapsing phase, the earthly poet is emulating God in creating fictive worlds of collapse. He realizes this theme principally by means of characters who journey into the "hypnagogic state," spiraling inward toward void, stasis, and unity, letting go of the turmoil of the conscious, earthly world. Wilbur writes principally of the dream motif of the poems. By this construct, however, the dream imagery of *The Narrative of Arthur Gordon Pym*—and the dream journey of Pym—is positive as well. Perhaps this kind of "affirmative" reading differs from the other main critical readings only in arbitrarily giving the same perceived structures and themes a positive connotation. Another (slightly Freudian) reading illustrates this critical problem: Pym's journey to the ends of the earth is at last to warm and milky waters; he sails an amniotic sea toward reabsorption into the great womb of the world. Or—alternately—he is buried alive in eternal unbeing.

Structuralist and deconstructionist criticism has suggested that Pym's journey is metafictional, creating fictional word-worlds in a way different from the creation of mythic worlds. Similar to Wilbur's thesis, the postmodernist thesis is that *The Narrative of Arthur Gordon Pym* is about the process of artistic creation; but it does not refer to the objective world. The novel by this reading is a fiction about fictionality: the creation of fiction is part of the definition of the self, and words are the self. These critical approaches represent various biases and assumptions of historical eras in criticism. Other less-cogent readings include biographical interpretations along a more or less Freudian line, emphasizing themes of maternal loss and latent homosexuality, sometimes connecting them with the motifs of cannibalism and disease in the book. (Not long before her death, Poe's mother starred in Theodore Hook's melodrama *Tekeli,* a word eerily parallel to the birds' cry of *Tekeli-li* at the South Pole; Poe's older brother, with whom he may have shared a suspicious bed in youth, died of a rotting gangrenous infection). Yet they all point to certain stable recurring elements that generate a haunting ambiguity in the book. *The Narrative of Arthur Gordon Pym* is a major text over which the critical waters of controversy break. The book has been the subject not only of a continuing stream of articles but also of new annotated editions and book-length publications. In the 1990s three interpretative books were published on this work that was once considered an aberration in the author's career: one, a systematic, analytic survey of critical approaches to the novel; another, a collection of essays from a conference

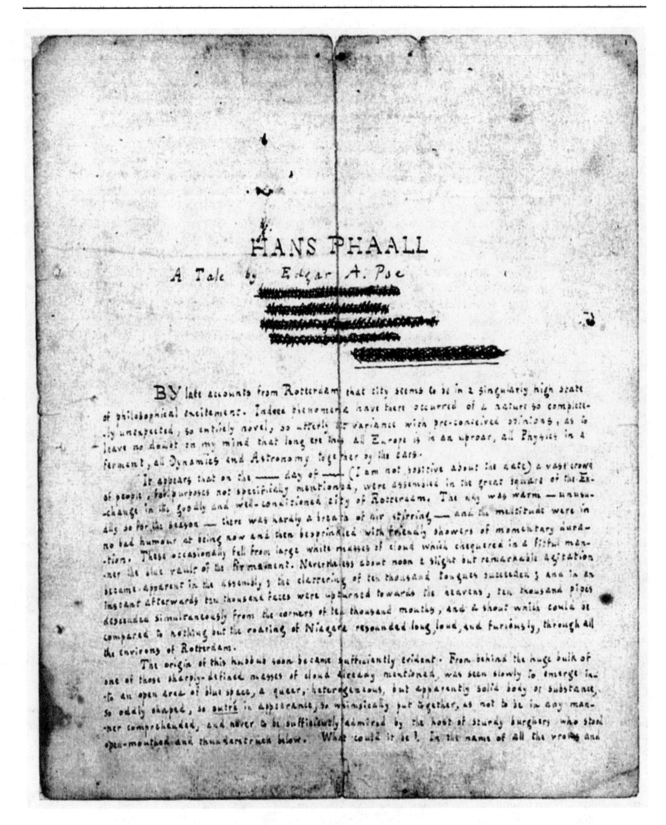

*First page of the manuscript for Poe's 1835 story about space travel by balloon (Pierpont Morgan Library)*

devoted to the work, attended by more than eighty scholars from several countries, held on Nantucket Island in 1988; and another one, a critique of various critical approaches.

Simultaneously with the publication of *The Narrative of Arthur Gordon Pym* early in July, Poe moved his family to Philadelphia, where he lived for the next five years. Presumably, he thought the literary opportunities better than in New York. Little is known of his life during the rest of 1838. The only other notable publications during the year were "Ligeia" in the September issue of a new Baltimore magazine, the *American Museum of Science, Literature and the Arts,* and "How to Write a Blackwood Article" and "The Scythe of Time" (retitled "A Predicament") in the November issue of the same journal.

In "How to Write a Blackwood Article" Mr. Blackwood Blackwood, editor of an influential British journal, advises a Bluestocking litterateur about the publishing situation of the day; and his recommendations constitute Poe's burlesque assessment of the formulas of *Blackwood's Magazine.* An author must get his protagonist into an impossible predicament and have him analyze his or her sensations. Blackwood comments on the "tone didactic," the "tone enthusiastic," the "tone metaphysical," and the "tone elevated, diffusive and interjectional." In the last of these the "words must be all in a whirl, like a humming-top, and make a noise very similar, which answers remarkably well instead of meaning . . . the best of all possible styles where the writer is in too great a hurry to think." Blackwood gives the young lady (whose name is either Suky Snobbs or Psyche Zenobia, depending on the precision of one's pronunciation) several "piquant facts for similes" and "piquant expressions" that she is to introduce into the narrative. The companion tale is her attempt to write in the *Blackwood's* style, replete with badly garbled versions of the Blackwood's expressions. She tells of her sensations when her head gets caught in a steeple clock. The clock hand comes down upon her neck as she is looking out of a hole in the clock face. While she is inextricably caught in this predicament, her head is severed from her body—a circumstance that gives rise to profound thoughts on the nature of identity.

By early 1839 Poe had become associated with Peter S. Duval and Professor Thomas Wyatt, author of *A Manual of Conchology,* published the previous year. Since Poe had achieved a degree of fame, he was paid $50 to allow his name to appear on the title page of a new and cheaper edition of Wyatt's book in order to increase sales. Poe revised the introduction and paraphrased portions of the text. He seems to have accepted a second such job for Wyatt's *Synopsis of Natural History* (1839). *The Conchologist's First Book,* with Poe's name as author, includes pages of material plagiarized by Wyatt from a Scottish text, and the whole enterprise later muddied Poe's reputation.

Poe continued to publish humorous and satiric works meanwhile. "The Devil in the Belfry" is a comic imitation of the kinds of Germanic and Dutch characters made fun of by Thomas Carlyle and Washington Irving, and one may detect a poke at the Pennsylvania Dutch among whom Poe was living. A playful devil enters the overly neat, perfectly regulated village of Vondervottei-mittis and causes the town clock to strike thirteen, thereby driving the fussy villagers to distraction. Poe's comic treatment of an increasingly major theme in his serious fiction—that of time—is both overt and covert, for the village is laid out like a clock with sixty houses, each with twenty-four cabbages; the clock has seven faces, and the taller devil and the fat belfry man are like minute and hour hands.

In the spring of 1839 Poe was living in a small house with a garden and had obtained a black cat, Catterina. On 10 May William E. Burton, a British comic actor and playwright, offered Poe co-editorship of his new journal, *Burton's Gentleman's Magazine,* at a salary of $10 per week. Poe accepted, but what happened immediately thereafter is unclear. He resigned in anger, apparently because Burton asked him to tone down the severity of his reviews. Burton mollified him, however, and for the July issue Poe contributed at least one review and reprinted two of his oldest poems. For August Poe reprinted three more poems and contributed a satire, "The Man That Was Used Up. A Tale of the Late Bugaboo and Kickapoo Campaign." In this sketch Brevet Brigadier General A. B. C. Smith, severely wounded in the Indian Wars, has been fully reconstructed by American technological know-how. He is fitted up with artificial limbs, shoulders, chest, hair, eyes, teeth, and palate. When put altogether, the general is a handsome figure of a man, more than six feet tall. The tale may be a comic version of a question that Poe was obsessed by, the principle of individual identity, treated in "Ligeia" and other stories; but it seems as well to be a political satire aimed at the campaign ploys of Richard M. Johnson, vice president under Martin Van Buren.

For the next year, from July 1839 to June 1840, Poe wrote most of the reviews in *Burton's.* The more important ones are easily recognized. Three reviews are of interest for Poe's comments about American writers: his August 1839 review of N. P. Willis's *Tortesa, the Usurer* (in which he discusses "inconsequential" plotting); his February 1840 charge that Henry Wadsworth Longfellow plagiarized from Alfred Tennyson; and his May 1840 overview of William Cullen Bryant. Two reviews show Poe working out his theoretical principles. For September 1839 he reviewed Baron de la Motte Fouqué's *Undine,* a romance about the love of a water spirit, a fay,

THE NARRATIVE

OF

ARTHUR GORDON PYM.

OF NANTUCKET.

COMPRISING THE DETAILS OF A MUTINY AND ATROCIOUS BUTCHERY
ON BOARD THE AMERICAN BRIG GRAMPUS, ON HER WAY TO
THE SOUTH SEAS, IN THE MONTH OF JUNE, 1827.

WITH AN ACCOUNT OF THE RECAPTURE OF THE VESSEL BY THE
SURVIVERS; THEIR SHIPWRECK AND SUBSEQUENT HORRIBLE
SUFFERINGS FROM FAMINE; THEIR DELIVERANCE BY
MEANS OF THE BRITISH SCHOONER JANE GUY; THE
BRIEF CRUISE OF THIS LATTER VESSEL IN THE
ANTARCTIC OCEAN; HER CAPTURE, AND THE
MASSACRE OF HER CREW AMONG A
GROUP OF ISLANDS IN THE

EIGHTY-FOURTH PARALLEL OF SOUTHERN LATITUDE;

TOGETHER WITH THE INCREDIBLE ADVENTURES AND
DISCOVERIES

STILL FARTHER SOUTH

TO WHICH THAT DISTRESSING CALAMITY GAVE RISE.

NEW-YORK:

HARPER & BROTHERS, 82 CLIFF-ST.

1838.

*Title page for Poe's novel, a hoax account of a series of fantastic sea adventures (Library of the University of Pennsylvania)*

for a mortal man. It is significant that Undine's race has no soul. Whereas men "awake" after death to a higher and purer state, her race simply dissolves into the elements. Poe says that he gathers from "internal evidence" of the book that the author suffered "the ills of an ill-assorted marriage" and gives a psychological interpretation of the marriage motif of *Undine*. Poe approves of this sort of implied meaning in the narrative or of any "mystic or under current of meaning," which is "simple" yet "richly philsophical," so long as it is "distinct from allegory." He finds allegory objectionable because it dissipates the effect of indefinitiveness, of suggestiveness, and tends toward heavy-handed didacticism. Fouqué, he says, has managed to make what would ordinarily be a blemish (this near approach to allegory) a beauty.

In his review of Thomas Moore's *Alciphron* (January 1840), Poe further develops his concept of the proper function of an "undercurrent" of meaning. Revising his earlier opinion in his Drake-Halleck review, he now criticizes Coleridge's distinction in the *Biographia Literaria* between Fancy and Imagination.

He defines a "*mystic*" work according to the concept of A. W. Schlegel and "most other German critics" as "that class of composition in which there lies beneath the transparent upper current of meaning an under or *suggestive* one. What we vaguely term the *moral* of any sentiment is its mythic or secondary expression." These remarks are consistent with his early attempt to create suggestive, indefinite poems. His concept of *how* this effect of suggestivity and indefinitiveness is to be achieved goes in an opposite direction from the theoretical effect. The artist patiently combines, by logic and laborious attention to detail, in order to create a work suggesting the ideal. Therefore Coleridge's distinction between the lower faculty of Fancy and the higher of Imagination ("the fancy combines, the imagination creates") Poe claims is a distinction "without a difference." Neither really creates, for the artist is not a literal God.

Throughout 1838–1839 Poe published a remarkable sequence of tales of the double: "Ligeia" (*American Museum,* September 1838), "The Fall of the House of Usher" (*Burton's,* September 1839), and "William Wilson" (*The Gift,* an annual for 1840, published December 1839). Poe experimented with different kinds of doubles: two opposite women in "Ligeia," a man and a woman in "Usher," and two men in "William Wilson." All three tales deal with the duality of the will: Ligeia has too strong a will, Usher too weak a will, and William Wilson an exactly counterbalanced will, as the repetition of *will* in his name suggests. Poe also experimented with doublings in setting, imagery, time sequence, and structure. In addition, the three stories reveal a consummate mastery of point of view well beyond that of any of his contemporaries and considerably antedating Henry James.

"Ligeia" is overtly a supernatural tale of metempsychosis, with the appropriate themes of the nature of identity and the potential power of the will over death. The narrator, somewhat cloudy of memory, conjures up visions of Ligeia, his dead wife. At her death she had exclaimed that it is only the feebleness of the will that prevents mortals from living forever. Both structurally and arithmetically by bulk of pages, the tale at this point is exactly half told. In the second half the distraught narrator leaves Germany and travels to England, where he buys a ruined abbey and a titled bride, the blonde and blue-eyed Lady Rowena Trevanion of Tremaine, who is the opposite of Ligeia. Whereas he loved Ligeia, he hates Rowena, though for no specific reason. He decorates her pentagonal bridal chamber with images of black magic and death. She dies; three nights later, at midnight, sitting by her shrouded body, the narrator thinks he sees her move as though struggling to life again. Then the body seems to relapse into death, only to show movement again later. Finally, he sees it stand, the cerements falling away. The figure is much taller than Rowena in life, the hair now raven-black, and the dark eyes those of his lost Ligeia.

The narrator's final reaction is left ambiguous; although one may assume that he would be glad to have his lost love back, shocked horror is equally appropriate. The reader's response is more important; Poe presumably built the story so that the reader, not having such an obsession with the lady, is awed and frightened by this return from the dead. Since narration is in first person throughout, some critics have argued that the entire work can be read as the ravings of a madman and is so distorted that the reader does not know that anything has happened as told. The tale seems calculated to achieve counterpoise between affirmation and negation, beatitude and horror, the supernatural and the psychological.

Poe's concern for the frail rationality of the mind was given remarkable form in a poem published in the *American Museum* in April 1839. Despite his strictures on the mode, Poe cast "The Haunted Palace" as an allegory. It proceeds by a single basic metaphor worked out in terms of two major images, a castellated palace and a human head, along with a subsidiary metaphor of sound (with two aspects each, music and voice, harmony and discord). In the first half of the poem the palace takes on features of a human face (the banners are hair; the windows are eyes; the door, a mouth) so that when "evil things" assail the palace of "Thought" the image of the castle/face changes from harmony to disharmony. Poe wrote in a letter sometime later that by the palace he meant "to imply a mind haunted by phantoms—a disordered brain (to R. W. Griswold, 29 May 1841)." Poe "embodied" (as he said) the poem at the center of the second of three episodes in "The Fall of the House of Usher," dividing the central episode and the tale exactly in half.

In "The Fall of the House of Usher," however, no overt allegory structures the tale. Instead all is suggestive, under the surface and even "mystic." It is a beautifully crafted tale of the last descendants, twin brother and sister, of a cursed family decaying in a haunted mansion that may be preternaturally alive. In fact, all things, organic and inorganic, may be linked in one identity. The house, the brother, and the sister seem to share a single soul, and they meet their common dissolution at the same time. But underneath, or around, the supernatural fatality that the story evokes is a structure of realistic psychological explanations. The struggle between the forces of life and death is paralleled by the struggle between the forces of reason and madness in a complex pattern of doubling. One clue to the pervasiveness of the pattern is the structure of resemblances between Usher's face and the face of the house, redoubled in Usher's poem about his fear of going mad, "The Haunted Palace," with its house/face analogy. Poe makes of the stock story of the haunted house (replete with hints of incest, burial alive, and a return from the grave) an elaborate architectural symbol of the frail rationality of the mind, of moral and psychological decay. He does so without sacrificing the sense of the supernatural; and he does so from the subjective point of view of the sick protagonist without sacrificing the occult vision of that protagonist. Moreover, Poe achieves these effects through an apparently objective first-person narrator, who corroborates, seemingly, the preternatural events of the narrative. If one accepts such a reading, the tale is a brilliant tour de force in point of view and the next logical step from "Ligeia."

"William Wilson" is a study of the psychology of interior conscience; the question of the physical existence of the second Wilson is not crucial because, whether a physical entity or not, Wilson's double is morally and psychologically real for him. As in "The Fall of the House of Usher," architecture is symbolic of the mind. The three different schools Wilson attends represent stages of moral and psychological growth (or regression). The first is Dr. Bransby's Academy for Boys, the middle is Eton, the last is Oxford, each identified with a building and more specifically a room. Mirroring the setting, the time sequence is in three episodes. The first and last episodes are developed at length, while the middle one is developed briefly and divides the story exactly in half—exhibiting the same pattern as "The Fall of the House of Usher." Inverting the presentation of merely implied doubles in "Ligeia," Poe begins with an overt identification of the second character as a traditional double—another being who physically duplicates the protagonist—although the alert reader will remember that the tale is told in the first person by the central (and therefore subjective) participant. This being intrudes into the life of the narrator at crucial moral junctures (like cheating at cards) to act as a reminder of conscience, always speaking in a whisper, even though at these times in the story he is apparently another human being. Poe then casts a double perspective (supernatural and psychological) upon the supposedly real physical doubles. At the end of the story the first Wilson is told, by the mirror image of either the first or second, or both, that it is his own "soul" that he has "murdered" by thrusting his rapier at his own image.

Obviously the double need not be supernatural at all; he may be the construct of the guilty or perverse mind of the narrator. As in "Ligeia," the world that readers perceive is filtered through the mind of the narrator; and he, in fact, calls attention in the opening of the story to his "family character." He is the descendent of a family of "imaginative and easily excitable temperament." He is "addicted to the wildest caprices" and says in a bla-

was never out of his mind. These problems of unity and duality are also apparent in the collection of previously published tales that Poe was at long last able to get published as a book: *Tales of the Grotesque and Arabesque* (1840). Critics have generally thought that the title indicates a division between the comic stories (grotesques) and the serious stories (arabesques). Although there is some basis for this distinction, the matter is not so simple. Each term carries a double meaning, and each definition shares some of the properties of the other. In the famous preface Poe defends himself from "Germanism": "If in many of my productions terror has been the thesis, I maintain that terror is not of Germany, but of the soul—that I have deduced this terror only from its legitimate sources, and urged it only to its legitimate results."

Poe's obsession with terror of the soul, duality, and doubling also finds expression in one of the few poems he wrote during these years. In "Sonnet—Silence" (1840), the speaker says that there are some qualities and things that are double and are the type of the duality that "springs / From matter and light, evinced in solid and shade." There is, for example, a "two-fold *Silence,*" comparable to the sea and shore, one solid, one not, like body and soul. One kind of silence is "corporate," associated with graves; it holds no real terrors. The other silence (of soul) is like a shadow that haunts places no living man knows. Should one be so unfortunate as to meet this incorporate silence, this image of void, then "commend thyself to God!"

Poe also was writing a column on various events in the city for *Alexander's Weekly Messenger* (a Philadelphia paper edited by Burton's printer). He attracted a good deal of attention by challenging readers of both *Alexander's* and *Burton's* to stump him with cryptograms and later wrote papers on "Secret Writing." Just as had happened during his association with the *Messenger,* the circulation of *Burton's* began to increase, despite the fact that Poe was not putting as much effort into the magazine because he did not respect Burton's standards. Poe claimed to have dramatically increased the subscriptions to all the magazines with which he had an editorial position. He took credit, for example, for increasing the paid circulation of the *Southern Literary Messenger* from about 600 to 700 to nearly 5,000, and of *Graham's* from 6,000 to more than 40,000. Although these claims are grossly exaggerated (the *Messenger,* for example, exceeded sales of 2,500 only once through 1845), he played an important role in gaining them national attention.

In January 1840 Poe's second longest fiction, "The Journal of Julius Rodman," began serial publication in *Burton's.* It is a tale of the exploration of the Far West, beyond the Rockies, based in part on his review of Irving's *Astoria* (1836). It shares some similarities with *The Narrative of Arthur Gordon Pym* in the excitement Rodman

TALES

OF THE

GROTESQUE AND ARABESQUE.

BY EDGAR A. POE.

Seltsamen tochter Jovis
Seinem schosskinde
Der *Phantasie.*
                    GOETHE.

IN TWO VOLUMES.
VOL. I.

PHILADELPHIA:
LEA AND BLANCHARD.
1840.

*Title page for volume one of the first edition of Poe's collected stories*
*(Library of the University of Pennsylvania)*

tant pun that he is "self-willed." Such seems to be the psychological meaning of the concluding image of Wilson staring at his image in the mirror and talking to himself. He has perversely willed his self-destruction. Poe would make use of doubles and structures of doubling again (as in, among others, in "Eleonora," "The Black Cat," "The Tell-Tale Heart," and "The Cask of Amontillado"), just as he had from the start of his career (in such works as "Metzengerstein," "Loss of Breath," "Morella"). In "Ligeia," "The Fall of the House of Usher," and "William Wilson" Poe's art of portraying psychological states reaches its first apogee.

In another kind of doubling, "The Man That Was Used Up" presents a comic version of the double, and its first four paragraphs parody point for point the opening paragraphs of "Ligeia." Poe's doublings extend to other complex pairings of tales, both serious and comic, and suggests that the "book-unity" he originally sought with "Tales of the Arabesque" and "Tales of the Folio Club"

feels in exploring country never before seen by civilized man, and in its apparent intent of hoaxing the public as to the actuality of the narrative. Also toward the end they discover, as in *The Narrative of Arthur Gordon Pym,* gigantic rock walls carved (by erosion) into hieroglyphics. This unfinished story has received comparatively little critical attention, and imaginative structures such as those that fascinate critics in Poe's novel have not been detected.

In February, Poe published a satire, "Peter Pendulum. The Businessman," in *Burton's.* Peter Profit owes his sense of business to his old Irish nurse, who cured him of crying by swinging him by the heels and hitting his head against a bedpost, raising the phrenological bump of "order." His business is mainly that of the con man; he is a minor extortionist who shines boots for those whose boots his dog muddies, and who for a charge delivers letters he has forged. It appears to be a parody of J. C. Neal's *Charcoal Sketches* (1838), but it may also reflect Poe's contempt for money-minded editors and creditors.

In May 1840 Poe and Burton quarreled. One version of what happened says that Poe drank too much, for which Burton criticized him. Poe resented any criticism from Burton, regarding him as a con artist and a fool (as in Poe's letters for 1840–1841). Another version is that Poe simply thought Burton lacked standards and chafed under Burton's heavy-handed editorial control. In addition, he may have resented his low salary and not being paid for extra contributions of fiction and poetry to the magazine. In any event he walked out. For some time he had been planning to establish his own publication; the *Penn Magazine,* as he was calling it, would be expensive and of high quality. He was already soliciting subscriptions. Burton demanded that Poe return $100 of salary advanced for work as yet undone and wanted to know his plans for concluding the "Rodman" serial. Poe said he owed Burton only about $60 and that whether he continued "The Journal of Julius Rodman" or not depended on Burton's behavior.

In November 1840 Burton sold his magazine to George Rex Graham, who united it with his own magazine, the *Casket,* to form *Graham's Magazine.* Despite his quarrel with Poe earlier in the year Burton seems to have recommended Poe to Graham. Financial support for the *Penn Magazine* had not been sufficient to bring it into existence, and he went to work for Graham. He contributed his tale "The Man of the Crowd" to the last issue of *Burton's,* which was really the first issue of the new magazine. Poe's name did not appear under the masthead of *Graham's* until April 1841. In "The Man of the Crowd" (1840) the narrator, recovering from illness and in a somewhat disoriented state of mind, comments that he can classify the various strata of the crowds passing by a café in London by their appearance or behavior. Through the smoke-darkened glass of the window

appears an old man of peculiar aspect who is unclassifiable. The narrator follows him through the streets of London all night until dawn. He notices that the man follows the flow of the crowd. The narrator arbitrarily concludes that he must be "the type and genius of deep crime. He refuses to be alone." The tale has been admired for its "urban" Gothic qualities, for its presentation of the modern city's glare of gaslight and its creation of the archetype of city restlessness in the old man. While these qualities are certainly part of the appeal of the story, the narrator's attribution of supernatural significance to the old man is suspect. He may be following an old drunk from one bistro to another (as suggested by certain resemblances to Dickens's "Gin Shops"). Most telling in this regard is that the narrator, in attributing sinister and mysterious significance to the old man, compares him to a mysterious German book that "would not allow itself to be read." The joke is that this particular book could not be read because it was so badly printed, not because of the inscrutable mystery it features.

Poe contributed four reviews to *Graham's* from January to March, the most notable of which is that of Bulwer-Lytton's *Night and Morning* (1841). While he was working on the April issue, a young Baptist minister named Rufus Wilmot Griswold asked him for a selection of work for an anthology of *Poets and Poetry of America;* Poe was also invited to contribute his own biographical sketch, which he did, altering his age and inventing some international adventures.

Poe now began what he called a new kind of thing, though it can be seen as the logical development of his interest in mysteries, puzzles, cryptograms, and the rational faculties. In *Burton's* the year before there had appeared the "Unpublished Passages in the Life of Vidocq, the French Minister of Police." Vidocq was a criminal turned detective who "solved" mysterious crimes committed in Paris. In April 1841 Poe published "The Murders in the Rue Morgue" in *Graham's.* The tale opens with C. Auguste Dupin and the narrator walking along a Paris street. When his friend slips on a cobblestone, Dupin with lightning quickness of mind follows the stream of probable associations in his friend's mind during the last quarter hour's walk. Reasoning back through seven stages, he comments about his friend's opinion of an amateur actor. His companion is amazed that Dupin knows his precise thought at the precise moment.

Dupin's instinctual analytic powers are next exhibited in the solution of a crime. He reads of the case in the newspaper. It is a sealed-room mystery. A mother and daughter have been murdered in a particularly violent fashion. Dupin examines the room and discovers that one of the nails in the windows has rusted through and that the two halves fit perfectly but imperceptibly. He

my 30                                    36 Carter's Alley, Philadelphia.

# PROSPECTUS OF THE PENN MAGA-ZINE, A MONTHLY LITERARY JOURNAL,

TO BE EDITED AND PUBLISHED IN THE CITY OF PHILADEL-PHIA, BY EDGAR A. POE.— *To the Public.*—Since re-signing the conduct of The Southern Literary Messenger, at the commencement of its third year, I have constantly held in view the establishment of a Magazine which should retain some of the chief features of that Journal, abandoning the rest. Delay, however, has been occa-sioned by a variety of causes, and not until now have I felt fully prepared to execute the intention.

I will be pardoned for speaking more directly of The Messenger. Having in it no proprietary right, my objects too, in many respects, being at variance with those of its very worthy owner, I found difficulty in stamping upon its pages that *individuality* which I believe essential to the perfect success of all similar publications. In regard to their permanent interest and influence, it has appeared to me that a continuous and definite character, with a marked certainty of purpose, was of the most vital impor-tance; and these desiderata, it is obvious, can never be surely attained where more than one mind has the general direction of the undertaking. This consideration has been an inducement to found a Magazine of my own, as the only chance of carrying out to full completion what-ever peculiar designs I may have entertained.

To those who remember the early years of the Messen-ger, it will be scarcely necessary to say that its main feature was somewhat overdone causticity in its depart-ment of Critical Notices. The Penn Magazine will retain this trait of severity in so much only as the calmest and sternest sense of literary justice will permit. One or two years, since elapsed, may have mellowed down the petu-lance, without interfering with the rigor of the critic. Most surely they have not yet taught him to read through the medium of a publisher's interest, nor convinced him of the impolicy of speaking the truth. It shall be the first and chief purpose of the Magazine now proposed, to become known as one where may be found, at all times, and upon all subjects, an honest and a fearless opinion. This is a purpose of which no man need be ashamed It it one, moreover, whose novelty at least will give it in terest. For assurance that I will fulfil it in its best spirit

*Prospectus, from the* Saturday Evening Post *(6 June 1840), for the* Penn Magazine, *one of Poe's unsuccessful plans to found a literary journal*

further discovers that the hair clenched in one victim's hands is not human and reasons that the force required to thrust one of the women upside down up the chimney was not human either. He places an ad in the papers to the effect that a large hairy animal has been found. When a sailor comes to claim the animal, Dupin confronts him with the "facts"; the sailor confesses that his pet orangutan escaped with his razor and swung up a pole to the women's apartment. The sailor is an acrobat and so was able to follow the animal up the side of the building and into the apartment. He could not recapture the animal, however, who fled out the window again; the sash slid back in place after the sailor fled. The embarrassed police are forced to release a bank clerk they have precipitously arrested.

Dupin's companion is slow of mind and must have everything explained. Obviously, the explanation is also for the reader and shows off the brilliance of the detective, who sees the clues, which so baffle the police, in a new way that leads to the solution. By such meticulousness of plot and detail, Poe created what he called the tale of ratiocination, in which the interest is in logically following the process of solution. With the use of the sealed room, the brilliant amateur sleuth, the bumbling police, and the naive sidekick, Poe perfected at one stroke the archetype of the detective story.

For the next four years Poe wrote permutations of the ratiocinative story, just as he had done with that of the double, incorporating the double motif in them. Poe's detective story proper is easily recognized: Dupin is the central character of both "The Mystery of Marie Roget" (1843) and "The Purloined Letter" (1845), and the method is the same as "The Murders in the Rue Morgue." In "'Thou Art the Man'" (1844) Poe even offers a comic burlesque of the genre he has just perfected. Several of the other tales of the early 1840s are clearly in the ratiocinative mode as well, though to varying degrees. "The Gold-Bug" (1843) is the most obvious of these, for the main reader interest is following Legrand as he deciphers Captain Kidd's map and steps out its directions, which include the dropping of a death's-head scarab through the eye of a skull for a precise measurement. Two stories of escape, "The Pit and the Pendulum" (1842) and "A Descent into the Maelström" (1841), and a story of metempsychosis, "A Tale of the Ragged Mountains" (1844), also employ the ratiocinative motif.

Poe builds a double mystery into "A Tale of the Ragged Mountains," in which a series of coincidences leads the characters to suspect metempsychosis. Augustus Bedloe, in a dream possibly induced by morphine, remembers being killed in a city in the Orient, his description exactly duplicating the experience of a Mr. Oldeb, a friend of Dr. Templeton, Bedloe's physician.

Templeton shows Bedloe Oldeb's miniature, noting the strong resemblance between the two. Later the narrator learns Bedloe has died and remarks that the newspaper spelling of his name without the final "e" is "Oldeb" spelled backward. Like Dupin's Watson figure, the narrator may have missed the full significance of the events, however, for his attention is focused elsewhere–on the supernatural possibilities of the experience. A pattern of subtle clues suggests that Templeton may possibly have obsessively, though perhaps unconsciously, reenacted the murder of his friend and taken Bedloe's life.

Most of these tales have other complex meanings as well. Both "A Descent into the Maelström" and "The Pit and the Pendulum" strongly suggest that the ratiocinative faculties have little or nothing to do with the final escape or salvation of the protagonists. In the former story Poe emphasizes the traditional Western themes of transcendence from a petty involvement with self and the need for submission to the larger design of Nature. Giving up all sense of mere individual importance, the narrator feels a positive wish to see what lies at the bottom of the whirlpool. Although he survives, it is probably by mere accident rather than by his careful observation of and submission to Nature (the mechanics of the hydraulic effect on geometric forms is a hoax). His incomplete confrontation with the void at the center of the whirlpool (a "manifestation of God's power") turns his hair prematurely white. The tale calls into question traditional Western belief: is the narrator's mystical experience of the magnificence of God one of horror or one of beatitude?

The narrator of "The Pit and the Pendulum" is thrown into a dungeon by the Spanish Inquisition. He is saved just as he is about to fall into the pit he has so long avoided by means of careful rational calculation. This ratiocinative tale is one of Poe's clearest dramatizations of the futile efforts of man's will to survive the malevolent perversity of the world and to make order out of chaos. The tale has sometimes been read as the escape from madness through a descent into madness. Although the hero is mentally tortured until he confesses to himself that "all is madness" and that his mind has been "nearly annihilated," he learns like Pym to rely on primal cunning and an instinctive sense of danger. Under the razor edge of the pendulum, he recovers his ratiocinative power: "for the first time during many hours–or perhaps days–I thought." Yet, when his release finally comes, it is a rescue from the outside coming unexpectedly, independently, unconnected with his own personal fate, and at the last moment of his despair and defeat. Both "A Descent into the Maelström" and "The Pit and the Pendulum" are apocalyptic in ways compatible with a failure of the rational mind to effect its own salvation. Furthermore, specific echoes of the Book of Revelation come

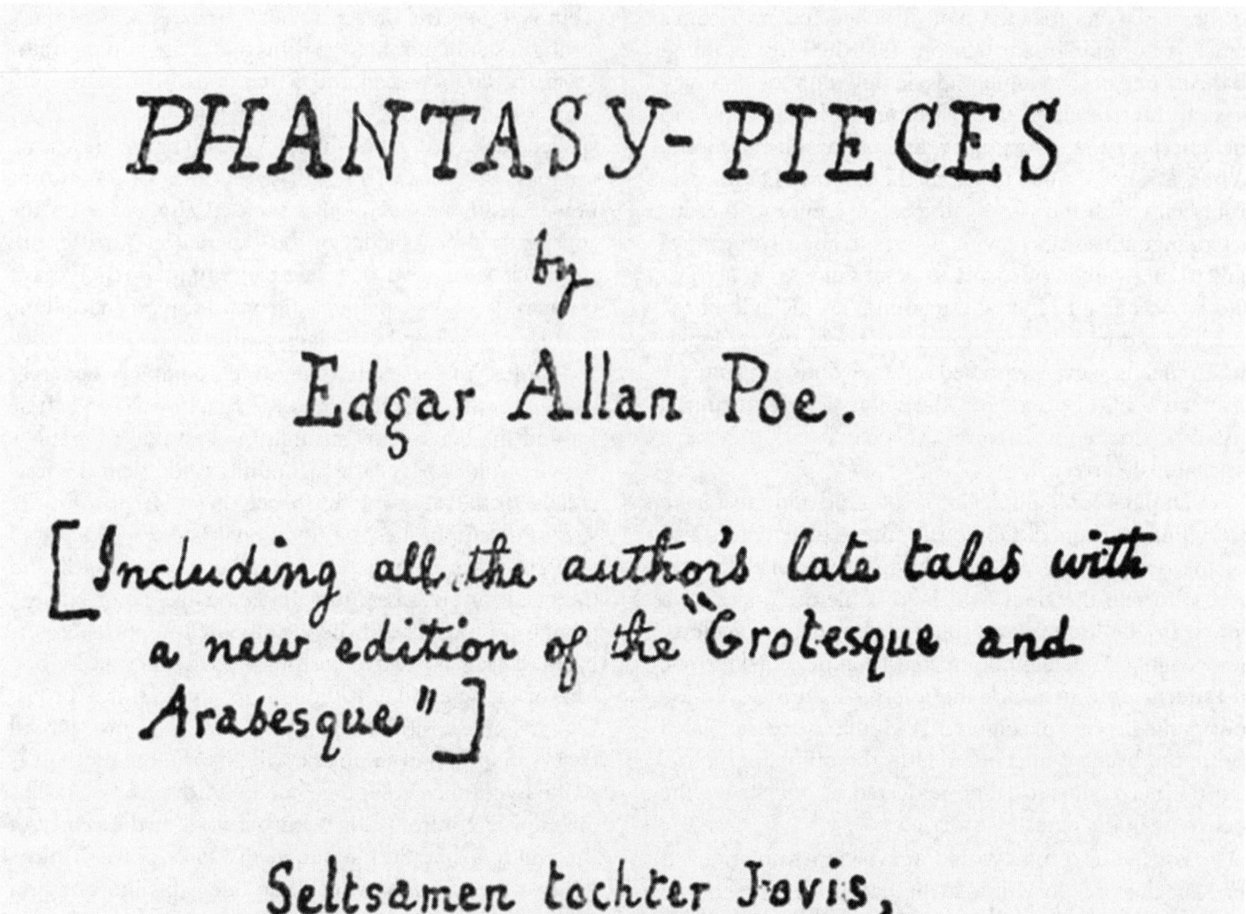

PHANTASY-PIECES

by

Edgar Allan Poe.

[Including all the author's late tales with a new edition of the "Grotesque and Arabesque"]

Seltsamen tochter Jovis,
Seinem schosskinde,
Der Phantasie.

Göthe

Two
~~Three~~ Volumes.

*Title page, designed by Poe, for the new collected edition of his tales he unsuccessfully proposed in 1842*
*(Stephen H. Wakeman Sale Catalogue, American Art Association, 28–29 April 1924)*

into play at both the opening and the conclusion of "The Pit and the Pendulum."

For most readers, the major interest of "The Gold-Bug" lies in the discovery of treasure and in following the cryptographic solution Poe offers. Recent criticism has uncovered a richer vein of meaning. A structure of East-West polarities parallels a theological split, and the tale may embody a coded scriptural message somewhat in the manner of *The Narrative of Arthur Gordon Pym,* though the meaning of this message is unclear. More concrete is the integrated pattern of alchemical symbolism in the tale. Tin and gold, both important alchemical elements, and the number seven play important parts. The particular tree from which the scarab must be dropped is specifically a golden tree having seven branches. There are seven stages in the alchemical process to transmute tin into gold. Legrand's servant is named Jupiter, and his dog, Wolf. Tin is associated with the planet Jupiter in alchemy, and a wolf or large dog symbolizes the active agent in the alchemical process that produces gold. One reading is that, thematically, the transformation is one of the "Americanizations" of the tradition. Poe's Faust becomes an American cryptographer; the Philosopher's Stone, Captain Kidd's treasure; and Mercurius, the spirit of ominous revelation, the shadowy Captain Kidd. A final ironic twist is that, like *The Narrative of Arthur Gordon Pym,* "The Gold-Bug" is filled with what may be calculated errors and chance discoveries. The code is inconsistent; the telescope is pointed at the wrong angle; the ink is specifically the wrong type; the invisible secret writing is revealed only by accident. Poe's ratiocinative tales are double-edged. Having once taken the reader through the ratiocinative process, he seems to mock it at the same time.

In Dupin this process is carried even further. In "The Mystery of Marie Rogêt" Dupin reasons that the police are wrong in believing the girl's death to be the work of a gang; the murderer is instead her lover. The Dupin type of mentality assumes a godlike omniscience, with the narrator and the reader playing the role of the dull-witted dupes. The setup in the Dupin stories is based on the discrepancy between appearance and actuality, the ease of Dupin's solutions contrasting with the readers' mystification.

The mystification goes deeper, however. Dupin's role in "The Purloined Letter" is complex and suspect. The tale is predicated on a perverse observation about human behavior: what is blatantly obvious often goes unobserved. Dupin hides the letter in the open, confounding the police and criminal. But the tale exhibits a complicated system of duplicative structures. Dupin and D–– (the minister) are moral doubles, each having a talent for duplicity and malice. Dupin's interest in the case is morally dubious, for it may be based on a desire for revenge or a love of game or even of financial profit and the acquisition of power. D–– duplicates all these traits. In both the strategies of sizing up one's opponent by identifying oneself with his mind and of deceiving, especially in the method of stealing the letter, are the same. Dupin and D–– may even be literal twin brothers, as a series of details suggests, especially the concluding reference to Crébillon's *Atrée,* a play about the fatal opposition between two brothers. Yet because enough calculated ambiguity about literal fraternity exists, a more symbolic meaning emerges. Dupin and D–– may constitute a single composite being, even one mind, each part the rival double of the other. For example, one character is said to go out only at night, the other only by day. Furthermore, D–– is never presented directly; his actions are reported by Dupin. In its total ambiguity of multiple structures, the double elements of the tale come to symbolize a basic opposition within a single human mind. The tale has become a favorite of various more or less psychological critics, including provocative exchanges among Jacques Lacan, Jacques Derrida, Barbara Johnson, John T. Irwin, and others.

While Poe developed the motif of the double and the technique of the ratiocinative story in the early 1840s, he also continued in other modes. In the second half of 1841 he published two "landscape" tales involving the death or dissolution of a female figure, another tale of apocalypse, and two comic works. Some of these incorporate the figure of the double. "Eleonora" (published in *The Gift*), for example, explores the nature of identity by means of two women, wives of the visionary narrator. One reading of the story is that Eleonora has a dual personality, one melancholy, one cheerful, and actually returns as the second wife. Other readings stress the narrator's unreliability ("men have called me mad"). An Undine-like figure in "The Island of the Fay" seems to be the last of her race, and she finally fades away into shadow and nothingness. Fading into nothingness is the major theme of "The Colloquy of Monos and Una" (*Graham's,* August 1841), which presents another of Poe's versions of apocalypse. Poe had theorized in "The Conversation of Eiros and Charmion" (*Burton's,* December 1839) that a large comet passing through the earth's atmosphere would draw out all the nitrogen, leaving such dense oxygen that it would ignite and engulf the world in flames. "The Colloquy Monos and Una" is supposedly an "affirmative" dialogue between two disembodied spirits beyond death who merge toward oneness. The revelation of what is beyond shows the merging of the body with the elements in the slow process of decay, while the spirit is, all the while, aware of this decay as its own energy fades away to a mere "glow" and silence. "The sense of being at length utterly departed, and there reigned in its stead . . . dominant and perpetual–the auto-

*The earliest known daguerrotype of Poe, taken sometime before 1843 ( from* The Critic, *46 [April 1905])*

crats *Place* and *Time*. . . . For all this nothingness, yet for all this immortality, the grave was still a home, and the corrosive hours co-mates."

Typically, Poe followed this gloomy tale with a comic and satiric piece: "Never Bet Your Head. A Moral Tale" (*Graham's,* September 1841; later titled "Never Bet the Devil Your Head"). With this tale Poe answers the charge that his works are unmoral–only the "moral" of this tale is a satiric slap at the high moralizing of the transcendentalists and at their journal, the *Dial.* The shocking conclusion of the tale, wherein the narrator coldly plans to have the body of his friend Toby Dammit dug up for "dog's meat," has been pointed to by some critics as an example of the fierce uncongeniality of humor in Poe, but the joke is that the "dissolute" life of the "immoral" but transcendentally gifted Dammit is merely the story of a boy (the narrator) and his dog (Dammit).

Such was the multiplicity of plots, characters, and themes taking shape in Poe's mind in 1841, ones he developed in a great outpouring of creative work in the next few years. His journalistic sense was also at a peak. His renewed "Autography" series (beginning September 1841) and his solutions of cryptograms (he solved all but one of a hundred sent in and demonstrated that that one was unsolvable) were popular, and the circulation of *Graham's* was increasing. Things had never been better for Poe: on the eve of his thirty-third birthday, he seems to have had

his drinking under control; he was secure in his job; he was decently paid; he had editorial authority; he was productive; and he was well-known and respected. Then in mid January 1842, while singing, Virginia Poe hemorrhaged from the lungs and throat, beginning the last phase of the tuberculosis that took her life five years later.

After some frantic watchful weeks, Poe moved his family farther out toward the country, where he began once more to act in an erratic manner. Nevertheless, during the first five months of 1842 he contributed an extraordinarily acute sequence of important reviews to *Graham's* (presumably drawn from the reservoir of the previous year's work). In the January issue Poe published a "Review of New Books," better known as "Exordium to Critical Notices," an essay on the art of reviewing. Here he reiterates his dismay that American criticism has gone to the "opposite extreme" of "subserviency to the *dicta* of Great Britain" and now calls for a "national literature!–as if any true literature *could be* 'national'–as if the world at large were not the only proper stage. . . ." He observes that a review used to give "an analysis of the contents" of a book and pass "judgment upon its merits or defects." Now reviews are merely "digests" with "copious extracts" or essays in which the book under review is merely a pretext for a difference of "opinion with the author." He compares American with British, French, and German reviews. He attacks Cornelius Mathews's "frantic spirit of *generalization,*" which goes counter to true criticism. Literary criticism should be limited to "comment upon *Art* . . . it is only *as the book* that we subject it to review." It is not the opinion but "*the mode*" that should be criticized. In these remarks Poe anticipates Henry James and mid-twentieth-century formalist criticism.

In the February issue he published a revised version of his *Post* article on *Barnaby Rudge* of the year before, adding that in the actual outcome of his mystery Dickens had not played fair with the reader. In March he met Dickens, who expressed admiration for his ability to forecast his plot. In the March and April issues he published a two-part review of Longfellow's *Ballads and Other Poems,* in which he says "his conception of the *aims* of poetry is all wrong. . . . His didactics are all *out of place.*" In the next installment he distinguishes between "the truthful and the poetical modes" of inculcating a moral. He places "taste" (beauty) between the "intellect" (truth) and the "moral sense" (duty): the paradigm of the German philosopher, Immanuel Kant. Man's sense of immortality is "a wild effort to reach the beauty above. It is a forethought of the loveliness to come. . . ." Novel combinations in poetry attempt to satisfy "the thirst for supernal Beauty . . . not offered the soul by any existing collocation of earth's forms. . . ." Although music most nearly approaches this ideal beauty, it needs the addition of words to make "song." Therefore, "the Poetry of words" is "*the Rhythmical Creation of Beauty*," in which the "sole arbiter is Taste," not duty or truth. It is clear from such reviews that Poe's concept of the aims of poetry is different from his concept of the aim and effect of prose fiction.

This point is made even more emphatic by another review beginning in the April 1842 *Graham's*, "Twice-Told Tales. By Nathaniel Hawthorne." In the May number he expanded his comments. Seeing Hawthorne as extraordinarily "original," Poe praises the "strong undercurrent of *suggestion*" that runs "continuously beneath the upper stream of the tranquil thesis." He mentions the "constitutional melancholy," the "fastidiousness of taste," and the sense of "indolence" in the tales. He develops a thesis of unity of impact around reading at "one sitting" a "short prose narrative, requiring from a half-hour to one or two hours in its perusal." He distinguishes between the aim of a poem and that of a tale: whereas an artificially rhythmic poem suggests the idea of indefinite Beauty, a tale frequently aims at Truth. Poe emphasizes the predesigned effect which is intransitive:

> During the hour of perusal the soul of the reader is at the writer's control. There are no external or extrinsic influences—resulting from weariness or interruption.

> A skilful literary artist has constructed a tale. If wise, he has not fashioned his thoughts to accommodate his incidents; but having conceived, with deliberate care, a certain unique or single *effect* to be wrought out, he then invents such incidents—he then combines such events as may best aid him in establishing this preconceived effect. If his very initial sentence tend not to the outbringing of this effect, then he has failed in his first step. In the whole composition there should be no word written, of which the tendency, direct or indirect, is not to the one pre-established design.

Poe also categorizes the types of the short tale as "the ratiocinative, for example, the sarcastic, or the humorous."

Because of his work for the Whigs and his acquaintance with President John Tyler's son, Robert, Poe at this time had persuaded himself that he was in line for a political appointment to a customhouse position, but it did not materialize. He became ill and, after recovering, found that *Graham's* other editor, C. J. Peterson, had assumed control. Poe promptly quit. Griswold then took Poe's job. Expecting to lose Virginia at any moment, Poe became distracted and melancholy—a change noted by Graham and others.

Poe's personal concerns seem to be reflected in two tales about the triumph of death. These contrast strongly with a new tale about an idyllic garden, of interest because Poe and others regarded landscape gardening as a kind of poetry. Perhaps "Life in Death" (*Graham's*,

April 1842; retitled "The Oval Portrait") reflects Poe's concern for Virginia's fading health, as some biographical critics maintain. Certainly the theme of the death of a beautiful woman intensified after Poe married his frail bride. But this tale about the transfer of life from a living person to a painting owes as much to literary convention as to anything else. Moreover, a carefully constructed dramatic frame surrounds it, so that the tale can also read as the dream of a man delirious from pain and lack of sleep, although the conclusion is left ambiguous. Similarly, "The Mask of the Red Death" (*Graham's*, May 1842), a tale of the supernatural visitation of Death himself, can also be read as a tone poem about hysteria engendered by mood and setting. The seven chambers extending from East to West, each lighted by a different colored window, suggest the progress from youth to death. Prince Prospero's sinister stronghold, of course, contrasts directly with the enchanted island of his namesake, Prospero, the magician in Shakespeare's *The Tempest* (1611). The theme of Poe's tale focuses on the grimly perverse joke of Prospero's having walled in death in a frenetic attempt to wall it out. In 1845 the word "mask" in the title was changed to "masque" to emphasize the tale's danse macabre fatality, and possibly to insinuate a "moral" undercurrent, as in *Comus*.

In contrast, "The Landscape Garden" (*Ladies' Companion*, October 1842) reads almost like a fantasy dream of wish fulfillment. Mr. Ellison inherits $450,000,000. He wants to create, by art, an earthly paradise. He embarks on a man-made landscape garden of vast proportions, which will be "Nature" and yet not "God" or an "emanation of God." Still, this project has "high spirituality." Ellison attempts by combination of novel physical forms in nature to emulate the Poet of words and the God of nature. The sketch concludes by observing that Ellison was able to obtain "an exemption from the ordinary cares of Humanity" through "the companionship and sympathy of a devoted wife." Poe was to revise this piece in 1847, the year of Virginia's death, in a melancholy way by adding a passage in which Ellison cannot contend with "geological upheavals" that prevent him from making the earth's surface (in other words, the earthly) fulfill "at all points man's sense of perfection in the beautiful. . . ." This intention is frustrated by rocky outcroppings, which Ellison now finds "prognostic of *death*." Whether or not man suffered a Fall, the Garden of Eden of his dreams is circumscribed, and these obtrusive rocks (as in *The Narrative of Arthur Gordon Pym*) are symbolic of God's "subsequently conceived deathful condition" for the earth. Ellison wants to parallel God's Creation and thus become Godlike himself. In the later version he dies, however.

In September 1842 Poe was able to meet with his new friend, F. W. Thomas, at a political rally in Philadel-

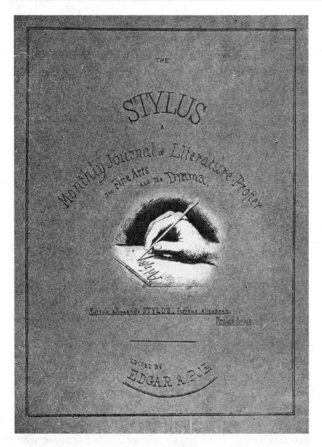

*Poe's original cover design for the literary magazine he unsuccessfully tried to found in 1843 (from Mary E. Phillips,* Edgar Allan Poe, the Man, *1926)*

phia, just before "The Mystery of Marie Rogêt" and "The Pit and the Pendulum" were published (in *Snowden's* and *The Gift*). About this time Poe collected and reorganized his tales under a new title, "Phantasy-Pieces," but he was unable to secure a publisher. He was also at this time corresponding with a Georgia physician, Thomas Holley Chivers, who later produced some highly rhythmic poems resembling Poe's; they discussed starting their own magazine. James Russell Lowell had just begun a magazine called the *Pioneer* and needed copy. Poe offered to contribute to the *Pioneer* regularly; and in January 1843 Lowell printed "The Tell-Tale Heart." In this story Poe improves upon Dickens's "A Madman's MS.," which he had singled out for praise years before. Poe's story is a study in obsessive paranoia, yet another story of the mind watching itself disintegrate under the stresses of delusion in an alienated world. It is the perverse fortune of the narrator to become fearful of the grotesque eye of a kindly old man, whom he says he loves. With a double perversity he gives himself away to the police at the moment of success. The narrator is caught in a weird world in which he loves the old man yet displays no real emotion toward him, in which he cannot let the

"beloved" old man live and yet cannot kill him without remorse, in which he cannot expose his crime and yet must do so. The two almost merge identities. He mistakes the apparent beating of his own heart as the beating of the still-living heart of the old man, which becomes an emblem of his own guilt (and which, finally, compels him to confess).

By February, Poe had taken a partner in his effort to establish his own magazine, now to be called the *Stylus*. In March he decided to go to Washington to inquire about a government appointment, but when he arrived he went on a weeklong drunk. He presented himself to President Tyler with his cloak turned inside out; he got into a fight with Thomas Dunn English; and he finally had to be sent home by friends. Poe had completed "The Gold-Bug" by this time and had given it to Graham; but when the *Dollar Newspaper* announced a $100 prize contest, Poe retrieved his story from Graham with a promise to make it up with reviews and other matter, beginning in the March number with a new series, "Our Amateur Poets." Meanwhile, Lowell's *Pioneer* was not doing well and soon ceased publication. Before it folded, however, Poe contributed "Lenore" (February) and "Notes on English Verse" (March; revised in 1848 as "The Rationale of Verse"). "Lenore" is a revision of the 1831 "A Paean," the angry lament of a young bridegroom for his lost bride; the speaker asserts she is lucky to die young and escape the jealousies of earthly life. Poe visited New York about this time and published an attack on "The Magazines" under a pseudonym. He had asked Lowell to contribute a poem to the *Stylus* and also asked him to persuade Hawthorne to contribute a story. But by May Poe had quarreled with his partner and the *Stylus* no longer had its funding.

"The Gold-Bug" won the $100 prize and was published in the *Dollar Newspaper* in June. It created a stir and was immediately reprinted; a dramatic adaptation was produced the next month in the famous Walnut Street theater. Also in August "The Black Cat" appeared in the *Saturday Evening Post*. Another development of the themes of guilt and perversity, it details the irrational desire to act against one's own self-interest. An ambiguous conclusion suggests the agency of malevolent fate at the same time that it suggests subconscious self-punishment. The motif of the double now takes the form of two black cats, representing different stages of the narrator's guilty conscience. In a drunken rage the narrator kills his first cat after mistreating it. A second cat manifests itself (suspiciously, on top of a wine barrel) and follows him everywhere. The second cat may be the hallucination of the narrator, a manifestation of his guilty conscience and alcohol-soaked brain. What the precise object of this guilt is becomes ambiguous, since, in a reenactment of his impulsive violence toward the first cat, he suddenly turns on his wife and cleaves her head in two with the ax he had intended to use on the second cat. The final manifestation of repressed guilt may be that he intentionally, though unconsciously, walls up the cat with the body of his wife so that its screaming will lead the police to discover the murder. Although in its details and atmosphere "The Black Cat" differs from "The Tell-Tale Heart," it shares with that tale similar plot structure, characterization, and theme.

Following his pattern, Poe's next published work, "Raising the Wind; or, Diddling Considered as One of the Exact Sciences" in the October *Saturday Courier,* was comic. In it Poe returns to the theme of the con artist, detailing several methods of swindling and comically asserting that the essential element of a successful "diddle" is the satisfaction that the con man feels afterward—summed up in the element of "Grin." Perhaps the same concerns, hoaxing and the juxtaposition of humor and horror, are behind the "uniform serial edition" of *The Prose Romances of Edgar A. Poe,* the first number of which appeared in the late summer or early fall of 1843. There were to be no other numbers, however; and the two "romances" were the unlikely duo of "The Murders in the Rue Morgue" and "The Man That Was Used Up."

In January 1844, at the age of thirty-five, Poe began lecturing, an enterprise that had made good money for other authors. He lectured on American poets in several cities, including Baltimore on 31 January and Reading, Pennsylvania on 13 March. At this time he got rid of his unbecoming side-whiskers and grew the dashing mustache generally associated with him. He published a nature sketch, "Morning on the Wissahiccon" (retitled "The Elk") in the gift annual *The Opal* early in 1844. In the March *Dollar Newspaper* he published "The Spectacles," a comic sketch about a man who, too vain to wear his glasses, is overwhelmed with the beauty of a woman who turns out not only to be quite elderly but also to be his own grandmother. These were followed in April by "A Tale of the Ragged Mountains" in *Godey's Lady's Book.*

His reviewing for *Graham's* had dwindled to nothing, and he still owed Graham money for "The Gold-Bug." Poe felt he had exhausted the possibilities of Philadelphia. Making arrangements with a Pennsylvania paper called the *Spy* to contribute a series of reports on the "Gotham" city, Poe moved his family in April to New York once again. He timed his arrival with one of his best hoaxes. What is now known as "The Balloon Hoax" appeared as a report of an actual transatlantic crossing in the 13 April extra issue of the *New York Sun,* causing such a commotion that the paper sold a record number at inflated prices. In May, Poe's "Doings of Gotham" began in the *Spy;* he describes various sections of New York and their people and comments on archi-

tecture, sports, city government, and the New York magazines. Poe then rented quarters in a farmhouse in the countryside just outside the city.

In June 1844 he published the poem "Dream-Land" in *Graham's.* In it he returns to the visionary experience of his earliest poems. The otherworldly landscape, as seen in a world of dreams, is a kind of "ultimate" in such visions in Poe's poetry: a "wild weird clime" that lies "Out of Space—out of Time." Its landscape is of

> Bottomless vales and boundless floods
> . . . . . . . . . . . . . . . . . . . . . . . . . . . .
> Mountains toppling evermore
> Into seas without a shore;
> Seas that restlessly aspire,
> Surging, unto skies of fire. . . .

This world is inhabited with "ghouls" and a fantastic amalgam of the dead and the living, of memories and realities, which may be viewed only obliquely through closed eyes (that is, as a dream vision). Such visions, such insights, come at that point of equipoise between sleeping and waking, Poe was to argue momentarily; and it was this moment of visionary experience that so intrigued him about the relatively new phenomenon of hypnotic sleep or mesmeric trance. Directly related is the cosmological theory Poe was developing at this time.

Lowell had agreed to write a biographical notice of Poe for the "Contributors" column of *Graham's.* On 2 July 1844, in response to a request, Poe wrote to Lowell about his life and philosophy. In this letter he outlines a theory of existence in terms of the infinite gradations of matter and denies the separate existence of spirit. It is a concise précis of the cosmology dramatized in the tale "Mesmeric Revelation" (published the next month in the *Columbian*) and expounded in his lectures on "The Universe" (1847–1848) that resulted in the book-length essay, *Eureka* (1848). Poe says he perceives "the vanity of the human or temporal life" and thus lives "continually in a reverie of the future": "I have no faith in human perfectibility. . . . Man is now only more active—not more happy—nor more wise, than he was 6000 years ago. . . . I cannot agree to lose sight of the individual, in man in the mass.—I have no belief in spirituality. I think the word a *mere* word. No one has really a conception of spirit. We cannot imagine what is not." He goes on to define what is called "spirit" monistically; it is infinitely rarefied matter. "Matter escapes the senses by degrees—a stone—a metal—a liquid—the atmosphere—a gas—the luminiferous ether."

How serious these philosophical musings are cannot be exactly determined, for Poe was out to make a name for himself by overturning traditional concepts; and to deny the existence of the spirit in nineteenth-century America was not only to contradict Christian orthodoxy but also to dismiss Ralph Waldo Emerson and the transcendentalists. Moreover, Poe elsewhere makes fun of these ideas. "Mesmeric Revelation," in which a man under hypnotism reveals this design of the universe (one that denies the existence of the spirit) before dying happily into his new "life," has been seen by some critics as a deadpan parody. In his characteristic pairing of tales, a year later Poe published another tale of mesmeric revelation, "The Facts of M. Valdemar's Case" (*American Review,* December 1845), in which the "sleep-waker" comes to a revolting end rather than expiring with a beatific smile. Valdemar's life is prolonged beyond the proper point of death by the new science of mesmerism; but the last horrible details suggest the grim finality of death as his whole body lapses rapidly into a disgusting liquid putridity. Poe was bemused with the success of these tales as hoaxes and remarked sarcastically on the gullibility of the public.

The seriocomic is a major feature of "The Premature Burial" (*Dollar Newspaper,* July 1844). The hero, an avid reader of Gothic books about burial alive, relates horrifying "factual" histories for three-quarters of the tale. Terrified of being buried alive himself, especially since he is subject to cataleptic fits, the protagonist arranges for a special sepulchre, easily opened from within, and a special coffin, with a spring lid and a hole through which a bellpull is to be tied to the hand of his "corpse." When he awakes in a cramped, dark, earthy-smelling place, he is convinced that he has fallen into a trance while among strangers and that he has been "thrust, deep, deep, and for ever, into some ordinary and nameless *grave*." It turns out that the hero has fallen asleep in the narrow berth of a ship, where he has sought refuge for the night, and he is rousted out of his bunk by the sailors he has awakened with his horrible cry of fear. The experience strikes the narrator as so ludicrous that he is shocked into sanity, and he reads no more "'Night Thoughts'—no fustian about churchyards—no bugaboo tales—*such as this.*"

Macabre humor also is at work in "The Oblong Box," published in the September 1844 issue of *Godey's.* An artist brings aboard a ship an oversized box that presumably contains his paintings. The passengers are forced to abandon ship in a storm, but the artist lashes himself to the box and sinks with it into the sea. The captain remarks puzzlingly that they will recover the box when the salt melts. This mystery is then explained: the box contained the body of the man's wife packed in salt; knowing the "superstitions" of his passengers, the captain had concealed the true contents from them, but he is haunted by a "hysterical laugh which will forever ring within my ears." This piece was followed in October by "The Angel of the Odd—an Extravaganza" (*Columbian Magazine*). When the narrator expresses his annoyance with improbable coincidences in the stories, the Angel of the Odd manifests himself. He causes a series of comic improbabilities to happen to the narrator, culminating in a fall from a balloon down his own chimney. There is a strong suspicion that the narrator has dreamed it all in a drunken haze. In a similar mood, Poe's parody of the detective story, "'Thou Art the Man,'" followed in the November issue of *Godey's.* The narrator catches a murderer by packing a wine case with the corpse of the victim and placing a length of whalebone down the throat and bending it so that the corpse seems to sit up when the case is opened at a party; at this point the narrator by ventriloquism says "Thou art the man," and Old Charley Goodfellow, in fright, confesses.

In the December 1844 *Southern Literary Messenger* Poe turned to satire of contemporary magazines and their editors, especially Lewis Gaylord Clark and possibly Graham. It is not hard to see Poe's firsthand experiences in the profession in "The Literary Life of Thingum Bob, Esq., Late Editor of the 'Goosetherumfoodle.'" The editor of the *Lollipop,* one Crab, criticizes the editor of the *Gad-Fly* and suggests that Thingum Bob write an attack on the *Lollipop* editor, though he makes it clear he cannot pay Thingum Bob for his work. Crab also suggests that he make a new "name" for himself as "Thomas Hawk," the "tomahawking" reviewer. Thingum Bob then proceeds to fashion reviews by physically cutting up texts and shaking them onto a glued surface; he eventually becomes a supereditor by merging four warring magazines together.

In the latter part of 1844 Poe had become a regular contributor to N. P. Willis's *New York Mirror* and had been contributing "Marginalia" notes to the *Democratic Review.* In December, Lowell put Poe in touch with Charles F. Briggs, author of *The Adventures of Harry Franco* (1839). Briggs began publishing a new magazine, the *Broadway Journal,* in January 1845; and the next month, Poe became Briggs's co-editor, sharing the profits equally with Briggs and John Bisco. Perhaps Poe was able to negotiate, for the first time, such an arrangement because his fame had taken another leap at the end of January with the publication of "The Raven."

"The Raven" appeared in the *New York Mirror,* the *American Review,* and several other papers and was an instant success, even more so than "The Gold-Bug." Poe seems to have had divided feelings about it—as he did about so many things—for he both touted it as the most original poem ever composed and downplayed it as written "for the express of running—just as . . . the 'Gold-Bug.'" In terms of public favor, he wrote F. W. Thomas that "the bird beat the bug . . . all hollow." The poem was widely reprinted in the United States and in Europe, where it caught the attention of Elizabeth Barrett. It is simultaneously an eerie and a comic psychological study of perversity. On a stormy December night a student reads curious volumes of ancient lore in an effort to forget his lost love, Lenore. A raven taps at his window, and for a wild moment (as in "Ligeia") he thinks it might be the ghost of his lady returned. Amused at himself and at the ungainly appearance of the raven, he lets the bird in; it perches ludicrously on the head of his bust of Pallas Athena, goddess of wisdom. Discovering that the bird has a one-word vocabulary, "Nevermore," he bemusedly puts to it questions capable of being answered by that word—until he asks (for whatever perverse reason) the ultimate question: Will he ever see his lost love Lenore in heaven? At the foreknown answer of "Nevermore," he shrieks his anguish at the bird—yet sets up a still deeper twisting of pain. In response to his injunction to the raven to depart and "Take thy beak from out my heart," the anticipated reply comes: "Nevermore." The student concludes (perhaps with satisfaction) that the shadow cast by this bird on his soul "shall be lifted—nevermore."

The poem is dramatically conceived. Poe carefully balances an atmosphere of the supernatural with the presentation of abnormal psychology, just as in the short stories, and the poem is to a degree a departure from his rigid distinction between poetry and fiction. The next year in "The Philosophy of Composition" (*Graham's*, April 1846), a half-serious, half tongue-in-cheek explanation of how he wrote "The Raven" step by step, Poe characterizes the student as one "impelled . . . by the human thirst for self-torture." He asks the bird questions he anticipates the answer to, so as to "bring him . . . the most of a luxury of sorrow." Other elements of the "philosophy" of composition are articulated in the essay that relate directly to the short story. The essay begins by asserting that "every plot, worth the name, must be elaborated in its *dénouement* before anything be attempted with the pen. It is only with the *dénouement* constantly in view that we can give a plot its indispensable air of consequence, or causation, by making the incidents, and especially the tone at all points, tend to the development of the intention." The denouement is tied to an "effect":

> Keeping originality *always* in view . . . I say to myself, in the first place, "Of the innumerable effects, or impressions, of which the heart, the intellect, or (more generally) the soul is susceptible, what one shall I, on the present occasion, select?" Having chosen a novel, first, and secondly a vivid effect, I consider whether it can best be wrought by incident or tone—whether by ordinary incidents and peculiar tone, or the converse, or by peculiarity both of incident and tone—afterward looking about me (or rather within) for such combinations of event, or tone, as shall best aid me in the construction of the effect.

*Portrait of Poe by A. C. Smith, 1843 or 1844 (Huntington Library)*

Effect is then a consequence of combinations of "tone" and "incident." The combinations specified are especially revealing: ordinary events plus peculiar tone; peculiar events plus ordinary tone; and peculiar events plus peculiar tone. These constitute a program for the heightened, romantic tale; the combination Poe omits is ordinary events plus ordinary tone, a formula for later nineteenth-century realism. Despite such heightening, however, "every thing is within the limits of the accountable—of the real." The storyteller's task is to bring the lover and the raven together in some reasonable way that yet creates intensity, which Poe achieved by choosing a locale that provides "close circumscription of space" and by emphasizing "the force of contrast, with a view of deepening the ultimate impression." An "air," a suggestion, of "the fantastic—approaching as nearly to the ludicrous as was admissible—is given to the Raven's entrance." This intensified, predesigned effect, Poe writes, is carefully calculated for "universal" appeal. The aesthetic effects of poetry, not prose, enable the soul to attain its most intense and pure elevation. For in poetry the adjuncts of repetition—of rhythm, measure, sound—help to create a hypnotic tone. Of the poetic devices, the most universal is the use of a refrain; Poe's is to be one of variable applicability that will bear repetition and deepen the effect. The word "Nevermore" itself is appropriate to the creation of a dominant tone of melancholy—the universal sense of loss of the ideal. Of all earthly subjects, he asks, what is the most melancholy? The death of a beautiful woman—the calculated subject of his poem. In it the raven comes to symbolize mournful and never-ending remembrance. Poe implies that at last someone has done an "*original thing*" in poetry.

In his review of N. P. Willis in the *Broadway Journal* (18 January 1845) two weeks before the publication of "The Raven" in February, Poe developed some similar concepts of "novelty" and "combination," distinguishing between *fancy, imagination, fantasy,* and *humor* but placing these four major categories on a continuum of effects. He concludes that the imagination selects for the creation of artistic works equally "from either beauty or deformity." In August of the same year, in his review of the "American Drama" (*American Review*), Poe defined plot as integrated structure and suggested that the "contemplation of unity" in a work of art partakes of the "ideal." In 1849, in an expansion of his essay on "Song Writing" in *Burton's* ten years before, he linked the ethereal, dream-like sense of indefinitiveness in poetry not only with "melody" but also with the mathematical measurement of music—even to the point of asserting that mathematical equality is the root of all beauty.

Meanwhile, in 1845, Poe continued his more-journalistic essays, commenting on new developments in printing, criticizing the state of reviewing and editorial practices of magazines, calling for an international copyright law to protect both American and foreign authors (in "Some Secrets of the Magazine Prison-House"). He continued his "Marginalia" and "Suggestions" series, and, in a curious sequence of events, he became involved in what is now known as "The Longfellow War." To understand this episode, one must be aware of several extenuating matters: Poe was trying to create publicity for himself and the new magazine. The literary warfare among the magazines of the time was acrimonious, personal, and characterized by almost instinctive aggressive reflexes. Further, Poe really did detest the power of the literary cliques and the abuse of the artistic gift. He felt Longfellow had sold out to popularity with his mechanical verse forms and easy didacticism.

Longfellow had in 1845 published an anthology he had edited of minor poems by minor writers, called *The Waif.* Poe charged him with avoiding "all American poets who may be supposed especially to interfere with the claims of Mr. Longfellow." Put more bluntly, Poe was saying Longfellow had failed to include poets he had plagiarized. Several magazines entered the fray, and early in March 1845 a defense of Longfellow and an attack on Poe appeared in the *New York Weekly Mirror* by one "Outis" ("Nobody"). Outis said by employing the kind of argument made by Poe about Longfellow's "borrow-

ings," one could accuse Poe of stealing "The Raven" from other poems about birds. Poe responded in five lengthy installments in the *Broadway Journal* from 8 March to 5 April, attacking not only Longfellow but also the Northern literati in general, and especially the clique around the *Knickerbocker,* then under the editorship of Lewis Gaylord Clark. The *Knickerbocker* responded with a parody of "The Raven." There is some reason to believe that Outis was none other than Poe himself, stirring up controversy and hoaxing friends and public alike; but the matter cannot be proved.

At the end of February 1845 Poe gave a lecture on American poetry, during the course of which he praised the poetry of Frances Sargent Osgood, a beautiful woman of thirty-four, two years younger than himself. She met with him sometime in the spring and carried on a "romantic friendship" that caused a great deal of criticism of Poe for "deserting a dying wife" in favor of a flirtatious poetess. Osgood was also frequently in the company of Griswold and another man; these flirtations may all have been her stratagem to win back an errant husband. In any event, Virginia Poe liked her; she seemed to think the relationship platonic and Fanny Osgood a good influence on Poe. Yet Poe was once again drinking, and, almost as if he were acting according to a script, his association with Briggs on the *Broadway Journal* began to break down. Poe wrote Thomas in May that he felt like "a slave" to the journal. At this time, Lowell was traveling through New York and wanted to see Poe, whom he had never met. When he called he found Poe "not tipsy," but certainly "a little soggy with drink"; the encounter ended their relationship. The Georgia poet Chivers called on Poe, and they seem to have gone drinking together repeatedly. On the way home from the office of the *Broadway Journal* one evening they ran into Clark of the *Knickerbocker,* and Poe offered to knock him down, but Clark avoided him.

In June, Evert A. Duyckinck, editor at Wiley and Putnam, selected twelve of Poe's stories for publication in a volume known simply as *Tales*. By July, Poe was being feted as a literary lion at the famous soirees of Anne Charlotte Lynch in Greenwich Village, where he met some of the most famous literary people of the day, and whom he gently satirized in "The Literati of New York City" in the May issue of *Godey's* the following year. He was noted for charm and for both reticence and brilliance in conversation. Briggs meanwhile had maneuvered to wrest the *Broadway Journal* from Poe and Bisco, its publisher. Bisco retained the magazine and renegotiated Poe's contract in July; he was to be in complete editorial control and to share all profits equally. To fill pages Poe reprinted most of his fiction and poetry in revised versions, sometimes under the pseudonym of "Littleton

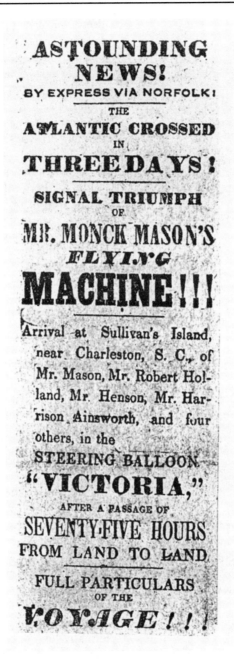

*Headline for Poe's "Balloon Hoax," which appeared in the 13 April 1844 edition of the*
New York Sun *(from* Edgar Allan Poe, the Man, *1926)*

Barry," apparently so his name would not appear too often.

Poe had been publishing works in a variety of other journals as well. In February 1845 "The Thousand-and-Second Tale of Scheherazade" had appeared in *Godey's;* in April "Some Words with a Mummy" in the *American Review*. Both satirize the penchant of Americans for gadgetry and patent medicines and are sprinkled with sarcastic observations on clothing styles and the democratic "experiment." In the first tale, after listening to all sorts of incredible stories of weird beings and devices from the future (in other words, the nineteenth century), the Arab potentate's credulity is stretched too far when Scheherazade tells him women wear contraptions called bustles. He has her executed. Poe reversed the basic frame in the second tale; instead of a medieval Arab hearing the wonders of the nineteenth century, the nineteenth century hears of ancient Egypt. "Some Words with a Mummy" comically presents Poe's dissatisfaction with mobocracy, with American technology, and with

THE RAVEN

AND

OTHER POEMS.

BY

EDGAR A. POE.

NEW YORK:
WILEY AND PUTNAM, 161 BROADWAY.

1845.

*Title page for Poe's fourth poetry collection, featuring his best-known poem (Library of the University of Pennsylvania)*

the concept of progress that had become by 1845 dear to the hearts of his countrymen. The narrator, deeply disturbed by the inability of modern Americans to demonstrate the superiority of their culture to that of ancient Egyptians, may mirror Poe's feelings when he comments: "The truth is, I am heartily sick of this life and of the nineteenth century in general. I am convinced that everything is going wrong."

Poe returned to the cosmological dialogue after death in "The Power of Words" (*United States Magazine and Democratic Review,* June 1845), which seems to take as its text the opening of the New Testament–"In the beginning was the word"–only literally. The spirit Oinos (whose name suggests "one" and "wine") discusses with the spirit Agathon (who in Plato's *Symposium* ends up drunk under the table) the nature of existence. Quite different is "The Imp of the Perverse," published in *Graham's* the next month. Almost more an essay than a tale, it is a dark comedy of errors that clearly spells out Poe's fundamental conception that man's fate is to act against his own best interests. The dissertation on perversity has its dramatic irony, however. The narrator commits the perfect murder, but his rationality merely enmeshes him

deeper in anxiety, as he absurdly, helplessly, uses his imaginative intellect to will his own destruction by means of a mere whimsical thought. What if he were to confess to the first person he met on the street?

By fall 1845 Bisco wanted out from the *Broadway Journal.* Poe had for years sought his own magazine; he borrowed what he could and signed a note to pay all outstanding debts against the journal. The 25 October issue carried the words "Edgar A. Poe, Editor and Proprietor." In October, Poe was supposed to read a new poem before the Boston Lyceum for $50, a considerable sum; but he was unable to compose an occasional poem and instead discoursed on the nature of poetry and read "Al Aaraaf." Some thought it was a good performance; others were outraged. Poe, who had gotten tipsy afterward, said in his *Broadway Journal* that he had hoaxed the Bostonians with a poem written when he was ten years old, delivering it to them while drunk. Meanwhile, since the *Tales* volume had been selling well (bringing Poe a royalty of 8¢ a copy), Wiley and Putnam brought out *The Raven and Other Poems* late in November. In his preface to this volume he claimed that, had he not been forced by worldly considerations to devote his energies to the somewhat more-profitable pursuits of editing, criticism, and tale writing, poetry would have been his first choice for a career. He remarked that the volume contained nothing "of much value to the public or very creditable to myself." The preface concludes with the observation that "with me poetry has been not a purpose, but a passion; and the passions should be held in reverence; they must not–they cannot at will be excited with an eye to the paltry compensations, or the more paltry commendations, of mankind." His prefatory deprecation of his efforts in poetry is actually an exaltation of the Poetic Ideal above the mundane considerations of deadlines and commerce.

Two tales closed out the year: "The Facts of M. Valdemar's Case" and "The System of Dr. Tarr and Professor Fether" (*Graham's,* November). In the latter Poe combines architectural symbolism with political satire in a comic grotesque and literary burlesque. Traveling through the South of France, the narrator encounters in the insane asylum of M. Maillard a conflict between the "soothing system" of treating patients (in which they are allowed to act out their delusions) and the "new" system of Professors Tarr and Fether (in which delusion is not tolerated). Under the old system inmates could even act out the delusion that the keepers were the insane and the insane the keepers. At a party that night, while the orchestra plays "Yankee Doodle," a troop of what appear to be black baboons bursts in. They turn out to be the keepers, tarred and feathered by the insane M. Maillard. They have escaped from their basement prison. As in other of Poe's works the irrational has welled up from

The System of Doctor Tarr and Professor Fether.

By Edgar A. Poe.

During the autumn of 18—, while on a tour through the extreme Southern provinces of France, my route led me within a few miles of a certain Maison de Santé, or private Mad-House, about which I had heard much, in Paris, from my medical friends. As I had never visited a place of the kind, I thought the opportunity too good to be lost; and so proposed to my travelling companion (a gentleman with whom I had made casual acquaintance, a few days before) that we should turn aside, for an hour or so, and look through the establishment. To this he objected; pleading haste, in the first place, and, in the second, a very usual horror at the sight of a lunatic.

*First page of the fair-copy manuscript for Poe's 1845 story "The System of Doctor Tarr and Professor Fether"*
*(from Donald G. Mitchell,* American Lands and Letters, *volume two [New York: Scribners, 1878–1998, 1899])*

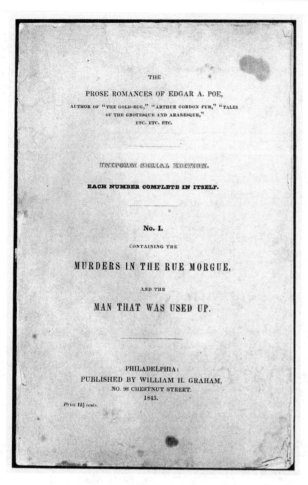

*Front wrapper of the first and only volume of an intended "uniform serial edition" of* The Prose Romances of Edgar A. Poe *(Pierpont Morgan Library)*

below to overwhelm the rational faculties, to be followed by another revolution. Both Dickens and Willis had commented on the conditions of asylums for the insane and are caricatured in the tale. The story seems, as well, to present satiric commentary on the political relations of the North and the South in the United States.

Earlier in the year, Poe seems to have contributed reviews to the *Aristidean,* edited by Thomas Dunn English. Until the latter part of the year he got along well enough with English. Poe was being manipulated by Elizabeth F. Ellet, however, who wanted him to puff her poems in his magazine. He got into a complicated argument with English over certain letters of both Osgood and Ellet. About the same time the note for the debts against the *Broadway Journal,* which had steadily lost money, came due. Poe got intoxicated and got into a fistfight with English. Poe's *Broadway Journal* ceased publication on 3 January 1846.

The years 1846–1847 were, for several reasons, Poe's least productive. Virginia Poe's health had seri-

ously deteriorated, and Poe became embroiled in personal, professional, and legal turmoil. One of the major literary wars was that between the *Knickerbocker* clique and another group calling themselves (after the model of the German Romanticists) Young America. Poe, without a clique of his own and now without a magazine, was caught in the middle. In January 1846 the *Knickerbocker* viciously attacked not only Poe's poetry and criticism, but also his character. Poe's ally Willis resigned from the *New York Mirror,* and his new enemy, Briggs, joined its staff. Poe had a chance to strike back hard in the "Literati" series, which ran in installments in *Godey's* during 1846, but he contented himself with occasional potshots. He seems to have been blacklisted in several of the new magazines. When "The Sphinx" appeared in the January number of *Arthur's Ladies' Magazine,* Poe felt degraded by being forced to publish in such a low-quality journal. The tale is one of his slighter pieces, but of interest for its remarks on the American ego and for its hoaxlike technique. It comes to a comic conclusion after a frightening and weird, but absurdly deceptive, vision of a monster that turns out to be a bug dangling only a fraction of an inch from the eye.

In February, Virginia wrote Poe a valentine poem, in which the first letters of each line spell out his name; she asks for "a cottage for my home" and says that "Love shall heal my weakened lungs." He first moved them to a farmhouse, later to a cottage at Fordham. In between he visited Baltimore, drank frequently, and became quite ill. In May the *New York Mirror* parodied Poe's first "Literati" sketch by viciously caricaturing Poe, both professionally and personally. In mid June, Poe retaliated halfheartedly in his "Literati" sketches of James Aldrich and English, suggesting that Aldrich was a plagiarist and that English's English was so bad that he needed some "private instruction." On 23 June the *Mirror* printed another scurrilous personal attack, "War of the Literati: Mr. English's Reply to Mr. Poe." English went too far; among other things he accused Poe of slander, forgery, and monetary fraud. In response Poe sued the *Mirror* for libel. He continued the literary war, though, being careful not to commit any blunders like English's. He had to publish his "Rejoinder" in a Philadelphia paper, however, because Godey was wary of getting embroiled with the factions. English's "Reply to Mr. Poe's Rejoinder" gleefully noted that "Mr. Poe had some difficulty in obtaining a respectable journal" for his article. The battle continued through the fall of 1846. Poe's August "Literati" sketch of Clark, the editor of the *Knickerbocker,* claimed that "as the editor has no precise character, the magazine, as a matter of course, can have none." In October the *Knickerbocker* repeated English's story of the fistfight with Poe. In the October "Literati" Poe inserted a tongue-in-cheek lament for the casting of the *Knickerbocker* under the editorship of

Clark to "outer darkness" and "utter and unconceivable dunderheadism," calling Clark "King Log the Second." The *Mirror* meanwhile was serializing English's *1844; or the Power of the S. F.,* in which Poe is satirized as one "Marmaduke Hammerhead." This attack was followed in November by Briggs's *Mirror* serial, *The Tripping of Tom Pepper,* in which Poe was caricatured (in February) as "Austin Wicks," who gets drunk on one glass of wine, picks fights, has to be carried home, and is eventually buried at public expense.

In the November *Godey's* Poe published one of his finest tales, "The Cask of Amontillado," notable for its compression and crisp dialogue, not to mention its structural symmetry and resonant symbolism. Tales such as "The Black Cat," "The Tell-Tale Heart," and "The Imp of the Perverse" involve a dramatized confessional element, wherein a first-person narrator seems calmly or gleefully to recount horrible deeds, but which generally implies a listener to whom the agonized soul is revealing his torment. The characterization of Montresor in "The Cask of Amontillado" is perhaps the ultimate in such strategy. In the surface story Montresor seems to be chuckling over his flawlessly executed revenge upon unfortunate "Fortunato" fifty years before. A moment's reflection, however, suggests that the indistinct "you" whom Montresor addresses in the first paragraph is probably his deathbed confessor—for if Montresor has murdered Fortunato fifty years before, he must now be some seventy to eighty years of age, having suffered the ravages of conscience for the entire time. As in "The Tell-Tale Heart," the murderer and the murdered merge their identities into one.

Virginia by this time required nursing, and Poe himself was ill. A kindly lady, Marie Louise Shew, was brought in to help; Poe wrote a couple of poems to her in gratitude. Things were in a bad way for the Poe family. Poe was out of work and out of money. Two weeks before Christmas, another friend, Mary Hewett, got the *New York Morning Express* to publish an appeal for money; the appeal was copied in other papers, and many people responded, to whom Poe wrote embarrassed notes of thanks. Shew noticed that Poe had an "intermittent pulse," which suggested heart trouble and a brain lesion of some kind, confirmed in some degree by Poe's recurrent feverishness. Virginia sent for Shew on 29 January 1847, when she felt her end was near. The next day Virginia Poe died.

According to tradition, Poe became distraught, morose, nervous, unable to sleep, given to solitary walks that would end at Virginia's grave, though the last may have been exaggerated by acquaintances to explain the poem "Ulalume," not published until December 1847 (*American Review*). The only other works of note published during the year were a cooler but still approving

*Poe's wife, Virginia Clemm Poe, in 1847*
*(Collection of Ridgely Bond Jr.)*

review of Hawthorne (*Graham's,* November) and "The Domain of Arnheim" (*Columbian,* March), a revision of "The Landscape Garden" of five years before. Whereas in the earlier tale there had been no withered leaves, not a single patch of barren ground, Poe now inserted the rocky facts of death and imperfection.

"Ulalume" has attracted a good deal of critical commentary—and the familiar controversies. It has been admired for its imagery and its hypnotic, incantatory repetition. But is it visionary and affirmative at the end, or is it a revelation of repressed grief over the triumph of death? The title itself includes an ambiguity. It is a made-up word suggesting "wailing" (*ululare*) and "light" (*lumen*), and one reading is that it means "light out of sorrow" and is thus affirmative; but it can equally as well mean "sorrowful light." In the latter reading it refers to the sad star or plant that brings painful remembrance of loss. The speaker remembers walking down an avenue of cypress trees one night in October, under ashen skies, conversing with himself. The other part of himself is personified as female, Psyche, his soul. The landscape is subjective; life has died out of the leaves; mist obscures vision; and the woods seem haunted by "ghouls." Toward dawn a nebulous light appears at the end of the path, and from this the crescent of Astarte (the planet

# Ulalume — A Ballad.
## By Edgar A. Poe.

The skies they were ashen and sober;
    The leaves they were crispèd and sere —
    The leaves they were withering and sere:
It was night, in the lonesome October
    Of my most immemorial year:
It was hard by the dim lake of Auber,
    In the misty mid region of Weir: —
It was down by the dank tarn of Auber,
    In the ghoul-haunted woodland of Weir.

Here once, through an alley Titanic,
    Of cypress, I roamed with my Soul —
    Of cypress, with Psyche, my Soul.
These were days when my heart was volcanic
    As the scoriac rivers that roll —.
    As the lavas that restlessly roll
Their sulphurous currents down Yaanek,
    In the ultimate climes of the Pole —
That groan as they roll down Mount Yaanek,
    In the realms of the Boreal Pole.

Our talk had been serious and sober,
    But our thoughts they were palsied and sere —
    Our memories were treacherous and sere;

*Autograph copy of Poe's 1847 poem, presented by the author to Susan V. C. Ingram (Pierpont Morgan Library)*

Venus) arises. The speaker says that this star-goddess (of sensual love) is warmer than the chaste moon-goddess, Diana (evoking Poe's "Evening Star"). She has, he says, "come past the stars of the Lion." Astrologically, the love goddess Venus has left the sign of Leo, which seems to hint of some vague hopefulness to the speaker, since Venus in Leo is unfavorable to marriage. Moreover, Venus seems to promise the peace of forgetfulness. The other part of the self, Psyche, does not trust this hopeful sign. The speaker insists, however, that the sky is full of beauty and hope, and that they follow the starlight to the end of the path. There they find a tomb inscribed with the name of his lost love, Ulalume. He then remembers that a year ago he had brought "a dread burden" to the tomb and wonders what demon has prompted him to return, to reawaken the painful memory of his lost love. The question is not answered.

Despite all this sorrowfulness, Poe was willing to use the poem in a little game of literary politics—to reestablish himself, as he said, in the literary scene. In December, Poe asked Willis to reprint "Ulalume" and speculate about the identity of the author so as to create a stir. Willis did as Poe asked on New Year's Day, 1848. Three weeks later Henry Hirst argued in the *Philadelphia Saturday Courier* that Poe was the author. Meanwhile, Poe scheduled a lecture on "The Universe" (later expanded as *Eureka*) for the New York Historical Society. Simultaneously he sent Godey the satire "Mellonta Tauta," not published until a year later, in February 1849. The title means "That Which Is to Come." Reminiscent of "Hans Phaall," the story is about a balloon voyage across the Atlantic Ocean, on 1 April 2848, a thousand years into the future. The manuscript had been found, the epigraph states, in a bottle floating in the *Mare Tenebrarum,* the Dark Sea, visited mainly by transcendentalists and "divers for crochets." The dim-witted female narrator, Pundita, may represent Margaret Fuller, and the man addressed as Pundit may represent Emerson. In any event, the types of transcendentalist thinkers are burlesqued. Poe used the opening of the tale as part of the opening of the ostensibly deadly serious *Eureka*.

The reception of the February lecture on "The Universe," which lasted two hours, was a little mixed, though generally favorable. One reviewer, a theological student, had been well impressed with the lecture. He became distressed, however, when the next month he looked over the manuscript for *Eureka* in the office of G. P. Putnam, which planned to publish it in the summer. He discovered to his shock that Poe actually denied the spirit and that the argument was based on a material pantheism. The underlying ideas of *Eureka* are much the same as outlined in Poe's letter to Lowell in 1844 and in "Mesmeric Revelation," but there is a good deal of word-play and philosophical joking in it well beyond any hoax-

*Annie Richmond, whom Poe met in 1848 and pursued romantically even though she was married at the time (University of Lowell Library)*

ing. Poe called it a "Poem," rather than a scientific treatise, but he also intended it to be a synthesis of modern scientific and philosophical thinking about the origin and nature of the universe, logic and consciousness, man, destiny, and God.

Poe suggests that the cycle of the birth, death, and resurrection of the universe operates through two forces: attraction (gravity) and repulsion (electricity). Matter as it is sensed is in a midregion between these two poles. Originally all was one whole; God then willed matter to become particulate and diffused through space; when it reaches its ultimate point of dispersal, it will collapse again into unity. Because the basic proposition of *Eureka* declares that inevitable annihilation is built into the structure of the universe, man's belief in a designed cosmos has to be reconciled with oblivion. Romantic literary analogies of God as an artist, shaping the cosmos with divine symmetry to his own end, provide Poe the answer. He says the universe is like a fictive romance; it is a "plot of God"; and the plot is for "novel universes" to swell into "objectless" existence and then subside into nothingness. If it were not for this grand design, Poe suggests, then "We should have been forced to regard the Universe with some such sense of dissatisfaction as we experience in contemplating an unnecessarily complex work

*Poe on 9 November 1848, the day after he had possibly suffered a stroke (Richard Gimbel Collection, Philadelphia Free Library)*

of human art. Creation would have affected us as an imperfect *plot* in a romance, where the *denoument* [*sic*] is awkwardly brought about by interposed incidents external and foreign to the main subject." The endlessly repeated cycles of creation, destruction, and re-creation make an aesthetic design that gives humankind some hope. The point is crucial, Poe argues, because only if there is aesthetic design does the "evil" manifest in the universe become "intelligible" and "endurable"; only then can one "comprehend the riddles of Divine Injustice." Some readers sense in the protestations Poe's real suspicion that his life, along with all existence, is like badly contrived fiction, riddled with injustice. The majority of readers, however, see *Eureka* as an affirmation of order and meaning in the universe.

In March 1848 two complimentary verses, addressed to ladies who had helped Poe through Virginia's last illness, appeared. "An Enigma" (*Union Magazine*) spells out the name Sarah Anna Lewis, beginning with the first letter of the first line, the second letter of the second line, and so on. Lewis was a poetess who bedeviled Poe for critical puffery in his last years. "To——" (*Columbian*) is another poem for Shew, given to her by Poe the year before along with "The Beloved Physician," extant only in fragments, which is supposed to have re-

created her diagnosis of his heart condition and brain lesion. According to tradition Poe visited her one Sunday, overwrought, and complained about the noise of the bells from Grace Church. To calm him she wrote on a piece of paper "The Bells, by E. A. Poe. The little silver bells." Poe wrote a few lines, she suggested iron bells, and he wrote several more lines. Although she seemed to have real affection for him, Shew allowed herself to be persuaded by friends that Poe's religion was unorthodox. He wrote her an anxiety-ridden letter saying that on his last visit she had been more cordial to the cat than to him. She never saw him again.

Poe's general health was poor, and he suffered from growing mental disorientation—apparently not only from drink, but from what seems to have been a series of strokes. He may have had diabetes as well. Again he sought a woman to keep him steady. A poetess, Sarah Helen Whitman, began to show interest in him; they exchanged poems, and eventually Poe wrote her some sixty lines (later titled "To Helen" by Griswold). Then Jane Locke of Lowell, Massachusetts, was taken with him and arranged a lecture in July. "The Poets and Poetry of America" was a great success and earned Poe a fair amount of money. While in Lowell, he met twenty-eight-year-old Nancy ("Annie") Richmond. Although she was still married, Poe decided he was in love with her.

Poe had really wanted to lecture in the South in an effort to resurrect the *Stylus* by subscription. He set out for Richmond, Virginia, and while there began drinking in a waterfront tavern, subsequent to which he seems to have challenged the editor of the *Richmond Examiner* to a duel. He spent the summer in Richmond, where he received a batch of poems from Sarah Helen Whitman. She turned out to be a well-to-do widow of forty-five (some six years older than Poe). As well as being a hypochondriac, she was something of a spiritualist, and used ether to veil the "grossness" of the world from her vision. Poe decided to pursue what started out as a literary flirtation, and late in September 1848 he called on her in Providence, Rhode Island. He claimed that he now loved "for the first and only time" and asked her to marry him. He wrote her that he would gladly die with her. She, however, had heard disturbing gossip about him, some of it from Ellet regarding Frances Osgood. Moreover, she said, her friends feared Poe wanted to marry her for her money.

Although Poe denied this, and reiterated his love for her, he went to Lowell in November and declared his love for Annie Richmond and begged her to leave her husband. Her refusal is said to have been gentle, but in a letter, in which it is hard to separate truth from fiction, Poe says that he fully intended to commit suicide because of her refusal. He claims that he bought two ounces of laudanum and took half of it. Apparently, he was so ignorant about the use of drugs that he did not know how to use the opiate properly and went into spasms of vomiting that left him debilitated for days. Despite his weakened condition he went to Providence to renew his suit with Whitman. She showed him written warnings from friends about his character, and Poe went away. But the next day he called her name repeatedly outside her house. He was let in, disoriented, and a doctor was called; the physician said that Poe had some kind of cerebral congestion. A neighbor seized the opportunity and forced Poe to pose for a now-famous daguerreotype, in which his face is puffy and lined, constricted and lopsided, as though he had just suffered a stroke.

Apparently Poe's woeful condition moved Whitman. She agreed to marry—on the condition that she would call off the marriage if he indulged in any of the excesses she had been warned about. In the middle of November 1848 he returned to New York by steamboat, where he promptly wrote a letter to Richmond asking her to come to him, if only for a week. Whitman sent him a poem, "Arcturus," along with more reports of his bad character received from friends. She had two legal documents drawn, the purpose of which was to make sure Poe could not get his hands on any of her money. Poe wrote that they could discuss the matter when he came to Providence to lecture on "The Poetic Principle" (posthumously published in the *Home Journal*, August 1850).

This lecture was a summary of the poetic theory he had been developing over the last twenty years, though it did not go into the technicalities of quantification, accentual stress, and strategies of rhythm of "The Rationale of Verse" (*Southern Literary Messenger*, October–November 1848). In "The Poetic Principle" he asserts that a poem must be brief or the totality of effect will be lost; yet, "undue brevity" is also a fault. The idea that the "ultimate object of all Poetry is Truth" and that every poem should "inculcate a moral" is, he says, "the heresy of the didactic." A poem conveys whatever "truth" it has through its art, through the poetic experience itself. Nothing more dignified or supremely noble exists than a "poem written solely for the poem's sake." The sense of the Beautiful is an immortal instinct, and the "Poetic Sentiment" attempts to apprehend "supernal Loveliness." It may take various modes: painting, sculpture, dance, especially music, and also landscape gardening. Only in the "contemplation of Beauty" can the "elevating excitement of the Soul" be attained. For such contemplation, rhythm and song are essential. Poe ends with a catalogue of elements that induce in the poet the "true poetical effect," moving from the stars, through objects of nature—especially indefinite sights, smells, and gentle tactile sensations such as wind—to the sense of the undiscovered, the distant, the unworldly, and concluding with

*Poe's literary executor, Rufus W. Griswold (New York Public Library)*

"the beauty of woman," especially the divinity of "her love."

Poe gave this lecture to a large audience of some two thousand people on 20 December. Two days later he signed the documents Whitman wanted and showed up at her house that evening a little tipsy. After a scene he promised never to touch a drop more. The next morning he had wine with breakfast, and Whitman broke the engagement amid some awkward complications.

In 1849 Poe arranged to contribute regularly to the *Flag of Our Union*, a Boston weekly of large circulation. He hoped as well to continue contributing to *Graham's* and *Godey's;* and he had connections with the *American Review*, the *Whig Review*, the *Democratic Review*, and *Sartain's Union*. After his return from Providence he arranged to contribute several pages of "Marginalia" to the *Southern Literary Messenger*. "Mellonta Tauta" appeared in *Godey's* in February, and "A Dream within a Dream" in the *Flag* in March. Also in the March *Flag* was Poe's ludicrous tale of horrible revenge told in fairy-tale style, "Hop-Frog, or the Eight Chained Orangoutangs." A hunchbacked dwarf is jester to a king who loves practical jokes. The king loves to torment Hop-Frog, especially by forcing a glass of wine on him, for he knows a single glass maddens the dwarf. The tale has been read as a parody of the fairy tale, as a story of the terrible darkness of the human soul, and as symbolic biography.

In the April *Flag* Poe published two poems, "For Annie" and "A Valentine" (retitled "Eldorado"), along

New-York. Feb. 24. 1845.

My Dear Griswold,

Soon after seeing you I sent you, through Zeiber, all my poems worth re-publishing, & I presume they reached you. With this I send you another package; also through Zeiber, by Burgess & Stringer. It contains in the way of Essay "Mesmeric Revelation" which I would like to go in, even if something else is omitted. I send also a portion of the "Marginalia" in which I have marked some of the most pointed passages. In the matter of criticism I cannot put my hand upon anything that suits me — but I believe that in "funny" criticism (if you wish any such) Flaccus will convey a tolerable idea of my style, and of my serious manner Barnaby Rudge is a good specimen. In "Graham" you will find these. In the tale line I send you "The Murders in the Rue Morgue" and "The Man that was Used Up" — far more than enough, you will say — but you can select to suit yourself. I would prefer having in the "Gold Bug" to the "Murders in the R. M", but have not a copy just now. If there is no immediate hurry for it, however, I will get one & send it you corrected. Please write & let me know if you get this. — I have taken a 3d interest in the "Broadway Journal" & will be glad if you could send me anything, at any time, in the way of "Literary Intelligence".

Truly yours. Poe.

*Letter from Poe to Griswold; as Poe's literary executor Griswold edited this letter
and others to portray Poe in an unflattering light (Boston Public Library)*

with a story, "Von Kempelen and His Discovery." The story is in the nature of a hoax; it is told as a newspaper account implying that Von Kempelen has discovered a way of scientifically transmuting base metals into gold; Poe apparently thought to capitalize on the California "gold fever." "Eldorado" is similarly conceived on one level, but it deepens into one of Poe's most effective ironic poems. The gold seeker becomes a "gallant knight" who grows old searching for the mythic City of Gold, Eldorado. He asks directions from a shadow pilgrim, who tells him that the treasure is beyond the mountains of the moon and "Down the Valley of the Shadow." "Ride, boldly ride!" the shadow says, not fully in derision. The quest leads, as always, to death.

"For Annie" is a highly ambiguous poem about the fever called living, which is over at last–though whether for the speaker or for Annie or for both is unclear. The speaker lies calmly in what some might call a narrow bed; some might fancy him dead now that the throbbing, nausea, and agony are quiescent; he himself fancies he smells the odor of funeral flowers; but he dreams of the bright Annie, who bathes him with her hair and kisses him. Others may fancy him dead, but he still feels Annie's love. The blurring of subjective and objective, of life and death, of dream and reality, is obvious. The biographical reading of this poem is considerably strengthened by the fact that Poe sent it to Richmond in March. In May he went to visit her, ran out of money, and, in her presence, had a bank draft drawn against *Graham's* rejected.

In May and June two stories appeared in the *Flag.* "X-ing a Paragrab" is another comic piece on printing and magazine editing. One rival paper attacks another in a paragraph with too many *O*s. The other paper wishes to reply by making fun of its rival's style; but the printer discovers all his *O*s have been stolen; so he substitutes *X*s–so that they can hardly "bxw-wxw-wxw" back at the other paper. "Landor's Cottage" is subtitled "pendant" to "The Domain of Arnheim." Here the landscape gardening is all naturalized, so that Arnheim's glittering, bejeweled, semi-Gothic, semi-Saracenic architecture becomes a simple country cottage. In July a touching tribute to Maria Clemm appeared in the *Flag,* "Sonnet–To My Mother," in which the lady is said to be twice a mother, once to the speaker and once to his wife.

In mid spring Poe received a delayed letter from E. H. N. Patterson of Illinois that renewed his hopes of establishing his own literary magazine. Patterson had been given a paper by his father, and he offered Poe entire editorial control of the literary department if they could get a thousand advance subscriptions. Poe wrote that he was going on a lecture tour from New England to the South, and he asked Patterson for a $50 advance, to be sent to him in Richmond. At the end of June, Poe left

E U R E K A :

A   P R O S E   P O E M

BY

EDGAR A. POE.

NEW-YORK:
GEO. P. PUTNAM,
OF LATE FIRM OF "WILEY & PUTNAM,"
155 BROADWAY.
MDCCCXLVIII.

*Title page for Poe's last published work, a book-length philosophical speculation (Library of the University of Pennsylvania)*

Mrs. Clemm to go to Philadelphia. Nearly two weeks went by without a word from him; then a letter dated 7 July arrived. Poe wrote that he had been ill with "the cholera, or spasms quite as bad." He spoke of wanting to die with her, of having been subject to fits of insanity, and of having "been taken to prison once since I came here for getting drunk; but *then* I was not. It was about Virginia."

Later in the month Poe went to John Sartain's office and insisted on protection from two men who were out to kill him. He had been on his way home; but when he noticed his pursuers, he had gotten off the train and returned to Philadelphia to confuse them. He wanted Sartain to shave off his mustache for him so he would not be recognized. He told Sartain he had been in prison and had had a dream about a radiant female figure on top of a tower speaking to him across a great distance. Few can object strongly to the biographical reading of this event as referring to Virginia and the other idolized

*Daguerreotype of Poe taken in late September 1849, within a few weeks of his death ( from George Edward Woodberry,* The Life of Edgar Allan Poe, Personal and Literary, *1909)*

In this summer of 1849 Poe called on his childhood sweetheart, Sarah Elmira Royster Shelton, now a wealthy widow in her late thirties. In their talk they discovered that two decades ago John Allan had refused to promise her father that Poe would be his heir. Royster therefore had thought it a bad match with Poe and sent his daughter out of the city and intercepted Poe's letters. Poe now courted her all over again. Even while engaged in this pursuit, however, he wrote Mrs. Clemm not to tell him anything about Annie Richmond—"unless you can tell me that Mr. R. is dead." He added that after his marriage to Elmira he did not want to live in Richmond: "I want to live *near Annie.*"

In September he lectured in Norfolk, Virginia, returning on 17 September to Richmond. His paranoid feelings were returning. He wrote Mrs. Clemm not to sign her next letter, but to address it to "E. S. T. Grey, Esq.," of Philadelphia. He lectured again with success, although people were beginning to remark on his paleness and nervousness. One evening at the home of Susan Talley, after talking enthusiastically of his future, when Poe took his leave (according to Talley), "a brilliant meteor appeared in the sky directly over his head, and vanished in the east." Poe and his hosts laughed, and he disappeared into the darkness. The next night he told Elmira Royster that he had a feeling he would never see her again. He stayed up all night at a local tavern without taking a drink and at dawn rushed down to the dock to catch the steamboat for Baltimore.

A week later, during election time, he was found lying unconscious in Lombard Street near the Fourth Ward polling place. According to one tradition, apparently fabricated, Poe had been plied with liquor by an unscrupulous element of one of the political parties and taken from one polling place to another to vote over and over again. Another more recent suggestion is that he suffered a bite from a rabid animal, possibly a bat. This speculation, in view of what was probably an apoplectic stroke late in 1848 (shortly after his supposedly bungled suicide attempt with laudanum) and his generally deteriorated physical condition, seems rather fanciful. A compositor for the *Baltimore Sun* dragged Poe into Gunner's Tavern and sent a note to J. E. Snodgrass, an acquaintance of Poe's for fifteen years, and Henry Herring, who had been married to Poe's deceased aunt, Eliza. Both men came.

Poe's jacket was ripped at the seams, and the trousers looked as though they belonged to someone else. He seemed to Snodgrass not so much to be in a drunken stupor as in a delirium from some sort of fever. When a physician, John J. Moran, examined Poe, in the hospital tower room where the drunks were taken, he too thought Poe in a much worse state than a drunken stupor. Cousin Neilson Poe arrived. He commented on the

lost women of his life calling to him across the void of death. Poe, Sartain said, was afraid to be left alone or in the dark. Two days later he had sufficiently recovered to say that the whole business was a delusion; he told Sartain he had been arrested on suspicion of passing counterfeit money but had been recognized as a poet and released. Fact and fancy are impossible to sort out. Two friends, Chauncey Burr and George Lippard, saw that Poe got on a train for Baltimore. From Baltimore he headed "home" to Richmond, where his sister, Rosalie, and her foster parents, the Mackenzies, cared for him. He had been scheduled to lecture on poetry in Richmond, but his valise had mysteriously disappeared at the train station in Philadelphia. So he had to set about rewriting the entire text of "The Poetic Principle," he claimed. The lectures were successful, and Poe's spirits picked up. As a protective measure against his weakness for drink, he joined the Shockoe Hill Division of the Sons of Temperance. As in the summer before he was once again accepted into Richmond society, and there are testimonies to his quiet grace, charm, and kindness to children.

"weakness" of the "bad streak" in the family and left with a promise to send some clean linen. At 3:00 A.M. Poe came back to consciousness and muttered incoherently about a wife, Richmond or the Richmonds, and death.

Poe remained in a semicoma for three days. Saturday night he called out "Reynolds! Oh, Reynolds!" Then, Sunday at 3:00 A.M., 7 October 1849, Poe died, "of congestion of the brain"–a brain lesion of some sort, possibly the result of his stroke, possibly complicated by intestinal inflammation, a weak heart, and diabetes. One of the more-persuasive suggestions is that Poe suffered from a progressive form of diabetes that gradually came to cause a single glass of wine to send him into states of excitation or into a semistupor that appeared to contemporaries to be a drunken state. (The breath of a person in an insulin coma sometimes has a wine-sweet odor.) Although Poe had a drinking problem, the charge that he was a hopeless alcoholic is belied by the volume of editorial, analytic, and creative work he turned out day after day, year after year. It would be hard to write so much and edit magazines of such high quality and be drunk all day long. Tippler or not, manic depressive or not, Poe had what might be called a poetics of professionalism, to which he was dedicated.

Among the obituaries was one in the *New York Tribune,* signed "Ludwig." The article was unsympathetic and critical; worse, it distorted his character and life mercilessly. "Few will be grieved," Ludwig said, for Poe "had few or no friends." The mysterious Ludwig seemed to know Poe's life and writings well, despite his distortions; he was the man chosen to be Poe's literary executor, Rufus Wilmot Griswold. He prepared an edition of Poe's collected works as rapidly as possible and published portions of Poe's correspondence, not only with deletions, but also with additions of his own, mostly designed to make Poe look bad. Perhaps he had some grudge over Poe's hoaxing reviews of his anthology of the *Poets of America* years before, or perhaps he thought to sensationalize Poe's character in order to create sales. He is said also, for some inexplicable reason, to have destroyed many letters and papers.

Several authors, including Willis and Longfellow, tried to defend Poe's reputation–but to no avail. The Griswold, *Mirror,* and *Knickerbocker* version of Poe took hold and grew. Poe the on-again, off-again alcoholic became Poe the drug addict. Poe who tried to preserve a fragmented family became Poe the luster after little girls. Poe the fighting journalist became the hypocrite and backbiter, the untrustworthy self-serving pretender, the liar, and the madman. Doubtless it made good copy and good material for romanticized biography. Even Poe's last publications were a bit melodramatic. His death was followed almost immediately by publication of two of what came to be his best-loved poems, both dealing with

*Portrait of Poe used as the frontispiece for volume one of*
The Works of the Late Edgar Allan Poe,
*1850 (engraving by John Sartain)*

the final triumph of death: "Annabel Lee" (*Richmond Examiner* and the *New York Tribune*) and "The Bells" (*Sartain's Union,* November). "Annabel Lee" is yet another lament for the death of a beloved woman, a wife, a child bride. She was taken away, the lover says, by jealous angels who envied their earthly love. But the speaker defies the power of either heaven or hell to "dissever my soul from the soul / Of the beautiful Annabel Lee," and he lies down by her side in her tomb by the sounding sea. "The Bells," a tour de force in onomatopoeia, traces the progress of life through four major stages signaled by different bells: silvery sleigh bells of childhood, golden wedding bells of youth, brass "alarum" bells of adulthood, iron funeral bells of age. Each section is developed at one more increment, so that the derisive triumph of the ghouls of death is nearly four times the length of the first section. Both poems are highly incantatory. Poe left little in manuscript: the opening paragraphs of a tale called "The Lighthouse" and a nearly complete draft of a satire on himself, "A Reviewer Reviewed."

Poe was to have a remarkable influence on the rest of his century. The French poet Charles Baudelaire became obsessed with Poe as his own alter ego. He saw Poe as the *poète maudit,* the blighted (and even, conventionally, evil) poet of genius buried alive in a materialistic

*Poe's gravesite, Westminster Graveyard, Baltimore*

society of insensitive Philistines. He undertook a series of translations of Poe's prose. Some readers say that the somber works are better in Baudelaire's French than in Poe's English, though the internal nuances of bizarre humor are lost or muted. For Baudelaire, Poe was heroic and therefore quite the opposite of Griswold's version. Yet, reflecting Baudelaire's own tormented personality, his Poe was as eccentric as Griswold's. Thus, the negative and the positive images of Poe grew together into an uneasy and grotesque composite of Griswold/Baudelaire and Puritan America/Bohemian France. Even in death Poe was destined to be split in two within a paradoxical union. In the Art-for-Art's-Sake, Symbolist, and Surrealist movements at the end of the nineteenth century and the beginning of the twentieth, Poe was reconstructed into the image required. For Mallarmé he was a culture hero; for Valéry, a stunning skeptic.

The vogue of Poe in France has continued, with Poe's works holding special fascination for the structuralist, poststructuralist, and deconstructionist cliques of avant-garde criticism. In Russia his major influence was on Fyodor Dostoyevsky. In German and Scandinavian countries Poe's influence is relatively recent, and he is regarded generally as a writer caught between Romanticism and modernism. In Britain, and even in the United States, Poe presents a puzzle; the nuances of his style and the narrow obsessiveness of his focus on the death/life

paradox seem to put him outside the mainstream of the Anglo-American tradition, though his affinities with Charles Brockden Brown, Washington Irving, Nathaniel Hawthorne, and Herman Melville have come to be more widely acknowledged.

As a poet Poe developed a mode of dramatized interior monologue and a lyric incantatory style aimed at suggesting a visionary state of "supernal beauty" to be sought "out of space—out of time." He tried to achieve this dreamlike perception through precise manipulation of sound and rhythm by means of hypnotic repetition. Poe developed a poetics that sought to reconcile the material and mental medium of language as sensuous sound. At the same time that he sought a visionary spiritual beauty (tinged with loss and melancholy and glimpsed but indefinitely), he emphasized meticulous craftsmanship based on a preestablished pattern of total integration of all elements of a work.

As a practical critic of contemporary letters Poe exposed carelessness, fraud, and literary theft while recognizing the talent of a writer such as Hawthorne. As a practicing journalist he took a stand against the literary cliques that promoted inferior regional writing, especially those centered around the Northern periodicals. Poe defended not only the cause of Southern letters but also the American quest for literary independence from Europe. Yet, at the same time that he attacked slavish imitation of European models he opposed the excesses of the American literary nationalism that forced critics into the dilemma of liking a stupid book because its stupidity was American. Although deeply involved in the literary warfare of his times, Poe's driving force was to establish an eminent magazine of letters and culture freed from petty conflict, social prejudice, and the prevailing moral bias of the age. Regarding the latter, he even went so far as to formulate the "heresy of the didactic." An overriding moral concern in a work of art he said, was to be regarded as an offense against the ideals of art as Art.

It is Poe's achievement in the short story for which he is best remembered. As with poetry, he codified an affective theory of the short story that aimed at an almost subliminal effect through a carefully predesigned and unified pattern. He considered the opening word through every piece of punctuation and every sentence as important to the impact of the whole structure on the conscious and unconscious responses of the reader. He exemplified his theory in his practice, while experimenting with proto-science-fiction, visionary prose-poems, multileveled satire, and developing, if not outright inventing, the detective story. Simultaneously, he perfected the Gothic tale of terror, horror, and mystery. Poe is an acknowledged master of Gothic atmosphere, but he is equally the master of the interior monologue of a profoundly disturbed mind. His fictional dramatizations of mental turmoil operate on several levels, from gruesome physical shock, to spiritual anguish, to subtle manipulation of narrative point of view. The stories exhibit an architectural symmetry and proportion and careful integration of details of setting, plot, and character into an indivisible whole.

Poe's life and career were strongly marked by self-division. Yet, in theory and practice he is a major exponent of one version of the Romantic ideal of the organic wholeness of art. As a consequence of this aesthetic he ventured into philosophical Romantic cosmology. In his creative, critical, and philosophical writings his Romantic program was nothing less than to resolve all apparent contraries of the world into unity: the life and death impulses of existence; the apparent irradiation and collapse of a pulsating universe; the paradoxes of time and space, of matter and energy, of the rational and irrational; the seeming oppositions of the material and the immaterial, of the serious and the comic, of logic and imagination, of science and poetry. His works and his career are the brilliant record of that inconclusive quest. Throughout his career Edgar Allan Poe continued to seek the vocation of a poet but was derailed by such worldly concerns as earning a living. He brought to the profession of magazine editing, reviewing, and fiction writing the same idealism he brought to his preferred genre of poetry. In his role as a hardworking journalist,

*Poe monument, Westminster Graveyard, Baltimore*

literary critic, and theorist Poe redefined the chivalric ideal in terms of a committed professionalism—precisely what the antebellum South and the United States at large was calling for. Yet, he seems perfectly serious in his claims that with him poetry was the all-consuming passion and that he would have chosen to have pursued a literary career as a poet. The irony of this ambition is that Poe was not a first-rate poet, though he is historically interesting. He was, however, a first-rate editor and critic and a highly effective and innovative writer of fiction. His grotesque and Gothic fictions are world famous; his literary criticism was unequalled by any American of his day; and he was one of the great magazinists of the nineteenth century. In his own mind, he may have missed his true calling, but he found it anyway, somewhat lower on the slopes of his visionary Parnassus.

## Letters:

*Poe and His Friends: Letters Relating to Poe,* volume 18 of *The Complete Works of Edgar Allan Poe,* edited by James A. Harrison (New York: Crowell, 1902);

*The Letters of Edgar Allan Poe,* 2 volumes, edited by John Ward Ostrom (Cambridge, Mass.: Harvard University Press, 1948); republished with three supplements (New York: Gordian, 1966); fourth supplement, *American Literature,* 45 (January 1974): 513–536.

## Bibliographies:

John W. Robertson, *Bibliography of the Writings of Edgar A. Poe* and *Commentary on the Bibliography of Edgar A. Poe* (San Francisco: Russian Hill Private Press, Edwin & Robert Grabhorn, 1934);

William D. Hull, "A Canon of the Critical Works of Edgar Allan Poe with a Study of Edgar Allan Poe the Magazinist," dissertation, University of Virginia, 1941;

John Cook Wylie, "A List of the Texts of Poe's Tales," in *Humanistic Studies in Honor of John Calvin Metcalf* (New York: Columbia University Press, 1941), pp. 322–338;

Charles F. Heartman and James R. Canny, *A Bibliography of First Printings of the Writings of Edgar Allan Poe,* revised edition (Hattiesburg, Miss.: Book Farm, 1943);

Haldeen Braddy, *Glorious Incense: The Fulfillment of Edgar Allan Poe* (New York: Scarecrow Press, 1953);

Jay B. Hubbell, "Poe," in *Eight American Authors: A Review of Research and Criticism,* edited by Floyd Stovall (New York: Modern Language Association, 1956), pp. 1–46;

William B. Todd, "The Early Issues of Poe's Tales (1845)," *Library Chronicle of the University of Texas,* 7 (Fall 1961): 13–17;

G. Thomas Tanselle, "The State of Poe Bibliography," *Poe Newsletter,* 2 (January 1969): 1–3;

Hubbell, "Poe," in *Eight American Authors: A Review of Research and Criticism,* revised edition, edited by James Woodress (New York: Norton, 1971), pp. 3–36;

J. Lasley Dameron, "Thomas Ollive Mabbott on the Canon of Poe's Reviews," *Poe Studies,* 5 (December 1972): 56–57;

Esther K. Hyneman, *Edgar Allan Poe: An Annotated Bibliography of Books and Articles in English, 1827–1973* (Boston: Hall, 1974);

Dameron and Irby B. Cauthen Jr., *Edgar Allan Poe: A Bibliography of Criticism 1827–1967* (Charlottesville: University Press of Virginia, 1974);

Pollin, "Poe 'Viewed and Reviewed': An Annotated Checklist of Contemporary Notices," *Poe Studies,* 13 (December 1980): 17–28;

John Ward Ostrum, "Revised Check List of the Correspondence of Edgar Allan Poe," *Studies in the American Renaissance 1981,* edited by Joel Myerson (Boston: Twayne, 1981), pp. 169–255;

Kent P. Ljunquist, "Poe," *Prospects for the Study of American Literature,* edited by Richard Kaplan (New York: New York University Press, 1997), pp. 39–57.

## Biographies:

Rufus Wilmot Griswold, "Memoir of the Author," in *The Works of the Late Edgar Allan Poe* (New York: Redfield, 1850), III: vii–xxxix;

Sarah Helen Whitman, *Edgar Poe and His Critics* (New York: Rudd & Carleton, 1860);

William Fearing Gill, *The Life of Edgar Allan Poe* (New York: Dillingham, 1877);

John H. Ingram, *Edgar Allan Poe: His Life, Letters and Opinions,* 2 volumes (London: John Hogg, 1880);

George Edward Woodberry, *The Life of Edgar Allan Poe, Personal and Literary,* 2 volumes (Boston: Houghton, Mifflin, 1909);

Hervey Allen, *Israfel: The Life and Times of Edgar Allan Poe,* 2 volumes (New York: Doran, 1926);

Joseph Wood Krutch, *Edgar Allan Poe: A Study in Genius* (New York: Knopf, 1926);

Mary E. Phillips, *Edgar Allan Poe, the Man,* 2 volumes (Chicago: John C. Winston, 1926);

Una Pope-Hennessy, *Edgar Allan Poe, 1809–1849: A Critical Biography* (London: Macmillan, 1934);

Arthur Hobson Quinn, *Edgar Allan Poe: A Critical Biography* (New York: Appleton-Century, 1941);

Marie Bonaparte, *The Life and Works of Edgar Allan Poe: A Psycho-analytic Interpretation,* translated by John Rodker (London: Imago, 1949);

Perry Miller, *The Raven and the Whale: The War of Words and Wits in the Era of Poe and Melville* (New York: Harcourt, Brace, 1956);

Frances Winwar, *The Haunted Palace: A Life of Edgar Allan Poe* (New York: Harper, 1959);

William Bittner, *Poe: A Biography* (Boston: Little, Brown, 1962);

Edward Wagenknecht, *Edgar Allan Poe: The Man Behind the Legend* (New York: Oxford University Press, 1963);

Sidney P. Moss, *Poe's Literary Battles: The Critic in the Context of His Literary Milieu* (Durham, N.C.: Duke University Press, 1963);

John Evangelist Walsh, *Poe the Detective: The Curious Circumstances behind "The Mystery of Marie Roget"* (New Brunswick, N.J.: Rutgers University Press, 1967);

Moss, *Poe's Major Crisis: His Libel Suit and New York's Literary World* (Durham, N.C.: Duke University Press, 1970);

John C. Miller, *Building Poe Biography* (Baton Rouge: Louisiana State University Press, 1977);

Wolf Mankowitz, *The Extraordinary Mr. Poe* (New York: Simon & Schuster, 1978);

Julian Symons, *The Tell-Tale Heart: The Life and Works of Edgar Allan Poe* (New York: Harper & Row, 1978);

Dwight R. Thomas, "Poe in Philadelphia, 1838–1844: A Documentary Record," dissertation, University of Pennsylvania, 1978;

John Carl Miller, ed., *Poe's Helen Remembers* (Charlottesville: University Press of Virginia, 1979);

David K. Jackson and Dwight Thomas, *The Poe Log: A Documentary Life of Edgar Allan Poe, 1809–1849* (Boston: Hall, 1987);

David Ketterer, *Edgar Allan Poe: Life, Work, and Criticism* (Fredericton, New Brunswick: York, 1989);

Michael J. Deas, *The Portraits and Daguerreotypes of Edgar Allan Poe* (Charlottesville: University of Virginia Press, 1989);

Kenneth Silverman, *Edgar A. Poe: Mournful and Never-ending Remembrance* (New York: HarperCollins, 1991);

Jeffrey Meyers, *Edgar Allan Poe: His Life and Legacy* (New York: Scribners, 1992);

J. R. Hammond, *An Edgar Allan Poe Chronology* (New York: Macmillan, 1998);

Walsh, *Midnight Dreary: The Mysterious Death of Edgar Allan Poe* (New Brunswick, N.J.: Rutgers University Press, 1998).

**References:**

Jean Alexander, ed., *Affidavits of Genius. Edgar Allan Poe and the French Critics, 1847–1924* (Port Washington, N.Y.: Kennikat Press, 1971);

Michael Allen, *Poe and the British Magazine Tradition* (New York: Oxford University Press, 1969);

Margaret Alterton, *The Origins of Poe's Critical Theory* (Iowa City: University of Iowa, 1925);

Carl L. Anderson, *Poe in Northlight: The Scandinavian Response to His Life and Work* (Durham, N.C.: Duke University Press, 1973);

Charles Baudelaire, *Baudelaire on Poe: Critical Papers,* edited by Lois and Francis Hyslop (State College, Pa.: Bald Eagle, 1952);

Baudelaire, *Edgar Allan Poe, sa vie et ses ouvrages,* edited by W. T. Bandy (Toronto: University of Toronto Press, 1973);

Richard P. Benton, ed., *New Approaches to Poe: A Symposium* (Hartford, Conn.: Transcendental Books, 1970);

Benton, ed., *Poe as Literary Cosmologer: Studies on Eureka. A Symposium* (Hartford, Conn.: Transcendental Books, 1975);

Clive Bloom, *Reading Poe, Reading Freud: The Romantic Imagination in Crisis* (New York: St. Martin's Press, 1988);

Bradford A. Booth and Claude E. Jones, *A Concordance to the Poetical Works of Edgar Allan Poe* (Baltimore: Johns Hopkins Press, 1941);

Vincent Buranelli, *Edgar Allan Poe* (Boston: Twayne, 1961; revised edition, 1977);

Michael L. Burduck, *Grim Phantasms: Fear in Poe's Fiction* (New York: Garland, 1992);

Célestin Cambiaire, *The Influence of Edgar Allan Poe in France* (New York: Stechert, 1927);

Killis Campbell, *The Mind of Poe and Other Studies* (Cambridge, Mass.: Harvard University Press, 1933);

Eric W. Carlson, ed., *A Companion to Poe Studies* (Westport, Conn.: Greenwood Press, 1996);

Carlson, ed., *Critical Essays on Poe* (Boston: Hall, 1987);

Carlson, ed., *The Recognition of Edgar Allan Poe: Selected Criticism since 1829* (Ann Arbor: University of Michigan Press, 1966);

Graham Clarke, ed., *Edgar Allan Poe: Critical Assessment,* 4 volumes (London: Routledge, 1992);

J. Lasley Dameron and Louis Charles Stagg, *An Index to Poe's Critical Vocabulary* (Hartford, Conn.: Transcendental Books, 1966);

Edward H. Davidson, *Poe: A Critical Study* (Cambridge, Mass.: Harvard University Press, 1957);

Joan Dayan, *Fables of Mind: An Inquiry into Poe's Fiction* (New York: Oxford University Press, 1987);

Jeffrey DeShell, *The Peculiarity of Literature: An Allegorical Approach to Poe's Fiction* (Madison, N.J.: Fairleigh Dickinson University Press / London & Cranbury, N.J.: Associated University Presses, 1997);

Dennis W. Eddings, ed., *The Naiad Voice: Essays on Poe's Satiric Hoaxing* (Port Washington, N.Y.: Associated Faculty Press, 1983);

Jonathan Elmer, *Reading at the Social Limit: Affect, Mass Culture, and Edgar Allan Poe* (Stanford, Cal.: Stanford University Press, 1995);

N. Bryllion Fagin, *The Histrionic Mr. Poe* (Baltimore: Johns Hopkins Press, 1949);

Benjamin Franklin Fisher IV, ed., *Poe and His Times: The Artist and His Milieu* (Baltimore: Edgar Allan Poe Society, 1990);

Fisher, ed., *Poe and Our Times: Influences and Affinities* (Baltimore: Edgar Allan Poe Society, 1986);

Fisher, ed., *Poe at Work: Seven Textual Studies* (Baltimore: Edgar Allan Poe Society, 1978);

Richard M. Fletcher, *The Stylistic Development of Edgar Allan Poe* (The Hague: Mouton, 1973);

Roger Forclaz, *Le Monde d'Edgar Poe* (Berne: Herbert Lang / Frankfurt: Peter Lang, 1974);

Frederick R. Frank and Anthony Magistrale, eds., *The Poe Encyclopedia* (Westport, Conn.: Greenwood Press, 1997);

John Phelps Fruit, *The Mind and Art of Poe's Poetry* (New York: Barnes, 1899);

David Halliburton, *Edgar Allan Poe: A Phenomenological View* (Princeton: Princeton University Press, 1973);

J. R. Hammond, *An Edgar Allan Poe Companion: A Guide to the Short Stories, Romances and Essays* (London: Macmillan, 1981);

Thomas Hansen with Burton R. Pollin, *The German Face of Edgar Allan Poe* (Columbia, S.C.: Camden House, 1995);

Ronald Harvey, *The Critical History of Edgar Allan Poe's "The Narrative of Arthur Gordon Pym": A Dialogue with Unreason* (New York: Garland, 1998);

Daniel Hoffman, *Poe Poe Poe Poe Poe Poe Poe* (Garden City, N.Y.: Doubleday, 1972);

John T. Irwin, *American Hieroglyphics: The Symbol of Egyptian Hieroglyphics in the American Renaissance* (Baltimore: Johns Hopkins University Press, 1980), pp. 41–235;

Irwin, *The Mystery to a Solution: Poe, Borges, and the Analytic Detective Story* (Baltimore: Johns Hopkins University Press, 1994);

Robert D. Jacobs, *Poe: Journalist & Critic* (Baton Rouge: Louisiana State University Press, 1969);

J. Gerald Kennedy, ed., *A Historical Guide to Edgar Allan Poe* (New York: Oxford University Press, 2001);

Kennedy, *"The Narrative of Arthur Gordon Pym" and the Abyss of Interpretation* (New York: Twayne, 1995);

Kennedy, *Poe, Death, and the Life of Writing* (New Haven: Yale University Press, 1987);

Kennedy and Liliane Weissberg, eds., *Romancing the Shadow: Poe and Race* (New York: Oxford University Press, 2001);

David Ketterer, *The Rationale of Deception in Poe* (Baton Rouge: Louisiana State University Press, 1979);

Richard Kopley, ed., *Poe's "Pym": Critical Explorations* (Durham, N.C.: Duke University Press, 1992);

A. Robert Lee, *Edgar A. Poe: The Design of Order* (New York: Barnes & Noble, 1987);

Harry Levin, *The Power of Blackness: Hawthorne, Poe, Melville* (New York: Knopf, 1958);

Stuart G. Levine, *Edgar Poe: Seer and Craftsman* (Deland, Fla.: Everett/Edwards, 1972);

Franz H. Link, *Edgar Allan Poe: Ein Dichter zwischen Romantik und Moderne* (Frankfurt am Main: Athenaum Verlag, 1968);

Kent Ljungquist, *The Grand and the Fair: Poe's Landscape Aesthetics and Pictorial Techniques* (Potomac, Md.: Scripta Humanistica, 1984);

Charles May, *Edgar Allan Poe: A Study of the Short Fiction* (Boston: Twayne, 1991);

John P. Muller and William J. Richardson, eds., *The Purloined Poe: Lacan, Derrida, and Psychoanalytic Reading* (Baltimore: Johns Hopkins University Press, 1988);

Edd Winfield Parks, *Edgar Allan Poe as a Literary Critic* (Athens: University of Georgia Press, 1964);

Scott Peeples, *Edgar Allan Poe Revisited* (New York: Twayne, 1998);

Elizabeth Philips, *Edgar Allan Poe, An American Imagination: Three Essays* (Port Washington, N.Y.: Kennikat Press, 1979);

Pollin, *Dictionary of Names and Titles in Poe's Collected Works* (New York: Da Capo, 1968);

Pollin, *Discoveries in Poe* (Notre Dame: University of Notre Dame Press, 1970);

Pollin, *Word Index to Poe's Fiction* (New York: Gordian, 1982);

Pollin, comp., *Images of Poe's Works: A Comprehensive Descriptive Catalogue of Illustrations* (New York: Greenwood Press, 1989);

Patrick F. Quinn, *The French Face of Edgar Poe* (Carbondale: Southern Illinois University Press, 1957);

D. Ramakrishna, ed., *Perspectives on Poe* (New Delhi: APC, 1996);

Geoffrey Rans, *Edgar Allan Poe* (Edinburgh & London: Oliver & Boyd, 1965);

Arthur Ransome, *Edgar Allan Poe: A Critical Study* (London: Stephen Swift, 1912);

Claude Richard, *Edgar Allan Poe écrivain,* edited by Henri Justin (Montpellier: Delta, 1990);

Richard, *Edgar Allan Poe journalise et critique* (Paris: Klincksieck, 1978);

Richard, ed., *Edgar Allan Poe* (Paris: Edition de l'Herne, 1974);

Shawn Rosenheim, *The Cryptographic Imagination: Secret Writing from Edgar Poe to the Internet* (Baltimore: Johns Hopkins University Press, 1997);

Rosenheim and Stephen Rachman, eds., *The American Face of Edgar Poe* (Baltimore: Johns Hopkins University Press, 1995);

David R. Saliba, *The Psychology of Fear: The Nightmare Formula of Edgar Allan Poe* (New York: McGraw-Hill, 1971);

Kenneth Silverman, ed., *New Essays on Poe's Major Tales* (New York: Cambridge University Press, 1993);

Don G. Smith, *The Poe Cinema: A Critical Filmography of Theatrical Releases Based on the Works of Edgar Allan Poe* (Jefferson, N.C.: McFarland, 1999);

Floyd Stovall, *Edgar Poe the Poet: Essays Old and New on the Man and His Work* (Charlottesville: University Press of Virginia, 1969);

G. R. Thompson, *Poe's Fiction: Romantic Irony in the Gothic Tales* (Madison: University of Wisconsin Press, 1973);

Thompson and Virgil L. Lokke, eds., *Ruined Eden of the Present: Hawthorne, Melville, Poe* (West Lafayette, Ind.: Purdue University Press, 1981), pp. 283–374;

Richard P. Veler, ed., *Papers on Poe: Essays in Honor of John Ward Ostrom* (Springfield, Ohio: Chantry Music Press at Wittenberg University, 1972);

Lois Davis Vines, *Poe Abroad: Influence, Reputation, Affinities* (Iowa City: University of Iowa Press, 1999);

I. M. Walker, ed., *Edgar Allan Poe: The Critical Heritage* (London: Routledge, 1986);

Terence Whalen, *Poe and the Masses: The Political Economy of Literature in Antebellum America* (Princeton: Princeton University Press, 1999);

Richard Wilbur, "The House of Poe," in *Anniversary Lectures 1959* (Washington, D.C.: Reference Department of the Library of Congress, 1959), pp. 21–38;

Wilbur, "Introduction" and "Notes" to *Poe,* The Laurel Poetry Series (New York: Dell, 1959);

Elizabeth Wiley, *Concordance to the Poetry of Edgar Allan Poe* (Selinsgrove, Pa.: Susquehanna University Press, 1989);

Michael J. S. Williams, *A World of Words: Language and Displacement in the Fiction of Edgar Allan Poe* (Durham, N.C.: Duke University Press, 1988).

**Papers:**

Significant collections of Edgar Allan Poe's papers are located at the University of Texas (M. L. Stark Library and Humanities Research Center–the Koerster Collection); Pierpont Morgan Library, New York; Free Library of Philadelphia (the Richard Gimbel Collection); Henry E. Huntington Library and Art Gallery, San Marino, California; Indiana University (Lilly Collection); New York Public Library (Manuscript Division and the Berg Collection); University of Virginia (Ingram Collection); Enoch Pratt Free Library, Baltimore; Poe Foundation, Richmond (State Library of Virginia); Boston Public Library (Griswold Papers); Library of Congress (Ellis and Allan Papers); Columbia University Libraries; Duke University Library (Whitty Collection); Yale University, Beinecke Rare Book and Manuscript Library; also the private collection of H. Bradley Martin, New York City, which can be viewed in the Pierpont Morgan Library.

# Margaret Junkin Preston

*(19 May 1820 – 28 March 1897)*

Kim Ingram Jameson
*University of Central Oklahoma*

See also the Preston entry in *DLB 239: American Women Prose Writers: 1820–1870*.

BOOKS: *Silverwood: A Book of Memories* (New York: Derby & Jackson, 1856);

*Dirge for Ashby* (N.p., 1862?);

*Beechenbrook; A Rhyme of the War* (Richmond: Randolph, 1865; revised, Baltimore: Kelly & Piet, 1867);

*The Young Ruler's Question* (Philadelphia: Presbyterian Board of Publication, 1869);

*Old Song and New* (Philadelphia: Lippincott, 1870);

*Cartoons* (Boston: Roberts Brothers, 1875; revised, 1881);

*Epithalamium, 1878. October 10th* (Lexington, Va., 1878?);

*Centennial Poem for Washington and Lee University, Lexington, Virginia, 1775–1885* (New York & London: Putnam, 1885);

*A Handful of Monographs, Continental and English* (New York: Randolph, 1886);

*For Love's Sake; Poems of Faith and Comfort* (New York: Randolph, 1886);

*Colonial Ballads, Sonnets, and Other Verse* (Boston & New York: Houghton, Mifflin, 1887);

*Chimes for Church-Children* (Philadelphia: Presbyterian Board of Publication and Sabbath-school Work, 1889);

*Semi-Centennial Ode for the Virginia Military Institute, Lexington, Virginia, 1839–1889* (New York & London: Putnam, 1889);

*Aunt Dorothy; An Old Virginia Plantation-Story* (New York: Randolph, 1890);

*Leonardo's Bird-Cages* (Lexington, Va., n.d.).

OTHER: "How Beautiful the Flowers Are," in *The Two Cousins, or, How to Be Loved,* by Francis Channing Woodworth as Theodore Thinker (New York: Clark, Austin & Smith, 1853), pp. 77–79.

SELECTED PERIODICAL PUBLICATIONS–
UNCOLLECTED: "Last Meeting of Pocahontas and the Great Captain," *Harper's,* 66 (1883): 281;

"Personal Reminiscences of Stonewall Jackson," *Century,* 50 (October 1886): 927–936;

*Margaret J. Preston*

"General Lee after the War," *Century,* 38 (June 1889): 271–276;

"Phryne's Test," *Atlantic Monthly,* 64 (1889): 314.

Margaret Junkin Preston was highly respected by her peers as a woman of notable literary talent and sensitivity toward others. Although Preston wrote prose, poetry, sonnets, ballads, and travel sketches, she was best known for her verse. Being closely connected to the military and military life through her husband and brother-in-law, Preston's work reflects events and feelings emphasizing a period beginning immediately prior to the Civil War and following the war to its close. She successfully conveys in her writing the emotions that she encountered in dealing with the hardships and losses inflicted upon her and her family during the war, including the loss of siblings and parents to death and political differences.

Born in Philadelphia, Pennsylvania, to one of the most distinguished educators and Presbyterian clergymen of his day, Reverend George Junkin, and Julia Rush (Miller) Junkin, Margaret Junkin's childhood years were inundated by education. When her parents married on 1 June 1819, her father was a minister of the Associate Reformed Church but soon moved to Milton, Pennsylvania, to take charge of the parish. His clerical and educational career developed swiftly. George Junkin served as the principal of the Manual Labor Academy of Pennsylvania at Germantown in 1830–1831; as first president of Lafayette College at Easton, Pennsylvania, from 1832 to 1840 and again from 1845 to 1848; as president of Miami University at Oxford, Ohio, from 1841 to 1844; and as president of Washington College (later Washington and Lee University) at Lexington, Virginia, from 1848 until the outbreak of the war, at which time he returned to Pennsylvania.

George Junkin's deeply devoted interest in the positive benefits of early and earnest learning resulted in an extensive educational background for his daughter, encompassing Latin, Greek, Hebrew, English literature, and theology. Margaret Junkin, affectionately called Maggie by her father, was the firstborn and favorite of his eight children. Because of his limited time away from his busy career, she would "rise at five o'clock in the morning to read the classics with her father." She was learning the Hebrew alphabet at the age of three years; she read Latin at age ten and Greek at twelve, as well as continuing her reading of the classics. This extensive literary exposure during her formative years cemented her lifetime involvement with literature.

Junkin began publishing verse and short stories in magazines and newspapers while still residing in her father's home. Unmarried at age twenty-eight, she relocated with her father and family to Lexington, Virginia, where she continued caring for the household. In 1856, at the age of thirty-six, she published anonymously her first book, *Silverwood: A Book of Memories*. Despite offers of additional payments by her New York publisher, Derby and Jackson, Junkin refused to allow her name to be published on her novel. *Silverwood* tells a simple story of Southern life, imparting to young women readers the "lesson of resignation"—one that was often difficult to accept and adhere to by Junkin and her peers. Although somewhat autobio-graphical, *Silverwood* follows the pattern of the domestic and sentimental novels popular at the time.

Junkin's excessive devotion to the pleasurable pursuits of reading and writing and the necessary task of sewing, combined with the lingering effects of a childhood illness, caused serious damage to her vision. She refused to allow this physical impairment to deter her, however, and instead used a writing device created for the blind or recruited someone to write for her when her sight interfered with her pursuits. Although Junkin never ceased to write, she eventually selected the customary path of marriage and motherhood and permitted nearly a decade to pass before her second book was published.

When Junkin married Major John T. L. Preston on 3 August 1857, she immediately accepted the role of a professor's wife and mother of seven children ranging in age from five years to twenty-two. Major Preston was a professor of Latin at the Virginia Military Institute in Lexington and later served as adjutant general on the staff of his brother-in-law, General Thomas "Stonewall" Jackson. Junkin's sister Eleanor married Jackson when he was a professor of mathematics at the Virginia Military Institute. Prior to the outbreak of the war, Preston and her husband had two children of their own, George Junkin and Herbert Rush. With a combined total of nine children Preston had little time to devote to writing and literature. Her marriage and associations developed while residing among this military establishment determined her loyalties during the war and influenced the sentiments reflected in her writing. Despite Preston's upbringing in the North, Eleanor's death merely a year after her marriage to Jackson, her father's return to Pennsylvania, and a brother's enlistment in the Union Army, Preston remained loyal to her husband, the South, and the Confederacy.

Although Preston recorded in her diary the anguish resulting from the split in her family caused by the war, these sentiments were not the topic of her wartime poetry. The war resulted in her husband being away from home for long periods of time and Preston spending years maintaining a home and raising their children alone. She wrote *Beechenbrook; A Rhyme of the War* "by firelight during the evenings of one week" late in the war. The first edition, published in Richmond in 1865, was printed on poor paper because of war shortages, and when the city was evacuated a short time later "nearly the whole edition was burned." Just as her first book expresses personal sentiments that paralleled her life, *Beechenbrook* portrays "the suffering and heroism of a Southern wife whose husband dies while fighting for the Confederacy." Preston drew on her early theological

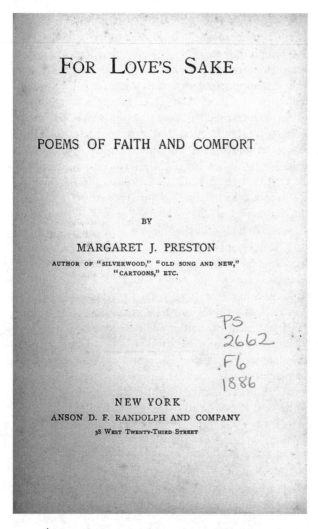

FOR LOVE'S SAKE

POEMS OF FAITH AND COMFORT

BY

MARGARET J. PRESTON

AUTHOR OF "SILVERWOOD," "OLD SONG AND NEW,"
"CARTOONS," ETC.

NEW YORK

ANSON D. F. RANDOLPH AND COMPANY

38 WEST TWENTY-THIRD STREET

*Title page for Preston's collection of theologically based verse
(Thomas Cooper Library, University of South Carolina)*

and classical training, filling the poem with an abundance of biblical imagery and classical allusions. The story "centered on love, duty, and sacrifice for family and state"—sacrifices that Preston knew well. In 1866 and 1867 the volume was republished in Baltimore and drew great interest throughout the South.

In 1870 Preston published *Old Song and New*, a collection of "poems from Hebrew and Greek story, and verses on a variety of subjects." The volume deals with familiar subjects from the author's childhood. Although her verse was widely popular, Preston was not deceived as to its quality. In a letter to Charleston poet Paul Hamilton Hayne, she spoke of her writing as being composed "amid a 'thousand petty house-wifely distractions.'" After spending five more years stealing moments away from the daily rigors of caring for her home and children to write verse, Preston eventually published *Cartoons* in 1875.

Preston again described her talent as a writer as one among many: "one cricket chirping in the grass." The verse in *Cartoons* deals with familiar subjects of the time: nature, history, war, and a woman's life.

The *New York Evening Post* characterized her poetry as belonging "to the school of Mrs. Browning" and stated: "No American woman has evinced a truer appreciation of what a poet owes to the art of poetry . . . from the most unstudied expression of susceptibility to the beautiful in the external world, and to the dramatic presentation of ideal and historic characters they touch the whole circle of art." While Preston's poetry was by her own admission common, it was that ordinariness that attracted her loyal readers. She wrote of a life and subjects with which her audience could identify.

When the war ended, Preston's husband returned to Lexington and his teaching. As Preston accustomed herself again to the daily duties of a busy academician's wife, the publication of her work nearly ceased. Not until after her husband's retirement did she again seek an outlet for writing. She traveled to Europe in 1884 with her husband and other members of her family and in 1886 completed a book of travel sketches, *A Handful of Monographs, Continental and English,* reflecting her experiences abroad. With John Preston's retirement, the couple devoted their summers to staying in Baltimore with one of their daughters and maintained contact with those formerly attached to the Confederacy.

As a result of a less restrictive schedule and diminished household duties, Preston again began writing for publication. Through her direct knowledge of former high-ranking officers of the Confederacy such as Jackson and Robert E. Lee, she wrote articles for magazines in which she commended these soldiers' efforts. "Personal Reminiscences of Stonewall Jackson" and "General Lee after the War" appeared in *Century Magazine* in October 1886 and June 1889. She was also honored as poet laureate of the two institutions of higher learning in Lexington, Washington and Lee and the Virginia Military Institute, for her commemorative odes to the schools.

Preston's later works are informed by her experiences and knowledge gained from a lifetime devoted to learning and helping others. *For Love's Sake; Poems of Faith and Comfort* (1886), a collection based on the theology she had learned as a child from her father, was described as being "full of spiritual insight and a religious feeling without cant or affectation." In 1887 she published a collection of her verses pertaining to early American life, *Colonial Ballads, Sonnets, and Other Verse,* that also demonstrates her gift for striking imagery. *Aunt Dorothy; An Old Vir-*

*ginia Plantation-Story* (1890) again draws on Preston's childhood memories and details the life of a Southerner. In this last work, which includes "comic scenes, the somewhat ambitious structure, and the mixture of black dialect with artificial and formal white speech," Preston appears to be attempting to challenge her literary abilities.

Although Margaret Junkin Preston's daily routines did not afford her the time to devote herself to her writing, her literary talents remained highly respected by her peers. During her later years she participated in the effort to sustain and advance Southern literature by offering her editing skills to many writers. Preston devoted herself to others and in return received the admiration and respect of all who knew or knew of her. Hayne considered Preston one of the best writers of sonnets in the United States and asked that she write the biographical sketch for the 1882 edition of his collected poems. When Preston died on 28 March 1897, two years after her husband's death, the South lost one of its most resolute patrons.

**Biographies:**

Elizabeth Preston Allen, *The Life and Letters of Margaret Junkin Preston* (Boston & New York: Houghton, Mifflin, 1903);

Rose Elizabeth Williams, "Margaret Junkin Preston, Poetess of Virginia," M.A. thesis, Duke University, Durham, N.C., 1940;

Mary Price Coulling, *Margaret Junkin Preston: A Biography* (Winston-Salem, N.C.: Blair, 1993).

**References:**

Jay B. Hubbell, *The South in American Literature, 1607–1900* (Durham, N.C.: Duke University Press, 1954), pp. 617–621;

Joyce B. MacAllister, "Margaret Junkin Preston: A Biography by Mary Price Coulling," *Virginia Magazine of History and Biography,* 102 (April 1994): 281–282;

Rayburn S. Moore, "'Courtesies of the Guild and More': Paul Hamilton Hayne and Margaret Junkin Preston," *Mississippi Quarterly,* 43 (Fall 1990): 485–493;

John Mackay Shaw, comp., *Childhood in Poetry: A Catalogue, with Biographical and Critical Annotations, of the Books of English and American Poets Comprising the Shaw Childhood in Poetry Collection in the Library of the Florida State University,* 5 volumes (Detroit: Gale, 1967–1968), II: 1186.

**Papers:**

The William R. Perkins Library, Duke University, holds in archive Preston's correspondence with Paul Hamilton Hayne.

# Anne Newport Royall

*(11 June 1769 – 1 October 1854)*

Margaret B. Moore

See also the Royall entry in *DLB 43: American Newspaper Journalists, 1690–1872.*

BOOKS: *Sketches of History, Life, and Manners in the United States by a Traveler,* anonymous (New Haven: Printed for the Author, 1826);

*The Tennessean; A Novel, Founded on Facts* (New Haven: Printed for the Author, 1827);

*The Black Book; or, a Continuation of Travels, in the United States,* 3 volumes (Washington, D.C.: Printed for the Author, 1828–1829);

*Mrs. Royall's Pennsylvania; or Travels Continued in the United States,* 2 volumes (Washington, D.C.: Printed for the Author, 1829);

*Mrs. Royall's Southern Tour, or, Second Series of the Black Book,* 3 volumes (Washington, D.C.: Printed for the Author, 1830–1831);

*Letters from Alabama on Various Subjects: to Which Is Added, an Appendix, Containing Remarks on Sundry Members of the 20th and 21st Congress, and Other High Characters, &c., &c. at the Seat of Government* (Washington, D.C.: Printed for the Author, 1830); republished, Southern Historical Publications No. 14, with notes and introduction by Lucille Griffith (University: University of Alabama Press, 1969).

PLAY PRODUCTION: *The Cabinet, or Large Parties in Washington,* Washington, D.C., Masonic Hall, 5, 12 March 1833.

OTHER: *Paul Pry,* edited by Royall (1831–1836); *The Huntress,* edited by Royall (1836–1854).

Anne Newport Royall, although largely forgotten, was well known in the first half of the nineteenth century as a writer of ten volumes of travel sketches and a novel and as a "holy terror" to those who crossed her. She was indicted and convicted of being a "common scold" in the summer of 1829. She took on all whom she felt were guilty of corruption in the national capital. She was adamant against the evangelical Presbyterians, who were, she thought, engaged in a giant conspiracy to make a church-state party that would run the country. She was against the banking interests and spoke out fearlessly against all who did not represent the sovereign people. She was caustic and biting, and her works, with all their faults, resonate as the productions of an authentic female voice.

Born near Baltimore on 11 June 1769, Anne was the daughter of William and Mary Newport, who moved to the frontier in Pennsylvania before the Revolutionary War. Her father taught her to read, but he died or disappeared when she was a young child. Her mother then married Patrick Butler, who died soon after. After an Indian attack on Hanna's Town and fort in July 1782, Anne, her mother, and her younger brother, James Butler, escaped to Virginia in late summer 1782. Her mother was hired as a housekeeper by William Royall, who was originally from the Tidewater region but had moved to Western Virginia, and built a large house on Peter's Mountain near Sweet Springs, one of the oldest of the springs that made Western Virginia famous.

Anne received an extensive education in Royall's personal library and from his ideas about the Enlightenment and freemasonry. After ten or so years she married the much older Royall; he died in 1812, leaving her his estate. The Royall relatives contested the will, and though it was upheld in 1817, they appealed. While waiting for a new trial, Royall set off for Alabama, and from there she wrote letters to a young friend, Matthew Dunbar, about her experiences. In 1822, however, William Royall's will was finally broken by members of his family, who accused his wife of being his concubine and of mistreating him. Royall was left penniless at the age of fifty-four.

As she journeyed back to Virginia, she noted the Scotch-Irish idiom in what is now West Virginia, reflecting the patterns of speech of the original settlers. This interest in language is present in all her works. With the help of Dunbar, a lawyer, she decided to go to Richmond to apply for the pension due Revolutionary War widows. No records of her husband's service could be found, despite his friendship with George Washington and the Marquis de Lafayette. She traveled to Washington, D.C., with the aid of Mason associates but had no luck there. She did have the support of John Quincy Adams, who petitioned for her pension for twenty-four years.

One of the frequently told stories about Royall concerns Adams. It has been said that she knew that he bathed nude in the Potomac in the mornings. She discovered the place and sat on his clothes on the bank until he agreed to be interviewed. The story is not true, but the Adamses did help her. When the pension was not immediately forthcoming, Royall decided to travel and to write about her excursions, selling her books, as did Parson Weems, along the way. Adams's wife, Louisa, when she saw Royall's thin coat, retrieved her own cloak and gave it to her for the trip.

Royall wrote ten travel books (counting each volume separately) in which she described with vivid detail places, people, and events. In her travels she always relied on the Masonic associations she had made through her husband. She tended to write kind descriptions of those who assisted her and the opposite of those who did not. She had strong convictions about everything, but none as strong as her belief that Presbyterian "blackcoats" were, in her opinion, trying to take over the country. She was often outrageous in her comments. Her style is breathless; her punctuation is erratic and her spelling amiss, but her meaning is clear.

Her first published book, and probably her best, is *Sketches of History, Life, and Manners in the United States by a Traveler* (1826). She began her tour in Richmond and Fredericksburg. With no luck there, she spent some time in Washington interviewing people and seeing sights. She wrote of John Randolph in the Senate with his hunting dog at his feet, his eyes blazing as he spoke; of the kindness of Adams and his wife; of Lafayette, who wrote for her a laudatory note about her husband's military service. She left Washington in the fall of 1824 and went to Baltimore, Philadelphia, New York, Hartford, Boston, and Salem. She traveled on foot only with the clothes on her back, and tried to sell her book. Her method was not only to record her impressions but also to sell subscriptions to her next book. Her impressions of Lydia Sigourney ("one of the brightest ornaments of the present age"), Jared Sparks ("as meek as Moses"), Hannah Adams ("the glory of New England's females"), and Noah Webster ("pompous blockhead") delighted some and infuriated many. She found a printer for the book in New Haven. During her travels she met editors and writers all over the middle states and the Northeast, which stood her in good stead later. Her reception as she traveled convinced her to write

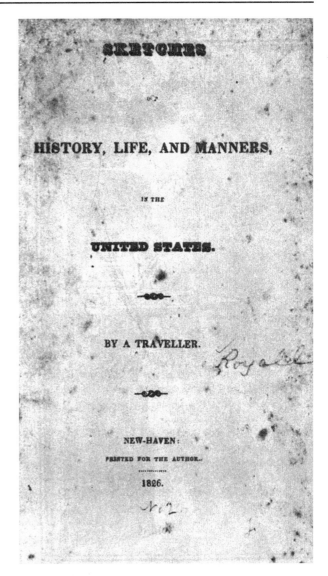

*Title page for Royall's first book, a collection of travel sketches and descriptions of the author's acquaintance with notable figures of the day (Library of Congress)*

three volumes of *The Black Book; or, a Continuation of Travels, in the United States* (1828–1829) to "bring terror to evil doers."

Meanwhile in 1827, "having sold out my first book of travels," as she remarked in the first volume of *The Black Book,* she published her only novel, *The Tennessean; A Novel, Founded on Facts,* called by one critic, Helen Beal Woodward, "the worst American novel of all time." It is the story of a group of Tennesseans who make a secret deal with Spain, based on stories told her by a man from that state while she was in Alabama. The novel was not well received, and Royall abandoned long fiction and ventured to writing travel literature.

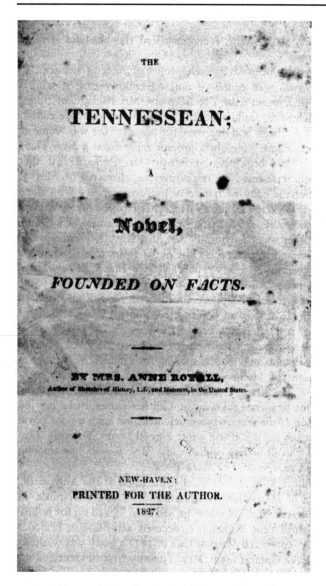

*Title page for Royall's only novel (Library of Congress)*

The Black Book is, as its subtitle announces, a continuation of Royall's popular travel sketches. In a way all of her works represent an extension of a single project. She then traveled through New York, Massachusetts, Connecticut, Rhode Island, and back to Virginia. Several themes emerge forcefully in volume one: her defense of the Masons, who were under extreme attack in 1827; her hatred of missionaries; and her preference for New England in some aspects. As is true of all her books, she reveals memories of her life in scattered passages.

In volume two of *The Black Book* Royall announces that she intends to take "a new route through New-York and New-England, sell books in the meantime, to bear my expences—see the people, and watch the missionaries." Since 1828 was a presidential election year, and she greatly

admired Andrew Jackson, many people thought she was campaigning for him; she also admired Adams, however. She went to see the latter on one occasion, and he wrote in his diary on 9 August 1827 that she

> continues to make herself noxious to many persons; tolerated by some and feared by others, by her deportment and her books; treating all with a familiarity which often passes for impudence, insulting those who treat her with incivility, and then lampooning them in her books. Stipped of all her sex's delicacy, but unable to forfeit its privilege of gentle treatment from the other, she goes about like a virago-errant in enchanted armor, and redeems herself from the cravings of indigence by the notoriety of her eccentricities and the forced currency they give to her publications.

Royall does indeed exhibit a curious mixture in her writing, demanding certain "ladylike" standards in women and yet hoping "to see the day when women will learn to respect themselves and command the respect of enlightened and generous men.

In volume three she relates the circumstances on 17 December 1827 in Burlington, Vermont, when she was thrown down the steps of a bookstore and left in the snow with a dislocated ankle, fractured leg bones, and a sprained knee. She did not walk again until June 1828. She describes in riveting detail her trip back to Washington: she constantly changed from boat to stagecoach and generally was left to fend for herself, often crawling up stairs and, at one point, getting stuck in the New Jersey mud when the stage she was traveling in tipped over. After she finally returned to Washington, she was cared for by her friend Sally Stack, who remained with her for the rest of her life. The balance of the volume is filled with her account of senators as she sees them from the Senate gallery, into which she had to be carried. Never quite free from fear again, Royall intensified her feelings against Presbyterian evangelicals.

Nevertheless, she did not stop either her travels or her writings. She began her two-volume work, *Mrs. Royall's Pennsylvania; or Travels Continued in the United States* (1829), with the words: "That the chain of my tour may not be broken, I commence my third series of travels precisely where I left off in the third volume of the Black Book, and, as usual, without preface or apology." She describes her trips to Lancaster, Harrisburg, Carlisle, and Pittsburgh, and she also continues her attack on the "blackcoats." She found that in Pennsylvania the evangelicals were also called "blueskins," "graybacks," "roundheads," and "bluestockings."

Again she describes serious disputes with Presbyterian antagonists, in this case with Royall's neighbors in Washington, the members of the Columbia Engine House Presbyterian Church. Their children threw stones at her windows and the members prayed loudly outside. Royall retaliated by referring in print to the leader of the church, John Coyle Sr., as "Holy Willie," "a d___d old bald-headed son of a b___h." The church brought suit against her, and she was indicted and convicted as a "common scold." The authorities had built a ducking stool, which, according to an old English law, was used to administer the penalty for her offense, but Judge William Cranch instead fined her $10. Two newspapermen paid her bail. James Gordon Bennett, founder and editor of the *New York Herald,* had sat by her through the trial and felt strongly that the case represented a threat to the freedom of the press. Royall's account of the trial takes up the last twenty-four pages of *Mrs. Royall's Pennsylvania.*

Before she started her southern tour, Royall went to Richmond to visit the Virginia Constitutional Convention, which had been called to decide the issue of proportionate representation. She walked "perhaps three miles" to see Dolley Madison, who enchanted her as she washed the mud from Royall's shoes. She started her tour on 30 January 1830, gathering the material for the three volumes of *Mrs. Royall's Southern Tour, or, Second Series of the Black Book* (1830–1831). In Charlottesville she was serenaded by a hostile mob of students. She discovered that Presbyterians were called "red-necks" in Fayetteville, North Carolina. Her favorite people in Charleston, South Carolina, were the wealthy "Israelites." In the third volume she relates her time in New Orleans, which she thoroughly canvassed. A river steamer took her up the Mississippi River to St. Louis, where she could not find a place to stay and was convinced that the people were antagonistic. The family that finally took her in thought she was almost paranoid but arranged for her to take a ferry across the river. Royall now blamed the power of the Second Bank of the United States as well as the Presbyterians for her difficulties. She was afraid most of the time. After visiting her brother in Indiana and her mother in Illinois, she went to Cincinnati and then back to Washington. She never ventured on long trips again, but she still rarely flinched from expressing her opinions.

Her last published book, *Letters from Alabama on Various Subjects: to Which Is Added, an Appendix, Containing Remarks on Sundry Members of the 20th and 21st Congress, and Other High Characters, &c., &c. at the Seat of Government* (1830), was the first written, comprising the letters written to Dunbar between 1817 and 1826, when she still had money and had not suffered the vicissitudes of her later life. Her first meetings with Jackson are detailed, and the Alabama country before statehood is described. The tone is genial, more curious and less fearful than in her later-written works.

From 1831 to her death in 1854, Royall owned and edited two newspapers from her house in Washington, in which she kept a sharp eye on the doings in the capital.

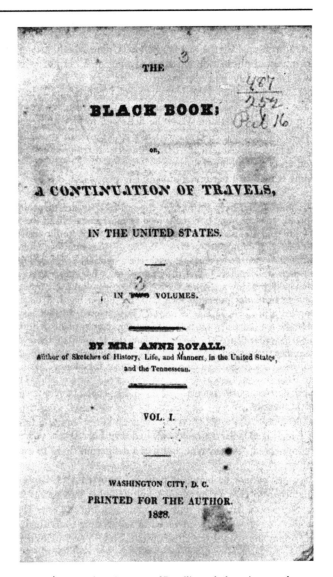

Title page for volume one of Royall's work that mixes travel descriptions with defenses of Freemasonry and attacks on Presbyterianism (Library of Congress)

She procured a discarded Ramage press and begged a set of type from Duff Green, editor of the *United States Telegraph.* From 1831 to 1836 she edited a weekly newspaper called *Paul Pry,* from a character in a comedy in the 1820s by John Poole. The purpose of the paper was to expose political evil. She sided with Andrew Jackson and Peggy Eaton; she took on the anti-Masons and the banking interests. During the Nullification crisis she was vehement for the preservation of the Union, though she was in favor of states' rights on the abolitionism issue. She gradually grew disenchanted with Jackson and did not like Martin Van Buren at first.

Royall's financial situation became more difficult in the years leading up to the panic of 1837. She traveled north to collect funds and advice for *The Huntress,* a continuation of *Paul Pry.* "The only difference between *The Hunt-ress* and *Paul Pry*," she wrote in the former, "will be the introduction of amusing tales, dialogues, and essays upon general subjects." She wrote the editorial page and had her printers select the fiction and advertising in the rest of the paper. The tone of her writings became somewhat quieter. Even so, she subjected P. T. Barnum to a tirade in 1836. "Anne was the most garrulous old woman I ever saw," he wrote later in *The Life of P. T. Barnum Written by Himself,* "Her tongue ran like wildfire." He offered her a lecture tour, which she declined. She continued to lecture against "gospel-spreading" evangelicals and anti-Masonry in her newspaper, however. She was also against the Locofoco faction of the Democratic Party, abolitionism of any kind, the Native American Party (those Americans who wanted to restrict immigration), Sunday blue laws, and intolerance in general. She felt nostalgia for the past, however, and more and more she begged for money, food, or wood. In July 1848 the pension law was finally changed and she received a modest sum, but after Major Royall's family got its share, after her debts were paid, and after Sally Stack accepted part, Anne ended up with $10. At the end of her long life, she wrote that she had 31¢ and no money for rent.

She died on 1 October 1854 and was buried in a then unmarked grave in the Congressional Cemetery in Washington, accompanied by Masonic pallbearers. Her grave was not marked until 1914. Yet, she was one of America's first female travel writers, one of the first female newspaper editors in the country, and one of the most vocal early critics of the government. Her lively writings and the rebuttals they incited have contributed signifi-cantly to what is known of the nation and the people of her time.

**Biographies:**

Sarah Harvey Porter, *The Life and Times of Anne Royall* (Cedar Rapids, Iowa: Torch Press, 1909);

George Stuyvesant Jackson, *Uncommon Scold: The Story of Anne Royall* (Boston: Humphries, 1937);

Louise Griffith, Introduction to Royall's *Letters from Ala-bama, 1817–1822* (University: University of Ala-bama Press, 1969);

Bessie Rowland James, *Anne Royall's U.S.A.* (New Bruns-wick, N.J.: Rutgers University Press, 1972);

Alice S. Maxwell and Marion B. Dunlevy, *Virago! The Story of Anne Newport Royall (1769–1854)* (Jefferson, N.C.: McFarland, 1985).

**References:**

Charles Francis Adams, ed., *Memoirs of John Quincy Adams Comprising Portions of His Diary from 1795 to 1849,* 12

volumes (Philadelphia: Lippincott, 1874–1877), VII: 321;

Phineas T. Barnum, *The Life of P. T. Barnum Written by Him-self* (New York: Redfield, 1855), pp. 163–166;

Maurine Beasley, "The Curious Career of Anne Royall," *Journalism History,* 3 (Winter 1976–1977): 98–102, 136;

Heber Blankenhorn, "The Grandma of Muckrakers," *American Mercury,* 12 (September 1927): 87–93;

Thomas D. Clark, ed., *Travels in the Old South: A Bibliogra-phy,* 3 volumes (Norman: University of Oklahoma Press, 1959), III: 80–83;

Ruth Woods Dayton, *Pioneers and Their Homes in Upper Kanawha* (Charleston: West Virginia Publishing, 1947), pp. 161–175;

Don Dodd and Ben Williams, "'A Common Scold': Anne Royall," *American History Illustrated,* 10 (January 1976): 32–38;

Pat Ferguson, "The Royall Treatment," *Mid-Atlantic Coun-try,* 17 (March 1996): 24–27, 82, 84;

Margaret B. Moore, "Anne Newport Royall: The Dreaded Power Within," paper presented to the Philological Association of the Carolinas, East Caro-lina University, 8 March 1997;

Madelon Golden Schilpp and Sharon M. Murphy, *Great Women of the Press* (Carbondale: Southern Illinois University Press, 1983), pp. 21–36;

Irving Wallace, *The Square Pegs: Some Americans Who Dared to Be Different* (New York: Knopf, 1957), pp. 243–266;

Lucille Watson, "Lynchburg's First Historian: Anne Roy-all, Pioneer Journalist (1769–1854)," *Iron Worker,* 20 (1955–1956): 1–15;

Helen Beal Woodward, *The Bold Women* (New York: Farrar, Straus & Young, 1953), pp. 8–23;

Richardson Wright, *Forgotten Ladies: Nine Portraits from the American Family Album* (Philadelphia: Lippincott, 1928), pp. 156–186.

**Papers:**

Scattered manuscripts of Anne Newport Royall's letters may be found in the Library of Congress, Washington, D.C.; the Historical Society of Pennsylvania, Philadelphia; the Newberry Library, Chicago; Vassar College, Pough-keepsie, N.Y.; the Wollman Library, Barnard College, Columbia University, New York; the Huntington Library, San Marino, Cal.; Beinecke Library, Yale University, New Haven; Boston Public Library, Boston; New York Historical Society, New York; the Perkins Library, Duke University; the Morristown National Historical Park, Morristown, N.J.; the Lipscomb Library, Ran-dolph-Macon Library, Lynchburg, Va.; the Alderman Library, University of Virginia, Charlottesville.

# William Gilmore Simms

*(17 April 1806 – 11 June 1870)*

James Everett Kibler
*University of Georgia*

See also the Simms entries in *DLB 3: Antebellum Writers in New York and the South; DLB 30: American Historians, 1607–1865; DLB 59: American Literary Critics and Scholars, 1800–1850;* and *DLB 73: American Magazine Journalists, 1741–1850.*

BOOKS: *Monody, on the Death of Gen. Charles Cotesworth Pinckney,* anonymous (Charleston, S.C.: Gray & Ellis, 1825);

*Lyrical and Other Poems* (Charleston, S.C.: Ellis & Neufville, 1827);

*Early Lays* (Charleston, S.C.: A. E. Miller, 1827);

*The Vision of Cortes, Cain, and Other Poems* (Charleston, S.C.: James S. Burges, 1829);

*The Tri-Color; or The Three Days of Blood, in Paris. With Some Other Pieces,* anonymous (London: Wigfall & Davis, 1830 [Charleston, S.C.: James S. Burges, 1831]);

*Atalantis. A Story of the Sea: In Three Parts,* anonymous (New York: Harper, 1832; enlarged edition, Philadelphia: Carey & Hart, 1848 [i.e., 1849]);

*Martin Faber; The Story of a Criminal* (New York: Harper, 1833; London: Limbird, 1834);

*The Book of My Lady. A Melange,* anonymous (Philadelphia: Key & Biddle, 1833; Boston: Allen & Ticknor, 1833);

*Guy Rivers: A Tale of Georgia,* 2 volumes (New York: Harper, 1834; London: Harper, 1834);

*The Yemassee. A Romance of Carolina,* 2 volumes (New York: Harper, 1835; London: [likely Harper], 1835);

*The Partisan: A Tale of the Revolution,* 2 volumes (New York: Harper, 1835);

*Mellichampe. A Legend of the Santee,* 2 volumes (New York: Harper, 1836);

*Martin Faber, The Story of a Criminal; and Other Tales,* 2 volumes (New York: Harper, 1837);

*Slavery in America, Being a Brief Review of Miss Martineau on That Subject,* anonymous (Richmond, Va.: Thomas W. White, 1838);

*William Gilmore Simms, circa 1859 (South Caroliniana Library, University of South Carolina)*

*Richard Hurdis; Or, The Avenger of Blood. A Tale of Alabama,* 2 volumes, anonymous (Philadelphia: Carey & Hart, 1838);

*Pelayo: A Story of the Goth,* 2 volumes (New York: Harper, 1838);

*Carl Werner, An Imaginative Story; With Other Tales of Imagination,* 2 volumes (New York: George Adlard, 1838); republished as *Young Ladies' Book of Romantic Tales* (Boston: E. Littlefield, 1839); *Carl Werner* republished as *Matilda: The Spectre of the Castle* (Boston: Gleason, 1846);

*Southern Passages and Pictures* (New York: George Adlard, 1839 [i.e., 1838]);

*The Damsel of Darien,* 2 volumes (Philadelphia: Lea & Blanchard, 1839; London: N. Bruce, 1843);

*The History of South Carolina, from Its First European Discovery to Its Erection into a Republic: With a Supplementary Chronicle of Events to the Present Time* (Charleston, S.C.: S. Babcock, 1840; revised, 1842); revised again (Charleston, S.C.: Russell & Jones / New York: Redfield, 1860);

*Border Beagles; A Tale of Mississippi,* 2 volumes (Philadelphia: Carey & Hart, 1840);

*The Kinsmen: Or The Black Riders of Congaree,* 2 volumes (Philadelphia: Lea & Blanchard, 1841; London: John Cunningham, 1841); revised as *The Scout or The Black Riders of Congaree* (New York: Redfield, 1854);

*Confession; Or, The Blind Heart. A Domestic Story,* 2 volumes (Philadelphia: Lea & Blanchard 1841; London: J. Cunningham, 1841);

*Beauchampe: Or The Kentucky Tragedy. A Tale of Passion,* 2 volumes (Philadelphia: Lea & Blanchard 1842; London: N. Bruce, 1842); volume 1 revised as *Charlemont or the Pride of the Village. A Tale of Kentucky* (New York: Redfield, 1856); volume 2 revised as *Beauchampe or the Kentucky Tragedy. A Sequel to Charlemont* (New York: Redfield, 1856);

*The Social Principle: The True Source of National Permanence. An Oration, Delivered before the Erosophic Society of the University of Alabama, at Its Twelfth Anniversary, December 13, 1842* (Tuscaloosa: The Society, 1843);

*The Geography of South Carolina: Being a Companion to the History of That State* (Charleston, S.C.: Babcock, 1843);

*Donna Florida: A Tale* (Charleston, S.C.: Burges & James, 1843);

*The Prima Donna: A Passage from City Life* (Philadelphia: Louis A. Godey, 1844);

*The Sources of American Independence. An Oration, on the Sixty-ninth Anniversary of American Independence; Delivered at Aiken, South Carolina, before the Town Council and Citizens Thereof* (Aiken: Town Council, 1844);

*The Life of Francis Marion* (New York: Henry G. Langley, 1844);

*Castle Dismal: Or, The Bachelor's Christmas. A Domestic Legend* (New York: Burgess, Stringer, 1844);

*Helen Halsey: Or, The Swamp State of Conelachita. A Tale of the Borders* (New York: Burgess, Stringer, 1845);

*Grouped Thoughts and Scattered Fancies. A Collection of Sonnets* (Richmond, Va.: W. Macfarlane, 1845);

*The Wigwam and the Cabin . . . First Series* (New York: Wiley & Putnam, 1845; London: Wiley & Putnam, 1845); enlarged as *Life in America* (Aberdeen, Scotland: George Clark, 1848);

*The Wigwam and the Cabin . . . Second Series* (New York: Wiley & Putnam, 1845; London: Wiley & Putnam, 1846);

*Count Julian; Or, the Last Days of the Goth. A Historical Romance* (Baltimore & New York: William Taylor, 1845; London: Bruce & Wyld, 1846);

*Views and Reviews in American Literature, History and Fiction . . . First Series* (New York: Wiley & Putnam, 1845; London: Wiley & Putnam, 1846);

*Views and Reviews in American Literature, History and Fiction . . . Second Series* (New York: Wiley & Putnam, 1845; London: Wiley & Putnam, 1846);

*Areytos: Or, Songs of the South* (Charleston, S.C.: John Russell, 1846);

*The Life of Captain John Smith. The Founder of Virginia* (New York: Cooledge, 1846);

*The Life of Chevalier Bayard: "The Good Knight," "sans peur et sans reproche"* (New York: Harper, 1847);

*Self-Development. An Oration Delivered before the Literary Societies of Oglethorpe University, Georgia; November 10, 1847* (Milledgeville, Ga.: Thalian Society, 1847);

*Lays of the Palmetto: A Tribute to the South Carolina Regiment, in the War with Mexico* (Charleston, S.C.: John Russell, 1848);

*Charleston, and Her Satirists; A Scribblement* (Charleston, S.C.: James S. Burges, 1848);

*Charleston and Her Satirists; A Scribblement . . . No. 2 (Conclusion)* (Charleston, S.C.: James S. Burges, 1848);

*The Cassique of Accabee. A Tale of Ashley River. With Other Pieces* (Charleston, S.C.: John Russell, 1849; New York: Harper, 1849);

*Father Abbot, Or, the Home Tourist; A Medley* (Charleston, S.C.: Miller & Browne, 1849);

*The Life of Nathanael Greene, Major-General in the Army of the Revolution* (New York: Cooledge, 1849);

*Sabbath Lyrics; Or, Songs from Scripture* (Charleston, S.C.: Walker & James, 1849);

*The Lily and the Totem, or, The Huguenots in Florida. A Series of Sketches, Picturesque and Historical, of the Colonies of Coligni, in North America* (New York: Baker & Scribner, 1850);

*Flirtation at the Moultrie House: In a Series of Letters, from Miss Georgiana Appleby, to her Friends in Georgia, Showing the Doings at the Moultrie House, and the Events Which Took Place at the Grand Costume Ball, on the 29th August, 1850; With Other Letters,* anonymous (Charleston, S.C.: Edward C. Councell, 1850);

*The City of the Silent: A Poem* (Charleston, S.C.: Walker & James, 1850 [i.e., 1851]);

*Katharine Walton: Or, The Rebel of Dorchester. An Historical Romance of the Revolution in Carolina* (Philadelphia: A. Hart, 1851);

*Norman Maurice; Or, The Man of the People. An American Drama* (Richmond, Va.: Thompson, 1851;

revised edition, Charleston, S.C.: Walker & Richards, 1852);

*The Golden Christmas: A Chronicle of St. John's, Berkeley. Compiled from the Notes of a Briefless Barrister* (Charleston, S.C.: Walker & Richards, 1852);

*The Sword and the Distaff; Or, "Fair, Fat and Forty," a Story of the South, at the Close of the Revolution* (Charleston, S.C.: Walker & Richards, 1852); republished as *Woodcraft or Hawks about the Dovecote* (New York: Redfield, 1854);

*As Good as a Comedy: Or, The Tennessean's Story,* anonymous (Philadelphia: A. Hart, 1852);

*Michael Bonham: Or, The Fall of Bexar. A Tale of Texas,* anonymous (Richmond, Va.: Thompson, 1852);

*South-Carolina in the Revolutionary War: Being a Reply to Certain Misrepresentations and Mistakes of Recent Writers, in Relation to the Course and Conduct of This State* (Charleston, S.C.: Walker & James, 1853; Charleston, S.C.: Courtenay, 1853);

*Marie de Berniere: A Tale of the Crescent City, Etc. Etc. Etc.* (Philadelphia: Lippincott, Grambo, 1853); republished as *The Maroon: A Legend of the Caribbees, and Other Tales* (Philadelphia: Lippincott, Grambo, 1855); "The Maroon" republished as *The Ghost of My Husband* (New York: Chapman, 1866);

*Egeria: Or, Voices of Thought and Counsel, for the Woods and Wayside* (Philadelphia: E. H. Butler, 1853);

*Vasconcelos. A Romance of the New World,* as Frank Cooper (New York: Redfield, 1853);

*Poems, Descriptive, Dramatic, Legendary and Contemplative,* 2 volumes (New York: Redfield, 1853 [i.e., 1854]; Charleston, S.C.: John Russell, 1853 [i.e., 1854]);

*Southward Ho! A Spell of Sunshine* (New York: Redfield, 1854);

*The Forayers or The Raid of the Dog-Days* (New York: Redfield, 1855);

*Eutaw: A Sequel to the Forayers, or The Raid of the Dog-Days* (New York: Redfield, 1856);

*The Cassique of Kiawah: A Colonial Romance* (New York: Redfield, 1859);

*Simms's Poems Areytos or Songs and Ballads of the South with Other Poems* (Charleston, S.C.: Russell & Jones, 1860);

*Sack and Destruction of the City of Columbia, S.C. to Which Is Added a List of the Property Destroyed,* anonymous (Columbia, S.C.: Power Press of Daily Phoenix, 1865);

*The Sense of the Beautiful. An Address, Delivered by W. Gilmore Simms, before the Charleston County Agricultural and Horticultural Association . . . , May 3, 1870* (Charleston, S.C.: The Society, 1870);

*Voltmeier Or The Mountain Men,* volume 1 of *The Writings of William Gilmore Simms Centennial Edition,* edited by James B. Meriwether (Columbia: University of South Carolina Press, 1969);

*As Good as a Comedy: Or the Tennessean's Story. And Paddy McGann; Or The Demon of the Stump,* volume 3 of *The Writings of William Gilmore Simms Centennial Edition,* edited by Meriwether (Columbia: University of South Carolina Press, 1972);

*Stories and Tales,* volume 5 of *The Writings of William Gilmore Simms Centennial Edition,* edited by John Caldwell Guilds (Columbia: University of South Carolina Press, 1974);

*Joscelyn A Tale of the Revolution,* volume 16 of *The Writings of William Gilmore Simms Centennial Edition,* edited by Keen Butterworth (Columbia: University of South Carolina Press, 1975);

*Selected Poems of William Gilmore Simms,* edited by James Everett Kibler (Athens: University of Georgia Press, 1990);

*Tales of the South by William Gilmore Simms,* edited by Mary Ann Wimsatt (Columbia: University of South Carolina Press, 1996);

*Poetry and the Practical,* edited by Kibler (Fayetteville: University of Arkansas Press, 1996);

*The Cub of the Panther. A Hunter Legend of the "Old North State,"* edited by Miriam Jones Shillingsburg (Fayetteville: University of Arkansas Press, 1997);

*The Simms Reader: Selections from the Writings of William Gilmore Simms,* edited by Guilds (Charlottesville: University Press of Virginia, 2001).

**Edition:** *Works of William Gilmore Simms,* Redfield edition, 20 volumes (New York: Widdleton, 1853–1866).

OTHER: *The Remains of Maynard Davis Richardson, With a Memoir of His Life,* edited anonymously by Simms (Charleston, S.C.: O. A. Roorbach, 1833);

*The Charleston Book. A Miscellany in Prose and Verse,* edited anonymously by Simms (Charleston, S.C.: Samuel Hart, 1845);

*A Supplement to the Plays of William Shakespeare,* edited by Simms (New York: Cooledge, 1848);

*War Poetry of the South,* edited by Simms (New York: Richardson, 1866);

*Selections from the Letters and Speeches of the Hon. James H. Hammond, of South Carolina,* edited by Simms (New York: John F. Trow, 1866);

*The Army Correspondence of Colonel John Laurens in the Years 1777–8. Now First Printed from Original Letters . . . ,* edited by Simms (New York: Bradford Club, 1867); republished as *A Succinct Memoir of* the *Life and Public Services of Colonel John Laurens* (Albany, N.Y.: Williamstadt, 1867).

## SELECTED PERIODICAL PUBLICATIONS– UNCOLLECTED:

### FICTION

"Chronicles of Ashley River," anonymous, *Southern Literary Gazette,* 1 (15 July 1829): 115–116; (1 September 1829): 129–130; (15 September 1829): 176–178; (15 October 1829): 208–210; (1 November 1829): 247–252, 278–280;

"The Spectre Chief of Accabee," *Literary World,* 11 (31 July 1852): 74–76;

"The Pirate Hoard. A Long Shore Legend," *Graham's* 48 (January 1856): 54–59; (February 1856): 124–131; (March 1856): 224–229; (April 1856): 344–351;

"Major Martinet; or, the Last Half Hour. The Record of a City Bachelor," *Cosmopolitan Monthly,* 9 (January 1870): 1–6.

### NONFICTION

"The Philosophy of the Omnibus," *American Monthly,* 3 (May 1834): 153–159; "The Progress of Civilization," *American Monthly,* 3 (August 1834): 361–372;

"American Criticism and Critics," *Southern Literary Journal,* 2 (July 1836): 393–404;

"Shakspeariana," *Southern Literary Journal,* new series 4 (September 1838): 184–192; (October 1838): 253–256;

"The Ages of Gold and Iron," *Ladies' Companion,* 15 (May 1841): 12–14;

"The Good Farmer," *Ladies' Companion,* 15 (August 1841): 154–157;

"Ancient and Modern Culture," *Magnolia,* 4 (May 1842): 308–311;

"Philosophy of Debt and Dunning," *Magnolia,* new series 1 (September 1842): 141–145;

"The Writing of Washington Allston," *Southern Quarterly Review,* 4 (October 1843): 363–414;

"The Broken Arrow. An Authentic Passage from Unwritten American History," *Ladies' Companion,* 18 (January 1844): 110–119;

"A Chapter on the Supernatural," *Orion,* 3 (February 1844): 227–238;

"The Moral Character of Hamlet," *Orion,* 4 (March 1844): 41–51; (April 1844): 76–89; (May 1844): 105–115; (June 1844): 179–194;

"Literature of the Bible," *Southern Quarterly Review,* 7 (January 1845): 103–123;

"Literature in Ancient Rome," *Southern and Western,* 1 (January 1845): 17–25;

"Bayard, the Chevalier," *Southern and Western,* 2 (August 1845): 73–85; (September 1845): 193–200;

"*Poems* by William W. Lord," *Southern and Western,* 2 (August 1845): 133–137;

"The Humorous in American and British Literature," *Southern and Western,* 2 (September 1845): 142–184;

"Poe's Poetry," *Charleston Southern Patriot,* 10 November 1845;

"The Hermitage," *Charleston Southern Patriot,* December 1846;

"*Carolina Sports* by William Elliott," *Southern Quarterly Review,* 12 (July 1847): 67–90;

"Fanny Kemble Butler's *A Year of Consolation,*" *Southern Quarterly Review,* 12 (July 1847): 191–236;

"Carlyle's Works," *Southern Quarterly Review,* 14 (July 1848): 77–101;

"Religious Instructions of Slaves," *Southern Quarterly Review,* 14 (July 1848): 170–183;

"Modern Prose Fiction," *Southern Quarterly Review,* 15 (April 1848): 41–83;

"The Poetical Works of Wordsworth," *Southern Quarterly Review,* new series 2 (September 1850): 1–23;

"Summer Travel in the South," *Southern Quarterly Review,* new series 2 (September 1850): 24–65;

"The Genius and Writings of Thackeray," *Southern Quarterly Review,* new series 3 (January 1851): 74–100;

"What Moves the Table," *Southern Quarterly Review,* new series 8 (October 1853): 480–501;

"Dickens' *Bleak House,*" *Southern Quarterly Review,* new series 9 (January 1854): 224–228;

"Charleston: The Palmetto City," *Harper's Monthy,* 15 (June 1857): 1–22;

"Look at Home," *Columbia Phoenix,* 16 June 1865;

"Flights to Florida," *Charleston Courier,* 27 February 1867; 5, 8, 14, 20, 28 March 1867; 5, 12, 16, 25 April 1867; 2, 9 May 1867;

"Bird's Eye View in Short Flights," *Charleston Courier,* 7, 11, 12, 24, 25, 27 June 1867.

Unquestionably the author with the best claim to being the Honoré de Balzac of American literature, William Gilmore Simms was in fact more prolific and wide-ranging than the great Frenchman himself. The page count of work published in book form alone runs to an amazing twenty-five thousand. If uncollected stories, poems, essays, and reviews were added, this figure would be increased by half. What wonder that at his death in 1870, his fingers could not be straightened from the position of holding the pen. No author has written so widely in so many different genres. The fact that he did so with skill and competence makes his achievement all the more impressive. He wrote 24 novels; 110 short stories; 2,000 poems (lyric, dramatic, and narrative, some of them book-length, and only half appearing in collections, the other 1,000 scattered through scores of nineteenth-century periodicals); several plays; scores of essays; 4 biographies; a significant number of speeches and lectures; a volume of history; and 6 editions as diverse as a William Shakespeare apocrypha and a volume of Southern war poetry.

Simms, however, is much more than a writer of great quantity. What is clear from his canon is that he did not possess energy alone, but unmistakable genius. His talent displayed itself not in understatement, tightness, and polish but in passion, expansiveness, flamboyance, dramatic vitality, the rush of a vigorous prose style of impressive verbal energy, and restless innovations that left their mark on American letters. That he achieved these literary accomplishments while editing one periodical or another throughout half of his career (twenty-four of the forty-five years from 1825 to 1870) should ensure him a position of high honor in the annals of early American literature and at least a modest place worldwide. Despite being one of the major American writers of the nineteenth century and the central figure of Southern letters, however, he has been largely neglected by literary history. Even though there has been a large growing interest since the late twentieth century, he is still excluded from major consideration by scholars, partly because of sectional bias. Mary Ann Wimsatt, in the most recent treatment of his short fiction, *The Major Fiction of William Gilmore Simms: Cultural Traditions and Literary Forms* (1989), has, in fact, called Simms a "national scapegoat." In 1865, the year Northern troops burned his home, an officer under General William T. Sherman, in his memoirs, reported that Simms now had "no home" and that, in the "glorious future of this country," he will likewise have "no name." Some manner of Simms's neglect seems thus to have been premeditated along sectional and political lines. With this same bias, even Edgar Allan Poe was neglected in the adulation of lesser New England lights. While Poe has finally been revived in the United States, Simms is only beginning to be. His works were allowed to go out of print around 1900, and until the last decades of the twentieth century few of his books have been available to the reading public. Consequently, Simms's reputation has suffered accordingly. His best work in poetry, fiction, and prose remains vital, however; a reflection of Simms's great energy, passion, and insight into experience.

Simms made major contributions to American letters. As a short-story writer he should be included with Washington Irving and Poe as one of the fathers of the genre, which he did much to define. Thus, the only distinctive American literary form owes a large part to his endeavor. Beginning his short-story writing in the 1820s, he exerted a direct influence upon Poe that was

*Simms's wife, Chevillette Eliza Roach Simms, whom he married in November 1836 (from volume one of* The Letters of William Gilmore Simms, *1952–1982)*

noteworthy. Poe felt that Simms's "Grayling" (1841) was the finest ghost story ever written. Among his best short works are "The Lazy Crow" (1839), "The Arm-Chair of Tustenugee" (1840), "Caloya, or the Loves of the Driver" (1841), "The Two Camps" (1843), "Maize in Milk" (1847), "Sharp Snaffles" (1870), and "Bald-Head Bill Bauldy" (1870). His story collection *The Wigwam and the Cabin* (1845) is particularly significant, owing to its effective realism and close thematic arrangement that provides a novelistic unity somewhat in the manner of James Joyce's *Dubliners* (1914), Sherwood Anderson's *Winesburg, Ohio* (1919), and William Faulkner's *The Unvanquished* (1938) and *Go Down, Moses* (1942). Its gritty realism elicited comment from Walt Whitman, who felt it too sexually explicit.

As a novelist Simms may have lacked the precise polish of Nathaniel Hawthorne, but he was a better craftsman than James Fenimore Cooper and had a better sense of form. His versatility allowed for several different types of novels, from Gothic tales such as *Castle*

*Dismal: Or, The Bachelor's Christmas. A Domestic Legend* (1844) to novels of manners such as *The Golden Christmas: A Chronicle of St. John's, Berkeley. Compiled from the Notes of a Briefless Barrister* (1852). He wrote short novels narrated in the first person, the primary purpose of which is to explore that narrator's psychology (for instance, *Martin Faber, The Story of a Criminal* [1837], and *Carl Werner, An Imaginative Story* [1838]). Understandably, Poe preferred this branch of Simms's fictional writing, particularly when Simms's narrator suffers from dementia, is a criminal, or both. A major influence on Poe was *Martin Faber,* a novel he reviewed favorably.

Simms was better known, however, for his romances. He was the first major American writer to define the genre as distinct from the novel in his preface to *The Yemassee. A Romance of Carolina* in 1835, thus predating by sixteen years Hawthorne's famous similar definition in *The House of Seven Gables.* Hawthorne reviewed Simms, so did not likely develop the idea independently. *Woodcraft or Hawks about the Dovecote* (1854; originally published as *The Sword and the Distaff; Or, "Fair, Fat and Forty," a Story of the South, at the Close of the Revolution,* 1852) deserves to be read as a major novel of the American Renaissance decade of the 1850s. What is particularly interesting about the novel is that it is the only work of the period that is predominantly humorous. Its literary descendants include such important Southern masterpieces as Mark Twain's *The Adventures of Huckleberry Finn* (1884) and Faulkner's *As I Lay Dying* (1930) and *The Hamlet* (1940).

*The Yemassee* has been celebrated for its balanced, realistic portrayal of the American Indian, which critics have long considered the best in early American literature, and it is a particularly notable achievement when compared to Cooper's less convincing treatment. Simms knew the Indian (Creek, Choctaw, Catawba, and Cherokee) from firsthand experience on the Southern frontier in the 1820s and 1830s. He lived among them in their camps and witnessed them in their degraded condition in the new towns of the border; Cooper got his portrayal from books. Simms's short stories "Indian Sketch" (1828) and "Oakatibbe" (1841), and his little-known poem "The Indian Village" (1837) present even more coolly realistic treatments of Indian character than *The Yemassee.* In all, Simms wrote three novels that treated the Indian, along with at least forty-nine poems, twenty-eight stories, and twenty-three essays—an accomplishment unmatched in his century.

In the novels as a whole Simms shows an innovativeness that points the way to later fiction. This energy of mind and originality are in fact often the hallmarks of his writing. From his earliest short stories and novels of the 1820s on, there is a strong impulse to graphic realism (including matters of sex and unpleasantly grim particulars) that is far ahead of its time. This strain offended Poe and even made the young Whitman uncomfortable. Whitman, in an essay in his *Brooklyn Eagle* (9 March 1846), called Simms's realism "coarse and indelicate in its details." In these ways, in fact, Simms was being much more realistic than most of the realists of the 1880s and 1890s—particularly such an author as William Dean Howells, whose dictum was to write nothing that might cause a blush. One has to wait until the twentieth century to see again the frank and unflinching realism of parts of such works as *The Yemassee, Woodcraft, The Wigwam and the Cabin,* and the border romances.

Simms peoples his fictional world with a parade of grotesque characters such as "Goggle" Blonay, Blodgits, Mother Blonay, and Bostwick, somewhat reminiscent of Dickensian characters but more closely akin to the physically deformed and spiritually incomplete people of Flannery O'Connor. This creation of the grotesque character is another way that Simms stands at the door opening to later fiction, in this instance, the haunted Southern grotesques of Poe, Faulkner, Carson McCullers, O'Connor, Cormac McCarthy, and Harry Crews.

Significantly, in the 1820s Simms opted to set his works in the United States. His philosophy as expressed in periodicals he edited during this period was that the nation could never establish its own literature until it stopped imitating British models. He calls for American literary independence. From 1825 to 1829 Simms strongly and consistently voiced a view that only became widespread nationwide in the "Young America" journals of New York after 1837. In the 1820s he had unequivocally stated the principles of "Young America," which a decade later were regarded as "radical" heresy by the *Knickerbocker,* the *North American Review,* the *New England Magazine,* the *New York Review,* and the *American Quarterly.* This demand for freedom from the literary bondage to England expressed itself in Simms's use of American setting, dialect, distinctively American character, style, and form—a realism that fit art to place and relied upon the genius loci. Simms therefore deserves recognition as precursor of the "Young America" movement that he joined and helped to promote through fiction, essays, and criticism.

Simms, however, took one important step beyond "Young America" and in so doing, he stands as the premier spokesman for this idea. This important realization was that "for one to be National in literature, he must first of necessity be Sectional"—that an author must write of his *patria,* his own little area that he knows best, and that the literature of various sections, then, when taken collectively, would produce a literature of national "Illustration" and universal import. This

*Illustration depicting Woodlands, near Bamberg, South Carolina, Simms's home from 1837 until his death (from* Homes of American Authors *[New York: Putnam, 1853])*

intense focus on the immediate locale (its evocation of place) yielded a quintessentially Southern literature, which found expression in the Southern local-color movement of the late nineteenth century and then blossomed in the twentieth century with scores of gifted Southern writers, the most celebrated of which was Faulkner. Simms's famous dictum on sectionalism in literature as a springboard to the universal has been proven prophetic by Faulkner, the American author most celebrated worldwide. The close similarities between the two writers have generated scholarly interest and occasioned a symposium on the subject in New Orleans in December 1997.

Simms must likewise be given credit for being the first to create a panoramic complex legend of the place and its people. He in fact called his romances collectively an epic, saga, or fable of the South. Simms's fiction is always engaged in the process of articulating Southern character and Southernness. He attempts to define his region in terms of its past and how that past shapes its present and will carry into its future. Many of his best poems and his several historical novels, of which *Woodcraft* and *The Cassique of Kiawah: A Colonial Romance* (1859) are examples, display that sense of time, mood, evocation of place and character that the mod-

ern reader perhaps understands best through the word "Faulknerian." Simms's character Porgy in *Woodcraft* is himself a representative of the Southern people as a whole, a veritable embodiment of the South, its hospitality, scorn of materialism, genial good-naturedness, tolerance, individualism, warmth, and neighborliness.

In *Woodcraft,* as in most of Simms's fiction, one has the sense of the Southern land as a place where ideals are high-toned but tempered by down-to-earth simplicity and common sense. Above all, relations are on a personal rather than a business level. Human contact undercuts and replaces abstraction. The practical and utilitarian purpose must be kept in check by a focus on the human and humane element. In other words, "poetry," beauty, spirituality, and all they represent must not be replaced by the starkly practical and materialistic. Place itself becomes spiritualized and humanized and becomes a character in its own right.

Critic Donald Davidson correctly noted that the oral quality of saga and epic is strong in Simms's work as a whole. The sense of the tale recounted is responsible for much of the effectiveness of the border romances as well as backwoods humor stories such as "Sharp Snaffles" and "Bald-Head Bill Bauldy." The narrative voice telling the tale anticipates the best of Southern writing from Mark Twain to Thomas Wolfe, Eudora Welty, Faulkner, Wendell Berry, and Fred Chappell.

As literary critic, Simms deserves more than passing note. He was remarkable for the accuracy of his assessments of his contemporaries in both the United States and Europe. He was among the most widely read authors in American literary history. His pronouncements upon literary value are closely in line with modern judgments. After more than a century and a half, he still has written one of the best essays on Cooper. He quickly saw the genius of the Brontë sisters. He judged Samuel Taylor Coleridge's talents superior to William Wordsworth's, though he was not disciplined enough to make him greater, and he preferred John Keats to Percy Bysshe Shelley and Robert Browning to the more popular Elizabeth Barrett Browning. He was the first in the United States to praise Keats in his essays. He similarly was among the first to see Poe's genius, and he aided, defended, and encouraged him when few did. He understood Poe's mysticism, spirituality, and disdain for the concrete perhaps better than any critic of the nineteenth century. Ralph Waldo Emerson he did not like so well, but he admired Hawthorne. Simms's judgments were not always prescient: Herman Melville's *Moby-Dick* (1851) he did not like at all except for its realistic depiction of whaling, and he found Ahab and his ravings a "monstrous bore." His essays on Wordsworth are always full of good sense, as are his comments on Charles Dickens, Sir Walter Scott, William Makepeace Thackeray, George Eliot, Thomas Carlyle, and Alfred Tennyson. He was also as well versed in the writers of Germany, France, and Spain as any American author of his day.

In the periodicals he edited, or as the author of the book column for the *Charleston Courier* and *Mercury,* he commented on nearly two thousand books during his lifetime. Even with so large a number, however, he was able to hit with precision the essential quality of the book and pronounce upon it, even if limited to a sentence or two. (Henry David Thoreau's *Walden,* 1854, for instance, he summarized as that curious volume of Yankee philosophy written in good prose, one aim of which was to make a virtue of stinginess.) His criticism was composed with the wit, dash, flare, and verve of his fiction. Many of his critical essays make for enjoyable, stimulating reading—as do his formal essays on literature and social matters. Several of the more significant ones are "Sectional Literature," "Americanism in Literature," "The Social Principle" (in which he states that if the United States is to produce great art and a high culture, her people must be rooted, rather than nomadic), and "The Philosophy of the Omnibus" (in which, in 1834, he outlined his attack on an industrial, technically

oriented society and criticizes Benjamin Franklin's materialism as too heavily influencing Americans to the point that the country had prostituted high art by mating it to the marketplace, thus making money the new measure of all things). He wrote against the "levelling" spirit of the age when that leveling results in the loss of quality. An incisive social and literary critic, Simms could hold his own with the best writers of his day.

As an editor he rivaled if not surpassed in color, energy, competence, and accomplishment the careers of his literary contemporaries. He formulated pioneering ideas in American literature in the pages of his journals and was excellent as an effective, practical editor. He received little remuneration from this work, so it was not done for monetary gain. He saw this endeavor as a kind of missionary service to letters. Simms, through his other writing, however, did make a living for himself. He was among the first professional authors in America to do so, no small achievement in itself during his day.

It has been shown that as a poet he penned some excellent personal lyrics quite modern in concept. He wrote effective narrative poems as well. His verse descriptive of nature is strikingly accurate. He used local setting and legend to anchor his poetry effectively in a sense of place. As early as the 1820s his use of the external landscape to mirror the mind of the viewer was an innovative and effective technique. His use of Coleridgean romanticism (particularly the concept of nature being formed through the consciousness of the person who views it) predated both Emerson's and Poe's and may be its earliest expression in the United States. In the study of American romanticism, Simms should hold a key position. As well, in poems such as "The Indian Village," he is a precursor of Realism.

Simms considered poetry his forte; and no American writer has written more, or has had a grander conception of its value—particularly as "minister to man," which would free him from the literal and scientifically empirical response to life in an era of increasing technology. Unlike his contemporaries from New England, he (like Poe) never joined what he called the cult of the didactic. His poems do not have a moral imprinted on their surface. Their subtlety is refreshing when compared to the preachy verse of John Greenleaf Whittier, Henry Wadsworth Longfellow, Emerson, and even William Cullen Bryant, who was a close personal friend of Simms. Simms's own moving defense of poetry as the most practical of pursuits against a growing empirically utilitarian world is dramatically rendered in his *Poetry and the Practical* (written between 1851 and 1854). *Poetry and the Practical,* which stands in the line of literary defenses from Edmund Spenser to Shelley, has the power to bridge the gap between poetry and a material-

[LITERARY CIRCULAR.]

# THE MAGNOLIA;
## OR, SOUTHERN APALACHIAN.
### A Literary Magazine and Monthly Review.

The Subscribers, publishers and proprietors of the MAGNOLIA MAGA- ZINE, have great pleasure in informing its friends and readers that, with the close of the present volume, or June number of this periodical, its publication will be transferred from the city of Savannah to that of Charleston. This arrangement is made in compliance with numerous suggestions from both cities, and is one which recommends itself, at a glance, to the judgments of most persons. The literary facilities of Charleston are, in some respects, superior to those of Savannah. It lies more conveniently in the line of the great thoroughfares, East and West; and its population, being so much larger, it necessarily combines the prospect of greater literary and pecuniary patronage in behalf of the work. The very considerable increase of its subscribers within the last two months, particularly in South-Carolina, naturally prompts its pro- prietors to a greater outlay of effort in promoting,—along with the wishes of its friends,—the extension of its own facilities and means of influence. This change of the place of publication, however, will imply no prefer- ence in favor of Charleston over our former publishing city. The work will be delivered to subscribers on the same day in both cities. The new arrangement will also effect that desideratum in the business de- partment of all periodicals, the punctual delivery of the journal to sub- scribers when due;—an object which has hitherto eluded all our efforts, and has been so frequently productive of mortification to ourselves, and dissatisfaction among our friends and readers. It is proposed to publish the Magazine, simultaneously, in the four cities of Savannah, Charles- ton, Columbia and Augusta, in each of which agents of character will be established, who will always be prepared with the adequate supply for subscribers, in sufficient season for delivery, on or before, the first day in every month. It will be a subject of congratulation to our friends to hear, as it is of great pride and pleasure with ourselves to state, that the MAGNOLIA, like its noble namesake, having triumphed over the first discouraging circumstances under which it was planted, has taken per- manent root, and is now in a condition of vigor and promise, which justifies the hope that it will bring forth goodliest fruit, and attain all the green honors of a hardy growth, a long life, and a perennial freshness to the last. Its subscribers are increasing daily, its typographical garments will soon be as flowing and beautiful as the best among its contempora- ries; and among the fine intellects assembled and secured to maintain its internal character, may be enumerated many of the most accomplished names of which the South can boast. It may be enough to say that we are still assured of the co-operation of all those who have heretofore written for our pages; to which we shall add, with each successive issue of the Magazine, other names no less able, by which we shall furnish to our readers a fortunate variety and most liberal supply, of the intellec- tual edibles which they desire. The Editorial duties will chiefly devolve upon Mr. W. GILMORE SIMMS, whose services we have secured to a greater degree than before. The Editorial bureau will be entirely sur- rendered to his control, and his general supervision of the work is here- after certain. He will nevertheless be assisted by the same gentlemen whose labors heretofore have contributed so largely to endow this par- ticular department of the MAGNOLIA, with the influence which it con- fessedly asserts.

It might be enough for our present purposes to end here. We rejoice to believe that the day of Southern lukewarmness to the necessity of mental culture, in our own land, has gone by forever. There is a glo- rious awakening. We have daily signs that a Southern literature is demanded. The MAGNOLIA is demanded. We are proud in detecting, in the progress of each day's events, the decisive proofs that our people need, and are determined to have, a periodical, which shall speak justly and fear not;—which shall be equally true and bold; in which criticism shall be free from cant, and opinion shall be unbiassed either by fear or favor;—a work in which the tone shall be manly, and the character and sentiment essentially and only Southern. It is very doubtful whether another word need be said on this subject. We feel the sentiment of Southern intellectual independence, every where, beginning to breath and burn around us. It will be no fault of ours if we do not maintain its fires.

Mr. P. C. PENDLETON will devote the remainder of the year to travel. He will visit our friends in the interior of South, and North-Carolina, and Georgia, during the present summer. The winter he will give to Alabama, Mississippi, and Louisiana. The superintendence of the mechanical department will fall to the charge of BURGES & JAMES, who pledge themselves that the MAGNOLIA, in typographic air and costume, shall be worthy of the noble name it bears. In this respect large im- provements are needed, and are contemplated. The general plan of the work will resemble that of the Southern Literary Messenger,—a journal confessedly among the neatest in this or in any country. These improve- ments will be made visible in the first number (July) of the next vol- ume and new series; but still farther improvements will take place in the two following numbers. On this head we will not enlarge: let the MAGNOLIA be judged by its fruits.

Our terms are as before—five dollars per annum,—payable half yearly in advance. No subscribers for less than a year. Each number will con'ain, at least sixty-four pages, which circumstances may occasion- ally induce us to increase. The press of matter, or the reception of any article of great present interest, will prompt always the addition of the necessary pages. With this summary we conclude our address to the friends of the South, Southern Literature and Southern Institutions.— It is not necessary to say how much the institutions of a country depend upon its literature. We appeal to our citizens in their own behalf, no less than ours. The creation of a national literature is, next to the actual defence of a country, by arms, against the invader, one of the first duties of patriotism. We are probably feeble now from the too long neglect of this duty. But it is not too late to reform the error, and the time is approaching fast, when the intellect of the whole South will be needed for the conflict.

P. C. PENDLETON, } *Proprietors*
BURGES & JAMES, }

CHARLESTON, JUNE 1, 1842.

☞ All communications for the MAGNOLIA should hereafter be ad- dressed to "the Publishers of the MAGNOLIA, Charleston, S. C."

*Prospectus for the magazine that Simms began editing when it moved to Charleston in 1842*

istic society as perhaps no other work in American literature. It is among Simms's highest achievements. It remained in manuscript for a century and a half, until published in 1996.

Prolific author of short stories, novels, essays, speeches, biographies, plays, and poetry, effective and devoted editor and social critic, Simms made an important mark on the literary scene that is just now being charted. His innovations and their influence were significant contributions and stand as the fountainhead of many literary traditions that developed after him. Within a career in which he never doubted the primary importance of art and its practical value to humankind, he fought hard and long for the creation of a distinctive, local, native literature free from the imitation of foreign models, either European or Northern. His own literary productions provided examples of the manner in which it could be done; and his magazines supplied him a place to voice such theories, to publish works that exemplified them, and to encourage their widespread production by adventurous new authors native to the place. It was a grand vision, a totally unselfish one, and one that, in the final analysis, triumphed.

Simms was born in Charleston, South Carolina, on 17 April 1806. His father, William Gilmore Simms Sr., was an Irish immigrant from the seaport town of Larne, near Belfast, in County Antrim. The extended Simms family of merchants in Belfast had gotten into trouble as supporters of the Irish freedom movement. Richard Simms, merchant kinsman and editor of a pro-liberation newspaper in Belfast, had in fact been banished from the country by English authorities. He had befriended and supported Wolfe Tone. The senior Simms had come to America as a young lad with his older brothers shortly after the American Revolution. He established himself as a merchant on King Street in Charleston and in 1804 married Harriet Singleton, whose paternal grandfather had migrated to Charleston from Virginia sometime before the Revolution and had become a tobacco factor and prominent citizen of the city. All the Singletons were patriots in the struggle for American independence. The Simmses and Singletons would thus have had common ground in their complaints against the English.

Simms Jr. was the second of three children and the only one to survive infancy. The first child, John, had died before Simms was born, and the third died in childbirth along with his mother in 1808 when Simms was two years old. His father's business had fallen on bad times, and the deaths of his wife and children caused him so much distress that he left for Mississippi, entrusting his remaining property and infant son in the care of his mother-in-law, Jane Miller Singleton, who, after the death of her first husband, had married Jacob

Gates. Although Simms later said that his father was bankrupt when he left, both his property and slaves remained with Jane Gates. Simms Sr. planned to have his son and Gates move to Mississippi with him after he had established himself. When he sent for them several years later, however, she refused either to leave Charleston or to relinquish the boy. Subsequently, the father sent his brother James to get Simms, but she again refused to give him up. When James attempted to abduct him on the street, Simms fought and resisted. Neighbors came to his rescue and the matter had to be settled in court with a custody trial. The judge left the decision up to the ten-year-old lad, who decided to remain in the city of his birth.

Simms's childhood in Charleston was a lonely one without parents or siblings. Throughout his life he was to reflect on this loneliness in poetry and remembrances. Nature was his solace. He describes taking long solitary walks in the lush moss-draped forests around Charleston and along the local rivers. He also found company and consolation in his reading. Gates sent Simms to school at the age of six, and he learned early to love poetry. He was soon reading so voraciously that she had to try to curb his reading time. Furthermore, Gates, who was an excellent storyteller, narrated many wonderful stories of the family and of Charleston history—particularly of the Revolution, which she had witnessed as a girl. Her own father had been killed at the Battle of Hanging Rock in 1780 and her uncle near Augusta in 1779. Her first husband, John Singleton, had been kept aboard a British prison ship. These stories lived and grew in Simms's imagination, later to be nourished by his knowledge of history, until they found artistic expression in his poetry and fiction.

As a boy Simms frequently loitered about Bull's Head Tavern, where wagoners camped after driving their long trains from upcountry South Carolina, Georgia, and the mountains of North Carolina and Tennessee. Here Simms heard the lively stories of the frontier and backcountry. There were also the Catawba Indians who brought their pottery and trading goods to market. All these experiences stirred an interest that was later manifested in his tales, romances, and poems. When Simms's father visited his son in around 1817, he regaled his listeners with tales of the Southwest, of his exploits with Andrew Jackson in 1813 and 1814, and the Indians of the Creek, Chickasaw, and Choctaw nations.

Although the boy was fascinated by these stories, he again chose to stay in Charleston rather than go with his father. Simms remained in the school that was sponsored by the College of Charleston and learned the rudiments of Latin, French, Spanish, and German and cultivated a lasting interest in language. Soon, however, his grandmother Gates had him apprenticed in a local pharmacist's shop. He had studied some medicine, and evidently she hoped he would become a doctor. But Simms had different ideas, for when his term of apprenticeship ended six years later, he entered the office of his family's friend Charles R. Carroll to study law. Like the Simmses, Carroll was also from an immigrant family of Northern Ireland.

During these years of training for a profession Simms had maintained a constant interest in literature. During long periods of illness in his youth he continued to read omnivorously, and as early as age eight he had begun to write poetry, largely in the manner of the English romantics, particularly Lord Byron. By age sixteen he was a published poet in the Charleston newspapers. By seventeen he had been praised by the well-known Hugh Swinton Legaré for a long poem written about the Ashley River. In 1825, at the age of nineteen, he published his first book, a poem in the neoclassical tradition of heroic couplets, *Monody, on the Death of Gen. Charles Cotesworth Pinckney.*

In 1824 Simms had made the first of several trips to his father's plantation on the Pearl River, near Columbia, Mississippi, where he spent several months observing life in the area. In 1825 he, his father, and uncle James traveled through the Indian territory west of the Mississippi. These firsthand experiences, particularly of backcountry and Indian life, served as the basis for several realistic poems, *The Wigwam and the Cabin,* his border romances, and, to some extent, his colonial romances in which Indians play a large part. Simms was fascinated by the variety and vitality of life in this raw new country; but when his father once again tried to convince him to stay, promising wealth, social prominence, and a political career, Simms refused and returned to Charleston. He preferred staying in the place of his birth to the rootlessness of wandering because, as he said, high culture can only be generated from the continuum of tradition. His first letters ("Letters from the West," first published in 1987) describe the frontier and its materialistic, crass new towns and give his rationale for not joining the rush for easy wealth and gain. He already knew he wanted to be a writer. When he returned home in 1825, he and a coterie of young Charleston gentlemen founded and edited the *Album,* the first periodical exclusively devoted to literature in the South, which lasted two volumes until 1826. Many of Simms's early works were published here. Early in 1826 he made his second trip west to see his father. His writings home prove that his disgust with greed on the frontier and the negative force it had on the forming of American culture found their way into his mature critique of American society. His theories were thus already formed at this early age.

Again Simms resisted his father's attempts to persuade him to stay west.

Another reason for Simms's desire to return home was Anna Malcolm Giles, whom he married later in 1826. Anna's father, Othniel Giles, was a city clerk, and the marriage was a love match. In 1827 their only child, Anna Augusta Singleton Simms, was born; and on his twenty-first birthday Simms was admitted to the bar. He became a lawyer, one of whose specialties was "cases arising on contract . . . and to the trials of Negroes and persons of colour." Even the responsibilities of marriage, fatherhood, and his new career could not keep Simms from his writing, however, as the publication of two collections of verse attests. These were *Lyrical and Other Poems* (1827) and *Early Lays* (1827), volumes that were romantic in the manner of Keats, Byron, and Coleridge. In 1828 Simms edited his second periodical, the *Southern Literary Gazette,* to further the cause of local literature. The magazine placed too much financial strain on him, and like the *Album* it was discontinued after two volumes. In the next two years Simms published two more volumes of poetry: *The Vision of Cortes, Cain, and Other Poems* (1829) and *The Tri-Color; or The Three Days of Blood, in Paris. With Some Other Pieces* (1830). Byron was a major influence in both.

Fellow authors such as Bryant and John Neal were praising his poetry rather effusively and widely at this time; and his successes indicated that he might make a career of writing and editing. Consequently, he gave up his law practice, and when the *Charleston City Gazette* was offered for sale in 1829, he invested in the publishing venture with money that had come through his mother's estate, forming a partnership with Duryea, a local printer. The first issue under Simms's editorship appeared on the first day of 1830. The death of Simms's father in that same year, however, necessitated a third journey to Mississippi in 1831 for Simms to oversee his financial interests there. In another important series of letters from the West, published in the *City Gazette* in spring 1831, he describes his journey through Georgia, Alabama, Mississippi, and Louisiana. He returned home to renew his editorship of the paper, but his firm stand against Nullification caused a political mob to gather outside the offices of the newspaper in the fall of 1831. Although Simms was threatened with injury to himself and property, he confronted the mob, defied it, and eventually the group dispersed. Although he continued to edit the paper until June 1832, his political stand obviously had crippled the paper financially. Even after his wife's death in February 1832, Simms refused to give up; but his partner's death later that spring hastened the end, and Simms was forced to sell the paper at a heavy loss.

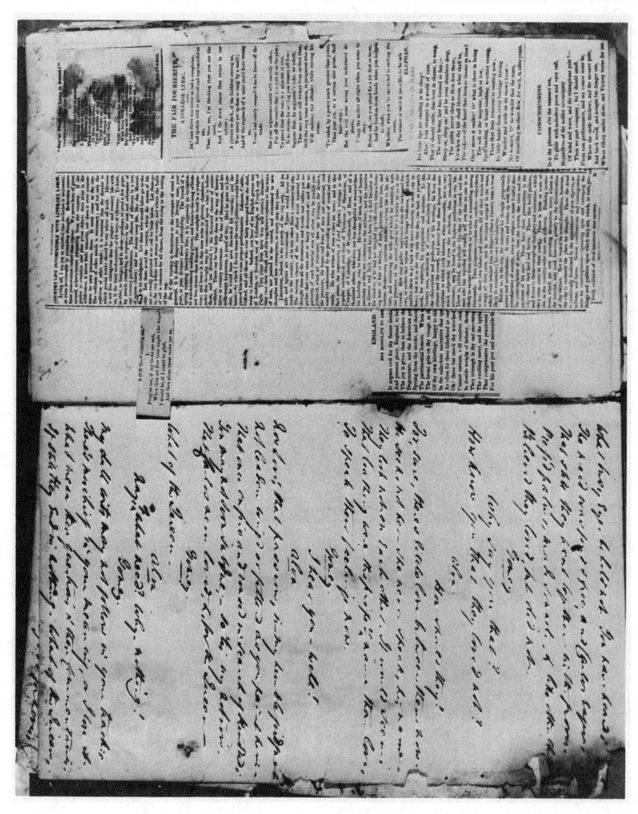

*Leaves from the manuscript for Simms's unfinished drama, "Don Carlos"; on the verso of the manuscript pages he attached clippings of his poems and sketches from various periodicals (Collection of Mary C. Simms Oliphant and the South Caroliniana Library, University of South Carolina)*

Thus, at age twenty-six, still mourning the deaths of his wife, father, and grandmother, having rejected careers in medicine and law, having failed financially as an editor, and heavily in debt, Simms was despondent. He decided to travel to the North, where literary men appeared to prosper a little better. He went first to Massachusetts and then to New York, where he made friends, among them Bryant, Timothy Flint, Evert Duyckinck, and James Lawson, who, as friend and correspondent, was later to act as a kind of literary agent for Simms in the North. He took with him the manuscript of *Atalantis. A Story of the Sea: In Three Parts,* a dramatic poem of high Romantic invention and imagination, which was published by Harper toward the end of 1832. It showed Simms's considerable talent and facility with the language and was well received both in the United States and England, where Thomas Campbell reviewed it favorably in the *London Metropolitan Magazine.*

Both Simms's homesickness and his understanding that the South was the wellspring of his art caused him to return to Charleston in October 1832. As he wrote in his "The Philosophy of the Omnibus" in 1834, he realized that the North was intent upon materialism and "levelism," forces that would eventually undermine and diminish all the achievements of Western high culture. The next year, 1833, he was back in Charleston, hard at work on a short novel, *Martin Faber; The Story of a Criminal,* which Harper accepted and published later that year. Here, Simms made use of his firsthand experiences as a trial lawyer. It is a gothic story of seduction and murder, told by the murderer, an unreliable narrator whose psychology seems chillingly accurate in his devious attempt to prove himself the victim instead of the victimizer. It achieved an immediate success in the United States and was published several times in England. Also in 1833, in Philadelphia, he visited with his friend Timothy Flint. Back home again, he collaborated on an occasional, *The Cosmopolitan,* which appeared in two numbers in Charleston.

Encouraged by his growing success, Simms went on in the next year to write his first major novel, *Guy Rivers: A Tale of Georgia* (1834), another story involving a criminal. The novel is the first of his border romances and is set in the frontier backcountry of north Georgia, through which Simms had traveled. Here he proved that he had vivid descriptive and narrative powers. *Guy Rivers* seized the public imagination and was praised by critics around the country. It was published in London, where it was also touted. Simms's reputation was now established, and in the next few years he enjoyed a success even he must have found hard to believe, receiving as much as $6,000 a year in royalties (more than $100,000 in today's currency)—more than he was ever to earn again by his pen.

In 1835 he published two major works of fiction, *The Yemassee. A Romance of Carolina,* the first of his colonial romances, and *The Partisan: A Tale of the Revolution,* the first of his Revolutionary War romances. *Mellichampe. A Legend of the Santee,* the second Revolutionary romance, appeared in 1836. All three were great popular successes. *The Yemassee* has been judged decidedly the superior, and although it is not as good as several of his later works, it is the one that, until recently, was the novel by which readers knew him best, largely because it was most widely available in several paperback editions. Like *Guy Rivers,* it has some wooden characters, but other characters, especially some of the backwoodsmen, are vivid and fully realized; and the Indians—Sanutee, Matiwan, and Occonestoga—are more realistically drawn than any of Cooper's. Simms also showed that he can keep various complicated strands of a plot going simultaneously and bring them together satisfactorily at the end—something Cooper failed to learn. The most impressive aspect of the book, however, and perhaps the reason for its modern popularity, is the sympathy with which Simms treats the Indians' plight in the face of encroaching civilization. The Indians' tragedy is absorbing and moving. *The Partisan* and *Mellichampe* have several minor characters—Porgy, Frampton, Blonay, Mother Blonay, and Thumbscrew Witherspoon—who demonstrate Simms's ability to create memorable characters, particularly deranged, obsessive, or grotesque ones. The primary interest of these romances is in Simms's descriptions of landscapes (similar to those in his poetry), his exciting battle scenes, his vigor as a narrator, and his imaginative and accurate recreation of the Revolutionary War experience.

With this unbroken string of popular and critical successes, Simms found himself one of the few men in America making a respectable living by his writing. He had survived the failures of a few years earlier and was back on his feet financially. More importantly, however, he was now a man with a national reputation and a following in Britain. The English reviewers, in particular, clearly understood the strengths of his art, as James Everett Kibler surveyed in "Some Unrecorded English Reviews of W. G. Simms" (1994). They found they "never read a better told story" and praised his "rough vigor of description," his courage to portray "terrible features," his vital "flesh and blood" characterization, his creation of the "dark" or grotesque character, and his "startling fidelity" to "life as it is." English reviewers also generally grasped Simms's realism, an aspect for which even the modern critic has sometimes failed to credit him.

Simms's talent, courage, and energy had never been in doubt, but for a man with his sense of personal worth and integrity, it must have been especially grati-

*Caricature of Simms by Charles Martin, which appeared in the 5 December 1846 issue of* Yankee Doodle *(from volume two of* The Letters of William Gilmore Simms, *1956)*

fying to find success both at home and abroad. He must have felt secure in his prosperity, for in November 1836 he married Chevillette Eliza Roach, the only daughter of Nash Roach, a well-to-do planter. The couple settled at the bride's family home, Woodlands, near Bamberg, South Carolina. From what remains of the great-house today, one can get an idea of the size and beauty of the original. Surviving sketches and descriptions of the great-house indicate that it was large and commodious, and its grounds, landscaped by Simms with exotic plants that complemented the giant moss-hung live oaks native to the place, were in keeping with the best Lowcountry plantation styles. Simms loved Woodlands, and it was his home until it was destroyed in 1865. He eventually took over the management of the extensive plantations of his father-in-law and eventually their ownership. Thus, Simms became a planter and a host famous for his hospitality, entertaining in the next two decades such notable guests as the popular English novelist G. P. R. James and the poet Bryant. Accounts also indicate that Chevillette was his charming counterpart, a lady in the best Southern tradition.

Arrangements were made at Woodlands for Simms's literary pursuits. He was given the large library as his office, and, always a bibliophile, he filled it with more than eleven thousand volumes, creating one of the largest personal libraries on the continent. When his family included many small children, he did some of his writing in the little one-room, detached brick office to the side of the great-house. Here at Woodlands, among his books, Simms wrote most of his best work. Except for his annual trip to New York to see to his literary interests and his stays at his "Wigwam" on Smith Street in Charleston, he did not often leave his plantation sanctuary.

When in 1837 Simms returned to his fiction, he chose a European subject. The results were his two Spanish romances, *Pelayo: A Story of the Goth* (1838) and its sequel, *Count Julian; Or, the Last Days of the Goth* (which was not published until 1845 because parts of the book were lost in transit and not recovered until several years later). In these works he was forced to create entirely in the imagination, and Simms was usually better when his imagination was firmly rooted in places with which he was intimately familiar. Neither book was successful with critics or the public, and Simms himself admitted later that he had strayed in abandoning native materials. In his collection of poems *Southern Passages and Pictures* (1838) he effectively returned to the genius loci for inspiration in a volume that must stand as a landmark of nineteenth-century American verse. He had conceived of this volume as early as 1836 and began publishing poems separately in that year. In its following of Simms's consistent theory of "Localism"—in using folklore, setting, and character of a well-known place—the collection is more than surface "local color." It provides instead the realization of the oneness of people and place; it shows the full-blown sense of Southern memory and remembrance, a sense of mystic reverie, spiritualized setting, and tone of mystery. It celebrates a reverence of place as being essential to the creation of high culture and of keeping mankind humane and human. Its spiritual center is an understanding that life cannot be reduced to the empirical and utilitarian, that such diminishment would be the direst kind of poverty.

In his next romance, *Richard Hurdis; Or, The Avenger of Blood. A Tale of Alabama* (1838), Simms stayed with his Southern settings, using materials he had gathered on his trips to Alabama and Mississippi. Again, the story involves a criminal and is a tale of love, jealousy, obsession, murder, and revenge. Clement Foster is patterned after the outlaw Murrell, whose history Simms had learned firsthand from Virgil Stewart, the man who had captured him. Simms continued the story of Foster-Murrell in *Border Beagles; A Tale of Mississippi* (1840). Both are considerable improvements over *Guy Rivers*, his first border romance. Their narrative excitement and vivid depiction of life constitute for some critics some of Simms's best fiction. Between *Richard Hurdis*

*Page from the manuscript for Simms's unpublished poem "The Mission" (Collection of Mary C. Simms Oliphant and the South Caroliniana Library, University of South Carolina)*

THE

# GOLDEN CHRISTMAS:

A

## CHRONICLE OF ST. JOHN'S, BERKELEY.

COMPILED FROM THE

NOTES OF A BRIEFLESS BARRISTER,

BY THE AUTHOR OF

"THE YEMASSEE," "GUY RIVERS," "KATHARINE WALTON," ETC.

CHARLESTON:
WALKER, RICHARDS AND CO.
1852.

*Title page for the first edition of Simms's 1852 novel of manners
(Collection of Dr. David Aiken)*

and *Border Beagles,* he wrote a Spanish colonial romance, *The Damsel of Darien* (1839), about Vasco Núñez de Balboa's American expedition, which was deemed so weak that even his friend James Lawson published a negative review of it. In the decade of the 1850s, when Simms was publishing his best romances of the Revolution, he also took time to write *Vasconcelos. A Romance of the New World* (1853), about Hernando de Soto's explorations, a better book than some have credited it. Simms is reputed to have had one of the best private collections of Spanish colonial literature and history in the world, and his great historical interest in Spanish colonialism obviously prompted these works. His view was that the Spanish failure to leave lasting colonies, as did the English, stemmed from their impulse to seek gold rather than make a new home.

The 1840s were the most productive years of Simms's career. During this decade he published thirty-one separate titles; contributed stories, poems, essays, and reviews to various periodicals; edited three magazines; served a term in the state legislature from 1844 to 1846; ran unsuccessfully for lieutenant governor in 1846; took hunting trips to the Carolina mountains, which he recorded in a journal that was the source of later fiction; and tended his duties as planter and head of a family that numbered nine children. He not only continued to write poetry, novels, short fiction, lectures, and essays, but also branched out into other areas: dramas, history, geography, and biography. In 1840, in addition to *Border Beagles,* Simms published his *The History of South Carolina, from its First European Discovery to Its Erection into a Republic: With a Supplementary Chronicle of Events to the Present Time,* which concentrates largely on the Revolution. In it he expounds the theme that is implicit in all his Revolutionary romances: that for South Carolina it had been civil war; as a result the state had suffered devastations to its property and population greater than the other colonies. The role of South Carolina in the war had been diminished by Northern historians, and he wanted to help set the historical record straight. To illustrate the internecine warfare in Carolina, he published in 1841 *The Kinsmen: Or The Black Riders of Congaree* (later revised and retitled *The Scout*), the third of his Revolutionary romances, in which two brothers take opposite sides in the conflict. Even though it has exciting scenes and a well-realized character in Jack Bannister, the book is not his best Revolutionary romance.

Also in 1841, Simms published *Confession; Or, The Blind Heart,* another effective psychological study in the vein of *Martin Faber.* It is a tale of jealously, in which Simms is essentially adapting Shakespeare's *Othello* to an American frontier setting. The book has generated much and growing current interest owing to its main female character, Margaret Cooper, a kind of Margaret Fuller on the frontier. In 1842, when Simms took up a similar subject in *Beauchampe: Or The Kentucky Tragedy. A Tale of Passion,* he was even more successful. When the romance was reissued in 1856, volume one was retitled *Charlemont or the Pride of the Village* and volume two retained the title *Beauchampe.* The source for the plot was the "Kentucky Tragedy," as Jereboam Beauchamp's murder of State Attorney General Solomon P. Sharp was popularly known, which had occurred some fifteen years earlier. Simms the former lawyer followed the reported details of the case and trial conscientiously and used his knowledge of the law and the border to make the novel realistic and powerful.

The factual nature of *Beauchampe* seems to signal an important change in Simms's literary career, for between it and *Katharine Walton: Or, The Rebel of Dorchester. An Historical Romance of the Revolution in Carolina* in 1851, Simms produced no extended works of fiction, only the novelettes *Castle Dismal,* which deals with the supernatural; *The Prima Donna: A Passage from City Life* (1844); *Helen Halsey: Or, The Swamp State of Conelachita. A*

*Tale of the Borders* (1845), another tale of the border; and the popular collection of short realistic fiction, *The Wigwam and the Cabin,* published to critical acclaim in the United States and England. Instead, he concentrated on poetry and nonfiction. In 1843 he produced *The Social Principle: The True Source of National Permanence, Donna Florida,* a tale in verse, and *The Geography of South Carolina: Being a Companion to the History of That State;* in 1845, *Grouped Thoughts and Scattered Fancies,* a collection of sixty-one sonnets, and his important collected literary essays, *Views and Reviews in American Literature, History and Fiction* (1845); and in 1846, his *Areytos: Or, Songs of the South.* Between 1844 and 1849 he published four biographies: lives of Francis Marion, Captain John Smith, Chevalier Bayard, and Nathanael Greene. The books on Smith and Bayard are readable popular biographies that at the same time delineate Southern culture and values. *The Life of Francis Marion* (1844) is good biography, using original materials, and remains even today an important source for the study of the Swamp Fox, one of the great heroes of the Revolution. As in the other biographies, Simms is here forging and defining the concept of a Southern people. Simms capped off the last two years of the decade with four collections of verse: *Lays of the Palmetto: A Tribute to the South Carolina Regiment, in the War with Mexico* (1848); *Charleston, and Her Satirists; a Scribblement* (1848), a satire on city society; *The Cassique of Accabee. A Tale of Ashley River* (1849), one of his finest collections, based on local lore and scenery; and *Sabbath Lyrics; Or, Songs from Scripture* (1849).

Simms had always been an advocate of Southern literature because he believed that only through sectional literature could a truly national literature be realized. One of the best ways to promote writing in the South, he felt, was through a Southern magazine that would encourage native talent and give native writers a place to publish. After a hiatus of ten years he decided to try his hand again. When the *Magnolia* moved to Charleston in 1842, he became its new editor. Then in 1845 Simms began his own *Southern and Western Magazine,* for which he had to write much of the copy himself, owing to the paucity of contributions. At the end of 1845 it was absorbed by the *Southern Literary Messenger,* and his editorship ended. In 1849, however, he took over the editorship of the *Southern Quarterly Review,* which under his direction became one of the best serious journals in the country. Often at odds with the owners, Simms quit in 1854.

If the 1840s were Simms's most productive period, the 1850s were the years during which he published his works of highest quality. His output was not as varied or as great, but during the decade he wrote some of his best fiction, notably in the four Revolutionary romances *Katharine Walton, The Sword and the Distaff*

(later retitled *Woodcraft),* and *The Forayers or The Raid of the Dog-Days* (1855) and its sequel, *Eutaw* (1856); an excellent novel of manners, *The Golden Christmas,* one of his best short works, which serves as a paired thematic counterpart to *Woodcraft;* and finally the colonial romance *The Cassique of Kiawah. Katharine Walton* again takes up the story of Colonel Walton (based on the Charleston patriot-martyr Isaac Hayne). A large part of the book concerns the local social scene during British occupation. As Mary Ann Wimsatt has pointed out, it is as much a novel of manners as a romance.

Most critics consider *Woodcraft* Simms's best book; some have even called it the first realistic novel in American literature. Jan Bakker argues this case most persuasively. The novel features Porgy, who first appeared as a minor character in *The Partisan,* considered by some to be Simms's finest fictional creation. Essentially, *Woodcraft* is a "soldier's pay" novel about a war-ravaged society attempting to come back to normality. It is also a realistic picture of plantation life in the Lowcountry and a portrayal of Southern ideals as set against Southern realities. Even though Porgy represents these ideals, he is at the same time a believable individual whose strengths and weaknesses yield an interesting and richly complex character. In fact, Porgy is one of the most likable individuals in the fiction of the American Renaissance. He bustles about as the affable, chivalric, middle-aged bachelor knight, dressing to meet his would-be fiancée. Having but recently returned home from war to a burned-out plantation, he must wear clothes that are old and shabby. He has also gained weight, and after his ride to court his lady fair, and in her presence, he begins splitting the seat of his pants. As a chevalier he is thus burlesqued, but his ideas are revered. He is not merely a Don Quixote or a Falstaff but his own distinctive self.

All the major characters in the novel tolerate one another's foibles with good nature, and the novel concludes with the status quo reaffirmed. Porgy remains a bachelor. His intended, the Widow Eveleigh, does not want to remarry. She enjoys the freedom to manage her plantation, which she does efficiently and effectively, having strength of character and intellect equal to any man in the novel. Interestingly, Simms's female characters run the gamut from the fainting damsel common in Cooper's novels to women of such strength as the widow, thus reflecting the spectrum of antebellum womanhood. The complexity of the conclusion of the novel causes the reader to question whether, despite Porgy's and the Widow's admirable traits, they are really living up to the Southern ideal after all. As recent criticism has pointed out, one of the main themes in the book is freedom, its value, cost, and meaning. Both Porgy and Eveleigh figure centrally in it. Another theme is that a proper way of seeing involves more than the empirical and "practical." "Impractical" Porgy is more sympathetic than the ever-busy, utilitarian Millhouse, said to be "born in a hurry," having not even waited for the midwife.

*The Forayers* and *Eutaw* were conceived and executed as a whole by Simms. They concern the final days of the war in Carolina. Again the conflicts are based on internal division and partisan warfare; and here Simms is at the height of his powers: he has full control over his language and characterization. His descriptions of action and scenery are among the best in his romances. A few critics have even gone so far as to consider the two taken together to be his greatest work.

*The Cassique of Kiawah* was Simms's last romance to receive book publication during his lifetime. Like *The Yemassee* of two decades before, it concerns South Carolina in the colonial era, but earlier, in 1684, when Charleston had only recently been founded. There are Indians, pirates, galleons, an intriguing heroine, love triangles, and a strong story. Here Simms reaches the height of his narrative powers. The book has a mature, serious, philosophic base and an effective tone that Simms manages to sustain throughout. He had just lost two of his young sons to fever, and the experience devastated him. The sober tone of the novel is undoubtedly a result of his loss. Another strength of the novel is the portrayal of the character Zulieme, which has garnered Simms much recent critical praise. The novel further demonstrates Simms's mature view of universal truths about life, love, fate, loss, responsibility, and destiny. It has the tight artistic unity lacking in some of his more sprawling, looser novels, without losing their energy and vitality. Until a reprint appeared in 1989, however, the book had been virtually unknown to both critics and readers. The plates from the 1859 first printing were sold and rented to Dodd, Mead for reprinting around 1860 and lost, so the romance does not appear in any of the subsequent reprintings from the Redfield settings. It has thus simply not been read except in the rarefied atmosphere of a few select rare-book rooms of major libraries. Of the major American works of the century, it is among the scarcest.

Also during the 1850s Simms published two plays, *Norman Maurice; Or, The Man of the People. An American Drama* (1851) and *Michael Bonham: Or, The Fall of Bexar. A Tale of Texas* (1852), and *As Good as a Comedy: Or, The Tennessean's Story* (1852), a work of short fiction rather tamely in the tradition of backwoods humor. In 1853 he brought out his two-volume *Poems, Descriptive, Dramatic, Legendary and Contemplative*, among the most significant poetic collections of its day. In 1854 he published a collection of related short fiction, *Southward Ho! A Spell of Sunshine*—a much-neglected, significant,

strong work that is still awaiting proper serious critical study and discovery. Another similar collection, *The Lily and the Totem, or, The Huguenots in Florida. A Series of Sketches, Picturesque and Historical, of the Colonies of Coligni, in North America* (1850), comprises historical fiction of the colonial era concerning the Huguenots and French settlements of North America, and has generated renewed critical interest. Rounding out this prolific decade was the poem *The City of the Silent* (1850–1851), a kind of ultimate graveyard poem; *Marie de Berniere: A Tale of the Crescent City* (1853), a collection of imaginative tales; and *Egeria: Or, Voices of Thought and Counsel, for the Woods and Wayside* (1853), poems, jottings, sayings, epigrams, and philosophic essays in miniature coming out of Simms's mature view of life, politics, society, death, virtue, morality, and wholeness. *Egeria* is an underutilized volume that holds the key to many of Simms's concepts. The most important publishing venture of the decade and of Simms's entire career, however, was the twenty-volume Redfield collected edition of his major works, published from 1853 to 1859. Simms revised nearly all the books published by Redfield, some of them extensively, and stereotyped plates were made for the edition. These plates were passed from publisher to publisher for the various reprintings that appeared through the entire rest of the century, thus assuring the availability of his works until the plates were so battered with wear around 1900 that they could no longer be used.

With the publication of *The Cassique of Kiawah* as the last volume of the Redfield edition in 1859, Simms's career was to begin its decline nationwide. The strain of national division was already occurring, even though the war had not begun. Simms had felt it strongly as early as 1856 when he was forced to cancel his Northern lecture tour after several engagements. His subject, "South Carolina in the Revolution," was his favorite, but because of Simms's defense of the South therein, he met with hostility from extremists in both public and press in Buffalo and Rochester, New York. He returned home dejected and even more convinced that secession was the only course for Southern survival. The revised edition of *Areytos*, published as *Simms's Poems Areytos or Songs and Ballads of the South with Other Poems* (1860), was his last collection of verse. Here he revised some of the best of his old poems and added new ones. With the outbreak of war the following year Simms was cut off from his publishers and much of his market. He received no royalties; and now in the South, publishing ventures were not priorities when the region was in a life-and-death struggle for existence. Simms himself turned his energies to the war effort. Other than poems, his only work of note during the war is *Paddy McGann; Or The Demon of the Stump* (1863). It appeared serially in the *Southern Illustrated News* and did not come out in book form until 1972. Since its republication the work has received considerable critical praise and attention.

Although Simms's son Gilmore Jr. went off to fight for the South, Simms himself was too old for soldiering. He stayed at home to manage the plantation and contribute what he could to the cause. He wrote letters making suggestions for coastal defenses and bought heavily in Confederate bonds. He gave Gilmore excellent fatherly advice in affectionate letters to the front. He wrote poems of encouragement, tribute, and mourning in the Southern press. Home itself was not safe, however. In 1862 Woodlands accidentally burned. As a sign of their respect and concern for Simms, neighbors and friends raised funds for its reconstruction. In the next year Simms suffered a much greater blow in the death of his wife from appendicitis. And in 1865 Woodlands burned again, this time at the hands of stragglers from Sherman's army, who looted and burned his large library and art collection and even destroyed the landscaped grounds on which Simms had lavished so much attention before the war. The home in which he was living in Columbia while he was working on a newspaper there would no doubt have been burned also had not a Union officer who admired his work sought him out and saved his property.

Thus, Simms lost much of what he owned except the few personal possessions he had with him in his temporary lodgings. He managed to save a trunk of his manuscripts and scrapbooks, subsequently housed at the South Caroliniana Library and the source of much primary knowledge of his career. Significant works to come out of Simms's witness of war were excellent poems such as "Among the Ruins," "Elegiac," "Ode—Our City by the Sea," and "The Voice of Memory in Exile from a Home in Ashes," and the strong narrative *Sack and Destruction of the City of Columbia, S.C. to Which Is Added a List of the Property Destroyed* (1865), among the most vivid pieces of writing by an American author-journalist. Gilmore Jr. was wounded, but his father went to him, nursed him, and brought him safely home.

The last five years of Simms's life were a struggle to support his family and the friends (such as Henry Timrod) who could not support themselves. Life at this point was a desperate battle for survival. As poet Sidney Lanier wrote, the story of these years for those of their generation in the South was largely a matter of not dying. Simms entered upon a four-book contract with a northern publisher, saying he would "die in harness." He was able to complete three of them but broke down before beginning the fourth. These works, published serially, feature some excellent writing: *Joscelyn A Tale of the Revolution* (1867), the last of the Revolutionary

romances, *The Cub of the Panther. A Hunter Legend of the "Old North State"* (1869), and *Voltmeier Or The Mountain Men* (1869). These works were first published in book form in 1975, 1997, and 1969, respectively. Simms wrote his two best stories during the last months of his life, in 1870: "Sharp Snaffles" and "Bald-Head Bill Bauldy." Besides overseeing his ruined plantation and writing, he also edited and helped edit three newspapers during these five years: the *Columbia Phoenix* (1865), the *Daily South Carolinian* (1866), and the *Charleston Courier* (1870). He was overburdened and aging, but as always Simms kept working. He practiced in his own life the great theme of endurance that appears often in his poems and fiction. Simms took his last ride in Charleston Harbor and died on 11 June 1870 from cancer and heart failure at the home of his first child, Anna, at 13 Society Street, Charleston, in the circle of family and friends. He thus departed life in the city of his birth, having resisted the nomadism he felt to be antipathetic to true culture.

An error frequently made by commentators on Simms's career is that his reception in the North and in the South during his lifetime was generally unfavorable. The mistake is caused, probably, by a familiarity with only a few often-reprinted negative reviews. Recent systematic studies of contemporary periodicals have shown that this view is completely unfounded. Simms was well received—generally praised and often in glowing terms—by reviewers in the North and South and in England. In the South he was praised by the *Southern Literary Messenger, Russell's,* and *De Bow's,* as well as lesser magazines. Contrary to the thesis of William Peterfield Trent in his *William Gilmore Simms* (1892), Charleston newspapers, critics, and reviewers always praised and supported Simms. In the North *Godey's,* the *New York Mirror,* the *American Review,* the *Democratic Review, Graham's,* and the *Broadway Journal* all praised Simms's best work and usually treated even his lesser work kindly. Only a few magazines, notably the *Knickerbocker,* the *North American Review,* and the *Harbinger,* were consistently hostile, for the most part because of literary politics. Simms had made an enemy of Lewis Gaylord Clark, and Clark took every opportunity to condemn Simms and the "Young America" movement, of which Simms was a predecessor, major member, and founder. Bryant, Henry W. Herbert, James Lawson, and Duyckinck stood by Simms almost without reservation. Poe, too, who was not always kind to his contemporaries, was usually his defender and praised his vitality, imagination, and powers of invention. The most objective contemporary commentaries at home and abroad applauded his realistic descriptions of scenery and action, the powerful kinetic energy of his style at its best, the fertility of his imagination, and the essential

*Simms, later in life (South Caroliniana Library, University of South Carolina)*

passion of his creation. Contemporaries usually placed Simms in the top rank of American writers, and Simms maintained this reputation until the outbreak of war.

Simms's reputation has never regained that early acclaim. In the age of realism that followed the war he was lumped summarily with other romancers and pronounced lacking. Although he had his defenders, his books, which were still read, were thought suitable only for children by, for example, John W. DeForest and William Dean Howells. Consequently, Simms was ignored by serious critics and literary historians into the twentieth century. In 1892 Trent published his biography of Simms. Charles Dudley Warner, the anti-Southern editor of the series in which this biography appeared, chose Trent to write this work, which would at the same time excoriate the chivalric Old South civilization that produced him.

Trent wrote what amounts to a hatchet job on Simms. "Chivalry was a fine thing in its own day, but modern civilization is a much higher thing," he wrote. He found Simms to be a product of his environment and heredity and therefore doomed to failure. Forgetting Homer and Virgil, Trent wrote that no slaveholding society could produce great art, thus making Simms a pretext for damning the Old South and praising "pro-

gressive" democratic America. Trent's volume made excellent propaganda for the brand of American Realism-Naturalism that had come into vogue, and Simms was effectively put aside. The Simms family, who had loaned Trent their papers, letters, and documents and had spent many hours aiding and being hospitable to him, felt betrayed by the biography. Trent also used Simms as a case in point to show that the South had always stifled her men of genius. Simms the man is treated sympathetically, if with an implicit condescension; but his works are admired only for their occasional rise above mediocrity. For the next thirty-five years, literary historians merely repeated Trent's pronouncements, most without bothering to seek out and read Simms's works.

In 1927 Vernon Louis Parrington in his *Main Currents in American Thought* altered Trent's thesis somewhat. Instead of seeing Simms as a natural romancer, he believed he was instinctively a realist who had been thwarted by a culture demanding romance. This view was not entirely new—James Scherer had foreshadowed Parrington in his essay on Simms in the *Library of Southern Literature* (1908–1913)—but Parrington gave the thesis a wide currency. His opinions were largely the ones followed for the next twenty-five years and have continued to influence Simms scholarship. A. H. Quinn, however, in his *American Fiction: An Historical and Critical Survey* (1936) appears to have actually read Simms and gives the work a balanced and sympathetic treatment, largely free from theses, propaganda, and gimmicks.

The publication of the first five volumes of *The Letters of William Gilmore Simms* (1952–1956) began a new era in Simms criticism and scholarship. Volume one includes an excellent introduction by Donald Davidson emphasizing the humor, realism, and the strength Simms drew from Southern culture as its bardic "saga man." The letters themselves made manifest for many scholars for the first time Simms's wide range and humanity and provided material not only for the literary scholar but also for the cultural historian as well. Another important contribution of the time was Jay B. Hubbell's essay in his *The South in American Literature, 1607–1900* (1954). A new interest in Simms, based on primary materials, thus began to bear fruit in the late 1960s.

The Centennial Edition of Simms's works, which published its first volume, *Voltmeier*, in 1969, gave some impetus to the trend. Four volumes in this edition appeared before the project lost its National Endowment for the Humanities funding. The Centennial Edition has been superseded by the Arkansas Press edition of the works of Simms, which has brought back into print (through 2001) seven more volumes—*Guy Rivers, The Yemassee, Richard Hurdis, Border Beagles, The Cub of the*

*Panther, Helen Halsey,* and *The Wigwam and the Cabin*—with many more titles projected. In 1976 all of Simms's Revolutionary romances were republished, complete with scholarly notes and introductions, in a handsome hardback edition. University press editions of Simms's best poems, his previously unpublished lecture *Poetry and the Practical,* and a collection of his best short fiction have made these works available to the modern reader. Limited press editions of *The Cassique of Kiawah* and *The Golden Christmas* also came out in the 1990s. As a result, Simms's works are being read again, and a rapidly increasing number of articles on him are appearing in the scholarly journals.

Several scholarly books on Simms were published in the last decade, including two volumes of collected essays, a bibliography of his two thousand poems, and a new biography that replaces the propagandistic and thesis-ridden Trent biography that has damaged Simms since its publication. With the founding of the William Gilmore Simms Society in spring 1993, its periodical, the *Simms Review,* devoted to publishing scholarship on the writer's canon and life, has appeared twice yearly. Its seventeenth issue was published in the summer of 2001. The Simms Society sponsors symposia and conferences every two years that provide a forum for the presentation of the latest Simms research. These meetings have been held in Arkansas, Mississippi, North Carolina, Louisiana, and South Carolina. In part through the efforts of the society, Simms is at last being celebrated worldwide, from Japan to Russia, for his important role in the history of American literature. As John Caldwell Guilds accurately concluded in his *Simms: A Literary Life* (1992), William Gilmore Simms "deserves place as a *major* American writer."

**Letters:**

*The Letters of William Gilmore Simms,* 6 volumes, volume 1–5 edited by Mary C. Simms Oliphant, Alfred Taylor Odell, and T. C. Duncan Eaves, volume 6 edited by Oliphant and Eaves (Columbia: University of South Carolina Press, 1952–1982);

James Everett Kibler, "The First Simms Letters: 'Letters from the West,'" *Southern Literary Journal,* 19 (Spring 1987): 81–91;

Anne B. Meriwether, "An Unpublished Letter of 1862 from Simms to W. J. Rivers," *Simms Review,* 3 (Summer 1995): 1–4;

Kibler, "Two New Simms Letters," *Simms Review,* 5 (Winter 1997): 3–6.

**Bibliographies:**

Alexander S. Salley Jr., *Catalogue of the Salley Collection of the Works of Wm. Gilmore Simms* (Columbia, S.C.: State Company, 1943);

James Everett Kibler, *Pseudonymous Publications of William Gilmore Simms* (Athens: University of Georgia Press, 1976);

Betty Jo Strickland, "The Short Fiction of William Gilmore Simms: A Checklist," *Mississippi Quarterly,* 29 (Fall 1976): 591–608;

Keen Butterworth, "William Gilmore Simms," in *First Printings of American Authors* (Detroit: Gale Research, 1977), I: 325–334;

Kibler, *The Poetry of William Gilmore Simms: An Introduction and Bibliography* (Spartanburg, S.C.: Reprint Company, 1979);

Butterworth and Kibler, *William Gilmore Simms: A Reference Guide* (Boston: Hall, 1980).

**Biographies:**

William Peterfield Trent, *William Gilmore Simms* (Boston: Houghton, Mifflin, 1892);

John Caldwell Guilds, *Simms: A Literary Life* (Fayetteville: University of Arkansas Press, 1992);

Miriam J. Shillingsburg, "The Senior Simmses—Mississippi Unshrouded," *Simms Review,* 6 (Summer 1998): 24–28;

David Aiken, "William Gilmore Simms," in *Fire in the Cradle: Charleston's Literary Heritage* (Charleston, S.C.: Charleston Press, 1999), pp. 15–32.

**References:**

David Aiken, Introduction to Simms's *The Cassique of Kiawah* (Gainesville, Ga.: Magnolia, 1989), pp. iii–xxix;

Aiken, "The Mock Trial in *The Golden Christmas* and the Theme of Reconciliation," *Simms Review,* 2 (Spring 1994): 17–20;

Aiken, Introduction to Simms's *The Golden Christmas* (Charleston, S.C.: Fletcher, 1994), pp. i–viii;

Aiken, "Simms's War Poetry: A Battle Cry of Freedom," *Simms Review,* 2 (Winter 1994): 11–17;

Aiken, "*The Wigwam* and *the Cabin:* An Artistic Response to Abolitionist Slander," *Simms Review,* 3 (Winter 1995): 16–21;

Jan Bakker, "The Pastoral Pessimism of William Gilmore Simms," *Studies in American Fiction,* 11 (Spring 1983): 81–90;

Lewis Bush, "Werther on the Alabama Frontier: A Reinterpretation of Simms's *Confession,*" *Mississippi Quarterly,* 21 (Spring 1968): 119–130;

Robert Bush, Introduction to Simms's *As Good as a Comedy: Or the Tennessean's Story. And Paddy McGann; Or the Demond of the Stump,* edited by James B. Meriwether (Columbia: University of South Carolina Press, 1972), pp. ix–xxx;

William Lamar Cawthorn, "The Mother Lend: The Southern Nationalism of William Gilmore Simms," *Simms Review,* 8 (Winter 2000): 3–19;

Corinne Dale, "William Gilmore Simms's Porgy as Domestic Hero," *Southern Literary Journal,* 13 (Winter 1980): 55–71;

Donald Davidson, Introduction to *The Letters of William Gilmore Simms,* volume 1, edited by Mary C. Simms Oliphant, Alfred Taylor Odell, and T. C. Duncan Eaves (Columbia: University of South Carolina Press, 1952), pp. xxi–lviii;

Davidson and Oliphant, Introduction to Simms's *Voltmeier* (Columbia: University of South Carolina Press, 1969), pp. xi–xxix;

Renée Dye, "A Sociology of the Civil War: Simms's *Paddy McGann,*" *Southern Literary Journal,* 28 (Spring 1996): 3–23;

Benjamin F. Fisher, "Simms Looks at Poe," *Simms Review,* 5 (Winter 1997): 13–19;

John Caldwell Guilds, ed., *"Long Years of Neglect": The Work and Reputation of William Gilmore Simms* (Fayetteville: University of Arkansas Press, 1988);

Guilds and Caroline Collins, eds., *William Gilmore Simms and the American Frontier* (Athens: University of Georgia Press, 1997);

Lynn Hogue, "The Presentation of Post-Revolutionary Law in *Woodcraft,*" *Mississippi Quarterly,* 31 (Spring 1978): 201–210;

C. Hugh Holman, Introduction to Simms's *Views and Reviews* (Cambridge, Mass.: Belknap Press of the Harvard University Press, 1962), pp. vii–xliii;

Holman, Introduction to Simms's *The Yemassee* (Boston: Houghton Mifflin, 1961), pp. vii–xxvii;

Holman, "The Present State of Simms Scholarship," *Southern Literary Journal,* 10 (Fall 1977): 92–97;

Elmo Howell, "The Concept of Character in Simms's Border Romances," *Mississippi Quarterly,* 22 (Fall 1969): 303–312;

Jay B. Hubbell, "William Gilmore Simms," in his *The South in American Literature, 1607–1900* (Durham, N.C.: Duke University Press, 1954), pp. 572–602, 958–961;

James Everett Kibler, *"The Album* (1826): The Significance of the Recently Discovered Second Volume," *Studies in Bibliography,* 39 (1986): 62–78;

Kibler, Introduction to *Poetry and the Practical* (Fayetteville: University of Arkansas Press, 1996), pp. xi–xlvii;

Kibler, Introduction to *The Poetry of William Gilmore Simms* (Spartanburg, S.C.: Reprint Company, 1979), pp. 1–51;

Kibler, Introduction to *Selected Poems of William Gilmore Simms* (Athens: University of Georgia Press, 1990), pp. xi–xxii;

Kibler, "The Major Fiction of W. G. Simms," *Mississippi Quarterly,* 43 (Winter 1990): 85–95;

Kibler, "On the Pairing of *Woodcraft* and *The Golden Christmas,*" *Simms Review,* 2 (Spring 1994): 13–16;

Kibler, "Simms as Naturalist: Lowcountry Landscape in His Revolutionary Novels," *Mississippi Quarterly,* 31 (Fall 1978): 501–518;

Kibler, "Simms Indebtedness to Folk Tradition in 'Sharp Snaffles,'" *Southern Literary Journal,* 4 (Spring 1972): 55–68;

Kibler, "Simms the Gardener, Reconstructing the Gardens at Woodlands," *Simms Review,* 1 (Summer 1993): 17–26;

Kibler, "Simms's First Published Fiction," *Studies in Bibliography,* 43 (1990): 376–380;

Kibler, "Simms's Poem for the Opening of the New Charleston Theatre," *Southern Literary Journal,* 28 (Spring 1996): 24–31;

Kibler, "Simms's Prophetic Muse," *Mississippi Quarterly,* 49 (Winter 1996): 109–113;

Kibler, "Some Unrecorded English Reviews of W. G. Simms," *Mississippi Quarterly,* 47 (Fall 1994): 557–566;

Kibler, "The Unpublished Preface to W. G. Simms's Collected Poems," *Studies in Bibliography,* 49 (1996): 291–293;

Annette Kolodny, "The Unchanging Landscape: The Pastoral Impulse in Simms's Revolutionary War Romances," *Southern Literary Journal,* 5 (Fall 1972): 46–67;

Ian Marshall, "The American Dreams of Sam Snaffles," *Southern Literary Journal,* 18 (Spring 1986): 96–107;

John McCardell, "Trent's *Simms:* The Making of a Biography," in *A Master's Due: Essays in Honor of David Herbert Donald,* edited by William J. Cooper Jr., Michael F. Holt, and John McCardell (Baton Rouge: Louisiana State University Press, 1985), pp. 179–203;

Stephen Meats, "Bald-Head Bill Bauldy: Simms's Unredeemed Captive," *Studies in American Humor,* new series 3 (Winter 1984): 321–329;

Meats, Introduction to Simms's *Joscelyn* (Columbia: University of South Carolina Press, 1975), pp. vii–xxx;

James B. Meriwether, "Simms's 'Sharp Snaffles' and 'Bald-Head Bill Bauldy': Two Views of Men–and of Woman," *South Carolina Review,* 16 (Spring 1984): 66–71;

E. A. Morozhina, "Simms's Views and Works as Looked upon from Russia," *Simms Review,* 9 (Summer 2001): 13–16;

Charmaine Mosby, "William Hinkley/Calvert: The Key to *Charlemont* and *Beauchamps,*" *Southern Literary Journal,* 16 (Spring 1984): 21–29;

Edd Winfield Parks, *William Gilmore Simms as Literary Critic* (Athens: University of Georgia Press, 1961);

Marietta Patrick, "The Dream Sequences in Simms's *Castle Dismal*," *Southern Quarterly*, 35 (Fall 1996): 7–11;

J. V. Ridgely, *William Gilmore Simms* (New York: Twayne, 1962);

Louis D. Rubin, "The Romance of the Colonial Frontier: Simms, Cooper, the Indians, and the Wilderness," in *American Letters and the Historical Consciousness: Essays in Honor of Lewis P. Simpson*, edited by J. Gerald Kennedy and Daniel Mark Fogel (Baton Rouge: Louisiana State University Press, 1987), pp. 112–136;

Miriam J. Shillingsburg, "From Notes to Novel," *Southern Literary Journal*, 5 (Fall 1972): 89–107;

Shillingsburg, "'The Idylls of the Apalachian': An Unpublished Lecture," *Appalachian Journal*, 1 (Autumn 1972): 147–160;

Shillingsburg, "The Influence of Sectionalism on the Revisions in Simms's Revolutionary Romances," *Mississippi Quarterly*, 29 (Fall 1976): 526–538;

Shillingsburg, "Maturing of Simms's Short Fiction–The Example of 'Oakatibbe,'" *Mississippi Quarterly*, 38 (Spring 1985): 99–117;

Shillingsburg, "Simms and the Myth of Appalachia," *Appalachian Journal*, 6 (Winter 1979): 111–119;

Shillingsburg, "Simms's Last Novel, *The Cub of the Panther*," *Southern Literary Journal*, 17 (Spring 1985): 108–119;

*Simms Review*, 1– (Spring 1993–   );

Arlin Turner, "Poe and Simms," in *Papers on Poe: Essays in Honor of John Ward Ostrom*, edited by Richard P. Veler (Springfield, Ohio: Chantry Music Press, 1972), pp. 140–160;

R. T. Valentine, "William Gilmore Simms, Episcopalian," *Simms Review*, 8 (Summer 2000): 2–14;

Simone Vauthier, "Of Time and the Old South: The Fiction of Simms," *Southern Literary Journal*, 5 (Fall 1972): 3–45;

Vauthier, "Une aventure du récit fantastique: *Paddy McGann*," *RANAM*, 6 (1973): 78–104;

Frederick Wagner, "Simms's Editing of The Life of Nathanael Greene," *Southern Literary Journal*, 11 (Fall 1978): 40–43;

Jon L. Wakelyn, *The Politics of a Literary Man: William Gilmore Simms* (Westport, Conn.: Greenwood Press, 1973);

Charles S. Watson, *From Nationalism to Secessionism: The Changing Fiction of William Gilmore Simms* (Westport, Conn.: Greenwood Press, 1993);

Watson, "Introduction" to Simms's *Woodcraft* (New Haven: New College & University Press, 1983), pp. 9–28;

Watson, "A New Approach to Simms: Imagery and Meaning in *The Yemassee*," *Mississippi Quarterly*, 26 (Spring 1973): 155–163;

Watson, "Simms and the American Revolution," *Mississippi Quarterly*, 29 (Fall 1976): 498–500;

Watson, "Simms and the Beginnings of Local Color," *Mississippi Quarterly*, 35 (Winter 1981): 25–39;

Watson, "Simms's *Richard Hurdis*: A Probable Source for Mark Twain's Grangerfords," *Simms Review*, 3 (Summer 1995): 23–27;

Clyde N. Wilson, "Tiger's Meat: Simms and the History of the Revolution," *Simms Review*, 8 (Winter 2000): 22–31;

Mary Ann Wimsatt, *The Major Fiction of William Gilmore Simms: Cultural Traditions and Literary Forms* (Baton Rouge: Louisiana State University Press, 1989);

Wimsatt, "William Gilmore Simms," in *The History of Southern Literature*, edited by Rubin and others (Baton Rouge: Louisiana State University Press, 1985), pp. 108–126.

## Papers:

The most important collection of William Gilmore Simms's manuscripts, which includes unpublished letters, writings, notebooks, and scrapbooks, is in the South Caroliniana Library, University of South Carolina, particularly in the Charles Carroll Simms Collection.

# Margaret Bayard Smith

*(20 February 1778 – 7 June 1844)*

Fredrika J. Teute

*Omohundro Institute of Early American History and Culture*

BOOKS: *The Diversions of Sidney, by a Friend of Youth* (Washington, D.C., 1805);

*American Mother; or, The Seymour Family,* anonymous (Washington, D.C.: Davis & Force, 1823);

*Winter in Washington, or Memoirs of the Seymour Family,* anonymous (New York: Bliss & White, 1824; London: Newman, 1824);

*What Is Gentility? A Moral Tale,* anonymous (Washington, D.C.: Pishey Thompson, 1828).

OTHER: Jean-Nicolas Bouilly, "Estelle Aubert. A Tale," translated by Smith, *Ladies' Magazine, and Literary Gazette,* 7 (July 1834): 308–326;

Madame de Genlis, "The Deaf and Blind: A Tale of Truth," translated by Smith, *Ladies' Magazine, and Literary Gazette,* 9 (March 1836): 149–159;

"Mrs. Madison," by Smith as "M.H.S.," in *National Portrait Gallery of Distinguished Americans,* compiled by James Herring and James B. Longacre, volume 3 (New York: Hermon Bancroft, 1836), n.p.

## SELECTED PERIODICAL PUBLICATIONS– UNCOLLECTED:

### POETRY

"Lines by a Young Lady. Written at the Falls of the Passaick, July, 1800," as M., *Monthly Magazine, and American Review,* 3 (November 1800): 399;

"To the Poppy," as S., *Ladies Magazine, and Literary Gazette,* 6 (July 1833): 217–218;

"To Harriet Martineau," as M. H. S., *Daily National Intelligencer,* 7 February 1835, p. 2;

"'No Time to Pray,'" as S****, *Ladies' Magazine, and Literary Gazette,* 8 (July 1835): 388;

"The Fairy's Flight," as S****, *Ladies' Magazine, and Literary Gazette,* 9 (November 1836): 652–654;

"The Marys," anonymous, *Southern Literary Messenger,* 3 (June 1837): 344;

"The Season of Flowers," as Mrs. Harrison Smith, *Godey's Lady's Book,* 15 (July 1837): 12.

### FICTION

"The Evils of Reserve in Marriage," as N., *Monthly Magazine, and American Review,* 2 (June 1800): 409–411;

*Margaret Bayard Smith (after the portrait by Charles Bird King; from* The First Forty Years of Washington Society, *1906)*

"Presence of Mind. Illustrated by Examples from Life," as S., *Ladies' Magazine, and Literary Gazette,* 4 (July 1831): 307–316;

"A Sketch," as S., *Ladies' Magazine, and Literary Gazette,* 4 (August 1831): 368–371;

"The Deserted Child, or Blessings of a Sunday School," anonymous, *Ladies' Magazine, and Literary Gazette,* 5 (February 1832): 79–86; (March 1832): 97–110;

"A Winter-Day's Ramble," as S., *Ladies' Magazine, and Literary Gazette,* 6 (May 1833): 204–213;

"Humble Life," as a Southern Lady, *Ladies' Magazine, and Literary Gazette,* 7 (June 1834): 254–258;

"Poor Mary.–A Mother's Story," as S., 8 (September 1835): 477–486;

"Recollections," as a Southern Writer, *Ladies' Magazine, and Literary Gazette,* 9 (September 1836): 491–501;

"The Young Wife," *Godey's Lady's Book,* 14 (May 1837): 196–209;

"Who Is Happy?" *Godey's Lady's Book,* 18 (March 1839): 97–102; (April 1839): 157–161; (May 1839): 214–218.

NONFICTION

"Recollections of a Visit to Monticello," anonymous, *Richmond Enquirer,* 18 January 1823, pp. 1–2;

"The Birthplace of Washington. Visited 1829," as S., *Ladies' Magazine, and Literary Gazette,* 4 (May 1831): 199–204;

"The Grave of Jefferson. Visited in August, 1828," as S., *Ladies' Magazine, and Literary Gazette,* 4 (May 1831): 204–206;

"My Books," as S****, Washington, 1831," *Ladies' Magazine, and Literary Gazette,* 4 (September 1831): 404–412;

"Presidential Inaugurations. Washington–1789. Adams–1797," as S****, *Ladies' Magazine, and Literary Gazette,* 4 (October 1831): 435–441;

"Presidential Inaugurations. Jefferson–1801," as S****, *Ladies' Magazine, and Literary Gazette,* 4 (November 1831): 481–485;

"Presidential Inaugurations. Madison–1806 [*sic*]," as S****, *Ladies' Magazine, and Literary Gazette,* 4 (December 1831): 529–537;

"Presidential Inaugurations. Jackson–1829," as S****, *Ladies' Magazine, and Literary Gazette,* 5 (March 1832): 112–117;

"The Three Cornelias," as S****, *Ladies' Magazine, and Literary Gazette,* 5 (May 1832): 217–221; (June 1832): 241–244;

"Arria, Or The Heroism of Affection," anonymous, *Ladies' Magazine, and Literary Gazette,* 5 (July 1832): 289–297;

"Roman Sketches. Poetus Thrasea, or the Closing of a Good Man's Life," anonymous, *Ladies' Magazine, and Literary Gazette,* 5 (August 1832): 337–352;

"Sophinisba: Or Love, the Conqueror, Conquered," anonymous, *Ladies' Magazine, and Literary Gazette,* 5 (September 1832): 385–396;

"Roman Sketches. Servilia, Or The Roman Daughter," as A Lady of Washington, *Ladies' Magazine, and Literary Gazette,* 6 (January 1833): 6–22;

"Domestic Sketches . . . No. I," as A Southern Pen, *Ladies' Magazine, and Literary Gazette,* 7 (January 1834): 21–35;

"Domestic Sketches . . . No. II," as A Southern Pen, *Ladies' Magazine, and Literary Gazette,* 7 (February 1834): 54–65;

"Domestic Sketches . . . No. III," as S****, *Ladies' Magazine, and Literary Gazette,* 7 (March 1834): 120–126;

"Roman Sketches.–Fannia," as Our Correspondent at Washington, *Ladies' Magazine, and Literary Gazette,* 8 (March 1835): 133–142; (April 1835): 193–204; (May 1835): 251–261; (June 1835): 323–330;

"Sketches of Private Life and Character of William H. Crawford," *Southern Literary Messenger,* 3 (April 1837): 262–265; (May 1837): 273–280;

"Constantine: Or, The Rejected Throne," as Mrs. Harrison Smith, *Southern Literary Messenger,* 3 (June 1837): 360–367; (July 1837): 447–454; (August 1837): 499–504; (September 1837): 579–582; (October 1837): 637–639; (November 1837): 669–673; (December 1837): 721–725;

"The Falls of Passaic," as Mrs. Harrison Smith, *Godey's Lady's Book,* 14 (June 1837): 265–268;

"The President's House Forty Years Ago," as Mrs. Harrison Smith, *Godey's Lady's Book,* 27 (November 1843): 212–218.

Margaret Bayard Smith is best known for her commentary on society in early national Washington, D.C., and for her character sketches of public figures in the capital city in the first four decades of the nineteenth century. Gaillard Hunt published an edited selection from her letters and journals in *The First Forty Years of Washington Society. Portrayed by the Family Letters of Mrs. Samuel Harrison (Margaret Bayard) Smith from the Collection of Her Grandson J. Henley Smith* (1906), a publication that has shaped twentieth-century perceptions of Smith. In editing her letters, Hunt omitted her discussions of her literary undertakings and of her discontent with women's status. Smith's letters portray her as a lively participant in and intelligent observer of the formative years of politics in the federal city. Her intimate vignettes of Thomas Jefferson during and after his presidency; her depiction of the burning of Washington and fear of slave insurrection during the War of 1812; and her critical portrayal of Andrew Jackson's presidential administration have particularly influenced historians interpreting the Jeffersonian era and the rise of Jacksonian democracy. Less recognized have been how consciously involved she and other women in Washington were as molders of national political culture and how deeply engaged they were as partisans in party politics. Smith's reputation in her own day was as one of "the distinguished literary ladies" of the United States and as the "authoress" of *Winter in Washington, or Memoirs of the Seymour Family* (1824), *What Is Gentility? A Moral Tale* (1828), and articles in periodicals. There is no complete bibliography of Smith's published works; many of her writings are anonymous or signed "S.," until the later 1830s, when she began signing herself "Mrs. Harrison

*Smith's father, Colonel John Bayard (from* The First Forty Years of Washington Society, *1906)*

Smith" or "M. H. S." Smith's importance lies in her doubled vision as an elite white woman. Living between the Revolution and the antebellum eras she was both an active participant in constructing the political and social structures of the new republic and an acute observer of those structures' exclusionary limitations.

Bayard descended from a long, prolific, and well-connected line of Huguenot immigrants. Her great-great-great grandmother was Anna Stuyvesant Bayard, who, along with her children, joined her brother, Director-General Peter Stuyvesant, in New Amsterdam in the 1650s. Her advantageously positioned sons and their children made strategic marriages with other rising colonial families of English, French Huguenot, and Dutch origin, building estates, wealth, and status as they formed a colonial elite of almost dynastic dimensions between New York and Maryland. As a result Bayard's heritage included a set of accomplished, well-educated women of socially prominent and powerful families.

Born on 20 February 1778 outside Philadelphia, Margaret Bayard entered the world in the midst of the Revolution. The upheaval of the war and the dislocation of her family marked the first years of her life. Her parents were Colonel John Bubenheim Bayard and

Margaret Hodge, daughter of Andrew Hodge, Bayard's mercantile partner. In 1780 Bayard's mother died, leaving eight living children, of whom Margaret was second from last. A prominent merchant, leading patriot, and later Federalist, Colonel Bayard served as a Revolutionary officer, speaker of the Pennsylvania Assembly, member of the Continental Congress, New Jersey jurist, and elder in the Presbyterian Church. As his daughter and as niece, cousin, and in-law of other legislators, lawyers, and judges, Bayard was born and bred into a political family. Her father's home was a salon for the Whig social and political leaders of the Revolutionary era. She certainly grew in an environment where intellectual conversation and political discussion were the common currency of social exchange. Her active involvement in forming a continental political and social coterie in Washington, D.C., was a natural move for a woman with her cosmopolitan background in Philadelphia, New Jersey, and New York.

By the time she was ten years old, she had lost her mother and a stepmother, Mary Grant Hodgson, and had acquired a second stepmother, Johannah White. In 1789 her father sent her and her younger sister, Anna Maria, to the Moravian Young Ladies Seminary in Bethlehem, Pennsylvania. The school was the premier female academy in the country. Bayard's taste for serious reading, writing, and intellectual discourse derived from her education there as well as in the homes of various family members where she resided during the 1790s. Particularly under the guidance of her older sister Jane Bayard Kirkpatrick and her husband in New Brunswick, New Jersey, she turned her attention from novels to Enlightenment reading in moral philosophy, history, and religion, including the works of Sir Isaac Newton; William Robertson's *The History of Scotland* (1761) and *The History of the Reign of the Emperor Charles V* (1769); Jean-Jacques Rousseau's *Julie, ou La Nouvelle Héloïse* (1761) and *Emile* (1762); biographies of Madame de Maintenon, the second wife of Louis XIV; the letters of author Marquise de Sévigné; Edward Young's *The Complaint; or Night-Thoughts* (1742–1746); and Hugh Blair's sermons. Her habits of extensive reading and critical thinking matured during the years she spent with the Kirkpatricks and in extended visits to her grandparents, the Presbyterian clergyman John Rodgers and his wife, in New York.

In New York between 1795 and 1800, Bayard fell in with a circle of young intellectual men and women. Among them were Elihu Hubbard Smith, Samuel Latham Mitchill, Anthony Bleecker, Samuel Miller, Edward Miller, William Johnson, Charles Brockden Brown, Maria Templeton, Maria Nicholson, and Margaretta Mason. The men were members of the Friendly Club, a weekly discussion group. Filled with

Enlightenment zeal for individual and social improvement, the women and men visited together in the evenings, reading, walking, and conversing. In their company Bayard's intellectual ambition took flight. During this period she came to question the strict Calvinist principles of her family, leaning instead toward a Universalist religious outlook. Influenced by Mary Wollstonecraft's *A Vindication of the Rights of Woman* (1792), Bayard became convinced of the importance and inadequacies of female education, the inhibitions against women's intellectual advancement, and the necessity for women's ability to support themselves economically. These concerns were recurrent themes in her writings in later years.

At the same time that she was expanding her intellectual horizons, she became engaged in 1797 to her second cousin Samuel Harrison Smith, a Philadelphia publisher and Jeffersonian Republican. They carried on a three-year courtship largely through correspondence. Bayard outlined in her letters to Smith her ideals for a companionate marriage based on friendship and intellectual esteem. Although anticipating future happiness with Smith, Bayard's writings on the eve of her marriage also reveal anxiety about conjugal bonds. Personal experience and several young women's fates in New York made Bayard keenly aware of middle-class women's dependence on the institution of marriage as the only viable option for those who lacked family or independent means of support. Recording her reflections on the potential pitfalls of the married state, she read extracts from her journals in the spring of 1800 to her New York friends, among them Johnson and Brown, who had just begun publication of the *Monthly Magazine, and American Review*. Impressed with her "correct" style and "just" sentiments, they requested a copy. Bayard found their praise "more highly gratifying than any I have ever received." "The Evils of Reserve in Marriage" appeared in the June 1800 issue. This first assay in print gave her a taste of the pleasures of commendation and recognition to be gained through intellectual production; it planted the seeds of ambition.

Although Bayard in "The Evils of Reserve in Marriage" may have meant to purvey positive advice (to herself, as well as to others) for felicity in marriage, in a word, "candour," her cautionary tale focused on the dangers of withholding love and support from one's spouse out of an excessive sensibility to the spouse's reserve. At a time when middle-class Americans were embracing the ideology of companionate marriage, Bayard's moral tale deconstructed the premises of affectional marriage and exposed the unequal power equation underlying it. At the beginning of the nineteenth century, Bayard's darker take on the irrationality of

human emotions more closely fit the emerging Romantic view of individual passions.

In November 1800, now a newlywed, Smith published her second piece in the *Monthly Magazine*. She had written "Lines by a Young Lady. Written at the Falls of Passaick, July, 1800," on an outing with her New York friends. In this poem Smith looses her passionate yearnings for transcendence. She equates nature's force with the force of her own desires. In the poetry's measured verse she both releases and controls her emotional and intellectual striving. This theme of aspiration and resignation to duty, of bursting bounds and submitting to a higher authority, runs through her diary entries and finds voice in the female protagonists in her novels and short stories. Years later, she recast both these pieces for publication as "A Sketch," appearing in Sarah Josepha Hale's *Ladies' Magazine, and Literary Gazette* (1831) and as "The Falls of Passaick," in Louis Godey's *Lady's Book* (1837). "Lines by a Young Lady" appeared in print a month after her marriage at the end of September 1800. The Smiths immediately departed Philadelphia to take up residence in Washington, D.C. With the encouragement of Jefferson, Smith had decided to move his Republican newspaper, the *National Intelligencer,* to the new capital with the intent of obtaining the government's printing business upon Jefferson's election to the presidency.

With anticipation and trepidation, Smith accompanied her husband to the federal city under construction on the banks of the Potomac. Coming from a staunch Federalist, Calvinist Presbyterian family, she experienced the stress both of parting with her relations and of feeling their disapproval of her connections with a man of Republican and deist principles. Upon meeting Jefferson soon after their arrival, however, she quickly became an ardent supporter of the president. Through her social background and her husband's public business, the Smiths' home became a center for Washington society. Smith, along with Secretary of State James Madison's wife, Dolley, generated an informal sociability that facilitated political intercourse and the formation of a continental leadership in the nation's capital. Thriving in this public environment, Smith found adjustment to marital obligations difficult. Her contact with politicians and eminent visitors to the capital stimulated the intellectual aspirations publicized in Brown's *Monthly Magazine,* while the constricted sphere of her new station thwarted her ambitions.

For the first decade of Smith's life in Washington, the tedium of domestic duties oppressed her. Supervising a household of servants, laborers, and a growing brood of children, she seldom saw her husband, who was preoccupied with his publishing business. Out of fifteen pregnancies in twenty years, she bore four living

*Smith's husband, Philadelphia publisher Samuel Harrison Smith (after the portrait by Charles Bird King; from* The First Forty Years of Washington Society, *1906)*

children: Julia in 1801, Susan in 1804, Jonathan Bayard in 1810, and Anna Maria in 1811. Smith did not have the time she wanted for reading and writing. Only one publication from this period has been identified, a children's story, *The Diversions of Sidney, by a Friend of Youth* (1805). Presenting a day in the life of Julia, the story was a missive to Julia's cousins in New Jersey, inviting them to share in the bucolic life led by the Smiths in their country retreat, Sidney, outside Washington. Beneath the surface calm of the story, however, Smith pointed to trouble brewing within nuclear families organized around affections. The absent father could not be held at home with promises of love, and the selfish child lacked consideration for others. Only the enslaved child servant, Matty, demonstrates genuine regard in her care for those around her. In *The Diversions of Sidney* Smith expresses her sense of isolation from both New Jersey and her immediate family. She felt for the intelligent and responsive Matty an interest and affinity that were lacking in her relations with her own daughter Julia.

The Smiths were antislavery in their sentiments. They refused to purchase slaves in their first decade in Washington, hiring them instead and in several instances intervening on their behalf with their owners. Smith sympathized with enslaved blacks, identifying with their aspirations for freedom and understanding their recalcitrance as legitimate resentment against those who had no superior claim to their obedience. She recorded black servants' personal histories in her diaries of the early 1800s, and when she began publishing in the 1820s she inserted their accounts into her stories and novels. Most notably, she incorporated along with Matty the characters of two other blacks in the neighborhood of Sidney into her children's stories in *American Mother; or, The Seymour Family* (1823). In the first story, "The Bees," Dick is a knowledgeable, hardworking husbandman whose common sense about bees and life reveals the ignorance of middle-class city folk come to the country. In another story, Old Betty is given her freedom and wanders about in the vicinity of Sidney, living off the charity of the poor farmers in the neighborhood. Her history portrays a black woman's defiant assertion of her right to love her husband and baby, her resistance to white oppression, and her Christian forbearance. Smith used children's stories as a vehicle for expressing the injustice of slavery and the moral superiority of enslaved blacks over whites. Along with the benevolent white Mrs. Seymour, Old Betty stands as an exemplar of an American mother. As a woman whose aspirations were truncated by gendered constraints, Smith was able to cross lines and articulate a different vision of what constituted American national identity. The cover of juvenile literature allowed her to assert most openly her critical commentary on the mores of her own class and race.

In the intervening period between about 1810 and 1822 Smith was silent on the topic of slavery. During the 1810s the Smiths had purchased slaves to assist with the domestic tasks and farmwork. The War of 1812, with the threat of British invasion and fear of slave insurrections, must have magnified her unease with claiming possession over blacks. In the early 1820s, following the war, the Missouri Compromise, and the end of the Virginia dynasty of presidents, a crisis over national leadership made slavery a pressing issue. The American Colonization Society, organized in Washington in 1816, attempted to form a national consensus on resolving the problem. Samuel Smith belonged to the organization and over time freed the slaves in his possession. Smith's *American Mother* was a contribution to the national dialogue in the early 1820s concerning the melioration and gradual elimination of the institution of slavery from the United States. Of the few American antislavery books for children, it was one of the earliest.

The following year Lydia Maria Child published an antislavery children's story, "The Little Master and

His Little Slave," in *Evenings in New England* (1824), which she had extracted from Smith's novel *Winter in Washington,* published the same year. Child, like Smith at this time, was advocating a gradualist solution to slavery. She uses the story to emphasize a common culture of humane values uniting North and South. Smith has a nationalist agenda in her novel as well. She disseminates a view of the social life at the heart of the nation, promoting "this rising metropolis of our wide-extended empire" and its president, Jefferson. Her firsthand descriptions of the presidential drawing room and Dolley Madison's salon paint a Republican society with simple but educated manners that eschewed European fashions. Threaded through the depictions of this Republican court society were two entwined plots. Mrs. Seymour, a perfect Republican mother and wife, wages a debate over the proper role of women with her protofeminist cousin Harriet Mortimer. Mortimer is Smith's alter ego and expresses many of her discontents with the constriction of women within the home. A second narrative revolves around a seduction drama and Mr. Seymour's defense of an accused murderer. Smith tucks in between the main story lines vignettes of poor whites, blacks, and Native Americans marginalized in a society that privileged middle-class white men.

Throughout her works, Smith employs this technique of incorporating opposition voices through antagonists who offer critical versions of prevailing social mores. Though her writings seem to bolster a conservative moral standard of normative family life, she consistently critiques the imposition of those values on white middle-class women, blacks, and the poor. By including lower-class characters who articulate alternative views, Smith expands the definition of American rights to freedom and pursuit of self-interest and broadens the sense of who had a claim to them. Her goal was to provide realistic depictions of people, especially women, in all walks of life. She wrote two other novels, "Lucy" and "Julia," that were never published, possibly because they were too realistic for middle-class taste in the 1820s.

In her second published novel, *What Is Gentility?,* Smith portrays honest working people, as well as the newly rich. In the fates of Charles and Catharine McCarty, she analyzes the effects of education on men and women and considers what was appropriate to each. The superficial boarding-school education proffered well-to-do young women turns Catharine into a useless, thoughtless being, whereas Charles's university training makes him into a sensitive, democratic man. His choice of Lydia, a self-educated carpenter's daughter, as his wife reflects his equalitarianism and sound judgment. In Lydia, whose social and intellectual accomplishments advance as Charles becomes an ambassador, Smith inscribes woman's importance as social mediator. Rather than proselytizing for equal education, she lampoons social and gender distinctions based on status rather than genuine merit. She argued from her own experience, believing women's accomplishments grew out of sociability and practical knowledge grounded in their station. Smith expresses most eloquently the importance she placed on women's intellectual fulfillment in "My Books" a few years later in the *Ladies' Magazine, and Literary Gazette* (September 1831). She donated the proceeds from *What Is Gentility?* to the Female Orphan Asylum in Washington. Her benevolent intentions and the merits of the work brought her to the attention of Sarah Josepha Hale, editor of the *Ladies' Magazine* in Boston.

Beginning in the early 1830s, Smith regularly contributed articles on a variety of topics to the journal. Involved in forming political society in Washington between 1800 and 1828 and in partisan politics during the 1820s, she reacted severely to the election of Andrew Jackson in 1828. The triumph of his Democratic Party brought the displacement of a thirty-year reign of Republican administrators and bureaucrats in the city, people who were part of the Smiths' social and political networks. Smith mounted a rear-guard attack in print, even as she joined the other women in Washington in ostracizing Peggy Eaton, the allegedly disreputable wife of Jackson's secretary of war, John Henry Eaton. Adopting the same mode she had in *Winter in Washington,* Smith constructed a history of Republican society and politics that emphasized amity above party differences in order to preserve national union.

In her series "Presidential Inaugurations" (1831–1832) Smith asserts the important function of levees and presidential drawing rooms in coalescing political interests and of women's roles there as power brokers. She carries forward the idea of women as social negotiators and exemplars of political virtue in her series "Roman Sketches" (1832–1833, 1835), in which she recounts the lives of powerful Roman women, most of whom lived during the tumultuous times of the early empire. In a serial story, "Constantine: Or, The Rejected Throne," published in the *Southern Literary Messenger* from June to December 1837, she analyzes the influence of women in the court society of another empire, Russia. In these writings Smith casts in negative relief the discomposed avidity of Jacksonian politics with the decorum of a self-disciplined ruling class presided over by disinterested women. Smith gives her fullest interpretation of the early Republican administrations and women as negotiators of power relations in Washington in her biographical sketch, "Mrs. Madison," in *National Portrait Gallery of Distinguished Americans* (1836).

Smith attributed the equitable cordiality and sociability that Dolley Madison established in her salon to a form of Southern hospitality. In another set of essays, "Domestic Sketches" (1834), in the *Ladies' Magazine,* she took on the Philadelphia author Eliza Leslie's prescriptions for formal, segregated social affairs. From the vantage point of a "Southern Pen," she defended informal gatherings of men and women within the home for generating social and intellectual exchange. As a Jeffersonian Republican and resident in an essentially southern city, Smith, through her publications in first the *Ladies' Magazine* and then *Godey's Lady's Book* and the *Southern Literary Messenger,* interpreted to a national audience life and politics in the capital.

From her perspective the Republican Party, led by a series of illustrious Southerners, had represented the best interests of the union. In the 1824 presidential election, the Smiths had supported William H. Crawford, the national candidate bearing the Republican mantle. After his defeat the Smiths' hope of political appointment faded, and with Jackson's election they withdrew from the political fray. Smith, through her publications, elevated the characters of many Southern leaders as national icons. She included Crawford in her pantheon, providing the *Southern Literary Messenger* with her "Sketches of Private Life and Character of William H. Crawford" (April–May 1837). Fittingly, her last known published work is about the man she revered the most, Thomas Jefferson. In "The President's House Forty Years Ago" (*Godey's Lady's Book,* November 1843), she reminisces about the scenes and characters who had enlivened her own ambition to the point of consigning her words to print. She saw Jefferson in his integrity as a private man able to unite the public in one family. In Smith's opinion Dolley Madison and Crawford carried on this essential national task.

Smith injected into the private sphere an essential function of public social formation. She, however, was always conflicted about women's ambitions and duties. The themes that she developed in her 1820s novels she explored in her short fiction and moral pieces during the 1830s. The boredom of young, intelligent wives leads to discontent, temptation, and resignation in two

pieces for *Godey's Lady's Book,* for example, "The Young Wife" (May 1837) and "Who Is Happy?" (March–May 1839). She addressed conditions of blacks and poor whites, social ambition, and class prejudice in stories for the *Ladies' Magazine, and Literary Gazette,* such as "The Deserted Child, or Blessings of a Sunday School" (February–March 1832), "A Winter-Day's Ramble" (May 1833), and "Recollections" (September 1836). She wrote little in the last years of her life, publishing "The President's House Forty Years Ago" in *Godey's Lady's Book* in November 1843. Smith died on 7 June 1844 at age sixty-six.

Margaret Bayard Smith wrote from observing her life and the life around her. Because the new nation was in the process of formation, American lives were full of contradictions. Smith, as an elite white woman, gave voice to the contrary impulses for individual expansion and social stability in the early republic.

**Letters:**

*The First Forty Years of Washington Society. Portrayed by the Family Letters of Mrs. Samuel Harrison (Margaret Bayard) Smith from the Collection of Her Grandson J. Henley Smith,* edited by Gaillard Hunt (New York: Scribners, 1906).

**References:**

Nina Baym, *American Women Writers and the Work of History, 1790–1860* (New Brunswick, N.J.: Rutgers University Press, 1995);

Baym, *Women's Fiction: A Guide to Novels by and about Women in America, 1820–1870,* second edition (Urbana & Chicago: University of Illinois Press, 1993).

**Papers:**

The primary source of material relating to Margaret Bayard Smith is the large collection of letters, journals, and manuscripts in the Margaret Bayard Smith Papers, Library of Congress, Washington, D.C. The Jonathan Bayard Smith Papers and William Thornton Papers at the Library of Congress also include related family papers and some of her manuscripts.

# David Hunter Strother
## (Porte Crayon)
### (26 September 1816 – 8 March 1888)

Robert C. Kennedy

See also the Strother entry in *DLB 3: Antebellum Writers in New York and the South.*

BOOKS: *Virginia Illustrated: Containing a Visit to the Virginia Canaan, and the Adventures of Porte Crayon and His Cousins, Illustrated from Drawings by Porte Crayon,* as Porte Crayon (New York: Harper, 1857);

*The Capital of West Virginia and the Great Kanawha Valley: Advantages, Resources and Prospects* (Charleston, W.Va.: Journal Office, 1872);

*Historical Address Delivered by Gen. D. H. Strother, at Berkeley Springs, W. Va., at the Centennial Celebrations, July 4, 1876* (Washington, D.C.: M'Gill & Witherow, 1876);

*The Old South Illustrated,* edited, with an introduction, by Cecil D. Eby Jr. (Chapel Hill: University of North Carolina Press, 1959);

*A Virginia Yankee in the Civil War: The Diaries of David Hunter Strother,* edited, with an introduction, by Eby (Chapel Hill: University of North Carolina Press, 1961).

SELECTED PERIODICAL PUBLICATIONS–
UNCOLLECTED: "Pen and Ink Sketches of an Artist," (Martinsburg, Va.) *Gazette,* 18 February 1841, 25 February 1841, 20 May 1841, 8 July 1841, 15 July 1841, 30 September 1841, 10 March 1842, 7 April 1842, 21 April 1842, 29 September 1842, 6 October 1842, 13 October 1842, 23 February 1843;

"The Bear and the Basketmaker," *Harper's Monthly* (June 1856);

"The Dismal Swamp," *Harper's Monthly* (September 1856);

"North Carolina Illustrated," *Harper's Monthly* (March 1857, May 1857, July 1857, August 1857);

"The Jamestown Celebration," *Harper's Weekly* (27 June 1857);

*David Hunter Strother (collection of Emily Strother Kreuttner)*

"A Winter in the South," *Harper's Monthly* (September–November 1857, January 1858, May 1858, August 1858, December 1858);

"A Reminiscence of Rome," *Harper's Monthly* (November 1857);

"Artist's Excursion on the Baltimore and Ohio Railroad," *Harper's Monthly* (June 1859);

"The Late Invasion at Harper's Ferry," *Harper's Weekly* (5 November 1859);

"The Trial of the Conspirators," *Harper's Weekly* (12 November 1859);

"Rural Pictures," *Harper's Monthly* (January 1860);

"A Summer in New England," *Harper's Monthly* (June 1860, September 1860, November 1860, May 1861, July 1861);

"Narrative of an Eye-Witness," *Harper's Weekly* (11 May 1861);

"Personal Recollections of the War by a Virginian," *Harper's Monthly* (June 1866, July 1866, September 1866, October 1866, January 1867, March 1867, May 1867, August 1867, November 1867, February 1868, April 1868);

"The Little Broom," *Riverside Magazine* (December 1867);

"The Young Virginians," *Riverside Magazine* (February 1868, March 1868, May 1868, June 1868, August 1868, April 1869, May 1869, September 1869, April 1870, June 1870, August 1870, December 1870);

"An Excursion to Watkin's Glen," *Harper's Monthly* (June 1871);

"The Mountains," *Harper's Monthly* (April–June 1872, August 1872, September 1872, November 1872, April 1873, November 1873, July 1874, September 1875);

"Notes from My Garden," *Horticulturist* (March 1873);

"Our Negro Schools," *Harper's Monthly* (September 1874);

"Confessions of a Candidate," *Harper's Monthly* (February 1876);

"The Baby," *Harper's Monthly* (March 1876);

"Sitting Bull–Autobiography of the Famous Indian Chief," *Harper's Weekly* (29 July 1876);

"Boys and Girls," *Harper's Monthly* (December 1876);

"Old Time Militia Musters," *Harper's Monthly* (July 1878);

"Old Fort Frederick," *Baltimore Sun*, 6 December 1878;

"General Averell's Last Ride," *Philadelphia Weekly Times*, 18 January 1879;

"Home," *Harper's Monthly* (January 1879);

"Banks in Louisiana," *Philadelphia Weekly Times*, 29 March 1879;

"The Port Hudson Expedition," *Philadelphia Weekly Times*, 5 April 1879;

"A Visit to the Shrines of Old Virginia," *Lippincott's Magazine* (April 1879);

"Edmund Pendleton of Virginia," *Pennsylvania Magazine*, no. 3 (1879).

The writer and graphic artist David Hunter Strother was perhaps the best-known and most well-regarded illustrator in the United States in the 1850s. His illustrated stories appeared mainly in *Harper's Monthly,* the most popular literary magazine of its time, and his pen name, Porte Crayon, was immediately recognizable in homes across the country. His work infused the fashionable travel genre with colloquial humor and local color, primarily through the vivid descriptions and characters of his native South and its people. While Strother's writings are usually no longer read, they remain valuable to literary, cultural, and social historians.

Strother was born on 26 September 1816 into a well-regarded family in Martinsburg, Virginia (now West Virginia). His father, John Strother, a former militia colonel, was assistant county clerk, and his mother, Elizabeth Hunter Strother, was a member of one of the elite "first families" of Virginia. During his first twelve years Strother stayed at home and studied at the local school. Because he showed a keen interest in art, his family transferred him in 1829 to the Pennsylvania Academy of Fine Arts in Philadelphia. There he briefly studied under Luigi Persico, an Italian-born sculptor and painter of miniatures, before becoming a student of another Italian artist, Pietro Ancora.

While at the academy, Strother organized a volunteer militia unit among the students, which raised his father's hopes that his son would receive a West Point education. The ascendancy of Jacksonian Democrats, however, blocked the path for Strother, as a member of a partisan Whig family, to enter the United States Military Academy.

Instead, young Strother matriculated at the Whiggish Jefferson College in Canonsburg, Pennsylvania, during the 1832–1833 academic year. He dropped out at the end of the year and returned to Martinsburg. For three years he unsuccessfully importuned Secretary of War Lewis Cass for admission to West Point. His time was otherwise spent as a courthouse subclerk and in the haphazard study of law and medicine.

Although a sickly child, as an adult Strother had robust health and became a keen outdoorsman. In the autumn of 1835 he joined his friend James Ranson for a five-hundred-mile trek across the Blue Ridge Mountains into the Piedmont area of Virginia. A year later he began a two-year program of art instruction at the University of the City of New York (now New York University) under the auspices of Samuel F. B. Morse, the renowned painter and inventor. Although the training was important to the development of his skill, he also learned that art was not a lucrative profession, unless one specialized in formal portraiture. Yet, even with that knowledge his commitment to a career in art was undeterred. In 1838–1839 he first combined his love of travel with his art by making his way along the Ohio River to St. Louis, painting and selling landscapes and portraits to support the journey.

In the autumn of 1840 Strother embarked on a three-year grand tour of Europe, a common rite of passage for the sons of elite families, especially those with artistic or literary inclinations. During his stay in Paris, Naples, Florence, and Rome he studied great works of art and sketched and painted to refine his own skills. It was not so much the great masters, however, who influenced Strother but painters such as Leopold Robert and G. Dura, whose popular works depicted the common people of Italy. While on his grand tour Strother unintentionally became a published writer. His father had the Martinsburg newspaper print his son's letters, which were full of descriptions and commentary about the people and places he had seen in Europe.

Upon returning to the United States in the autumn of 1843 Strother spent a year in Martinsburg, painting sporadically and descending into pessimism concerning his career prospects. In November 1844 he traveled to Baltimore to visit his older cousin, John Pendleton Kennedy, the popular author of *Swallow Barn* (1832) and *Horse-Shoe Robinson* (1835) and a politician of some influence. Strother's friend, John Gadsby Chapman, convinced him to move to New York City, which he did in 1845, to work in the growing field of illustrated publications—magazines, books, pamphlets, and tracts. Strother's first big break came in 1850 when Kennedy asked him to illustrate the revised edition of *Swallow Barn*.

The year before, on 15 May 1849, Strother married Ann Doyne Wolff, and they had one daughter, Emily. In November 1859 his first wife died. He married a cousin, May Eliot Hunter, on 6 May 1861, by whom he had two sons, David, who died in childhood, and John.

During the summer of 1851 Strother joined several friends, including Philip Pendleton Kennedy, the youngest brother of John, on a fishing, hunting, and hiking expedition in the Blackwater Falls region of Virginia (now West Virginia). In 1853 the younger Kennedy published their exploits as *The Blackwater Chronicle,* which included illustrations by Strother.

In the spring of 1852 Strother planned and led a second outing to the same region, during which he made many sketches and completed drawings. Prompted by a friend, Charles Edmond, Strother showed his sketches to Fletcher Harper of the prestigious Harper and Brothers publishing house. The Harpers firm commissioned him to re-create his sketches on wood blocks, used in making illustrations, and to write a corresponding narrative of the trip.

The piece, "The Virginian Canaan," appeared in *Harper's Monthly* in December 1853 and received positive critical and public notice. This work was the first of a long and mutually profitable relationship between

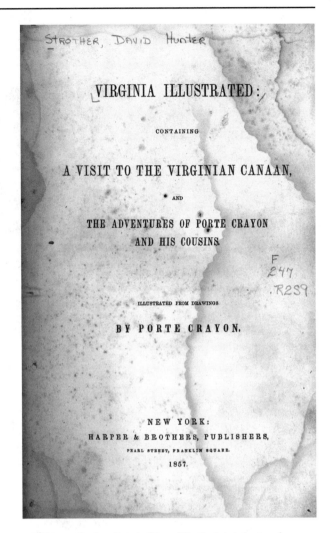

*Title page for the collected edition of Strother's popular travel essays, which first appeared in* Harper's Monthly Magazine *(Thomas Cooper Library, University of South Carolina)*

Strother and Harpers. The story also introduced what became the artist-author's pseudonym, Porte Crayon, as a character modeled after Strother himself. The name was probably adapted from the pen name "Geoffrey Crayon" used by Washington Irving, a literary influence on Strother and an acquaintance. Another character in "The Virginian Canaan," Conway the guide, is a prototype of the yarn-spinning, fiddle-playing, independent mountain man who would become popular again with twentieth-century folklorists and scholars.

Pleased with the success of "The Virginian Canaan," Harpers commissioned Strother to develop a series based on his other travels in the Virginia backcountry. The resulting five articles, collectively titled "Virginia Illustrated: Adventures of Porte Crayon and His Cousins," appeared in *Harper's Monthly* between December 1854 and August 1856. The stories and sketches depict a fictionalized version of an 1853 jour-

THE STORMING OF THE ENGINE-HOUSE BY THE UNITED STATES MARINES.—[SKETCHED BY PORTE CRAYON.]

*Depiction of the raid on Harper's Ferry by Strother (as Porte Crayon) for the 5 November 1859 issue of* Harper's Weekly

ney he took with three women ("cousins" in the tale)—his wife, sister, another woman (possibly a real cousin)—and a black servant.

The articles describe the flora and fauna of various sights of natural beauty and wonder in Virginia—such as the Natural Bridge, Allegheny Springs, Weyer's Cave, and the Peaks of Otter—as well as the adventures and local characters the travelers encounter along the way. These articles were also immensely popular and, together with "The Virginian Canaan," were published in 1857 as Strother's only book, *Virginia Illustrated: Containing a Visit to the Virginia Canaan, and the Adventures of Porte Crayon and His Cousins, Illustrated from Drawings by Porte Crayon.* While Strother's writing style is often identified with that of Irving, it has also been compared to that of other Virginia travel writers, such as Andrew Burnaby, William Burke, and Samuel Kercheval.

To ensure that Strother continued his successful work for *Harper's Monthly,* the publisher made him one of its highest-paid contributors during the 1850s, with an open-ended assignment to write about and draw scenes from his travels for the magazine. An account of his solo journey into North Carolina appeared serially in *Harper's Monthly* from September 1856 through August 1857 as "Dismal Swamp" and the four-part "North Carolina Illustrated."

Strother decided to return to his previous template of multiple characters in order to advance the plot

through conversation and interaction. In "A Winter in the South," which ran from September 1857 through December 1858, Bob Larkin and the family of Squire Broadacre wander from Virginia through several other Southern states—Tennessee, Alabama, and Mississippi—until they arrive at New Orleans. A companion piece, "A Summer in New England," appeared between June 1860 and July 1861. This piece is a mildly satiric look at the folkways and foibles of New England Yankees from the point of view of four Southerners.

Although a Southerner, Strother was a strong Unionist and cast his lot with the Union army when the Civil War began. With his intimate knowledge of the Southern landscape and his obvious drawing talent, Strother was assigned to the topographical corps. As an assistant adjutant general he served on the staffs of several Union generals. He worked in Virginia under Generals George McClellan and John Pope, then served with General Nathaniel Banks in New Orleans and the Red River campaign. He was next recalled to duty with the Third West Virginia Cavalry and was finally made chief of staff to General David Hunter, a cousin. Having survived thirty battles unwounded, he retired on 10 September 1864 and was subsequently granted the honorary rank of brigadier general.

At the war's end in 1865 Strother was appointed to the staff of Virginia governor Francis Pierpont as adjutant general of the Virginia State Militia. Both men favored a mild Reconstruction policy, which was rejected by the Radical Republicans in Congress. In frustration, Strother resigned his position with the Virginia government in December 1865.

Strother returned to his family home in Berkeley Springs and contacted the editors at Harpers to restart his literary career. During his Civil War service he had sketched pictures and written his impressions in notebooks. Unlike his previous submissions to *Harper's Monthly,* Strother's "Personal Recollections of the War by a Virginian" was a serious examination of the causes and experiences of the war. The series ran for eleven installments from June 1866 through April 1868 and is valued by Civil War historians.

The reading preferences of the public in postwar America had moved away from the diary-type writing style of Strother, and he was never to regain the popularity he held in the antebellum period. Financial problems and a larger family to support kept him writing, though. In the early years of his career he had provided illustrations for children's books. Now he tried his hand at an illustrated children's story, titled "The Young Virginians," that appeared as twelve chapters in *Riverside Magazine* from February 1868 to December 1870.

Strother's last major publication was a ten-part *Harper's Monthly* series, "The Mountains," which ran from April 1872 to September 1875. Short on plot, it was an evocative look at the people and land of his beloved West Virginia, imparting in the process information about the natural history, social history, and material culture of the new state.

After attempting to earn money as a public lecturer, Strother briefly worked as editor of the *Charleston* (W.Va.) *Herald* in 1870. In 1878 President Rutherford B.

Hayes appointed him consul general in Mexico City, where he learned Spanish and served successfully. Upon the election of a Democratic president, Grover Cleveland, six years later, the Republican Strother resigned his post. He returned to West Virginia, spending the summers in Berkeley Springs and the winters in Charleston. David Hunter Strother died on 8 March 1888 of pneumonia.

**Biography:**

Cecil D. Eby, *"Porte Crayon": The Life of David Hunter Strother* (Chapel Hill: University of North Carolina Press, 1960).

**References:**

John A. Cuthbert and Jessie Poesch, *David Hunter Strother: "One of the Best Draughtsmen the Country Possesses"* (Morgantown: West Virginia University Press, 1997);

Gregg D. Kimball, "'The South As It Was': Social Order, Slavery, and Illustrations in Virginia, 1830–1877," in *Graphic Arts & The South: Proceedings of the 1990 North American Print Conference,* edited by Judy L. Larson (Fayetteville: University of Arkansas Press, 1993), pp. 128–157;

Jessie J. Poesch, "David Hunter Strother: Mountain People, Mountain Images," in *Graphic Arts & The South: Proceedings of the 1990 North American Print Conference,* pp. 62–99;

Dana F. White, "Two Perspectives on the Cotton Kingdom: 'Yeoman' and 'Porte Crayon,'" in *Graphic Arts & The South: Proceedings of the 1990 North American Print Conference,* pp. 100–127.

# John Reuben Thompson

*(23 October 1823 – 30 April 1873)*

Richard Fusco
*Saint Joseph's University*

See also the Thompson entries in *DLB 3: Antebellum Writers in New York and the South* and *DLB 73: American Magazine Journalists, 1741–1850.*

BOOKS: *Across the Atlantic* (New York: Derby & Jackson, 1857);
*Poems of John R. Thompson,* edited by John S. Patton (New York: Scribner, 1920);
*The Genius and Character of Edgar Allan Poe,* edited by J. H. Whitty and James Henry Rindfleisch (Richmond: Garrett & Massie, 1929).

SELECTED PERIODICAL PUBLICATIONS–UNCOLLECTED: "The Late Edgar A. Poe," *Southern Literary Messenger,* 15 (November 1849): 694–697;
"Notice of New Works," *Southern Literary Messenger,* 18 (October 1852): 630–638.

*John Reuben Thompson*

The modern reputation of John Reuben Thompson has three facets. As a poet he remains a curious, almost forgotten figure among nineteenth-century Southern men of letters. Twice since his death scholars tried to find him a place in the American canon, but both attempts failed to take hold. As an editor, journalist, and reviewer he earned a modest place among publishing luminaries of the nineteenth century, a status acquired chiefly through his efforts for the *Southern Literary Messenger.* As a biographical source Thompson provided testimony that aided both sides in the intense debate between detractors and defenders of Edgar Allan Poe regarding the character of the man before his death.

Thompson essentially lived the sort of existence that Poe had at one time imagined for himself. As a youth Poe expected to enter a life of Virginian quasi aristocracy, only to have his hopes dashed by his estrangement from and disinheritance by his foster father, John Allan. In contrast Thompson enjoyed an indulgent and nurturing relationship with his father. Poe wanted the life of a Southern gentleman; Thompson lived it. Poe had to withdraw from the University of Virginia by 1827 because of finances; Thompson finished his degree in 1842. Throughout his adult life Poe scrambled for opportunities to own a literary journal. Thompson's father bought the *Southern Literary Messenger* for his son. During the 1820s Poe entertained the notion that composing poetry would be his primary creative endeavor; later, however, he migrated to other genres. Like Poe, Thompson had to deal with the professional responsibility of churning out reviews and essays; otherwise, he devoted more of his artistic energies to poetry. Poe's habitual battles with art and life created vibrant texts that ascend in status with every generation. Thompson's tendency to appease and to please produced a body of work that has plunged into obscurity.

John Reuben Thompson was born in Richmond, Virginia, on 23 October 1823 to John and Sarah Thompson. His father, a native of New Hampshire, met and married Sarah Dyckman in New York and then moved to Richmond, where he set up a lucrative business retailing hats and furs. As his fortunes improved he was able to do well for his three surviving children. (A fourth had died in infancy.) Young Thompson proved to be a studious child, one who savored Charles Lamb's essays but also one who cultivated popularity with his peers. In 1836 his father sent him to a Connecticut preparatory school, where the boy composed his first poem, a short, juvenile piece for a friend's album. He returned to Virginia in 1837 and graduated from the Richmond Academy in 1840.

That same year he enrolled at the University of Virginia, which at the time boasted a small but renowned faculty. During Thompson's first year tensions between a strict administration and a rebellious student body erupted into a demonstration and ended in a teacher's death. The gambling and drinking so prevalent in campus life were reminiscent of Poe's experience fourteen years earlier. By the start of the following semester, however, the academic situation and campus climate improved. Thompson was an unenthusiastic student. He missed classes often and found those that he attended uninspiring. For instance, he studied Latin with Gessner Harrison, a linguist of national repute. Thompson recorded his displeasure in this excerpt from "Verses of a Collegiate Historian":

End at last! Gloria in Excelsis!!
Eight minutes of eleven o'clock, Jan. 30th, 1841.

Farewell! farewell to thee, old Latin History!
(Thus warbled a student, who once read it through.)
Thou art so profoundly enveloped in mystery
That with feelings of pleasure I bid you adieu.

Notwithstanding, along with his study of German and French, Thompson's familiarity with classical languages and linguistics served him well later in life, especially in securing acceptance into literary circles. He did well enough in his final examinations to earn a degree in chemistry.

Thompson also composed poems in college. Several were printed in *The Collegian,* an organ for the school literary club, the Jefferson Society. Another effort, "You bid me wake my slumbering muse," was written for an acquaintance and provides an early

example of a poetic variety he returned to throughout his career—occasional poetry. Probably through reading contemporary French literature, Thompson became acquainted with the philosophical dimensions of the dandy. Even in college he dressed himself as a method of artistic self-expression. He refused to wear his uniform on campus but would parade himself in it while on holiday in Richmond. In both the academic and lay worlds he seemed intent more to be noticed than to confront. Inspired by a Virginia professor, Thompson indulged his fondness for clothing throughout the rest of his life, often impressing his acquaintances as a gentle dandy.

Back in Richmond he dabbled in law and later returned to the university to secure a Bachelor of Law degree in 1845. His father's prosperity allowed the son to pursue that profession without vigor. For the bulk of the 1840s Thompson honed the affability that later gained him access to a variety of social and literary circles. A polished storyteller, a "delightful reader," a companion full of good humor and taste, this "small" and "delicate" man belonged, according to an article from *Hearth and Home* (20 December 1873) by a friend, writer John Esten Cooke, in a Paris salon to "become famous among the wits of the wittiest city in Europe."

Toward the end of the decade, Thompson's wish to write professionally prompted a trip to New York. Hoping to keep his son in Virginia, the elder Thompson purchased the *Southern Literary Messenger* from B. B. Minor in 1847. As the editor of the best literary magazine in the South, young Thompson found, to his delight, that his social opportunities increased. Gerald M. Garmon, in *John Reuben Thompson* (1979), the best biography about the author, identified Thompson's three aims during his thirteen-year editorship. First, he wanted to cultivate a readership in the South by promoting its own literature. At the opposite end, he wanted the *Messenger* to be respected by the literati in the North. These competing audiences thus compelled the third and most difficult goal—to remain apolitical during a decade when sectional polemics threatened secession and civil war. Beset with financial woes at the magazine, complicated by his father's recent business setbacks, Thompson somehow managed to solicit contributions from writers as diverse as Richard Henry Stoddard, Henry Wadsworth Longfellow, Thomas Bailey Aldrich, and William Gilmore Simms.

In 1848 Thompson met a Southern writer he greatly admired, one of the former editors of the *Messenger,* Edgar Allan Poe. His response to his predecessor was quintessentially ambivalent. He reported to Philip Pendleton Cooke (whose own death shortly after Poe's acutely agitated Thompson) that a habitually inebriated Poe had been "discoursing 'Eureka' to barroom audi-

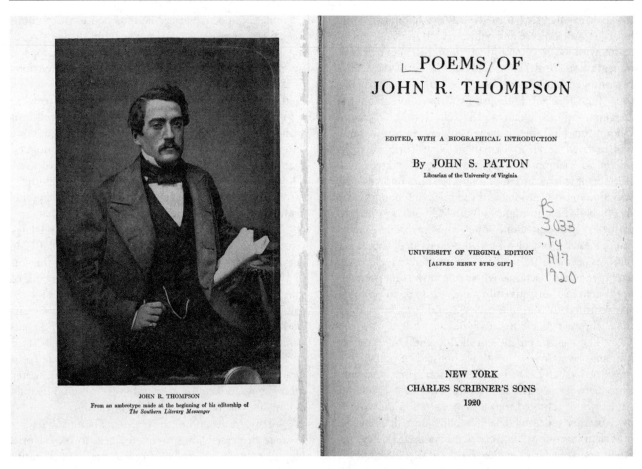

JOHN R. THOMPSON
From an ambrotype made at the beginning of his editorship of
*The Southern Literary Messenger*

POEMS/OF
JOHN R. THOMPSON

EDITED, WITH A BIOGRAPHICAL INTRODUCTION

By JOHN S. PATTON
Librarian of the University of Virginia

UNIVERSITY OF VIRGINIA EDITION
[ALFRED HENRY BYRD GIFT]

NEW YORK
CHARLES SCRIBNER'S SONS
1920

*Frontispiece and title page for the posthumous edition of Thompson's collected poems*

ences" in Richmond. Ever one to note such matters, Thompson observed how poverty had impinged upon the innate taste and decorum in Poe's dress. But to Thompson, Poe was a "distinctly . . . original writer and thinker," and so he extended to him several kindnesses and charities. By the time of Poe's death in 1849 Thompson had privately come to the harsh view of his personal life held by a new acquaintance, Rufus Griswold. The editor's personal dealings with Poe likely reinforced Griswold's perspective in his infamous biography. In public, however, Thompson remained generous and pacifying, especially in evaluating Poe's literary talents. This outward stance helped to assuage some of the harm propagated by Griswold. For instance, as W. T. Bandy demonstrates in the introduction to his 1973 translation of Charles Baudelaire's *Edgar Allan Poe, sa vie et ses ouvrages,* Baudelaire cribbed from Thompson's obituary in his laudatory 1852 essay.

Later, in 1859, perhaps responding belatedly to a personal appeal from Elizabeth Barrett Browning to repair Poe's reputation, Thompson composed a lecture, "The Genius and Character of Edgar Allan Poe," in which he moved away from the Griswold view. After the passage of a decade, Thompson had begun to dissociate the name Poe from the unhappy man he remembered and instead equated it to the body of work he bequeathed to humanity: "For while he moved about this planet, struggled, suffered, aspired here, owned an American citizenship and was set down in the New York Directory as 'Poe, Edgar A., editor, house Fordham,' he was at the same time an inhabitant of that shadowy realm of ideas in which the scene of his story was laid and where the music of his verses w[as] borne on the wind."

During the 1850s Thompson's tenure at the *Messenger* was plagued by a variety of difficulties. Because he composed reviews with a gentler pen, unlike the "tomahawk" wielded by Poe, the best writers in the nation reacted favorably to his inquiries for material and to other professional requests. The inability of the *Messenger* to sustain itself through subscription revenues, however, forced Thompson to pay contributors less than the going rate in the North. His father's continued business woes eliminated him as a resource from which to bail out the magazine. These financial problems forced several significant changes in the editorial latitude of the publication, including the physical restructuring of its size and format for the sake of economy. Nevertheless, Thompson used the *Messenger* to advance the careers of many young writers from both the North and the South, including Philip Pendleton Cooke, Henry Timrod, Frank R. Stockton, Joseph Glover Baldwin, and George Washington Harris.

More taxing than his struggles to keep the *Messenger* afloat was Thompson's battle to maintain the apolitical position of the magazine. The sectional quarrels that had been momentarily quelled by the Compromise of 1850 still burned emotionally. Opposing the institution of slavery itself, Thompson privately believed that the "peculiar institution" would end in the far future. A closet gradualist in a state where many engaged in the open sophistry that slavery benefited all, including the slave, Thompson for the most part resisted pressures from friends and colleagues and tried to keep the *Messenger* literary. On occasion, however, he did violate his own restrictions. When Harriet Beecher Stowe, whom he called a "vile witch in petticoats," published *Uncle Tom's Cabin* in 1852, Thompson orchestrated a campaign of vitriolic reviews about the novel, including his own "Notice of New Works."

On the other hand, perhaps in response to his father's New Hampshire heritage, Thompson offered a conciliatory hand upon the death of Daniel Webster. The New England politician had died shortly after being vilified by Northern liberals for his instrumental support of the Compromise of 1850. Whereas John Greenleaf Whittier in "Ichabod!" had denounced Webster's political maneuver as moral treason, Thompson offered a three-sonnet elegy in 1852, including this second stanza:

> If he had foibles, let us kindly fling
> Oblivion's mantle here above them all,
> And in this hour of grief alone recall
> Those nobler virtues that can ever spring
> From littleness of soul; and let us bring
> Some flowers as fadeless to bedeck his pall
> As those on which his fancy's sunbeams fall,—
> And let our future poets learn to sing
> How in the Senate house he stood erect,
>    And battled always for his Country's cause,—
>    Her shrines, her Constitution and her laws,—
> And how, when treason rose from Faction's sect,
>    He turned Columbia's aegis on the crime
>    And froze it into silence for all time!

"Webster" typifies many of the poems he wrote for the *Messenger* and other publications, which included the prestigious Northern periodicals the *Literary World* and the *Knickerbocker Magazine*. He often composed to respond to an event or to honor a person (such as Jenny Lind and Edward Bulwer-Lytton), employing conventional poetic forms and imbuing points of view with sentimentality.

Thompson's tuberculosis forced him to relinquish temporarily the editorial reins of the *Messenger* in 1854. He traveled to London, where he renewed his friendship with William Makepeace Thackeray, and then toured the European continent. His pleasant and convivial manner ingratiated him to literary luminaries along the way, including Bulwer-Lytton and Browning. Bandy speculates that Thompson possibly met Baudelaire. The American recorded his observations for publication under the title *Across the Atlantic,* but a fire at a New York bindery destroyed every copy save one, which is now owned by the University of Virginia Library.

Upon returning to the United States, he resumed control of the *Messenger,* but economic conditions proved increasingly debilitating. By 1860 he was forced to sell the magazine and to cease all other association with it. After a brief and dispiriting editorial stint with *Southern Field and Fireside* in Georgia, Thompson returned to Richmond and served the state government of Virginia in several capacities during the Civil War, including assistant secretary of state and assistant state librarian. Despite his misgivings regarding secession, Thompson devoted most of his tuberculosis-limited energies to the war effort, which also involved a variety of literary endeavors. He maintained sundry published correspondence with the *Memphis Daily Appeal*, the *Louisville Journal*, the *New Orleans Picayune*, the *Crescent Monthly*, and the *(New Orleans) Cosmopolitan.*

Thompson also published about a dozen poems that either anticipated the war or reacted to it. Like most of his verse, his war poetry is occasional, often pushing romantic values toward sentimental ends. In an 1862 issue of the *Messenger* he offered "The Burial of Latané," which elegizes the heroic death of Confederate captain William Latané under J. E. B. Stuart's command. At the heart of Thompson's theme is the old conceit that poetry ennobles individual sacrifice to exalted heights:

> One moment on the battle's edge he stood,
>    Hope's halo like a helmet round his hair,
> The next beheld him, dabbed in his blood,
>    Prostrate in death, and yet in death how fair!
> Even thus he passed through the red gate of strife,
> From earthly crowns and palms to an immortal life.

The eight sestets of the poem enshrine the entrenched romanticism of the South. Early in the war junior officers such as Latané could still be singled out and commemorated.

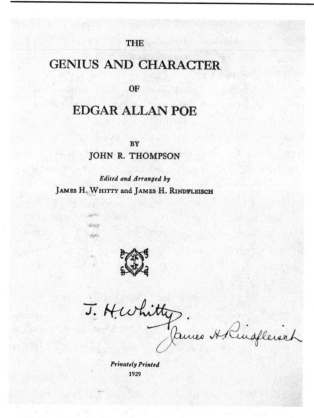

THE

GENIUS AND CHARACTER

OF

EDGAR ALLAN POE

BY

JOHN R. THOMPSON

*Edited and Arranged by*
JAMES H. WHITTY and JAMES H. RINDFLEISCH

*Privately Printed*
1929

*Title page for the first publication of Thompson's 1859 lecture in
which he attempted to revive Poe's tarnished reputation
(The Lilly Library, Indiana University)*

The continued savagery and weariness of later years curtailed such attention, however. Thus, Thompson's subjects shifted from the historically obscure Latané to the more renowned Stuart (about whom he composed the elegy "General J. E. B. Stuart" in 1864) and Robert E. Lee. "Lee to the Rear" testifies to the odd situation that the general's fame had placed him in while rallying his troops during the battle of the Wilderness:

> The grand old grey-beard rode to the space
> Where death and his victims stood face to face,
> And silently waved his old slouched hat—
> A world of meaning there was in that!
>
> "Follow me! Steady! We'll save the day!"
> This is what he seemed to say;
> And to the light of his glorious eye
> The bold brigades thus made reply—
>
> "We'll go forward, but you must go back"—
> And they moved not an inch in the perilous track:
> "Go to the rear, and we'll send them to h–!"
> And the sound of the battle was lost in their yell.
> Turning his bridle, Robert Lee
> Rode to the rear. Like the waves of the sea,

> Bursting the dikes in their overflow,
> Madly his veterans dashed on the foe.

In Thompson's assessment the "grey-bearded man in the black slouched hat" had become the iconic nexus of Southern identity, which forced the general to act against several basic command instincts. Both "The Burial of Latané" and "Lee to the Rear" were staples in Southern classrooms up to the early decades of the twentieth century. Other war poems that gained popularity among Southern readers included "Ashby" (1862), "Music in Camp," and "On to Richmond." Perhaps to mollify his own despair, Thompson also penned a few comic efforts during the war.

The war exacted an enormous physical toll upon Thompson. Despite his impairment he undertook a variety of extra projects. His journalism skills earned him a reputation as one of the better reporters in the South. He assembled a collection of Southern poetry for publication abroad in book form, but the manuscript did not make it through the Union blockade. As usual, he remained an essential cog in the machinery of Richmond society.

Suffering a relapse of his tuberculosis in 1863, Thompson could not endure another summer in Richmond. Consequently, he moved to London in 1864, where he continued to advance the Confederate cause with both his affability and his writing, chiefly through the *Index,* the Confederate propaganda organ in England. He found himself accepted by an even larger literary circle that included Charles Dickens, Wilkie Collins, and Alfred Tennyson. He cultivated an earnest friendship with Thomas Carlyle. Another close friend was Anne Thackeray, daughter of the recently deceased novelist. After the war ended, Thompson provided some material relief from London for his impoverished family in Virginia. Homesickness compelled him to risk his health by returning to the United States in 1866. As a goodbye gift Thackeray presented him with the copy of her father's novel *Henry Esmond* (1852) that he had inscribed for her family. Thompson treasured the volume for the rest of his life.

The scarcity of literary work in postwar Virginia motivated Thompson to seek employment in New York in 1867, which began the financially leanest year in his life. Tuberculosis continued to emaciate him, and his decline was hastened by the quantities of alcohol that his doctors prescribed to alleviate the symptoms. William Cullen Bryant generously hired Thompson to be the literary editor for the *New York Evening Post* (a position that at differing times William Dean Howells and Benjamin Park had sought but had been denied). To his credit, Thompson realized how the war had rendered Southern Romanticism inappropriate and archaic, especially in the face of emerging American Realism. His book reviews, however, were pedestrian at best. Nevertheless, he charmed his way into the good graces of the staff, who regarded him as the "Rebel to be loved." Illness forced unsuccessful recuperative trips to Cuba and Colorado. Sensing his impending death, he asked Richard Henry Stoddard to be his literary executor. John Reuben Thompson died on 30 April 1873. On his marker in a Virginia graveyard is engraved: "The graceful poet, the brilliant writer, the steadfast friend, the loyal Virginian."

Stoddard was not a conscientious executor. He quickly dispersed Thompson's library and failed to see any of the manuscripts into print, losing many in his carelessness. In 1920 John S. Patton gathered the extant material and edited the only book-length collection of Thompson's poetry. Thompson's lecture on Poe was printed privately at the end of that decade. Aside from Garmon's excellent volume in Twayne's United States Authors Series, Thompson has received only cursory treatment among recent scholars, perhaps for good reason. For all his talent and facility with language, he lacked the imagination to go beyond dying conventions. He wrote to please an audience that was mired in place, in time, in values, and in aesthetics. Successive generations of potential readers have found little of themselves with which to identify and thus have consigned Thompson's oeuvre to the depths of historical curios.

## References:

Hervey Allen, *Israfel, the Life and Times of Edgar Allan Poe* (New York: Farrar & Rinehart, 1934), pp. 40–45, 609–613;

J. Cutler Andrews, *The South Reports the Civil War* (Princeton: Princeton University Press, 1970), pp. 34, 59;

W. T. Bandy, Introduction to Charles Baudelaire, *Edgar Allan Poe, sa vie et ses ouvrages* (Toronto: University of Toronto Press, 1973), pp. xxix–xxxvi;

Gerald M. Garmon, *John Reuben Thompson* (Boston: Twayne, 1979);

Jay. B. Hubbell, *The South in American Literature, 1607–1900* (Durham, N.C.: Duke University Press, 1954), pp. 521–528;

Joseph Roddey Miller, "John Reuben Thompson: His Place in Southern Life and Literature," dissertation, University of Virginia, Charlottesville, 1930;

Benjamin B. Minor, *The Southern Literary Messenger, 1834–1864* (New York: Neale, 1905), pp. 161–209;

William Moss, "Walt Whitman in Dixie," *Southern Literary Journal,* 22 (1990): 98–118;

Allan Nevins, *The Evening Post: A Century of Journalism* (New York: Russell & Russell, 1968), pp. 353–354, 407–411;

Arthur H. Quinn, *Edgar Allan Poe: A Critical Biography* (New York: Appleton-Century-Crofts, 1941), pp. 569, 660;

Edward L. Tucker, "A Rash and Perilous Enterprise: *The Southern Literary Messenger* and the Men Who Made It," *Virginia Cavalcade,* 21 (1971): 14–20.

## Papers:

The University of Virginia Library possesses a significant collection of John Reuben Thompson's correspondence, manuscripts, and other archival materials. The Boston Public Library holds several biographically significant letters.

# William Tappan Thompson

## (31 August 1812 – 24 March 1882)

### Scott Slawinski
*University of South Carolina*

See also the Thompson entries in *DLB 3: Antebellum Writers in New York and the South* and *DLB 11: American Humorists, 1800–1950.*

BOOKS: *Major Jones's Courtship: Detailed, with Other Scenes, Incidents, and Adventures, in a Series of Letters, by Himself. To Which is Added, The "Great Attraction!"* (Madison, Ga.: Hanleiter, 1843; revised and enlarged, Philadelphia: Carey & Hart, 1844; revised and enlarged, New York: Appleton, 1872);

*Chronicles of Pineville: Embracing Sketches of Georgia Scenes, Incidents, and Characters,* anonymous (Philadelphia: Carey & Hart, 1845);

*John's Alive; Or, The Bride of a Ghost,* anonymous (Baltimore: Taylor, Wilde, 1846);

*Major Jones's Sketches of Travel, Comprising the Scenes, Incidents, and Adventures in His Tour from Georgia to Canada* as Major Jones (Philadelphia: Carey & Hart, 1848);

*Major Jones's Courtship; or Adventures of a Christmas Eve: A Domestic Comedy in Two Acts* as Major Jones (Savannah: Purse, 1850);

*Truth at the Bottom of a Well, or How Billy Williams Escaped from the Deserters* (Augusta, Ga.: Augusta Constitutionalist, 1865);

*Rancy Cottem's Courtship. Detailed, with Other Humorous Sketches and Adventures* (Philadelphia: Peterson, 1879);

*John's Alive; or, The Bride of a Ghost, and Other Sketches,* edited by Mary Augusta Wade (Philadelphia: McKay, 1883).

PLAY PRODUCTION: *Major Jones's Courtship; or Adventures of a Christmas Eve,* Baltimore Museum, Baltimore, 7 July 1848.

OTHER: A. B. Longstreet, *A Voice from the South: Comprising Letters from Georgia to Massachusetts, and to the Southern States,* introduction by Thompson (Baltimore: Western Continent Press, 1847), pp. 5–8.

The revised publication of *Major Jones's Courtship: Detailed, with Other Scenes, Incidents, and Adventures, in a Series of Letters, by Himself. To Which is Added, The "Great Attraction!"* in 1844 immediately brought Georgia journalist and editor William Tappan Thompson national recognition as a new voice in the growing profession of American authorship. Thompson's extremely popular book chronicles Major Jones's courtship of and marriage to his sweetheart, Mary Stallings, and depicts the birth of their son. Presented as a series of letters written by the major, the book also records the humor, mannerisms, and middle-class, Whig values of central Georgia residents during the antebellum period. Though Thompson abandoned the epistolary format for *Chronicles of Pineville: Embracing Sketches of Georgia Scenes, Incidents, and Characters* (1845), he returned to it in 1848 for *Major Jones's Sketches of Travel, Comprising the Scenes, Incidents, and Adventures in His Tour from Georgia to Canada as Major Jones* and by the close of the decade had firmly secured his reputation as a significant American humorist.

While Thompson resided in Georgia nearly all of his life, he was born in Ravenna, Portage County, Ohio. His father was David Thompson, a Virginian, and his mother was Catherine Kerney, a native of Dublin, Ireland. Thompson's mother died when William was about eleven years old. His father remarried, and friction with his stepmother caused him to leave home at the age of fourteen. Shortly thereafter his father died, leaving Thompson to earn his own way.

Thompson moved to Philadelphia and acquired a job with the *Daily Chronicle,* a nonpartisan newspaper that regularly printed stories, poetry, and theater information. In Philadelphia, Thompson resumed the schooling he had begun in Ohio. He also acquired an appreciation for the theater, eventually joining an amateur acting company. During this time he formed important friendships with Morton McMichael, future mayor of the city and eventual owner of the *North American,* a national Whig newspaper, and James Diament Westcott, recently appointed secretary of the Territory of Florida. Westcott employed Thompson as his private secretary and allowed the young man to read law under him. Florida provided Thompson with material for the sketches he soon began writing; it also witnessed the publication of his earliest known works, two poems in the *Tallahassee Floridian.*

After Westcott's term ended in 1834, Thompson left Florida for Augusta, Georgia, where he found employment at the *States' Rights Sentinel,* the newspaper owned and edited by Augustus Baldwin Longstreet, author of *Georgia Scenes* (1835). In addition to his duties at the *Sentinel,* Thompson continued to study law, this time under Longstreet. When war broke out with the Seminole Indians in 1836, Thompson volunteered for duty with the Richmond Blues, and the *Sentinel* employed him as its war correspondent. At this time Thompson met General Donald L. Clinch, to whom he dedicated *Major Jones's Courtship,* and Lieutenant Ebenezer Starnes, to whom he dedicated *Chronicles of Pineville.*

Thompson's unit returned to Augusta on 27 April 1836, and he was mustered out on 5 May. The *Sentinel* published Thompson's first sketch, "The Seminole Dance," in July 1836. Longstreet sold the paper the same month to William E. Jones, who merged it with the *Augusta Chronicle* and continued to employ the aspiring author. Longstreet's entrance into the Methodist ministry ended Thompson's law studies and confirmed his commitment to a lifetime career in journalism.

The following year Thompson married Augusta native Caroline Love Carrie. The couple faced many hardships during their long marriage. Six of their ten children died before reaching adulthood, and Thompson suffered chronically from bouts of a fever he acquired during his Florida military service. Moreover, they had consistent financial difficulties because the periodicals employing Thompson were unreliable sources of income.

On 5 May 1838 Thompson and James McCafferty founded the *Augusta Mirror,* one of the earliest Georgia periodicals dedicated solely to literature. Though it claimed A. B. Longstreet among its contributors and initially saw a rapid increase in subscriptions, the *Mirror* failed to maintain popular interest and constantly experienced financial troubles because it had difficulty collecting payments from subscribers. Thompson soon realized that southerners were not prepared to support a periodical exclusively dedicated to publishing literary pieces. Moreover, an increasing number of other periodicals forced Thompson to share his contributors with them. While the *Mirror* did experience some triumphs, such as the praise it received from future Confederate vice president Alexander H. Stephens during his 1839 Fourth of July speech, it also experienced a shutdown during the yellow fever epidemic of August 1839, and its offices were flooded when the Savannah River overflowed in May 1840. Eventually, Thompson had to sell his press, and though he kept the *Mirror* in print through 1841, he later merged it with the *Family Companion and Ladies' Mirror,* published in Macon. The publisher of the *Family Companion,* Benjamin F. Griffin, hired Thompson to serve as co-editor with Griffin's wife. Thompson also contributed pieces, including the first Pineville, Georgia, sketch, "Great Attraction! or The Doctor 'Most Oudaciously Tuck In.' A Sketch from Real Life" (March 1842), and the first Major Jones letter (June 1842). Relations with the Griffins, however, were troubled. Thompson criticized some anonymous pieces the periodical published, only to discover Mrs. Griffin was their author. He battled the Griffins over the terms of his contract; they expected him to work in the pressroom, while he maintained that the negotiations had eliminated presswork from his duties on account of his health. Thompson eventually withdrew from the *Family Companion* and gained employment as editor of the *Southern Miscellany,* where he was able to respond to the Griffins' accusations. The battle cooled over time, but Thompson remained bitter for at least two decades.

The first issue of the *Southern Miscellany* Thompson edited appeared on 20 August 1842. His editorial

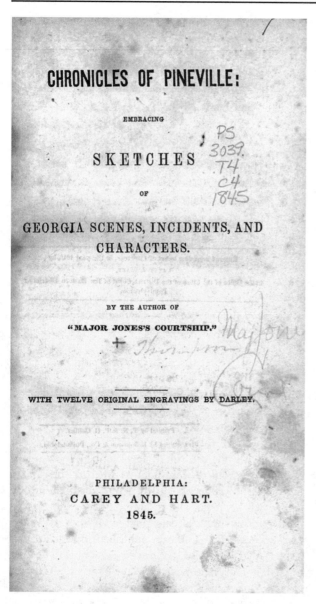

CHRONICLES OF PINEVILLE:

EMBRACING

SKETCHES

OF

GEORGIA SCENES, INCIDENTS, AND
CHARACTERS.

BY THE AUTHOR OF

"MAJOR JONES'S COURTSHIP."

WITH TWELVE ORIGINAL ENGRAVINGS BY DARLEY.

PHILADELPHIA:
CAREY AND HART.
1845.

*Title page for Thompson's collection of humorous sketches about
life in rural Georgia near Augusta (Thomas Cooper Library,
University of South Carolina)*

the paper, Cornelius R. Hanleiter, did him a great service by publishing *Major Jones's Courtship* in 1843. The collection appeared as a pamphlet and included the first sixteen Major Jones letters with "Great Attraction!" appended to them. Hanleiter and Thompson presented the pamphlet as a gift to new subscribers who paid $2.50 in advance for the second volume of the paper. The book sold rapidly. Soon after Thompson had left the *Miscellany,* Philadelphia publishers Carey and Hart brought out a second edition in May 1844. Thompson had revised the letters for Hanleiter's edition; he did so again for Carey and Hart, omitting many of the local references and expanding the edition to include twenty-six of the major's letters. This edition also included sketches by F. O. C. Darley and quickly became popular. Among the periodicals reviewing the second edition favorably was *Godey's Lady's Book,* perhaps because at the time Thompson's friend McMichael was one of its editors. Thompson had agreed to a royalty of only five cents for every copy sold, however, and at the end of the first year, thinking the book had had its run, he sold the entire copyright to Carey and Hart for $250.

At about the same time the second edition was coming off the press, Thompson moved back to Augusta. Here he collected eight of his sketches and contracted with Carey and Hart to print *Chronicles of Pineville.* The book appeared in spring 1845, and William Trotter Porter, who earlier had provided Thompson with national exposure by reprinting the letter featuring Major Jones's marriage proposal in the New York periodical *Spirit of the Times,* told the rising author that *Chronicles of Pineville* would greatly enhance his reputation.

Needing to support his family, Thompson went to New York City in 1845 and fell back on his legal training, preparing William A. Hotchkiss's *A Codification of the Statute Law of Georgia.* The job took seven months and required Thompson to write the analysis, headnotes, and footnotes for the book. Though not much is known about Thompson's life in New York, it is likely he traveled—to Lowell, Massachusetts; Boston; Niagara Falls; Montreal; and Quebec—collecting material for his next Major Jones book.

Sometime in 1845 Thompson met Park Benjamin, and with publisher William Taylor they founded the *Western Continent,* a new Baltimore-based periodical. Thompson was assistant editor, making his debut in the editorial columns of the second edition. Dedicated to the printing of literature, the *Western Continent* published many original pieces in a variety of genres. The paper claimed among its contributors Longstreet, T. S. Arthur, John Pendleton Kennedy, and William Gilmore Simms. Mixed in with these authors' works were the

duties allowed him to review other contemporary periodicals and literary works, and he continued the series of Major Jones letters begun at the *Family Companion.* Thompson's career with the *Miscellany* did not offer him financial security, however. In February 1843 he withdrew as editor because the paper was not drawing in enough money to pay him. The paper quickly rehired him, but when it endorsed Whig candidate Henry Clay for president on 24 November 1843 it lost many of its Democratic subscribers, and Thompson found he had edited his last issue on 9 February 1844.

Though the *Southern Miscellany* maintained an unstable relationship with Thompson, the publisher of

first four installments of Thompson's *John's Alive; Or, The Bride of a Ghost*. Soon after their appearance, the publishing firm of Taylor, Wilde, and Company brought out a book edition in 1846.

Within the pages of the *Western Continent* also appeared the first travel letter from Major Jones. Eventually, Thompson wrote and published twenty-two more letters and then collected all of them except for one into *Major Jones's Sketches of Travel*. This latest edition of letters from the major was again published by Carey and Hart. The tone of this book differed from the earlier installments. Sectional differences among the states stand in the foreground and the attitude of the book is more pro-Southern than *Major Jones's Courtship*. Even in the short span of five years times had changed, and *Major Jones's Sketches of Travel* reflects the increasing animosity between North and South. In addition to the major's travel sketches, Thompson also published several other pieces in the Baltimore periodical. He reprinted two works—"The Doomed Maiden" and an excerpt from "How to Kill Two Birds with One Stone"—and presented new Major Jones material in a regular feature column called "Humourous Department. Edited by Major Jos. Jones, of Pineville." By this time Thompson had become editor and proprietor of the *Western Continent*. Benjamin had withdrawn from the periodical on 11 July 1846 over disagreements concerning editorial views. Almost all of the sketches that appeared were eventually collected into the 1872 edition of *Major Jones's Courtship*.

As assistant editor and then co-editor (along with William H. Carpenter after Benjamin's exit) Thompson took a clearly pro-Southern tone in his editorials. At one point he had to rescue Benjamin from the wrath of the Northern press, pointing out that he and not Benjamin had written the editorials defending the South and attacking abolitionists. Thompson felt he was not attacking the North so much as he was giving voice to a South whose attitudes had not found full representation elsewhere. His pro-Southern stance also allowed him to write the introduction to *A Voice from the South: Comprising Letters from Georgia to Massachusetts, and to the Southern States* (1847), a collection of proslavery letters pseudonymously addressed to Massachusetts from "Georgia," written by A. B. Longstreet for the *Western Continent*. Thompson's ownership of the periodical was nevertheless short-lived, because debts he incurred while building up the paper forced him to sell it in 1848.

In addition to the pieces Thompson printed in his paper, he also wrote three plays, only the first of which was published—*Major Jones's Courtship, or Adventures of a Christmas Eve: A Domestic Comedy in Two Acts as Major Jones;* "The Live Indian"; and "The Vicar of Wakefield" (a dramatic adaptation of Oliver Goldsmith's

1766 novel). For the first of these plays Thompson adapted the first fifteen letters of his book, and the play was performed at the Baltimore Museum on 7 July 1848. He eventually published his adaptation as well. Both *The Live Indian* and *The Vicar of Wakefield* were also performed, but they never made it into print, and overall Thompson never profited much from his plays.

Thompson worked steadily throughout 1849, producing two more sketches for the *Spirit of the Times,* contributing pieces to the *Baltimore Clipper,* and serving as editor to the *Baltimore American*. By the end of the year, though, he was ready to move on. He relocated to Savannah, Georgia, and with printer and bookseller John M. Cooper began a new daily newspaper—the *Daily Morning News*. They modeled their creation after the cheap papers available in the North, including in it editorials, advertisements, daily news, and extracts from other papers. Remembering the lesson he learned from the *Augusta Mirror,* Thompson was not about to found another literary periodical. Nor did he intend to make the paper polemical; the *Daily Morning News* remained politically neutral. Its first issue appeared on 15 January 1850 and immediately faced fierce competition from the two established, successful Savannah newspapers, the *Savannah Republican* and the *Georgian*. Despite its competitors, Thompson's paper survived to become one of the most influential newspapers in the South.

In addition to his duties at the paper, Thompson continued to produce literary pieces. He revised his Major Jones play for *The Friend of the Family,* a Savannah literary periodical founded the year before Thompson's paper, and eventually published three other newly written pieces in it, two of which he collected for an 1872 revised edition of *Major Jones's Courtship*. Thompson also began a new column in the *Daily Morning News,* one written by Mrs. Stallings, the major's mother-in-law, in which she comments on the latest news.

After 1852 Thompson's literary production tapered off until 1857 because he was primarily interested in political matters. He supported expanding the railroads to connect Savannah with the inner regions of Georgia and with areas west. He also served as part of a local committee charged to raise money for Georgians settling Kansas and was chairman of the board of health for 1858, post warden for Savannah, city printer for 1857 and 1858, and a member of the board of managers for the Bethesda orphanage. These were also difficult years for Thompson's family. On 9 August 1854 he lost his two-year-old son Cooper to a yellow fever epidemic. Thompson moved the rest of his family to Augusta and then over the Savannah River into South Carolina, but he, too, eventually took ill and could not return to his editorial duties until October. Four years

MAJOR JONES' COURTSHIP;

OR

*Adventures of a Christmas Eve,*

A DOMESTIC COMEDY,

IN TWO ACTS.

BY MAJOR JOSEPH JONES.

SAVANNAH:
EDWARD J. PURSE, BOOK & JOB PRINTER,
No. 102 Bryan-Street—Up Stairs
1850.

*Title page for Thompson's play featuring his most popular comic character (University of Georgia Library)*

Thompson also went to Charleston, South Carolina, immediately after he had heard that troops had fired on Fort Sumter. He witnessed the shelling, and the next day he gained permission to board a steamer that anchored close to the fort while terms of surrender were negotiated, all of which he reported to the *Daily Morning News.* Throughout the war Thompson supported the South, serving as aide-de-camp and later as colonel in the Georgia militia and organizing recruitment efforts for the Confederate army. He was present for some of the fighting surrounding Savannah, observed an ironclad attack on Fort McAllister, and even remained hopeful after the Confederates lost Fort Pulaski. He also gained material for his editorials from his son, Joseph C. Thompson, who was serving in the Confederate army and could provide firsthand details of the war. Thompson condemned the North at every turn, which ultimately may have forced his removal as editor once Atlanta fell to General Sherman in 1864 and the proprietors wished to position the paper favorably should Union troops take Savannah. Thompson's removal as editor, however, did not change his views, and he joined Confederate General Hardee's retreat from Savannah, eventually joining General Joseph E. Johnston as a volunteer soldier. He was camped near Greensboro, North Carolina, when Johnston surrendered to Sherman in 1865 and the war ended.

The war years had also been difficult for Thompson: in 1862 he lost his four-year-old daughter, Carrie, to scarlet fever, and in 1865 the son who had provided him with news for his editorials was shot in the face, which cost him an eye, disfigured his face, and impeded his speech. After the war Thompson returned to Savannah from North Carolina ill, jobless, and homeless. Not long after his return, however, he accepted an offer from Union journalist Samuel W. Mason to become the assistant editor at the *Savannah Daily Herald,* which was soon to be known as the *Daily News and Herald.* Back in the role of journalist, Thompson journeyed to Philadelphia in August 1866 to report on the National Union Convention, designed to oppose Radical Reconstruction. Though he vehemently stood against Radical Republicans in his editorials, he had also accepted the outcome of the war and urged reconciliation with the North.

The war had weakened Thompson's health, and in autumn 1866 he sickened again. To ease his condition he decided to visit Europe; Mason encouraged him to write editorials for the paper while he toured the Old World. Thompson also hoped to gather material for a new Major Jones book and to negotiate for a British edition of *Major Jones's Courtship.* Heading to Europe without his family, he endured a stormy Atlantic crossing during which he revised *Major Jones's Courtship.* His

later, Thompson's family suffered the loss of another son, Pierce, also at the age of two.

The ever-increasing political debate between North and South also drew much of Thompson's attention. His editorials in the *Daily Morning News* reveal his strong pro-Southern views; yet, he at first opposed secession. While he vehemently disliked the Compromise of 1850 and the Fugitive Slave Law, feeling them insults to Southerners, he continued to favor resistance to Northern policies over outright secession. By 1860, however, he had evolved into a zealous secessionist, supporting those Democrats who walked out of the national convention in Charleston that year and participating in a plot to seize Fort Pulaski, Fort Jackson, and the Savannah Custom House. He went to Milledgeville in January 1861 to observe the Georgia secession convention and the next month traveled to Montgomery, Alabama, to report on the formation of the provisional Confederate government. His editorials include descriptions of Jefferson Davis's inauguration and the first sessions of the Confederate Congress.

ship made port 30 May 1867 in Liverpool, which awed him so much that he exhausted himself touring the city on his first day there. He eventually made his way to London and negotiated his book deal, only to see it disintegrate after his publisher, J. Warne, discovered the existence of recently pirated editions of both *Major Jones's Courtship* and *Major Jones's Travels* and backed away from publishing an authorized edition. Besides England, Thompson's tour encompassed several cities in Scotland, Ireland, France, and Italy and placed him in proximity to many members of the nobility. In Italy he climbed Mount Vesuvius and dined on eggs roasted in lava.

On 16 September 1867 he left for home, having taken many notes for his envisioned edition of "Major Jones in Europe," a book he never published. He actually composed four chapters of his new work, but apparently the 1869 appearance of Mark Twain's *The Innocents Abroad* discouraged him from publishing a similar book, and the heated debate over Radical Reconstruction distracted him. Nearly a year after Thompson's return from Europe, John Holbrook Estell acquired complete control over the *Daily News and Herald*. He promoted his assistant editor to editor, a position Thompson held for the rest of his life. In September 1868 the name of the paper changed again, this time to the *Savannah Morning News*. With Estell as manager, Thompson as editor, and eventually Joel Chandler Harris as a contributing writer and assistant editor the paper became one of the most influential in the South.

Despite his abandonment of "Major Jones in Europe," Thompson did maintain an interest in his fiction. New congressional legislation allowed him in 1872 to renew his copyright of *Major Jones's Courtship*. T. B. Peterson of Philadelphia had acquired the copyright from Carey and Hart and had made a sizable profit from Thompson's book. He distrusted this publisher, however, so when he regained control of his work he published his revised and expanded edition with D. Appleton and Company of New York City. Thompson lessened the amount of dialect in the new edition and added thirteen sketches, many of which had appeared in the *Western Continent*. Peterson did not stop selling its edition, however, and in frustration Appleton stopped paying royalties until Thompson halted the sales of the unauthorized edition. Eventually the author sold his copyright back to Peterson, who divided the Appleton edition into two volumes, one featuring the original set of letters from the 1844 edition of *Major Jones's Courtship*, the other including the added thirteen sketches and a revised version of *Truth at the Bottom of a Well*, a sketch by Thompson originally published as a pamphlet in 1865. This second volume Peterson titled *Rancy Cottem's Court-*

*ship. Detailed, with Other Humorous Sketches and Adventures* (1879). The last Jones letter Thompson ever wrote appeared on 25 August 1873 in the *Morning News*.

As the 1860s came to a close and Reconstruction moved forward, Thompson's assaults on the policy became more aggressive. He vehemently attacked General John Pope, the commander of the military district that included Georgia, and his successor, General George Meade, who removed the conservative governor of the state. Thompson also displayed his displeasure with the constitutional convention of blacks and whites that was taking place in Atlanta. The *Morning News* stood firmly for white supremacy and strongly opposed blacks in the legislature. When the Democrats regained control in December 1870, Thompson was elated, and he enthusiastically supported the Bourbon leadership in Georgia.

Thompson's political role was not limited to his editorial duties. In 1868 he traveled to New York City as a delegate to the National Democratic Convention and delivered a speech at his return encouraging fellow Georgians to vote for the Democratic ticket. Naturally, he was deeply disappointed with the election of Ulysses S. Grant as president, lamenting in his column the loss of liberty, law, and good government in the South. In 1875 some Georgians encouraged Thompson to run for governor, but he declined. He also was a delegate to the 1877 Constitutional Convention taking place in Atlanta. He served as chairman of the Committee on Amendments of the Constitution and Miscellaneous Provisions and as a member of three others—the Committee of Final Revision, the Committee on Printing, and the Committee on Education. In 1879 several Georgia newspapers advocated that Thompson be named to complete the term of Congressman Julian Hartridge, who had died in office, but the convention considering the matter failed to select him for the job. In 1880 Thompson found himself a delegate to the State Democratic Convention in Atlanta, and throughout the postwar years he remained active in local and county politics.

Thompson also supported the economic development of both Savannah and Georgia. Involved in furthering the growth of trade and industry, he stood behind the establishment of a steamship line connecting Savannah directly to Liverpool. He participated in designing the route for the transcontinental line of the Southern Pacific Railroad, favoring a route through the South to aid its depressed regions. Finally, he formed part of a Georgia delegation in June 1879 to the National Board of Trade Convention in New York City, and his columns promoted agriculture whenever possible.

38

*in your life, on one condition*

May.— What are the conditions.

Major.— Why you must promise me, that youll keep the present I give you for ever, as long as you live, for better or for worse,
in sickness or in health, and that you wont never have any other
like it.

Caroline.— aside. Webster's dictionary has brightened his ideas enough since

Mayor— And you say its a good present

Major.— Its very valuable to me, but I'd rather you would have it than keep it myself.

May— Well I'll promise to comply with your conditions.

Major.— You will, Miss May. Do you hear that, Carry. Now
hang up your bag! I've got her word (aside)

Caroline— I'm a witness & the bargain

May— Where shall I hang it

Major. On the back porch, and you'll find the present in
it in the morning (aside I've done the business this time.)

May— Well, the bag shall be there.

Major— Remember your promise miss May.— Good night

May and Caroline— Good night    Exit the Major & W.L.

Caroline. Come sister its very late. Exit Caroline and May

I've just —

Scene 14.

A wood — Stage dark

Enter Cutchell L.H.

Cutchell. Its past the time, and yet I do not see her. Something may
have detained her. I have horses ready to take us to the stage road, and

---

*Manuscript page from Thompson's play adaptation of* Major Jones's Courtship *(Collection of Mr. and Mrs. W. B. Williams Jr. and the Georgia College Library)*

Though Thompson remained active during these years, his health had been in a steady decline. He was ill during the 1876 yellow fever epidemic that ravaged Savannah. To improve his health he traveled to Florida in 1881 and to St. Paul, Minnesota, in 1882. Despite Thompson's poor health, the governor of Georgia recommended him to serve as a commissioner to the International Exhibition, which was to take place in New York City to celebrate the centennial of the 1783 Treaty of Paris. Thompson, however, died at his Savannah home on 24 March 1882. Tributes appeared throughout the South in various newspapers, which the *Savannah Morning News* reprinted, and Thompson's daughter, Mary Augusta Wade, gathered some of her father's uncollected pieces into *John's Alive; or, The Bride of a Ghost, and Other Sketches,* which appeared in 1883. Funeral services for Thompson were held at Trinity Methodist Church, and he was buried in Laurel Grove Cemetery. His wife, Caroline, joined him there on 25 May 1886.

Journalist, editor, author, husband, father, soldier, secessionist, white supremacist, political activist—Thompson was all of these things. Though he will probably be remembered best for his creation of Major Jones, he was primarily a newspaperman, and his writing career encompasses more than just one popular book.

## References:

George R. Ellison, "William Tappan Thompson and the *Southern Miscellany,* 1842–1844," *Mississippi Quarterly,* 23 (Spring 1970): 155–168;

David C. Estes, "Major Jones Defends Himself: An Uncollected Letter," *Mississippi Quarterly,* 33 (Winter 1979–1980): 79–84;

Laura Doster Holbrook, "Georgia Scenes and Life in the Works of William Tappan Thompson," M.A. thesis, University of Georgia, 1967;

Henry Prentice Miller, "The Authorship of *The Slaveholder Abroad,*" *Journal of Southern History,* 10 (February 1944): 92–94;

Miller, "The Background and Significance of *Major Jones's Courtship,*" *Georgia Historical Quarterly,* 30 (December 1946): 267–296;

Miller, "The Life and Works of William Tappan Thompson," dissertation, University of Chicago, 1942;

Carl R. Osthaus, "From the Old South to the New South: The Editorial Career of William Tappan Thompson of the *Savannah Morning News,*" *Southern Quarterly,* 14 (April 1976): 237–260;

Herbert P. Shippey, "William Tappan Thompson: A Biography and Uncollected Fictional Writings," dissertation, University of South Carolina, 1991;

Shippey, "William Tappan Thompson as Playwright," in *Gyascutus: Studies in Antebellum Southern Humorous and Sporting Writing,* edited by James L. W. West III (Atlantic Highlands, N.J.: Humanities Press, 1978), pp. 51–80.

## Papers:

Though some materials are in private hands, the two major sets of William Tappan Thompson papers are located at the University of Georgia and the Ina Dillard Russell Library at Georgia College.

# Thomas Bangs Thorpe

### (1 March 1815 – 20 September 1878)

## David C. Estes
### *Loyola University New Orleans*

See also the Thorpe entries in *DLB 3: Antebellum Writers in New York and the South* and *DLB 11: American Humorists, 1800–1950.*

BOOKS: *The Mysteries of the Backwoods; or, Sketches of the Southwest: Including Character, Scenery, and Rural Sports* (Philadelphia: Carey & Hart, 1846);

*Our Army on the Rio Grande. Being a Short Account of the Important Events Transpiring from the Time of the Removal of the "Army of Occupation" from Corpus Christi, to the Surrender of Matamoros; with Descriptions of the Battles of Palo Alto and Resaca de la Palma, the Bombardment of Fort Brown, and the Ceremonies of the Surrender of Matamoros* (Philadelphia: Carey & Hart, 1846);

*Our Army at Monterey. Being a Correct Account of the Proceedings and Events Which Occurred to the "Army of Occupation" under the Command of Major General Taylor, from the Time of Leaving Matamoros to the Surrender of Monterey* (Philadelphia: Carey & Hart, 1847);

*The Taylor Anecdote Book: Anecdotes and Letters of Zachary Taylor* (New York: Appleton, 1848);

*The Hive of "The Bee-Hunter": A Repository of Sketches, Including Peculiar American Characters, Scenery, and Rural Sports* (New York: Appleton, 1854);

*The Master's House; A Tale of Southern Life,* as Logan (New York: McElrath, 1854).

**Edition:** *A New Collection of Thomas Bangs Thorpe's Sketches of the Old Southwest: A Critical Edition,* edited by David C. Estes (Baton Rouge: Louisiana State University Press, 1989).

OTHER: "The Big Bear of Arkansas," in *The Big Bear of Arkansas and Other Sketches, Illustrative of Characters and Incidents in the South and South-West,* edited by William Trotter Porter (Philadelphia: Carey & Hart, 1845).

SELECTED PERIODICAL PUBLICATIONS–
UNCOLLECTED:

NONFICTION

"The Mississippi," *Knickerbocker Magazine,* 16 (December 1840): 161–164;

*Thomas Bangs Thorpe*

"The Spectator and Simon Suggs," *Spirit of the Times,* 15 (29 November 1845): 29;

"Reminiscences of Tom Owen the Bee Hunter," *Spirit of the Times,* 29 (26 February 1859): 30;

"The New York Custom-House," *Harper's New Monthly Magazine,* 43 (June 1871): 11–26.

Thomas Bangs Thorpe is best known for his contribution to American humor as the author of "The Big Bear of Arkansas" (1841). This classic tall tale features the comic backwoodsman, language, and situations that characterize many sketches by the humorists of the Old Southwest. Scholars have speculated whether Thorpe's story influenced William Faulkner in writing his masterpiece "The Bear" (1942), and Faulkner complimented "The Big Bear of Arkansas" by saying, "A writer is afraid of a story like that. He's afraid he'll try to rewrite it. A writer has to learn when to run from a story." Thorpe contributed both humorous and sporting sketches to William Trotter Porter's New York *Spirit of the Times,* the first national weekly devoted to sports. His accounts of wild animals and field sports were highly regarded for their polish and accuracy. Five of them were selected for the first American edition of the popular British manual *Instructions to Young Sportsmen* (1846). Thorpe revised many of his humorous and sporting sketches for two books of his own.

During the 1840s Thorpe was a respected newspaper editor in several Louisiana towns. He remained active as a painter throughout much of his life. While in Louisiana from 1837 to 1854 he became involved in politics. During the last twenty years of his life he held political appointments in the New York Custom House and at the same time continued to write, publishing more than 150 articles in national magazines on art and drama, wildlife, and the culture and picturesque scenery of Louisiana.

Thorpe was born on 1 March 1815 in Westfield, Massachusetts, the oldest child of Rebecca Farnham and Thomas Thorp. The Thorps (as the writer's ancestors spelled their name) were descended from a literate bond servant who had arrived in Connecticut before 1639. Thorpe's father, however, was born in New Brunswick, Canada, where his father, a Loyalist, had resettled during the Revolutionary War. Following this grandfather's death, his grandmother returned to Connecticut to raise their children. There, Thorpe's father became a Methodist circuit rider, moving his family to several towns in that state before settling in New York City in 1818. He died in 1819, a few days before Rebecca gave birth to their third child. Within a few months she moved to Albany, New York, to live with her parents. Thorpe later recalled the Dutch architecture and culture that surrounded him there.

By May 1827 Thorpe's mother had moved the family back to New York City, where he completed his secondary education. About 1830 he began studying painting with John Quidor, a bohemian who earned an unconventional living by painting the panels of fire engines. Thorpe and Quidor shared a love of Washington Irving's works, and the first painting that Thorpe exhibited, in 1833 at the American Academy of Fine Arts, was of Irving's Ichabod Crane dancing. Later in life, Thorpe recalled learning to appreciate oral humor by attending Quidor's storytelling sessions with other artists, including Gilbert Stuart and Henry Inman. Early in 1832 Thorpe's mother married Charles Albert Hinckley, a

bookbinder and gilder. Thorpe was then still living at home, according to the New York City directory for 1833, in which he listed himself as a portrait painter.

Unable to finance the training in portrait painting that Thorpe wanted in Europe, his family sent him to Wesleyan University in Middletown, Connecticut, in the fall of 1834. There he became friends with several sons of plantation owners from Mississippi and Louisiana. Although Thorpe would have graduated in 1837, he withdrew after the summer term in 1836 because of illness. Early in 1837 he journeyed by stagecoach and steamboat to Louisiana to visit one of his friends. Thorpe may have intended to find employment in the South because in September he was living in Baton Rouge and corresponding with a friend in Mississippi about plans to establish himself as a painter in New Orleans.

Although that dream was not realized, he did become an itinerant painter of portraits of plantation families in the Feliciana parishes along the Mississippi River between Baton Rouge and Natchez. John James Audubon had sketched birds in this same region in the 1820s. Despite the differences in financial circumstances between Thorpe and the Louisiana planters, the stocky, red-haired painter with a distinguishing large nose had a reputation for being good-humored and enjoyed dinners, entertainments, and hunting trips with them. He married, probably in 1838, Anne Maria Hinckley, who was perhaps the daughter of his stepfather. In 1840, after the birth of the first of their three children, they settled in St. Francisville. By 1842 they had moved into the neighboring parish, where Thorpe began his lifelong interest in politics by being elected to the East Feliciana Parish Police Jury, a post equivalent to county commissioner.

Thorpe's literary career commenced inauspiciously in the Feliciana parishes in the autumn of 1839. Out riding with local planters, he met Tom Owen, a fifty-year-old local character with a reputation for tracking wild bees and harvesting honey. Thorpe's friends encouraged him to memorialize the ensuing adventure by sending an account of it to the local weekly. The editor kept the manuscript for three months, then returned it. Sometime later a planter who read the *Spirit of the Times* suggested that Thorpe send it there. The sketch, "Tom Owen, the Bee-Hunter," was immediately and enthusiastically printed. It proved to be one of Thorpe's most popular sketches in the nineteenth century and was reprinted in major anthologies by Rufus Wilmot Griswold, George and Evert Duyckinck, and Edmund Clarence Stedman. The humor in the sketch derives largely from the bee hunter's incongruous apparel—his outlandish hat that resembles a

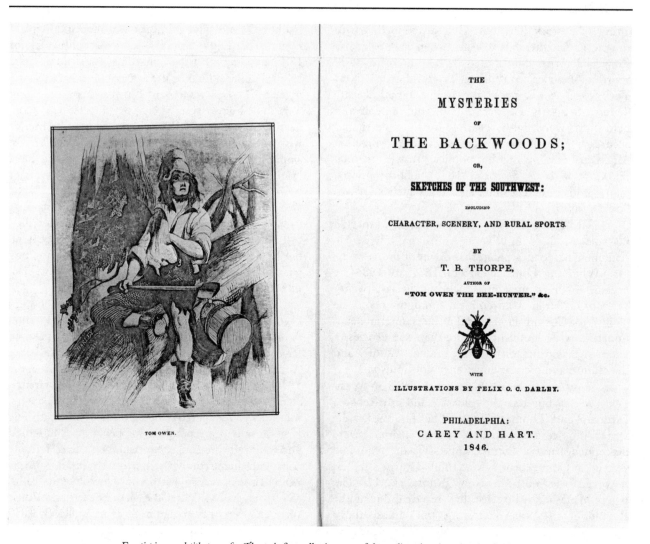

TOM OWEN.

THE

MYSTERIES

OF

THE BACKWOODS;

OR,

SKETCHES OF THE SOUTHWEST:

INCLUDING

CHARACTER, SCENERY, AND RURAL SPORTS.

BY

T. B. THORPE,

AUTHOR OF

"TOM OWEN THE BEE-HUNTER." &c.

WITH

ILLUSTRATIONS BY FELIX O. C. DARLEY.

PHILADELPHIA:
CAREY AND HART.
1846.

*Frontispiece and title page for Thorpe's first collection, one of the earliest American sporting books*

hive and the "pair of inexpressible," or undergarments, that were fully visible—his vernacular language, and the mock heroic tone with which the narrator describes Tom's successful hunt for honey. The comic contrast between an urbane narrator and a backwoodsman found in this sketch was a conventional technique in the writings of the Southern humorists who began publishing in newspapers during the 1840s.

Before Thorpe left the Felicianas in March 1843 to begin a career editing newspapers, he had published a piece in the London *New Sporting Magazine,* three articles in Lewis Gaylord Clark's *Knickerbocker Magazine,* and nearly twenty additional sketches in the *Spirit of the Times.* Two of these *Spirit of the Times* pieces are reminiscences of the New York of his youth, but the others are about animals, hunting, natural scenery, and Native Americans in the lower Mississippi valley. Descriptions of Native Americans

vary from the noble Osage, who tames wild horses in "Romance of the Woods. The Wild Horses of the Western Prairies" (9 April 1842), to the melancholy and brutish Seminoles who are being removed from their homeland by government officers in "Scenes on the Mississippi" (4 September 1841), "The Disgraced Scalp Lock, or Incidents on the Western Waters" (16 July 1842) tells of the renegade Proud Joe, who seeks vengeance when his scalp lock is shot off by Mike Fink, the legendary keelboat pilot of Jacksonian America widely immortalized in popular literature of the day. Thorpe exhibited his knowledge of natural history in writing about the black bears, wildcats, and wild turkeys of the region and the distinctive ways of hunting them. "Woodcock Fire Hunting" (1 May 1841), however, was regarded by some readers as a hoax both because of Thorpe's reputation as a humorist and because this method of killing broke the rules of sportsmanship with abandon. Thorpe

FALL OF MAJOR RINGGOLD.

OUR ARMY

ON

THE RIO GRANDE.

INTERIOR OF FORT BROWN.

The Graves of Major Brown and Lieut. Stevens at the foot of the Flag-staff.

PHILADELPHIA:
CAREY AND HART.
1846.

*Title page for Thorpe's history of the Mexican American War, based in part on his own experiences serving with the Louisiana Volunteers (Thomas Cooper Library, University of South Carolina)*

was forced to publish a defense of his veracity in reporting that hunters in fields adjacent to the swamps of Louisiana and Mississippi blind the migratory woodcocks by carrying a torch and then pick them off before they can escape.

In the 27 March 1841 issue of the *Spirit of the Times* Thorpe published "The Big Bear of Arkansas." This piece has secured his place in American literary history since 1930, when Franklin J. Meine reprinted it in *Tall Tales of the Southwest*. Traveling upriver on the steamer *Invincible,* the urbane narrator, whose voice dominates the frame of the sketch, happens to overhear the loquacious backwoodsman Jim Doggett telling whoppers to a crowd in the bar. The narrator asks

Doggett for the story of a bear hunt, and he agrees to "give you an idea of a hunt, in which the greatest bar was killed that ever lived, *none excepted;* about an old fellow that I hunted, more or less, for two or three years, and if that ain't a *particular bar hunt,* I ain't got one to tell you." Charmed by Doggett's singular style, "the great peculiarity of which was, the happy manner he had of emphasizing the prominent parts of his conversation," the narrator takes care to present the story in Doggett's own words, never realizing that he has swallowed a tall tale of epic proportions. Doggett calls his adversary "a creation bar" and respects him for his enormous size, cunning, and endurance in the chase. As the tale progresses, Doggett masterfully escalates the exaggerations while simultaneously giving them the air of truth even in the outlandish climax. One morning the "unhuntable bar" gives himself up just as Doggett is squatting in the woods for a bowel movement. Doggett shoots, but when he tries to run after the mortally wounded bear, he is tripped by the undergarments around his heels. Walter Blair and Hamlin Hill have observed that "this combination of the earthy with the fantastic makes for a superb anticlimax." The gentleman auditor mistakes Doggett's "grave silence" at the conclusion of the tale for childlike awe before nature's mysteries—never realizing that Doggett, assuming a pose that is part of the tall-tale tradition, deceptively pretends to believe his own lies.

In 1929 Bernard DeVoto suggested Thorpe's preeminence among antebellum Southern humorists by dubbing them the "Big Bear school of literature." The editors of the *New Orleans Picayune* in 1844, however, reserved that theme for him alone: "It has generally been conceded that Thorpe . . . is the only man entitled to tell a *'bar'* story." Stylistically, "The Big Bear of Arkansas" is a masterful literary re-creation of both the tall-tale form and the vernacular voice of oral storytellers. Thematically, it is a meditation on the complex relationship between the wilderness and American civilization. "The Big Bear of Arkansas" is a comic yet disturbing reflection on the hunters and their field sports that Thorpe generally celebrated in his writings.

From 1843 to 1847 Thorpe edited six newspapers in Louisiana, using his position to espouse Whig causes. These newspapers were the *New Orleans Southern Sportsman,* from 18 March 1843 to 5 June 1843; the *Vidalia Concordia Intelligencer,* from mid June 1843 to 20 June 1845; the *New Orleans Daily Commercial Times,* from November 1845 to spring 1846; the *New Orleans Daily Tropic* from 1 April 1846 to September 1846; the *Baton Rouge Louisiana Conservator,* from November 1846 to spring 1847; and the *New Orleans Daily National,* from June 1847 to 10 December 1847. The position of editor allowed Thorpe to pursue his interest in writing as well as to dabble in politics by supporting Whig causes in Louisiana.

Although short-lived, the *Southern Sportsman* is significant because it was launched to compete against Porter's *Spirit of the Times,* which had a significant southern readership. Thorpe's weekly similarly carried original sporting sketches, reports from jockey clubs, humorous contributions from correspondents, and discussions of drama. Porter immediately perceived the threat to his own enterprise if a regional sporting press should develop and countered with the *American Sporting Chronicle.* It included news of boxing, a disreputable sport that was not then regularly covered by the press. Six months after Thorpe's paper failed, Porter discontinued his second weekly as well.

As editor of the *Concordia Intelligencer,* at the time the largest Louisiana newspaper outside of New Orleans, Thorpe published a hoax that succeeded in gulling some readers, including the editors of the *Picayune.* This series of satiric letters enhanced his reputation as a humorist. "Letters from the Far West" appeared irregularly in twelve installments between August 1843 and February 1844 and were reprinted in the *Spirit of the Times.* These tongue-in-cheek sporting epistles burlesque the rather dull reports submitted to the *Picayune* by its assistant editor, Matthew C. Field, who was traveling along the Oregon Trail with the hunting expedition of Scotchman Sir William Drummond Stewart. Thorpe, who had made a hunting trip to the western Louisiana prairies that summer, had been invited to join the group. He chose instead to draw on his own experiences to write letters in which P.O.F., a genteel sportsman with romantic illusions about the West, recounts his painful and demoralizing encounter with the bewildering brutality of frontiersmen and nature. Thorpe's critique of the national myth of the frontier recalls Irving's in *A Tour on the Prairies* (1835).

In March 1844 Thorpe wrote to Porter, seeking assistance in publishing a collection of sketches. The *Spirit* editor recommended Thorpe to the firm of Carey and Hart but did so only a full year later after having edited a book for that firm that exploited the humorist's fame. In spring 1845 Porter used Thorpe's most famous sketch as the title and leading piece for *The Big Bear of Arkansas* (1845), an anthology of humor from the *Spirit of the Times.* This incident, along with Porter's earlier response to the *Southern Sportsman,* qualifies his self-proclaimed pose of being a helpful "literary god-father" to Thorpe and other humorists, who contributed to the *Spirit of the Times* without remuneration.

Despite Porter's delay, Thorpe contracted with A. Ackerman, a publisher of sporting journals in London, to write a book, but the firm failed before his one-hundred-page manuscript arrived. Carey and Hart were nevertheless interested and published *The Mysteries of the Backwoods; or, Sketches of the Southwest: Including Character, Scenery, and Rural Sports* in January 1846. It is important as one of the first American sporting books. For the most part its sixteen sketches, five of them written especially for the volume, describe natural scenery and hunting realistically rather than comically. Thorpe's stylistic debt to travel writing and his democratic view of field sports in *Mysteries of the Backwoods* contrast with William

*Thorpe's 1860 painting* Niagara As It Is *(Vose Galleries, Boston)*

Elliott's *Carolina Sports by Land and Water,* also published in 1846, which emphasizes the pleasures that gentleman plantation owners find in hunting on their own property.

Despite an initial press run of four thousand copies (the same as *The Big Bear of Arkansas*), sales of *Mysteries of the Backwoods* were disappointing, possibly because it was not a book of humor. Carey and Hart clearly wanted Thorpe to produce such a book, and the firm rejected his proposals for a romance set on the western frontier at the turn of the century, a book about northern California, and another of the correspondence of a revolutionary general. The latter two were to be based on manuscript materials Thorpe had purchased. Acceding to the wishes of his publishers, in the spring of 1846 Thorpe began soliciting humorous sketches from contributors. He soon became involved in other projects instead of capitalizing on his national reputation as a humorist, however.

The Mexican American War, which began in April 1846, offered Thorpe two opportunities for which he was more eager—to write histories and to secure an influential political position. He received a temporary commission in the Louisiana Volunteers and retained the title of "Colonel" for the rest of his life. He carried dispatches to the front and, while there, gathered materials for two books. Carey and Hart published the two resulting histories, *Our Army on the Rio Grande. Being a Short Account of the Important*

*Events Transpiring from the Time of the Removal of the "Army of Occupation" from Corpus Christi, to the Surrender of Matamoros; with Descriptions of the Battles of Palo Alto and Resaca de la Palma, the Bombardment of Fort Brown, and the Ceremonies of the Surrender of Matamoros* (1846) and *Our Army at Monterey. Being a Correct Account of the Proceedings and Events Which Occurred to the "Army of Occupation" under the Command of Major General Taylor, from the Time of Leaving Matamoros to the Surrender of Monterey* (1847). Undoubtedly sensing the growing dissatisfaction of the firm with the inferiority of these books and their poor sales, when sending the manuscript "Anecdotes of the War" in April 1848 Thorpe offered "to give you a volume for your humorous library soon, if you wish it." Instead, his association with Carey and Hart abruptly ended with the rejection of both "Anecdotes" and also his plans to complete the series on the Mexican American War with a book on the Battle of Buena Vista and another on General Zachary Taylor, whom Thorpe had met briefly. In hopes of supporting his family with these projects, he had already stopped working as a newspaper editor.

Next, Thorpe turned to political activity in support of Taylor as the Whig candidate for the presidency. D. Appleton and Company published his war anecdotes as *The Taylor Anecdote Book: Anecdotes and Letters of Zachary Taylor* (1848), a campaign biography of the general. Taylor was residing in Baton Rouge throughout much of 1848, and he posed for Thorpe, also living there at the time, who painted two portraits of the successful candidate. Thorpe's hopes for an appointment in the foreign service were dashed when he was offered the minor position of register of the Land Office at New Orleans, which he refused. The larger of his portraits of Taylor was, however, purchased by the Louisiana legislature in 1852 for $1,000. Thorpe toured central Louisiana in the fall of 1852, speaking in behalf of General Winfield Scott's presidential candidacy. The Whigs not only failed to carry Louisiana for Scott, but Thorpe was also defeated in his campaign for state superintendent of schools by the Democratic candidate.

Thorpe's interest in writing was apparently reawakened in the summer of 1852 when Henry Carey Baird offered to sell him the copyright and plates of *The Mysteries of the Backwoods*. After protracted negotiations Thorpe selected fourteen sketches from it for inclusion in *The Hive of "The Bee-Hunter": A Repository of Sketches, Including Peculiar American Characters, Scenery, and Rural Sports,* which was published in the spring of 1854. The contents included twenty-three sketches by Thorpe and one, "The Great Four-Mile Day," by A. C. Bullitt, editor of the *New Orleans Bee*. Thorpe wrote no new pieces for *The Hive of "The Bee-Hunter,"* but he did meticulously revise what he selected from *Mysteries of the Backwoods* and various newspapers. F. O. C. Darley's illustrations for *Mysteries of the Backwoods* were reused, and several others were added. *The Hive of "The Bee-Hunter"* includes all of Thorpe's most popular humorous pieces except "Letters from the Far West." At last, he had published what can be considered primarily a book of humor, and it was reviewed widely and favorably.

Less than three months later, Thorpe's only novel, *The Master's House; A Tale of Southern Life* (1854), appeared under the pseudonym "Logan." It tells the story of Graham Mildmay, a young North Carolina gentleman with both a New England education and a New England bride, who settles on a Louisiana plantation, where he must defend his abolitionist views. The climax is a duel in which Mildmay kills his neighbor, leading to the decline of both families. Several scholars have mistakenly classified it as a proslavery novel. Although at times ambiguous on the sensitive issues of the day, it expresses Thorpe's opinions about the evils fostered by slavery. The novel is Whiggish in its politics, preaching preservation of the Union and the need for the South to diversify its economy. Rather surprisingly, the narrative lacks a humorous subplot or even a comic character. One chapter, "Cinderella Negro-

typed," in which a slave adapts the fairy tale to a plantation setting for her master's children, was reprinted in William Burton's *Cyclopedia of Wit and Humor* (1858). Nevertheless, reviewers did not praise the book.

Probably because of the death of his stepfather in the summer of 1852, the birth of his third child sometime during 1853, and his declining literary and political prospects in Louisiana, Thorpe decided to return to New York City to seek his fortune. By the fall of 1854 and at the age of thirty-nine, he had completed the move. On 4 October 1854 his wife died. During the first several years in New York, Thorpe was busy writing. *Harper's* published nineteen articles by him between 1853 and 1857, many of them about southern topics, including the cultivation of sugar, cotton, and tobacco. He married Jane Fosdick in November 1857, and their daughter was born sometime before 1860. Also in 1857 Thorpe joined the editorial staff of *Frank Leslie's Illustrated Newspaper*. Although lacking the proper training, he operated a law office for three years beginning in 1858. From February 1859 to March 1861 he was part owner and an editor of the *Spirit of the Times,* for which he wrote about art, including a series of critiques of paintings exhibited at the National Academy of Design. In 1860 he completed a monumental view of Niagara Falls, which received favorable attention when it was exhibited, and in 1862 he exhibited two canvases at the National Academy of Design. One of them was titled *Washington Irving's Grave*.

Thorpe returned to New Orleans in June 1862 following its capture by Union forces. He traveled there with an appointment as a customs officer but quickly became surveyor in the city government at a salary of $5,000. He was in charge of sanitation, an important task that he handled ably in the disease-ridden city. Thorpe also held appointments in the New Orleans Custom House and served in the Louisiana Constitutional Convention. He went back to New York City in the summer of 1866 under a cloud of suspicion for misappropriating funds while holding those public positions.

Following this sojourn Thorpe was a city surveyor in New York before returning in 1869 to the New York Custom House, where he had previously served from 1858 to 1862. There he rapidly jumped to increasingly lucrative posts, finally becoming a weigher at the salary of $2,500. At this time the New York Custom House collected three-fourths of the revenues of the federal government and was notoriously corrupt. Apparently, Thorpe became involved in such schemes because, during a reform campaign in 1877, he was to be fired. The order, however, was eventually rescinded, allowing him to resign and thereby avoid any imputation of corrupt behavior. Relying on political connections, six months later Thorpe was reappointed to the Custom House as a minor clerk at less than half his former salary.

While serving in the Custom House, Thorpe was active in local Republican politics. He also published informative articles on a wide variety of topics—ten in *Harper's* and more than thirty in *Appleton's Journal. Forest and Stream* carried his weekly reviews of art and drama from August 1873 to January 1874. His last project was a series on American painters for *Baldwin's Monthly* that ran from November 1875 up until his death three years later. Thorpe had suffered from chronic Bright's disease, but he was unable to withstand the shocking sudden deaths of his youngest daughter and her year-old son in September 1878. Thorpe died on 20 September and was buried in Green-Wood Cemetery in Brooklyn.

Thorpe wrote steadily throughout his life, seldom producing anything other than hackwork for newspapers and magazines. Only at the start of his career in the early 1840s did he find subjects about which he was temperamentally suited to write memorably. Thorpe had an ear for the vocabulary and rhythms of vernacular speech, and therefore the best of his humorous and sporting sketches describe fascinating characters, wildlife, and scenes from the southwestern frontier in prose that remains fresh and vibrant.

**References:**

Walter Blair and Hamlin Hill, *America's Humor: From Poor Richard to Doonesbury* (New York: Oxford University Press, 1978), pp. 200–212;

Stanton Garner, "Thomas Bangs Thorpe in the Gilded Age: Shifty in a New Country," *Mississippi Quarterly,* 36 (1982–1983): 35–52;

Barrie Hayne, "Yankee in the Patriarchy: T. B. Thorpe's Reply to *Uncle Tom's Cabin,*" *American Quarterly,* 20 (Summer 1968): 180–195;

J. A. Leo Lemay, "The Text, Tradition, and Themes of 'The Big Bear of Arkansas,'" *American Literature,* 47 (November 1975): 321–342;

Alice Hall Petry, "The Common Doom: Thorpe's 'The Big Bear of Arkansas,'" *Southern Quarterly,* 21 (Winter 1983): 24–31;

Milton Rickels, "The Grotesque Body of Southwestern Humor," in *Critical Essays on American Humor,* edited by William Bedford Clark and Craig W. Turner (Boston: Hall, 1984), pp. 155–166;

Rickels, *Thomas Bangs Thorpe: Humorist of the Old Southwest* (Baton Rouge: Louisiana State University Press, 1962).

**Papers:**

Thomas Bangs Thorpe's only extant manuscript of a sketch is in the Thomas Bangs Thorpe Collection, Barrett Library, University of Virginia, Charlottesville. His letters can be found among the Carey and Hart Papers, New York Historical Society; the Edward Carey Gardner Collection and the Simon Gratz Collection, Historical Society of Pennsylvania, Philadelphia; the Griswold Manuscripts, Boston Public Library; the Bancroft Papers, Massachusetts Historical Society, Boston; and the Charles Robers Autograph Letters Collection, Haverford College Library, Haverford, Pennsylvania.

# Henry Timrod

*(8 December 1828 – 7 October 1867)*

Rayburn S. Moore
*University of Georgia*

See also the Timrod entry in *DLB 3: Antebellum Writers in New York and the South.*

BOOKS: *Poems* (Boston: Ticknor & Fields, 1860);
*The Poems of Henry Timrod,* edited by Paul Hamilton Hayne (New York: Hale, 1873);
*Katie* (New York: Hale, 1884);
*Poems of Henry Timrod; With Memoir and Portrait* (Boston: Houghton, Mifflin, 1899);
*The Uncollected Poems of Henry Timrod,* edited by Guy A. Cardwell Jr. (Athens: University of Georgia Press, 1942);
*The Essays of Henry Timrod,* edited by Edd Winfield Parks (Athens: University of Georgia Press, 1942);
*The Collected Poems: A Variorum Edition,* edited by Parks and Aileen Wells Parks (Athens: University of Georgia Press, 1965).

*Henry Timrod*

Since Henry Timrod's output before the Civil War was limited to verse sufficient only for a single volume–published in December 1859–his literary reputation at the time was modest. The political activities surrounding the formation of a new nation and the impact of the war itself aroused Timrod's poetic imagination, however, and he quickly became widely known as the literary spokesman and eventually as the so-called poet laureate of the Confederacy, an unofficial title he has retained ever since. After the war, poor health associated with the complications of tuberculosis and abject poverty related to political and social conditions in South Carolina during Reconstruction made it impossible for Timrod to fulfill the promise or equal the achievement of his wartime performance, and he died in 1867, two months before his thirty-ninth birthday.

Henry Timrod was born in Charleston, South Carolina, on 8 December 1828 to Thyrza Prince and William Henry Timrod, a bookbinder and amateur poet whose shop was a gathering place for lawyers, politicians, editors, and writers–some of the keenest minds of the city. Henry was educated at the Classical School of Christopher Cotes, generally considered to be the best available, where Paul Hamilton Hayne, the poet, and Basil L. Gildersleeve, the classical scholar, were his classmates and where he was offered a sound grounding in such traditional subjects as Greek, Latin, French, history, and mathematics. Later, with help from a Charleston merchant, he attended the University of Georgia for three terms in 1845–1846, continuing his classical studies but dropping out when financial difficulties occurred. Returning home, he read law with James Louis Petigru, a distinguished lawyer and former attorney general of the state, and in the 1850s he devoted himself to teaching school and tutoring on Carolina plantations.

Meanwhile he had begun contributing poems in 1846 to the *Charleston Evening News* and in 1849 to periodicals such as the *Southern Literary Messenger.* When *Russell's Magazine,* under the editorship of his old friend Hayne, began appearing in Charleston in April 1857, Timrod found a substantial outlet for his poetry and criticism. During the three-year life of *Russell's,* Timrod contributed thirty-seven poems, including several of his best of the period–"The Arctic Voyager" (April 1857), "Dreams" (May 1857), "Praeceptor Amat" (February 1858), and "Sonnet: At Last, Beloved Nature" (February 1859). These pieces suggest Timrod's versatility with subject, line, and form. "The Arctic Voyager," in blank verse, follows the experience of Captain Elisha Kent Kane, an Arctic explorer, who tells about his third attempt to reach the North Pole in a Tennysonian dramatic monologue fashioned after "Ulysses" (1842). In the last twelve lines he addresses his "hardy shipmates" directly, urging them not "to count the chances" but to do all that "bold and patient hearts can do." "Dreams," on the other hand, deals with the power of intuitive reverie in seven quatrains with an *abab* rhyme scheme and concludes that "our dreams" are "allegories with deep hearts of truth / That tell us solemn secrets of ourselves." Yet another approach is taken in "Praeceptor Amat," in which a tutor is halfway in love with one of the pupils who is studying Greek and reading Homer with him. The lines are long to suggest the Greek, and the heroic couplet provides dignity for a topic that is not to be taken too seriously, a fairly rare situation in Timrod's canon. This poem is based upon his own experience in 1856 with one of his favorite students, Felicia Robinson, as Edd Winfield Parks and others have pointed out. Finally, the sonnet "At Last, Beloved Nature!" finds him working in a favorite genre–one of his most impressive essays is "The Character and Scope of the Sonnet," which also appeared in *Russell's* (May 1857). Though the lyric is basically Italian in pattern, the rhyme scheme of the second quatrain is different from the norm and the sestet is turned upside down, with the couplet appearing in the first two lines instead of the last two; consequently, the resolution of the poem is in the sestet and not in the couplet. Altogether, there is an interesting variety in subject and technique in some of his best verse for *Russell's.*

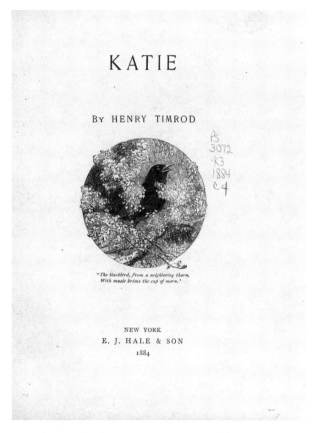

KATIE

By HENRY TIMROD

"The blackbird, from a neighboring thorn,
With music brims the cup of morn."

NEW YORK
E. J. HALE & SON
1884

*Title page for Timrod's poem about his wife (Thomas Cooper Library, University of South Carolina)*

Timrod also contributed some of his best prose to the monthly, a total of four essays, including "The Character and Scope of the Sonnet" and two others deserving of mention: "What Is Poetry?" (October 1857) and "Literature in the South" (August 1859). The piece on the sonnet defends the form–and William Wordsworth–from the attacks of a "large body of depreciators" and shows that poetry is far more than the "result of a sort of mystical inspiration," for it also requires the artistry of "patient and elaborate execution." "What Is Poetry?" is a response to an essay of the same title by William J. Grayson, a well-known lawyer and former member of Congress, who had presented a neoclassical view of the topic. Timrod, on the contrary, offers a romantic interpretation that concentrates on unusual sensibility, powerful emotion, and beautiful language. The last article in *Russell's,* "Literature in the South," is, as Jay B. Hubbell has pointed out in *The South in American Literature, 1607–1900* (1954), "the most penetrating analysis of the difficulties of the Southern author." Timrod sees the writer in the South as "the Pariah of modern literature," an artist without honor in his own country and ridiculed in the North as a representative (and often defender) of

*The last known photograph of Timrod, taken a few months before his death in 1867*

an outmoded and immoral way of life. The Southern author, then, has a limited audience and serious difficulties that may seldom be resolved.

Timrod's contributions to *Russell's,* especially those in verse, led to the publication of the only collection that appeared during his lifetime, *Poems,* in December 1859, an event that seemed to presage a certain kind of literary career; but the coming of the war changed his poetic focus and charged his imagination in a different way. The establishment of the new government in Montgomery provided him with his first topic, and he responded with "Ode on Occasion of the Meeting of the Southern Congress" (*Charleston Daily Courier,* 23 February 1861; later retitled "Ethnogenesis"), an announcement by a narrator of the arrival of a new "nation among nations," warning "our foes" of the North that the Confederates shall "Go forth / To meet them, marshaled by the Lord of Hosts," and prophesying that in the future the young country would share the blessings of "wealth, and power, and peace" with the "whole sad planet o'er."

Later in the year and in spite of the abortive nature of his first military experience (he enlisted, but poor health quickly led to his discharge), Timrod, still imbued with patriotism and sanguine about the future of the country, sought again to celebrate the virtues of the Confederate state and to examine its future in a second laureate poem, "The Cotton Boll" (*Charleston Mercury,* 3 September 1861). Once more a speaker looks out over the natural world of the South, notes that it is blessed with "all the common gifts of God," and concludes that "no fairer land hath fired a poet's lay, / Or given a home to man." The Confederacy will not only share its wealth with the rest of the world, but it will also "Revive the half-dead dream of universal peace." In the meantime, however, the foe must be overcome and forced to return to "his own blasted altar-stones, and crave / Mercy," which, in due course, will be granted. These odes and ten other lyrics of this period—"I Know Not Why," "A Cry to Arms," "Carolina," "Charleston," "Christmas," "Spring," "The Two Armies," "Carmen Triumphale," "The Unknown Dead," and "Ode Sung on the Occasion of Decorating the Graves of the Confederate Dead"—constitute the core of Timrod's poetic tribute and contribution to the Confederacy and commentary on the war in all its manifestations of glory and horror.

The poems Timrod wrote during the war years reflect and express his moods and his views on the new nation and its progress and on the war and its results. In "Ethnogenesis" and "The Cotton Boll" the mood is hopeful, but, concurrently, there is a feeling of melancholy and foreboding in "I Know Not Why," a sonnet written in August 1861 and published in the *Charleston Mercury* (7 October 1861), the period during which "The Cotton Boll" was composed. The speaker's allusions to "this weary day," to "sad fancies" and a "vessel losing way," to "a banner drooping in the rain, / And meadows beaten into bloody clay" suggest something more than a personal response to surroundings, for the "bloody clay" may refer not only to the battles already fought, chiefly the first battle of Bull Run, but to future conflicts as well, such as those that led in 1862 to the loss of Forts Henry and Donelson in Tennessee and of Roanoke Island and a sizable portion of eastern North Carolina, leaving Charleston with dim prospects for the days to come.

Timrod responded to these developments with "A Cry to Arms" (*Charleston Mercury* and *Daily Courier,* 4 March 1862), "Carolina" (*Charleston Daily Courier,* 8 March 1862), and "Charleston" (*Charleston Mercury,* 3 December 1862). The first two lyrics exhort Southerners and Carolinians to meet and defeat the foe, described in "A Cry to Arms" as "the despot" who "roves your fairest lands" and in "Carolina" as the "Huns" who "tread thy sacred sands." "We Battle for our Country's sake," the speaker maintains in the first poem, and in the second he calls upon Carolinians to "Rouse all thy strength and all thy skill" and "All shall be safe beneath thy sod." In "Charleston" the city "bides the foe" and "a thousand guns" "wait and watch for blood," but the issue is in doubt and the city "waits the triumph or the tomb." Only a few weeks later, in "Christmas" (*Charleston Mercury,* 25 December 1862), the narrator, with the experience of the aftermath of Shiloh in April behind him (Timrod had been there as a correspondent) and despite the Confederate victory at Fredericksburg on 13 December, questions the propriety of battle in the midst of "this hallowed day" and wonders how "we bear the mirth" while remembering the death "a year ago" of someone who now "keeps his mute Christmas" in "cold Virginian earth." He cries therefore for "peace, peace in all our homes / And peace in all our hearts!"

In 1863 Timrod expresses and anticipates a modern view of war and its consequences in four poems published in the *Southern Illustrated News:* "Spring" (4 April), "The Two Armies" (30 May), "Carmen Triumphale" (7 June), and "The Unknown Dead" (4 July). These pieces were prepared in the early part of the year when the Confederacy was holding its own in the East; they celebrate the important Southern victory of Chancellorsville and mourn the unexpected death of General Thomas "Stonewall" Jackson. In "Spring" the eternal return of life represented by the blooming jasmine and crocus brings with it "thoughts of war and crime," "the call of Death," and the rousing of a "million men to arms." In such circumstances spring can only encourage nature "To fall and crush the tyrants and the slaves / Who turn her meads to graves." In "Carmen Triumphale" the charge is even more emphatic. "Our foes" have "fought as tyrants fight," the speaker asserts, and they have rightly "fallen," their bones "bleaching on the sands, / Or mouldering slow in shallow graves." Nevertheless, he concludes, "Lord! Bid the frenzied tempest cease." "The Two Armies" celebrates, as Walt Whitman did concurrently in his poem of the same name, those on the front line and those on the home front, concluding that when "triumph" has been achieved and "freedom" won, "each shall see its dearest prize / gleam softly from the other's eyes." Spring appears again in "The Unknown Dead" as the narrator, speaking in the first person, counts the cost of victory and of battles "nobly lost"; he imagines "myriad unknown heroes" in "nameless graves" who fought "for free-

*Bronze bust of Timrod located on Washington Square in Charleston, South Carolina*

dom and for right" but whose graves arouse an ironic response from "Nature's self": "Oblivious of the crimson debt / To which she owes her April grace," she only "laughs gaily o'er their burial place." Such poems, though they may lack the bite and disillusionment of World War I poetry as explored in the works of Alan Seeger, Siegfried Sassoon, or Wilfred Owen, nevertheless look forward to it in use of irony, tone, and in a searing sense of loss.

Timrod's ultimate poetic contribution on the war and its result is his "Ode Sung on the Occasion of Decorating the Graves of the Confederate Dead, at Magnolia Cemetery, Charleston, S.C., 1866" (*Charleston Daily Courier,* 18 June 1866; revised, 23 July 1866). The poem is a tribute to those who have given their lives for a "fallen cause," those in "humble graves" who wait for stone monuments and are honored with "memorial blooms" by their "sisters for the years," who, by remembering these "martyrs" with their tears and flowers, share in this public recognition. The ode is Timrod's most perfect poem, worthy of those whom it celebrates, a testimonial to the poet's own work, and deserving of high rank among all Horatian odes in English.

Although Timrod's most important poetry is related to the war, he also composed other notable verse during the period, including "Our Willie," "A Mother's Wail," "Katie," and "La Belle Juive." "Katie" (printed concurrently in the *Charleston Mercury* and the *Charleston Daily Courier*, 28 December 1861) is a tribute to Katie S. Goodwin, later his wife but at the time of composition only one of several women Timrod found particularly interesting. He was "anxious" about the piece because, as he expressed it in a letter of 25 December 1861 to Rachel Lyons, another of his close female friends, it "was so purely an inspiration" with only "small recourse to art in the execution"; enough readers liked it for it to appear in a separate publication in 1884, however. Initially titled "Rachel," "La Belle Juive" (*Charleston Daily Courier*, 23 January 1862) honors Lyons only a month after the tribute to Goodwin. More concentrated and less flowery in diction than "Katie," "La Belle Juive" offers a brief narrative in triplets that describes the poet's response to the beauty of one of "the noblest women of your race" and characterizes their relationship in the scriptural context of that of Boaz and Ruth, although at the end the image of Ruth lying at the feet of Boaz is reversed to that of the poet lying at the feet of Rachel. These love poems and the pair of lyrics about the death of his son, William Henry Timrod, demonstrate that Timrod could readily manage nonmartial themes and topics, but the war and the Confederacy stirred his imagination in special ways and furnished him with material for his most memorable poetry.

The war also provided Timrod with an occasion to write another important essay. In 1863 he was asked to deliver a lecture before the Methodist Female College in Columbia in aid of Confederate soldiers, and he took as his topic "A Theory of Poetry" (eventually published in the *Independent*, 28 March, 4 April, and 11 April 1901). In arriving at his own view of poetry, he disagrees with Edgar Allan Poe's ideas that a long poem (the epic in particular) is a contradiction in terms and that poetry is limited in subject to "the sense of the beautiful." Timrod maintains, on the contrary, that John Milton's *Paradise Lost* (1667), for example, has a cumulative effect and a general harmony and unity and that poetry, while including beauty as a source, must also have power and truth and embody great moral and philosophical lessons.

After the cessation of hostilities in 1865, Timrod had little time to write poems. He tried to support his family—he had married Goodwin, his sister Emily's sister-in-law, on 16 February 1864, and their only child, William Henry or "Willie", was born the following

Christmas Eve—but his work as an editor and journalist paid little, frequently not at all, and they lived from hand to mouth, selling family furniture and silver and reluctantly accepting money from friends, including William Gilmore Simms and Hayne. During this period Timrod had recurrent hemorrhages, but he managed to write a few poems and work on a manuscript of a new edition of his verse. In two of these pieces, "Our Willie" (September 1866) and "A Mother's Wail" (October 1866), both published in *Scott's Monthly* and both about the death of Willie on 23 October 1865, the agony of loss is imparted with little aesthetic distance. Less than two years later, Timrod died of tuberculosis on 7 October 1867, eighteen years to the day after the death of Poe.

Timrod is, after Poe, the most important Southern poet of the nineteenth century. The quality of his best work, though small in bulk, exceeds that of Sidney Lanier and Hayne, and his contributions to war and nature poetry also exceed theirs. He is not a major poet, but he is a significant minor poet.

**Letters:**

"Some Letters of Henry Timrod," edited by Thomas O. Mabbott, *American Collector*, 3 (February 1927): 191–195;

"Unpublished Letters of Henry Timrod," edited by William Fidler, *Southern Literary Messenger*, 2 (October 1940): 527–535; (November 1940): 605–611; (December 1940): 645–651;

*The Last Years of Henry Timrod, 1864–1867, Including Letters of Timrod to Paul Hamilton Hayne and Letters about Timrod by William Gilmore Simms, John R. Thompson, John Greenleaf Whittier, and Others*, edited by Jay B. Hubbell (Durham, N.C.: Duke University Press, 1941);

"Seven Unpublished Letters of Henry Timrod," edited by Fidler, *Alabama Review*, 2 (April 1949): 139–149;

"Two Timrod Letters," edited by Douglas J. Robillard, *North Carolina Review*, 39 (Autumn 1962): 549–553.

**Bibliography:**

Jack De Bellis, *Sidney Lanier, Henry Timrod and Paul Hamilton Hayne: A Reference Guide* (Boston: Hall, 1978), pp. 107–137.

**Biographies:**

Paul Hamilton Hayne, "Memoir," in Timrod's *The Poems*, edited by Hayne (New York: Hale, 1873): 7–69;

John P. K. Bryan, Introduction to *Poems*, Memorial Edition (Boston: Houghton, Mifflin, 1899): vii–xxxviii;

George A. Wauchope, *Henry Timrod: Man and Poet, a Critical Study* (Columbia: University of South Carolina Press, 1915);

Henry T. Thompson, *Henry Timrod: Laureate of the Confederacy* (Columbia, S.C.: *The State,* 1928).

**References:**

John Dickson Bruns, "A Lecture on Timrod," *Charleston Sunday News,* 30 April 1899;

Jack De Bellis, "Henry Timrod," in *Fifty Southern Writers before 1900: A Bio-Bibliographical Sourcebook,* edited by Robert Bain, Joseph M. Flora, and Louis D. Rubin Jr. (Westport, Conn.: Greenwood Press, 1987), pp. 464–472;

Claud B. Green, "Henry Timrod and the South," *South Carolina Review* 2 (May 1970): 27–33;

Jay B. Hubbell, *The South in American Literature, 1607–1900* (Durham, N.C.: Duke University Press, 1954), pp. 466–474;

Ludwig Lewisohn, "Books We Have Made," *Charleston News and Courier,* 5 July–20 September 1903 (Chapter 12);

Edd Winfield Parks, *Ante-Bellum Southern Literary Critics* (Athens: University of Georgia Press, 1962), pp. 193–226;

Parks, *Henry Timrod* (New York: Twayne, 1964);

Rubin, "Henry Timrod and the Dying of the Light," *Mississippi Quarterly,* 11 (Summer 1958): 101–111;

Rubin, "The Poet Laureate of the Confederacy," in his *The Edge of the Swamp: A Study in the Literature and Society of the Old South* (Baton Rouge: Louisiana State University Press, 1989), pp. 190–225;

Milledge B. Seigler, "Henry Timrod and Sophie Sosnowski," *Georgia Historical Quarterly,* 31 (September 1947): 172–180;

Rupert Taylor, "Henry Timrod's Ancestress, Hannah Caesar," *American Literature,* 9 (January 1938): 419–430;

G. P. Voigt, "New Light on Timrod's 'Memorial Ode,'" *American Literature,* 4 (January 1933): 395–396;

Voigt, "Timrod in the Light of Newly Revealed Letters," *South Atlantic Quarterly,* 37 (July 1938): 263–269;

Voigt, "Timrod's Essays and Literary Criticism," *American Literature,* 6 (May 1934): 163–167.

**Papers:**

The four major sources of Henry Timrod manuscripts are the William R. Perkins Library, Duke University (Paul Hamilton Hayne Collection); the Charleston Library Society (especially the William A. Courtenay Collection); South Caroliniana Library, University of South Carolina (especially the Goodwin Collection); and the University of Alabama Library.

# George Tucker

*(29 August 1775 – 10 April 1861)*

Donald R. Noble Jr.
*University of Alabama*

See also the Tucker entries in *DLB 3: Antebellum Writers in New York and the South;* and *DLB 30: American Historians, 1607–1865.*

BOOKS: *Letter to a Member of the General Assembly of Virginia on the Subject of the Late Conspiracy of the Slaves: With a Proposal for their Colonization* (Baltimore: Bonsal & Niles, 1801);

*A Letter to a Member of the General Assembly of North Carolina on the Navigation of the Roanoke and Its Branches,* anonymous (Richmond, Va.: Lynch, 1811);

*Letters from Virginia, Translated from the French,* anonymous (Baltimore: Lucas, 1816);

*Recollections of the Life of Eleanor Rosalie Tucker, Addressed to Her Surviving Sisters by Their Father* (Lynchburg, Va.: Boyce, 1818);

*Speech of Mr. Tucker, of Virginia, on the Restriction of Slavery in Missouri, Delivered in the United States House of Representatives of the United States, February 25, 1820* (Washington, D.C., 1820);

*Essays on Various Subjects of Taste, Morals, and National Policy,* as A Citizen of Virginia (Georgetown, D.C.: Milligan, 1822);

*To the Freeholders of the Counties of Campbell, Pittsylvania, and Halifax* (Lynchburg, Va., 1824);

*The Valley of Shenandoah; or, Memoirs of the Graysons,* as A Citizen of Virginia, 2 volumes (New York: Wiley, 1824);

*A Voyage to the Moon: With Some Account of the Manners and Customs, Science and Philosophy, of the People of Morosofia and Other Lunarians,* as Joseph Atterley (New York: Bliss, 1827);

*A Discourse on the Progress of Philosophy and Its Influence on the Intellectual and Moral Character of Man* (Richmond, Va.: White, 1835);

*The Laws of Wages, Profits and Rent Investigated* (Philadelphia: Carey & Hart, 1837);

*The Life of Thomas Jefferson, Third President of the United States. With Parts of His Correspondence Never Before Published, and Notices of His Opinions on Questions of Civil Government, National Policy, and Constitutional*

*George Tucker (New-York Historical Society)*

*Law,* 2 volumes (Philadelphia: Carey, Lea & Blanchard, 1837);

*Defence of the Character of Thomas Jefferson Against a Writer in the New-York Review and Quarterly Church Journal,* anonymous (New York: Osborn, 1838);

*Theory of Money and Banks Investigated* (Boston: Little & Brown, 1839);

*Progress of the United States in Population and Wealth in Fifty Years, as Exhibited by the Decennial Census* (New York: Press of *Hunt's Merchant's Magazine* / Boston: Little

& Brown, 1843); augmented as *Progress of the United States . . . Containing an Abstract of the Census of 1850* (New York: Press of *Hunt's Merchant's Magazine,* 1855);

*Public Discourse on the Dangers Most Threatening the United States* (Washington, D.C., 1843);

*Memoir of the Life and Character of John P. Emmet, M. D.* (Philadelphia: Sherman, 1845);

*An Essay on Cause and Effect, Being an Examination of Hume's Doctrine That We Can Perceive No Necessary Connexion Between Them* (Philadelphia: Lea & Blanchard, 1850);

*A History of the United States from Their Colonization to the End of the Twenty-Sixth Congress, in 1841,* 4 volumes (Philadelphia: Lippincott, 1856–1857);

*Political Economy for the People* (Philadelphia: Sherman, 1859);

*Essays, Moral and Metaphysical* (Philadelphia: Lippincott, 1860);

*A Century Hence Or, A Romance of 1941,* edited, with an introduction, by Donald R. Noble Jr. (Charlottesville: University Press of Virginia, 1977).

**Edition:** *The Valley of Shenandoah; or, Memoirs of the Graysons,* introduction by Donald R. Noble Jr. (Chapel Hill: University of North Carolina Press, 1970).

OTHER: "United States of North America," in *America and the West Indies, Geographically Described,* by George Long, George R. Porter, Tucker, and Wilhelm Wittich (London: Knight, 1845), pp. 198–352.

SELECTED PERIODICAL PUBLICATIONS–
UNCOLLECTED: "Discourse on the Progress of Philosophy, and its Influence on the Intellectual and Moral Character of Man," *Southern Literary Messenger,* 1 (April 1835): 405–421;

"Discourse on American Literature: Delivered Before the Charlottesville Lyceum, Dec. 19, 1837," *Southern Literary Messenger,* 4 (February 1838): 81–88;

"Autobiography of George Tucker," *Bermuda Historical Quarterly,* 18 (Autumn–Winter 1961): 82–159.

George Tucker was a novelist, member of the U.S. Congress, historian, biographer, statistician, political economist, and professor at the University of Virginia. His work in history and political science has always been familiar to scholars in those fields, but only since the last decades of the twentieth century has his fiction received serious critical interest for its role in the tradition of southern plantation literature.

George Tucker, the son of Daniel Tucker, was born 29 August 1775 on St. George's Island in the Bermudas into a prosperous and well-established merchant family. He was tutored privately and read law. After the death of his mother, Elizabeth Tucker, in 1795 Tucker immigrated to the United States to further his education and to begin his career. Upon arriving in the United States, Tucker first visited Philadelphia and then traveled to see his kinsman St. George Tucker, a wealthy landowner, a poet of some reputation, and a judge in the Virginia court system. St. George advised him to enroll at the College of William and Mary. Tucker took this advice and spent two years at the college. He was an indifferent student but an assiduous socializer. He was graduated *ex speciali gratia* after one year as a general student and one year studying law.

Tucker's family connections were extensive and impressive. Besides St. George, Tucker was related to Thomas Tudor Tucker, a congressman and later treasurer of the United States, and Nathaniel Beverley Tucker, St. George's son and a promising novelist. In October 1797 he married Mary Byrd Farley, herself from a wealthy family, the great-granddaughter of William Byrd II of Westover. The couple lived in Williamsburg but the marriage was short, as Mary died of consumption on 25 May 1799 after a trip to Bermuda failed to improve her health. She bequeathed a large estate to Tucker, but legal complications in the will kept him from ever receiving much of it. Tucker faced financial difficulties all his life.

In the summer of 1800 Tucker moved to Richmond to combine a career in law with his avocation, literature. He published verse, and in 1801 his pamphlet *Letter to a Member of the General Assembly of Virginia on the Subject of the Late Conspiracy of the Slaves: With a Proposal for Their Colonization* was well received. Published anonymously, the work was thought by many readers to be by the popular novelist, essayist, and biographer William Wirt. In it Tucker advocated the federal purchase of land west of the Mississippi River as a place for the colonization of freed slaves. By the 1820s Tucker had abandoned the idea of colonization and was in favor of the Missouri Compromise. By 1841 he assumed that slavery would be abolished voluntarily in the South and would not exist in the twentieth century.

In Richmond, Tucker was also a success as a man-about-town, and in February 1802 he married Maria Ball Carter, seventeen years of age, the great-niece of George Washington. A participant in the Rainbow Society, he published essays in the *Richmond Enquirer,* a Jeffersonian newspaper edited by Thomas Ritchie. He served for one year as commissioner of bankruptcy.

Tucker in these years was a profligate spender, an unsuccessful gambler, a land speculator, and a poor lawyer during a time when law was not a particularly lucrative profession. He became insolvent and in 1806 was forced to move with his family to his father-in-law's house, Woodbridge, in Frederick County, in the

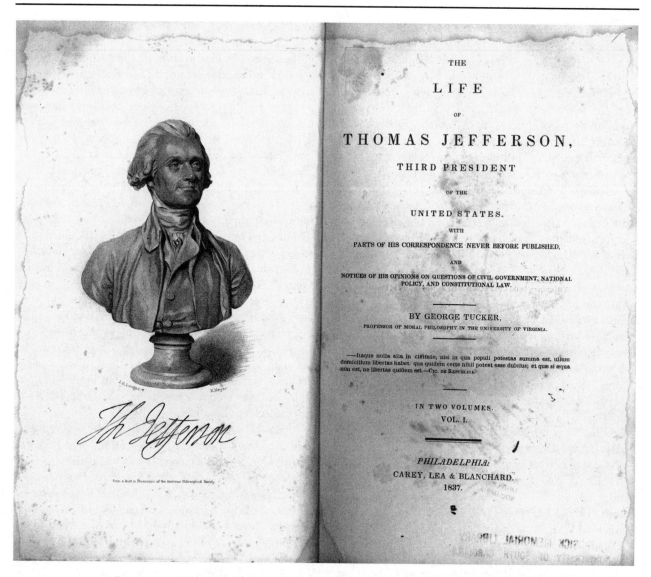

*Frontispiece and title page for Tucker's 1837 book, the first authorized biography of the third president*
*(Thomas Cooper Library, University of South Carolina)*

Shenandoah Valley of Virginia, near Danville. In 1808 he moved south to Pittsylvania County, built a new house, and purchased slaves. In 1814–1815 his essays appeared under the title "Thoughts of a Hermit" in the *Philadelphia Port Folio,* edited by North Carolinian Charles Caldwell. In Virginia he socialized less, worked harder at law, became a more competent attorney, and got his finances in order. He moved to Lynchburg, Virginia, and in 1819, after several failed attempts, was elected to the U.S. House of Representatives.

Tucker served three terms but was not a distinguished congressman, perhaps because of the distraction of personal problems. His father-in-law went bankrupt; his wife, Maria, died in 1823 during pregnancy; his daughter Harriet had died in 1817 and his daughter Rosalie in 1818; and his son was showing signs of

increasing mental instability. Despite his work and his personal difficulties, however, Tucker wrote steadily. He published *Letters from Virginia, Translated from the French* in 1816. These "letters" purport to be the reflections of a traveling Frenchman and make amusing satirical remarks about such contemporary topics as the decayed condition of Williamsburg, the pretensions of the Virginia middle class, and the newly rich. The "Thoughts of a Hermit" essays were incorporated into *Essays on Various Subjects of Taste, Morals, and National Policy* (1822). These essays were widely admired, by James Madison among others, and may have been responsible for Tucker's being offered a professorship at Thomas Jefferson's newly formed University of Virginia in 1824.

Tucker at first hesitated to accept this lucrative, secure position, even though it looked like the answer to his problems. He had just finished his first novel, *The Valley of Shenandoah; or, Memoirs of the Graysons,* and he had high hopes for it financially. As he noted in a letter to Joseph C. Cabell, "I have for more than a year conceived the project & indulge in the hope that I might pursue the business of authorship as a profitable calling–I have . . . actually essayed the public favor in a novel just published in New York and should I meet with any thing like the success which has attended Cooper, I think my prospects of profit much greater than any professorship might hold out." Despite his hope to rival the author of the Leather-Stocking Tales, the novel did not sell well, and Tucker wrote to Cabell and accepted the position Jefferson offered. He became the professor of moral philosophy at the University of Virginia until his retirement in 1845.

Tucker's optimism about *The Valley of Shenandoah* was not wholly misplaced, however. It is his most important book and has subsequently received a great deal of critical attention. Fulfilling Tucker's stated purpose to offer a "faithful picture of the manners and habits which have lately prevailed in one of the most distinguished states of our confederacy," it is a reasonably realistic portrayal of plantation life. The Graysons are in financial difficulties and thus live rather modestly, with the widowed Mrs. Grayson forced to take an active hand in the kitchen. There is a strong middle-class family in the novel, the Fawkners; young Edward Grayson, a "Cavalier," is in love with Matilda Fawkner, and the union is deemed appropriate. A New Yorker, James Gildon, a college friend of Edward, comes to visit, which prompts some frank debates on the ethics of slavery, exchanges that are heightened by a slave auction. Gildon seduces and abandons young Louisa Grayson, which, given the Graysons' keen sense of honor, necessitates a duel in which Edward is killed. The novel gives an accurate picture of the demographics of Virginia at the time, with large numbers of Scotch-Irish and German immigrants, and warns throughout of the dangers of financial irresponsibility. The novel is generally a creditable first effort.

All through his academic years Tucker wrote constantly, and in many different fields: philosophy, poetics, aesthetics, economics, and literature. In 1832 he published pseudonymously a science-fiction satire, *A Voyage to the Moon: With Some Account of the Manners and Customs, Science and Philosophy, of the People of Morosofia and Other Lunarians,* sometimes called the first American science-fiction novel. The novel pokes fun at standard objects of satire such as quack physicians, incompetent and greedy lawyers, and fashion-crazy females. It has been suggested that passages in *A Voyage to the Moon* provided material for Edgar Allan Poe's lunar fantasy, "The Unparalleled Adventure of One Hans Pfaall" (*Southern Literary Messenger,* June 1835). In 1841 he wrote a futuristic novel of manners, *A Century Hence Or, A Romance of 1941,* which remained unpublished until 1977. This work features Tucker's amazingly prescient ideas on where civilization was headed. He predicts a worldwide overpopulation problem, something akin to the women's liberation movement, and triangular international tensions among China, Russia, and the United States.

In the fields of biography, history, economics, statistics, and political science Tucker had even more success than in fiction. He wrote *The Life of Thomas Jefferson, Third President of the United States. With Parts of His Correspondence Never Before Published, and Notices of His Opinions on Questions of Civil Government, National Policy, and Constitutional Law* (1837), the first authorized biography of the former president; *A History of the United States from Their Colonization to the End of the Twenty-Sixth Congress, in 1841* (1856–1857), the first real history of the nation; and important studies into the theories of money, banks, wages, profits, and rents. He also published important statistical works on the growth of the population of the United States and on the wealth and productivity of the nation. Tucker's academic career was, in the main, successful. He was the first chairman of the faculty of the University of Virginia and was respected by his students and colleagues, although it has been noted that he was sometimes rambling in class and aloof, testy, and irritable in his private life. In 1839 he made his only trip abroad, to England, but despite meeting distinguished people (including the statistician Charles Babbage, the historian Henry Hallam, and the economist Thomas Tooke), he was not pleased with his visit. He found the English unfriendly and the island overcrowded. His visit intensified his interest in the problem of global overpopulation, and his speculations on the subject were incorporated into *A Century Hence* as well as into *Progress of the United States in Population and Wealth in Fifty Years, as Exhibited by the Decennial Census* (1943). Chapters of this work had appeared in *Hunt's Merchants'* magazine in 1842 and 1843.

In 1845 Tucker retired, freed his slaves, and moved to Philadelphia with his third wife, Louisa A. Thompson, whom he had married in December 1827. He moved there in hopes of enjoying the intellectual society of a northern metropolis, but he was disappointed. He may have become disillusioned with the way in which the profession of authorship had been degraded by commerical values in the literary marketplace. As he noted in his essay "Mental Industry" in *Political Economy for the People* (1859),

> But of all the intellectual labors, those of authors are, in general, the worst rewarded. Now and then, indeed, a popular author receives a liberal remuneration; but for one of this description, there are probably fifty failures, and perhaps twenty who do not receive

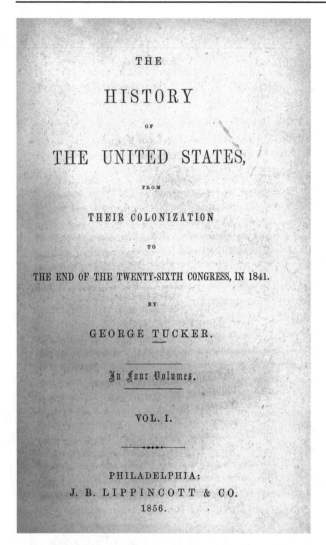

THE

HISTORY

OF

THE UNITED STATES,

FROM

THEIR COLONIZATION

TO

THE END OF THE TWENTY-SIXTH CONGRESS, IN 1841.

BY

GEORGE TUCKER.

In Four Volumes.

VOL. I.

PHILADELPHIA:
J. B. LIPPINCOTT & CO.
1856.

*Title page for volume one of Tucker's four-volume national history
(Thomas Cooper Library, University of South Carolina)*

for their efforts in this way the pay of a common laborer. . . .
Men pay more freely and liberally for pleasure than for
instruction; and there are probably a hundred readers of
an interesting romance for one of an eloquent sermon.

Abolitionist fever and anti-Southern sentiment were
rising, and though Tucker had written many times of the
evils of slavery, he remained convinced that emancipation
would bring chaos to the South and would work enormous hardships on the illiterate and unskilled masses of
blacks set free. After his wife's death in 1858 Tucker spent
his winters in the South to escape the severe Philadelphia
winters. On one such trip he was struck and seriously
injured by a falling bale of cotton while standing on the
deck of a ship in Mobile Bay. He died in Virginia three
months later.

An amateur novelist, George Tucker, perhaps
sensing that his real contributions to society lay in
teaching, the law, and public service, may have published fiction as a gentlemanly avocation. He was, nevertheless, a sophisticated, erudite man who mastered
many genres. He has risen in esteem as scholars and
readers learn more about the thoughts and imaginings
of this antebellum man of letters.

**References:**

J. O. Bailey, "Sources of Poe's *Arthur Gordon Pym* 'Hans
Pfaall,' and Other Pieces," *PMLA*, 57 (June 1942):
513–535;

Guy Cardwell, "The Duel in the Old South: Crux of a
Concept," *South Atlantic Quarterly*, 66 (Winter 1967):
50–69;

Elizabeth Simmons Chamberlain, "The Virginia Historical Novel to 1835," dissertation, University of
North Carolina, Chapel Hill, 1980;

Joseph Dorfman, "George Tucker: Hamiltonian in Disguise," "George Tucker: A Southern Anachro-
nism," in his *The Economic Mind in American
Civilization, 1606–1865,* volume 2 (New York:
Viking, 1946), pp. 539–551, 881–889;

L. C. Helderman, "A Satirist in Old Virginia," *American
Scholar,* 6 (August 1937): 481–497;

Helderman, "A Social Scientist of the Old South," *Journal
of Southern History,* 2 (May 1936): 148–174;

Jay B. Hubbell, *The South in American Literature* (Durham,
N.C.: Duke University Press), pp. 243–255;

Michael Kreyling, *Figures of the Hero in Southern Narrative*
(Baton Rouge: Louisiana State University Press,
1987);

Kreyling, "The Hero in Antebellum Southern Literature," *Southern Literary Journal,* 16 (Spring 1984): 3–
20;

Robert Colin McLean, *George Tucker: Moral Philosopher and
Man of Letters* (Chapel Hill: University of North
Carolina Press, 1961);

Donald R. Noble Jr., "A Century Hence: George
Tucker's Vision of the Future," *Virginia Cavalcade,* 25
(Spring 1976): 184–191;

Louis D. Rubin Jr. and others, *The History of Southern Literature* (Baton Rouge: Louisiana State University
Press, 1985);

Tipton R. Snavely, *George Tucker as Political Economist* (Charlottesville: University Press of Virginia, 1964);

William L. Van Deburg, "Slave Imagery in the Literature
of the Early Republic," *Mississippi Quarterly,* 36 (Winter 1982–1983): 21–33;

Ritchie Devon Watson Jr., *The Cavalier in Virginia Fiction:
The Making of a Myth* (Baton Rouge: Louisiana State
University Press, 1985);

Bertram Wyatt-Brown, *Southern Honor: Ethics and Behavior in the Old South* (New York: Oxford University
Press, 1982).

# Nathaniel Beverley Tucker

*(6 September 1784 – 26 August 1851)*

David A. Rawson
*Worcester State College*

See also the Tucker entry in *DLB 3: Antebellum Writers in New York and the South.*

BOOKS: *A Lecture on the Study of the Law; Being an Introduction to a Course of Lectures on That Subject, in the College of William and Mary.* (Richmond, Va.: White, 1834);

*George Balcombe: A Novel,* 2 volumes, anonymous (New York: Harper, 1836);

*The Partisan Leader; A Tale of the Future,* as Edward William Sidney (Washington, D.C.: Green, 1836);

*A Discourse on the Genius of the Federative System of the United States* (Richmond, Va.: White, 1839);

*A Discourse on the Importance of the Study of Political Science, as a Branch of Academic Education in the United States.* (Richmond, Va.: Bernard, 1840);

*A Discourse on the Dangers That Threaten the Free Institutions of the United States, Being an Address to the Literary Societies of Hampden Sidney College, Virginia, Read on the 22nd of September, 1841, at the Request of the Philanthropic Society of That College* (Richmond, Va.: Martin, 1841);

*An Address Delivered Before the Society of the Alumni of William and Mary College, Upon the 5th of July, 1842.* (Richmond, Va.: Bernard, 1842);

*A Series of Lectures on the Science of Government; Intended to Prepare the Student for the Study of the Constitution of the United States* (Philadelphia: Carey & Hart, 1845);

*The Principles of Pleading* (Boston: Little, Brown, 1846);

*Southern Convention. Remarks of the Hon. Beverley Tucker of Virginia* (Richmond, Va.: Colin, Baptist & Howland, 1850);

*Address of Beverley Tucker, Esq.* (Montreal: Longmoore, 1865).

## SELECTED PERIODICAL PUBLICATIONS– UNCOLLECTED:

### NONFICTION

Untitled letters, as "Hampden." *Missouri Gazette & Public Advertiser,* 22 April, 5 May, 16 June 1819;

Untitled letters, as "A Friend to State Rights," *Western Monitor,* 25 August, 15 September, 13 October, 3 November, 24 November, 1 December 1830;

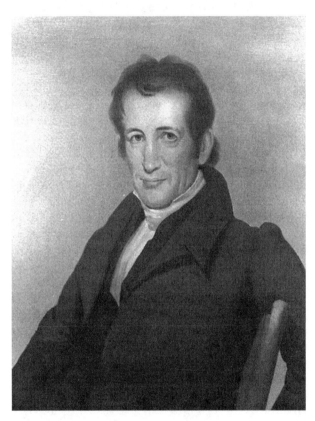

*Nathaniel Beverley Tucker ( from a portrait by Betuel Moore; College of William and Mary)*

"Note to Blackstone's Commentaries, Vol. 1. Page 423. Being the Substance of Remarks on the Subject of Domestic Slavery, Delivered to the Law Class of William and Mary College, December 2d, 1834," *Southern Literary Messenger,* 1 (January 1835): 227–231;

"Christian Education," *Southern Literary Messenger,* 1 (April 1835): 432–435;

"Professor Beverley Tucker's Valedictory Address to His Class," *Southern Literary Messenger,* 1 (July 1835): 597–602;

"Judge Tucker's Address," *Southern Literary Messenger,* 13 (September 1847): 568–570;

Untitled letters, as "A Son of Virginia," *Richmond Semi-Weekly Examiner,* 18 January, 1 February, 5 February, 15 February, 22 February, 8 March, 12 March, 19 March, 26 March 1850;

"South Carolina: Her Present Attitude and Future Action," anonymous, *Southern Quarterly Review,* 20 (October 1851): 273–298.

FICTION

"Gertrude; An Original Novel," *Southern Literary Messenger,* 10 (September 1844): 513–519; (November 1844): 641–647; (December 1844): 705–713; 11 (March 1845): 178–186; (April 1845): 219–230; (May 1845): 257–265; (June 1845): 377–382; (July 1845): 434–441; (November 1845): 690–694; (December 1845): 705–712.

Nathaniel Beverley Tucker is best known as a major intellectual voice for the proslavery perspective in antebellum America. His ideas were founded upon a classical/legal education acquired among the political leadership of Virginia at the zenith of Jeffersonian republicanism. Those ideas were applied in a long legal career that helped shape the constitutions and laws of early-Republic Virginia and Missouri, a career that established him as a leading advocate of states' rights in the Jeffersonian tradition. As slavery came under increasing attack in the 1830s and 1840s, Tucker turned to magazine commentaries and fictional narratives in an effort to reach a more universal audience than did his many legal writings. He hoped to counter antislavery moralism and abolitionist propaganda with what he considered to be realistic portrayals of plantation life in the American South and of the ill effects that the destruction of slavery would bring to his beloved Virginia, both socially and economically. Tucker's novels in a sense anticipate Harriet Beecher Stowe's *Uncle Tom's Cabin* (1852) in that they seek an emotional response among his readers by appealing to their common sense and experience. Yet, his novels were not well received in their time, even in the South, and thus did not have the impact he and other advocates of states' rights had hoped. His inability to reach that goal makes him a marginal character in the history of events that led to the Civil War. Yet, during the war, a decade after his death, Tucker achieved his greatest popularity. His memory was used by Confederate leaders to build national unity among white Southerners, transforming him into the great prophet of the antebellum period. His novels and writings were reprinted and taken as evidence of his prescience and genius. Even that recognition was fleeting, however, given the catastrophic result of that lengthy war on the plantation culture he had cherished. Tucker has been little remembered subsequently, having faded into the mists of history along with his proslavery ideals.

Tucker was born into a prominent Virginia family on 6 September 1784. His father was St. George Tucker, who had established himself as an eminent attorney and legal scholar by the time of Beverley's birth. St. George immigrated to Virginia from Bermuda as a young man and immediately found himself in the center of the American Revolution. He studied law with George Wythe, principal legal theorist among the revolutionary leadership of Virginia and mentor of Thomas Jefferson. He then served with the state militia during the Revolutionary War, witnessing the surrender of Lord Cornwallis at Yorktown in 1781. In 1778 he married Frances Bland Randolph, a young widow who brought with her both social connections and considerable property. She had three sons from her first marriage and a sizeable estate that included a large plantation on the Appomattox River west of Petersburg–Matoax–which became the new Tucker family home. There her established social prominence complemented Tucker's newfound political and judicial reputation. Four children were born from their union, of which Beverley was the last.

Frances Tucker died in January 1788 when Beverley was four years old. Within a month of her death, St. George Tucker had taken an appointment as a judge on the newly formed Virginia circuit court and had moved the family to Williamsburg. These events marked a dramatic change for Beverley, moving from the informal rurality of the farm to the formal urbanity of the late colonial capital. They also marked the ascendancy of the elder Tucker to the elite tier of the Virginia judiciary, which culminated in his appointment to George Wythe's chair as the professor of law at the College of William and Mary in 1790. From this position he guided his sons and stepsons into the legal profession, while trying to instill in them the same faculties of rigorous reasoning that were the hallmarks of his writing and teaching.

Tucker thus found himself in competition with his father's ideals and achievements for the rest of his life. In adolescence he rebelled at the constraints imposed on him by the extensive reading required of him as a student at the College of William and Mary, where he matriculated from 1799 to 1802, though he did take a particular liking to the works of John Locke, Jean-Jacques Rousseau, William Paley, William Duncan, Thomas Read, Hugh Blair, and Dugald Stewart. These preferences reflect his affinity for the "Scottish common sense school" of Enlightenment thinking with its fundamental concepts of natural law, rational religion, and contractual government, an affinity shared by many in the Virginia gentry elite. For a time he persevered in his education with the tutorial assistance of his eldest brother, Henry St. George Tucker, who also went on to a distinguished legal career.

During this period Tucker's views of states' rights took their firm root, largely through his proximity to his father and his father's Revolutionary colleagues. Tucker's father withdrew him from college in 1802 and set him to reading intensively in the law, particularly among those writers that the elder Tucker felt best suited a practicing attorney in the new American republic. These were writers, such as William Blackstone, whose legal commentaries St. George Tucker edited for American publication in 1803, that focused on the guiding hand of the common law rather than that of legislation as the proper form of government. This perspective made St. George an antifederalist in the Virginia Constitutional Convention of 1788. His objections focused on centralization of powers in the hands of a national government, at the expense of the individual states and their essential judicial systems; he wanted the decentralized power structure of government under the Articles of Confederation continued, even while recognizing the need for improvements to that earlier form of national union. He was only one of many who believed in this concept of the sovereign authority of states within the United States; it was wholly consistent with his earlier views. Apparently, Beverley Tucker was attentive to this controversy, coming as it did during his Williamsburg years, as this conception of the law and states' rights appears in his writings throughout his life.

Tucker's chance to promote and advance his perspective on states' rights came with his majority, but only after a considerable struggle to establish himself independently. Practicing law in Tidewater Virginia and, briefly, in Staunton under John Coalter proved financially unrewarding. He thus moved to rural Charlotte County in 1806, at the recommendation of his eldest stepbrother, John Randolph. There, he practiced law in the county and state courts of the upper James River Valley. His association with Randolph put him in the orbit of the Tertium Quids, dissident members of Jefferson's own party who objected to Jefferson's use of the powers of the federal government in a manner contrary to the ideals he had previously professed, powers that these men believed were unconstitutional. Even while living among such ideologically compatible friends and associates, however, Tucker's legal practice did not improve his financial fortunes; it did allow him enough sustenance to contemplate marriage, though. In February 1809 he mar-

*Tucker's mother, Frances Randolph Tucker, who died when he was four years old (Collection of Dr. Janet C. Kimbrough)*

ried Polly Coalter, daughter of his legal mentor in Staunton. In the next two years they had two children, Frances and Jack, named respectively for his mother and stepbrother. When war broke out with Britain in 1812, Tucker joined the Virginia militia; he saw no action though, serving only on garrison duty. At the end of the war he was in debt, with a family to support and few prospects, despite his impeccable legal and social pedigree.

In the winter of 1815–1816 he moved his practice and his family to St. Louis, Missouri, in hopes of finding better opportunities there. They were not long in coming. His legal practice thrived. By December 1817 the growth of the territory and the dearth of trained lawyers led to Tucker's appointment to a seat on the bench of the Northern Circuit Court of Missouri. From this seat he became a visible and influential leader in the rapidly growing territory, and thus he became heavily involved in the controversy surrounding the admission of Missouri as a state in the federal union in 1819–1820. In particular he debated Northern congressmen in the pages of Missouri and Virginia newspapers over their objections to the existence of slavery in the proposed new state. Tucker built his case on the principles of property rights and contract law that were the basis of the common law and thus of the new American jurisprudence system. These principles were the foundation of the new state constitution of Missouri and the basis of Tucker's advocacy of states' rights; in his mind, the two were inseparable. His advocacy of these principles, as well as the predominant southern immigrant population in the territory, sustained slavery in Missouri and forced Congress to forge the Missouri Compromise of 1820.

Tucker's celebrity was now national, not just regional, but he remained in Missouri rather than returning to the East to seek a continuing role on the national stage. Instead, he involved himself in building something of a utopian community in northern Missouri. Dardenne, near St. Charles, was a place designed to build upon the best of Southern, and especially Virginian, culture. Dissension soon crept in, however, and the original unity of purpose was diffused. Moreover, Tucker encountered ample personal heartache in the venture. His two young children had died of fever at the outset of the Missouri adventure in September 1816; lingering illness now plagued him, as well, particularly in the winter of 1825–1826; in the fall of 1826 his father died in Williamsburg; and in fall 1827 his wife, Polly, died. A year later he married Polly's niece, Elizabeth Naylor, but by March 1829 she too was dead. He turned to writing about his religious feelings as solace for his losses, producing several pieces he intended to publish. Only one of them was published, though, as an article in the fourth issue of the *Southern Literary Messenger* in 1835. "Christian Education" draws on his early religious training and the Presbyterian piety of his beloved Polly. He challenges others to understand the mysterious workings of God by a careful study of the classics of Episcopal and Presbyterian devotional literature, not through the illiterate emotionalism of the new evangelical Christian faiths then gaining adherents.

As a result of this personal anguish and the decline of the Dardenne community, Tucker decided to start over again further west. In February 1830 he moved to Saline County, Missouri, to a plantation he called Ardmore. There he married again, this time to Judy Smith, the young daughter of his close friend General Thomas Smith. Events on the national stage soon called him back into print, however, this time to challenge the unfettered use of federal power by another president, Andrew Jackson. A new tariff on imported goods had been enacted at Jackson's insistence and South Carolina had refused to collect it. The venerated South Carolina senator, John C. Calhoun, declared that any state could nullify any federal law that hurt the interests of the state, applying the

states' rights perspective. Jackson responded with plans to force the collection of those tariffs at gunpoint in the port of Charleston. Once again, Tucker argued that the president was usurping the rights of the individual states by this use of force. He also argued that Calhoun's Nullification process was not the proper means for a state to resist an unconstitutional act, however. Instead, Tucker argued, a state was constitutionally obliged and allowed to secede from the union if it objected to unconstitutional acts against the interests of the state. He made this argument in a series of letters in Virginia newspapers, usually signed "A Friend of States' Rights," infuriating both sides in the dispute in the process. His argument, whatever its historical merit, was consistent logically with everything he had said before, as well as everything he said subsequently. With the existing federal constitution in place, Tucker believed that states had only two options: accept their subservient status to the national government or else leave the union. There was no middle ground.

Early in 1833 Tucker traveled to Virginia to attend his mortally ill stepbrother, John Randolph. While in the East he met with likeminded political leaders, men who saw the growing power of the federal government as a threat to the independence of the individual states in the union. These meetings put him in contact with the editors of several new southern periodicals, who were determined to counteract the abolitionist influences of northern periodicals on the people and government of the United States; Tucker proved a reliable source of publishable material. After Randolph's death in June, Tucker moved back to Virginia permanently, taking up residence at Randolph's estate. The following winter, with the help of his new political allies, he was appointed the professor of law at the College of William and Mary, the post his father had held in Tucker's adolescence. Now he was the intellectual voice of the Virginian political elite, like his father before him; he used that position to advance his vision of states' rights for the rest of his life.

The bulk of his public writing was henceforth found in the pages of the *Southern Literary Messenger*. Indeed, many of the early issues of the magazine included two or three pieces from the pen of Tucker, most anonymous. The readily identifiable essays were, for the largest part, drawn from his lectures to his law students, starting with his inaugural lectures in the fall of 1834. Frequently these published lectures were reprinted by the owner and founder of the *Messenger,* Thomas Willis White, in pamphlet form, and many of them were later reprinted again in book-length collections of his lectures. The theme in these lectures was the common law, the body of American legal precedent, as it had been throughout his career. Tucker contended that the common law amply justified the states' rights perspective, providing many details in support of his argument. Given this set of precedents, the nation was now faced with the vexing problem that certain northern interests did not want to live by those precedents. Instead, they were using the powers of the federal legislature to create unprecedented and inconsistent laws that fundamentally changed the terms of the contract between the individual states and the nation that were built into the common law. The logical conclusion was that if the terms of the contract were changed by one party, then the other party was no longer bound by the terms of that contract; the constitutional union of the sovereign states of the United States would be thereby dissolved.

These complex legal arguments brought considerable reaction among White's readers. The next largest part of Tucker's writings for the *Messenger* were responses to those letters critiquing his earlier essays, responses that themselves often generated further comment and criticism, and thus further responses on his part. This dialogue is exactly what Tucker, White, and other Southern thinkers sought to achieve by publishing magazines like the *Messenger*. These magazines—including the *Southern Literary Messenger,* the *Southern Quarterly Review,* the *Southern and Western Monthly Magazine,* the *Farmer's Register,* the *Southern Times,* the *Magnolia,* and *De Bow's Review*—were conscious attempts in the years after 1830 to present a southern answer to the increasingly strident anti-southern and antislavery tone of the northern magazines that dominated the field at the time.

Tucker was, as a result of his many travels and connections, part of an informal cadre of Southern intellectuals that included William Gilmore Simms, George Frederick Holmes, Edmund Ruffin, and James Henry Hammond—men who dominated this new dialogue. They were men who longed for an idealized past, now seemingly lost. In many respects they were hopeless romantics, believers in the heroism of resistance to tyranny exemplified in Sir Walter Scott's novels, such as *Ivanhoe* (1819), a Tucker favorite. They believed that their beloved country had been brought to the verge of ruin by self-interested politicians, illiterate and unpropertied voters, and unscrupulous businessmen. To them the North was a lost cause; now the South needed to return to the virtuous models of its heroic past, to return to the values of the Revolutionary generation by recognizing the genius of men such as themselves and then democratically and gracefully submitting to their disinterested governance. These men tried to use these southern maga-

*Tucker in 1828 (painting by Joseph Wood; Collection of Dr. Janet C. Kimbrough)*

zines to reinvigorate southern pride and reestablish their own waning social primacy. Tucker was, unsurprisingly in this context, one of the most generous early contributors to the *Messenger*.

Yet, these learned lectures and commentaries were not Tucker's only contributions to the journal. He often wrote reviews of literary and historical works that came into White's hands, though not without losing sight of his larger purpose. One notable example is his 1838 review of Charles Dickens's *Oliver Twist* (1838), in which Tucker uses Dickens's flawless depictions of the misfortunes of the English working class as a means for commenting on the similar degradation then emerging in the American North. When not so occupied, he was complimentary of romantic novels, finding works in the style of Sir Walter Scott especially pleasing. He also wrote a few anonymous travelogues that depicted favorably the places in the southern interior through which he had traveled and in which he had lived. These articles are a minor part of his literary output, but they remain instructive for those wanting to understand what Tucker thought everyday life in America should be, a perspective usually overshadowed by his enormous legalistic production.

This familiarity with the literary world presented Tucker with an alternative way to present his states' rights arguments. He reasoned that if he wrote for the novel-reading public, rather than simply a legal one, he could reach a far-wider audience and have a far-greater effect on public opinion. He thus turned to fiction, creating accounts of a United States wherein the virtuous ways of the past had been forgotten, where the rights of the states had been usurped, but which was still salvageable. While his novels were certainly political, they were also romantic works, with heroes, villains, and damsels in distress, in the best tradition of Scott. In early 1836, less than two years into his professorship at the College of William and Mary, he produced two such novels, *George Balcombe* and *The Partisan Leader; A Tale of the Future,* works that one Tucker biographer, Robert J. Brugger, notes gave him "minor claim to a novelist's reputation." Both novels appeared anonymously and were apparently timed to have some effect on public opinion during the pivotal election year that determined the successor to the problematic Jackson; both were received indifferently, however, with the only unqualified acclaim coming from the pen of Edgar Allan Poe, the new assistant editor at White's *Southern Literary Messenger,* raising questions of the young editor's literary judgment in the process.

*George Balcombe,* published in spring 1836, is a tale in the style of Scott's *Waverley* romances. The title character is an aging Indian fighter and planter on the Missouri frontier who befriends the Virginia-born narrator of the book, John Napier, during the latter's travels in Missouri. There Napier discovers that he has been swindled out of his Virginia patrimony by an unscrupulous speculator named Montague, who is also, it turns out, a sworn enemy of Balcombe's. The two pursue Montague through the Missouri countryside–among the Indian raids and revival meetings–and the rudimentary courts of the state before he escapes eastward to Virginia and they follow. Tucker paints an idealized view of plantation life in his depiction of Napier's ensuing reunion with his family near Fredericksburg, and then an unflattering picture of the fluid chaos of Missouri against the established order of Virginia. In the end the two men's character, particularly that of Balcombe, wins the day for the Napier family, in a properly run court, and regains them their tidewater lands from the vile Montague. Thus, although the book was intended as a tale of inspiration, suggesting what could yet be achieved in the South, it also seems to be a lament for what was and could never be again. The tidewater region of Virginia ends up as the only place where virtuous men retain their social authority, and then only with great difficulty.

In the fall of 1836 *The Partisan Leader* was published. Intended as a warning to voters about the future of the country under a Martin Van Buren presidency, it reached bookstores too late to have had any real impact upon the presidential election. That tardiness has been ascribed to its publisher, Duff Green, another in the growing ranks of pro-Southern editors; ensconced in Washington, Green failed to distribute the book in sufficient numbers and in the right places to have achieved Tucker's ends, and he received considerable criticism from Tucker's friends and associates for this failure. The novel itself is futuristic. It was published under a pseudonym–Edward William Sidney–with a fictitious imprint date of 1856, twenty years into the future, and describes events of 1848 and 1849, some dozen years into the future. The plot revolves around the secession of the states of the Deep South, which have formed an independent league of states after withdrawing from the Union; Van Buren has subverted the 1848 election, with the help of the military, thereby gaining an unprecedented and unconstitutional fourth term in office. The state of Virginia has resolved to join this new southern league, but federal troops have invaded the Old Dominion to prevent this defection, and a guerrilla war against the federal troops is in progress as the book opens. By the book's end the resolution of this brutal war is still in doubt, but Tucker has presented to his readers everything he sees as wrong in the character and motives of the northern aggressors, everything right in those of the southern guerrillas, the wrenching agony that this conflict has caused in dividing families and communities, and the utter cowardice of those who try to play both sides to their own advantage. *The Partisan Leader* is a book about honor and identity as much as a planned political tract about the dangers of a Van Buren administration. Its blatantly political nature apparently gained it little serious notice, and once again, the only positive notices it received were in the southern magazines that were the outlets for Tucker's friends and associates.

In the wake of these disappointments Tucker returned to his students and to legal writing. He published fiction only once more in his life, serializing a sentimental novel, "Gertrude," in the pages of the *Messenger* during the final months of the magazine. Benjamin Blake Minor, a former student of Tucker's, had replaced White as editor of the *Messenger* after the latter's death in 1843. In the wake of White's death the magazine suffered a decline in subscriptions and thus faltering finances. Minor turned to Tucker for help in improving the content of the magazine, in hopes of reviving its fortunes. Tucker responded with "Gertrude," published in fits and starts between September 1844 and December 1845. It was a work in progress that had to compete with the other demands in Tucker's life–teaching and legal publishing–and with his extended illness in the fall of 1844. Yet, it was a rousing success with readers, raising Minor's hopes, if only temporarily, for the revival of the magazine. Gertrude, a female counterpart of the virtuous heroes of *George Balcombe* and *The Partisan Leader,* is a Virginia woman living among the temptations of Washington, D.C., all of which she conquers. The novel is a morality play in which Tucker critiques all the mores of the modern urban United States. While the rest of the characters are hurt by their encounters with modernity, Gertrude remains true to the virtues of old that have always served women: piety, modesty, charity, simplicity, passivity, obedience, and honor. Again, Tucker's conservatism is readily apparent; his meaning is clear, and his purpose is consistent.

Much the same can be said for the balance of his legal writings as well. Tucker gained some clout in Washington in 1841 when his longtime friend, John Tyler, became president. Tyler's cabinet included several of his associates, including his friend Abel P. Upshur, a conservative justice from the Eastern Shore of Virginia. At this point Tucker became something of a senior adviser, operating behind the scenes among the officials of Tyler's administration. As a consequence of his new status he was asked to publish several speeches and lectures over the course of 1841 that laid out for the public what he had already said to Tyler in private. These articles continued his rather frequent publication during the Van Buren years, when he critiqued the president from New York for the faults of his policies and the failings of his administration. He wrote a particularly biting commentary, published in the midst of the 1840 election, that chastised Van Buren's supporters for their lack of understanding of the fundamental principles behind the American systems of government and jurisprudence. Now with a friendly ear in the White House, Tucker tried to help build public support via the press for his suggestions to Tyler. With the coming of the Mexican-American War, however, and with Tyler increasingly embroiled in that controversy, Tucker's ideas and suggestions were moved to the back burner. His influence in Washington quickly waned, as did Tyler's power as both the Whig and Democratic parties renounced his accidental presidency.

Tucker was left to promote his views the way he had when he first returned to Virginia: in the classroom and in pamphlets. To a certain extent this reversion embittered him. For nearly thirty years he had

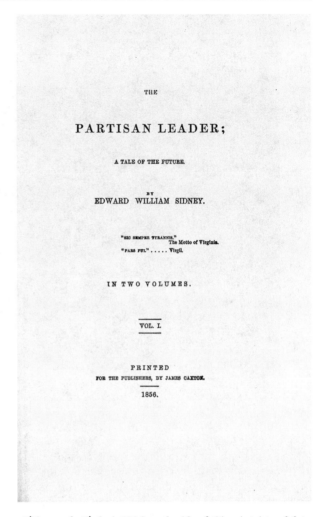

*Title page for Tucker's 1836 novel, with a fictitious imprint and date indicating that it was published twenty years later (Special Collections, Thomas Cooper Library, University of South Carolina)*

been fighting for the cause of states' rights, and success was now even further away from his grasp than it had been when he was in Missouri. Students and admirers pressed him to produce collections of his lectures and speeches to help reinvigorate the cause he had championed. Tucker agreed, but the result, *A Series of Lectures on the Science of Government; Intended to Prepare the Student for the Study of the Constitution of the United States* (1845), was another disappointment. Production problems in Philadelphia created many errors, which were impossible to fix in Williamsburg; his late 1844 illness had sapped his strength to the point that he had not been able to refine and rewrite as much of the original material that provided the foundation of the collection as he had hoped; thus, the entire work lacked the intellectual cohesion he had hoped for, a fault magnified by the many errata.

Still, Tucker remained the intellectual progenitor of a growing family of disaffected Southern leaders. In the

*The Tucker House, in Williamsburg, Virginia*

1840s, especially after the controversies surrounding the Mexican-American War, these men began organizing what came to be known as the Southern Commercial Conventions, meetings of southern business and political leaders designed both to build political unity among them and to institute programs that would advance southern commerce in the face of a northern economic onslaught brought on by industrialization. Tucker had not been a part of these conventions in the late 1840s, but events surrounding the so-called Compromise of 1850 brought him back to center stage. He was elected as a delegate to the 1850 convention in Nashville. There he found a convention willing to reconcile itself to the North, in the spirit of the last national compromise forged by Henry Clay—a convention controlled by Whigs ratifying a Whig compromise. The aging Democrat could not see any use in such a reconciliation; instead Tucker reintroduced his call for disunion. A southern confederation could loose itself from the tyrannical grip of northern businessmen, and with an economical government that confederacy could exploit the trade of the world without having to share the bounty with northern merchants. The South could reestablish the kind of society that had been evaporating since the introduction of the federal constitution. The rule of common law could be made to prevail at last.

Given the composition of the convention, Tucker's words and logic carried little weight in Nashville. In the Democratic centers of the South, however, his words rang out as a clarion call. His speech and its subsequent publication, as *Southern Convention. Remarks of the Hon. Beverley Tucker of Virginia* (1850), created for the first time a real debate over the concept and constitutionality of secession. Even though he had first raised the idea during the Nullification crisis, secession had not been given as much serious consideration then. Indeed, some have argued that Tucker set the tone for the entire 1850s with his speech. Moreover, sensing that he was nearing the end of his life, he saw the situation as more desperate; action needed to be taken immediately, before the leaders of this movement, those who remembered the Revolutionary generation and its ideals, were gone. This overwhelming sense of urgency infected the debates of the 1850s as well.

Tucker died on 26 August 1851, while he still held the professorship of law at the College of William and Mary. He was buried in the yard of Williamsburg's Bruton Parish Church, near many of those he had held up as examples of virtue and honor. His legacy lived on in the debates over states' rights that followed his death, however. When the South finally embraced secession in the spring of 1861, they embraced his common-law perspective, seeking to give it legitimacy. The decentralized government they created, and which Tucker had longed for much of his life, was unable to compel Southerners to fight its war of independence with as many resources and as many men as the centralized government in Washington did in its war against rebellion. Tucker's ideas may have been theoretically correct in the context of the courtroom and lecture hall, but they were pragmatically impaired in the context of defending that now properly constituted nation.

The government of the Confederacy produced several editions of *The Partisan Leader* during the war as a tool for building Southern nationalism and patriotism. Fighting the well-equipped armies of the North with guerrilla tactics became a reality, even if Tucker's posited causes for that war were inaccurate. This posthumous use of his work as prophecy transformed him as well into a Moses figure who had seen the great changes coming but would not be among the living when those changes came to pass. Tucker recognized that the changes altered the fundamental contract of the American constitution and would inevitably alter the life of Southerners and the operation of their government. What Nathaniel Beverley Tucker did not see, or perhaps would not see, was that democracy had the ability to alter the status quo, and that no single person could reverse what had already changed, despite the precedent of common law.

**Biographies:**

Jane Ellis Tucker, *Beverley Tucker. A Memoir by His Wife* ([Richmond, Va.: Frank Baptist, 1893?]);

Robert J. Brugger, *Beverley Tucker: Heart over Head in the Old South* (Baltimore: Johns Hopkins University Press, 1978);

Beverley D. Tucker, *Nathaniel Beverley Tucker, Prophet of the Confederacy, 1784–1851* (Tokyo: Nanbundo, 1979).

**Reference:**

Drew Gilpin Faust, *A Sacred Circle: The Dilemma of the Intellectual in the Old South, 1840–1860* (Baltimore: Johns Hopkins University Press, 1977);

Arthur Wrobel, "Romantic Realism: Nathaniel Beverley Tucker," *American Literature,* 42 (November 1976): 325–335.

**Papers:**

The majority of the surviving Nathaniel Beverley Tucker papers can be found in the Swem Library of the College of William and Mary. Other repositories with significant Tucker papers include the Alderman Library at the University of Virginia, the Library of Virginia in Richmond, the Virginia Historical Society, the Library of Congress, the Perkins Library at Duke University, and the Southern Historical Collection at the University of North Carolina at Chapel Hill.

# Catherine Ann Warfield

### (6 June 1816 – 21 May 1877)

Larry W. Gibbs
*East Georgia College*

BOOKS: *The Wife of Leon, and Other Poems by Two Sisters of the West,* by Warfield and Eleanor P. Lee (Cincinnati: Morgan, 1843);

*The Indian Chamber, and Other Poems,* by Warfield and Lee (New York: Derby & Jackson, 1846);

*The Household of Bouverie, or The Elixir of Gold,* 2 volumes (New York: Derby & Jackson, 1860);

*The Romance of the Green Seal* (New York: Beadle, 1866);

*The Romance of Beauseincourt* (New York: Carleton, 1867);

*Miriam Monfort, A Novel* (New York: Appleton, 1873);

*A Double Wedding; or, How She Was Won* (Philadelphia: Peterson, 1875);

*Hester Howard's Temptation: A Soul's Story* (Philadelphia: Peterson, 1875);

*Lady Ernestine, or, The Absent Lord of Rocheforte* (Philadelphia: Peterson, 1875);

*Miriam's Memoirs* (Philadelphia: Peterson, 1876);

*Sea and Shore* (Philadelphia: Peterson, 1876);

*The Cardinal's Daughter* (Philadelphia: Peterson, 1877);

*Ferne Fleming, A Novel* (Philadelphia: Peterson, 1877).

OTHER: "You Can Never Win Us Back" [song], music by J. E. Smith, lyrics by Warfield (Richmond, Va.: Davies, 1864).

Born into the Southern planter aristocracy, Catherine Ann Warfield led a life that was, on the surface, one of privilege and relative luxury. Beneath that surface, however, persisted an underlying anxiety and sadness resulting from her often absent, yet domineering father and from her mother's family history of mental illness and tragedy. These became common motifs in the two volumes of poetry and eleven novels that Warfield published in her lifetime, as was her cautious critique of a woman's role in Southern society.

Catherine Ann Ware was born 6 June 1816 to Sarah and Major Nathaniel Ware in Natchez, Mississippi. Sarah Percy Ware, left alone with two young children in 1808 by the death of her first husband, Judge John Ellis, married Ware in 1814. Ware was an active participant in the political life of the Mississippi Territory, serving for a time as secretary of state and as acting governor from 1815 to 1816. The wealth he had acquired from his law practice and land speculation, combined with Sarah's social prominence and inherited wealth, facilitated his political ambitions. Those ambitions came to an end, however, with the birth of his second daughter and the resulting mental collapse of his wife.

Catherine Ware was three years old when her sister, Eleanor, was born. During this delivery, Sarah Ware, who was thirty-nine years old at this time, contracted puerperal fever and slipped into an unstable mental condition recognized in modern times as depression psychosis. This condition had contributed to the suicide of Sarah's father, Charles, and left its mark on other members of the Percy family. Her depression ultimately required that Sarah Ware be institutionalized for most of the next eleven years and dominated her life and the lives of her family until her death in 1835.

Knowing that satisfactory medical facilities were unavailable for his wife in frontier Mississippi, Ware moved his family to Philadelphia, where Sarah Ware's daughter by her first marriage lived. Mary Jane Ellis married into the prominent colony of French aristocratic refugees in that city. Her husband, Rene LaRoche, was a doctor at the prestigious Pennsylvania Hospital, where Sarah Ware was to be a long-term resident until 1831. Thomas Ellis, Sarah's only son, was also in the vicinity, studying at Princeton University.

As Ware settled his daughters into the LaRoche household and his wife into the Pennsylvania Hospital's mental ward, he became ill at ease in his new environs and began a series of business trips and relocations that continued until near the end of his life. During one such absence, Ware served as land commissioner for the federal government in Pensacola, Florida, in 1822. While on these sojourns he often left his two young daughters for several months with relatives or friends in Philadelphia. Ware possessed a talent for land speculation and development and amassed a considerable estate by the time of his death in 1853. His frequent absences from his daughters generated much criticism from members of his wife's family. The major's solution was, rather than remaining in Philadelphia, to take Catherine and Eleanor with him as he visited his land holdings in Mississippi, Florida, and elsewhere in the South. He also took them with him as he toured Europe in 1821. The trio often spent winters on Ware's plantations near Natchez, Mississippi, and in the Florida panhandle.

When they were not traveling with their father, the Ware sisters benefited from the best formal education the major could provide. Like the daughters of many Southern planters, they were enrolled in Madame Sigoigne's French-speaking academy. Catherine, however, refused to stay and ran away to her half sister's nearby home to hide. Giving in to his daughter's apprehensions, the major, with the help of tutors, personally undertook her education in classical French and English and allowed her free rein in his extensive library. There Catherine was first exposed to the Gothic romances that were so prevalent in the late eighteenth and early nineteenth centuries. She remarked later in life that William Beckford's *Vathek: An Arabian Tale* (1786) was her favorite among the many such Gothic horror stories in the major's library. In her novel *Ferne Fleming* (1877) Warfield has a character recall that Beckford's novel had "saddened her for days, . . . and left its imprint of mournful warning on her heart for life."

In 1831 Ware removed Sarah from her Philadelphia hospital and sent her to live on her son Thomas's plantation near Natchez. Here Sarah occasionally wandered around the grounds or worked in her flower garden. Most often she remained in her room on the upper floor of her son's house, where it was occasionally necessary for her to be restrained. During summer visits by Catherine and Eleanor, Sarah Ware was unable to recognize her daughters. She died in May 1835.

On 3 January 1833, at the age of sixteen, Ware married Robert Elisha Warfield of Kentucky in Cincinnati, Ohio, her father's most recent temporary home. Her dowry was composed of "sixty-six slaves, a quantity of land in Arkansas, bank stock, and half-interest in Utopia plantation on Black Bayou, in Washington County, Mississippi, the total valued at more than $100,000," according to Bertram Wyatt-Brown in *The House of Percy: Honor, Melancholy, and Imagination in a Southern Family* (1994). Her father maintained control of this property, however, refusing to transfer it into the control of his new son-in-law. The Warfield family was prominent in thoroughbred racehorse breeding and were the founders of the Lexington Association Race Course. Catherine Warfield's father-in-law taught medi-

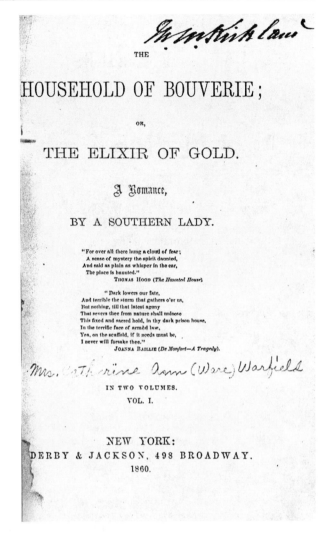

*Title page for Catherine Ann Warfield's first novel, a Gothic romance (Special Collections, Thomas Cooper Library, University of South Carolina)*

cine at the Transylvania Medical School; her husband, however, pursued no such professional interest, preferring to involve himself in the equine interests of the family. This decision eventually led to financial difficulties for the Warfields and their six children, and in 1857 they were forced to relocate to the Pee Wee Valley near Louisville, Kentucky. Little else is known of Warfield's married life.

Warfield's literary life, however, started when she and her sister began writing poetry for each other's pleasure, as well as to please their father. Their father, impressed by his daughters' literary efforts, convinced them to collect and publish a volume of their poems. The major made arrangements for a Cincinnati printer to publish *The Wife of Leon, and Other Poems by Two Sisters of the West* in 1843. The volume was so well received that a second printing was brought out in 1845. Wil-

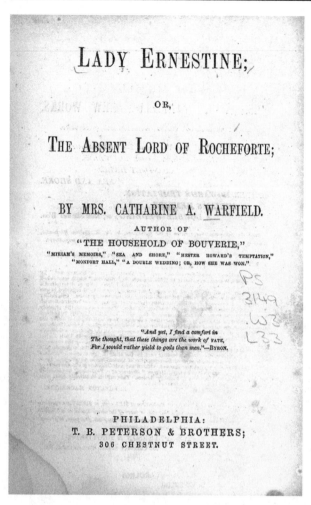

LADY ERNESTINE;

OR,

THE ABSENT LORD OF ROCHEFORTE;

BY MRS. CATHARINE A. WARFIELD.

AUTHOR OF

"THE HOUSEHOLD OF BOUVERIE,"

"MIRIAM'S MEMOIRS," "SEA AND SHORE," "HESTER HOWARD'S TEMPTATION,"
"MONFORT HALL," "A DOUBLE WEDDING; OR, HOW SHE WAS WON."

"And yet, I find a comfort in
The thought, that these things are the work of FATE,
For I would rather yield to gods than men."—BYRON.

PHILADELPHIA:

T. B. PETERSON & BROTHERS;

306 CHESTNUT STREET.

Title page for Warfield's 1875 novel, set in revolutionary France
(Thomas Cooper Library, University of South Carolina)

liam Cullen Bryant praised the *The Wife of Leon* in a personal letter to the sisters, and the sisters dedicated their second volume of poetry, *The Indian Chamber, and Other Poems,* to him when it was published in 1846.

In these two volumes of poetry the sisters lament the loss of their mother, whom they elevated to saintlike status, and their lack of a relationship with her. In the title poem of their first volume their mother's voice speaks to her child of being "the fairest daughter of our line" but then "darkly, darkly hurl'd / From that rich summit, in my glorious prime, / How have I bathed with tears the sorrowful feet of time!" In "The Forsaken" they write that "the cold sickness of her brain / Seemed to have frozen every vein, / And fixed her limbs, and chilled her breath / Into a mockery of death." Other poems betray the women's displeasure at their father's absenteeism and dominance. "The Wanderer" warns of the impact of "ambition, boundless, uncontroll'd" and the desire to escape the confines of

home and family. In general the poems reflected the poetic conventions of the times and, as Wyatt-Brown notes, "celebrated the code of honor and gentility that undergirded Southern social discourse."

A third volume of poems was being planned when Eleanor died in a yellow fever epidemic in Natchez in 1849. So painful was her sister's death for Warfield that she put aside her literary efforts for the next eleven years. Her grief was compounded when her father, having purchased large tracts of property in the booming Galveston, Texas, market as well as his first permanent home in many years, also died of yellow fever in 1853.

In 1860, after an eleven-year hiatus and at the prompting of her family, Warfield once more took up her pen and published her first work of fiction, *The Household of Bouverie, or The Elixir of Gold.* Written in the tradition of Gothic fiction, this romance elicited a favorable review from *Harper's New Monthly Magazine,* in which it was acclaimed for its "unquestionable imaginative power." Warfield was complimented by the reviewer as "a female novel-writer who displays the unmistakable fire of genius, however terrific its brightness." *The Household of Bouverie* reflects much of Warfield's personal life as well as the Southern cultural influences she experienced. Set in an indeterminate locale, the two-volume novel explores issues of familial displacement, manic depression, abusive relationships, and the dependent status of married women. Warfield also employs such mainstays of Gothic romances as alchemy, gloomy mansions with locked rooms and secret passageways, and mysterious, evil presences. Significantly, *The Household of Bouverie* makes no reference to slavery, the foremost social issue in the United States in 1860. The Bouverie household is maintained through the employment of only a few servants of European origins.

Despite the positive reception of *The Household of Bouverie,* Warfield's "fire of genius" was refocused as she shifted her attention to the sectional conflict of the Civil War. Although her adopted state of Kentucky did not secede from the Union, Warfield wrote in support of the Confederacy. During the war she wrote several poems that were published in various Southern newspapers, expressing her commitment to the Southern cause. In 1864 she wrote the lyrics for a patriotic song, "You Can Never Win Us Back," which was dedicated to Confederate heroes John Singleton Mosby and his men. Nine of Warfield's wartime poems were included in *The Southern Poems of the War,* published in 1867.

Shortly after the conclusion of the Civil War, Warfield published her second novel, *The Romance of the Green Seal* (1866), a short fiction about an abused Southern wife who carries on a secret correspondence with an unknown admirer of her poetry. In 1867 she extracted a portion of a larger work in progress, obviously begun during the war, and published it as *The Romance of Beauseincourt*. This novel, set in the antebellum South, is written more in the vein of the plantation novel and represents a significant shift in thematic emphasis for Warfield into the realm of historical fiction.

Warfield did not publish again until 1873, revising *The Romance of Beauseincourt* and restoring the earlier excised material to tell the complete story in *Miriam Monfort*. Between 1875 and her death on 21 May 1877 Warfield published seven other works of fiction, although none of her later works enjoyed the same popularity or critical success as *The Household of Bouverie*. Of her latter novels, only *Lady Ernestine, or, The Absent Lord of Rocheforte* (1875) and *Ferne Fleming* are historically based, the former set in revolutionary France and the latter in the antebellum South. The novels set in the prewar South demonstrate Warfield's continuing commitment to both the political and racial ideologies of her Southern heritage.

Warfield's postwar fiction, however, recognizes the changing role of women in the South. Her heroines and other female characters gradually become more assertive, taking greater control over their own lives and the lives of others around them. Many are shown rejecting the social conventions for women in the antebellum South and becoming active participants in society.

Other than the *Harper's* review of her first novel, there is no extant critical response to Catherine Ann Warfield's fiction. Whether because of the racial views expressed in her earlier works, her continuing allegiance to the defeated Confederacy, or shifting public preferences, Warfield's body of fiction has fallen into disfavor. Her unreconstructed views on politics, race, and slavery must be juxtaposed against her representation of the expanded role of women in the postwar South, however. Whatever the previously perceived merits of Warfield's fiction, her novels reflect the shifting attitudes of Southern women about their functions in society after the destruction of the paternalistic antebellum social system and thus deserve modern critical attention.

**References:**

Mary Forrest, *Women of the South Distinguished in Literature* (New York: Derby & Jackson, 1861), pp. 114–117;

Janet Gray, *She Wields a Pen* (Iowa City: University of Iowa Press, 1997), pp. 64–66;

James B. Lloyd, ed., *Lives of Mississippi Authors, 1817–1967* (Jackson: University Press of Mississippi, 1981), pp. 452–454;

Emily V. Mason, ed., *The Southern Poems of the War* (Baltimore: John Murphy, 1867);

Mildred Lewis Rutherford, *The South in History and Literature: A Handbook of Southern Authors* (Atlanta: Franklin-Turner, 1906), p. 223;

Sydney Louise Smith, "A Critical Study of the Life and Novels of Catherine Ann Warfield," dissertation, University of Mississippi, Oxford, 1929;

Mary T. Tardy, *The Living Female Writers of the South* (Philadelphia: Claxton, Remsen & Haffelbinger, 1872), pp. 17–28;

James Wilson Townsend, *Kentucky in American Letters* (Cedar Rapids, Iowa: Torch Press, 1913), pp. 197–200;

Bertram Wyatt-Brown, *The House of Percy: Honor, Melancholy, and Imagination in a Southern Family* (Oxford: Oxford University Press, 1994), pp. 87–169.

# Books for Further Reading

The following selective list should be of interest to those who want to read further about antebellum literature in New York and the South. The list is limited, for the most part, to works that deal with American literature from 1815 to 1865. Those who wish additional suggestions may consult *Eight American Authors*, edited by James Woodress; *Fifteen American Authors Before 1900*, edited by Robert A. Rees and Earl N. Harbert; *Articles in American Literature*, 3 volumes, edited by Lewis Leary; the annual *PMLA* bibliography; the annual bibliography in *Mississippi Quarterly*; and *American Literary Scholarship: An Annual*.

Aaron, Daniel. *The Unwritten War: American Writers and the Civil War*. New York: Knopf, 1973.

Adams, Grace and Edward Hutter. *The Mad Forties*. New York: Harper, 1942.

Alderman, Edwin A. and Joel Chandler Harris, eds. *A Library of Southern Literature*, 17 volumes. New Orleans & Atlanta: Martin & Hoyt, 1908–1923.

Bain, Robert, Joseph M. Flora, and Louis D. Rubin Jr. *Southern Writers: A Biographical Dictionary*. Baton Rouge: Louisiana State University Press, 1979.

Barnes, James J. *Authors, Publishers and Politicians: The Quest for an Anglo-American Copyright Agreement 1815–1854*. Columbus: Ohio State University Press, 1974.

Bartlett, Irving H. *The American Mind in the Mid-Nineteenth Century*. New York: Crowell, 1967.

Baym, Nina. *American Women Writers and the Work of History, 1790–1860*. New Brunswick, N.J.: Rutgers University Press, 1995.

Baym. *Novels, Readers, and Reviewers: Responses to Fiction in Antebellum America*. Ithaca, N.Y.: Cornell University Press, 1984.

Baym. *Woman's Fiction: A Guide to Novels by and about Women in America, 1820–1870*, second edition. Urbana: University of Illinois Press, 1993.

Bell, Michael Davitt. *The Development of American Romance: The Sacrifice of Relation*. Chicago: University of Chicago Press, 1980.

Bender, Thomas. *New York Intellect: A History of Intellectual Life in New York City, from 1750 to the Beginnings of Our Own Time*. Baltimore: Johns Hopkins University Press, 1988.

Bender. *Toward an Urban Vision: Ideas and Institutions in Nineteenth-Century America*. Lexington: University of Kentucky Press, 1975.

Blair, Walter. *Native American Humor*. San Francisco: Chandler, 1960.

Bode, Carl. *Antebellum Culture*. Carbondale, Ill.: Southern Illinois University Press, 1969.

Bradbury, Malcolm. *Dangerous Pilgrimages: Transatlantic Mythologies and the Novel*. New York: Viking, 1996.

Braden, W. W., ed. *Oratory in the Old South: 1828–1860*. Baton Rouge: Louisiana State University Press, 1970.

Bradshaw, S. E. *On Southern Poetry Prior to 1860*. Richmond: B. F. Johnson, 1900.

Branch, E. Douglas. *The Sentimental Years 1836–1860*. New York: Appleton-Century, 1934.

Brooks, Van Wyck. *Chilmark Miscellany*. New York: Dutton, 1948.

Brooks. *The Times of Melville and Whitman*. New York: Dutton, 1947.

Brooks. *The World of Washington Irving*. New York: Dutton, 1944.

Brown, Herbert Ross. *The Sentimental Novel in America, 1789–1860*. Durham: Duke University Press, 1940.

Callow, James T. *Kindred Spirits: Knickerbocker Writers and American Artists, 1807–1855*. Chapel Hill: University of North Carolina Press, 1967.

Calverton, V. F. *The Liberation of American Literature*. New York: Scribners, 1932.

Camfield, Gregg. *Necessary Madness: The Humor of Domesticity in Nineteenth-Century American Literature*. New York: Oxford University Press, 1997.

Cash, W. J. *The Mind of the South*. New York: Knopf, 1941.

Chai, Leon. *The Romantic Foundations of the American Renaissance*. Ithaca, N.Y.: Cornell University Press, 1987.

Charvat, William. *Literary Publishing in America: 1790–1850*. Philadelphia: University of Pennsylvania Press, 1959.

Charvat. *The Profession of Authorship in America, 1800–1870,* edited by Matthew J. Bruccoli. New York: Columbia University Press, 1992.

Chielens, Edward, ed. *American Literary Magazines: The Eighteenth and Nineteenth Centuries*. New York: Greenwood Press, 1986.

Coultrap-McQuin, Susan. *Doing Literary Business: American Women Writers in the Nineteenth Century*. Chapel Hill: University of North Carolina Press, 1990.

Cunliffe, Marcus. *The Literature of the United States*. London & Baltimore: Penguin, 1954.

Current-Garcia, Eugene. *The American Short Story through 1850*. Boston: Twayne, 1985.

Davidson, James Wood. *The Living Writers of the South*. New York: Carleton, 1869.

Day, Martin S. *History of American Literature from the Beginning to 1900*. Garden City, N.Y.: Doubleday, 1970.

Dekker, George. *The American Historical Romance*. Cambridge: Cambridge University Press, 1987.

Derby, J. C. *Fifty Years among Authors, Books, and Publishers*. New York: Carleton, 1884.

Dormon, James H., Jr. *Theater in the Antebellum South*. Chapel Hill: University of North Carolina Press, 1967.

Douglas, Ann. *The Feminization of American Culture*. New York: Knopf, 1977.

Duyckinck, Evert A. and George L. Duyckinck, eds. *Cyclopaedia of American Literature,* 2 volumes. New York: Scribner, 1855.

Eaton, Clement. *The Growth of Southern Civilization, 1790–1860.* New York: Harper, 1961.

Eaton. *The Mind of the Old South,* revised edition. Baton Rouge: Louisiana State University Press, 1967.

Eggleston, George Cary. *Recollections of a Varied Life.* New York: Holt, 1910.

Ekirch, Arthur A., Jr. *The Idea of Progress in America, 1815–1860.* New York: Columbia University Press, 1944.

Elliott, Emory, ed. *Columbia Literary History of the United States.* New York: Columbia University Press, 1988.

Faust, Drew Gilpin. *A Sacred Circle: The Dilemma of the Intellectual in the Old South, 1840–1860.* Baltimore: Johns Hopkins University Press, 1978.

Feidelson, Charles. *Symbolism and American Literature.* Chicago: University of Chicago Press, 1953.

Feller, Daniel. *The Jacksonian Promise: America, 1815–1840.* Baltimore: Johns Hopkins University Press, 1995.

Ferguson, Robert A. *Law and Letters in American Culture.* Cambridge, Mass.: Harvard University Press, 1984.

Floan, Howard R. *The South in Northern Eyes 1831 to 1861.* Austin: University of Texas Press, 1958.

Flora and Bain. *Fifty Southern Writers Before 1900: A Bio-Bibliographical Sourcebook.* New York: Greenwood Press, 1987.

Foster, Edward Halsey. *The Civilized Wilderness: Backgrounds to American Romantic Literature, 1817–1860.* New York: Free Press, 1975.

Freidel, Frank, ed. *Harvard Guide to American History,* revised edition, 2 volumes. Cambridge, Mass.: Harvard University Press, 1974.

Gaines, Francis Pendleton. *The Southern Plantation: A Study in the Development and the Accuracy of a Tradition.* New York: Columbia University Press, 1924.

Garvin, Harry R. and Peter C. Cariofol, eds. *American Renaissance: New Dimensions.* Lewisburg, Pa.: Bucknell University Press, 1983.

Gilmore, Michael T. *American Romanticism and the Marketplace.* Chicago: University of Chicago Press, 1985.

Gohdes, Clarence. *American Literature in Nineteenth-Century England.* New York: Columbia University Press, 1944.

Goldfarb, Russell M. and Clare R. *Spiritualism and Nineteenth-Century Letters.* Rutherford, N.J.: Fairleigh Dickinson University Press, 1978.

Grammer, John M. *Pastoral and Politics in the Old South.* Baton Rouge: Louisiana University Press, 1996.

Grey, Robin. *The Complicity of Imagination: The American Renaissance, Contests of Authority, and Seventeenth-Century English Culture.* New York: Cambridge University Press, 1997.

Gross, Theodore L. *The Heroic Ideal in American Literature.* New York: Free Press, 1971.

Guarneri, Carl J. *The Utopian Alternative: Fourierism in Nineteenth-Century America.* Ithaca, N.Y.: Cornell University Press, 1991.

Gustafson, Thomas. *Representative Words: Politics, Literature, and the American Language, 1776–1865*. New York: Cambridge University Press, 1992.

Haralson, Eric L., ed. *Encyclopedia of American Poetry: The Nineteenth Century*. New York: Garland, 1998.

Harris, Neil. *The Artist in American Society; The Formative Years, 1790–1860*. New York: Braziller, 1966.

Harris, Susan K. *19th-Century American Women's Novels: Interpretive Strategies*. New York: Cambridge University Press, 1990.

Hart, James D. *The Popular Book: A History of America's Literary Taste*. New York: Oxford University Press, 1950.

Hoffman, Daniel. *Form and Fable in American Fiction*. New York: Oxford University Press, 1961.

Holliday, Carl. *A History of Southern Literature*. New York: Neale, 1906.

Holman, C. Hugh. *The Immoderate Past: The Southern Writer and History*. Athens: University of Georgia Press, 1977.

Howard, Leon. *Literature and the American Tradition*. Garden City, N.Y.: Doubleday, 1960.

Howe, Daniel Walker. *The Political Culture of the American Whigs*. Chicago: University of Chicago Press, 1979.

Hubbell, Jay B. *The South in American Literature, 1607–1900*. Durham: Duke University Press, 1954.

Hubbell. *Southern Life in Fiction*. Athens: University of Georgia Press, 1960.

Hudson, Arthur Palmer. *Humor of the Old Deep South*. New York: Macmillan, 1936.

Inge, M. Thomas, ed. *The Frontier Humorists: Critical Views*. Hamden, Conn.: Archon, 1975.

Jehlen, Myra. *American Incarnation: The Individual, the Nation, and the Continent*. Cambridge, Mass.: Harvard University Press, 1986.

Jones, Howard Mumford. *O Strange New World: American Culture, The Formative Years*. New York: Viking, 1967.

Joyce, William L., David D. Hall, and John B. Hench, eds. *Printing and Society in Early America*. Worcester, Mass.: American Antiquarian Society, 1983.

Kammen, Michael. *A Season of Youth: The American Revolution and the Historical Imagination*. New York: Knopf, 1978.

Kasson, Joy S. *Artistic Voyagers: Europe and the American Imagination in the Works of Irving, Allston, Cole, Cooper, and Hawthorne*. Westport, Conn.: Greenwood Press, 1982.

Kaul, A. N. *The American Vision: Actual and Ideal Society in Nineteenth-Century Fiction*. New Haven: Yale University Press, 1963.

Kelley, Mary. *Private Woman, Public Stage: Literary Domesticity in Nineteenth-Century America*. New York: Oxford University Press, 1984.

Kerr, Howard, John W. Crowley, and Charles L. Crow. *The Haunted Dusk: American Supernatural Fiction, 1820–1920*. Athens: University of Georgia Press, 1983.

Knight, Denise, ed. *Nineteenth-Century American Women Writers: A Bio-Bibliographical Sourcebook*. Westport, Conn.: Greenwood Press, 1997.

Knight, Grant C. *American Literature and Culture*. New York: Long & Smith, 1932.

Kolb, Harold H., Jr. *A Field Guide to the Study of American Literature*. Charlottesville: University Press of Virginia, 1976.

Kramer, Aaron. *The Prophetic Tradition in American Poetry, 1835–1900*. Rutherford, N.J.: Fairleigh Dickinson University Press, 1968.

Kramer, Michael P. *Imagining Language in America: From the Revolution to the Civil War*. Princeton: Princeton University Press, 1992.

Lavernier, James and Douglas R. Wilmes. *American Writers Before 1900: A Biographical and Critical Dictionary*. Westport, Conn.: Greenwood Press, 1983.

Lawrence, D. H. *Studies in Classic American Literature*. New York: Viking, 1961.

Leary, Lewis. *American Literature: A Study and Research Guide*. New York: St. Martin's Press, 1976.

Lee, A. Robert, ed. *The Nineteenth-Century American Short Story*. New York: Barnes & Noble, 1986.

Lehmann-Haupt, Hellmut, and others, *The Book in America: A History of the Making and Selling of Books in the United States*, second edition. New York: R. R. Bowker, 1951.

Leisy, Ernest Erwin. *American Literature: An Interpretative Survey*. New York: Crowell, 1929.

Lemelin, Robert E. *Pathway to the National Character, 1830–1861*. Port Washington, N.Y.: Kennikat, 1974.

Leverenz, David. *Manhood and the American Renaissance*. Ithaca, N.Y.: Cornell University Press, 1989.

Levin, Harry. *The Power of Blackness: Hawthorne, Poe, Melville*. New York: Vintage, 1950.

Levine, Lawrence. *Highbrow/Lowbrow: The Emergence of Cultural Hierarchy in America*. Cambridge, Mass.: Harvard University Press, 1988.

Lewis, R. W. B. *The American Adam: Innocence, Tragedy and Tradition in the Nineteenth Century*. Chicago: University of Chicago Press, 1955.

Lively, Robert A. *Fiction Fights the Civil War: An Unfinished Chapter in the Literary History of the American People*. Chapel Hill: University of North Carolina Press, 1957.

Loving, Jerome. *Lost in the Customhouse: Authorship in the American Renaissance*. Iowa City: University of Iowa Press, 1995.

Marchalonis, Shirley, ed. *Patrons and Protégées: Gender, Friendship, and Writing in Nineteenth-Century America*. New Brunswick, N.J.: Rutgers University Press, 1988.

Martin, Terence. *The Instructed Vision: Scottish Common Sense Philosophy and the Origins of American Fiction*. Bloomington: Indiana University Press, 1961.

Martin. *Parables of Possibility: The American Need for Beginnings*. New York: Columbia University Press, 1995.

Marx, Leo. *The Machine in the Garden: Technology and the Pastoral Ideal in American Culture*. New York: Oxford University Press, 1964.

Matthiessen, F. O. *American Renaissance: Art and Expression in the Age of Emerson and Whitman*. New York: Oxford University Press, 1941.

Michaels, Walter Benn and Donald Pease, eds. *The American Renaissance Reconsidered*. Baltimore: Johns Hopkins University Press, 1989.

Miller, Perry. *Nature's Nation*. Cambridge, Mass.: Harvard University Press, 1967.

Miller. *The Raven and the Whale: Poe, Melville, and the New York Literary Scene*. Baltimore: Johns Hopkins University Press, 1997.

Minnigerode, Meade. *The Fabulous Forties, 1840–1850*. Garden City, N.Y.: Garden City Publishing Company, 1924.

Mitchell, Donald Grant. *American Lands and Letters—Leather-Stocking to Poe's "Raven."* New York: Scribners, 1899.

Moses, Montrose J. *The Literature of the South*. New York: Crowell, 1910.

Moss, Elizabeth. *Domestic Novelists in the Old South: Defenders of Southern Culture*. Baton Rouge: Louisiana State University Press, 1992.

Mott, Frank Luther. *Golden Multitudes: The Story of Best Sellers in the United States*. New York: Macmillan, 1947.

Mott. *A History of American Magazines,* 5 volumes. Cambridge, Mass.: Harvard University Press, 1938–1968.

Nilon, Charles. *Bibliography of Bibliographies in American Literature*. New York: R. R. Bowker, 1970.

Nye, Russel Blaine. *Society and Culture in America, 1830–1860*. New York: Harper & Row, 1974.

Osterweis, Rollin G. *Romanticism and Nationalism in the Old South*. New Haven: Yale University Press, 1949.

Paine, Gregory L., ed. *Southern Prose Writers: Representative Selections*. New York: American Book Company, 1947.

Papashvily, Helen Waite. *All the Happy Endings: A Study of the Domestic Novel in America*. New York: Harper, 1956.

Parks, Edd Winfield. *Antebellum Southern Literary Critics*. Athens: University of Georgia Press, 1962.

Parks. *Segments of Southern Thought*. Athens: University of Georgia Press, 1938.

Parks, ed. *Southern Poets: Representative Selections*. New York: American Book Company, 1936.

Parrington, Vernon Louis. *The Romantic Revolution in America, 1800–1860*. New York: Harcourt, Brace, 1927.

Pattee, Fred Lewis. *The Development of the American Short Story: An Historical Survey*. New York: Harper, 1935.

Pattee. *The Feminine Fifties*. New York: Appleton-Century, 1940.

Pattee. *The First Century of American Literature, 1770–1870*. New York: Appleton-Century, 1935.

Pearce, Roy Harvey. *The Continuity of American Poetry*. Princeton: Princeton University Press, 1961.

Pearce. *Savagism and Civilization: A Study of the Indian and the American Mind*. Baltimore: Johns Hopkins University Press, 1967.

Pease. *Visionary Compacts: American Renaissance Writings in Cultural Context*. Madison: University of Wisconsin Press, 1987.

Petter, Henri. *The Early American Novel*. Columbus: Ohio State University Press, 1971.

Porte, Joel. *The Romance in America: Studies in Cooper, Poe, Hawthorne, and James*. Middletown, Conn.: Wesleyan University Press, 1969.

Price, Kenneth and Susan Belasco Smith, eds. *Periodical Literature in Nineteenth-Century America*. Charlottesville: University Press of Virginia, 1995.

Pritchard, John Paul. *Literary Wise Men of Gotham: Criticism in New York, 1815–1860*. Baton Rouge: Louisiana State University Press, 1963.

Quinn, Arthur Hobson. *American Fiction: An Historical and Critical Survey*. New York: Appleton-Century, 1936.

Quinn, ed. *The Literature of the American People: An Historical and Critical Survey*. New York: Appleton-Century-Crofts, 1951.

Reynolds, David S. *Beneath the American Renaissance: The Subversive Imagination in the Age of Emerson and Melville*. New York: Knopf, 1988.

Reynolds, Larry. *European Revolutions and the American Literary Renaissance*. New Haven: Yale University Press, 1988.

Richardson, Robert, Jr. *Myth and Literature in the American Renaissance*. Bloomington: Indiana University Press, 1978.

Riegel, Robert E. *Young America 1830–1840*. Norman: University of Oklahoma Press, 1949.

Riley, Sam G. *Magazines of the American South*. New York: Greenwood Press, 1986.

Ringe, Donald A. *American Gothic: Imagination and Reason in Nineteenth-Century Fiction*. Lexington: University of Kentucky Press, 1982.

Rogers, Edward R. *Four Southern Magazines*. Richmond, Va.: Williams, 1902.

Rosenthal, Bernard. *City of Nature: Journeys to Nature in the Age of American Romanticism*. Newark: University of Delaware Press, 1980.

Rourke, Constance. *American Humor: A Study of the National Character*. New York: Harcourt, Brace, 1931.

Rowe, John Carlos. *Through the Custom-House: Nineteenth-Century American Fiction and Modern Theory*. Baltimore: Johns Hopkins University Press, 1982.

Rubin, Louis D., Jr., ed. *A Bibliographical Guide to the Study of Southern Literature*. Baton Rouge: Louisiana State University Press, 1969.

Rubin, ed. *A History of Southern Literature*. Baton Rouge: Louisiana State University Press, 1985.

Rubin and Holman, eds., *Southern Literary Study: Problems and Possibilities*. Chapel Hill: University of North Carolina Press, 1975.

Rutherford, Mildred L. *The South in History and Literature*. Atlanta: Franklin-Turner, 1907.

Samuels, Shirley. *Romances of the Republic: Women, the Family, and Violence in the Literature of the Early American Nation*. New York: Oxford University Press, 1996.

Sanford, Charles L. *The Quest for Paradise: Europe and the American Moral Imagination*. Urbana: University of Illinois Press, 1961.

Sartain, John. *Reminiscences of a Very Old Man 1808–1897*. New York: Appleton, 1899.

Saum, Lewis. *The Popular Mood of Pre-Civil War America*. Westport, Conn.: Greenwood Press, 1980.

Seldes, Gilbert. *The Stammering Century*. New York: John Day, 1928.

Simpson, David. *The Politics of American English 1776–1850*. New York: Oxford University Press, 1986.

Simpson, Lewis. *The Man of Letters in New England and the South: Essays on the History of the Literary Vocation in the United States*. Baton Rouge: Louisiana State University Press, 1973.

Slotkin, Richard. *Regeneration Through Violence: The Mythology of the American Frontier*. Middletown, Conn.: Wesleyan University Press, 1973.

Smith, Henry Nash. *Democracy and the Novel: Popular Resistance to Classic American Writers*. New York: Oxford University Press, 1978.

Smith. *Virgin Land: The American West as Symbol and Myth*. Cambridge, Mass.: Harvard University Press, 1970.

Spencer, Benjamin T. *The Quest for Nationality: An American Literary Campaign*. Syracuse: Syracuse University Press, 1957.

Spengemann, William C. *The Adventurous Muse: The Poetics of American Fiction, 1789–1900*. New Haven: Yale University Press, 1977.

Spiller, Robert E. and others, *Literary History of the United States,* fourth edition, revised. New York: Macmillan, 1974.

Spiller, ed. *The American Literary Revolution, 1783–1837*. Garden City, N.Y.: Anchor, 1967.

Stafford, John. *The Literary Criticism of "Young America": A Study in the Relationship of Politics and Literature 1837–1850*. Berkeley: University of California Press, 1952.

Stauffer, Donald Barlow. *A Short History of American Poetry*. New York: Dutton, 1974.

Stem, Madeleine B. *Heads & Headlines: The Phrenological Fowlers*. Norman: University of Oklahoma Press, 1971.

Strong, George Templeton. *The Diary of George Templeton Strong,* edited by Allan Nevins and Milton Halsey Thomas, 4 volumes. New York: Macmillan, 1952.

Sundquist, Eric. *To Wake the Nations: Race in the Making of American Literature*. Cambridge, Mass.: Harvard University Press, 1993.

Taft, Kendall B., ed. *Minor Knickerbockers*. New York: American Book Company, 1947.

Taylor, William R. *Cavalier and Yankee: The Old South and the American National Character*. New York: Braziller, 1961.

Tompkins, Jane. *Sensational Designs: The Cultural Work of American Fiction, 1790–1860*. New York: Oxford University Press, 1985.

Trent, William P. *A History of American Literature 1607–1865*. New York: Appleton, 1903.

Tyler, Alice Felt. *Freedom's Ferment: Phases of American Social History from the Colonial Period to the Outbreak of the Civil War*. Minneapolis: University of Minnesota Press, 1944.

Van Doren, Carl. *The American Novel, 1789–1939*. New York: Macmillan, 1955.

Von Frank, Albert J. *The Sacred Game: Provincialism and Frontier Consciousness in American Literature*. Cambridge: Cambridge University Press, 1985.

Voss, Arthur. *The American Short Story: A Critical Survey*. Norman: University of Oklahoma Press, 1973.

Waggoner, Hyatt H. *American Poets from the Puritans to the Present*. Boston: Houghton Mifflin, 1968.

Walker, Cheryl. *The Nightingale's Burden: Women Poets and American Culture Before 1900*. Bloomington: Indiana University Press, 1982.

Watson, Ritchie Devon. *The Cavalier in Virginia Fiction*. Baton Rouge: Louisiana State University Press, 1985.

Watts, Emily Stipes. *The Poetry of American Women from 1632 to 1945*. Austin: University of Texas Press, 1977.

Weisbuch, Robert. *Atlantic Double-Cross: American Literature and British Influence in the Age of Emerson*. Chicago: University of Chicago Press, 1986.

Welter, Barbara. *Dimity Convictions: The American Woman in the Nineteenth Century*. Athens: Ohio University Press, 1976.

Welter, Rush. *The Mind of America, 1820–1860*. New York: Columbia University Press, 1975.

Wendell, Barrett. *A Literary History of America*. New York: Scribners, 1900.

Widmer, Edward L. *Young America: The Flowering of Democracy in New York City*. Oxford: Oxford University Press, 1999.

Williams, Stanley T. *The Beginnings of American Poetry (1620–1855)*. Uppsala, Sweden: Airnquist & Wiksells, 1951.

Wilson, Edmund. *Patriotic Gore: Studies in the Literature of the American Civil War*. New York: Oxford University Press, 1962.

Woodward, C. Vann. *The Burden of Southern History*, revised edition. Baton Rouge: Louisiana State University Press, 1968.

Yellin, Jean Fagan. *The Intricate Knot: Black Figures in American Literature, 1776–1863*. New York: New York University Press, 1972.

Zboray, Ronald J. *A Fictive People: Antebellum Economic Development and the American Reading Public*. New York: Oxford University Press, 1993.

Ziff, Larzer. *Literary Democracy: The Declaration of Cultural Independence in America*. New York: Viking, 1981.

# Contributors

J. Robert Baker . . . . . . . . . . . . . . . . . . . . . . . . . . . . . . . . . . . . . . . *Fairmont State College*

Dorri R. Beam . . . . . . . . . . . . . . . . . . . . . . . . . . . . . . . . *University of California, Berkeley*

Boyd Childress . . . . . . . . . . . . . . . . . . . . . . . . . . . . . . . . . . . . . . *Auburn University*

Peter A. Dorsey . . . . . . . . . . . . . . . . . . . . . . . . . . . . . . . . . *Mount Saint Mary's College*

David C. Estes . . . . . . . . . . . . . . . . . . . . . . . . . . . . . . . . . *Loyola University, New Orleans*

Richard Fusco . . . . . . . . . . . . . . . . . . . . . . . . . . . . . . . . . . . . *Saint Joseph's University*

Larry W. Gibbs . . . . . . . . . . . . . . . . . . . . . . . . . . . . . . . . . . *University of Mississippi*

Robert D. Habich . . . . . . . . . . . . . . . . . . . . . . . . . . . . . . . . . . . *Ball State University*

Thomas S. Hansen . . . . . . . . . . . . . . . . . . . . . . . . . . . . . . . . . . . *Wellesley College*

Bert Hitchcock . . . . . . . . . . . . . . . . . . . . . . . . . . . . . . . . . . . . . . *Auburn University*

Kim Ingram Jameson . . . . . . . . . . . . . . . . . . . . . . . . . . . . . *University of Central Oklahoma*

Robert C. Kennedy . . . . . . . . . . . . . . . . . . . . . . . . . . . . . . . . . . . . *Norfolk, Virginia*

David B. Kesterson . . . . . . . . . . . . . . . . . . . . . . . . . . . . . . . . *University of North Texas*

James Everett Kibler . . . . . . . . . . . . . . . . . . . . . . . . . . . . . . . *University of Georgia*

Judy Logan . . . . . . . . . . . . . . . . . . . . . . . . . . . . . . . . . . . . *Eastern Washington University*

Esther Lopez . . . . . . . . . . . . . . . . . . . . . . . . . . . . . . . . . . . . *University of Rochester*

Richard C. Lounsbury . . . . . . . . . . . . . . . . . . . . . . . . . . . . . . *Brigham Young University*

Jennings R. Mace . . . . . . . . . . . . . . . . . . . . . . . . . . . . . . . . *Eastern Kentucky University*

James W. Mathews . . . . . . . . . . . . . . . . . . . . *State University of West Georgia Emeritus*

Kathryn B. McKee . . . . . . . . . . . . . . . . . . . . . . . . . . . . . . . . *University of Mississippi*

Margaret B. Moore . . . . . . . . . . . . . . . . . . . . . . . . . . . . . . . . . . . *Athens, Georgia*

Rayburn S. Moore . . . . . . . . . . . . . . . . . . . . . . . . . . . . . . . . . . *University of Georgia*

Donald R. Noble Jr. . . . . . . . . . . . . . . . . . . . . . . . . . . . . . . . . . *University of Alabama*

David A. Rawson . . . . . . . . . . . . . . . . . . . . . . . . . . . . . . . . . . *Worcester State College*

Miriam Shillingsburg . . . . . . . . . . . . . . . . . . . . . . . . . . *Indiana University, South Bend*

Scott Slawinski . . . . . . . . . . . . . . . . . . . . . . . . . . . . . . . . . *University of South Carolina*

E. Kate Stewart . . . . . . . . . . . . . . . . . . . . . . . . . . . *University of Arkansas at Monticello*

Lane Stiles . . . . . . . . . . . . . . . . . . . . . . . . . . . . . . . . . . . . . *University of Minnesota*

Fredrika J. Teute . . . . . . . . . . . . . . . *Omohundro Institute of Early American History and Culture*

G. R. Thompson . . . . . . . . . . . . . . . . . . . . . . . . . . . . . . . . . . . . *Purdue University*

Edward L. Tucker . . . . . . . . . . . . . . . . . . . . *Virginia Polytechnic Institute and State University*

Robert W. Weathersby II . . . . . . . . . . . . . . . . . . . . . . . . . . . . . . . . *Dalton State College*

C. P. Seabrook Wilkinson . . . . . . . . . . . . . . . . . . . . . . . . . . . . . *College of Charleston*

Jack C. Wills . . . . . . . . . . . . . . . . . . . . . . . . . . . . . . . . . . . . . . *Fairmont State College*

Clyde N. Wilson . . . . . . . . . . . . . . . . . . . . . . . . . . . . . . . *University of South Carolina*

Arthur Wrobel . . . . . . . . . . . . . . . . . . . . . . . . . . . . . . . . . . . *University of Kentucky*

# Cumulative Index

*Dictionary of Literary Biography,* Volumes 1-248
*Dictionary of Literary Biography Yearbook,* 1980-2000
*Dictionary of Literary Biography Documentary Series,* Volumes 1-19
*Concise Dictionary of American Literary Biography,* Volumes 1-7
*Concise Dictionary of British Literary Biography,* Volumes 1-8
*Concise Dictionary of World Literary Biography,* Volumes 1-4

# Cumulative Index

**DLB** before number: *Dictionary of Literary Biography,* Volumes 1-248
**Y** before number: *Dictionary of Literary Biography Yearbook,* 1980-2000
**DS** before number: *Dictionary of Literary Biography Documentary Series,* Volumes 1-19
**CDALB** before number: *Concise Dictionary of American Literary Biography,* Volumes 1-7
**CDBLB** before number: *Concise Dictionary of British Literary Biography,* Volumes 1-8
**CDWLB** before number: *Concise Dictionary of World Literary Biography,* Volumes 1-4

# C

# D

Cumulative Index

# H

# J

# L

# M

# N

# S

# T

ISBN 0-7876-4665-2

90000

9 780787 646653